Aging in Canada

VICTOR W. MARSHALL

Aging in Canada: Social Perspectives

Second Edition

Fitzhenry & Whiteside

for Joanne Gard Marshall

© Fitzhenry & Whiteside 1987

Fitzhenry & Whiteside
91 Granton Drive
Richmond Hill, Ontario
L4B 2N5

Canadian Cataloguing in Publication Data

Main entry under title:

Aging in Canada

Bibliography: p.

Includes index.

ISBN 0-88902-879-6

1. Aging — Social aspects — Canada.   2. Aged — Canada   I. Marshall, Victor W.

HQ1064.C3A35 1986   305.2'6   C86-093982-0

Contents

Preface

Aging in Canada, Second Edition is completely new. Therefore, it does not replace the original edition. While the basic organization of this edition is similar to that of its predecessor, every chapter is new and all contain information not to be found in the original edition. By implication, the first edition contains many chapters which I consider to be of enduring value. Indeed, my pleasure at the favourable reception of the original volume prompted me to edit this new edition.

As with the initial edition, this book is aimed at a diverse audience of social and health science students, social service and health-care personnel, policy makers and research-oriented scholars, advocates of and activists for and among the aged. The chapters commissioned for the book accordingly represent diverse interests but are united by a common concern with the social aspects of aging.

The principal changes, at a general level, in this edition are an expansion of the treatment of retirement and health and social policy issues. This should enhance the usefulness of the book for general reference purposes in a wider field of gerontology, health sciences and policy studies. In more specific areas, this book contains increased amounts of basic reference material in several areas related to aging: ethnicity, health status, the health-care delivery system, housing and social support networks. To a considerable extent, the ability to be more comprehensive reflects tremendous maturation of the research community in aging and the social sciences. In all chapters, authors have used the latest demographic and epidemiological data as appropriate.

In many, but not all chapters, authors have been asked to bring together a report of their own current research with a discussion of the wider knowledge base in that area. My intent in this request has been to add greater interest to "review of the literature" discussions, without sacrificing the value of the book as a basic reference source.

I offer my thanks to the authors whose work is represented here, for their research efforts and for their spirited cooperation in making this book a reality. It has been a pleasure working with them. I worked initially with Murray Lamb, formerly of Fitzhenry and Whiteside, on the development of this *Second Edition*, and would like to thank him for his efforts. It has been a pleasure, in the later editorial stages, working with Holly Fitzhenry as Managing Editor for this book. I would like to thank Joanne Daciuk for compiling the name index.

My own contribution to the book has been facilitated by support received as a National Health Scientist from The National Health Research Development Program of Health and Welfare Canada and by a generous award from The Laidlaw Foundation in support of my gerontological research activities. My immediate intellectual homes, The Department of Behavioural Science and the Programme in Gerontology of The University of Toronto, represent optimal environments for work and reflection in this area.

With the passage of years, some things change, and some things stay the same. I find the closing paragraph of the Preface to the original, 1980 edition of this book continues to reflect my sentiments, and therefore close this Preface with the same words: My daughter Emily has been bemused by this activity and has been patient with her dad. I am fortunate in having support, encouragement, critical judgment and tolerance from Joanne Gard Marshall. I would like to dedicate this book to her. May we grow old together.

TORONTO, 10 May, 1986

1
Introduction:
Social Perspectives on Aging

Victor W. Marshall
Department of Behavioural Science
University of Toronto

In the world context, Canada is an "old" society, with about one in ten Canadians aged 65 or more. It is also an "aging society" insofar as the average age of the population is rising and the proportion of Canadians in the older age categories is increasing. The aging of Canadian society is impossible to ignore, as the very tenor of social life is affected by the changing age structure. Societies, like humans, grow older in a way: they accumulate experience, develop a character, partake of history. Aging is not simply of societal interest to the old: people of all ages are affected by the aging of the population.

The changing age structure of the Canadian population has raised questions about the provision of income security for the aged, the increased demands on the health-care system, housing, transportation and other service needs. It has also led to a re-examination of the family. The nature of family life in its own right, as affected by the fact that people are more likely to live to advanced ages, and the relationship of younger family members to the oldest generations have both received increasing attention by bureaucrats, policy makers and social scientists.

Population aging, as it differentially affects men and women, has profound implications not only for income, health and family reasons, but also for the use of leisure time, the organization of work and the planning of communities. For example, if we ghettoize the old in institutions, high-rise apartments for the elderly and the like, we necessarily ghettoize the young elsewhere. If we continue to use seniority as a major basis of job protection and remuneration, we necessarily privilege the old over the young. If we target social services on the basis of age rather than need, we risk reinforcing negatively consequential stereotypes of the aged.

We need to know more about the aging of the society: what are the patterns, what is the present like and what future do we envision? We are already in an unprecedented situation, in the Canadian context, with respect to the age structure of our population, and we face even greater population aging. Yet we know very little about the social consequences, or even the causes, of population aging. We also need to know what kind of present and future we *want* to have, because nothing is inexorable. The future is at least partially within our power to shape.

At the individual and interpersonal level, aging also touches us all. We are born, grow up, grow old and die. Others preceded us. Society will go on after our death. We take an interest in our past and our future and in that which will be experienced by our successors. The interweaving of biography and social history is the stuff of individual life and also the manner in which societies endure. There is a "micro" and a "macro" side to aging, a personal and a social side, an inside and an outside view. Policy concerns about the aging of the society are not experienced abstractly, but they touch us and our loved ones. The kind of life older people are able to live is the kind of life we will ourselves live. Aging, then, concerns us all.

The personal experience of aging is profoundly social psychological. That is, the individual life course cannot properly be appreciated in isolation. As an individual grows older, his or her parents and children simultaneously grow older. As a worker gains experience and seniority, the experience and seniority mix of co-workers is also likely to reflect the passage of time. More generally, the very meaning of age categories and the transitions from life stage to life stage are socially constructed. For example, "old age" in Canadian society is principally defined as a consequence of our developing (or adopting) a social institution called retirement.

By extension of the idea that the personal experience of aging is conditioned by the social context, it is critical to recognize that there are numerous ways of growing up and growing old. Age itself is only a very crude marker of one's life situation. If we knew *only* a person's age, we might predict some things with moderate success (a twelve-year-old is not likely to be married, a ninety-year-old is likely to be widowed; a twenty-five-year-old is likely to be employed in paid labour, a sixty-eight-year-old is not). However, our success at prediction would be much less than what we could obtain if we also knew the person's social-class position, gender and health status. The experience of aging itself interacts with other socially relevant factors, such as gender, social class and ethnicity, in some instances increasing and in other instances decreasing their impact. For example, social-class differences may become less consequential in advanced age, while there may be a resurgence of ethnic identity in very old people.

Such considerations should be tempered with the realization that aging also increases people's stores of experiences and often, as a result, their competencies. People do not passively experience aging, but rather they take part in creating their life course. This is no less true of the very old than it is of the very young. Social scientists have long ago abandoned an "oversocialized" conception of human nature in which people's life experiences are seen as wholly constrained or determined by external forces or the internalization of social norms.

The Scope of the Book

This is a book on the social aspects of aging. The study of aging in all its aspects is defined as the field of gerontology. Gerontology is not a scientific discipline, but rather a focal point that draws the attention of many disciplines, such as economics, demography, political science, sociology, anthropology, epidemiology, psychology and biology. It is viewed by many, in fact, as inherently interdisciplinary by virtue of its subject matter, although why the study of individual or population aging should be thought uniquely or more strongly interdisciplinary than any other aspect of the social or human studies may well be questioned. At any rate, insofar as this is a book in gerontology, it should be qualified as a book in social gerontology. No claim is made to comprehensiveness beyond the social sciences.

The book is, however, like the field of gerontology, highly applied in many places. Several applied disciplines, such as nursing, medicine, social work, health administration and social policy are represented. There is a strong sociological emphasis to the book that reflects its editor's own bent, but also the fact that sociologists have been active with others, often in applied areas, in the conduct of research. Gerontology is one of the least "ivory tower" of the academic areas. As noted above, its subject matter holds both long-range interest and immediate interest and relevance. Few gerontologists have the patience to remove themselves too far from either direct fields of application or the policy domain.

The emphasis of this book is on social perspectives to the exclusion of biological gerontology because in my view the social domain calls for a distinctively Canadian research contribution. The book is intended to bring together and to stimulate new Canadian research in the social aspects of aging, precisely because these aspects are not universal. It may fairly be assumed that the fundamental biological and even the psychological aspects of aging are largely universal. While these, too, are areas in great need of research, what is discovered about the biological and psychological processes of aging through research done in other countries can be "imported" with reasonable assurance that the same processes are operative in Canada. The Canadian research community should, of course, carry its weight internationally in the production of such knowledge (and in fact Canadian researchers have distinguished records in these areas), but there is no substitute for Canadian research in social gerontology.

We cannot rely for basic data about the social aspects of aging in Canada on research conducted in other countries, because, by definition, the social aspects of aging are context specific. This context is social and historical, and Canada is not demonstrably similar enough to any other society (even that of the United States) to allow direct translation of research findings from other countries into the Canadian context.

The articles in this book have been prepared especially for it and have not appeared elsewhere. In some cases, authors in the first edition of *Aging in Canada: Social Perspectives* have been asked to update their chapters for this edition. Most chapters are wholly new. My editorial goals have been multiple. I wanted to: (1) bring together a number of basic *facts* about age and aging in Canada; (2) illustrate the major and most important *theoretical approaches* that characterize social gerontological research in Canada; (3) provide examples of principal *sources of data* that could be used in studying aging, such as survey data, material from archives, ethnographies, participant observation, vital statistics and content analysis; (4) provide examples of different *research designs*; and (5) represent a *critical stance* towards social research, theory, methodology and policy in the field of aging.

These goals are identical to those pursued in the first edition of *Aging in Canada: Social Perspectives*. Their realization is, I think, more satisfactory. This reflects a significant growth in the size and scope of Canadian research in the social aspects of aging.

Canadian Research in the Social Aspects of Aging: Directions and Limitations

The major theoretical approaches to understanding aging and the aged that are found in this book probably quite fairly represent those found in Canadian scholarship. While this range is extensive, reflecting a large and diverse set of researchers and theoretical perspectives, the overall theoretical tone is dissimilar to that found in other texts in the field, particularly works emanating from the U.S.A. Social theorizing about age and aging takes something of a different tack in Canada than elsewhere. Canadian social scientists are influenced by currents of thought in the U.S.A., and one can read in this book about modernization theory and age-stratification theory, which dominate the macro-sociology of aging in that country, and about role theory and its derivatives, activity and disengagement theory, which have been the focus of so much theorizing in the U.S.A. These approaches, however, do not dominate the scholarship of Canadian social gerontologists, who, if anything, are for the most part highly critical of such approaches. On the other hand, European and British influences are apparent in work informed by various "political economy" approaches, by an explicit attention in many of the chapters to issues of social class and by the tendency to examine the broader social structural and historical contexts that shape the aging experience. As noted in the introduction to the first edition of this book, Canadian theory about aging is more structural, collectivist and historically grounded than the predominately attitudinal, individualistic and consensually oriented theorizing found south of the border. Marxian and Weberian strains combine with a healthy dose of British social-policy orientation. European phenomenologists are drawn together with American symbolic interactionists at the social psychological level. In these respects, in formulating social theory of aging or in drawing on it to guide specific research, Canadian social gerontologists have followed the orientations of Canadian social scientists in general. I pursue these theoretical matters in Chapter 3.

In the first edition, I noted that the sources of data available to Canadian social scientists interested in aging have been somewhat limited, with heavy reliance placed on official statistics. Many of the chapters in this second edition reflect a continuing reliance on official statistics, but a comparison of this edition with the first will reveal a dramatic increase in the number of investigators who have developed their own data sets. Chapters that, in the first edition, speculated about the Canadian situation based on data gathered in other nations, or that wove interpretive threads on a skeleton of official statistics, now draw on numerous Canadian studies conducted by a growing number of Canadian social scientists in the area of aging. There are also many more investigators conducting secondary analyses on large data sets, but also on smaller data sets. This reflects in part a move to a three-generational structure of researchers in which one now frequently sees active research programs conducted by the students of students of the first social scientists to conduct aging research in Canada. In turn, this reflects an exponential growth in the quantity, if not necessarily the quality, of research.

Sadly, an observation made in the introduction to the first edition of this book must be repeated. In Canada, political scientists in the university community have almost totally ignored issues of aging. Economists outside governmental circles have been almost as unlikely to become involved in such research. There is little historical research, except for a growing amount of historical sociology, and anthropological research is scattered. The philosophical aspects of individual and population aging, including ethical issues, remain largely unexplored in Canada or by Canadian scholars. Although the chapters in this book reflect remarkable progress in developing research on ethnic and geographical variability in aging in Canada, we cannot claim a large or authoritative data base in these areas, either.

Compared to our neighbour to the south, we in Canada still have a situation in which we have comparatively fewer nationwide studies, fewer longitudinal projects and fewer large, big-budget studies. Our research funding structure, while greatly improved, is not yet comparable to that in the United States on a per capita basis. Nonetheless, since publication of the first edition of *Aging in Canada: Social Perspectives,* the impact of continued support of research on aging by the National Health Research Development Program of Health and Welfare Canada (NHRDP), the initiation of the Gerontology Research Council of Ontario (GRCO) and, in particular, the full development of the Strategic Grants Program in Population Aging of the Social Sciences and Humanities Research Council of Canada (SSHRCC) has been remarkable.

Several gerontology research centres, many funded by the SSHRCC program, have been established in the past few years and are likely to survive their initial seed funding. Canada still has no centralized agency to support gerontological research in the health and social fields, comparable to the National Institute on Aging and the Administration on Aging in the U.S.A. The first Canadian social scientists trained in Canada in programs with strong gerontology interests have only recently graduated. Yet, when this catalogue of limitations has been recited, one can still recognize significant growth in scholarly productivity in aging and the social sciences. From an editorial point of view, this is painfully evident to me in the fact that I have been unable to include a number of productive researchers as chapter authors; this is a situation in sharp contrast to the one I faced when recruiting authors for the first edition.

Continuing Growth of Canadian Gerontology[1]

The same demographic pressures that contributed to initiating interest in gerontological research and study in the late 1960s continue, and indeed are more acutely felt as the year 2009 approaches. This is the year in which the first of the baby-boom generation begin to pass over into that age 65-and-over category that has come through social convention (and the institution of retirement) to represent old age. With the proportion of the Canadian population older than age 65 expected to double between now and the census of 2031, policy makers and social scientists continue to be concerned with a lack of knowledge about the processes of aging and the nature of a society with a radically different age structure.

What is different now compared to the late 1960s, and even to the 1980 publication date of the first edition of *Aging in Canada: Social Perspectives*, is the increasing institutionalization of our ability to produce and use such knowledge systematically. There are several indicators of this institutionalization, some of which were mentioned earlier. The Canadian Association on Gerontology, founded in 1971, had about 1,300 members on its fifteenth anniversary. It holds annual conferences and publishes *The Canadian Journal on Aging*, which is itself now in its fifth year of publication as a fully refereed journal. There are also provincial gerontology associations in every province, which take a more applied approach to gerontology, and there is a Canadian Association of Gerontological Nursing, as well as other specialized gerontology associations such as the Ontario Psychogeriatric Association.

Gerontology research centres or programs are now to be found scattered from Victoria, British Columbia, to St. John's, Newfoundland, and their emphasis is heavily on social science and health policy research. These are also playing an important part in the development of new scholars, as well as long-term projects and research programs.

Writing this introduction *after* the rest of the book has been completed, I have become optimistic about the future of social research on aging in Canada. Much is yet to be done, but discernible progress is being made. It is as fitting as ever to close this introductory chapter with the closing paragraph to my introduction to the original edition of *Aging in Canada: Social Perspectives:*

> As gerontologists, we are aware of the flow of generations, of the need to pass on what is known to our successors and, more important, of the need to have successors. My hope is that this book will nourish a new generation of students and stimulate them to try to fill the many gaps in our knowledge of the social aspects of aging in Canada. Thus, while the book reflects the growth of social gerontology in Canada, I hope it will contribute to its eventual maturity.

Note

[1] For additional historical details, see my article, "Gerontology," in *The Canadian Encyclopedia*, Vol. 2, p. 740 (1985).

I

Thinking Systematically About Aging

The three chapters of this section are intended to lay a groundwork for the entire book and, I expect, will be consulted from time to time as a context or foundation for reading other chapters. They can also stand on their own.

Denton, Feaver and Spencer provide in Chapter 2 a detailed account of Canadian population aging, both historically and projecting into the future. Interest in the social aspects of aging reflects, in many respects, the fact that we are an aging *society*. It is important to recognize how *many* older people there are in Canada, but also how *few*. More important, it is essential to have an understanding of the entire age structure of the population and to avoid simply dichotomizing the population into all those above and below age 65 or some other arbitrary age.

The various factors that come together to create population aging — birth, death, immigration and emigration — interact in ways that affect not only the aged but all segments of the age structure. They not only create an ever-changing age *structure*, but also affect population *growth*.

Denton, Feaver and Spencer introduce data relevant to the commonly employed concept of dependency ratio, but they also point to weaknesses in this concept. It does not provide historically sensitive measures of the relationship between productive and nonproductive members of a society, and in the current period it provides no more than a crude measure, as well. Nonetheless, because dependency ratios so frequently appear in the literature on aging, it is critical to understand how they are constructed and how they relate to labour-force participation.

Turning to the future, Denton, Feaver and Spencer provide two alternative population projections, which differ in terms of assumed fertility. It is noteworthy that the "high fertility" assumption suggests a move towards completed fertility of only 2.1, or about the rate of fertility required in the long run to avoid a decline in population. Until very recently, a completed fertility rate at the replacement level would have been deemed not even a moderate level but a low level. However, as the authors point out, with fertility in several European countries at or near 1.4, this choice is not unreasonable for projection purposes (alternative projections appear in this book in Chapter 28 by Denton, Li and Spencer and in Chapter 29 by Messenger and Powell).

Relating population projections to dependency ratios, Denton, Feaver and Spencer argue that under either of their projections, population aging will not create an unmanageable burden on the population of working age. A similar point is made by Messenger and Powell in Chapter 29.

The importance of understanding age-related phenomena is affected in no little measure by the number of older people in a society and by the overall age structure of the population. The changing demography of aging is, then, the essential foundation for the social study of aging, and demographic issues reappear throughout this book.

A second foundation for the book is provided in Chapter 3, by Marshall, which provides a brief sketch of theoretical approaches in the sociology and the social psychology of aging. A number of different theoretical approaches to aging are employed by the authors of various chapters in this book. It may be helpful, particularly for students, to have a theoretical framework in which to place these studies. Many of the chapters in this volume make no explicit reference to theory, but an implicit theoretical stance can unfailingly be drawn from them with sufficient effort. While Chapter 3 focusses on theoretical approaches from sociology and social psychology (these approaches vary in assumptions made about human motivation, the nature of social interaction and the importance of social structure.) any of the social sciences must make some assumptions within its domain about these issues (Are humans rational? Is conflict or consensus the normal state of affairs? How free are humans to build their own lives, or how constrained are they by social structure?).

Chapter 4, by Norris, is included to emphasize the place of the individual, as a social creature, aging in a social context. Norris, a psychologist, uses the life-span developmental perspective as a conceptual framework. This is similar to the life-course perspective in sociology (Hagestad and Neugarten, 1985; Ryff, 1986). She focusses on social interaction, which may be thought of as the most sociological focal point for a psychologist to address and the most psychological focal point for a sociologist to address.

Norris describes the historical antecedents of the life-span perspective in developmental psychology, including the interest of early developmental psychologists in social interaction.

To illustrate the value of the life-span approach, Norris pursues two specific areas of inquiry: the role of the social environment in producing a healthy sense of identity, and the concept of social competence. These are two areas of high current interest to psychologists of aging, which simultaneously interest scholars from other social science backgrounds. The social environment, at this micro-social or social psychological level, includes interaction contexts in the family and kinship domains, and Norris's discussion is complementary to subsequent analyses in chapters by Cape (Chapter 5), Rosenthal (Chapter 17), Martin Matthews (Chapter 18), Corin (Chapter 19) and Marshall (Chapter 23), all of which deal to some extent with social interaction domains in relation to social support. Social competence is a multifaceted construct both influenced by and influencing social factors. The concept of social competence moves us away from static analyses of the aging individual (e.g., in terms of personality traits), to look at *processes* of interaction in a life-span perspective.

Finally, Norris makes a plea for more qualitative research. This is a plea that is echoed many times by the authors in this volume.

While the chapters in this first section are presented to provide some conceptual and methodological tools to assist in confronting subsequent chapters of the book, additional theoretical and methodological discussions are found as appropriate in various chapters. There is no overriding theoretical approach for understanding the social aspects of aging. Attempts to produce one, such as disengagement theory, have not been highly successful. We should not expect to find an integrated theory of aging, because aging is part of life. The social study of aging, or as it is sometimes called, social gerontology, is not a discipline but a field of inquiry. The most appropriate theoretical approaches will be taken from the best existing theory in all the social sciences and will not be distinctively gerontological. Similarly, the methodological principles most appropriate for gaining an understanding of aging are the best principles of social science in general. There are different matters of emphasis, of course, but in general, any search for a specific gerontological methodology would be fruitless.

References

Hagestad, Gunhild O. and Bernice L. Neugarten
   1985   "Age and the life course." Chapter 2, pp. 35-61, in Robert H. Binstock and Ethel Shanas (eds.), *Handbook of Aging and the Social Sciences*. New York: Van Nostrand Reinhold.
Ryff, Carol D.
   1986   "The subjective construction of self and society: An agenda for life-span research." Chapter 2, pp. 33-74, in Victor W. Marshall (ed.), *Later Life: The Social Psychology of Aging*. Beverly Hills: Sage.

2

The Canadian Population and Labour Force: Retrospect and Prospect

Frank T. Denton, Christine H. Feaver
and Byron G. Spencer
Department of Economics
McMaster University

The long-term development of a nation, in all its social and economic aspects, is inextricably linked with changes in its population. With the passage of time, those who are born today become the school children, the young adults, the workers and, eventually, the elderly of the future. As they live their lives, their actions and decisions affect not only themselves and their contemporaries, but also the conditions under which future generations will live.

The "baby boom" that followed the Second World War, and the subsequent "baby bust," provide good illustration. The Canadian birth rate rose sharply in the 1940s and remained at a high level until the end of the 1950s. In consequence, a large bulge was created in the population age pyramid, and throughout the whole of their lives, those born during this period will be affected by the fact that they are part of this bulge. Much of their schooling took place under relatively crowded conditions, and as they have entered the labour force they have felt the influence of large numbers of their contemporaries competing for jobs at the same time. When they reach retirement age, the demands for support that they make on the economy, and hence on the working generations that follow them, will be relatively great, by virtue of their numbers. In contrast, those born since the latter part of the 1960s, when the birth rate has been low, will have experienced quite different circumstances or will experience them in the future. The experience will include less crowded classrooms as school children, less competition for jobs as adults, and smaller costs, in total, for their support in old age.

The wide variation of the birth rate during the twentieth century has been

The work on which this paper is based has been supported by the Social Sciences and Humanities Research Council of Canada under its grant program in the field of population aging. We acknowledge with gratitude the support of the SSHRCC and the computing and related assistance of Rosanna Giordano.

TABLE 1:
The Population, by Sex and Age, and the Labour Force, by Sex, Canada, Census Years 1901 to 1981

Sex and Age	1901	1911	1921	1931	1941	1951	1956	1961	1966	1971	1976	1981
						— Thousands —						
Population												
Males:												
0-19	1,219	1,557	1,930	2,184	2,184	2,700	3,250	3,895	4,302	4,338	4,216	3,994
20-64	1,394	2,095	2,384	2,895	3,325	3,837	4,279	4,650	5,036	5,676	6,358	7,063
65+	139	171	215	295	391	551	622	674	717	782	875	1,010
Females:												
0-19	1,186	1,506	1,898	2,137	2,134	2,608	3,137	3,729	4,128	4,157	4,025	3,803
20-64	1,302	1,715	2,155	2,584	3,095	3,777	4,170	4,573	5,010	5,653	6,391	7,121
65+	133	165	205	281	377	535	622	717	823	962	1,127	1,350
Total	5,371	7,207	8,788	10,377	11,507	14,009	16,081	18,238	20,015	21,568	22,993	24,342
Labour Force												
Total	1,855	2,744	3,236	3,955	4,545	5,274	5,826	6,556	7,503	8,649	10,203	11,904
Female	284	423	568	760	948	1,204	1,406	1,828	2,342	2,970	3,835	4,851

— Percent of Total —

Population												
Males:												
0-19	22.7	21.6	22.0	21.1	19.0	19.3	20.2	21.4	21.5	20.1	18.3	16.4
20-64	26.0	29.1	27.1	27.9	28.9	27.4	26.6	25.5	25.2	26.3	27.7	29.0
65+	2.6	2.4	2.4	2.8	3.4	3.9	3.9	3.7	3.6	3.6	3.8	4.2
Females:												
0-19	22.1	20.9	21.6	20.6	18.6	18.6	19.5	20.4	20.6	19.3	17.5	15.6
20-64	24.2	23.8	24.5	25.0	26.9	27.0	25.9	25.1	25.0	26.2	27.8	29.3
65+	2.5	2.3	2.3	2.7	3.3	3.8	3.9	3.9	4.1	4.5	4.9	5.5
Total	100.0	100.0	100.0	100.0	100.0	100.0	100.0	100.0	100.0	100.0	100.0	100.0
Labour Force:												
Female/Total	15.3	15.4	17.5	19.2	20.9	22.8	24.1	27.9	31.2	34.3	37.6	40.8

NOTE: All figures prior to 1951 exclude Newfoundland. The population figures relate to June 1 of each census year, while the labour force figures are annual averages. The labour force figures from 1951 to 1981 are based on estimates from the Statistics Canada Labour Force Survey. Labour force figures prior to 1951 are based on estimates from Denton and Ostry (1967). All labour force estimates prior to 1976 have been adjusted by the authors to make them consistent with new definitions introduced into the Labour Force Survey in the latter year. Components may not add precisely to totals because of rounding.

accompanied by marked fluctuations in the annual rate of immigration to Canada and by a long-term decline in death rates. All these changes have left their mark on the size and composition of the population and have had a major influence on the characteristics of our society and our economy. One of the most important facts to recognize in connection with demographic changes is that even though some of their effects are felt immediately, it takes many generations for all the effects to be realized fully.

It is not the purpose of this chapter to discuss the social and economic consequences of population change. That is the topic of other chapters, and one that has been treated elsewhere (e.g., Denton and Spencer, 1975, 1979, 1981, 1983, 1985; Foot, 1982; United Nations, 1973). Instead we limit ourselves to a review of the record of population and labour-force growth in Canada and some projections into the future. The material presented here may be of interest in its own right, but it is intended also to provide background for other papers in this volume.

The Growth of the Population and the Labour Force

In 1867, at the time of Confederation, the population of what is now Canada totalled about 3.5 million. By the time of the 1901 census it had

FIGURE 1:

Annual Birth, Death and Natural Increase Rates, Canada, 1876 to 1982

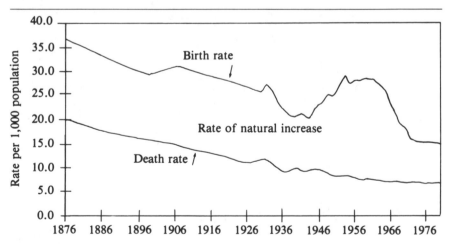

NOTE: Up to 1926, figures are intercensal decade averages, expressed at annual rates and plotted at the mid-years of the decades. From 1926 on, annual rates are plotted. Rates up to and including 1966 are from Table 4 of Denton (1970). Rates subsequent to 1966 are based on various Statistics Canada published sources; annual rates are on a census year (June 1 to May 31) basis.

reached 5.4 million, and by the 1981 census it was more than 24 million. In roughly eleven decades, the population has thus increased almost sevenfold.

Some of the major features of population and labour-force growth in this century are indicated in Table 1. The numbers of males and females in the population are recorded for each of three broad age groups, in each of the years in which a national census was taken from 1901 to 1981. Estimates of the total labour force and of the female labour force are provided, also.

As is evident from Table 1, the total population has grown from one census to the next, without exception. There were very large proportionate increases in the early part of the century, especially in the years prior to the First World War, when the Canadian West was being settled rapidly and immigrants were pouring into the country. There was rapid growth again in the decade and a half following the Second World War, when large-scale inflows of immigrants coincided with the sustained high rates of fertility associated with the baby boom. In the decade ending with the 1961 census, the

FIGURE 2:
Annual Immigration, Emigration and Net Immigration Rates, Canada, 1876 to 1983

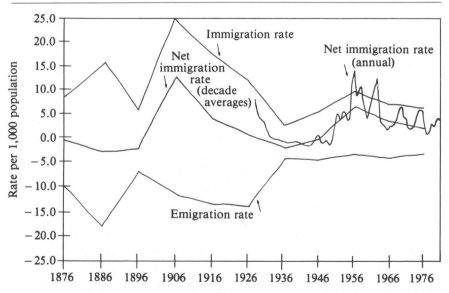

NOTE: Immigration and emigration figures are intercensal decade averages, expressed at annual rates and plotted at the mid-years of the decades. The decade averages are based on Denton (1970: Table 9) and Statistics Canada (1976: Table 3). Annual net immigration rates up to 1971 are from Statistics Canada (1976: Table 4); for subsequent years, they are based on various Statistics Canada published sources.

population increased by more than 30 percent. While the population has continued to grow since then, the rate of increase has fallen as a result of declines in both the birth rate and the rate of immigration. In the decade ending in 1981, the increase was only 13 percent.

Systematic attention is given to the components of population change in Figures 1 and 2. Figure 1 is concerned with the elements of "natural increase." Natural increase is calculated as the number of births less the number of deaths. It is convenient to express births, deaths and natural increase relative to population size, and this is what is done in Figure 1. Birth, death and natural increase rates per 1,000 population are plotted for the period from the 1870s to the 1980s.

There was an extended decline in the birth rate from the last quarter of the nineteenth century to the latter part of the 1930s. Observers of the day expected that this decline would continue, or at least that the birth rate would remain at a low level. However, that was not to be. Instead there was a sharp increase in the 1940s, followed by a period in which the rate remained at a consistently high level, year after year. This period lasted until the very end of the 1950s. The rate then decreased just as sharply as it had increased earlier, falling to the lowest levels ever recorded in Canadian demographic history by the late 1960s, and continuing to fall in the 1970s and the 1980s. Throughout the whole of the period from 1947 to 1959, the annual birth rate never fell below 27 per 1,000 population; in sharp contrast, the 1983 rate was only 15.0.

The story of the death rate is quite different. There have been no substantial fluctuations, but instead a rather steady and gradual decrease in the overall rate. The declines in infant mortality have been especially dramatic, but all groups have shared in the decrease, and average life expectancies have risen markedly over the decades. Based on 1931 mortality conditions, a newborn male would have been expected to live to an age of 60 years, on average, and a newborn female to an age of 62; based on 1981 conditions, their life expectancies would have been 72 and 79 respectively.

The net immigration component of population change represents the difference between the number of immigrants and the number of emigrants. Again it is convenient to express migration relative to population size, and this is done in Figure 2. The rates are plotted for intercensal decades from 1871-81 to 1971-81, and the net immigration rates are plotted annually, as well, from the end of the 1920s.

Taking the last hundred years as a whole, the gross immigration rate is characterized by generally high levels over long periods, and by substantial volatility over shorter ones. Prior to the Second World War, periods of high immigration coincided with periods of high emigration, as the figure indicates: many who came to Canada stayed for only short periods before moving on again, typically to the United States. Nevertheless, net immigration has been positive in most decades, and quite substantial in many. In the present century, the depressed decade of the 1930s represents the only extended period in which the numbers of people leaving Canada - exceeded the numbers arriving.

The short-run variation of immigration is evident in the series of annual net rates plotted in Figure 2 for the period since the late 1920s. As the series indicates, year-to-year fluctuations have been pronounced: immigration is much more volatile than an inspection of decade averages alone would suggest.

Changes in the size of a population and changes in its age composition go hand in hand: the factors that are responsible for the one are responsible, also, for the other. The distributions among the broad age groups 0-19, 20-64 and 65-and-over are recorded in Table 1, for males and females in each of the national census years since 1901. For these groups, there are only three instances in which the population failed to increase from one census to another: the 0-19 age group declined in size between 1931 and 1941 and, more recently, between 1971 and 1976 and again between 1976 and 1981. The earlier decreases were so small as to represent virtually no change; they were a consequence of the low birth rates of the 1930s and, to some extent, of the excess of emigration over immigration in that period. However, the more recent decreases were quite substantial, reflecting the very sharp drop in the numbers of births in the 1960s and 1970s.

With these exceptions, the historical pattern has been one of growth in each age group from census to census. Over the eighty-year period as a whole covered in Table 1, the number of people under the age of 20 — males and females combined — increased more than threefold, the number in the range 20-64 increased more than fivefold and the number 65-and-over increased almost ninefold.

In some very general respects, the composition of the population today is not greatly different from what it was twenty, fifty or eighty years ago. Somewhat more than half the population is in the 20-64 age range, and the overall numbers of males and females are about equal, as in past times. However, changes have taken place, and they are important ones. The proportion of young people has declined quite sharply in recent years, an inevitable consequence of the declining numbers of births. In 1966, people under 20 represented 42.1 percent of the total population; in 1976, they represented only 35.8 percent, and in 1981, only 32.0 percent. At the older end of the age spectrum, the proportion aged 65-and-over has risen over the long term. In 1901, when the Canadian population was a younger one on average, people 65-and-over represented 5.1 percent of the total; in 1976, they represented 8.7 percent, and in 1981, 9.7 percent. There have been changes in the sex composition of the population, too. It is a curious fact that males exceed females at birth. However, women tend to live longer than men, and the gap in life expectancies has widened. Largely for this reason, there were 1,350,000 women 65-and-over in 1981, compared with only 1,010,000 men.

The size of the labour force — the total number of persons with jobs or looking for jobs — is obviously related to the size of the population. But it is related, also, to the age composition of the population and to the labour force participation rates in individual male and female age groups — that is, to the proportions of people in these groups who wish to be employed. Labour force growth in Canada has been closely linked with population growth, and hence with all those factors that are responsible for population growth. In addition, though, there have been major changes in the patterns of participation. Men now retire much earlier, on average, than they did in previous decades. The average age of school leaving has risen, too, so that the male working life has been shortened at both ends. At the same time, female participation rates have risen markedly, in response to changing social and economic circumstances.

The long-run pattern of growth of the labour force is indicated in Table 1. In 1901, the Canadian labour force numbered some 1.9 million people; in 1981, it numbered about 12.0 million. In 1901, women represented a little over 15 percent of the total; in 1981, they represented over 40 percent. In round numbers, two out of every five members of the working population today are women. The growth of the female labour force has been especially rapid since the Second World War, and the growth continues at a brisk pace.

The age structure of the population has important implications for the economic burden that a society must bear in supporting its dependent members. Those who are economically "productive" are typically those in the conventional working-age range who provide the labour required to produce the national output and the national income. Others — the young and the old — are, in a basic sense, dependent on this group, and as the age structure of the population changes, the burden of dependency may change, also.

Various measures of dependency can be calculated, and a number are provided in Table 2. The upper part of the table provides measures based on the sizes of young and old age groups relative to the group aged 20 to 64, the latter taken as a rough approximation to the working-age population. The first measure is the "youth" dependency ratio — the ratio of the population aged 0-19 to the population 20-64. In 1901, the youth ratio was 0.89 — that is, there were 89 people under the age of 20 for every 100 people aged 20-64. In 1981, the ratio was 0.55, the lowest level recorded over the entire eighty-year period. However, the transition from the high 1901 level to the low 1981 one was not steady. Consistent with the general decline in the birth rate, the youth ratio fell in most of the decades before 1941; it then rose, as

TABLE 2:
Selected Dependency Ratios, Canada, Census Years 1901 to 1981

Type of Ratio	1901	1911	1921	1931	1941	1951	1956	1961	1966	1971	1976	1981
Ratio to Population 20-64												
Population: 0-19	0.89	0.80	0.84	0.79	0.67	0.70	0.76	0.83	0.84	0.75	0.65	0.55
65+	0.10	0.09	0.09	0.11	0.12	0.14	0.15	0.15	0.15	0.15	0.16	0.17
0-19 and 65+	0.99	0.89	0.93	0.90	0.79	0.84	0.91	0.98	0.99	0.90	0.81	0.72
Total Population	1.99	1.89	1.93	1.90	1.79	1.84	1.91	1.98	1.99	1.90	1.81	1.72
Ratio to Labour Force												
Population: 0-19	1.30	1.12	1.18	1.09	0.95	1.01	1.10	1.16	1.13	0.98	0.80	0.65
65+	0.15	0.12	0.13	0.15	0.17	0.21	0.21	0.21	0.21	0.20	0.19	0.20
0-19 and 65+	1.44	1.24	1.31	1.24	1.12	1.22	1.31	1.37	1.34	1.18	0.99	0.85
Non-Labour Force	1.63	1.63	1.72	1.62	1.53	1.68	1.78	1.80	1.69	1.49	1.23	1.03
Total Population	2.63	2.63	2.72	2.62	2.53	2.68	2.78	2.80	2.69	2.49	2.23	2.03

NOTE: Ratios are based on figures in Table 1. Components may not add precisely to totals because of rounding.

a result of the baby boom, until 1966, since which time it has declined sharply.

The second row of Table 2 displays values of the "elderly" dependency ratio — the ratio of those 65-and-over to those 20-64. In 1901, this ratio was 0.10. The ratio has increased considerably since then, and by 1981 it had risen to 0.17.

The sums of the foregoing two dependency ratios, which we may take as rough measures of the total "dependency burden," are provided in the third row. The figures in this row are less than one. They vary over the period, ranging from 0.99 in 1901 and again in 1966, to 0.79 in 1941. However, the 1981 ratio was only 0.72, the lowest level recorded in the table. By this rough measure, then, the population of today is characterized by a relatively low "dependency burden."

It will be evident that the dependency measures just considered are far from precise, especially when compared over long periods of time. For one thing, while the age group 20-64 may be adequate as a rough approximation to the working-age population today, its adequacy for the earlier decades of the century is questionable. The average age of entrance of men into the labour force was considerably younger in earlier periods, and the average age of retirement was considerably older. Moreover, the population-based ratios ignore the dependency implications of increases in the labour force participation of women. It is appropriate, therefore, to consider dependency measures that take account directly of the size of the labour force, rather than inferring it from the population. A few such measures are provided in the lower half of Table 2.

The picture is altered in detail when ratios of population to labour force are considered, but in broad terms it remains substantially the same. The levels of the ratios are higher than the ones in the top half of the table, but the patterns of change through time are generally similar, and it is these patterns that are of principal interest. Relative to earlier levels, the 1981 ratios are now seen to be even lower than before. The overall ratio of persons not in the labour force to persons in the labour force was 1.03 in 1981, and this is by far the lowest level of that ratio recorded in the table. As before, we conclude that the current dependency burden is a relatively light one, by historical standards.[1]

The Future Population

The baby boom of the 1940s and the 1950s accounted for much of the very rapid expansion of the labour force in the later 1960s and throughout the 1970s. Those who were born during the baby-boom period can be expected to remain in the labour force for several decades, of course, but eventually they will reach retirement age and become part of the dependent population. The children of the 1960s and the 1970s, and those born later, will become responsible, in the second and third decades of the next century, for the national income base that will support the baby-boom generation in its old age. The prospect of a large increase in the fraction of the population in the elderly dependent category has been a source of concern for many.[2] It is useful, therefore, to attempt to attach some numbers to the future size and age distribution of the population.

The population at the end of any period is equal to the population at the beginning of the period, plus births and immigration, minus deaths and emigration. We have made projections of fertility rates for females of different ages in the childbearing range[3] and of mortality rates for males and females of different ages. These projections, together with assumptions about the numbers and age-sex distributions of immigrants and emigrants, allow us to make projections of the population, both in total and for particular age-sex categories. The population is moved ahead one year at a time for as many years as there are in the projection period. Each year, the existing population is aged by one year, mortality rates are applied to calculate the numbers of deaths and fertility rates to calculate the number of births. Immigrants are added at each age, and emigrants are subtracted.

We report here two projections of the population based on particular sets of assumptions concerning the future course of fertility, mortality and rates of migration.[4] The projections differ only in terms of the assumption regarding future fertility. In the first projection the total fertility rate (the sum of the fertility rates for individual ages) is assumed to increase, in equal annual increments, from its 1983 level of about 1.7 births per woman, to a level of 2.1 births per woman by 1996, and to remain at that level thereafter to the end of the projection period.[5] (A rate of 2.1 is roughly equal to the natural replacement rate — the rate required, in the long run, for the population to be able to reproduce itself.) In the second projection the total fertility rate is assumed to continue to decrease, going from 1.7 in 1983 to 1.4 by 1996, and then to remain at the 1.4 level thereafter. (A rate as low as 1.4 is far below the natural replacement rate; by way of comparison, however, as of the early 1980s the rates in the Federal Republic of Germany and in Denmark were about 1.4, and the rates in Switzerland, Sweden, Finland, the Netherlands and Belgium were only slightly higher.)

Whichever total rate is assumed to apply, the fertility rate for women of each age is taken to be a constant proportion of the total rate throughout the projection period. The mortality rates for particular ages and sexes are assumed to decline in the future in accordance with recent experience. Taking into account the common view that the pace of decline must diminish in the longer run, it is assumed that the observed rates of change of mortality for all age-sex groups will decline gradually from what they were in the period 1961-81, and that after 2031 no further changes will occur. Annual immigration of 120,000 and emigration of 40,000 are assumed

TABLE 3:
Projected Population of Canada by Sex and Age, 1981 to 2051, Assuming the Total Fertility Rate to Increase to 2.1 by 1996

Sex and Age	1981	1986	1991	1996	2001	2011	2021	2031	2041	2051
					— Thousands —					
Males:										
0-19	3,994	3,811	3,916	4,119	4,285	4,386	4,548	4,807	4,931	5,139
20-64	7,063	7,747	8,185	8,528	8,869	9,537	9,776	9,708	10,173	10,647
65-69	390	416	482	511	515	660	882	994	811	869
70-74	281	327	351	407	434	465	698	830	733	702
75-79	180	213	250	269	314	340	440	589	662	542
80+	159	188	228	274	313	406	459	635	806	810
Females:										
0-19	3,803	3,624	3,723	3,917	4,074	4,168	4,321	4,566	4,684	4,882
20-64	7,121	7,797	8,222	8,575	8,935	9,620	9,801	9,672	10,124	10,595
65-69	454	495	576	587	590	764	1,044	1,139	928	993
70-74	352	418	460	537	550	595	903	1,077	926	887
75-79	252	306	368	408	480	500	654	895	976	796
80+	292	361	456	572	687	927	1,071	1,456	1,902	1,956
Total	24,342	25,703	27,215	28,705	30,044	32,368	34,597	36,370	37,656	38,819

	— Percent of Total —									
Males:										
0-19	16.4	14.8	14.4	14.3	14.3	13.5	13.1	13.2	13.1	13.2
20-64	29.0	30.1	30.1	29.7	29.5	29.5	28.3	26.7	27.0	27.4
65-69	1.6	1.6	1.8	1.8	1.7	2.0	2.5	2.7	2.2	2.2
70-74	1.2	1.3	1.3	1.4	1.4	1.4	2.0	2.3	1.9	1.8
75-79	0.7	0.8	0.9	0.9	1.0	1.1	1.3	1.6	1.8	1.4
80+	0.7	0.7	0.8	1.0	1.0	1.3	1.3	1.7	2.1	2.1
Females:										
0-19	15.6	14.1	13.7	13.6	13.6	12.9	12.5	12.6	12.4	12.6
20-64	29.3	30.3	30.2	29.9	29.7	29.7	28.3	26.6	26.9	27.3
65-69	1.9	1.9	2.1	2.0	2.0	2.4	3.0	3.1	2.5	2.6
70-74	1.4	1.6	1.7	1.9	1.8	1.8	2.6	3.0	2.5	2.3
75-79	1.0	1.2	1.4	1.4	1.6	1.5	1.9	2.5	2.6	2.1
80+	1.2	1.4	1.7	2.0	2.3	2.9	3.1	4.0	5.1	5.0
Total	100.0	100.0	100.0	100.0	100.0	100.0	100.0	100.0	100.0	100.0

NOTE: Components may not add precisely to totals because of rounding.

TABLE 4:
Projected Population of Canada by Sex and Age, 1981 to 2051, Assuming the Total Fertility Rate to Decrease to 1.4 by 1996

Sex and Age	1981	1986	1991	1996	2001	2011	2021	2031	2041	2051
					— Thousands —					
Males:										
0-19	3,994	3,798	3,751	3,654	3,464	2,996	2,808	2,564	2,324	2,177
20-64	7,063	7,747	8,185	8,528	8,869	9,375	8,970	8,188	7,687	7,022
65-69	390	416	482	511	515	660	882	994	811	858
70-74	281	327	351	407	434	465	698	830	733	702
75-79	180	213	249	269	314	340	440	589	662	542
80+	159	188	228	274	313	406	459	635	806	810
Females:										
0-19	3,803	3,611	3,566	3,475	3,294	2,848	2,669	2,436	2,208	2,068
20-64	7,121	7,797	8,222	8,575	8,935	9,465	9,026	8,207	7,719	7,064
65-69	454	495	576	587	590	764	1,044	1,139	928	981
70-74	352	418	460	537	550	595	903	1,077	926	887
75-79	252	306	368	408	480	500	654	895	976	796
80+	292	361	456	572	687	927	1,071	1,456	1,902	1,956
Total	24,342	25,677	26,894	27,798	28,443	29,341	29,623	29,012	27,683	25,864

	— Percent of Total —									
Males:										
0-19	16.4	14.8	13.9	13.1	12.2	10.2	9.5	8.8	8.4	8.4
20-64	29.0	30.2	30.4	30.7	31.2	32.0	30.3	28.2	27.8	27.1
65-69	1.6	1.6	1.8	1.8	1.8	2.2	3.0	3.4	2.9	3.3
70-74	1.2	1.3	1.3	1.5	1.5	1.6	2.4	2.9	2.6	2.7
75-79	0.7	0.8	0.9	1.0	1.1	1.2	1.5	2.0	2.4	2.1
80+	0.7	0.7	0.8	1.0	1.1	1.4	1.5	2.2	2.9	3.1
Females:										
0-19	15.6	14.1	13.3	12.5	11.6	9.7	9.0	8.4	8.0	8.0
20-64	29.3	30.4	30.6	30.8	31.4	32.3	30.5	28.3	27.9	27.3
65-69	1.9	1.9	2.1	2.1	2.1	2.6	3.5	3.9	3.4	3.8
70-74	1.4	1.6	1.7	1.9	1.9	2.0	3.0	3.7	3.4	3.4
75-79	1.0	1.2	1.4	1.5	1.7	1.7	2.2	3.1	3.5	3.1
80+	1.2	1.4	1.7	2.1	2.4	3.2	3.6	5.0	6.9	7.6
Total	100.0	100.0	100.0	100.0	100.0	100.0	100.0	100.0	100.0	100.0

NOTE: Components may not add precisely to totals because of rounding.

throughout the projection period, implying net immigration of 80,000 per year. The latter may be regarded as a "medium" level of net immigration: by historical standards, it is neither very high nor very low.

The above assumptions, in conjunction with the population reported in the 1981 census, allow us to calculate the size and age distributions of the population in future years. The results are summarized in Table 3 for the case in which the total fertility rate increases to 2.1, and in Table 4 for the case in which it decreases to 1.4. In each case the total population and its distribution among twelve age-sex groups are shown at five-year intervals for the period from 1981 to 2001, and at ten-year intervals thereafter, to the year 2051. The focus of attention is the older population, and greater age detail is therefore reported for this group than for the younger ones.

In the case of the higher fertility rate (Table 3), the total population is projected to grow throughout the entire period of seventy years, increasing by almost one-quarter between 1981 and 2001, and by another three-tenths between 2001 and 2051. The older population, however, increases much more rapidly, under the assumptions made here (and indeed, under a much wider range of assumptions). The population 65-and-over is projected to increase by more than 60 percent by the end of this century, and then almost to double in the fifty years following. In relation to the overall population, the population 65-and-over is projected to increase from about 9.7 percent of the total in 1981 to 12.8 percent by 2001, and to 19.5 percent by 2051. If the assumptions underlying this projection prove to be even roughly in accord with future developments, we can expect a very substantial relative increase in the older population in the decades ahead.

It is of interest to observe that the projected increases in the number of older women greatly exceed the projected increases in the number of older men. The reason is that mortality rates have fallen more sharply for women than for men in recent decades, and our projections assume that the trends will continue. Under the assumptions made, men 65-and-over will constitute 7.5 percent of the population in 2051 (compared with 4.2 in 1981), while women 65-and-over will constitute 12.0 percent (compared with 5.5 in 1981).

If fertility should continue to decline, as assumed in the second projection, which is reported in Table 4, the situation would look somewhat different. Even with fertility held well below the replacement level, the overall size of the population would continue to grow until the second or third decade of the next century: by 2021 it would be more than one-fifth larger than in 1981. The growth results mostly from the fact that the 1981 population is a relatively young one, with a large fraction of women still in their childbearing years; thus, even though women, on average, have very few children in this projection, the number of births still exceeds the number of deaths for a period of several decades. However, the growth proceeds at a much slower pace than in the previous projection, and ceases altogether by

2021. If the low fertility rate were realized, the number of births would continue to decline year after year, and by 2021 there would be only 70 percent as many people under the age of 20 as there were in 1981.

Whether the assumed future fertility rate is "low" or "high" has no impact on the size of the population 65-and-over until the very end of the projection period, of course, but it does have a major impact on the *proportions* of older people in the population. Even by 2001 the population 65-and-over accounts for 13.6 percent of the total in the second projection (compared to 12.8 percent in the first), and by 2051 the proportion is an unprecedented 29.1 percent (compared to 19.5 percent). The future course of fertility clearly has major implications for social and economic policies.

A visual impression of the impact of the two fertility assumptions on the future age distribution of the population is provided by Figure 3. This figure contains "population pyramids," showing the percentage distribution of the population by age, for males and females separately. (Age is measured in two-year intervals on the vertical axis, with the youngest age group at the base; males are shown to the left, females to the right.) The top pyramid shows the population age-sex distribution as of 1981. Below it are four more pyramids relating to the projections. The first two are for 2001 and the next two for 2051. Of these, two are based on the replacement-level fertility assumption underlying Table 3 and two are based on the assumption of sustained lower fertility underlying Table 4.

It is evident from Figure 3 that the future course of fertility has very important implications for the age distribution of the population over the longer term: a movement towards replacement-level fertility would lead to a rectangular age distribution by 2051 (the third of the pyramids relating to the projection), whereas a movement towards lower fertility would result in a pyramid with a narrow base and very high proportions of the population at older ages.

The Future Labour Force

The labour force is, of course, drawn from the population. It is possible, therefore, to project the labour force once we have projected the population, provided that we have labour-force participation rates for the various age-sex groups.

We have made a set of assumptions about future participation rates. These assumptions involve an extrapolation of historical trends in the rates for each of nine age groups, separately for each sex. Roughly speaking, we have assumed further declines in the participation rates of young men, and a continuation of the tendency towards earlier retirement among men over 55. In the case of women, we have assumed a continuation of the trend towards lower participation rates among those under 20 and 65-and-over. For women 20-65, though, we have assumed a continuation for some years

FIGURE 3:
Population Pyramids, 1981, 2001 and 2051, Under Alternative Fertility Assumptions

Projection P-1: Age Pyramid, 1981

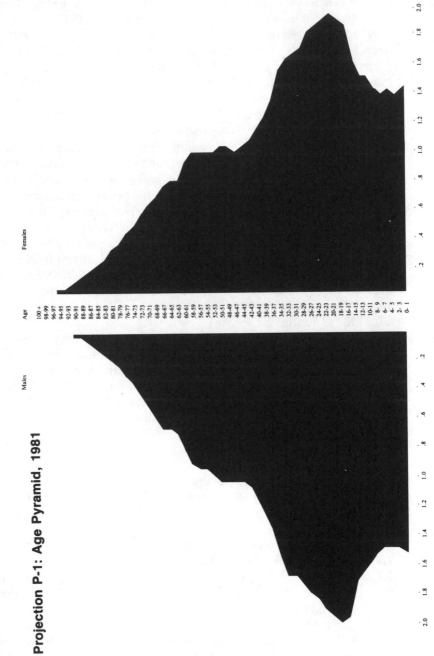

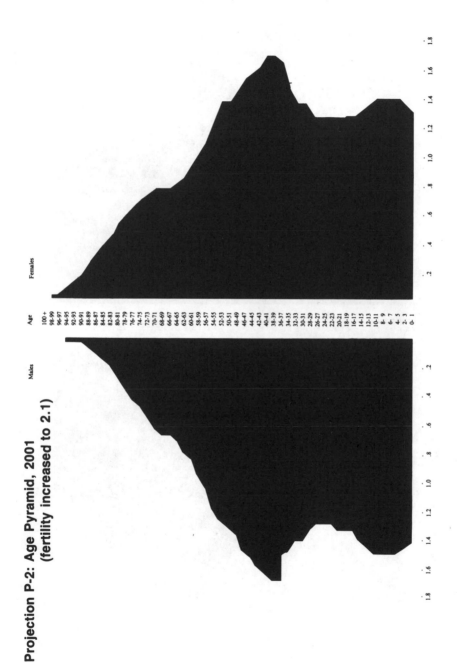

Projection P-2: Age Pyramid, 2001
(fertility increased to 2.1)

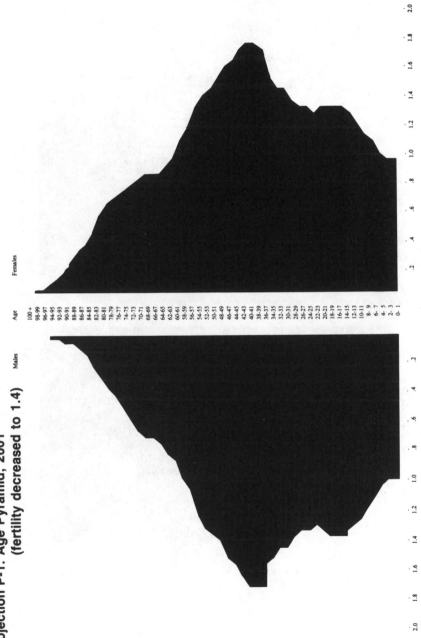

Projection P-1: Age Pyramid, 2001
(fertility decreased to 1.4)

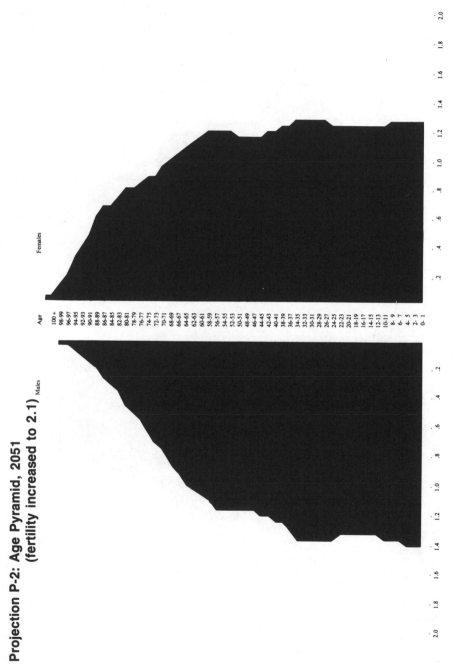

Projection P-2: Age Pyramid, 2051
(fertility increased to 2.1)

Projection P-1: Age Pyramid, 2051 (fertility decreased to 1.4)

Males

Females

Age

Fertility decreases to 1.4

NOTE: The horizontal scale indicates percent of total population.

to come of the recent strong increases in participation rates. For all ages and both sexes, the rates are assumed not to change after the year 2001.

The results of these assumptions, in terms of the size and age-sex distribution of the labour force, are reported in Table 5 for the case of a fertility increase and in Table 6 for the case of a decrease. With higher fertility the overall labour force is projected to grow by some 30 percent by 2001, and by a further 18 percent by 2051. In the earlier period, the female labour force is projected to grow by about 45 percent, the male labour force by about 20 percent; in the later period, the proportionate increases are 17 percent for females and 20 percent for males. The proportion of the labour force under age 45 decreases after 1986 in this projection, while that over 45 increases, at least until the end of the first decade of the next century, indicating an increase in the average age of members of the labour force. The labour force 65-and-over is projected to change little for some years, in spite of the projected increases in the number of older people, a consequence of the declining male participation rates in this age group. Only after the turn of the century, when (by assumption) the participation rates cease to decline, does the older component of the labour force start to grow.

The alternative fertility assumption has little impact on labour force size until early in the next century, but then the impact is substantial, and increases with time: by the end of the projection period the overall labour force is less than two-thirds as large under the lower fertility assumption as under the higher one. Furthermore, a larger proportion of the labour force is 45-and-over in the lower fertility case. It is evident that the future course of fertility does, in the longer term, have substantial implications for the overall size of the labour force, and hence for the overall productive capacity of the economy.

Dependency Implications of the Projections

The population and labour force projections have implications for the economic burden of dependency in future decades. To draw out these implications, we present, in Table 7, some calculated dependency ratios based on each of the projections.

Consider first the fertility-increase case. Much the same message is contained in both the ratios based on population and those based on the labour force. In general, the youth-dependency ratio declines between 1981 and 2011, and then remains roughly constant thereafter. The elderly-dependency ratio, however, rises sharply, more than doubling between 1981 and 2031, with most of the increase taking place after the year 2001. The net result of the fall in the youth ratio and the rise in the elderly one is a somewhat lower overall dependency ratio for the remainder of this century and through the first decade of the next, as compared with 1981, and then a pronounced increase in the following two decades. In spite of the increase, the

TABLE 5:
Projected Labour Force of Canada by Sex and Age, 1981 to 2051, Assuming the Total Fertility Rate to Increase to 2.1 by 1996

Sex and Age	1981	1986	1991	1996	2001	2011	2021	2031	2041	2051
	— Thousands —									
Males:										
15-24	1,667	1,509	1,337	1,291	1,334	1,533	1,517	1,573	1,691	1,700
25-44	3,397	3,895	4,288	4,322	4,226	3,879	4,164	4,391	4,453	4,696
45-64	1,921	1,991	2,169	2,499	2,858	3,546	3,412	3,194	3,459	3,600
65+	134	135	141	141	138	169	224	268	249	249
Females:										
15-24	1,432	1,338	1,199	1,172	1,227	1,409	1,394	1,444	1,553	1,561
25-44	2,314	2,924	3,436	3,626	3,645	3,320	3,563	3,753	3,804	4,010
45-64	1,065	1,217	1,418	1,778	2,147	2,617	2,425	2,289	2,495	2,567
65+	56	54	58	58	56	69	92	110	106	106
Total	11,985	13,063	14,046	14,885	15,632	16,541	16,791	17,021	17,811	18,489
	— Percent of Total —									
Males:										
15-24	13.9	11.6	9.5	8.7	8.5	9.3	9.0	9.2	9.5	9.2
25-44	28.3	29.8	30.5	29.0	27.0	23.5	24.8	25.8	25.0	25.4
45-64	16.0	15.2	15.4	16.8	18.3	21.4	20.3	18.8	19.4	19.5
65+	1.1	1.0	1.0	0.9	0.9	1.0	1.3	1.6	1.4	1.3
Females:										
15-24	12.0	10.2	8.5	7.9	7.8	8.5	8.3	8.5	8.7	8.4
25-44	19.3	22.4	24.5	24.4	23.3	20.1	21.2	22.0	21.4	21.7
45-64	8.9	9.3	10.1	11.9	13.7	15.8	14.4	13.4	14.0	13.9
65+	0.5	0.4	0.4	0.4	0.4	0.4	0.5	0.6	0.6	0.6
Total	100.0	100.0	100.0	100.0	100.0	100.0	100.0	100.0	100.0	100.0

NOTE: Components may not add precisely to totals because of rounding. The projected labour force figures include members of the armed forces; historical labour force figures presented in previous tables relate only to the civilian labour force.

TABLE 6:
Projected Labour Force of Canada by Sex and Age, 1981 to 2051, Assuming the Total Fertility Rate to Decrease to 1.4 by 1996

Sex and Age	1981	1986	1991	1996	2001	2011	2021	2031	2041	2051
					— Thousands —					
Males:										
15-24	1,667	1,509	1,337	1,291	1,329	1,257	1,039	1,020	923	833
25-44	3,397	3,895	4,288	4,322	4,226	3,866	3,737	3,328	3,031	2,864
45-64	1,921	1,991	2,169	2,499	2,858	3,546	3,412	3,182	3,060	2,712
65 +	134	135	141	141	138	169	224	268	249	248
Females:										
15-24	1,432	1,338	1,199	1,172	1,223	1,158	957	939	851	769
25-44	2,314	2,924	3,436	3,626	3,645	3,309	3,200	2,851	2,601	2,459
45-64	1,065	1,217	1,418	1,778	2,147	2,617	2,425	2,280	2,181	1,926
65 +	56	54	58	58	56	69	92	110	106	106
Total	11,985	13,063	14,046	14,885	15,623	15,991	15,085	13,977	13,002	11,916
					— Percent of Total —					
Males:										
15-24	13.9	11.6	9.5	8.7	8.5	7.9	6.9	7.3	7.1	7.0
25-44	28.3	29.8	30.5	29.0	27.0	24.2	24.8	23.8	23.3	24.0
45-64	16.0	15.2	15.4	16.8	18.3	22.2	22.6	22.8	23.5	22.8
65 +	1.1	1.0	1.0	0.9	0.9	1.1	1.5	1.9	1.9	2.1
Females:										
15-24	12.0	10.2	8.5	7.9	7.8	7.2	6.4	6.7	6.5	6.5
25-44	19.3	22.4	24.5	24.4	23.3	20.7	21.2	20.4	20.0	20.6
45-64	8.9	9.3	10.1	11.9	13.7	16.4	16.1	16.3	16.8	16.2
65 +	0.5	0.4	0.4	0.4	0.4	0.4	0.6	0.8	0.8	0.9
Total	100.0	100.0	100.0	100.0	100.0	100.0	100.0	100.0	100.0	100.0

NOTE: Components may not add precisely to totals because of rounding.

TABLE 7:
Projections of Selected Dependency Ratios, Canada, 1981 to 2051

Type of Ratio		1981	1986	1991	1996	2001	2011	2021	2031	2041	2051
Fertility Increases to 2.1											
Ratio to Population 20-64											
Population:	0-19	0.55	0.48	0.47	0.47	0.47	0.45	0.45	0.48	0.47	0.47
	65+	0.17	0.18	0.19	0.21	0.22	0.24	0.31	0.39	0.38	0.36
	0-19 and 65+	0.72	0.65	0.66	0.68	0.69	0.69	0.77	0.88	0.86	0.83
Ratio to Labour Force											
Population:	0-19	0.65	0.57	0.54	0.54	0.53	0.52	0.53	0.55	0.54	0.54
	65+	0.20	0.21	0.23	0.24	0.25	0.28	0.37	0.45	0.43	0.41
	0-19 and 65+	0.85	0.78	0.77	0.78	0.78	0.80	0.89	1.00	0.97	0.95
Non-Labour Force		1.03	0.97	0.94	0.93	0.92	0.96	1.06	1.14	1.11	1.10
Total Population		2.03	1.97	1.94	1.93	1.92	1.96	2.06	2.14	2.11	2.10
Fertility Decreases to 1.4											
Ratio to Population 20-64											
Population:	0-19	0.55	0.48	0.45	0.42	0.38	0.31	0.30	0.30	0.29	0.30
	65+	0.17	0.18	0.19	0.21	0.22	0.25	0.34	0.46	0.50	0.53
	0-19 and 65+	0.72	0.65	0.64	0.63	0.60	0.56	0.65	0.77	0.80	0.84
Ratio to Labour Force											
Population:	0-19	0.65	0.57	0.52	0.48	0.43	0.37	0.36	0.36	0.35	0.36
	65+	0.20	0.21	0.23	0.24	0.25	0.29	0.41	0.54	0.60	0.63
	0-19 and 65+	0.85	0.78	0.75	0.72	0.68	0.66	0.77	0.90	0.94	0.99
Non-Labour Force		1.03	0.97	0.91	0.87	0.82	0.83	0.96	1.08	1.13	1.17
Total Population		2.03	1.97	1.91	1.87	1.82	1.83	1.96	2.08	2.13	2.17

NOTE: Ratios are based on figures in Tables 3, 4, 5 and 6. Components may not add precisely to totals because of rounding.

overall dependency ratio at its projected peak in 2031 is no higher than it was in the early 1970s, whichever form of the ratio one looks at.

A movement towards sustained lower fertility would lead to a lower youth-dependency ratio in both the near-term future and beyond, and would cause the increase in the elderly-dependency ratio, which takes place after the turn of the century, to be considerably sharper than with sustained higher fertility. However, the decrease in the youth ratio more than offsets the increase in the elderly ratio until the fourth decade of the next century; a lower overall dependency ratio is the result.

While measures such as the ones we are looking at should be viewed merely as rough indicators of dependency, it appears that future increases in the older population of the order indicated in our projections would certainly not impose an unmanageable burden on the economy or on the working-age population.

Concluding Remarks

We have reviewed the growth of the population and the labour force over periods of many decades and have provided two sets of projections to the middle of the next century. The past eight decades have witnessed increases in the relative size of the older population, and in the years ahead we can expect further substantial increases. These increases will be especially pronounced in the first few decades of the next century if, as we have assumed in our projections, fertility rates do not again rise to high levels.

The impact on society and the economy of changes in the age distribution of the Canadian population is not investigated here. However, we note that, under the assumptions we have made, a projected decrease in the relative size of the youth population coincides with the projected increase in the relative size of the elderly component. Furthermore, the fraction in the middle years is projected to be slightly larger in the future than it has been in the past. These prospective changes, taken together, would seem to suggest that overall there will be no "crisis" associated with the expected general aging of the population, as some have suggested. Nonetheless, there are important implications in terms of educational, health care, pension and other requirements that should be anticipated as a basis for informed social planning and policy formulation.

Notes

[1]   It should be noted that even the more refined dependency ratios based on the labour force are not ideal. They neglect such considerations as differences in dependency costs among different non-labour force groups, differences in productivity among members of the labour force, the distinction between full-time and part-time workers, the size and composition of the nation's productive capital stock, changes in technology and productivity through time, and the omis-

sion of housework and volunteer work in the measurement of the labour force and the gross national product. Nevertheless, the ratios do serve a useful purpose when interpreted with appropriate caution.

2   There have, for example, been expressions of concern about the ability of pension funds, both public and private, to meet their future obligations, and concern, also, about the size of future health-care bills as the population grows older and increasing numbers of individuals reach ages that typically have high health-care requirements.

3   Fertility rates are the average numbers of births per woman of a given age. The childbearing range is taken to be from 15 to 49 years of age, inclusive.

4   The sets of assumptions are two of many on which projections might be based. For projections of the population based on other assumptions, see Denton and Spencer (1979, 1985) and Denton, Feaver and Spencer (1980).

5   The total fertility rate may be regarded as the average number of children per woman who would be born to a cohort of women by the end of their childbearing years, assuming none of the women was to die before the end of those years.

References

Denton, Frank T.
  1970   *The Growth of Manpower in Canada.* Ottawa: Statistics Canada.
Denton, Frank T., Christine H. Feaver and Byron G. Spencer
  1980   *The Future Population and Labour Force of Canada: Projections to the Year 2051.* Ottawa: Economic Council of Canada.
Denton, Frank T. and Byron G. Spencer
  1975   *Population and the Economy.* Toronto: D.C. Heath.
  1979   "Some economic and demographic implications of future population change." *Journal of Canadian Studies* 14(1): 81–93.
  1981   "A macroeconomic analysis of the effects of a public pension plan." *Canadian Journal of Economics* (November): 609–634.
  1983   "Population aging and future health costs in Canada." *Canadian Public Policy* 9(2): 155–163.
  1985   "Prospective changes in the population and their implications for government expenditures." In *Ottawa and the Provinces: The Distribution of Money and Power.* Toronto: Ontario Economic Council.
Denton, Frank T. and Sylvia Ostry
  1967   *Historical Estimates of the Canadian Labour Force.* Ottawa: Statistics Canada.
Foot, David K.
  1982   *Canada's Population Outlook: Demographic Futures and Economic Challenges.* Toronto: Lorimer.
Statistics Canada
  1976   *Population Growth in Canada.* Volume 5, Pt 1. 1971 Census Profile Studies, catalogue no. 99–701.
United Nations
  1973   *The Determinants and Consequences of Population Trends,* Vol. 1. New York.

3
Social Perspectives on Aging: Theoretical Notes

Victor W. Marshall
Department of Behavioural Science
University of Toronto

The word *theory* intimidates people and especially seems to intimidate students. This is a great misfortune because the term theory should really not instill fear in the hearts or minds of anyone. In our everyday life humans theorize all the time but we usually do so informally. We classify events and we form guesses about how different events "hang together." We use these guesses to make predictions about the future. Certain types of clouds and rain go together. If we note the accumulation of such clouds, we predict that it will soon rain. Many old people are religious. As people grow older, they will become more religious. Neither of these predictions is very good (and the second is almost certainly wrong), but they illustrate theoretical thinking on an everyday basis, that is perhaps not much less accurate than theorizing in the social sciences.

In our everyday theorizing, we are undisciplined. We learn a bit by experience but we don't really set our minds to the task of making our generalizations about relationships and our predictions precise. Theorizing in the social sciences is a lot like everyday theorizing but it puts a premium on precision. Coming up with theoretical ideas may be very undisciplined, but theoretical ideas, to be considered useful, have to be disciplined to precision.

In this chapter I provide some introductory notes on theory, mostly sociological, dealing with the social aspects of aging. A systematic or comprehensive coverage of theory is not intended. Reference is made to theoretical issues raised in various chapters of this book and to other theoretical work in this area. I attempt to describe the major theoretical foci that, in my judgment, currently characterize Canadian social science theory in aging. My own theoretical biases will be apparent. A simple classification scheme will emphasize the similarities and differences between major theoretical approaches. Selected individuals and theoretical foci will be placed in this scheme. All classification is arbitrary but this exercise will hopefully show the diversity and richness of theory and theorizing in Canadian gerontology. Prior to engaging in classification, however, some general comments will be made about theory.

What Is Theory?

Turner offers a useful discussion of what theory is. He says (1982:2) "theory is a mental activity. It is a process of developing ideas that can allow us to explain why events should occur." More formally, Gibbs (1972:5) describes a theory as "a set of logically interrelated statements in the form of empirical assertions about properties of infinite classes of events or things." There is a difference between Turner's and Gibbs' definitions of theory. Turner sees theory as an activity directed towards understanding. Gibbs is more restrictive. Understanding must unfailingly be tied to empirical statements, that is, to measured properties of the observed world. Gibbs is more purely "positivistic,"[1] resting his notion of theory on the natural sciences.

Sociology, however (and the same may be said for the social sciences in general), arose as part of but also in reaction to the natural sciences. Sociology is still split into two main groups, those who seek a "natural science of society" and those who believe such a quest is futile. This raises certain problems for the development of theory.

Sociology, Weber says,

> . . . is a science concerning itself with the interpretive understanding of social action and thereby with a causal explanation of its course and consequences. We shall speak of 'action' insofar as the acting individual attaches a subjective meaning to his behavior — be it overt or covert, omission or acquiescence. Action is 'social' insofar as its subjective meaning takes account of the behaviour of others and is thereby oriented in its course.
>
> (Weber, 1978:4)

If Weber's view of sociology is to be accepted (and I believe it should be accepted), then we want a science that is capable of providing *causal* accounts of *meaningful* behaviour. Attempts to develop a science have not been highly successful. For example, in regression analyses conducted by sociologists, the investigator is often happy if he or she is able to predict the outcome on some dependent variable (e.g., the decision to retire) successfully as often as 25 percent of the time. What are we to make of the failure to predict accurately 75 percent of the time? Is this failure due to the imprecision of our "science" or to the nature of that which is being studied?

If human social life cannot be reduced to law-like regularities and described with precision, the reason is not a failure of imagination on the part of social scientists but rather has to do with the subject matter. The problem is that human beings are creatures capable of exercising some degree of choice. Theories, to prove adequate to their subject matter, have to take into account this fact. People do not simply *react* to external stimuli; they *act* on the basis of meanings they attach to stimuli. Their action is social (in the Weberian sense) insofar as it takes account of the behaviour of others. This implies that any theory that assumes "strong" determinism is likely to be unfaithful to the social world.

There is no question, however, that social life is more patterned than not; else chaos would reign more pervasively than it does. The social sciences have been established on the assumption that there is at least some degree of patterning in social life. There is not in fact a Hobbesian "war of each against all." Anyone who has driven an automobile on a highway will recognize that there are aspects of a war of each against all in that form of social life but that, for the most part, people cooperate with one another sufficiently so that most people reach their destinations safely. When driving on the freeway, we *are* in fact interested in the unique conduct of others (the car that is now tailgaiting us) but for the most part our own driving actions and reactions rest on typified predictions that certain kinds of drivers are likely to behave in certain typical ways (most drivers will maintain safe driving distance, cars that are signalling a turn will eventually attempt to make a turn, etc.). Such typefications represent theorizing.

If theorizing is recognized as embodying typefication, then it is easy, and useful, to note the important use of metaphor in social theorizing. We try to understand social life by showing how it is like something we already understand. In the social sciences, this has led more positivistic scholars to see social life as "like" a machine or a biological organism or system; other scholars, who have emphasized that social life is shaped in part by human characteristics that are quite distinct from physical, chemical or biological nature (such as our ability to use language and to exercise choice), have looked elsewhere for metaphors. The anthropologist, Clifford Geertz, has put this well. He notes that

> . . . theory, scientific or otherwise, moves mainly by analogy, a 'seeing-as' comprehension of the less intelligible by the more (the earth is a magnet, the heart is a pump, light is a wave, the brain is a computer, and space is a balloon) . . . . the instruments of reasoning are changing and society is less and less represented as an elaborate machine or a quasi-organism and more as a serious game, a sidewalk drama, or a behavioral text. (Geertz, 1983:22-23)

Gibbs' definition of theory, noted above, is therefore too restricting in suggesting that theory makes *logical* statements about the relationship between concepts and *infinite classes of events*. The events we wish to understand through theory may be quite context-specific rather than infinite, and the logical relations between conceptual statements and statements about the empirical world may call for a wide variety of logics (certainly not just Aristotelian logic).

In a general sense we may say that a theory is a set of logically related statements that purports to describe the relationship between variables. But theories need not be stated in formal, deductive logic in order to be called theories. The building blocks of theories are concepts, variables and hypotheses. A *concept* "is an abstract generalized idea about an object or phenomenon" that "provides a common means of communication among scientists interested in a similar phenomenon" (McPherson, 1983:107). In social gerontology, terms such as "role," "disengagement" and "retirement" are concepts. Concepts are based on definitions but to be useful for theory they must be translated to *variables*. A variable is a concept to which more than one value can be assigned.[2] For example, disengagement might be defined as a variable in terms of the change in the number of social roles in which an individual is embedded. From a finite list (spouse, parent, worker, etc.), a number can be assigned to any individual that reflects the difference between role-embeddedness at two points in time.

A *hypothesis* is a statement that describes the relationship between two or more variables. An example would be "The greater the age, the greater the disengagement." A *theory* is a set of two or more logically related hypotheses. How the propositions are related to one another may be left quite open. Turner (1982) distinguishes three types of relationships between propositions: axiomatic, causal and typological. These are referred to as "formats" by Turner (1982:8-11), whose views are drawn on here.

Axiomatic formats begin by establishing scope — the conditions for which the theory applies (e.g., "in all modernized societies," "among women but not men)." Then, statements about the relationships between variables are stated in a hierarchical manner at the top of which are axioms, highly abstract statements from which all other statements (propositions) are logically derived. Axioms should be intuitively plausible and are assumed to be "law-like" in the sense that the derived propositions have not been disconfirmed by evidence. There are few attempts at axiomatic theorizing in social gerontology, although the activity theory of aging has been formulated in such terms by Lemon, Bengtson and Peterson (1972).

Causal formats are much more common in sociology and in social gerontology. Hypotheses asserting causal ordering are not themselves hierarchically ordered as derivatives of axioms. Causal formats are evident in the much-used path-analytic models frequently found in the literature and in regression models such as are employed by McDonald and Wanner in Chapter 14 of this volume to predict retirement. The model predicting future health care costs in Chapter 28 of this volume, by Denton, Li and Spencer, is a complex example of a causal format.

Typological or classificatory formats are not based on propositions (although they can lead to them) but instead attempt to understand a phenomenon by placing it in a comparative context, in categories that are ordered in relation to one another. Turner (1982:8) gives as examples the periodic table in chemistry or the Linnean classification of species in biology. While classification is, strictly speaking, solely descriptive, it often leads to theoretical questions and is antecedent to explanation (you have first to describe that which you wish to explain). Classification also contributes to explanation by enhancing "understanding," which Weber argues is as necessary to explanation as is causal ordering.

Classification almost always implies causation. For example, when Tindale classifies sources of job strain as either class-related or age (seniority) related, in Chapter 10 of this volume, he implies that class and age have discernibly different causal implications. When Rosenthal, in Chapter 17, uses a typology to organize information about aging and intergenerational relations, she inevitably evokes implicit, if not explicit, hypotheses to the effect that certain aspects of family life are causally linked.

If yet one more statement about the nature of theory may be permitted, it may be argued that, at a most general level, the term theory can be used to refer to *any disciplined* process of describing events in the world. The discipline need not stem from application of the rules of positivistic science but there must be adherence to standards of conceptual (definitional) and logical precision. In addition, in the social sciences, an empirical reference is necessary. There must be definable contact with a putatively real world. We are not spending our time speculating about unicorns or angels; rather we start with the *assumption* that a world exists independently of our consciousness of it. Theory becomes a way that we can all achieve a disciplined way of talking about that world.

The Scope of Theorizing in Aging

The social study of aging or, as it is sometimes called, social gerontology, should only incidentally deal with old people. The social study of aging deals properly with the ways in which age and changes in age become consequential for social life and, conversely, with the ways in which aspects of social life become consequential for aging. But aging can usefully be considered both as individual and as population aging. The passage of time leads to changes in individuals, referred to as aging. On the other hand, when we speak of the aging of a population we refer to changes in its age composition. We need, then, to deal with the ways in which both individual and population aging impact on other aspects of social life and the ways in which social life impacts on both individual and population aging.

An example may be useful. The single most important cause of changes in the age structure of a population has, throughout most of history, been changes in fertility; thus paradoxically, the study of aging cannot ignore those social processes related to fertility. If we wish to predict the age structure of a population thirty or forty years from now, we have to study current fertility behaviour. This extreme example underlines the point that aging and age-related processes cannot be adequately comprehended without taking a much broader focus than a focus on the aged alone.

It follows from this that any attempts to develop "theories of aging" are not likely to be highly successful. Rather, social scientists interested in aging are likely to do best if they draw on the most fruitful or the most promising theoretical developments in the social sciences. Old people are, after all, people. Special theories ought not to be required to account for their behaviour. Similarly, age structure is but an example of social structure. We ought to be able to gain insight into the nature and dynamics of age structure by turning to general theoretical insights about social structure available in the social sciences.

This is not to say that theorizing about aging and age structure has no place but only that it has no privileged place. We can hope, for example, that theoretical developments in the sociology or anthropology of aging will enrich general sociological and anthropological theory just as, for example, theorizing about the family and kinship or social class enriches general sociological and anthropological theory. But attempts to develop theories of age and aging in isolation from main currents of social science theorizing will no doubt prove fruitless.

The scope of our theorizing about age and aging should have to deal with both *age structures* and *aging processes*. Age structures can be characterized in a number of ways, as I will discuss below, but however characterized, they can be viewed as social contexts in which individuals live out their lives. The living out of those lives can be addressed through theories about the experience of aging to individuals as social beings (people grow old in the context of others who are also aging). Theories about such aging processes may be quite different from theories about the social causes or consequences of age structures, such as a theory that attempted to account for the rise of retirement as a social, age-related category or a theory that sought to account for the differential allocation of prestige or stigma to occupants of different age categories or groups.

A further differentiation might be identified. Much valuable theoretical work in aging deals with events and phenomena found in later life. Such work, while done by people who identify themselves as gerontologists, is not strictly speaking a theory of aging. Examples would be theorizing that attempts to predict depression or life satisfaction in older people, adjustment to retirement or geographical mobility among the aged. While we need theoretical understanding in such areas, such work can be distinguished from attempts to identify the ways in which age becomes an organizing principle in individual or in social life or to identify ways in which individuals or other social units change over time.

Probably few people, mainly in academia, take the study of aging, in the above sense, as their primary interest. Little of that work is reflected in this volume, which instead deals with very general social phenomena *in the contexts of an aging society and individual aging*. The chapters are tied together by their substantive focus on age and aging.

Major Theoretical Dimensions

Theories in the sociology of aging have been categorized in many different ways. For present purposes, a classification of theories along two distinct dimensions is useful. The first differentiates theories on a "macro" versus "micro" dimension; the second differentiates "normative" from "interpretive" theories. Any theory can be placed simultaneously in these two dimensions.

The micro level of analysis is concerned with the individual and with the individual in social interaction. The macro level of analysis is concerned with social structure that provides the context for individual lives and social interaction. Just where to draw the distinction is somewhat arbitrary. McPherson (1983) defines "macro" much more widely than I do, placing family relationships, for example, in the macro category. McPherson also includes within the micro category biological and physical systems which are not of direct concern to social scientists (although they are often brought into gerontology through interdisciplinary research).

While most theoretical approaches are confined in scope to either the micro or macro level of analysis, I would argue that ideally micro-level phenomena should be interpreted in terms of macro-level contextual features and that, conversely, macro-level phenomena should be viewed in light of their significance for and impact on micro-level phenomena. This is a point strongly made by C. Wright Mills (1959) who urged that the sociologist study the relationship between biography and history and private troubles and public issues. While social psychology is often identified as equivalent to "micro-sociology," again I would argue that good social psychology will relate individual behaviour and social interaction among small numbers of individuals to wider contexts and social structures.

Cross-cutting the macro-micro distinction is another continuum in which theories may be seen as ranging from "normative" to "interpretive." I have described this distinction at length elsewhere (Marshall, 1986a, 1985, 1980a, 1980b) and it has been described in a number of gerontological (Breytspraak, 1984; Dowd, 1980; McPherson, 1983) and general sociological (Bernard, 1983; Dawe, 1970; Wilson, 1970) sources. Therefore, the distinction will be only briefly made here. Wilson sees the normative perspective as consisting of two major ideas; that interaction is rule-governed and that sociological explanation is essentially deductive in form, following the model of the natural sciences (Wilson, 1970). These assumptions are not made in the interpretive perspective.

Various scholars see this contrast as rooted in different theoretical traditions in the social sciences, but most agree that structural-functionalism exemplifies the normative approach. The interpretive perspective draws strongly from Weber's definition of sociology as seeking to formulate *meaningful* explanations of causal relationships, seeking "interpretive understanding." The symbolic interactionist and phenomenological traditions are important foundations of the interpretive perspective.

Dawe (1970) has distinguished between the "sociology of order" and the "sociology of control," paralleling the normative-interpretive distinction. Structural functionalism again exemplifies the sociology of order. It gives priority to the social system over the individual, argues that widespread consensus over norms is typical in societies and that socialization processes are efficient enough to ensure adherence to societal norms, which become not just regulative but *constitutive* of the self. In contrast, the sociology of control views society as "the creation of its members; the product of their construction of meaning, and of the action and relationships through which they attempt to impose that meaning on their historical situations" (Dawe, 1970: 216).

Whereas people are viewed as "voluntaristic" or exercising choice within the interpretive perspective, in the normative perspective their choices are seen as highly constrained. Even within the interpretive perspective, people are not assumed to have high degrees of freedom of choice. Choice can only be made when there exists a field of options. Social structure places severe limits on choices — the class dimension of social structure being an obvious example — and, moreover, in any given field of choice more than one individual might seek to make the same choice in an environment of limited choices. Within the interpretive perspective, then, people are seen as "strategic" in their actions. They are viewed as goal-seeking, intendedly-rational creatures who actively pursue their goals using a variety of devices that often place them in conflict with others. While different interpretive theorists vary in the extent to which they see social life as smooth and consensual or characterized by conflict, most see conflict as a normal aspect of social life. For this reason, the interpretive perspective in social psychology is in assumptive agreement with the conflict perspective at the macro level of analysis.

Conflict theory takes many forms and is variously traced to Weber's sociology of domination and Marxian theory. Simmel's sociology, which is recognized as an important influence on symbolic interactionist thinking, is also described as a form of conflict theory (Bernard, 1983). All conflict theories, however, are likely to see conflict, rather than consensus, as the normal state of affairs. For a conflict theorist, consensus or stability would be deemed unusual, needing an explanation. The nature of that explanation usually postulates domination of one social unit (a group, class, faction or individual) by another. Such domination may result from brute force, the institutionalization of power (authority) or the manipulation of ideology (e.g., state-engineered fostering of "false consciousness" or control over information as a means of manipulation). As Collins (1985:47) notes of conflict theory,

> Its main argument is not simply that society consists of conflict, but the larger claim that what occurs when conflict is not openly taking place is a process of domination. Its vision of social order consists of social groups and individuals trying to advance their own interests over others whether overt outbreaks take place in this struggle for advantage.

In contemporary sociology, and in the sociological analysis of aging, tremendous diversity is found among those who share the above view. Some political economists, for example, suggest that the major forces that structure social life emanate from the dynamics of the mode of production, the ways in which social relations are structured by technology and the productive process. Others, who also see conflict and domination as pervasive features of social life, emphasize the role of ideology in the maintenance of domination.[3] Some political economists conduct their analyses only at the level of social structure while other conflict theorists seek to relate social structure to individual biography. If such bridging between macro and micro is attempted, the conflict theorist is likely to opt for a theoretical approach from the interpretive perspective because its assumptions of conflict at the micro level are consistent with the assumption of conflict at the macro level.

I have outlined two dimensions that classify social science theories, as applicable to the field of aging. Below, I divide each dimension into three categories. Classifying any analysis on these dimensions will place it in one of nine categories. Three cautions are in order about the use of such a classification. First, the typology is *heuristic* only. It is designed solely to facilitate understanding (it is a "typological or classificatory format" as discussed in an earlier section). Like all classifications, it is likely to be rough around the edges. Few analyses are couched "purely" in any one of these nine categories. This is particularly true since three of them are considered "linking" between the micro and macro levels of analysis and three of them are considered "bridging" between the normative and interpretive perspectives. Alternative formulations, even of these dimensions, might have employed fewer or more categories, leading to simpler or more complex typological formats.

As a second caution, a given analyst should not be assumed to be consistently classifiable over time. Some scholars are eclectic and shift theoretical perspectives as they move from topic to topic. Some fail to see logical inconsistencies (e.g., it is logically inconsistent to take a conflict theory position at the macro level and a normative position at the micro level, or vice versa). Some people change their mind. The better scholars sharpen and hone their theoretical analyses over their research careers and this is likely to lead to changes in theoretical approach.

CHART 1:
A Taxonomy of Theoretical Perspectives in Aging and the Social Sciences

	MICRO	LINKING	MACRO
N O R M A T I V E	Functionalist role/ socialization theory Activity theory Developmental Life Span theory	Disengagement theory Environmental theory Social Clock perspective	Modernization theory Age Stratification theory Conventional Social Anthropology, Macro-economic and Demographic theory
B R I D G I N G	Generational Solidarity framework Network theory Exchange theory Continuity theory	Life Course perspective Systems perspective	Interest Group theory
I N T E R P R E T I V E	Career and Status Passage theories Identity and Labelling theory Dramaturgical perspective Phenomenology	Critical theory Subculture of aging theory Generational Conflict perspective Symbolic Anthropology	Political Economy approaches Conflict theory

A third caution is that many specific empirical analyses are not readily classifiable because the link between theory and analysis is not always explicit[4] or the research may never have been formulated in theoretical terms. Several chapters in *Aging in Canada: Social Perspectives* are highly atheoretical in this explicit sense, although one can argue that an implicit theory can always, in principle, be drawn from such works.

With these cautions in mind, Chart 1 may be used to place some of the major social science theoretical approaches found in the field, many of which are also represented at various places in this book. It is not my intention to examine each cell of this typology in detail. Rather, the remainder of this chapter will be restricted to providing a sketch of major trends in Canadian theory, including a placement of some key Canadian works in terms of the typology.[5]

In the introduction to the first edition of *Aging in Canada: Social Perspectives* (Marshall, 1980b:3), I said that

> . . . theory in this country is, thankfully, taking something of a different tack than has been dominant in the major bastion of social gerontology, the United States. The little discussion in this book about such theoretical issues as the debate between "activity theory" and "disengagement theory," or the "role-less role of the aged" is, on the whole, critical of such theory. . . . In general, theory about aging in Canada is more structural, collectivisit and historically grounded than the predominately attitudinal, individualistic and consensually oriented theorizing south of the border. . . . We have drawn heavily on Marxist and Weberian strains in social economic theory, and on the European phenomenologists and American symbolic interactionists for our social psychology.

I believe that this characterization is still generally true. However, the tremendous growth in the number of people conducting research in aging has increased the diversity among Canadian social gerontologists. This partly reflects the fact that some scholars more structural-functionalist in orientation have been drawn into the field. It may also be that theory is less explicit in the burgeoning flood of research reports than it had been in the early days when the field was being established. Research which is atheoretical, that is, purely empiricist work, usually implicitly assumes a determinism more characteristic of the normative approach than the interpretive.

Where theory is explicit, however, it is usually oriented against normative approaches and frequently argues for interpretive approaches which, at the macro level, involve one form or another of conflict theory. For example, Marshall and Tindale (1978-79) and Marshall (1981) critiqued the "sociology of happiness" of activity and disengagement theory which seemed to find nothing more interesting to try to explain than how happy people are. Most Canadian scholars have tried to explain other dependent variables than happiness or, recognizing that happiness depends on good health and income security, they have been concerned with variability in those attributes.

At the micro level, Chappell, writing with Orbach, has recently provided a comprehensive outline of the potential of Meadian symbolic interactionism for studies in aging (Chappell and Orbach, 1986); and she has provided analyses within that framework (Chappell, 1978; Chappell, Strain and Blandford, 1986), drawing also on phenomenology.

Martin Matthews (1980) has employed the symbolic interactionist framework to understand identity in widowhood and in this volume she links this approach to the life course perspective. Tindale explicitly invokes the interpretive perspective in his account of seniority concerns among school teachers in Chapter 10 of this volume; in the first edition of *Aging in Canada*, he drew on identity theory and on the labeling perspective to enhance our understanding of old, poor men (Tindale, 1980). In both cases, he employs an interpretive perspective that emphasizes the place of individual aging in a wider, social class context.

Somewhat differently, Rosenthal and Marshall draw on phenomenological reasoning to describe the social reality of the "head of the family," a position that a majority of people say exists in their extended families and that has structural properties even though consensus on who occupies this position is not high (Rosenthal and Marshall, 1986; also see Rosenthal, 1985).

McPherson, in Chapter 12 of this volume, relates his findings to activity and disengagement theory, which are normative approaches at the micro and linking levels in my typology, but he moves towards the interpretive perspective when he favours continuity theory, an approach that emphasizes that people strive to provide meaning and continuity in their sense of identity as they move through the life course. Similarly, introducing a collection of original papers in the anthropology of aging and dying in Pacific societies, Counts and Counts note the usefulness of a variety of general theories, including disengagement theory, but they emphasize the interpretive position that ". . . old people are not passive recipients of the behaviour of others. The elderly people . . . negotiate their status; they attempt to exploit the advantages and minimize the weaknesses of old age; and they employ strategies designed to maintain and extend their authority" (Counts and Counts, 1985:20).

D'Arcy, in Chapter 21, presents a conceptualization of the "Mental Illness Process" that draws on the assumptions of the interpretive perspective, particularly the labelling theory of symbolic interaction. In the first edition, he described the interactionist perspective in greater detail as applied to mental illness labelling (D'Arcy, 1980).

The concept of career has been extensively employed by Canadian social gerontologists to understand age-related phenomena in the interpretive perspective. Marshall described the concept and argued its usefulness in the first edition of this book (Marshall, 1980b) and has applied it to understand the career of aging and dying (Marshall, 1980a, 1986b). Connidis (1982) used the concept, further specified by Spence and Lonner (1978-79; see also Spence, 1986) as the "career set," to examine the interaction of multiple careers engaged in by women, as they affect retirement adjustment.

The career notion provides a bridge to the macro level of analysis by way of the life course perspective (Marshall and Rosenthal, 1982, 1986). Gee examines the family life course, identifying structural changes in the family in relation to large-scale historical and structural factors, in Chapter 15; and Stone and Fletcher similarly invoke the life course perspective, particularly as it embodies aspects of historical demography, to understand changing household characteristics of the aged in Chapter 16.

Another bridge between micro and macro is found in the conceptualization of ethnic and aging subcultures. The question of whether the aged are a minority group has been examined by Abu-Laban and Abu-Laban in the first edition of this book (1980), and is reviewed again by Ujimoto in Chapter 7. In a broader context, as Ujimoto summarizes, age identification and ethnicity may interact in ways about which very little is known. Rosenthal (1983, 1986) and Holzberg (1982), as noted by Ujimoto in Chapter 7, have articulated the notion of ethnicity but Rosenthal in particular argues that both cultural (meaning identity) and structural aspects of ethnicity should be considered in any analysis.

Turning now to macro-theoretical considerations, despite a wide range of theoretical approaches, Canadian social gerontology has tended to ignore or to criticize normative approaches and to emphasize interpretive approaches such as conflict theory and the political economy perspective.

For example, modernization theory, an archetypically structural-functionalist and normative perspective that has been tremendously important for gerontology (see Cowgill, 1986, for a recent overview), is criticized in this volume by Vanderburgh (Chapter 6) as being too simplistic. Neysmith and Edwardh (1983) also criticized the modernization thesis and its use as an ideological formulation in the deliberations of the World Assembly on Aging held in 1982. Contrasting modernization theory with "dependency theory," a version of the political economy approach, they argue that modernization theory:

. . . blames underdevelopment on the characteristics of people, rather than on the economic and social relations which bind the Third World to the industrial world. We believe that it is dependency theory, which offers a global or world systems approach, that clarifies the dialectic among economic relations or capital accumulation, social organization and well-being or pathos in individual lives. It is the means by which we can understand why old people live as they do in Third World countries. (Neysmith and Edwardh, 1983:129-130)

Like modernization theory, the age stratification perspective has also come under criticism. This approach, centred on the work of Matilda White Riley and a number of associates, is rooted in structural functionalism (for reviews and critiques see Marshall, 1986a, 1981a; and for a recent systematic application of the approach see Foner 1986).

Marshall (1983 and Bengtson, Cutler, Mangen and Marshall, 1985) has criticized the age stratification perspective for failing to distinguish between cohorts and generations. The term cohort is best used methodologically to organize data by year of birth or some other marker, while generation refers to a set of adjacent cohorts who share a common encounter with historical factors. Such encounters shape their life chances and possibly their consciousness in ways that can be seen as qualitatively different from those of adjacent sets of cohorts. The generation concept, taken principally from the sociologist Karl Mannheim, is social structural, in dramatic contrast to the non-structural cohort notion that underlies age stratification theory. Generations exist concretely as acting social units; cohorts exist synthetically as analytical categories only.

Building on this distinction, Tindale and Marshall (1980) developed a "generational conflict" perspective that began with insights from the age stratification perspective but explicitly introduced the concept of generation in this socio-historical sense to arrive at a social structural model that explictly rested on an assumption that conflict is an endemic feature of social interaction at the group level. The same principles of *generational* conflict have been extended to look at conflict between *age groups* by Tindale in Chapter 10 of this volume and by Marshall (1981b).

Thus, while the two major theoretical approaches that dominate macro-sociology in the United States, modernization theory and the age stratification perspective, play an important role as influences on Canadian theorizing, this role is largely to stimulate critical reaction.

Much research at the macro level of analysis, perhaps especially in the economics and demography of aging, is explicitly atheoretical. However, were the theoretical assumptions to be drawn out from this research, the underlying approach would be structural-functionalist and essentially deterministic or, in the typology used in this chapter, normative.

Menzies has classified one set of social theories as "interest" theories. These theories "assume that individuals or social institutions (e.g., firms) pursue their own interests or seek to exploit every situation to their advantage" (Menzies, 1982:78). In his classification people are assumed to act as if they were rational but full rationality is not assumed. Nor are people thought necessarily to recognize their own interests:

> People are seen as acting to further their own interests, partly as a result of rational calculation, partly out of emotional feeling, and partly from a moral sense of the righteousness of their course of action. Where the analysis focuses on institutions like business firms or political parties, interest theory assumes that the institutions' actions benefit the institution in some specified way. . . . (Menzies, 1982:78-79).

In the typology of this chapter, I have placed interest theory midway between normative and interpretive approaches because it makes no assumptions about whether people or larger social units pursuing their own interests will interact with other people or social units in harmony or in conflict. Social interaction may or may not be highly constrained by rules.

The analysis of professional rivalry by Schwenger, in Chapter 25, might be classified as an interest group theory. Although Schwenger does not label it as such, his analysis does assume various interest groups pursuing their objectives in a field of other interest groups. The analysis of long-stay patients by Aronson, Marshall and Sulman, in Chapter 27 of this volume, may also be seen as an interest group theory, although the interpretive and conflict approaches are emphasized in noting that the definitions of the "problems" of long-stay patients are social constructions of reality that serve various and conflicting interests.

Several examples have been given above of interpretive theorizing at the macro level in reaction to modernization and age stratification theory. To these examples may be added a few others. Shapiro and Kaufert, like Neysmith and Edwardh, have developed a critique of the ideological underpinnings of the United Nations World Assembly on Aging. Their critique, however, rests on an analysis of politics as involving manipulation of symbols by elites so as to assure compliance and loyalty of the governed (Shapiro and Kaufert, 1983). Government-sponsored conferences on aging, they maintain, use experts to promote definitions of the social problems of the aged that ignore substantive issues of the economic and social marginalization of the aged in our political economy (Walker, 1981) and legitimate token gestures to the aged and band-aid solutions to their problems. Their approach draws heavily on Edelman's conception of "symbolic politics" (1977) and Guillemard's (1977) analysis of French governmental ideological manipulation of the aged (the ideology of the "third age") in a manner similar to that employed by Estes (1979) in her analysis of the symbolic politics of the Administration on Aging in the United States.

The political economy of aging is a perspective favoured by many Canadian sociologists. A major strain of such theorizing, exemplified in the work of Myles (1984), focusses on the role of the state that has assumed major responsibility for the welfare of the aged due to the institution of retirement and public pension systems. In a major book, Myles takes the viewpoint that

> . . . the social dynamic of modern Western societies is a product of what are ostensibly the two main pillars upon which these societies are built: a capitalist economy and a democratic polity. . . . these two forms of social organization represent contradictory rather than complementary principles of social participation and distribution. (Myles, 1984:4)

The inherent contradiction in the welfare state lies in the societal need to promote capital accumulation while maintaining democratic principles. There is no harmony and little normative regulation in this view; apparent stability emanates from the exercise of power. The state, however, is in a period of crisis in juggling its social welfare responsibilities against its service to capital accumulation. With respect to the aged, however, this crisis is not caused by demographic changes such as population aging but is rather determined by politics: "The social, legal and political constituency we now call the elderly was created and given form by social, political and economic forces. . . ."(Myles, 1984:120).

McDonald and Wanner review a range of political economy theory variants in Chapter 14 of this volume and their own analysis tests the "dual economy" thesis that is important in general political economy analyses and which Dowd (1980) first applied to the situation of aging and retirement. They conclude that retirement cannot be understood adequately from solely an individualistic perspective but that such explanations should be related to structural features that are addressed with partial success through political economy approaches.

Conclusion

I have not intended to review the entire range of social science theories, let alone their exemplars, in this chapter. However, the examples given will hopefully enrich the meaning of the typology that, in turn, will hopefully further understanding of specific theoretical approaches and analyses. Canadian aging research from the social science approach appears to have a vitality in relation to theory. There is a great deal of research conducted without explicit reference to theory but, at the same time, discernible theoretical developments are evident. There is a commendable critical stance, a reluctance to accept extant theories unquestioningly and a willingness to draw on the best recent theoretical developments in the social sciences. No "grand theory" of aging is likely to appear; nor does anyone appear to want one. Instead, theoretical strands from a variety of sources are applied to the social situation of the aged, to the process of aging or to the analysis of the societal causes and consequences of population aging.

I have argued for a very general approach to theorizing that is not restricted to axiomatic or even to causal formats. While both these formats bring a useful rigour to the service of explanation, they tend to promote a somewhat conservative approach to theory development in that hypotheses follow from first premises in the axiomatic format and deductive reasoning is the form of logic underlying both. Typological formats are more promoting of inductive reasoning and it is only through this means that truly novel theoretical formulations will be arrived at.

If Canadian theorizing in social gerontology is to be judged comparatively, it may be seen as faring well because both theory and theorizing are actively pursued, because the subject of this theorizing is not highly restricted and because a wide range of theoretical perspectives, including the most promising perspectives in the social sciences, are being employed.

Notes

1   According to Martindale (1960:53) positivism "refers to that tendency in thought which rigorously restricts all explanation of phenomena purely to phenomena themselves, preferring explanations strictly on the model of exact scientific procedure, and rejecting all tendencies, assumptions, and ideas which exceed the limits of scientific technique." He also defines positivism as "that movement in thought which rests all interpretation of the world exclusively on experience" (1960:56).

2   The most useful discussion of the translation of concepts into variables of which I am aware appears in Hage (1972: Chapter 1).

3   Some Marxists view the term "conflict theory" as pejorative, referring to a 'liberal,' watered down version of Marxist theory that they argue is more 'radical' in directing the theorists to examine the 'roots' of all social relationships and the structure of domination in the material world of production.

4   For example, in a recent book, Chappell, Strain and Blandford (1986: Preface) say of their book that "For those familiar with the discipline, the perspective is unmistakably symbolic interactionism. It is, though, a symbolic interactionism learned through the actual writings of George Herbert Mead. . ." However, the book itself is not evidently symbolic-interactionist and is largely devoted to theoretically-neutral presentations of research data.

5   By consulting the index to this book, readers can find the location of discussion of many of these approaches.

References

Abu-Laban, Sharon and Baha Abu-Laban
    1980   "Women and the aged as minority groups: A critique." Chapter 7, Pp.
        63-79 in Victor W. Marshall (ed.), *Aging in Canada: Social Perspectives.*
        Toronto: Fitzhenry & Whiteside.

Bengtson, V.L., N.E. Cutler, D.J. Mangen and V.W. Marshall
    1985   "Generations, cohorts and relations between age groups." Chapter 11, Pp.
        304-338 in R. Binstock and E. Shanas (eds.), *Handbook of Aging and the*
        Social Sciences, 2nd Edition. New York: Van Nostrand Reinhold.

Berger, Peter
    1963   *Invitation to Sociology.* Garden City, New York: Doubleday Anchor
        Books.

Bernard, Thomas J.
    1983   *The Consensus-Conflict Debate: Form and Content in Social Theories.*
        New York: Columbia University Press.

Breytspraak, Linda M.
    1984   *The Development of Self in Later Life.* Boston: Little, Brown.

Chappell, Neena L.
    1978   "Senility: Problems in communication." Pp. 65-86 in Jack Hass and
        William Shaffir (eds.), *Shaping Identity in Canadian Society.* Englewood
        Cliffs, New Jersey: Prentice-Hall.

Chappell, Neena L., and Harold L. Orbach
    1986   "Socialization in old age: A Meadian perspective. Chapter 3, Pp. 75-106 in
        Victor W. Marshall (Ed.), *Later Life: The Social Psychology of Aging.*
        Beverly Hills: Sage.

Chappell, Neena L., Laurel A. Strain and Audrey A. Blandford
    1986   Aging and Health Care: A Social Perspective. Toronto: Holt, Rinehart and
        Winston.

Collins, Randall
    1985   *Three Sociological Traditions.* New York: Oxford University Press.

Connidis, Ingrid
    1982   "Women and retirement: The effect of multiple careers on retirement ad-
        justment." *Canadian Journal on Aging*, 1 (3 and 4): 17-27.

Counts, Dorothy Ayers, and David R. Counts
    1985   "Introduction: Linking concepts aging and gender, aging and death."
        Chapter 1, Pp. 1-24 in D.A. Counts and D.R. Counts (eds.), *Aging and its*
        Transformations: Moving Toward Death in Pacific Societies. Lanham,
        New York and London: University Press of America.

Cowgill, David O.
    1986   *Aging Around the World.* Belmont, California: Wadsworth.

D'Arcy, Carl
    1980   "The manufacture and obsolescence of madness: Age, social policy and
        psychiatric morbidity in a prairie province." Chapter 16, Pp. 159-176 in
        Victor W. Marshall (Ed.), *Aging in Canada: Social Perspectives.* Toronto:
        Fitzhenry & Whiteside.

Dawe, Allan
   1970   "The two sociologies." *British Journal of Sociology,* 21 (207-218).
Dowd, James J.
   1980   *Stratification Among the Aged.* Monterey, California: Brooks/Cole.
Edelman, M.
   1977   *Political Language: Words that Succeed and Policies that Fail.* New York: Academic Press.
Estes, Carroll L.
   1979   *The Aging Enterprise.* San Francisco: Jossey-Bass.
Foner, Anne
   1986   *Aging and Old Age: New Perspectives.* Englewood Cliffs, New Jersey: Prentice-Hall.
Geertz, Clifford
   1983   *Local Knowledge.* New York: Basic Books.
Gibbs, Jack
   1972   *Sociological Theory Construction.* Hinsdale, Illinois: The Dryden Press.
Guillemard, Anne-Marie
   1977   "The call to activity amongst the old: Rehabilitation or regimentation." Pp. 80-88 in B. T. Wigdor (ed.), *Canadian Gerontological Collection* I. Winnipeg: Canadian Association on Gerontology.
Hage, Jerald
   1972   *Techniques and Problems of Theory Construction in Sociology.* New York: Wiley Interscience.
Holzberg, Carol S.
   1982   "Ethnicity and aging: anthropological perspectives on more than just the minority elderly." *The Gerontologist,* 22 (3): 240-257.
Kohli, Martin
   1986   "The world we forgot: A historical review of the life course." Chapter 9, Pp. 271-303 in Victor W. Marshall (ed.), *Later Life: The Social Psychology of Aging.* Beverly Hills: Sage.
Lemon, B.W., V.L. Bengtson and J.A. Peterson
   1972   "An exploration of the activity theory of aging: Activity types and life satisfaction among in-movers to a retirement community." *Journal of Gerontology,* 27 (4): 511-523.
Marshall, Victor W.
   1986a "Dominant and emerging paradigms in the social psychology of aging." Chapter 1, Pp. 9-31 in Victor W. Marshall (ed.), *Later Life: The Social Psychology of Aging.* Beverly Hills: Sage.
   1986b "A Sociological perspective on aging and dying," Chapter 5, Pp. 125-146 in Victor W. Marshall (ed.), *Later Life: The Social Psychology of Aging.* Beverly Hills: Sage.
   1985   "Aging and dying in pacific societies: implications for theory in social gerontology," Chapter 12, Pp. 251-274 in Dorothy Ayers Counts and

David R. Counts (eds.), *Aging and its Transformations: Moving Toward Death in Pacific Societies*. ASAO Monograph No. 10. Lanham, New York and London: University Press of America.

1983   "Generations, age groups and cohorts: Conceptual distinctions." *Canadian Journal on Aging*, 2 (2): 51-62.

1981a   "State of the art lecture: The sociology of aging." Pp. 76-144, in John Crawford (ed.), *Canadian Gerontological Collection III*. Winnipeg: Canadian Association on Gerontology.

1981b   "Societal toleration of aging: Sociological theory and social response to population aging." Pp. 85-104, in *Adaptability and Aging* 1 (Proceedings, IX International Conference on Social Gerontology). Paris: CIGS/ICGS.

1980a   *Last Chapters: A Sociology of Aging and Dying*. Monterey, California: Brooks/Cole.

1980b   "No exit: An interpretive perspective on aging." Chapter 6, Pp. 51-60 in Victor W. Marshall (ed.), *Aging in Canada: Social Perspectives*. Toronto: Fitzhenry & Whiteside.

Marshall, Victor W., and Carolyn J. Rosenthal

1986   "Aging and later life." Chapter 5, Pp. 133-162 in R. Hagedorn (ed.), *Sociology, 3rd Edition*. Toronto: Holt, Rinehart and Winston.

1982   "Parental death: A life course marker." *Generations*, 7 (Winter): 30-31, 39.

Marshall, Victor W., and Joseph A. Tindale

1978-   "Notes for a radical gerontology." *International Journal of Aging and Human Development*, 9 (2): 163-175.

79

Martindale, Don

1960   *The Nature and Types of Sociological Theory*. Boston: Houghton Mifflin

Martin Matthews, Anne

1980   "Women and widowhood." Chapter 15, Pp. 145-153 in Victor W. Marshall (ed.), *Aging in Canada: Social Perspectives*. Toronto: Fitzhenry & Whiteside.

McPherson, Barry D.

1983   *Aging as a Social Process*. Toronto: Butterworth.

Menzies, Ken

1982   *Sociological Theory in Use*. London: Routledge and Kegan Paul.

Mills, C. Wright

1959   *The Sociological Imagination*. New York: Oxford University Press.

Myles, John

1984   *Old Age in the Welfare State*. Boston: Little, Brown.

Neysmith, Sheila, and Joey Edwardh

1983   "Ideological underpinnings of the world assembly on aging." *Canadian Journal on Aging*, 2 (3): 125-136.

Rosenthal, Carolyn J.

1986   "Family supports in later life: Does ethnicity make a difference." *The Gerontologist*, 26 (1):19-24.

1985   "Kinkeeping in the familial division of labor." *Journal of Marriage and the Family*, 47 (4):965-974

1983   "Aging, ethnicity and the family: Beyond the modernization thesis." *Canadian Ethnic Studies*, 15 (3):2-16.

Rosenthal, Carolyn J., and Victor W. Marshall
1986   "The head of the family: Social meaning and structural variability." *Canadian Journal of Sociology*, 11 (2):183-198.

Shapiro, Evelyn, and Joseph Kaufert
1983   "The role of international conferences — a theoretical framework." *Canadian Journal on Aging*, 2 (2): 43-49.

Spence, Donald L.
1986   "Some contributions of symbolic interaction to the study of growing old." Chapter 4, Pp. 107-123 in Victor W. Marshall (ed.), *Later Life: The Social Psychology of Aging*. Beverly Hills: Sage.

Spence, Donald L., and T.D. Lonner
1978-   "Career set: A resource through transitions and crises." *International*
79   *Journal of Aging and Human Development*, 9: 51-65.

Tindale, Joseph A.
1980   "Identity maintenance processes of old poor men." Chapter 9, Pp. 88-94 in Victor W. Marshall (ed.), *Aging in Canada: Social Perspectives*. Toronto: Fitzhenry & Whiteside.

Tindale, Joseph A., and Victor W. Marshall
1980   "A Generational-conflict perspective for gerontology." Chapter 5, Pp. 43-50 in Victor W. Marshall (ed.), *Aging in Canada: Social Perspectives*. Toronto: Fitzhenry & Whiteside.

Turner, Jonathan H.
1982   *The Structure of Sociological Theory*. Georgetown, Ontario: Irwin-Dorsey Limited.

Walker, Alan
1981   "Towards a political economy of old age." *Ageing and Society*, 1 (Part 1, March): 73-94.

Weber, Max
1978   *Economy and Society, An Outline of Interpretive Sociology, Vol. 1*. Edited by Guenther Roth and Claus Wittich. Berkeley: University of California Press.

Wellman, Barry, and Alan Hall
1986   "Social networks and social support: Implications for later life." Chapter 7, Pp. 191-231 in Victor W. Marshall (ed.), *Later Life: The Social Psychology of Aging*. Beverly Hills: Sage

Wilson, T.P.
1970   "Normative and interpretive paradigms in sociology." Chapter 3, Pp. 57-79 in Jack D. Douglas (ed.), *Understanding Everyday Life*. Chicago: Aldine.

4

Psychological Processes in the Development of Late-Life Social Identity

Joan E. Norris
Department of Family Studies
and Gerontology Research Centre
University of Guelph

Gerontologists have devoted considerable research time and effort to explorations about social functioning in later life. The goal of this work has usually been to examine the relationship between social involvement and well-being. For example, a large body of literature concerns the connection between the size of an individual's social network and the extent of life satisfaction (e.g., Lowenthal and Robinson, 1976), and a number of studies examine the role of social support in promoting healthy adjustment to age-related life events (e.g., Kahn and Antonucci, 1980).

While such studies are useful in determining the predictors of global well-being in later life, they do little to further our understanding about social relationships themselves. This is particularly true if we are interested in the *developmental purpose* of social contact. We need to know more about how relationships develop and are maintained in old age, and more about the meaning and function of social interaction to normal psychological and social functioning in later life.

This chapter explores the issue of successful social functioning in later life by applying a life-span developmental perspective.

The Contextual Perspective of Life-Span Developmental Theory

An understanding of the basic themes of the life-span developmental perspective is necessary in order to determine how it can be used to create, as well as evaluate, research on social functioning in later life. This section explores the evolution of life-span developmental psychology from traditional developmental approaches.

The assistance of the Gerontology Research Centre, University of Guelph, and the Social Sciences and Humanities Research Council of Canada is gratefully acknowledged in the preparation of this chapter.

Traditionally, developmental theorists have stressed the importance of social experience for psychological growth (e.g., Piaget, 1967). Social interaction is thought to promote social, social-cognitive and cognitive skills (Hartup, 1983) by providing challenges to existing beliefs and knowledge. For example, early in their development, children regard others from their own egocentric perspective. For more socio-centred thinking to develop, there must be a stimulating social environment to provide accurate feedback about social judgments.

Despite this view that social contact promotes development, most developmentalists have remained firmly within an organismic theoretical framework. This proposes a "weak" interaction between internal and external factors to produce growth, but that the major contributors to such growth are biologically based mechanisms. Only when these are engaged can the social environment stimulate or modify the development of new ways of understanding the world, known as cognitive structures. Because of this theoretical position, researchers have hypothesized the existence of developmental invariants, patterns of growth that occur in a wide variety of cultures and contexts.

The search for invariance in social or psychological growth has proven frustrating. Researchers have often been unable to find evidence for hypothesized cognitive structures outside a particular context (Brandstadter, 1984), a problem of even greater concern recently as gerontologists have attempted to extend developmental theory to adulthood. As various researchers have discovered (e.g., Bielby and Papalia, 1975), older participants in studies of cognitive and social functioning tend to perform poorly, contrary to theories of irreversible, linear development. Indeed, their responses have at times been labelled "primitive," and questions about regression in abilities raised (Rubin, Attewell, Tierney and Tumolo, 1973).

Such problems with traditional developmental perspectives have contributed to advances in *life-span developmental psychology*. This view, as articulated by Baltes and colleagues (e.g., Baltes and Brim, 1979; Baltes, Reese and Lipsitt, 1980), states that individual growth cannot be considered in isolation from the social context. Further, it is proposed that development is the consequence of a "strong" interaction between intrinsic, biologically based factors and extrinsic, socially determined variables. Thus researchers are encouraged to consider the *complete* interdependence of individual factors, such as personality, and contextual variables, such as the social network, in understanding psychological functioning.

The life-span framework is particularly useful because it helps determine *which* variables may be most salient for development at a particular time. This explanatory power is accomplished, in part, by considering the events associated with chronological age. As Baltes et al. (1980) have noted, individuals must come to terms with various types of life events depending on their stage in the life course. Early in life, one must confront upheaval from age-graded life events, those that are strongly linked to chronological or biological age: for example, childbearing. Later one typically confronts history-graded events, those that are the product of a particular period in a particular culture: for example, wars. Finally, in late life one is often confronted with less typical, nonnormative events such as widowhood, and may be less susceptible either to biologically based developmental change or to widespread cultural influences.

The fact that different life events may change the course of development has also led life-span theorists to embrace the concept of "plasticity" (e.g., Brandstadter, 1984; Brim and Kagan, 1980; Pascual-Leone, 1983; Lerner and Busch-Rossnagel, 1981). This suggests that humans are, at any point in the life course, capable of a wide range of behaviours, provided that the necessary environmental conditions to elicit and support the behaviours are present. This viewpoint prevents a deficit focus on aging, where age differences are noted and losses tallied.

Implications for Social Development and Functioning

Within a dialectical, contextual perspective on development, there is understood to be a continual interplay between the needs and abilities of the organism and the demands and contributions of the environment (Riegel, 1973). This approach allows an analysis of the plasticity of social behaviour across various contexts; it also provides a means of understanding how older individuals can be the active producers of their own development (Lerner and Busch-Rossnagel, 1981). In this way Brim and Kagan's (1980) remark that "growth is more individualistic than was thought and it is more difficult to find general patterns" need not be seen as a barrier to understanding, but rather as affirming the use of a contextual perspective.

To understand social functioning in later life, the remainder of this chapter explores two general areas of research in the psychology of adult development and aging. In the first section the meaning and function of social relationships to older adults is examined, with a focus on the role of the social environment in producing a healthy sense of identity. The second section discusses the concept of social competence. Of particular concern will be the notions of behavioural flexibility and appropriateness across a variety of social settings.

The Meaning and Function of Social Relationships

In order to understand the nature and purpose of social interaction in later life, there must be a consideration of both family and nonfamily relationships within the framework of development across the life-span.

A large body of literature on the importance of social interaction in child-hood and adolescence underscores the importance of both peer and family relationships in promoting healthy cognitive, social and personality development. Work on parent-child relationships, for example, reveals that a secure bond between child and caregiver is vital to normal growth and the development of later relationships (see Maccoby and Masters, 1970, for a review of this literature). In fact, some theorists (e.g., Cairns and Hood, 1983) have proposed that this first significant attachment becomes the model for all subsequent relationships.

Researchers have also stressed the importance of nonfamily, peer rela-tionships in promoting development in childhood (see Norris and Rubin, 1984, for a review). Peers have been shown to enhance perspective-taking, mature moral judgment and communication skills early in life, as well as provide emotional security and support. Rejection by peers, or the inac-cessibility of peers, has been shown to predict a variety of developmental problems later in childhood and early adulthood (Hartup, 1983).

Family Relationships in Later Life

Attachment to family members in childhood, then, is obviously important, but what happens in later life? To understand the meaning and function of family interactions in later life, from a developmental point of view, two ex-amples of the literature on family relationships will be considered: the parent-child relationship, with particular reference to the frail elder and caregiving child, and the grandparent-grandchild relationship. Of particular concern is Hagestad's (1981) question "[How do] family members produce developmental milieux for one another?" In other words, how can the family promote or impede individual development?

1. The Parent-child relationship

In childhood, the major developmental issue within the family is the forma-tion and maintenance of secure attachment. In many ways, attachment is also the central issue to be considered in later life. With the onset of adolescence, the individual is faced with the task of separating from primary relationships with parents in order to become more autonomous. However, separation and individuation must not be a *total* process for the healthy development of self and social identity to occur. The adult must be prepared to maintain a delicate balance between personal independence and interdependence with others in the family network (Cohler, 1983).

In old age, this balance may be easily disturbed, especially if the indiv-idual becomes physically or mentally frail. The literature on caregiving families captures the ambivalence and strain that can result. On the one hand, families do not, contrary to popular belief, abandon their elders

(Shanas, 1979), but instead have considerable contact with them (Marcus and Jaeger, 1984). On the other hand, as Johnson (1983) has noted, there is a body of clinical literature that suggests that this contact can be burdensome.

Many recent studies reflect this latter view. The elderly are not seen to contribute to the developmental milieux of the family except to provide a problem to be "managed." The negative tinge of this research is apparent even from a cursory glance at its themes: strain among caregivers (Cantor, 1983); dealing with dependent elderly (Soldo and Myllyluoma, 1983); "helping" community-dwelling older adults with daily activities (Stoller and Earl, 1983); supplying financial aid to elders (Moon, 1983), and so on.

In view of the potential family problems associated with frailty in later life, it is not surprising that some older adults have difficulty preserving a strong and independent sense of self. As Kuypers and Bengtson (1983) have pointed out, the most difficult task for members of later-life families is to "maintain a sense of continuity in the face of fundamental changes in processes and structure." If conditions do not support an older family member's desire to remain "attached" to others, forced disengagement may result or, alternatively, the elder may begin to use less socially acceptable, but highly effective, techniques such as guilt induction in order to cement family bonds and restore feelings of power and control (Kalish and Knudtson, 1976).

A contextual theory compatible with life-span development, that of social construction (e.g., Wood, 1983), may shed further light on the meaning of withdrawn or manipulative behaviour in older family members. According to this perspective, certain social behaviours arise because of the need to maintain respect and esteem for oneself through the views of significant others. Esteem is the consequence of attaining a valued achieved position such as a career goal. Respect is the product of success in an ascribed position, such as family member, and as such is particularly important for older adults who may have lost access to achieved positions (Wood, 1983). Thus, if respect is variable or discontinuous, serious identity concerns may result: in this case, hollow or even empty identity following disengagement, or manipulative power-assertion tactics designed to force respect from family members.

A recent study on caregiving families (Forbes, 1985; Forbes and Norris, 1984) indicated that lack of respect is often a problem when multiple generations of a family cohabit. Families who managed to avoid or minimize such problems of identity were characterized by flexible boundaries. This flexibility permitted fluctuations in dependency and power, and input from other informal and formal support systems. Those with identity problems had rigid role relationships and accepted little assistance from outside the family system.

2. The grandparenting experience

Developmental issues involving social identity have been the focus of much of the grandparenting literature, as well. In fact, even in some of the very early literature, social scientists were concerned with the nature of the grandparenting relationship and its effects on individual development, usually the grandchild's (see Semple, 1985, for a review). In the early clinical literature, this effect was assumed to be negative; grandparents engendered family conflict. Indeed, one writer, Vollmer (1937) described the grandmother as a "pernicious influence." He did not speculate about the possible reciprocal influence of grandchild on grandmother, however!

More recent research reveals a varied pattern of perceived meaning and function on the part of the grandparent and grandchild. Now classic studies by Neugarten and Weinstein (1964) and Robertson (1977) have described older adults as having a number of possible reactions to the grandparenting role, ranging from emotional distance to a desire for surrogate parenting. Similarly, other researchers (Gladstone, 1985; Kahana and Kahana, 1970; Morgan, 1985; Pihlblad and Habenstein, 1964) have revealed that children's attitudes towards their grandparents are very much dependent on the family context and the children's developmental stage.

Studies in this area indicate that grandparenting can be potentially a significant, meaningful force in the lives of older adults — but they do little to explain variability in individual experiences. Some variability may be explained by easily quantifiable factors such as the sex of a grandparent (Fischer, 1983; McGreal, 1985) or the physical proximity of all family members (Harris, 1975). Nevertheless, general statements from such survey studies need further clarification. For example, Neugarten and Weinstein (1964) stated that "while 60 percent of respondents found the grandparenting role comfortable and pleasant, approximately one-third experienced difficulty in the role and expressed disappointment or referred to discomfort and strain or lack of positive rewards from the role." The researchers, however, did not attempt to account for this variability, or speculate about its effects on individual and family well-being.

Only by studying the individual in the social context of the family can we determine the developmental usefulness of the grandparenting experience. In a recent study (Norris and Tari, 1985), an attempt was made to understand grandparenting within a life-span developmental framework. In other words, what is the meaning of the experience within the context of other relationships, life events and activities? From a qualitatively focussed interview with recent grandparents, we found that many "young old" adults seemed to be in a period of psychosocial moratorium, rather like that experienced by adolescents (Erikson, 1963), and not actively engaged with children and grandchildren. They had strong ties to family members, but preferred to spend more time developing other interests than entertaining or teaching their grandchildren.

Seen from the contextual perspective of life-span development, this apparent complexity may tie together some of the disparate threads of earlier work. Many of today's healthy and relatively advantaged older people face the necessity of renegotiating roles and revising the self-concept as a means of coping with an extended period of old age (Hall, 1983). This would help to account for the variability attached to the grandparenting experience reported by other researchers. It is probable that at various points in later life, such as immediately postretirement, identity issues may be extremely salient. Thus, personal concerns may appear to have relatively more importance than family relationships.

The family is a potent influence in promoting or impeding development in old age. Beliefs about the self as a competent, social being may be undermined when issues of changing power and control are not negotiated successfully. It is clear that this often happens in caregiving families when older relatives become frail and dependent. However, it is also apparent that it might happen under more normal conditions — for example, when grandparents attempt to maintain some distance between themselves and their children and grandchildren. If family involvement is forced, other identity questions may remain unresolved. In the next section, the issue of resolving these social identity concerns through nonfamily, peer relationships will be addressed.

Peer Relationships in Later Life

As noted earlier, a large body of literature in child development stresses the importance of peers to healthy social functioning and the growth of the self, but the question of whether peers fulfill the same social developmental functions in adulthood as they do early in life has not been addressed directly. Nevertheless, there is suggestive evidence that peers are vital to well-being in later life (e.g., Shanas et al.,1968).

In an examination of the literature on peer relationships in old age, it is important to be clear about whom we regard as "peers." In the child-development literature, peers are considered to be age-mates, regardless of differences in demographic characteristics or in the nature of interactions. Research concerning early adulthood similarly indicates that age is still a significant factor in determining who are one's peers and one's friends (e.g., Newcomb, 1962). However, as young adults become less conforming and more independent in their thinking (Boyd, 1975), and as they experience a wider variety of life events, their peer group becomes increasingly differentiated and complex (Newcomb, 1962). Individuals who share similar interests, attitudes, occupations or histories may now be considered the young adult's peers.

Throughout most of the life course peers continue to be selected on the basis of similarity. For example, an age-graded event such as the birth of a child provides a new referent group: parents. Similarly, history-graded events such as war may create groups that adults consider as peers, even though they vary in age, sex or socio-economic status (Marshall, 1983). As well, nonnormative events such as divorce may provide an individual with peers of even greater variety. Only in late adulthood, when ties to former roles are weakened, may we see a return to considering age as the salient characteristic in defining one's peer group (Lowenthal and Robinson, 1976).

This reemergence of age as an important defining characteristic of peer relations may account for the tendency of gerontologists to focus on *age-mates* when investigating the social world of older adults. Early research in this area was primarily quantitative, focussing on the number of age-mates an individual reported having contact with, as well as the frequency of contact (see Lowenthal and Haven, 1968, and Snell, 1985, for reviews). The underlying assumption of this literature is that the more frequently an older person interacts with a broad range of peers, the more likely he or she is to have high morale. This assumption was apparently derived from activity theory (Maddox, 1963) in an effort to refute the less popular disengagement theory position (Cumming and Henry, 1961). The latter theory proposed that diminishing numbers of social contacts might be the best route to successful aging.

While this quantitatively oriented literature did not substantiate the basic tenets of disengagement theory, neither did it provide unequivocal support for the view that "more is better and closer is happier" (Kuypers and Bengtson, 1983). Attempts to account for variations in life satisfaction by assessing the magnitude of an individual's social world have generally been unsuccessful (Conner, Powers and Bultena, 1979). As Chappell (1983) has pointed out, these quantitative studies have been important in refuting the stereotypes of elderly people as alone, but have not been useful in determining which aspects of particular relationships are most rewarding.

Many gerontologists now concur with Conner et al. (1979) that "it is in the quality of the interactional experience that a broader understanding of adjustment to aging will ultimately be found." Early support for this position can be found in the often cited study by Lowenthal and Haven (1968) that suggested that having only one close friend or "confidant" is sufficient protection against some of the stresses of normal aging. This intriguing finding has spawned a recent body of research focussed specifically on *friendship* and its link to late-life morale and satisfaction. Generally this research has had two goals: to explore older adults' definitions of friendship and to investigate the connection between disclosure in a peer relationship and adjustment to old age.

Recently researchers have argued that too many studies have asked about friendship without clarifying this concept for older subjects or asking for *their* definitions. As Jerrome (1981) has noted, "even when carefully defined, the research worker's concept tends to be imposed on respondents in the context of a formal interview situation that takes little account of the range of subjective meanings attached to the terms." In view of this, a number of studies have focussed on the *function* of friendship as a means of understanding its *meaning* to the individual. Generally, findings indicate that friends fulfill two major functions: helping (e.g., Fischer and Oliker, 1983; Jerrome, 1981) and providing emotional support (e.g., Aries and Johnson, 1983; Luke, Norton and Denbigh, 1981; Perlman, Gerson and Spinner, 1978). As Matthews (1983) has indicated, many individuals, perhaps those best functioning, have friends who fulfill both major purposes.

The provision of emotional support by friends has been investigated in more detail in a small number of studies on the confidant relationship. Generally, this research supports Lowenthal and Haven's (1968) finding that having a friend to disclose intimate details of one's life to is positively related to satisfaction and adjustment in old age (e.g., Hess, 1979; Snell, 1985; Strain and Chappell, 1982; Weir, 1985).

The literature on friendship has also noted important differences among subgroups of the elderly, which may account for the varying reactions of older people to friendships in late life. The most significant findings suggest that there may be both age and sex differences in the meaning and function of friendships to older people. Recent work by Goldman and colleagues (Goldman, Cooper, Ahern and Corsini, 1981) and Richardson (1981) has indicated that older cohorts of elderly adults view intimacy as a less important feature of friendships than do younger cohorts. Other researchers (Aries and Johnson, 1983; Hess, 1979; Keith, Hill, Goudy and Powers, 1984) have reported that older men have less intimate relationships with friends than do women. Keith et al. (1984) have suggested that this sex difference indicates a preference for less intimacy on the part of older men.

There are still major gaps in our understanding of friendship relationships and their contribution to the maintenance of a healthy sense of self as a social being. Recent theoretical work on loneliness is helpful in filling in some of these gaps.

Loneliness has been characterized as a deficient social network (Perlman, forthcoming). Wood (forthcoming) has suggested that an individual's perception of his or her network as deficient is socially constructed—by the self and by society as a whole. The mechanism used in this construction is one of failed intersubjectivity: lonely people feel misunderstood and unable to understand others. This lack of shared understanding may lead to feelings of helplessness, isolation and loneliness. Compounding the problem may be the older person's interpretation of few social contacts as an indication that society *expects* the old to be lonely. Withdrawal, disengagement and further loneliness then become normative events (Kafer and Davis, 1984).

This contextual analysis, supported by other cognitively oriented approaches to social functioning (e.g., Olbrich and Thomae, 1978), helps to explain why a confidant is so important in later life, and why sheer numbers in a social network are unrelated to adjustment. As Mueller and Ross (1984) have theorized, changes in the self-schema with age (such as those caused by acceptance of the "lonely" label) may become exaggerated. The result may be avoidance of contact with less lonely peers, which further distorts the self-concept, making it consistent with a negative image of aging. This pattern of downwards-spiralling social competence has also been described as the social breakdown syndrome (Kuypers and Bengtson, 1973).

Social Competence in Old Age

The frequency of interaction is not sufficient to ensure healthy social functioning. Thus it would seem likely that socially competent individuals of any age should be better adjusted than their less competent peers because of more satisfying social interaction.

Defining social competence

Social competence has proven to be a difficult construct to describe and to operationalize (see Waters and Sroufe, 1983, for a review). Nevertheless, the phenomenon can be characterized as involving three related components (Norris and Rubin, 1984). First, the socially skilled person is one who can employ multiple behaviours successfully to achieve given social goals. Second, such an individual is cognizant of and sensitive to situational or contextual factors; this allows choice of the most appropriate response from among the multiple behaviours in his or her social repertoire. Third, the socially competent individual is one who is successful in meeting goals through culturally acceptable means.

Support for these factors as indicative of competence comes mainly from the child development literature (Norris and Rubin, 1984). Nevertheless, they also seem relevant to social functioning across the life span. Certainly adults also benefit from having a large repertoire of social behaviours, as well as from the ability to select those appropriate to differing situations. These characteristics appear to be especially important for the older adult whose social network may be diminishing. Work by Spence (1975) indicated that the ability to reinterpret changing social situations allows elderly individuals to adapt most quickly to novel settings. In support of this premise, Sequin (1973) found that the successful in-movers to a retirement community were those who adjusted previous role-related behaviours to suit their new situation.

Influencing competence: individual factors

Age-related changes in the ability to perceive and understand social situations may have a significant influence on the older adult's social performance. For example, deteriorating perceptual and memory functioning, which is often a result of organic illness (Moscovitch, 1982), may make it difficult to identify important social interactors. There may even be a problem in determining that certain situations require a social response (Burnside, 1980). While there is some uncertainty as to whether memory decline is a normal *developmental* process in later life (Craik and Byrd, 1982), most authors agree that some inefficiency in cognitive and perceptual processing is common (see, for example, Charness, 1984).

Changes in information-processing capacity clearly also have an impact on the ability to communicate with others. If oral communication is impeded, one of the most important aspects of social competence has been undermined (Norris, 1986; Norris and Rubin, 1984; North and Ulatowska, 1981). Work by various researchers has indicated that this may be the case in later life. Cohen (1979) has reported widespread declines in the ability to understand spoken and written discourse. More specifically, research by Davidson and colleagues (Davidson, Schonfield and Winkelaar, 1982) has indicated that older adults need more time to understand speech. Rubin (1974) found that older, versus younger, adults were poor at referential communication—the ability to describe something to another individual. Ryan (1986), however, has warned gerontologists to be alert for individual differences in these patterns of decline and to search for possible contextual causes. Otherwise we may inappropriately communicate with older adults as if they had regressed to a childlike state (Rubin and Brown, 1974).

Research discussed above suggests that any changes in social competence with age are likely to reflect declining abilities. It is possible, however, that researchers may have missed qualitative *improvements* in some forms of thinking (Norris and Rubin, 1984). Recent theoretical work on social cognition, the ability to understand a social situation, provides some support for this view. Various authors (e.g., Berg, 1985; Blanchard-Fields, 1985; Dolen and Bearison, 1982; Kramer, 1985) have put forward the idea that adult cognitive ability should be understood as arising out of meaningful adaptation to the social environment. If this is the case, the elderly, with their accumulated range of experiences, should show no declines in social cognitive ability, but instead be particularly skillful.

This viewpoint has not been confirmed by empirical research, but work by Norris (1979; Norris and Pratt, 1980) has indicated that older adults do possess sophisticated strategies for understanding their social world. In one study (Norris, 1979), elderly individuals perceived significant others in more complex and differentiated terms than did young adults. In another (Norris and Pratt, 1980), well-educated older adults outperformed young and middle-aged individuals in determining the motives of story characters. Further, in a study of moral judgment (Pratt, Golding, Hunter and Norris, in press), older adults were better able to assimilate social information into their own personal framework than were younger adults. Research on real social encounters is minimal; however, it seems likely that older adults are quite adept at using their social cognitive ability to respond appropriately (McGee and Barker, 1982).

Perhaps because of changes in social cognitive abilities, older adults also appear to perceive and understand their social relationships somewhat differently from younger adults (e.g., Tierney, Zwicker and Bush, 1982). This then may influence the type of contextual cues that are monitored in an interaction. There is evidence, for example, that older adults look for the highest payoff (i.e., best quality) for the lowest cost (i.e., least energy expenditure) when evaluating a relationship, whether it be with a family member (Snell, 1985) or friend (Duff and Hong, 1980). Thus, older, versus younger, adults seem to be more selective in their choice of social contacts, a decision that may provide high quality relationships, but also preclude the consideration of those potentially rewarding, but more effortful, contacts.

Part of the decision-making process in any social encounter is also linked to relatively stable individual personality factors. For example, overlearning of some social responses may inhibit flexibility in meeting the demands of a changing social environment (Botwinick, 1978). Adults who have lost important social relationships through death or separation may have difficulty forming new relationships. Instead they may enact outmoded "scripts" (Abelson, 1976) for social behaviour that lead to failure. In a vulnerable older adult, such failure may cause serious erosion in beliefs about personal power and control.

A note about contextual influences

Important as the individual factors are to successful social functioning, a life-span developmental perspective reminds us that they must be considered within the context of particular social situations. The maintenance of an adequate repertoire of social behaviours and the ability to use these strategies wisely are clearly affected by an older individual's social and physical environment.

A dramatic example of this may be seen by considering Looft's (1972) discussion of the development of egocentrism in old age. In old age, access to peers may be diminished because of normative life events such as retirement or relocation. Further restrictions in the social environment may then occur because of nonnormative events such as widowhood or ill health. According to Looft (1972), an important consequence of this increasing social isolation is the lack of feedback about competent social behaviours. Without others to provide information about the appropriateness of an older person's style of interaction, an increasingly internal focus is likely to develop. The result may be the loss of skills necessary for developing new relationships or maintaining existing ones.

Competence and identity

Through this review of factors that contribute to socially skilled behaviour, it is clear that social competence is an important contributor to a strong sense of self. Competence is an especially powerful concept if it is understood within a life-span developmental perspective. In this light, social skill can be seen as a *process* rather than a stable personal trait. This process is dialectical, subject to the interaction of varying individual and contextual factors. Thus social competence at any point in the life-span may be maximized or inhibited, depending on the source and type of variables interacting.

Summary and Conclusions

This chapter has discussed the importance of late-life social relationships to the maintenance of a strong sense of self. In the first section, we saw that the family is a critical contributor to healthy functioning at any point in the life span. Early bonds between parent and child lay an important foundation for the success of later relationships and they probably have an influence on how changes in the power structure of the family are negotiated in later life. It is likely, for example, that less parental and filial anxiety will occur in families where changes in role relationships and boundaries are expected. Similarly, a flexible family structure may aid grandparents in their transition to this role. Grandparents may need time to balance pressing identity concerns and a desire to preserve some distance with a need to remain involved in family affairs.

Peer relationships are also critical in preserving feelings of power and worth in later life, in providing models of appropriate behaviour in later life and in serving as buffers against aging-related stresses. Emotional support given by friends in later life may be particularly important to those with a shaky sense of self who are more susceptible to negative stereotypes of aging.

Social competence maximizes the benefits of a restricted social network in later life. There is some disagreement about whether older adults gain or lose skill because of normative life events. However, on balance it would

seem that if environmental and physiological factors remain ɪ
portive, there should be stability, and possibly improvement,
competence of older adults. Feelings of competence enhance well-being and
strengthen the self-concept.

Limitations of current research

This discussion has emphasized the importance of a life-span developmental
perspective on social relationships. Unfortunately, most researchers still
seem reluctant to employ the life-span view in their own work. Part of the
problem is the struggle that gerontologists have had in making complex life-
span developmental questions researchable. It is difficult to understand
how numerous factors interact to produce a social behaviour or
psychological state. It is easier to forge ahead with single-variable studies
using increasingly sophisticated quantitative techniques, while the meaning
of this variable to older adults is ignored.

How, then, can this research focus be altered? As one avenue of change,
it would seem that the use of more qualitative methods would be useful
(Norris, 1984). We assume that because we can identify an "issue" or
"problem" facing the elderly individual, we can also capture its meaning.
Instead, what we may have captured is *our* meaning; we have forgotten to
make our respondents partners in the research, and instead have relied on
our own beliefs and attitudes (Ryff, 1984). As Streib (1983) has suggested,
we need to pause for a moment and give "as much attention to initial observations in social research as we now give to analysis and statistical
methods."

There are various means of employing qualitative methods in life-span
developmental research (see Norris, 1984, and Norris and Rubin, 1984, for
reviews). Because of the importance of understanding the context of
development, however, the life history technique seems one of the most
useful. As Frank (1980) has noted, the life history approach seems an ideal
way to study older adults since they have "lived the longest, seen the most
and had more time than anyone to develop a personal outlook on the events
that have befallen them."

Generally, this method refers to a number of ethnomethodological
techniques designed to provide the researcher with a description of events in
an individual's life, both past and current (Langness and Frank, 1981). The
narrative that is produced may take many forms. Whatever the form, the
life history method provides a means of obtaining an individual's *own*
analysis of the events that have moulded his identity. The subject then
becomes a co-investigator in the research process.

The life history approach can also be used to examine the effect of peer
relationships on healthy social and psychological functioning. Ongoing
research by Norris and Rubin (1985) has examined the relationship of

qualitatively rich peer interactions with feelings of depression, social anxiety and disengagement. Preliminary results have indicated a link between competent social and psychological functioning.

It is clear, then, that researchers concerned with developmental issues in later life must be prepared to adopt a contextual perspective. A search for underlying developmental invariants is likely to prove fruitless. Instead, gerontologists must be prepared to accept a life-span developmental framework when dealing with complex, multiply determined patterns of functioning.

References

Abelson, R.P.
   1976   "Script processing attitudes, formation and decision making." In T.S. Carroll and T.W. Payne (eds.). *Cognition and Social Behavior*. Hillsdale, New Jersey: Erlbaum.
Aries, E. and F. Johnson
   1983   "Close friendships in adulthood: Conversational context between same-sex friends." *Sex Roles* 9(12):1183-1196.
Baltes, P.B. and O.G. Brim, Jr. (eds.)
   1979   *Life-Span Development and Behavior*. Vol. 2. New York: Academic Press.
Baltes, P.B., H.W. Reese and L.P. Lipsitt
   1980   "Life-span developmental psychology." *Annual Review of Psychology* 31:65-110.
Berg, C.A.
   1985   "The Role of Social Competence in a Contextual Theory of Adult Development." Paper presented at the annual meeting of the Gerontological Society of America, New Orleans, Louisiana.
Bielby, D.D.V. and D.E. Papalia
   1975   "Moral development and perceptual role-taking egocentricism: Their development and interrelationship across the life span." *International Journal of Aging and Human Development* 6(3):293-308.
Blanchard-Fields, F.
   1985   "Attributional Processes in Adult Development and Aging." Paper presented at the annual meeting of the Gerontological Society of America, New Orleans, Louisiana.
Botwinick, Jack
   1978   *Aging and Behavior*. 2nd ed. New York: Springer Publishing.
Boyd, R.E.
   1975   "Conformity reduction in adolescence." *Adolescence* 10:297-300.
Brandstadter, Jochen
   1984   "Personal and social control over development: Some implications of an action perspective in life-span developmental psychology." Pp. 1-32 in

Paul B. Baltes and Orville G. Brim, Jr. (eds.), *Life-Span Development and Behavior*. Vol. 6. Orlando, Florida: Academic Press.

Brim, O.G., Jr. and J. Kagan (eds.)
1980   *Constancy and Change in Human Development*. Cambridge, Mass.: Harvard University Press.

Burnside, I.M.
1980   "Symptomatic behaviors in the elderly." Pp. 719-744 in J.E. Birren and R.B. Sloane (eds.), *Handbook of Mental Health and Aging*. Englewood Cliffs, New Jersey: Prentice-Hall.

Cairns, Robert B. and Kathryn E. Hood
1983   "Continuity in social development: A comparative perspective on individual difference prediction." Pp. 301-358 in Paul B. Baltes and Orville G. Brim, Jr. (eds.), *Life-Span Development and Behavior*. Vol. 5. New York: Academic Press.

Cantor, Marjorie H.
1983   "Strain among caregivers: A study of experience in the United States." *The Gerontologist* 23(6):597-604.

Chappell, Neena
1983   "Informal support network among the elderly." *Research on Aging* 5(1):77-99.

Charness, Neil
1984   "Elementary Perceptual Processes: The Span of Apprehension in Adulthood." Paper presented at the annual meeting of the Canadian Association on Gerontology, Vancouver, B.C.

Cohen, G.
1979   "Language comprehension in old age." *Cognitive Psychology* 11:412-429.

Cohler, Bertram J.
1983   "Autonomy and interdependence in the family of adulthood: A psychological perspective." *The Gerontologist* 23(1):33-39.

Conner, K.A., E. Powers and G. Bultena
1979   "Social interaction and life satisfaction: An empirical assessment of late-life patterns." *Journal of Gerontology* 34(1):116-121.

Craik, Fergus, I.M. and Mark Byrd
1982   "Aging and cognitive deficits: The role of attentional resources." Pp. 191-212 in F.I.M. Craik and Sandra Trehub (eds.), *Advances in the Study of Communication and Affect*. Vol. 8. New York: Plenum Press.

Cumming, E. and W.E. Henry
1961   *Growing old*. New York: Basic Books.

Davidson, A., D. Schonfield and R. Winkelaar.
1982   "Age differences in the effects of reverberation and pause on sentence intelligibility." *Canadian Journal on Aging* 1(1 and 2):29-32.

Dolen, L.S. and D.T. Bearison
1982   "Social interaction and social cognition in aging: A contextual analysis." *Human Development* 25:430-442.

Duff, R.W. and L.K. Hong
1980   "Quality and Quantity of Social Interactions and the Life Satisfaction of

Older Americans." Paper presented at the annual meeting of the Gerontological Society, San Diego.

Erikson, Erik
1963 *Childhood and Society*. 2nd rev. ed. New York: Norton.

Fischer, C. and S. Oliker
1983 "A research note on friendship, gender and the life cycle." *Social Forces* 62(1):124-133.

Fischer, L.R.
1983 "Transition to grandmotherhood." *International Journal of Aging and Human Development* 16(1):67-68.

Forbes, Sandra J.
1985 "Families Coping with an Elder's Care and Related Decisions." Unpublished Master's thesis, University of Guelph, Guelph, Ontario.

Forbes, Sandra J. and Joan E. Norris
1984 "Family Coping with Caregiving Decisions." Paper presented at the annual meeting of the Canadian Association on Gerontology, Vancouver, B.C.

Frank, G.
1980 "Life histories in gerontology: The subjective side to aging." In C.L. Fry and J. Keith (eds.), *New Methods for Old Age Research*. Chicago: Loyala University.

Gladstone, J.
1985 "A Study of Grandparents Whose Children Have Separated or Divorced." Unpublished doctoral dissertation, University of Toronto, Toronto, Ontario.

Goldman, T., P. Cooper, K. Ahern and D. Corsini
1981 "Continuities and discontinuities in the friendship descriptions of women at six stages of the life cycle." *Genetic Psychology Monographs* 103(1):153-167.

Hagestad, G.O.
1981 "Problems and promises in the social psychology of intergenerational relations." Pp. 11-46 in R.W. Fogel, E. Hatfield, S.B. Kiesler and E. Shanas (eds.), *Aging: Stability and Change in the Family*. New York: Academic Press.

Hall, Elizabeth
1983 "A conversation with Erik Erikson." *Psychology Today* June:22-30.

Harris, L. and associates
1975 *The Myth and Reality of Aging in America*. Washington, D.C.: National Council on Aging.

Hartup, W.W.
1983 "The Peer System." In E.M. Hetherington (ed.), *Handbook of Child Psychology*. Vol. 3. *Social Development*. New York: Wiley.

Hess, B.B.
1979 "Sex roles, friendship and the life course." Research on Aging 1(4):494-515.

Jerrome, D.
1981 "The significance of friendship for women in later life." *Ageing and Society* 1(2):175-197.

Johnson, C.L.
  1983   "Dyadic family relations and social support." *The Gerontologist* 23(4):377-383.
Kafer, N.F. and D. Davies
  1984   "Vulnerability of self and interpersonal strategies: A study of the aged." *Journal of Psychology* 116:203-206.
Kahana, Boaz and Eva Kahana
  1970   "Grandparenthood from the perspective of the developing grandchild." *Developmental Psychology* 3(1):98-105.
Kahn, R.L. and T.C. Antonucci
  1980   "Convoys across the life course: Attachment, roles and social support." Pp. 253-286 in P.B. Baltes and O.G. Brim, Jr. (eds.), *Life-Span Development and Behavior*. Vol. 3. New York: Academic Press.
Kalish, R.A. and F.W. Knudtson
  1976   Attachment vs. disengagement: A lifespan conceptualization. *Human Development* 19:171-181.
Keith, P.M., K. Hill, W.T. Goudy and E.A. Powers
  1984   "Confidants and well-being: A note on male friendships in old age." *The Gerontologist* 24(3):318-320.
Kramer, D.A.
  1985   "A Life-Span View of Social Cognition." Paper presented at the annual meeting of the Gerontological Society of America, New Orleans, Louisiana.
Kuypers, J.A. and V.L. Bengtson
  1973   "Social breakdown and competence." *Human Development* 16:181-201.

  1983   "Toward competence in the older family." In T.H. Brubaker (ed.), *Family Relationships in Later Life*. Beverly Hills: Sage Publications.
Langness, L.L. and G. Frank
  1981   *Lives: An Anthropological Approach to Biography*. Novato, California: Chandler and Sharp.
Lerner, Richard M. and Nancy A. Busch-Rossnagel
  1981   "Individuals as producers of their own development." Pp. 1-36 in Richard M. Lerner and Nancy A. Busch-Rossnagel (eds.), *Individuals as Producers of Their Development: A Life Span Perspective*. New York: Academic Press.
Looft, William R.
  1972   "Egocentrism and social interaction across the life span." *Psychological Bulletin* 78(1):73-92.
Lowenthal, M.F. and C. Haven
  1968   "Interaction and adaptation: Intimacy as a critical variable." *American Sociological Review* 33(1):20-30.
Lowenthal, M.F. and B. Robinson
  1976   "Social networks and social isolation." Pp. 432-456 in R.H. Binstock and E. Shanas (eds.), *Handbook of Aging and the Social Sciences*. New York: Van Nostrand Reinhold.
Luke, E., W. Norton and K. Denbigh
  1981   "Medical and social factors associated with psychological distress in a sam-

ple of community aged." *Canadian Journal of Psychiatry* 26:244-250.

Maccoby, Eleanor E. and John C. Masters
  1970   "Attachment and dependency." Pp. 73-155 in P.H. Mussen (ed.), *Carmichael's Manual of Child Psychology*. 3rd ed. New York: Wiley.

Maddox, George
  1963   "Activity and morale: A longitudinal study of selected elderly subjects." *Social Forces* 42:195-204.

Marcus, Lotte and Valerie Jaeger
  1984   "The elderly as family caregivers." *Canadian Journal on Aging* 3(1):33-44.

Marshall, Victor W.
  1983   "Generations, age groups and cohorts: Conceptual distinctions." *Canadian Journal on Aging* 2(3):51-62.

Matthews, Sarah
  1983   "Definitions of friendship and their consequences in old age." *Ageing and Society* 3(2):141-155.

McGee, J. and M. Barker
  1982   "Deference and dominance in old age: An exploration in social theory." *International Journal of Aging and Human Development* 15(4):247-262.

McGreal, Cathleen
  1985   "Men's Perceptions of Grandparenthood." Paper presented at the annual meeting of the Canadian Association on Gerontology, Hamilton, Ontario.

Moon, M.
  1983   "The role of the family in the economic well-being of the elderly." *The Gerontologist* 23(1):45-50.

Morgan, Griffith A.
  1985   "The Meaning of Being a Grandparent." Paper presented at the annual meeting of the Ontario Psychological Association, Ottawa, Ontario.

Moscovitch, Morris
  1982   "A neuropsychological approach to perception and memory in normal and pathological aging." Pp. 55-78 in F.I.M. Craik and Sandra Trehub (eds.), *Advances in the Study of Communication and Affect*. Vol. 8. New York: Plenum Press.

Mueller, J.E. and M.J. Ross
  1984   "Uniqueness of the self-concept across the life span." *Bulletin of the Psychonomic Society* 22(2):83-86.

Neugarten, B.L. and K.K. Weinstein
  1964   "The changing American grandparent." *Journal of Marriage and the Family* 26:199-204.

Newcomb, T.M.
  1962   "Student peer group influence." In N. Sanford (ed.), *The American College*. New York: Wiley.

Norris, Joan E.
  1979   "Social Cognition. Perceiving the Complexity of Others." Paper presented at the annual meeting of the Gerontological Society, Washington, D.C.
  1984   "Qualitative Methods in the Study of Aging and Intergenerational Relations." Paper #84-3, Gerontology Research Centre Publication Series, University of Guelph.

1986   "Social Psychological Factors in Later Life Communication." Proceedings of the McMaster Summer Institute in Gerontology. Hamilton: McMaster University.

Norris, Joan E. and Michael Pratt
1980   "Adult Usage of Kelley's Causal Schemes." Paper presented at the annual meeting of the Canadian Association on Gerontology, Saskatoon, Saskatchewan.

Norris, Joan E. and Kenneth H. Rubin
1984   "Peer interaction and communication: A life-span perspective." Pp. 355-391 in P.B. Baltes and O.G. Brim, Jr. (eds.), *Life-Span Development and Behavior*. Vol. 6, Orlando, Florida: Academic Press.

1985   "Assessing Social Interaction and Social Skills Among the Elderly." Unpublished data, University of Guelph, Guelph, Ontario.

Norris, Joan E. and Andor J. Tari
1985   "A Qualitative Study of the Grandparenting Experience." Paper presented at the annual meeting of the Ontario Psychological Association, Ottawa, Ontario.

North, A.J. and H.K. Ulatowska
1981   "Competence in independently living older adults: Assessment and correlates." *Journal of Gerontology* 36(5):576-582.

Olbrich, E. and H. Thomae
1978   "Empirical findings to a cognitive theory of aging." *International Journal of Behavioural Development* 1(1):67-82.

Pascual-Leone, Juan
1983   "Growing into human maturity: Toward a metasubjective theory of adulthood stages." Pp. 118-157 in P.B. Baltes and O.G. Brim, Jr. (eds.), *Life-Span Development and Behavior*. Vol. 5. New York: Academic Press.

Perlman, Daniel
forthcoming: "Loneliness: A life-span family perspective." In R.M. Milardo (ed.), *Families and Social Networks*. Beverly Hills: Sage.

Perlman, D., A.C. Gerson and B. Spinner
1978   "Loneliness among senior citizens: An empirical report." *Essence* 2(4):239-248.

Piaget, Jean
1967   *Six Psychological Studies*. New York: Random House.

Pihlblad, C.T. and R.W. Habenstein
1964   "Social factors in grandparent orientation of high school youth." In A.M. Rose and W.A. Peterson (eds.), *Older People and Their Social World*. Philadelphia: F.A. Davis Co.

Pratt, Michael J., Gail Golding, William Hunter and Joan Norris
in press: "From inquiry to judgment: Age and sex differences in patterns of adult moral thinking and information-seeking." *International Journal of Aging and Human Development*.

Richardson, V.
1981   "Projective measurement of adult peer relations as a function of chronological age." *International Journal of Aging and Human Development* 19(1):11-20.

Riegel, K.F.
   1973   "Dialectical operations: The final period of cognitive development."
          Human Development 16:346-370.
Robertson, J.F.
   1977   "Grandmotherhood: A study of role conception." *Journal of Marriage
          and the Family* 33(1):165-174.
Rubin, Kenneth H.
   1974   "The relationship between spatial and communicative egocentrism in
          children and young and old adults." *Journal of Genetic Psychology*
          125:295-301.
Rubin, K.H., P.W. Attewell, M.C. Tierney, P.Tumolo
   1973   "Development of spatial egocentrism and conservation across the life
          span." *Developmental Psychology* 9(4):432.
Rubin, Kenneth H. and I.D.R. Brown
   1975   "A life-span look at person perception and its relationship to communica-
          tion interaction." *Journal of Gerontology* 30:461-468.
Ryan, Ellen B.
   1986   "Communication with Older Adults." Proceedings of the McMaster Sum-
          mer Institute in Gerontology. Hamilton: McMaster University.
Ryff, Carol
   1984   "Personality development from the inside: The subjective experience of
          change in adulthood and aging." Pp. 244-281 in P.B. Baltes and O.G.
          Brim, Jr. (eds.), *Life-Span Development and Behavior*. Vol. 6. Orlando,
          Florida: Academic Press.
Semple, Shirley J.
   1985   "A Generational Model of Child Care: Attitudes toward Child-Rearing
          Practices." Unpublished Master's thesis, University of Guelph, Guelph,
          Ontario.
Sequin, M.M.
   1973   "Opportunity for peer socialization in a retirement community." *The
          Gerontologist* 13(2):208-214.
Shanas, Ethel
   1979   "Social myth as hypothesis: The case of the family relations of old
          people." *The Gerontologist* 19(1):3-9.
Shanas, E., et al.
   1968   *Old People in Three Industrial Societies*. New York: Atherton.
Sinnott, T.D.
   1978   "Adult Intellectual Development as Social Cognitive Growth." Paper
          presented at the annual meeting of the Gerontological Society, Dallas,
          Texas.
Snell, Leslie
   1985   "Qualitative and Quantitative Aspects of Social Interaction in a Sample of
          Retired Men and Women." Unpublished Master's thesis, University of
          Guelph, Guelph, Ontario.
Soldo, B.J. and J. Myllyluoma
   1983   "Caregivers who live with dependent elderly." *The Gerontologist*
          23(6):605-611.

Spence, P.
  1975   "The meaning of engagement." *International Journal of Aging and Human Development* 6:193-198.
Stoller, E.P. and L.L. Earl
  1983   "Help with activities of everyday life: Sources of support for the non-institutionalized elderly." *The Gerontologist* 23(1):64-70.
Strain, L. and N. Chappell
  1982   "Confidants: Do they make a difference in quality of life?" *Research on Aging* 4:479-502.
Streib, G.
  1983   "The frail elderly: Research dilemmas and research opportunities." *The Gerontologist* 23(1):40-44.
Tierney, Mary C., C. Zwicker and B. Bush
  1982   "Conceptions of Friendship in Well-Adjusted Older People." Paper presented at the annual meeting of the Canadian Association on Gerontology, Winnipeg, Manitoba.
Vollmer, H.
  1937   "The grandmother: A problem in child-rearing." *American Journal of Orthopsychiatry* 7:378-382.
Waters, E. and L.A. Sroufe
  1983   "Social competence as a developmental construct." *Developmental Review* 3(1):79-97.
Weir, Nancy
  1985   "Friendship in Elderly People: A Further Exploration of Its Meaning and Its Relation to Levels of Self-Esteem." Unpublished undergraduate thesis, University of Guelph, Guelph, Ontario.
Wood, Linda A.
  1983   "Loneliness and social identity." Pp. 51-70 in T.R. Sarben and K.E. Scheibe (eds.), *Studies in Social Identity*. New York: Prager.
Wood, Linda A.
  forthcoming "The social construction of loneliness." In Rom Harre (ed.), *The Social Construction of Emotion*. Oxford: Basil Blackwell.

II

The Diverse Meanings
of Age and Aging

Contemporary Canadian society is stratified by age. In everyday life, Canadians of different age groups spend large proportions of their time with others who are similar to them in age. Children of school age are segregated in schools; many young adults are segregated from people of other ages in colleges and universities. In the work-place, neither the young, who are still being educated, nor the old, who have been retired, are to be found. In cultural life, different entertainments and events tend to attract people of different age groups. Many movies are targeted at teenagers. The price of some events discourages attendance by nonworking young and old people. Old people may avoid public transit or crowded shopping malls during periods when large numbers of young people are likely to be present. Some restaurants and bars gear their ambience and entertainment to specific age groups or even attract different age groups at different times of the day. Young people may be kept off the streets at night by anxious parents; old people may stay off the streets at night because of their own anxieties about street safety. It is not that laws or posted signs say *no old people here* (although laws and signs do restrict the young in that way and retirement policies exclude the old); nonetheless, many aspects of our lives are so structured that they diminish contact between old people and the young.

Aside from their own parents and grandparents, young adults may have little intimate and little routine contact with people who differ from them in age by more than ten years. As a result, their images of the old may be highly stereotypical and the stereotypes may be highly inaccurate.

To adapt a well-worn phrase in the social sciences, we would be well advised to try to ascertain the extent to which all old people are alike, the ways in which some old people are alike and the ways in which no old people are alike. In process terms, we want to understand how all people age in similar ways, how some types of people age in similar types of ways and how individuals age in unique ways. For the most part, the social sciences seek to articulate patterns of social behaviour. Thus, attention is diverted from individual differences. Yet, as noted in Chapter 3, it is possible to seek patterns without doing violence to individuality.

So conveniently do we talk about "the aged" or "the elderly" that we too easily fall into the assumption that all old people are alike. The four chapters of this section describe several axes or dimensions on which all old people are not alike; simultaneously, they allow us to ask how age and aging may transcend the potential for difference along each axis. In Chapter 5, the major axes are gender and rural-urban differences. In Chapter 6, the major axes are historical time and race. In Chapter 7, the ethnic mosaic of Canada is treated as an axis of possible differentiation in the aging experience, but again, historical time is a cross-cutting basis. In Chapter 8, sexual orientation is the analytical focus. In general, the chapters show that each dimension is itself more complex than might at first be assumed: there are different types of rurality, different racial and ethnic experiences, different ways of growing old gay. While the authors focus on different issues in the four chapters, ranging from social status to social support and life satisfaction, they all make the point that aging is not a uniform process leading to a uniform status. Other bases of differentiation are discussed in other chapters: class and health being dimensions of critical importance. But these chapters serve to sensitize us to differentiation itself.

Rural Canada, Cape points out in Chapter 5, is becoming less commercial and more residential. Increasingly, rural towns and villages are becoming "geriatric dormitories." Simple models of social change, such as the theory of "modernization and aging," are unable, Vanderburgh shows in Chapter 6, to capture the diversity of patterns of social change. Her account of the Anicinabe, as well as Ujimoto's depiction of the aged Japanese-Canadian, while tuning in to sociological theories, is, like Cape's chapter, sensitive to historical analysis, which is necessary to capture this diversity. Similarly, Lee finds it necessary, in understanding the situation of older gays, to take account of the "dreadful stereotypes of single gay life" that they experienced decades ago.

Taken together, the four chapters of this section show that there are many different ways to age. Patterns of aging described here reflect both constraint and the outcomes of choice, often of intense personal (Chapter 8) or collective (Chapters 6 and 7) struggle, working itself out over individual life times and simultaneously over historical times.

5
Aging Women in Rural Settings

Elizabeth Cape
Department of Behavioural Science
University of Toronto

In spite of the fact that the elderly are disproportionately represented in rural populations, and that a majority of these elders are female, little is known about the distaff side of rural aging. The lives of older rural women, like those of country people generally, tend to be obscured by the fallacy of ruralism — a misapprehension wedded to a stereotype. "Rural" is not a synonym for "farm," and country life today is not an evocation of the utopian world of illustrator Norman Rockwell — if it ever was. Less than 3 percent of Canada's rural elderly live on farms, and the nostalgic image of "grandmother's house" is just as much a part of the "myth of the golden years" (Gubrium, 1973) when it is pictured against a backdrop of fields and silos.

The tendency to equate rurality with agriculture fails to acknowledge the rapid decrease in the number of people directly involved with farming, the diversity of rural settings in Canada and the heterogeneity of rural populations. In particular, it does not take account of the growing number of city people who are retiring to the country. The assumption that all older women in rural settings are farm wives and grandmothers is even less tenable today than in the past.

Background

Rural populations in Canada have always had an excess of males, but the proportion of men to women has been steadily declining. Even though rural sex ratios continue to be somewhat higher than those of urban Canada, women now outnumber men in virtually every part of the country, and it is only in the North that one still finds any semblance of an excess of males (Kalbach and McVey, 1979:159). At the same time that rural sex ratios have been decreasing, Canada's population of rural elderly has been increasing, with the result that older females now comprise a numerically and proportionately larger group of rural residents than ever before.

This rising population of rural elderly women aging in place is being augmented by the female half of urban couples retiring to the country. During the past decade there has been an unprecedented out-migration from urban to rural areas both in the United States and in Canada. For the first time in history more people are moving from the city to the country than from the country to the city. In spite of the continuing exodus of rural youth, Canada's rural population has grown by 8.9 percent since 1976, compared with an urban growth rate of 5 percent (Statistics Canada, 1983:24). Some nonmetropolitan regions are attractive to industry, and population follows jobs, but it is the noncommercial rural areas that are experiencing an influx of older people in their retirement years. If this pattern continues, "it may have important impact on the future concentration of elderly in Canada" (Shulman, 1980:32).

More to the present point, such a trend would concentrate still more older women in small rural settlements that are already centres of aging females (Hodge and Qadeer, 1983:107). Relatively few elderly women continue into old age in open country settings, especially if they are widowed. Even for the country-bred, the harsh winters, the physical labour and the long distances between neighbours militate against an independent lifestyle in sparsely populated areas. Instead, aging women congregate in villages and small towns wherein a quarter to a third of the population may be over the age of 65.

In addition to a skewed age distribution, country settlements are changing in other ways. Typically they have become less commercial and more residential; less able to provide their inhabitants with the necessary mix of goods and services, and more dependent upon outside resources. In consequence, rural towns and villages are becoming geriatric dormitories where access to private transportation is a major determinant of the quality of life.

The decay of commercial life may be offset by the manageability of social interaction in rural communities and, in the lives of older women, the one may compensate for the other. Or it may not. If it is generally true that the elderly lead "invisible lives" (Unruh, 1983), older rural females have to be one of the most hidden of all subgroups of seniors. A few studies have looked at older Canadian women as a group (cf. Posner, 1977; Dulude, 1978; Martin Matthews, 1980; Abu-Laban and Abu-Laban, 1980), and two reports on women in rural life have focussed principally (McGhee, 1984) or entirely (Ireland, 1983) on younger farm women, but few data have been collected on elderly females in rural Canada. Nor has a feminist perspective been brought to bear on how it is to be old and female and rural — and Canadian.

The literature of rural sociology yields little information, and in Canada, as in the United States, studies of rural life typically have focussed on social, ethnic or cultural minorities (cf. Davidson and Davidson, 1969; Guemple, 1980; Ishwaran, 1980) and there are few data relating to the large majority of Canada's elderly population, which is of British ethnic origin.

Anthropology supplies a view of aging in cultures ranging from Afghanistan to Zambia (cf. Amoss and Harrell, 1981), but elderly rural women in our own culture remain largely out of sight and out of mind (Cape, 1982). At present they can be discerned principally in demographic silhouette.

Rurality adds an additional risk factor to the known hazards of being old and female. As a group, aging country women have even less money, less education and fewer services than their urban counterparts, and income data point to the "unequivocal conclusion" that the smaller the community, the lower the income (Hodge and Qadeer, 1983:57). By most objective indicators of socio-economic status, rural elderly women would appear to lead a marginal existence, minus the money and the access to services associated with a comfortable old age.

But in spite of these deficits there are positive aspects to country life that might be expected to contribute to well-being in later years. Life is slower paced and less frazzling. It is also more intimate; people know one another as individuals and not merely as role incumbents. Because the concept of neighbourhood is still operationalized in rural communities, the idea that country people look after their own continues to have many subscribers. Previous research suggests, however, that kinship and neighbourliness are doubtful supports, especially in cases of chronic incapacity (Cape, 1981a).

One factor that makes it difficult to evaluate the pluses and minuses of rural life for older women is the lack of specificity in present definitions of rurality (Martin Matthews and Vanden Heuvel, 1986). Rural tends to be seen only as a residual, i.e., whatever is nonurban, and the size and character of geographic units designated as rural vary from one study to another. This global view fails to discriminate among farm dwellers and the many kinds of nonmetropolitan nonfarm populations. Nor does it distinguish short-term from long-term rural residence, or the "native" from the urban "transplant." A study of aging women in rural Southern Ontario addresses some of these diversities, and this chapter is based on certain findings from that study relating to the informal support services available to elderly females in country settings.

Aging Women in Rural Society

The sample

Respondents were selected from two different kinds of rural regions in Southern Ontario: Haliburton County, a tourist area of lakes and forests; and the northern part of Northumberland County, which is fertile farmland. Both areas are beyond commuting distance from a metropolitan centre. Neither ethnicity nor poverty is a salient factor in any of the townships sampled: over 90 percent of the inhabitants of both counties are white and of United Kingdom background, and only 3 percent of the respondents reported serious financial concerns.

The sample is a purposive one and cases were selected as evenly as possible on the basis of county; type of location (open country or small settlement); age (under 70, 71-79, 80 and over); and predominant background (rural "natives" and urban "transplants"). Open country elders were oversampled in order to compensate for the preponderance of seniors in small towns and villages. In spite of the risks associated with nonprobability sampling, it is felt that the subjects fairly represent the overall population of aging women in this English-speaking, primarily middle-class part of rural Canada.

In order to lower the psychic barriers between rural respondents and "strangers" (Ontario Advisory Council on Senior Citizens, 1980:27), all of the interviewers were themselves older rural women living in one or the other of the two counties from which cases were drawn.

The settings

Rural towns and villages can differ qualitatively in ways that have relatively little to do with population size. In spite of the fact that the communities in both areas are officially categorized as small rural settlements, there are important differences that are likely to affect the lives of older female residents.

In tourist regions like Haliburton, aging "summer people" have become year-round residents, and cottage areas are turning into stable communities of winterized homes. In contrast, Northumberland County is almost entirely open country and agricultural. Forty percent of its population is located on the southern rim that borders Lake Ontario — an area that was not sampled in this study. The northern part of the county is a prosperous region of mixed farming and large dairy herds and a few widely dispersed villages.

The towns of Haliburton are somewhat larger and more urban in character, reflecting both their economic dependence on tourism and their role as market towns and meeting places for the growing numbers of urban transplants in the surrounding cottage communities. In contrast, the villages of Northumberland remain traditional farm settlements. As yet they lack a critical mass of urban transplants because most of the city people who have retired to the country have settled in towns adjacent to the Toronto-Montreal transportation corridor, and those who have pushed "inland" have opted for open country locations rather than the villages.

The subjects

Fifty-three percent of the cases were drawn from Haliburton County and 47 percent from Northumberland; 60 percent from villages and towns with populations ranging from a couple of hundred to 1,200, and 40 percent from open country. Not all of the open country elders live on farms, and in any case, the word "farm" has various connotations: it may be a working farm, a hobby farm, or land that is "let out" to a neighbour farmer. Some of the respondents do live in the kind of farmhouses conjured up by the word "rural." Others occupy new suburban-style homes that are appearing on country side roads throughout Southern Ontario.

Forty-two percent of the women in the sample were in their sixties, 37 percent in their seventies, and 21 percent were 80 or more. Just over half of the respondents were married; two-fifths were widowed, and only 7 percent were single. One woman was divorced; the other singles had never married. More than a third of the respondents had a grade school education or less; 41 percent had finished high school, and 23 percent had completed some form of postsecondary work, typically nursing or teacher training.

Forty percent of the sample was comprised of urban transplants. As a group, they were younger, more likely to be married and had significantly more formal education than their rural counterparts. More of the city women had been employed outside the home, but a majority of all the respondents had spent most of their lives being housewives.

No attempt was made to collect data on income. It was felt that questions about respondents' financial status would be unwelcome and would risk destroying the rapport between interviewer and subject. In order that the effects of rurality not be confounded with those of poverty, one important criterion for selecting the particular research areas was their relative prosperity and lack of rural slums. Nineteen percent of the respondents were "somewhat concerned" about money, but only a handful were obviously poor.

Living arrangements

Like most of Canada's elderly, the women lived in private households. Most of them had no choice; it is only in places with populations larger than 2,500 that the range of housing options broadens significantly (Hodge and Qadeer, 1983:188). Therefore, the ability to maintain an independent life-style was crucial, not only because the value orientations of their cultural heritage stress autonomy and self-reliance, but also because of the very practical problem of having no place to go. The only alternative accommodation in the same general neighbourhood was most likely to be a nursing home.

The older and frailer women, a large majority of them widows living alone, managed to stay on in their own homes by adopting the common country practice of closing off most of the house and confining themselves to a few downstairs rooms. But even this stratagem tends to be insufficient for continued independence in the open country. Life in the outlying areas of rural Canada is seldom a do-it-yourself project and the circumstances in which this may be possible are likely to be highly individual.

Only four of the respondents fell into this category. One was a wealthy widow who had built a country showplace and had the money to import whatever services she needed. A second widow lived in the kitchen of her dilapidated farmhouse and was almost completely dependent upon her farmer son across the road. A third was the prototypical rural recluse whose strange ways were tolerated by neighbours who had known her from girlhood. The fourth was a former schoolteacher who was preparing a country home for herself and her soon-to-be-retired sister — a rare example of joint female tenancy.

Contrary to popular mythology there was no indication that these rural elderly women were any more likely than their counterparts elsewhere to relish the idea of living with their children. Over 85 percent of the respondents said that this was not a preferred option, and only six of them actually did so. But apart from not wanting to be, as they saw it, a burden on their families, few of the women had any contingency plans to deal with increasing age and infirmity. Most of the farm women thought that in time they would move to a nearby village, and some of the urban transplants thought they might return to the city, but only a few had actually developed a fall-back position.

The unavailability of alternative accommodation undoubtedly contributed to the respondents' signal lack of contingency planning. Subsidized housing is a scarce resource in rural Ontario, and low population density areas are unattractive to private developers. Many of the women spoke of possibly moving to an apartment, but they were vague about where the apartment might be.

The Need For Service

The formal support services available to rural elders tend to be inferior both in quantity and in quality to those in urban areas (Taietz, 1975:145), particularly if the criterion is a continuum of care (Coward and Rathbone-McCuan, 1985:206). The medical specialties and paramedical personnel to be found in metropolitan centres are scarce or nonexistent in rural areas. In the circumstances, indigenous informal support networks involving family members, neighbours and friends are indispensable (Rowles, 1983:115), especially for those who are "failing" but are not technically "sick." Unfortunately, even though emergency aid is a rural tradition, chronic illness and functional incapacity are not well contained by the informal support system (Ward, 1978; Cape, 1981a).

Parenthetically, the absence of very elderly subjects in some of these same rural areas has been noted in previous research (Cape, 1981b), suggesting that rurality added to incapacity may lead to early institutionalization.

Less than 10 percent of the present respondents reported serious concerns about the state of their health, even though half of them had problems that were serious enough to interfere with activities of daily life. Nevertheless, all the subjects in this study were maintaining a more or less autonomous existence in the community at large, and the fact that they were there at all was the best indication that they were reasonably intact. The majority of rural elderly women have only two choices: either they must manage to stay in their own homes, or they must leave the neighbourhood altogether. As Table 1 indicates, they were determined to see themselves as independent and able to function on their own.

TABLE 1:
The Need For Service

"Do you have anyone (apart from a husband) who regularly gives you a hand . . . ?"

	With Indoor Work	With Outdoor Work
"Yes."	22.6	53.0
"No, but I wish I did."	14.3	9.5
"No, I don't need help."	63.1	37.5

Mental health needs were largely ignored by the women, even though 27 percent reported periods of serious depression during the past year, depression that went beyond just being blue or "down in the dumps." Typically, the respondents did not define these depressive episodes as a health problem, and only eight women had sought medical treatment. Since mental health specialists were practically unavailable in these rural areas, whatever help the women had with psychological problems was largely a function of the good offices of family and friends.

The Informal Support Network

The literature of rural gerontology tends to picture the informal support network as a kind of fourfold table, with practical assistance and companionship as the two dimensions of support, and family and neighbour-friends as the two main categories of service providers (cf. Powers, Keith and Goudy, 1975). For this sample, however, there was a third category of caregiver, one seldom remarked in the literature, but a major source of assistance for these respondents: the paid employee.

Table 2 is a summary of the amount of help available from these various sources for inside housework and outdoor maintenance. In total, relatives contributed the least amount of service, only 13 percent overall. Neighbours supplied 20 percent, and children and paid employees each contributed 38 percent. Widows and unmarried women were the principal beneficiaries of this extra help; for the married women, a husband was the single most important source of practical assistance and companionship.

TABLE 2:
Age and Sources of Household Help

"Do you have anyone (apart from a husband) who regularly gives you a hand . . . ?"

| | With Indoor Work | | | With Outdoor Work | | |
| | -70 | 71-79 | 80+ | -70 | 71-79 | 80+ |
	(n = 72)	(n = 62)	(n = 34)	(n = 72)	(n = 62)	(n = 34)
Kin						
Children	11.1	8.0	20.6	22.2	16.1	23.5
Other Relatives	—	4.8	14.7	2.8	8.1	17.7
Neighbours-Friends	5.6	3.2	2.9	9.7	19.4	23.5
Employees	5.6	16.1	32.4	16.7	25.8	29.4
No One	77.7	67.9	29.4	48.6	30.6	5.9

The marital relationship

Husbands were partners in household tasks, chauffeurs and, as Table 3 indicates, best friends. Affectional bonds with children, relatives and especially with neighbours were strengthened by widowhood, and the single women had particularly close ties with their kin, but the marital relationship was the linchpin of the married respondents' lives.

TABLE 3:
Marital Status and Friendship

"Who would you say is your closest friend?

	Single (n = 12)	Married (n = 87)	Widowed (n = 69)
Husband	—	77.9	—
Child	—	4.7	29.9
Relative	54.5	4.7	17.9
Neighbour	36.4	7.0	41.8
Other	9.1	5.7	10.4

The wives worried more about their husbands' health than about their own — a realistic concern in view of the fact that almost half of all women in Canada over age 65 are widows (Martin Matthews, 1980) — and the younger the wife, the greater the worry. Significantly more of the respondents in their sixties were concerned about their husbands than were the older wives, even though the younger women were less likely than their elders to see their husbands' health as poor.

This anomalous finding is partially explained by residential location. More of the younger couples were living in open country settings where rurality superimposes a gender-based division of labour on otherwise egalitarian marriages. Differences in rural sex roles may have a structural rather than a cultural explanation (Lee and Cassidy, 1985:157) even among the elderly and those not country-bred.

The influence of geography was especially clear in the lives of the urban women transplanted to agricultural Northumberland County. As a group, they had little relish for developing an intimate acquaintance with the tools of country property management; neither they nor their husbands felt that running a tractor or a chainsaw was suitable employment for an older woman. In any case, the outside work was the husband's chosen province, and very likely the principal reason for the couple's relocation. The decision to retire to the country was twice as likely to have been jointly made by the Haliburton couples than by their Northumberland counterparts, for whom their husbands' enthusiasm for the outdoor life was a salient factor in the choice of setting.

Elderly farm couples had followed rural tradition by retiring to small settlements where they were surrounded by neighbours and friends. The open country transplants not only lacked these supportive relationships, but they found themselves committed to a lifestyle that was largely dependent upon the health and vigour of their husbands.

Another area in which husbands made a vital contribution was that of transportation. Only about half of the women were drivers, and even fewer drove in the winter, so that quite apart from the emotional trauma of losing a spouse, widowhood was likely to be attended by physical as well as social immobility. None of the respondents had any real difficulty arranging necessary trips, but owning a car and being able to drive are essential components of rural self-sufficiency, and for the 50 percent of the sample who lacked this skill, the availability of a husband-chauffeur was crucial.

Driving went beyond the strictly utilitarian to become something of an occupation and a regular source of companionship, especially for retired farm couples, who appeared to spend a significant proportion of weekday time on motor junkets, euphemistically known as "going shopping."

Children

In spite of the declining fertility of Canadian women, rural families are larger than urban families; rural women marry earlier, divorce less frequently and have more children — a situation that would seem to ensure for an aging mother the assistance of at least one or two adult children. But as Powers et al. (1981:201) point out: "Nowhere is the mobility of the young more obvious than with the children of the rural aged," and the present data corroborate this demographic fact: only a fifth of these respondents had children living in the same townships.

It is commonly assumed that kinship bonds are stronger in rural than in urban families, although the evidence is "surprisingly equivocal" (Lee and Cassidy, 1985:159). What has been shown is that interaction with kin constitutes a greater proportion of the social contacts of rural than of urban women (Lee and Cassidy, 1981:61). For the women in this sample, neighbours provided more casual contacts, but planned social events primarily involved kinfolk, especially the children and their families. Apart from informal neighbouring, family get-togethers were the mainstay of the women's social lives, and the older the respondent, the greater the reliance on adult children for friendship and recreation. Yet in spite of the fact that relationships with offspring were the social core of the women's lives, their children were twice as likely to stay in contact with their mothers by phone than in person.

Female children are generally considered to be the principal caregivers for aging parents, but the present findings suggest that this assumption should not be stretched too far. The fact that younger generation women are more attentive than their male counterparts in times of illness does not necessarily mean that their contribution to routine domestic activities is correspondingly large, even in rural families. Twenty percent of the respondents could count on sons or sons-in-law for such outside chores as grass cutting and snow shovelling, but only 10 percent of the women had regular assistance from daughters or daughters-in-law with housecleaning and laundry work. Fifteen percent of the respondents said they wished they had more help with housework, but they did not expect this help to come from their daughters.

Relatives

The importance of other kinfolk in the lives of rural elders is unclear, although they are thought to be especially helpful to widows (Powers, Keith and Goudy, 1981:204). For this sample, however, it was the single women who were the principal recipients of kinship support both in terms of friendship and domestic labour. Even though the widows were older and in poorer health, the single women were more than twice as likely to receive help from their kin with their indoor housework, and almost five times more likely than the widows to have their outside chores looked after by relatives.

The number of single women in this sample is too small to draw any conclusions from these findings, but they suggest that other relatives may substitute for adult offspring in the lives of unmarried older females.

Neighbours and friends

Older women depend primarily on their age peers for friendship and a social life (Rosow, 1967), and the longer one has lived in the same community, the more extensive these bonds of friendship are likely to be (Riley and Foner, 1968:561). The present data generally support these claims, but they also suggest certain dysfunctions of rural residence even in the supposedly supportive environment of a small town or village.

Four-fifths of the lifelong country dwellers in this sample had lived in the same rural neighbourhood for more than twenty years, the oldest of them for most of their lives. The bonding of local families through intermarriage and lifelong association does produce a kind of cousinship that is the backbone of the rural support network. Less remarked, however, is the fact that this informal service network operates more successfully in built-up areas than in isolated locations (Kivett, 1985:182), and that a support system rooted in propinquity is more likely to sustain the rural native than the urban transplant.

Given the clustering of aging females in towns and villages, there is a strong probability that the friends and neighbours of a rural elderly woman are themselves elderly women living alone, and the amount of practical assistance that neighbours can offer one another is likely to be limited. Table 2 seems to confirm this social fact: neighbours contributed the least amount of service, even with such traditional neighbourly activities as cutting grass or shovelling walkways in winter.

Still, neighbours are an assurance of help in emergencies, and they are accessible for informal socializing. With the exception of the single women, whose strongest links were with kin, all the respondents had closer friendship ties with neighbours than with either their children or their other relatives. Confidant relationships, however, were of a different order.

The confidant relationship is especially important to the quality of life in old age (Strain and Chappell, 1982) and, in theory, women who have known one another for most of their lives should be able to fortify themselves with these nourishing friendships. This was not necessarily the case here, however. The likelihood of having a confidant declined with age, with widowhood, and with community residence, in spite of the concentration of elderly widows in small settlements where access was not a problem and the women were no strangers to one another.

Social isolation may be a serious concern in areas where the population is widely dispersed and transportation largely unavailable (Kivett, 1985:183), but these were not salient factors in the lives of the village widows. Nevertheless, these oldest women did report significantly more difficulty than their younger counterparts in keeping in touch with close friends. Overall, 78 percent of the respondents said that transportation was not a problem in maintaining personal friendships, but the oldest women were over four times more likely than the younger ones to cite lack of transportation as a problem in preserving their confidant relationships with other women — suggesting that even in the shrinking social world of aging females, confidant relationships may be qualitatively different from relationships with neighbours and other friends.

The close-knit quality of country neighbourhoods can be both an advantage and a drawback. Small communities offer a high degree of social stability and personal safety, but the obverse of these desirable attributes is that they are inward-looking and gossipy. Ever-watchful eyes are an excellent guarantee of assistance in time of need: neighbours are intimately acquainted with each other's personal habits, and any deviation is immediately noted. Depending upon one's age, health, life situation or personality, this monitoring can be a blessing or a tribulation.

In the same way, village life may be perceived as either tranquil or dull. The outside world can seem very far away, and the medium of social exchange is the small coin of daily trivia. Everyone knows everyone else's business — or thinks they do. Rural memories are long; nothing is ever forgotten (forgiven, yes; forgotten, no), and relationships that stretch back into childhood may not necessarily be the most rewarding sources of social intercourse in later life. Table 4 suggests that this darker side of rural life was a more salient factor in Northumberland's farm communities than in the mixed environment of Haliburton's tourist-cum-retirement towns.

TABLE 4:
Informal Visiting

"Do you have a neighbour with whom you exchange regular informal visits, such as dropping in for coffee?"

	County	
	Haliburton (n = 89)	Northumberland (n = 79)
"Yes."	65.2	50.6
"No, but I wish I did."	14.6	12.7
"No, and I'm just as glad I don't."	20.2	36.7

Clearly, friends may be neighbours, but not all neighbours are friends. Interestingly, there was no difference according to background: the responses of rural and urban women were virtually identical.

Employees

Paid employees provided significantly more household assistance than either relatives or neighbours, and the same overall amount as children. Fifteen percent of the women employed someone to help with indoor housework, and the older the respondent the more likely it was that this employee was a visiting homemaker who also provided meals and personal care. More than half of the women over 80 who employed someone to help them in the house were being looked after by visiting homemakers.

Overall, 53 percent of the respondents had some kind of practical assistance, mainly with their indoor work, and there was a strong association between age and the likelihood of having help. Children contributed mainly to the oldest women, especially the widows, and whatever support other relatives provided went primarily to the single women, regardless of their age. Neighbours and friends offered companionship but a minimal amount of physical labour, and paid employees were a major source of care.

Discussion

The *Gemeinschaft* characteristics of country life encourage stereotypical thinking about the goodness of fit between the needs of elderly women and the supportive nature of rural environments. Because rural communities are essentially aggregates of primary relationships, there is a tendency to assume that it is easier for aging women to maintain their independence and social contacts in a place where people know and help one another.

A study of elderly women in rural Southern Ontario generally supports this assumption but does raise some questions about the adequacy of a service network based on kinship and neighbourliness, especially in view of the increasing in-migration of urban elders who may or may not have close ties to their new community.

The shortage of formal support services in nonmetropolitan areas means that the health and well-being of older women are, to a considerable extent, dependent upon an informal network of family and friends. However, only so much can be done informally: the services of kinfolk and peers may be necessary, but they are not sufficient for meeting the dependency needs of old age and widowhood. They cannot compensate for the scarcity of housing alternatives and home-care services, or the general lack of organized community effort on behalf of the rural elderly.

The strong association between age and the likelihood of having household help would seem to indicate that the informal support network was working well for these particular respondents. However, a substantial proportion of this help came from paid employees, and the question does arise: had this kind of assistance not been available to the respondents, would their kinfolk be able, and willing, to make up the difference? Generally speaking, there is no one else. Country neighbours are an excellent resource in times of emergency and for transportation, and they also keep a weather eye on one another — although neighbourly solicitude is not without its cost. But routine care can scarcely be expected from neighbours and friends who are likely to be as old as oneself.

In sum, the practical assistance offered to these elderly women by their offspring and kinfolk and by neighbours and friends epitomized the rural support network in general: long on emergencies and short on routine care.

There is also the question of how much assistance is really needed, and on this point the data cannot judge. Most of the women maintained that they did not need additional assistance, and given the rural environment's intolerance of serious and chronic impairment, they were probably right. Had they been more incapacitated, it is unlikely they would have been able to remain in the community. However, the greater involvement of visiting homemakers with women in the two highest age categories attests to the rising incidence of medically defined incapacity and is a straw in the wind.

Advancing age had already compromised the respondents' ability to live alone in the open country. The fact that virtually all the widows were clustered in the towns and villages underlines a salient social fact of rural life: the ability to maintain an independent lifestyle in open country depends in large measure on the availability of vigorous males.

It has been suggested that the family is a reasonable alternative to the health and welfare organizations of modern society (Shanas and Sussman, 1981), but in spite of the larger size of rural families, consanguinity is not a guarantee of adequate support. Young adults continue to migrate out, and it is problematic whether those who are left have the ability to provide ongoing care, always assuming they have the inclination. "If the rural elderly really were uniquely advantaged by embeddedness in strong, supportive kin networks. . .their needs for public services might indeed be less. The fact is that they are not" (Lee and Cassidy, 1985:165).

The situation may be even more parlous for aging women who are not longtime country dwellers. Women in the country are not all "country women." During the past decade, out-migration from metropolitan areas has brought increasing numbers of retired urban couples to the country. How these city wives will cope with advancing age and widowhood remains to be seen. At the moment they are relatively young, healthy and married, and most of them have developed friendly relationships with their new neighbours. But their closest ties are to city friends, and the data suggest that the husbands of these women may be more enthusiastic about country life than they are themselves. Only time, and longitudinal research, will determine whether their rural roots have grown sufficiently strong to sustain them in a nonmetropolitan environment.

References

Abu-Laban, Sharon and Baha Abu-Laban
　1980　"Women and the aged as minority groups, A critique." Pp. 63-79 in Victor
　　　　W. Marshall (ed.), *Aging in Canada*. Toronto: Fitzhenry & Whiteside.
Amoss, Pamela T. and Stevan Harrell
　1981　*Other Ways of Growing Old*. Stanford, California: Stanford University
　　　　Press.

Cape, Elizabeth
    1981a "Social Change and the Rural Elderly." Paper presented at the Rural
        Sociological Society Annual Meeting, University of Guelph, Ontario.
    1981b "Health Beliefs and Practices of the Rural Aged." Paper presented at the
        Joint Meeting of the Gerontological Society of America and the Canadian
        Association on Gerontology, Toronto.
    1982   "Aging women in rural society: Out of sight, out of mind." Pp. 214-215 in
        Emily M. Nett (ed.), *Women As Elders*. Toronto: Resources for Feminist
        Research 11(2) July.
Coward, Raymond T. and Eloise Rathbone-McCuan
    1985   "Delivering health and human services to the elderly in rural society." Pp.
        197-222 in Raymond T. Coward and Gary R. Lee (eds.), *The Elderly in
        Rural Society*. New York: Springer Publishing Company.
Davidson, Kenneth R. and Elizabeth Davidson
    1969   "Healthways in seaward: A Nova Scotian fishing community." *Canadian
        Journal of Public Health* 48.
Dulude, Louise
    1978   *Women and Aging: A Report on the Rest of our Lives*. Ottawa: Advisory
        Council on the Status of Women.
Gubrium, Jaber F.
    1973   *The Myth of the Golden Years: A Socio-Environmental Theory of Aging*.
        Springfield: Charles C. Thomas.
Guemple, Lee
    1980   "Growing old in Inuit society." Pp. 95-101 in Victor W. Marshall (ed.),
        Aging in Canada. Toronto: Fitzhenry & Whiteside.
Hodge, Gerald and Mohammad A. Qadeer
    1983   *Towns and Villages in Canada*. Toronto: Butterworth.
Ireland, Giselle
    1983   *The Farmer Takes a Wife*. Chesley, Ontario: Concerned Farm Women.
Ishwaran, K.
    1980   *Canadian Families: Ethnic Variations*. Toronto: McGraw-Hill Ryerson.
Kalbach, Warren E. and Wayne W. McVey
    1979   *The Demographic Bases of Canadian Society*. Toronto: McGraw-Hill
        Ryerson.
Kivett, Vira R.
    1985   "Aging in rural society: Non-kin community relations and participation."
        Pp. 171-191 in Raymond T. Coward and Gary R. Lee (eds.), *The Elderly in
        Rural Society*. New York: Springer Publishing Company.
Lee, Gary R. and Margaret L. Cassidy
    1981   "Kinship systems and extended family ties." Pp. 57-71 in Raymond T.
        Coward and William M. Smith, Jr. (eds.), *The Family in Rural Society*.
        Boulder, Colorado: Westview Press, Inc.
    1985   "Family and kin relations of the rural elderly." Pp. 151-169 in Raymond
        T. Coward and Gary R. Lee (eds.), *The Elderly in Rural Society*. New
        York: Springer Publishing Company.
Martin Matthews, Anne
    1980   "Women and widowhood." Pp. 145-153 in Victor W. Marshall (ed.),
        Aging in Canada. Toronto: Fitzhenry & Whiteside.

Martin Matthews, Anne and Audrey Vanden Heuvel
   1985   *Conceptual methodological issues in research on aging in rural versus urban environments.* Guelph: Canadian Journal on Aging 5 (1):49-60.
McGhee, Molly
   1984   *Women in Rural Life: The Changing Scene.* Government of Ontario: Ministry of Agriculture and Food.
Ontario Advisory Council on Senior Citizens
   1980   *Towards An Understanding of the Rural Elderly.*
Posner, Judith
   1977   "Old and female: The double whammy." *Essence* 2(1):41-48.
Powers, Edward A., Patricia M. Keith and Willis J. Goudy
   1975   "Family relationships and friendships." Pp. 67-90 in Robert C. Atchley and Thomas O. Byerts (eds.), *Rural Environments and Aging.* Washington, D.C.: Gerontological Society.
   1981   "Family networks of the rural aged." Pp. 199–217 in Raymond T. Coward and William M. Smith, Jr. (eds.), *The Family in Rural Society.* Boulder, Colorado: Westview Press.
Riley, Matilda W. and Anne Foner
   1968   *Aging and Society.* Vol. 1. *An Inventory of Research Findings.* New York: Russell Sage Foundation.
Rosow, Irving
   1967   *Social Integration of the Aged.* New York: Free Press.
Rowles, Graham D.
   1983   "Geographical dimensions of social support in rural Appalachia." Pp. 111-130 in Graham D. Rowles and Russell J. Ohta (eds.), *Aging and Milieu.* New York: Academic Press.
Shanas, Ethel and Marvin B. Sussman
   1981   "The family in later life: Social structure and social policy." Pp. 211-231 in Robert W. Fogel et al. (eds.), *Aging: Stability and Change in the Family.* New York: Academic Press.
Shulman, Norman
   1980   "The aging of urban Canada." Pp. 27-34 in Victor W. Marshall (ed.), *Aging in Canada.* Toronto: Fitzhenry & Whiteside.
Statistics Canada
   1983   *Current Demographic Analysis*, Report on the Demographic Situation in Canada 1983. Catalogue 91-209E. Ottawa.
Strain, Laurel A. and Neena L. Chappell
   1982   "Confidants: Do they make a difference in quality of life?" *Research on Aging* 4 December (4):479-502.
Taietz, Philip
   1975   "Community facilities and social services." Pp. 145-156 in Robert C. Atchley and Thomas O. Byerts (eds.), *Rural Environments and Aging.* Washington, D.C.: Gerontological Society.
Unruh, David R.
   1983   *Invisible Lives.* Beverly Hills: Sage.
Ward, Russell A.
   1978   "Limitations of the family as a supportive institution in the lives of the aged." *Family Coordinator* 27 October (4):365-373.

6
Modernization and Aging in the Anicinabe Context

Rosamond M. Vanderburgh
Department of Anthropology
University of Toronto

The need for sensitivity to such differences as gender, ethnicity and socio-economic class among Canadian aged has been pointed out by Marshall (1980:62). Canada's Native population is characterized by a very different demographic situation from that prevalent in the larger Canadian society. While the larger society shows a distinct trend towards the aging of the population (Denton and Spencer, 1980), Canada's native Indian population is "younging"[1] (Frideres, 1983:138). This reversal of the national trend within a minority group has profound implications not only for the making and implementation of health care and social service policy, but also for the development of theory in social gerontology.

The search for patterns upon which to base theory is a complex problem. Holzberg (1981) has noted that ethnic categories themselves are seldom homogeneous, and certainly within the broad category of "Native Canadian" there exists tremendous diversity based upon various combinations of the cultural and historical dimensions (see Vanderburgh, 1982, for a more complete discussion of this point). The discussion below is concerned with a small portion of an Indian "nation," the Anicinabe of the Georgian Bay area in Ontario. The term *Anicinabe*, which means "original people," is used by these Native speakers themselves when referring to a population of mixed Ojibwe, Odawa (Ottawa) and Potawatomi origin. These three tribal groups share a common language and a similar traditional culture. As well, they were historically linked in the nineteenth century migrations, removals and resettlements of Native populations in the Great Lakes area. The research upon which this article is based has been conducted in Anicinabe reserve communities on the Bruce Peninsula and Manitoulin Island, as well as in the Native community in Toronto. The role of Anicinabe aged will be reviewed in both the historical and contemporary contexts, and the implica-

The research upon which this paper is based was supported by the Canada Council (Grant S74-0105, 1974-1975) and the Social Sciences and Humanities Research Council of Canada's Population Aging Program (Grant 492-82-0010, 1982-1983). As well, Erindale College, University of Toronto, has provided ongoing support in the form of travel grants.

tions of these data for the development of theory will be discussed. The data on traditional elderhood are drawn from the memories of aged informants, as well as from standard ethnographic and ethnohistorical writings on the Anicinabe (including, for example, Brown, 1952; Densmore, 1929; Dunning, 1959; Hallowell, 1960; Jenness, 1935; and Johnston, 1976).

One of the most widely used theoretical models of macro-level social change, the modernization model, has found considerable support among gerontologists. Cowgill and Holmes (1972) tested the modernization model against ethnographic data on the status and role of the elderly in fifteen very dissimilar societies. They concluded that as modernization increases the status of the elderly declines. Cowgill (1974:127) has tried to tighten and thus strengthen this theory with a more explicit definition of the general process of modernization. He emphasizes that the process is an unidirectional one, is international in scope and transforms a total society rather than effecting transformations in segments of a total society. Thus the definition of the process as international implies that wherever modernization is known to have occurred we would expect to be able to document an increasingly lower status for the elderly. Cowgill further notes that the development or introduction of modern health technology has important implications for the status and role of the aged. Although in the long run modern health technology leads to the aging of a society, in the short term the opposite trend, a "younging," should occur due to "a rapid increase of the child population" (Cowgill, 1974:129). This phenomenon could, he suggests, be a significant factor in determining patterns of intergenerational relations.

Certainly these insights seem to account for the demographic variance between Canada as a whole and the Canadian Indian minority, and in the discussion of the Anicinabe that follows, the proportion of young to old emerges as a significant dimension (though only one) in intergenerational relationships. However, the model of modernization as transforming a total society needs to be qualified and redrawn. The Canadian demographic statistics suggest that while modernization may transform a whole society, the *timing* of the transformation will vary across the segments of a plural society.

Recently Foner (1984) has reviewed both the modernization model and the arguments of those who have used historical data to criticize it. She notes that cross-cultural data from modernizing nonindustrial societies show that a decline in the status of the elderly is far from inevitable, and suggests that the model, even as revised by Cowgill in 1974, is too simplistic (Foner, 1984:203). It fails to take into account the multidimensionality of the overall status of the elderly.

Amoss (1981a, 1981b) has used data from the Coast Salish Indians of British Columbia and Washington State to challenge the application of the modernization model in gerontology. The status of the elderly in any society is, she feels, directly related to the balance between the cost of supporting them and the social contributions they are perceived as making. She shows that the high premodernization status of Coast Salish elders changed with modernization to approximate the low status of the aged in the larger North American society. However, with the "younging" of Coast Salish society that followed the introduction of modern health technology, the traditional knowledge of the elders came to be perceived as a major contribution to the maintenance of Salish identity.

The Anicinabe data presented below further challenge the validity of the modernization model of aging. Missionary influence in the Georgian Bay area began as early as 1825 (Graham, 1975), and the establishment of schools for Indian children was an important part of early missionary work here. Thus, erosion of the aboriginal culture has continued steadily for over a century and a half. This erosion has been especially severe in the linked areas of religion and healing,[2] as well as in the language. These are the very aspects of culture that relate most closely to what we know of the traditional role of Anicinabe elders.

Traditional Elderhood

In prereserve times, and prior to the influence of missionaries and schools, Anicinabe elder status was understood partly in terms of the individual's progress through the life-cycle statuses. Those who were grandparents, or who belonged to the grandparental generation, tended to be perceived (and to perceive themselves) as elders. However, the nature of the individual's contribution to the survival of the kin group was another important aspect of the meaning of elderhood.

The younger adult members of the group were busy with the daily subsistence round, based partly on hunting and gathering and partly on horticulture. Members of the parental generation had little time for child rearing. Those perceived as elders, on the other hand, played a major role in the socialization of new members of the group; this socialization role was their major contribution to group survival. Thus, any individual who was no longer actively involved in the subsistence round tended to be viewed, whatever his or her age, as an elder. Frequently the socializing elder was a grandparent, but the Anicinabe child referred to anyone in the grandparental generation, or who fulfilled an elder's role, as "grandparent."

"Grandparents" expected, and received, deference and respect from "grandchildren." Within these broad guidelines the relationship between elder and child was warm and almost fraternal. In contrast, the relationship between parent and child was patterned along authoritarian lines.

It is difficult to ascertain whether *any* person in the appropriate generation, and in a socializing role, was invariably perceived as an elder. Aged informants today mention the additional criteria of acquired wisdom and successful experience in surviving life's vicissitudes. At any rate, Anicinabe "grandparents" were repositories of knowledge, of essential cultural information, and they were responsible for transmitting that information to the "grandchildren."

This aspect of the elders' role is not unique to the Anicinabe; it has been widely documented in North American Native groups, and indeed among traditional cultures around the world. Amoss and Harrell (1981) use Lévi-Strauss's nature/culture distinction to explain why this should be so. The young represent "nature," and must be transformed into cultural beings; this transformation is achieved by the elderly, who represent "culture." The aged represent not only the general aspect of "culture" as opposed to "nature," but also they "embody" a specific culture:

> Whereas young children are unruly and unmannerly, without language, shame, instruction, or memory, the old are dignified, masters of their native language and its oral traditions, sensitive to honor, well versed in customary law. . . . They are also more fully committed [than young people] to their own cultural system, its modes of expressio, its technology, its dominant themes, and its aesthetic values" (Amoss and Harrell 1981:15).

Anicinabe elders in the Georgian Bay area were (and still are) experts on both mythic and local history, on Native language usage, on healing and (to a lesser extent today because of the depth of missionizing) on ritual. In sum, they controlled the core values of their culture as these were embodied in myths/legends and in the forms of their language. Anicinabe core values have always been concerned with what are perceived as the most basic aspects of survival: the control of social interaction and of the "supernatural," both essential for survival and success at the group and individual levels.

Social interaction involved not only human persons, but also the interaction of humans with "other-than-human" persons, i.e., animal and supernatural "persons" (Hallowell, 1960). In addition, the incremental building up of individual power during the life course through proper social relations with the supernatural was the major road to success and renown. Survival to elder status underlined and validated the existence of this personal power, and elders could transmit some of their power to children through the naming ceremony, as well as through the passing on of specific skills in dealing with the supernatural.

Teaching was done largely through oral narratives, and the functional model of elderhood is embodied in the two forms of Anicinabe elders' narratives (Hallowell, 1960). Anicinabe dialects distinguish between the myth or sacred tale and the anecdotal narrative (glossed by Hallowell as "news or tidings"). Myths deal with the exploits of culture heroes such as Nanabush, and "other-than-human" persons, and in these tales elders passed on the core values that control social interaction. The anecdotal (or experiential) narratives are based on real events in the lives of real people, either the narrator or someone he has known or heard of. Into this form of narrative the elders incorporated information about survival techniques of proven worth in both known and new situations. New situations called for new ways of coping, and elders transmitted not only received cultural information but also new information. Amoss (1981a, 1981b) has noted that Coast Salish elders not only pass on received cultural information (tradition), but that they also innovate freely, creating new ceremonies based on a combination of traditional and contemporary belief.

Erosion of Elders' Role

With the coming of Christian missions and schools the role of elders as transmitters of vital survival information began to break down. By the 1960s it had virtually disappeared. Missionaries and schoolteachers controlled the cultural information now perceived as vital to survival in the larger Canadian society. As the context of survival changed, so did the nature of the information. Traditional knowledge was denigrated by the new purveyors of cultural information as they transmitted Christian values, literacy and mathematics and the skills of manual training and domestic science.[3]

Not only was the elders' role usurped, but their prestige disappeared. Once vital, contributing members of Native society, they were reduced to the status of liability. Families no longer assigned to a fortunate grandchild or great-grandchild the coveted status of helper to a beloved elder. The physical toll of aging brought about a loss of autonomy for the elders, and many were forced into various non-Native care institutions. The bewilderment and resentment of such elders, many of whom had as children helped their own grandparents to remain independent, has a special pathos.

Anicinabe Elders Today

In searching for a model for the study of role adaptation under conditions of socio-cultural change, Landy (1974) has reviewed the data on the impact of Western medicine on traditional curers. He defines three categories of role adaptation to the process of modernization: "adaptive," "attenuated" and "emergent" roles (Landy, 1974:106). The "adaptive" role involves change in the direction of a new synthesis of tradition with modern science and technology. If we apply this concept to the study of elderhood, a traditional elder in the "adaptive" role would not only *receive* new information, but would *process* that information and *create* new cultural forms, while retaining the indigenous community as his major reference and membership group. Amoss's description of the contemporary role of Coast Salish elders closely approximates Landy's "adaptive" role (Amoss, 1981a, 1981b).

The category of "attenuated" role involves a conscious decision to maintain the traditional role within the indigenous community and the acceptance of diminishing prestige associated with an increasingly obsolete role. The modernizing community, in "attenuated" role adaptation, views the modern role as superior to the traditional role. This sort of attenuation of the Anicinabe elders role has been described above.

Landy's third category, the "emergent" role, involves the appearance of an entirely new role, not previously known in the indigenous society but having an analogue in the modern system. An elder who fills an "emergent" role retains his membership in the indigenous community, but the role reference group is the modern society, and he may find himself in competition with members of that system who fill the analogue roles. For example, Native elders who are involved in alcohol and drug-addiction counselling (an "emergent" role) are in competition with non-Native social workers.

Amoss notes that "a shift in the cultural climate" (Amoss, 1981b:50) during the 1960s and '70s has enabled contemporary Coast Salish elders to reestablish the high prestige held formerly. The shift she refers to is the increasing awareness of minority rights in the context of North American plural society. In Canada, one result of this shift is governmental support at federal, provincial and municipal levels for the policy of multiculturalism.

Canada's Native community has undergone a resurgence of political awareness, accompanied by a prolonged period of "consciousness raising" during the sixties and early seventies. Native demands, in conjunction with support for multiculturalism, have given rise to a federally supported Indian cultural renaissance through the Cultural/Educational Centres Program of the Department of Indian Affairs and Northern Development (DIAND). The foundation of this program is the belief that awareness and understanding of Native values and traditions will give Indian people a sense of pride in their Native identity and will improve the quality of their participation not only in their own communities, but also in the larger Canadian society.

Sixty of these Native Cultural/Educational Centres have been instituted across Canada, four of them in Ontario. As staff members of the various centres began the search for resources in the quest for cultural traditions, local elders took on new significance. They began to be perceived as being of major cultural value, as living links to tradition.

The Ojibwe Cultural Foundation (OCF) was started in 1974 on the West Bay Reserve of Manitoulin Island in Georgian Bay, with representation from twelve local reserve communities. OCF staff, initially concerned primarily with the development and implementation of a Native language curriculum in the elementary schools, soon discovered that local elders were their most important resource. As communication with other centres grew, so, too, did the full realization of the vital role elders had played in earlier times.

While each centre developed its own thrust and its own programs, based on local concerns, the mandate of the DIAND program in which they were rooted continued to emphasize the importance of Native traditions. On Manitoulin Island this emphasis led to a focus by the OCF on the revival of the traditional religious system, including ritual protocol. Since elders had been the traditional experts on these matters, the OCF began to articulate as one of its major goals the revival of the elders' role.

Due to the depth of the missionary experience there has been very little retention of traditional ritual in this area. A form of divination known as the "shaking tent" ritual seems to have persisted into the 1950s, but most local elders, as the OCF began its thrust to revive their traditional role, were unenthusiastic about participation in its programs. To be involved in teaching the Anicinabe language and legends in the schools seems to have been perfectly acceptable. However, belief in sorcery, and fear of accusations of sorcery, remain strong forces of social control in Anicinabe communities, and elders, the traditional repositories of spiritual power as well as knowledge, command fear as sorcerers as well as respect for the positive aspects of their role. For some years fear of being accused of sorcery as well as a strong commitment to Christianity kept most local elders from participating in the programs of the OCF. Searching for substitutes for local elders, OCF staff imported elders from the north and west, as well as from Michigan and Minnesota, and the revival of traditional ritual began in this area.

As local elders came into contact with the imported ritual experts and became aware of the survival of many elements of the traditional religious system in other Anicinabe areas, they began to lose their fear of sorcery accusations. Also, some of the imported elders belonged to other tribal groups (e.g., Cree, Sioux), and many of the rituals presented under the auspices of the OCF reflected a Pan-Indian ceremonialism rather than cultural specificity.

Not until the OCF staff began to work with the few remaining local "medicine people" (curers, both men and women), did they become aware of the amount of traditional information still controlled by their own elders. In addition, they discovered a strong storytelling tradition. Elders still recounted to one another the narratives they had heard in their youth from their elders. Some of these narratives dealt with local places of spiritual power, and these sacred places have become focal points for the reviving ceremonialism.

While it has taken some time for local elders to accept the OCF and its programs, an increasingly positive response is discernible from 1978 to the present. Today elders attend OCF board meetings where their opinions are sought in decision making. These opinions are frequently given in either mythic or anecdotal narratives, and while to a non-Native observer the elders' narrative answers to questions are frequently obscure, the points they are making are readily understood by their Native audience. Elders attend the summer art camps sponsored by the OCF, and use both types of narrative to acquaint the young artists with Anicinabe traditions. Elders attend the craft training programs, where they pass on specific skills (and incidentally acquire new skills, as well). The language skills of elders are still utilized in local schools. As the OCF has developed its elders program, and begun to sponsor conferences bringing together elders from across Canada and the United States, the positive aspects of elderhood are becoming more widely appreciated. The annual Elders Conference attracts more and more local people in the young and mid-life categories, and the OCF continues to feel that this "revival" of the elders' role is an important aspect in the fulfillment of its mandate.

However, it should be noted that what is taking place is not really a "revival." Although the elders are beginning to receive again the kind of respect and deference that was formerly their due, they are operating today in a new context and fulfilling a somewhat different function than in former days. These Anicinabe elders are no longer operating primarily in the familial context, but rather in the context of a voluntary association, the OCF. This is happening in the urban context, as well, with the Elders' Circle at the Toronto Native Centre. Parallels can be drawn with modernizing institutions in other parts of the world.

As well, there has been a conscious downplaying of the negative aspects of elders' power. The publicly articulated image of elders is of benevolence and wisdom; only in private gossip does the other side of elderhood still find expression. There has been a partial redefinition of the meaning of elderhood. Even though it is stated that absolute age is not a criterion for elder status, there seems to be a tendency to view anyone receiving the Old Age Security benefit, which begins at age sixty-five, as at least a potential elder. While successful experience in coping with and surviving life's traumas is still an important criterion of elderhood, the traumatic situations have been redefined to include dealing with the educational, social service, health care and legal systems, as well as with alcohol and drug abuse and the transition to urban living. While personal honesty and integrity have always been important attributes to the elders, today they are expanded to emphasize the need to be honest about one's mistakes, to discuss them openly so that others may learn from them. This new emphasis may be related to the acquaintance of many of today's elders with the methods of Alcoholics Anonymous.

Most importantly, those who would attain the status of elder today should have had significant socializing experiences with past elders in their own childhood. This is related to the major contemporary function of modern elders, their role as validators of Indian identity (Amoss, 1981b:59-62). The generation of Anicinabe elders who received cultural transmissions from traditional elders is rapidly disappearing. Each year the ranks of those who underwent socializing experiences with elders who had been "born free," prior to the setting up of reserves, dwindle.

The few remaining elders who touched the hands of grandparents acquainted with the vitality of full traditional elderhood constitute a precious resource for Native communities in Canada today. The current quest for Native self-government has been supported in the recent report of the Special Committee on Indian Self-Government (Canada, 1983), which recommends that each Indian "nation" work out its own governmental policy based on traditional forms of government. Indian "nations" are turning not only to recorded history for this information, but also to the oral narratives of the elders.

Anicinabe elders are still telling stories, although the institutional setting in which they operate has changed. Their stories still reflect the dual function of the elders' role inherent in the two categories of narratives recognized linguistically, maintenance and change, tradition and transformation. They pass on the core values of the old culture in the myths they heard in their childhood, but in their anecdotal narratives they share with today's youth their own experiences in survival, in coping with modernization. They look forward, at meetings organized by the OCF, to that part of the program when the tables are pushed back and the young people gather to listen. They are master storytellers, evoking breathless attention, laughter and sighs from their audience. That their messages are received and understood is obvious from the emphatic verbal punctuations of agreement and encouragement given by members of their audience.

Amoss has suggested that for the aged the critical issue in social change is the specific context of change, i.e., whether that context provides them with "opportunities to reestablish themselves in useful roles" (Amoss, 1980a:228). The context of social change for Anicinabe elders is marked by the same "younging" of the Native population, governmental support for multiculturalism and emphasis on Native identity that are felt in Native communities across Canada. What seems to be unique in the Georgian Bay area is the presence of an institution, the Ojibwe Cultural Foundation, that not only keeps the elders from local reserves in constant communication but also provides them with opportunities to meet with elders from other Indian "nations," and thus to reinforce on a wider level a positive image of elderhood. In addition, the OCF provides opportunities in its programs for today's elders to fulfill their "transformative" role, the role implicit in the anecdotal narrative mode. Their role today seems, in Landy's terms, to be strongly "adaptive."

Because, however, the context on which Anicinabe elderhood is operating is so ephemeral, one cannot but wonder what will happen when today's elders with their validating youthful experiences of traditional elderhood are gone. Tomorrow's elders will be one more generation removed from those experiences. Nevertheless, the flexibility of the oral narrative mode of cultural transmission, and the possibilities it offers for innovation and the introduction of change, would seem to suggest that as long as the elders tell stories they will retain some measure of significance in Anicinabe society.

Notes

1   The term "younging" is taken from Cowgill, 1974:129.
2   See Vecsey, 1983:144-159, for a review of the relationship between religion and healing.
3   See Vanderburgh, 1977, for a review of the curriculum in Anicinabe reserve schools.

References

Amoss, P.
   1981a "Coast Salish elders." In P. Amoss and S. Harrell (eds.), *Other Ways of Growing Old: Anthropological Perspectives*. Stanford: Stanford University Press.
   1981b "Cultural centrality and prestige for the elderly: The Coast Salish case." In C. Fry (ed.), *Dimensions: Aging, Culture, and Health*. New York: Praeger.
Amoss, P. and S. Harrell (eds.)
   1981 *Other Ways of Growing Old: Anthropological Perspectives*. Stanford: Stanford University Press.
Brown, Paula
   1952 "Changes in Ojibwa social control." *American Anthropologist* 54(1):57-70.
Canada, House of Commons
   1983 *Indian Self-Government in Canada. Report of the Special Committee on Indian Self-Government*. Ottawa: Queen's Printer.

Cowgill, D.O.
 1974 "Aging and modernization: A revision of the theory." In J.F. Gubrium (ed.), *Communities and Environmental Policy*. Springfield: Charles C. Thomas.
Cowgill, D.O. and L. Holmes (eds.)
 1972 *Aging and Modernization*. New York: Appleton-Century-Crofts.
Densmore, Frances
 1929 *Chippewa Customs*. Bureau of American Ethnology, Bulletin 86.
Denton, F.T. and B.G. Spencer
 1980 "Canada's population and labour force: Past, present and future." In V.W. Marshall (ed.), *Aging in Canada*. Toronto: Fitzhenry & Whiteside.
Dunning, R.W.
 1959 *Social and Economic Change Among the Northern Ojibwa*. Toronto: University of Toronto Press.
Foner, N.
 1984 "Age and social change." In D.I. Kertzer and J. Keith (eds.), *Age and Anthropological Theory*. Ithaca: Cornell University Press.
Frideres, J.S.
 1983 *Native People in Canada: Contemporary Conflicts*. Scarborough: Prentice-Hall Canada.
Graham, E.
 1975 *Medicine Man to Missionary*. Toronto: Peter Martin Associates Limited.
Hallowell, A.I.
 1960 "Ojibwa ontology, behavior and world view." In S. Diamond (ed.), *Culture in History: Essays in Honor of Paul Radin*. New York: Columbia University Press.
Holzberg, C.
 1981 "Cultural gerontology: Towards an understanding of ethnicity and aging." *Culture* 1(1):110-122.
Jenness, Diamond
 1935 The Ojibwa Indians of Parry Island: Their social and religious life. *National Museum of Canada Bulletin* 78, Anthropological Series 17.
Johnston, Basil
 1976 *Ojibwa Heritage*. Toronto: McClelland and Stewart.
Landy, D.
 1974 "Role adaptation: Traditional curers under the impact of Western medicine." *American Ethnologist* 1(1):103-127.
Marshall, V.W. (ed.)
 1980 *Aging in Canada: Social Perspectives*. Toronto: Fitzhenry & Whiteside.
Vanderburgh, R.M.
 1977 *I am Nokomis, too: The biography of Verna Patronella Johnston*. Don Mills: General Publishing.
 1982 "When legends fall silent our ways are lost: Some dimensions of the study of aging among Native Canadians." *Culture* II(1):21-28.
Vecsey, C.
 1983 *Traditional Ojibwa Religion and its Historical Changes*. Philadelphia: The American Philosophical Society.

7

The Ethnic Dimension of Aging in Canada

K. Victor Ujimoto
Department of Sociology and Anthropology
and Gerontology Research Centre
University of Guelph

In a multicultural society such as Canada, the aged population is not homogeneous and ethnic differences must be taken into account when considering solutions designed to alleviate some of the problems faced by our elderly. A better overview of the heterogeneity of our aging society can be obtained from the percentage age distribution of the elderly by ethnicity in Canada as shown in Table 1. It will be noted that the proportion of those in the 65 years of age and over category is particularly high among certain ethnic groups such as the Jewish, the Polish and the Ukrainian. Although the proportion of the elderly is low among the Chinese and the Italian, this condition may change in the years to come, as indicated by the percentage age distribution for foreign-born populations shown in Table 2. The population "bulge" in the 45 to 64 age category will eventually shift into the over 65 age category. The wide diversity of ethnic groups will continue to exist in Canadian society, however, the most significant aspect of this diversity is perhaps reflected in the recent Canadian immigration statistics for 1980, which are shown in Figure 1.

It will be noted from Figure 1 that in 1980 over 60 percent of the immigrants to Canada came from Asia, Africa, South America and the Caribbean. Future studies on any aspect of Canadian society must recognize that its changing demographic nature, and ethnic minority groups traditionally lumped together as "others" must be considered as an integral component of Canadian society. Jackson (1980:5) argues that for aged minorities, successful adjustment to aging is frequently compounded by their minority statuses, and therefore, examining the "effects of institutionalized victimization" will enable us to assist aged minorities in their adjustment to aging as well as correct some of the inequalities faced by them. In this chapter, some of the implications of this changing demographic profile will be explored with reference to aged ethnic minorities. We will begin by providing an overview of current Canadian literature on ethnicity and aging. This will be followed by an examination of ethnic relations and various patterns of aging in our multicultural Canadian society within the context of

TABLE 1:
Population 65 Years and Over as a Percentage of the Total
Population for Selected Ethnic Groups, Canada, 1981

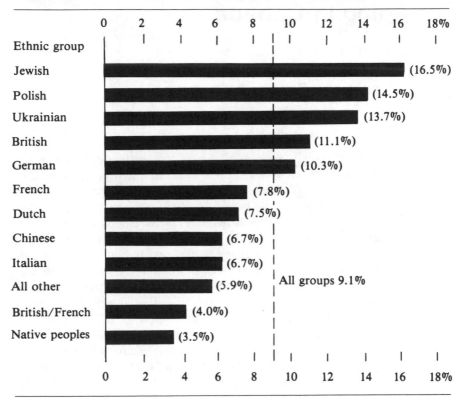

SOURCE: *Elderly in Canada.* Ottawa: Statistics Canada, 1984.

several well-known theories on aging. Several major theories on aging will be assessed in order to determine the extent to which each is appropriate for our study on ethnicity and aging. The key question to bear in mind is whether the theoretical inadequacies are due mainly to the level of abstraction or "fuzziness" of the main concepts, or are a result of the eurocentric biases implicit in the underlying assumptions of the theory. Finally, we provide an overview of our current research in progress that attempts to deal with some of these issues.

Ethnicity and Aging: Overview of Canadian Literature

The impact of ethnicity on aging is a relatively unexplored area of study in Canadian gerontology, but one to which greater significance is being attached. Variations in the ethnic social structure and their influence on

TABLE 2:
Percentage Age Distribution for Foreign-Born Populations
by Selected Birthplaces, Canada, 1981

	Age				
Birthplace	0-14	15-44	45-64	65+	Total
United Kingdom	5.37%	39.36%	29.52%	25.75%	100%
United States	12.14	42.59	21.44	23.83	100
Germany	5.93	48.00	35.42	10.65	100
Hungary	0.74	29.72	45.50	24.04	100
Poland	0.88	18.78	45.20	35.14	100
U.S.S.R.	1.26	10.99	39.93	47.82	100
Romania	2.46	22.56	44.80	30.18	100
Sweden	5.16	37.13	16.55	41.16	100
Finland	2.44	37.06	31.01	29.49	100
Austria	1.65	31.07	32.65	34.63	100
Czechoslovakia	3.43	36.78	38.65	21.13	100
China	3.98	36.27	32.37	27.38	100
Korea	18.09	62.70	14.73	4.43	100
Japan	8.06	56.11	17.05	18.82	100
Taiwan	4.45	48.99	31.56	15.00	100
India	9.06	67.85	17.81	5.28	100
Italy	1.66	51.27	36.35	10.72	100

SOURCE: 1981 Census of Canada, Population, Series 93-926.

expressions of age-related behaviour are gradually being recognized by various health practitioners such as doctors, nurses, social welfare workers and social policy analysts. In order to account for the variations in social and psychological behaviour of aged ethnic minorities, the limitations in the traditional ways of conceptualizing age-related issues must be recognized and basic assumptions that underlie existing theories must be modified or discarded entirely. Theories that are applicable to one ethnic group may not be applicable to another.

Isajiw (1974:124) examined the various definitions of ethnicity and listed the most common attributes of ethnic groups that were most frequently included in the definition. These were attributes such as ancestral origin, same culture or customs, cultural beliefs, common values, sense of ethnic group identity, race or physical characteristics and language. Since Canadian society is multicultural, it is obvious that the ethnicity factor, which is comprised of the various attributes noted by Isajiw, will also vary considerably throughout Canadian society. Therefore, when considering the ethnici-

FIGURE 1:
Landed Immigrants to Canada, 1981

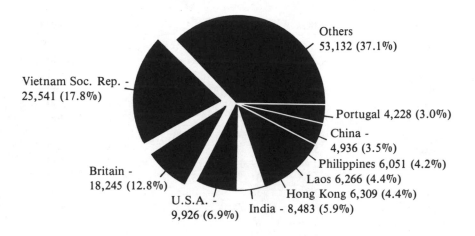

Major Source Countries

Others
53,132 (37.1%)

Vietnam Soc. Rep. -
25,541 (17.8%)

Portugal 4,228 (3.0%)

China -
4,936 (3.5%)

Philippines 6,051 (4.2%)

Britain -
18,245 (12.8%)

Laos 6,266 (4.4%)

Hong Kong 6,309 (4.4%)

U.S.A. -
9,926 (6.9%)   India - 8,483 (5.9%)

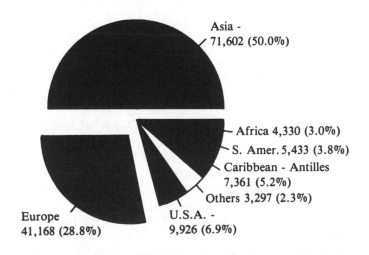

World Areas

Asia -
71,602 (50.0%)

Africa 4,330 (3.0%)

S. Amer. 5,433 (3.8%)

Caribbean - Antilles
7,361 (5.2%)

Others 3,297 (2.3%)

Europe
41,168 (28.8%)   U.S.A. -
9,926 (6.9%)

SOURCE: 1980 *Immigration Statistics*. Ottawa: Employment and Immigration
Canada, 1982:6.

ty dimension in relation to aging studies, there should be a clear understanding of the selected attributes that comprise ethnicity. As Anderson and Frideres (1981:45) have argued, ethnicity has been carelessly overemphasized in the literature and used interchangeably with ethnic groups.

The various ways in which ethnicity has been conceptualized in relation to aging studies may have prevented scholars from finding answers to fundamental questions concerning the influence of ethnicity on family relationships. Rosenthal (1983:2; 1986) has argued that ethnicity has been viewed in at least two different ways. In the first instance, ethnicity has been viewed primarily as immigrant culture. In this view, ethnic/nonethnic equates with traditional/modern. The ethnic family is neatly subsumed under the traditional label and the "Anglo" family at the modern end of the continuum. In the second perspective, ethnicity is viewed as a determinant of social inequality in which "differential access to societal rewards can be related to a model of ethnic change and persistence in families as explained by the relationship of ethnicity to social class and social conflict." Both perspectives overgeneralize and neither intergenerational nor cross-generational variations among ethnic groups are considered. Rosenthal (1983:2) attempts to clarify the ways in which modernization theory has been drawn into the study of aging, ethnicity and the family.

While previous studies on ethnic relations have tended to homogenize ethnic groups and to disregard intergenerational differences, Baar (1978:335) has argued for a generational approach to the analysis of ethnic relations, which differentiates between the various generations of a particular ethnic group. Such an approach may help untangle some of the problems faced in our study of ethnicity and aging. In the Japanese-Canadian case, for example, there are currently four well-defined generational groups: namely, the *Issei* (first or immigrant generation), the *Nisei* (second generation or Canadian born), the *Sansei* (third generation) and the *Yonsei* (fourth generation). As explained by Baar, the generational approach emphasizes the importance of the nature of the environment in which social relations occur. Thus, the degree of institutionalized social distance in the 1900s is considerably different from that of the 1980s, and consequently, ethnic relations between the minority ethnic group and the majority group in Canadian society during the span of these two periods will probably also be different.

One recent study that examines those factors that influence the attitudinal formation between the first or immigrant generation and the second or Canadian born generations is that by Sugiman and Nishio (1983:17). They examine the differences in the socialization process experienced by the *Issei* and *Nisei*. For the *Issei*, the initial period of adjustment to Canadian society is a period of adult socialization in which new values, new social roles and social behaviour must be learned. For the *Issei*, the traditional values may often be in conflict with that of the new society. Feelings of anxiety and insecurity may occur if value conflicts are not resolved. For the *Nisei*, in contrast, value conflict should not be an insurmountable problem depending on the degree of traditional socialization that may have occurred in the earlier formative years. The *Nisei* are often overidealized as a model minority and Sugiman and Nishio advance two hypotheses: (1) that this view is misleading for it rests on the assumption that childhood socialization about traditional Japanese age norms dominates the individual's behaviour throughout life, and (2) that it fails to see how belief systems are shaped by social structures. In order to examine these hypotheses, Sugiman and Nishio advance two contrasting models of old age, namely, the traditional Japanese model based on the Confucian ethic, and the other, the North American model based on individualism.

The traditional Japanese model of old age places primary emphasis on the concept of filial piety through which the children have a filial duty or obligation to look after their parents in old age. This constitutes a kind of social exchange relationship in which the children's debts are eventually repaid to their aged parents by providing comfort and security. Sugiman and Nishio found that the *Issei* did not rely solely upon their children for support and that the *Nisei* regarded dependency upon their own children as a negative option. This tends to support the view that the North American model of old age is preferred even by those who were instilled with the traditional Japanese value system during their early childhood. It cannot be assumed, therefore, that childhood socialization about traditional age norms and social values can be expected to dominate the individual's behaviour patterns over the life span. Social structural conditions or constraints such as social and geographic mobility, high rates of intermarriage and the lack of meaningful communications all appear to be more influential in shaping the belief system of the *Nisei*. While a cursory glance at the existing social gerontological literature may lead one to the conclusion that dependency or reciprocal relationship is not so pronounced between Canadian parents and their children because of the emphasis on independence and individualism, it remains for future studies to investigate intergenerational relationships in various Canadian ethnic groups.

There are several social structural factors to consider when examining intergenerational relationships between immigrants or first generation Canadians and their offspring, the second generation. The elderly today are living to a much older age than in previous generations and this has resulted in a concomitant increase in multigenerational families. The traditional view in some ethnic groups of maintaining filial or moral obligations to parents tends to become untenable from an economic perspective. Also, given the relatively well-developed social welfare system in Canada, there may be less need for the elderly to rely upon their children for economic support, thereby furthering independence for the elderly. Both longevity and the social welfare programs may have a greater impact on intergenerational relations than the traditional factors associated with ethnicity and aging. For many aged immigrants, difficulties with language and the inability to express their personal feelings erect formidable barriers that prevent them from easy access to the available social and economic support services.

Whether it is the lack of services available in one's own language or the cultural and language barriers that prevent ethnic minorities from utilizing them, the net result is the same: underutilization of available services. Chan (1983:43) found that while elderly Chinese women were generally aware of various medical and dental services as well as Chinese community organizations in the Montreal Chinatown, they had no knowledge of services and resources available for the elderly at other institutions and agencies outside the Chinese community. Both Chan (1983:38) and Sugiman and Nishio (1983:24) note the salience of the historical and cultural dimension of the aging process. They argue that research on ethnicity and aging must take into account the impact of the personal histories, the socialization experiences and the structural forces of prejudice and discrimination.

Another area of research on ethnicity and aging that is slowly gaining recognition is that of long-term care. More and more elderly ethnic minorities are being institutionalized in facilities that are essentially organized for the majority or dominant culture. MacLean and Bonar (1983:52) address several important issues that centre around the elderly people from one ethnic group who are placed in institutional settings organized for another cultural group. First generation aged ethnic minorities who are not completely fluent in English or who have an accent are perceived by staff members as recent arrivals to Canada, or at best, only as second-class Canadian citizens. Many institutional care staff members are not aware of the long history of prejudice and discrimination against members of many ethnic minorities such as the Blacks and Asian-Canadians. Elderly ethnic minorities are often placed in a hostile or indifferent environment that not only lacks essential social support, but also the emotional support and recognition for having survived many adversities during their life span. Consequently, a lowering of self-esteem impacts on the well-being and mental health of the aged ethnic minority.

The lack of understanding of ethnic group culture by staff members of hospitals and long-term care facilities also impacts on the relationship between staff and family members. Some ethnic groups such as the Japanese, Chinese, Koreans and Filipinos strongly value the emotional and symbolic support provided the aged members by their family. However, visits by family members to assist with eating, clothing, bathing, etc. are often viewed as interference with the tasks of the staff. The situation becomes even more acute if the aged patient has a communication problem and requires a translation of various instructions or medical directions provided by staff. Aged Japanese, Chinese, Korean and Filipino patients regard doctors as authority figures and seldom question them directly. Questions are often not asked or asked only through family members. Perhaps the aged Japanese patients are mostly at fault for not providing frank responses to doctors' queries concerning the state of the patient's health. There is a very strong tendency not to express feelings of pain or suffering even when a simple request for a pain suppressant may alleviate much of the pain. Indeed Takeuchi's (1984) study of a 250-bed acute care facility of mixed ethnic patients indicated that the aged Japanese patients very seldom utilized the call button because they "didn't want to bother the nurses." Takeuchi notes that it is extremely difficult for social workers and nurses to understand the Japanese patient's innermost feelings because, for some, suffering means strength. Therefore, social workers and nurses must be on a constant lookout for nonverbal signs regarding the care of their patients. The cultural aspects of nonverbal communication, differences in pain thresholds by ethnic groups and differences in the expression of both joy and grief are several vital areas yet to be explored in relation to ethnicity, aging and institutional care. There are, however, indications that a good start has been made to conduct research in some of these areas.

One particular research examines grieving in terms of the bereaved person's discovery patterns of a new culture (Disman, 1983:106). Disman argues that a loss of a mate is one of the major traumas of later life and that the experience parallels the immigrant experience. The central theme of her comparison is that of loss-related transition. Disman suggests that the immigrant experience is but one instance of the grief experience. Similarly, bereavement from a loss of a spouse is but one instance of a transitional experience. She does not agree with the commonly accepted "stage theories of grieving," as not all stages are experienced by the grieving person. Disman recognizes the limitations of her study and concludes by suggesting further exploration of the persistence of ethnic identity that may be a crucial intervening variable in the study of grieving behaviour.

Several studies explore the relationship among religion, ethnicity and aging. Naidoo (1981:84) compares the spiritual aspect of aging in India and in Canada. Although based on a very limited sample of South Asians residing in Toronto, the study permits us to observe some of the characteristics of a traditional South Asian family. Not only are the aged accorded great respect by all family members, they also enjoy the status, prestige and control of family wealth and family power. Family power centres on the ability to influence and control arranged marriages, on the ability to counsel the young and on the socialization of grandchildren. These characteristics are still strongly manifested because South Asian immigrants are still relatively recent arrivals to Canadian society. Naidoo observes that the basis for respect between the old and the young South Asians is cultural rather than religious, and that it arises from the feelings of mutual responsibility.

The spiritual way of life of aged South Asians cannot be easily generalized; however, Naidoo describes it in terms of visits to gurus, temples, mosques, or *Gudwara*, meditation, recitation of mantras, the giving away of material possessions, living in an ashram, worshipping at a shrine and reading sacred scriptures. Naidoo (1981:88) estimates that approximately 10 percent of older South Asians in Canada had moved away from traditional spiritual pursuits to a more permissive way of life. As can be expected, South Asian youth are also placing less emphasis on traditional values and religious practices. For South Asian parents, the erosion of traditional ways of thinking has created some fear in that they may yet find themselves all alone in old age. Manifestations of this are already present in many extended families where the aged are economically well taken care of but socially and culturally isolated, or as Naidoo describes the situation, they experience a "first class prisoner's life."

Another study examines the religious dimension of ethnicity and aging in rural Manitoba (Bond and Harvey, 1985). The role of religious practice in family support and social relationships was examined by asking pastors from the Lutheran and Mennonite congregations questions on (1) the theology or religious writings that relate to the support of the elderly parents by their middle-aged offspring, (2) activities in the church that foster parent/adult child relationships, (3) aspects of church support for the elderly, (4) perception of the congregation regarding parent-child interaction and support, and (5) strains and stress of church members regarding interaction and support between generations of adults. Although the Mennonites are organized into conferences (General Conference, Evangelical Mennonite Conference, Church of God in Christ-Mennonite), Bond and Harvey found that the religious leaders did not reveal any marked differences in their doctrinal dictates to care for the elderly family members. Lutheran respondents reported a lower level of religious practice than either the General Conference or Evangelical Mennonite Conference respondents. However, no differences were found between congregations in the burden reported in the provision of elderly care for family members. Regardless of religious denomination, persons reporting a greater degree of religious practice cited less burden in caring for their family members. The Christian community studied by Bond and Harvey had a common religious and ethnic heritage. However, they found that intradenominational differences appeared stronger than interdenominational differences in the care of elderly family members. The authors also report that despite all the commonalities, the perceptions of social support held by the elderly parents are not the same as those of their adult children.

Several articles on the multiple-jeopardy hypothesis of aging have appeared recently in the literature. The multiple-jeopardy hypothesis argues that members of ethnic minority groups experience the combined negative effects that stem from their minority status, sex and old age. An excellent overview and critique of the literature concerning the propriety of applying the minority label to women and the aged is given by Abu-Laban and Abu-Laban (1977:103-16). In the revised version of this article (1980:63), the authors summarize the various arguments that qualify or disqualify women for minority group status and also, the arguments for and against minority group status for the aged. They note problems based on discrepancies or disagreements in defining minority status characteristics, differential characteristics of women, and in the parameters of agedness. The authors conclude that the disagreements stem from several factors such as ideological considerations, experiential commonalities, social-structural components, conceptual ambiguities and measurement problems associated with concepts such as group consciousness and group identification.

Penning (1983:81) and Havens and Chappell (1983:119) provide further insights into the multiple jeopardy aspects of age, sex and ethnicity. Penning notes that while it has been generally acknowledged that differential status, opportunity and access to social and economic resources are dependent upon one's sex, age, or ethnicity, there is less agreement regarding their combined effects. Penning argues that previous analysis tended to be limited by the following. First, the focus was on single-indicator differentials in the quality of life. Second, there were assumptions about the homogeneity in oversimplified age and ethnic groupings. Third, little attention was paid to interactions among the jeopardy indicators and other relevant predictor variables. Penning provides an empirical assessment of the multiple jeopardy perspectives by utilizing both subjective and objective dimensions of such quality-of-life indicators as self-assessed health status, perceived economic security, and income. This differentiation of the commonly accepted quality of life indicators into the objective and subjective dimensions is an important first step towards a refinement in our analysis of the multiple jeopardy hypothesis. Furthermore, Penning uses four different age and seven ethnic groups for her analysis to examine the additive and interactive relationships of selected variables.

Penning's (1983:90) initial analysis indicated that neither age, sex, nor ethnic origin exerted an independent effect on perceived well-being. Furthermore, the combined effects of age and sex, age and ethnic origin, sex and ethnic origin, and age, sex and ethnic origin were not significantly related to perceptions of overall well-being. Thus, her findings clearly dispute the notion "that interactions between age, sex and ethnicity result in a situation of triple jeopardy, at least with reference to perceptions of well-being as a measure of quality of life." However, Penning found that different factors, such as perceived health status and perceived economic security, were important in determining general feelings of well-being, depending upon one's age and sex. The same variables are of differential significance to the well-being of different groups. As a result, Penning concludes that while the data do not confirm the existence of multiple jeopardy with regard to perceptions of well-being (subjective indicators), they do point out the differential effects of selective factors on various age and ethnic group cohorts. In contrast, multiple jeopardy was an accurate characterization with regard to the one objective indicator employed in the study. Penning's overall conclusion is that her data failed to provide strong support for a multiple jeopardy interpretation. However, in view of the fact that only one objective indicator was examined, she suggests further research that examines the qualitative and quantitative aspects of the aging experience within differing subgroups.

Another study that deals with triple jeopardy in terms of age, sex and ethnicity is by Havens and Chappell (1983:119). Their data are from the Aging in Manitoba Study that examined the unmet needs of 4,805 elderly Manitobans in nine areas: psycho-social functioning, housing, household maintenance, ethnocultural participation, physical health, mental health, economic well-being, accessibility to resources and availability of resources. The data reveal that the elderly in each ethnic group have unmet needs in each of the above noted need areas. Havens and Chappell demonstrate the existence of triple jeopardy for elderly women of Polish, Russian and Ukrainian descent with reference to the mental functioning dimension. The old-elderly women belonging to these ethnic groups emerge as being significantly worse off than the old-elderly men or the young elderly, both men and women, or the old-elderly women of other ethnic groups. As reported by Penning (1983:100), Havens and Chappell also found triple jeopardy confirmed at the objective level but not for subjective measures of well-being. In terms of health perceptions, Havens and Chappell found only ethnicity to be a significant predictor. The findings of both these studies regarding the subjective aspects of well-being should alert future researchers to exercise extreme caution in the measurement of subjective well-being. The psychological aspects of this issue, which centre on perceptions and the translation of perceptions according to one's life expectations, require further research. One possible avenue towards an explanation of the multiple effects of age, sex and ethnicity on the differences that emerge in subjective well-being is to examine the strengths of cultural and ethnic identity retention of the elderly ethnic members. In this regard, it may be instructive to consider some of the more recent studies on the subject of ethnic identity, for example, Driedger (1978:14), Isajiw (1981), Anderson and Frideres (1981:37) and Isajiw and Makabe (1982).

Differences in the reporting of subjective well-being may also be a function of the cultural aspects of ethnicity. Wong (1985:20) notes that Western culture emphasizes independence and individuality, whereas Eastern culture emphasizes social cohesion and dependence on the group for support and guidance. Wong studied elderly Chinese and Anglos to determine if there were any differences in coping, given various stressful events. Three categories of coping behaviour are developed. Internal strategies are those based on one's own instrumental efforts. External strategies include various forms of dependence on others, and palliative strategies are those that make one feel better but do not solve the problem. Given a common set of stressful events such as loss of spouse, worry about children's problems, in-law problems, health problems or income problems, Wong found that the internal strategy of "try various ways to solve the problems yourself" was used more often by the Chinese only in coping with health problems. In other areas of stress, the Chinese relied less on internal strategies than Anglos.

Wong provides two explanations for the preference for internal strategies by the Chinese in dealing with health problems. One is that health services are less accessible to the Chinese elderly. Another explanation is that the older Chinese consider themselves as possessing ancient Chinese secrets in the art of healing. There is also the long tradition of depending on homemade herbal remedies. An interesting finding in Wong's study was that although the Chinese employed more coping strategies, they felt less effective in coping than Anglos. Wong's study has shown that relative to the Anglos, "aging Chinese Canadians found growing old a more stressful experience, reported lower psychological well-being, depended more on external and palliative coping strategies and felt less effective in coping."

One final study on the multiple effects of aging, sex and ethnicity to be noted here is the study by Gerber (1983:62). Gerber notes that the conditions of the ethnic elderly are determined in part by the degree to which the aged are a significant component of each group. Examining Ontario data on Canadian census tapes, Gerber has shown that the elderly of Ontario's many ethnic groups are experiencing old age in different ways. The age of the group and its concentration in specific cities or rural areas determine its potential for meeting the social, economic and service needs of its members. Gerber's study of nineteen categories of ethnic elderly in terms of objective census indicators such as age composition, residence, marital status, fertility, household composition, religion, immigration and internal migration, language, education and income indicated that the aged of specific ethnic groups are disadvantaged in very different and unexpected ways. As Gerber herself has recognized, objective data alone will not provide any insights regarding the question of how much a given phenomenon is a function of ethnicity or culture and how much is a function of recency of immigration, linguistic assimilation, or some other characteristic associated with a given ethnic group. It is abundantly clear, as noted by Holzberg (1981:110), Ujimoto (1983:iv) and Wong (1985:29), that the cultural aspects of ethnicity must be taken into account in studies of aging. The failure to distinguish cultural factors from situational factors often leads to inaccurate assumptions and, at the same time, to questionable conceptualization of the aging process. With reference to ethnicity and aging, then, what are some of the theoretical inadequacies in existing gerontological theories? What aspects related to important life events and transitions must be taken into account in addition to the cultural aspects of ethnicity? We now examine some gerontological theories to determine how well they account for the cultural and situational aspects of ethnicity.

Principal Theories on Aging

At present, as Jackson (1980:8) has indicated, there is no specific theory on ethnicity and aging. Therefore, a fruitful beginning will be to examine some of the major theories on aging and to point out some of their inadequacies in applying the theory to aged ethnic groups, particularly aged ethnic minorities. This will force us to synthesize competing theoretical perspectives on aging and at the same time provide us with a much better understanding of ethnicity and aging.

Bengtson (1979), Chappell and Havens (1980), Havens and Chappell (1983) and Penning (1983) note the multiple jeopardy based on age, sex and ethnic variations. Havens and Chappell argue that to be a member of an ethnic group is to bring to the aging situation both the past history of disadvantage and discrimination based on gender. The key terms here are "past history" and "discrimination." To what extent are contemporary ethnic relations among the aged influenced by certain life events and a history of prejudice and discrimination? Does the process of aging have a modifying effect on prejudicial views and attitudes?

One way in which to investigate these questions is to examine the extent to which ethnic minorities were active participants in various sectors of society with members of other ethnic groups prior to retirement and then to determine if changes had occurred after retirement. The central idea here is based on the disengagement theory developed by Cumming and Henry (1961). The theory postulates the voluntary withdrawal from various activities and role relationships. However, some ethnic minority members, particularly ethnic minority women who were restricted to their traditional family roles, may not have had the opportunity for participation in social and organizational activities prior to retirement. As noted by Dowd (1980:7), "disengagement theory posits the social withdrawal of old people as a universal cultural process that occurs regardless of social-structure variation among societies." If this statement is to be examined with reference to certain minority groups in Canada, it can be shown that discrimination, prejudice and certain historical events that disrupted their earlier lives have had an impact that carried over into their later lives and that this has contributed to the situation of "double jeopardy" and other economic and social consequences in their subsequent patterns of aging. The term "double jeopardy" is issued by Dowd and Bengtson (1978:427) to describe a situation that arises from both age and race discrimination.

The social disorganization experienced by the Japanese-Canadians during World War II is a good example of this. It must be emphasized at the outset, however, that while the situational, historical, political and other social and cultural constraints experienced by "one minority within a minority group," such as the Japanese-Canadians, may not be directly applicable to other minority Asian Canadian groups such as the Chinese, East Indian, Pakistani, Korean and Filipino, the situational similarities faced by these minority ethnic groups today are much greater than the differences. Thus, it may be instructive to use the Japanese-Canadian experience, as an example, to illustrate the relationship between historical events, socio-cultural factors and intergenerational differences that greatly influenced their later lives as an aged ethnic minority in Canadian society.

If we examine the current situation of the aged Asian-Canadians in terms of disengagement theory, we must make the initial assumption that the Asian-Canadians were at one time active participants in the social system and that they were thus able to withdraw from it as they approached retirement. However, it is possible to argue that for the current group of Asian-Canadians, that is, those who are the first generation in Canada, their lack of fluency in the English language as well as differences in social values that they possessed never enabled them to participate fully in the various social and political activities in Canada. This lack of interaction with other ethnic groups could not only be blamed on the lack of fluency in English by the minority group, but also on the behaviour of the dominant or majority group towards the minority group based on subjective evaluations of limited vocabulary and speech style (Giles, 1977).

Another interesting aspect to note here in terms of the withdrawal or disengagement phenomenon most applicable to the Japanese-Canadian *Issei* (first generation Japanese-Canadian) and *Nisei* (second generation in Canada) is the self-imposed situation based on traditional patterns of thinking that centred on the notion of *shikata-ga-nai* or "it can't be helped." Such a withdrawal process initiated by the individual occurred long before reaching retirement and it was essentially based on traditional social values that emphasized complete obedience to authority. This nonchallenging or unquestioning outlook enabled both the *Issei* and *Nisei* to accept meekly whatever was demanded of them during the World War II evacuation period. It may be a gross oversimplification to state that it was the *shikata-ga-nai* mentality that prevented the *Issei* and *Nisei* from demanding a fair and equal return on the various services and tasks performed in relation to their Caucasian counterpart. Nevertheless, the loss in equal wages, the confiscation of land and personal property and the lack of access to higher education eventually exacted their toll before the *Issei* and *Nisei* reached retirement age.

Although it has been argued by many that the lack of *Issei* and *Nisei* aggressiveness was probably based on their respect for certain traditional cultural values, it is essential to recognize that the lack of fair play and the overt discriminatory political practices in British Columbia greatly contributed to and reinforced the *Issei* and *Nisei* feelings of inferiority and helplessness that were to remain with them for the rest of their lives. This is an important aspect to remember when examining the aged *Issei* and *Nisei* today in terms of the activity theory of gerontology.

The central thesis of the activity theory, as noted by Hendricks and Hendricks (1979:76), is that: "The greater the number of optional role resources with which the individual enters old age, the better he or she will stand the demoralizing effects of exit from the obligatory roles ordinarily given priority in adulthood." Aging ethnic minorities, and aged Asian-Canadians in particular, often lack this relative luxury of optional role resources, and thus, along with their communication problems in English, are faced with an alienating and lonely environment. In many old age residences, organized activities, whether social, cultural, or purely physical, neglect both the skills and interests held by the aged Asian-Canadians because of their minority status.

To participate effectively and enjoyably in any day-to-day activity is a skill that is developed continuously during one's lifetime. In a democratic and upwardly mobile society, it is therefore quite conceivable that many of our future aged persons will possess the optional role resources that can be effectively utilized to lead a much more meaningful post-retirement life. However, many aged foreign born were socialized for the future during a period in which they were denied their basic social and human rights. In the case of the Japanese-Canadians, for example, Canadian citizenship was denied to the *Issei* and *Nisei* until June 15, 1948. The British Columbia legislature had disenfranchised the Japanese, including naturalized Canadian citizens, in 1895. The Chinese were already deprived of the franchise in 1875. In 1896, the provincial disenfranchisement was extended to include municipal elections as both Chinese and Japanese were "declared ineligible to vote in municipal elections" (Woodsworth, 1941:42). The British Columbia legislature went even further in ensuring that the Chinese and Japanese were prevented from participating in the electoral processes by proposing an amendment to the naturalization laws so that a residency requirement of ten years had to be satisfied prior to naturalization. In 1897, the provincial legislature passed the Alien Labour Act, which "prohibited the employment of Chinese or Japanese on works authorized by the provincial government" (Woodsworth, 1941:42).

The 1895 act that denied the Japanese the right to a provincial vote had other extremely serious racist implications (Adachi, 1976:52) and the disenfranchisement of the Japanese prevented them from full participation in several areas of professional employment because of the eligibility requirement of having one's name on the voters' list. For example, to secure hand-logging licences required that the applicant be on the voters' list. To practise law or pharmacy, the applicant had to be twenty-one years of age and on the voters' list.

Disenfranchisement did not exempt the Japanese who were British subjects by naturalization or the Japanese-Canadian *Nisei* from certain obligations such as the Taxation Act or the Income Tax Act, and the Dominion Militia Act. Eventually, however, even enlistment in the Canadian Armed Services was denied to the Canadian Japanese. Provincial legislation applied to "racial groups rather than to aliens," and as Adachi (1976:53) has noted, the denial of basic rights such as the right to vote and employment in professional occupations meant that for the Japanese-Canadians, citizenship was meaningless, or at best, symbolized the "status of second class citizenship."

The historical aspects of prejudice, discrimination and concomitant racial segregation into concentration and internment camps experienced by the Japanese-Canadians minimized their optional role resources in their later life. A result was that as one aged and retired from the work force, compensatory activities did not take place readily. The central thesis of the activity theory is that by keeping active by exercising multiple social roles acquired during one's lifetime, the aged can remain socially and psychologically fit and, consequently, able to retain a positive self-concept that contributes to a higher degree of life satisfaction. The theory does not address the relationship between the social structural conditions and what aged ethnic minorities are or are not able to do. Dowd (1980:7) observes that "correlation between 'successful aging' and social class was apparently either unrecognized or considered irrelevant to the theory." This failure to recognize the social structural conditions as they impinged upon one's social interaction, for example, prevented social gerontologists from examining other factors that may have been responsible for the same phenomenon.

Although the hardships encountered because of institutional racism described above applied to all Japanese-Canadians, the impact was not the same on all individuals. In order to understand why some aged people experience difficulties while others do not, we must examine the interplay among biological, social and personal changes as one ages. This approach to the study of aging has been described by Hendricks and Hendricks (1979:198) as the personality theory of aging. With reference to the *Issei* and *Nisei* samples, the devastating effects of continued exposure to prejudice and discrimination on the psychological and personality developments of the victims have not been adequately researched. However, George (1978:840) argues that personality and social status factors are important explanatory variables in accounting for both individual differences in levels of activity and psychological well-being of the aged. George notes further that social status variables such as sex, race and social class are "relatively enduring individual characteristics thus providing a stable context for social interaction and fostering behavioral continuity." It is presumed that "individual differences in behavior reflect individual differences in relevant social status factors." George (1978:842) employs several standard measures for social status, such as education, occupational prestige, employment status and marital status. If we apply these measures to the aged ethnic minorities, both levels of education and occupational prestige scores will be low compared to other aged Canadians, given some of the historical problems briefly noted above.

Studies of older persons by Reichard et al. (1962) and by Neugarten et al. (1968) suggest that patterns of activity and psychological well-being in adulthood reflect underlying personality factors. A much more recent study, by George (1978:840), that examined the relative impact of both personality factors and social status variables upon levels of activity and psychological well-being of older persons revealed that "personality factors were better predictors of psychological well-being than were social status factors, while activity levels were better predicted by social status variables." The above results all suggest the importance of personality and social status factors. Indeed, Pearlin (1980:350) observes that "in order to capture fully the sources of stress, it is necessary to observe life conditions both as they are structured at any moment in time and as they change over time." An interesting aspect of stress and aging is the way in which different groups cope with the stress situation. In this regard, Wong (1985:29) observes that ethnicity is particularly relevant to the study of stress and coping in the ethnic minority elderly since culture may affect the selection of coping strategies.

One possible consequence of the lack of interethnic relations among the aged is the development of subcultural groups based on age and ethnicity. Rose (1965) argues that a distinctive aged subculture develops as "members of one category interact more among themselves than with people from other categories." Rose suggests that current demographic and social trends seem to support this view. However, in the case of the Asian-Canadians and other minority groups in Canada, the notion of a development of an aged subculture seems to be a little premature, as the minority ethnic group members are seldom able to experience a sense of group identity, which is an essential element for a subculture to exist. Furthermore, aged ethnic minorities such as the Blacks and Asian-Canadians over 65 years of age do not form an identifiable collectivity in any given location at present. This condition may soon change if present demographic trends continue and if residential segregation of the aged develops. The degree of ethnic institutional completeness (Breton, 1964) and the extent to which traditional ethnic cultures are maintained may have a modifying effect on the significance of such customs as filial piety and respect for the aged. The more highly developed or institutionally complete the ethnic community, the more likely will cultural characteristics of ethnicity become dynamic components of everyday life and not just convenient labels to be attached to ethnic minority groups.

In the case of the *Issei* and *Nisei* in Canada, there is some importance attached to the year one was born (*nan nen umare*), and also, in the case of the early immigrants, to the time one immigrated to Canada. In this regard, the emphasis placed on the hierarchy of age strata may enable sociologists to examine the aged *Issei* and *Nisei* in terms of the sociology of age stratification. As noted by Hendricks and Hendricks (1979:202), there are several conditions to be met when examining the age structure of society. These are as follows:

1. That there exist "a population of disparate individuals who can be grouped together on the basis of chronological age or other developmental criteria into a series of age strata";
2. That "each stratum, because of actual physical, social or psychological factors, differs from the others in terms of the contributions it makes to ongoing societal needs";
3. That there be "a patterning and distribution of social roles" according to age (age-graded roles); and
4. That there be "an element of age-related expectations intrinsic to the ways in which people react in the roles they perform."

This emphasis on the hierarchy of age strata and the assignment of age-graded roles based on age and experience may serve as a useful stimulus towards better mutual understanding as one ages, regardless of ethnicity. The differences in age-related expectations are culture bound, and it may be of interest to note some of the differences in the ways of thinking about our aged in North America, Europe and in Asia.

In contrasting the Western versus Eastern philosophical approaches to the study of human aging, the French philosopher and gerontologist Michel

Philibert (1979:384) summarizes the Western conceptions and attitudes as follows:

> Aging as biologically engineered; aging as decline and demotion; aging as an anticipation of death; aging as the failure or the enemy of growth, life, and happiness; the aged, feared, despised and discriminated against by the many, looked on as a different species, a minority group, a target population, to be cared for, controlled, segregated and investigated.

In contrast to the above, Philibert (1979:385) provides an outline for the Eastern philosophical view in which:

> . . . aging would be seen more as a cultural and spiritual process than a biologic one, and as a process of continued opportunity for further growth in knowledge, in experience, in wisdom, that is, in understanding the world and in self mastery; a growth, similarly, in social prestige and authority. The aged consequently would be obeyed, respected, consulted and envied.

Although our aged Japanese-Canadian *Issei* and *Nisei* were once exposed to the traditional Japanese family system, their later life experience in Canada contributed to erase whatever images or expectations they may have once held for their later life. This is a commonly held view that seems to agree with earlier studies on the Japanese-Americans, which argued that the impact of lowered status and authority seriously affected them in later life.

In contrast to this view, a study by Osako (1979:448) notes that aged Japanese-American elderly do not suffer from a sudden status loss in old age and that they adjust to it without losing self-esteem. Osako argues that "this is because of the continuity between traditional rural Japanese and contemporary American filial norms that facilitated the Japanese-Americans' adaptation to old age." Although Osako's study is based on a very small sample of 46 *Issei*, 50 *Nisei* and 18 other Japanese-Americans, from various age groups, the study points out the importance of cultural continuity, which influences aging as an adjustment process.

All of the above suggests that current theories on aging must be modified when studying ethnic groups so that socio-cultural differences as well as those aspects related to important life events and transitions are taken into account. One such approach to the study of the aging process is the "life-span developmental perspective" (Hultsch and Deutsch, 1981:216).

The life-span developmental perspective (in its more strictly sociological variant, referred to as the life-course perspective, see Chapter 3 by Marshall and Chapter 15 by Gee) draws attention to the importance of the socio-historical and cultural contexts in which certain life events occurred and how these events in turn influenced the subsequent aging process of the individual. Application of the life-span developmental perspective to the area of ethnicity and aging can be found in an article by Kalish and Moriwaki (1979:266) in which they argue that:

> The older Asian Americans [Asian-Canadians] cannot effectively be theorized about, understood, or provided for without a grasp of four factors: (a) their cultural origins and effects of earlier socialization; (b) their life history in the United States and Canada; (c) those age related changes that occur regardless of early learning or ethnicity; and (d) their experiences concerning what it means to be old.

Previous studies by Ujimoto (1976, 1979, 1982a, 1982b, 1985) examined only selective aspects of the Asian-Canadian experience. At present, we do not have any empirical data to indicate that the four factors noted above have influenced the process of aging as experienced by Asian-Canadians. Our current research project (K.V. Ujimoto, H. Nishio, P. Wong and L. Lam), entitled "Comparative Aspects of Aging Asian-Canadians: Social Networks and Time Budgets," attempts to provide the appropriate data. A very brief overview of our research currently in progress will now be provided.

Research in Progress

The degree to which the cultural aspects of ethnicity are retained can be observed in family or kinship interaction patterns, community participation and in other forms of social activities. From family and kinship interaction patterns, the retention of traditional roles and values by the aged can be observed if the aged still occupy positions of authority and prestige and they play a role in family decision making. Therefore, the extent to which Asian-Canadians, namely the Japanese-, Korean- and Chinese-Canadians, are able to maintain traditional beliefs and behavioural patterns may be associated with differences in the extent to which the family and social network ties are also maintained and the aged are socially integrated into both family and community activities. Another aspect of our research examines the well-being of the aged Asian-Canadians as manifested by their variable participation in daily activities.

Earlier aging studies that examined well-being and daily activities (for example, Neugarten, Havighurst and Tobin, 1968; Martin, 1973; and Longino and Kart, 1982) did not go beyond conventional methodologies and reported only the frequency of participation in selected activities. Our study employs both time-budget and life satisfaction instruments that will enable us to determine (1) the social context in which various activities occurred; (2) the duration and frequency of single and multiple activities; and (3) the general well-being or satisfaction of our aged respondents. By not having preselected activity categories, and by asking respondents to record their sequence of daily events, we will have the advantage of relative objectivity while at the same time preserving much of the content of daily life experiences (Moss and Lawton, 1982). In aging research, the duration of participation for some activities appears to be more important than the frequency of activity. For example, visits of several hours in duration by a relative may be more meaningful to the aged than ritualistic and much shorter regular visits.

One way in which we plan to improve on the utilization of our time-budget data is to determine those activities most predictive of well-being. There is now accumulating evidence that coping plays a central role in reducing stress-related illnesses and in promoting good health (Antonovsky, 1979; Coelho, Hamburg and Adams, 1974). Coping is particularly relevant to aging because many changes that come with advancing age require psycho-social adjustments (Renner and Birren, 1980). At the same time, to obtain a better understanding of coping in the elderly, we need to know the cultural context in which the adjustment process takes place (Holzberg, 1982; Rosenthal, 1983).

For our research, a coping inventory developed by Wong and Reker (1983, 1984) will be employed to differentiate those who are judged to be healthy and well-adjusted from those who are not. Subjects will be asked to nominate an event or problem that they find most stressful and to indicate how they cope with this stress using the rating scale of the coping inventory. Used in conjunction with time-budget and social network data, we will be able to pick out those individuals who resorted to external resources in order to cope with a given situation rather than through internal control. Another aspect of our research is that we draw attention to the importance of socio-historical and cultural contexts in which certain life events occur and show how these events in turn influence subsequent well-being.

At the theoretical level, our work is an extension of Chapin's (1974) study of obligatory versus discretionary time and of work associated with the activity theory of aging (Longino and Kart, 1982; Martin, 1973; McClelland, 1982; and Snow and Gordon, 1980). We hope to account for the general well-being of aged Asian-Canadians by examining (1) social networks of the respondents; (2) their general health conditions; (3) socio-cultural and demographic factors that may precondition action; and (4) culturally delineated coping strategies. Factors specifically identified as contributing to ethnic identity retention and socialization (Isajiw, 1981; Isajiw and Makabe, 1982) can be obtained from our time-budget data. As Holzberg (1981) has indicated, ethnic research results can be employed to service populations rather than relying on the current planning tendency to engage in "expedient planning" designed for the elderly middle-class White Anglo-Saxon Protestants. Our data can provide the basis for both longitudinal and social-policy-oriented research in areas related to an aging and multicultural population as in Canada. The study of the relationship between what people do in time and in space, their perceived well-being and their constraints as they relate to an ever changing population is an extremely important one that will have policy implications for the future, especially from an interethnic policy perspective.

Conclusion

In this chapter, we have indicated at the outset two significant aspects of our changing demography. First, the total Canadian population over the age of 65 years has a highly ethnic composition. Second, recent immigration statistics reveal that more than 60 percent of immigrants to Canada came from Asia, Africa, South America and the Caribbean. Future studies on any aspect of Canadian society must recognize its changing demographic nature and that minority groups traditionally categorized as "others" must be studied as a distinct and integral part of Canadian society.

We have shown that existing theories on aging, such as the disengagement and activity theories, are inadequate in their conceptualization because of the eurocentric biases implicit in their underlying assumptions. From the various examples provided to illustrate the adverse conditions many of our aged minorities have had to endure throughout their life span, one predominant characteristic of ethnic relations was that they involved a power relationship in which the dominant group systematically denied the minority groups equal access to educational, social, political and economic resources. In some cases, ethnic relations resulted in overt discrimination and conflict. Because of these factors, we have argued that certain life events may have left a permanent scar on the personality development of those affected that in turn may have had other negative consequences in terms of the aging process.

In our examination of other theories in the context of ethnicity and aging, the personality theory of aging, the aged as a subculture and age stratification theory, we found that empirical evidence is lacking at present to evaluate adequately their utility and applicability to the study of aged ethnic minorities. However, the various concepts and theoretical frame of reference do provide a useful starting point for future studies in that they all direct our attention to the importance of including socio-cultural differences, important life events and transitions in a life-span developmental perspective.

References

Abu-Laban, Sharon and Baha Abu-Laban
   1977   "Women and the aged as minority groups: a critique." *Canadian Review of Sociology and Anthropology* 14(1):103-16.
   1980   "Women and the aged as minority groups: A critique." Pp. 63-79 in Victor W. Marshall (ed.), *Aging in Canada.* Toronto: Fitzhenry & Whiteside.
Adachi, Ken
   1976   *The Enemy That Never Was.* Toronto: McClelland and Stewart.
Anderson, Alan B. and James S. Frideres
   1981   *Ethnicity in Canada.* Toronto: Butterworth.
Antonovsky, A.
   1979   *Health, Stress and Coping.* San Francisco: Jossey-Bass.
Atchley, Robert
   1980   *The Social Forces in Later Life: An Introduction to Social Gerontology.* Belmont, California: Wadsworth Publishing Company.
Baar, Ellen
   1978   "Issei, Nisei and Sansei." In Daniel Glenday, Hubert Guindon and Allan Turowetz (eds.), *Modernization and the Canadian State.* Toronto: Macmillan.
Bengtson, V.L.
   1979   "Ethnicity and aging: Problems and issues in current social science inquiry." In D.E. Gelfand and A.J. Kutzik (eds.), *Ethnicity and Aging: Theory, Research, and Policy.* New York: Springer.
Bond, John B., Jr. and Carol D.H. Harvey
   1985   "Familial Support of the Elderly in a Rural Mennonite Community." Paper presented at the 13th Conference of the International Congress of Gerontology, New York, N.Y.
Breton, Raymond
   1964   "Institutional completeness of ethnic communities and the personal relations of immigrants." *American Journal of Sociology* 70:193-205.
Chan, Kwok, B.
   1983   "Coping with aging and managing self-identity: The social world of the elderly Chinese women." *Canadian Ethnic Studies* 15(3):36-50.
Chapin, F. Stuart
   1974   *Human Activity Patterns in the City.* Toronto: John Wiley.
Chappell, Neena L. and Betty Havens
   1980   "Old and female: Testing the double jeopardy hypothesis." *The Sociological Quarterly* 21 (Spring) 157-171.
Coelho, G.V., D.A. Hamburg, and J.E. Adams (eds.)
   1974   *Coping and Adaptation.* New York: Basic Books.
Cumming, E. and W.E. Henry
   1961   *Growing Old: The Process of Disengagement.* New York: Basic Books.

Disman, Milada
    1983   "Immigrants and other grieving people: Anthropological insights for counselling practices and policy issues." *Canadian Ethnic Studies* 15(3):106-117.
Dowd, James J.
    1980   *Stratification Among the Aged.* Monterey, California: Brooks/Cole.
Dowd, James J. and Vern L. Bengtson
    1978   "Aging in minority populations: An examination of the double jeopardy hypothesis." *Journal of Gerontology* 33(3):427-436.
Driedger, Leo (ed.)
    1978   *The Canadian Ethnic Mosaic.* Toronto: McClelland and Stewart.
Employment and Immigration
    1982   *1980 Immigration Statistics.* Ottawa: Employment and Immigration.
Gelfand, Donald E.
    1982   *Aging: The Ethnic Factors.* Boston: Little, Brown.
George, Linda K.
    1978   "The impact of personality and social status factors upon levels of activity and psychological well-being." *Journal of Gerontology* 33(6):840-847.
Gerber, Linda M.
    1983   "Ethnicity still matters: Socio-demographic profiles of the ethnic elderly in Ontario." *Canadian Ethnic Studies* 15(3):60-80.
Giles, Howard
    1977   *Language, Ethnicity and Intergroup Relations.* London: Academic Press.
Havens, Betty and Neena L. Chappell
    1983   "Triple jeopardy: Age, sex and ethnic variations." *Canadian Ethnic Studies* 15(3).
Hendricks, Jon and C. Davis Hendricks
    1979   "Theories of gerontology." In Jon Hendricks and C. Davis Hendricks (eds.), *Dimensions of Aging.* Cambridge: Winthrop Publishers Inc.
Holzberg, Carol S.
    1981   "Cultural gerontology: Towards an understanding of ethnicity and aging." *Culture* 1(1):110-122.
    1982   "Ethnicity and aging: Anthropological perspectives on more than just the minority elderly." *The Gerontologist* 22(3):240-257.
Hultsch, David F. and Francine Deutsch
    1981   *Adult Development and Aging: A Life-Span Perspective.* Toronto: McGraw-Hill Ryerson.
Isajiw, Wsevolod W.
    1974   "Definitions of ethnicity." *Ethnicity* 1:111-124.
    1981   "Ethnic Identity Retention." Research Paper No. 125, Centre for Urban and Community Studies. Centre for Urban and Community Studies, University of Toronto, Toronto.
    1983   "Multiculturalism and the integration of the Canadian community." *Canadian Ethnic Studies* 15(2).
Isajiw, Wsevolod W. and Tomoko Makabe
    1982   "Socialization as a Factor in Ethnic Identity Retention." Research paper No. 134, Centre for Urban and Community Studies. Centre for Urban and Community Studies, University of Toronto, Toronto.

Jackson, Jacqueline Johnson
  1980   *Minorities and Aging.* Belmont, California: Wadsworth Publishing Company.
Kalish, Richard A. and Sharon Moriwaki
  1979   "The world of the elderly Asian American." In Jon Hendricks and C. Davis Hendricks (eds.), *Dimensions of Aging.* Cambridge: Winthrop Publishers Inc.
Longino, Charles F. and Cary S. Kart
  1982   "Explicating activity theory: A formal replication." *Journal of Gerontology* 37(6):713-722.
MacLean, Michael J. and Rita Bonar
  1983   "The ethnic elderly in a dominant culture long-term care facility." *Canadian Ethnic Studies* 15(3):51-59.
Martin, William C.
  1973   "Activity and disengagement: Life satisfaction of in-movers into a retirement community." *The Gerontologist* 13(2):224-227.
McClelland, Kent A.
  1982   "Self-conception and life satisfaction: Integrating aged subculture and activity theory." *Journal of Gerontology* 37(6):723-732.
Moss, Miriam S. and M. Powell Lawton
  1982   "Time budgets of older people: A window on four lifestyles." *Journal of Gerontology* 37(1):115-123.
Naidoo, Josephine C.
  1981   "The South-Asian experience of aging." Pp. 84-94 in K. Victor Ujimoto and Gordon Hirabayashi (eds.), *Asian Canadians: Regional Perspectives.* Selections from the Proceedings of the Asian Canadian Symposium V, Mount Saint Vincent University, Halifax, Nova Scotia. Ottawa: Canadian Asian Studies Association.
National Council of Welfare
  1984   *Sixty Five and Over.* Ottawa: National Council of Welfare.
Neugarten, B.L., R.J. Havighurst and S.S. Tobin
  1968   "Personality and patterns of aging." In B.L. Neugarten (ed.), *Middle Age and Aging.* Chicago: University of Chicago Press.
Osako, Masako M.
  1979   "Aging and family among Japanese Americans: The role of ethnic tradition in the adjustment to old age." *The Gerontologist* 19:448-455.
Pearlin, Leonard I.
  1980   "The life cycle and life strains." In Hubert M. Blalock, Jr. (ed.), *Sociological Theory and Research, A Critical Appraisal.* New York: The Free Press.
Penning, Margaret J.
  1983   "Multiple jeopardy: Age, sex and ethnic variations." *Canadian Ethnic Studies* 15(3).
Philibert, Michel
  1979   "Philosophical approach to gerontology." Pp. 379-394 in Jon Hendricks and C. Davis Hendricks (eds.), *Dimensions of Aging.* Cambridge: Winthrop Publishers Inc.
Reichard, S., F. Livson and P.G. Peterson

1962   *Aging and Personality.* New York: Wiley.

Renner, V.J. and Birren, J.E.
1980   "Stress: Physiological and psychological mechanisms." Pp. 310-331 in J.E. Birren and R.B. Sloane (eds.), *Handbook of Mental Health and Aging.* Englewood Cliffs, N.J.: Prentice-Hall.

Rose, A.M.
1965   "The subculture of the aging: A framework in social gerontology." In A.M. Rose and W.A. Peterson (eds.), *Older People and Their Social World.* Philadelphia: F.A. Davis Company.

Rosenthal, Carolyn J.
1983   "Aging, ethnicity and the family: Beyond the modernization thesis." *Canadian Ethnic Studies* 15(3):1-16.
1986   "Family supports in later life: Does ethnicity make a difference?" *The Gerontologist* 26 (1): 19–24.

Snow, David L. and Judith B. Gordon
1980   "Social network analysis and intervention with the elderly." *The Gerontologist* 20(4):463-467.

Statistics Canada
1976   *Canada's Elderly.* Ottawa: Statistics Canada Census Characteristics Division.
1981   *1981 Census of Canada.* Population, Series 93-926.

Sugiman, Pamela and Harry K. Nishio
1983   "Socialization and cultural duality among aging Japanese Canadians." *Canadian Ethnic Studies* 15(3):17-35.

Takeuchi, Janice
1984   "Serving an Aging Population having a Background of Different Cultures, Needs and Concerns." Paper presented at the 37th Annual Scientific Meeting of the Gerontological Society of America, San Antonio, Texas.

Ujimoto, K. Victor
1976   "Contrasts in the prewar and postwar Japanese community in British Columbia: Conflict and change." *Canadian Review of Sociology and Anthropology* 13(1):80-89.
1979   "Postwar Japanese immigrants in British Columbia: Japanese culture and job transferability." Pp. 338-357 in Jean Leonard Elliott (ed.), *Two Nations, Many Cultures: Ethnic Groups in Canada.* Scarborough: Prentice-Hall.
1982a   "Visible minorities and strategies for social change." *Journal of Canadian Studies* 17(1):111-121.
1982b   "Postwar Japanese immigrants: The allocation of time to organizational, social and leisure activities." In Zahari Staikov (ed.), *It's About Time.* Sophia: Institute of Sociology, Bulgarian Academy of Sciences, Bulgarian Sociological Association.
1983   "Introduction: Ethnicity and aging in Canada." *Canadian Ethnic Studies* 15(3)i-vii.
1985   "The allocation of time to social, organizational and leisure activities by aged Asian Canadians." *Tsukuba Journal of Sociology* 9 (1 and 2):55-68.

Woodsworth, Charles J.
  1941   *Canada and the Orient*. Toronto: Macmillan.
Wong, P.T.P. and G.T. Reker
  1983   "Face Validity of the Coping Inventory." Paper presented at the 12th
          Annual Meeting of the Canadian Association on Gerontology, Moncton,
          New Brunswick.
  1984   "Coping Behaviours of Successful Agers." Paper presented at the 30th
          Western Gerontological Society Annual Meeting, Anaheim, California.
Wong, Paul T.P.
  1985   "Stress, coping and well-being in Anglo and Chinese elderly." *Canadian
          Journal on Aging* 4(1):29-37.

8

The Invisible Lives of Canada's Gray Gays

John Alan Lee
Department of Sociology
Scarborough College, University of Toronto

Despite the recent surge in studies of the aged, Unruh (1983) argues that their social world is still one of "invisible lives." If this is true of hetero-sexual elders, how much truer for gays and lesbians. The vast majority of sociological studies of aging assume their subjects are heterosexual. While a few studies have paid attention to (assumed heterosexual) lifelong singles (e.g., Tunstall, 1966; Lowenthal and Haven, 1968), these "unfortunates" were often expected to show "very low morale in old age." (Kutner et al., 1956:77). When an aging bachelor was found to be quite happy, this was "ironic. . .as though he had a lifetime of practice in the self-reliance and autonomy required. . .and was spared the grief and loneliness of widowers" (Clark and Anderson, 1967:257).

A few studies of gay and lesbian aging have been published (e.g., Kelly, 1977; Levy, 1979; Berger, 1982), but authors of general studies of aging have remained largely oblivious to the existence of older homosexuals. It is not until Brecher (1984:147ff) that a general survey of aging includes some homosexual respondents, but they are still too few for meaningful com-parison with the huge heterosexual sample. One of Canada's recent and comprehensive texts on aging (Roadburg, 1985) contains no acknowledge-ment whatever that older homosexuals exist.

Small wonder. Even authors sympathetic to homosexuals have generally assumed that no one enjoys gay old age. In a subculture said to "put even more emphasis on youth than society in general" (Simon and Gagnon, 1967), where "virtually the sole criterion of value. . .is physical attractive-ness (Hoffman, 1968:155), "the fear of becoming old. . .with reduced opportunities for sexual liaison" (Lehne, 1974) is said to drive older gay men to "try desperately to preserve some semblance of youth" (West, 1968:57) to avoid being labelled an "old auntie" (Kelly, 1980:178). The media agree. The ridiculous antics of an old fairy in *La Cage aux Folles* are hardly more appealing than the pathetic end of an artist in *Death in Venice*, or the puerile backbiting of Rex Harrison and Richard Burton, playing two

This research was funded by the SSHRC of Canada. I am grateful to Professors Sheldon Ungar and Victor Marshall for their comments on an earlier version of this paper.

gay men who have been coupled for many years, in *The Staircase*. What sociologist would want to study the fate of such *misérables*?

In 1980, publicly gay and approaching 50 years of age, I decided it was time to discover what lay ahead for me. A study of gay aging might uncover ways to increase the well-being of older gays, and possibly of heterosexual singles, too. After all, the proportion of the aged who are single is rising (Tunstall, 1966; Stein, 1976; Brecher, 1984). Drawing on the existing literature and my own familiarity with gay life, I framed hypotheses about variables I expected would be related to the level of life satisfaction and adjustment to aging among older gay men. These variables included: number of years since "coming out," extent of participation in the gay community, acquaintance with still older gays as role models, continuity of relationships (close friends, lovers), proportion of social times spent with much younger gay men, level of secrecy about one's gayness, and so forth.

Methodology

Longitudinal design

Where possible, a longitudinal study of aging seems preferable (Maddox, 1963; Palmore, 1968). I began my four-year study with 54 respondents. Each was interviewed in depth in the first year, using the card sort technique (cf. Lee, 1973:240). Each respondent received a mailed questionnaire in the second and third years, and was again interviewed in the final year. During the four years I lost contact with several men and two died, leaving 47 in the final sample.

The investment in longitudinal research was amply rewarded. As time passed, most respondents became more candid and revealing. They telephoned or wrote to bring me up to date on their latest adventures. Some respondents, "in for a penny," went in for a pound by disclosing unexpected, derogatory data. A longitudinal study does tend to demonstrate that the researcher is really *interested* in the respondent, who becomes in fact a collaborator.

Sample

There is no such thing as a representative sample of gay Canadians. The best possible sample is by quotas, to represent a reasonable range of ages, incomes, educational levels and regions of Canada. Believing that women can best do studies of lesbians, and relying on my personal networks to recruit much of the sample, I sought only gay men. My 47 respondents ranged from 50 to 80 years of age, in the final year of the study. They lived from New Brunswick to Edmonton, with a few retired in Florida. They ranged from a recipient of one of the highest distinctions in Canadian public life, to a clerk who never finished high school and rarely left his small hometown, to an unemployed worker on welfare. Some married and later divorced; some led a double life with wife and family. Some had been actively homosexual since early childhood; others became aware of their gayness only in midlife. One is still reluctant to attempt his first act of gay sex with another man, and contents himself with masturbation using gay pornography.

As in many aging studies (e.g., Berger, 1982; Brecher, 1984), my sample contains proportionately more well-educated and professional men than the general population. Clearly my findings cannot be generalized to all older Canadian gay men, for I excluded obvious samples (e.g., French speaking, nonwhite).

Measures

To make my findings more comparable, interview and mail questions were based on existing sociological literature on aging. Life satisfaction is the key measure, and questions were drawn from Neugarten, Havighurst and Tobin (1961); Reichard, Livson and Petersen (1962); Simpson and McKinney (1966); Palmore (1968); and Butler (1977). Respondents selected from such statements as: "Each year of my life seems better than the year before," and "I was a lot happier when I was younger."

Other measures included self-image and self-description of personality (Kutner et al., 1956; Blau, 1957; Gough and Heilbrun, 1965; Kaplan and Pokorny, 1970); role count (Havighurst and Albrecht, 1953; Cumming and Henry, 1961); activities (Kutner et al., 1956; Bull and Aucoin, 1975; Atchley, 1977); family and friendship networks (Blau, 1957); achievement of career and personal goals (Simpson and McKinney, 1966); celebration of major festivals (Kimmel, 1979); and stressful events and crisis management (Huyck, 1974).

Questions relating to gay aspects of aging included self-identification as homosexual (Dank, 1971; Lumby, 1978); degree of openness about being gay (Lee, 1977); attitudes to younger and older gays (Weinberg, 1969; Minnigerode, 1976); attitudes to heterosexuals (Tripp, 1976); extent of gay vs. nongay personal networks (Weinberg and Williams, 1974); sexual attraction (age of preferred partners, type of preferred relationships: Bell and Weinberg, 1978); sexual practices and fantasies (Humphreys, 1970; Lehne, 1974; Kelly, 1977); sex partners, and lovers, if any (Kimmel and Ralph, 1978).

Findings

Variance in life satisfaction

Life satisfaction is not easily defined (Roadburg, 1985:139). George (1979:210) defines it as "a cognitive assessment of one's progress toward desired goals." This "progress" is obviously measured retroactively by reminiscence and life review. In this study, each participant was asked several times to select acceptable statements expressing his enjoyment of his life and his feelings about being an older man. The statements attempted a balance between happiness and adjustment (cf. Maclean, 1983).

After the initial round of interviews, each man's responses were weighed, and rank-ordered from "most satisfied" to "least satisfied." Of course the ranks did not proceed by exactly equal intervals; instead they tended to cluster. Five clusters were identified (cf. Axelrod, 1967). The middle cluster of scores was labelled the "average satisfaction category" — Category C. The most satisfied men became Category A, the least satisfied Category E. The remaining categories are, obviously, B and D. Men in Category A feel they have had more of the "breaks" in life than most people they know. Their life continues to get better each year and the future holds a lot worth living for. At the other extreme, men in Category E feel they never got much of what they wanted from life. Old age seems tougher for them than for most elders they know, and they feel there is little point in making any plans for next year.

Following the final round of interviews, the men were assessed again. Some men's life satisfaction had changed, causing them to move from one category to another. The categories reported here are those at the end of the study, and it is obvious that any man's rating is by no means immutable.

In the following sections, I test for a number of possible factors relating to life satisfaction. Obviously the sample sizes are small, especially Category E. My discussion is therefore indicative rather than conclusive. Since more significance is often imputed to correlation coefficients than is justified by the sample size, I have avoided such statistical calculations.

Age as a factor

The average age of the sample of 47 men is 60.5 years, but the average age of each category is not the same — the oldest men are more likely to be among the least satisfied with their lives (see Table 1). However, each category contains at least one man in each ten-year age group, and the most satisfied men (Category A) are older than Categories B and C.

Whether aging itself is a more potent factor in life satisfaction among homosexuals than heterosexuals is a debated question in the still scanty literature on older gays. Some argue that a feeling of being "old" arrives early among gay men because their subculture is "youth oriented" and makes even the age of thirty seem "over the hill" (e.g., Warren, 1974:54). Other researchers reject this theory of "accelerated gay aging," arguing that if gay men tend to feel older at any given age, it is because they are usually *single men*. Like the *comparable* heterosexual subculture (e.g., at singles' bars), gay men put greater emphasis on cosmetic appearance, but no more so than heterosexual singles (cf. Harry, 1978:200). Brecher (1984:145) found that age did *not* significantly affect the life satisfaction of his sample of 402 single old men, but unfortunately he does not report statistics for the 56 older gay men among his sample (ibid:272).

Table 1 neither proves nor disproves "accelerated gay aging." Since the issue remains in doubt, I control for age in some of the tests below, where it might be an intervening variable.

TABLE 1:
Satisfaction Category by Age Group
(Number of Men and % of Age Group)

	Satisfaction category										Total
	A		B		C		D		E		
	n	%	n	%	n	%	n	%	n	%	n
Age											
50-9	5	20	8	32	8	32	2	8	2	8	25
60-9	4	24	2	12	3	18	6	35	2	12	17
70+	1	20	1	20	1	20	1	20	1	20	5
Total men	**10**		**11**		**12**		**9**		**5**		**47**
Average age of category	61.4		57.9		58.8		63.2		65.4		*

* average age of whole sample is 60.5 years

Health as a factor

The questions on which my life satisfaction categories are based exclude questions about health, to avoid artifactual outcomes. Forty-seven percent of my respondents considered their health excellent throughout the four-year period, 34 percent good and 19 percent poor. Thus my sample does not differ remarkably from comparable heterosexual and homosexual samples. Brecher (1984:266), in a sexually mixed sample, reports a self-rating of health ranging from 69 percent excellent in the 50s group to 51 percent in the 70s. Berger (1982:138) reported 41 percent of his gay men considered their health excellent, 45 percent good, and 14 percent poor (he does not provide details by age group).

It is well-known in gerontology that health profoundly affects life satisfaction (Kutner, 1956:114; Atchley, 1977:200; Roadburg, 1985:145). The situation of older gay men seems no different from that of (assumed) nongays. The men in my sample reporting excellent health are much more likely to fall into the most satisfied categories (A and B). Berger's study of aging gay men (1982:175) reports the same relationship of health to life satisfaction.

Income

It is also well-known that income is related to life satisfaction among the aged (Blau, 1957:105; Simpson and McKinney, 1966:63; Rosow, 1974:3). When compared with all older Canadians (as reported by Roadburg, 1985:23), a smaller proportion of my older gay men are in the low-income range. But it is also true that a smaller proportion of my sample are in the highest income bracket than in the Canadian population. In short, my sample is more compressed into the middle-income category ($22,000 to $39,999) than the population in general.

Income per se is a relatively weak factor in life satisfaction among my older gay men. High income did not assure a place among the most satisfied men, but low satisfaction almost always included reports of low income. More significant was the *attitude towards one's income*. I asked each man to compare his standard of living to that which he believed others of his own age enjoyed. The men who believed their standard of living was above average (for their age) were much more likely to be satisfied with their lives, regardless of whether their income was statistically above the average for that age.

Education

Educational level achieved is related to income and, in turn, to life satisfaction. The 7 men with Ph.D.'s in my sample are all among the most satisfied (Categories A, B), but only a quarter of the men with less than a B.A. degree are among these happiest men, and half fell into the least satisfied (Categories D, E). Unfortunately Berger (1982) and Brecher (1984) do not provide comparable educational data.

Marital status

Marriage is one of the great havens of life, especially in old age. It is conventional wisdom in gerontology that older married people are happier than older singles (Brecher, 1984:145). Until the 1960s, remaining unmarried past the age of 30 raised questions in the minds of family, friends, employer, colleagues, neighbours. Many of my sample reached age 30 before 1960. Some decided to marry and lead a double life, usually keeping their homosexuality secret from wife and children. Such a life seemed to promise "insurance" against a lonely old age (Berger, 1982:9) despite the stress of duplicity and the fear of discovery (Plummer, 1975). Studies vary in their estimates of the number of gay men who married prior to "gay liberation." Hart and Richardson (1981) estimate 20 percent; Berger (1982) reports 29 percent married.

Thirty-eight percent (18 men) of my sample married at some time and 13 percent (6 men) were still living with their spouse during the time of the study. However, they all considered themselves *gay*, not bisexual. All passed the litmus test I have proposed elsewhere (Lee, 1977), by preferring sexual fantasies and pornography involving same-gender rather than cross-gender activity.

Many of these men made their marital choices in a time of dreadful stereotypes of single gay life, as epitomized by West (1968:57):

> Many aging homosexuals. . .find that they are left without family, roots or purpose. Some of them can be seen wearily trailing their old haunts, trying to bribe themselves back into the company of young men, or loitering pathetically around public lavatories. Others retire to a grimly isolated existence.

The choice of deceitful marriage is no one-shot solution to the dread of a lonely old age, even if one's mate remains alive and devoted throughout one's elder years. The deception is continuous, and often daily. Telephone calls and correspondence to several men in this study had to be extremely discreet, lest I be blamed for giving the spouse even the slightest clue to the long-hidden secret of my respondent.

Some men suspected that their wives had already guessed, but out of fear of the alternatives, "said nothing and let well enough alone." At least one wife had gone further, making home life miserable with accusations, each denied by the husband with great vigour, and each levelled again with greater rancour. "We're like the proverbial two scorpions in a bottle," my respondent complained, "but there's no way I want to break up and face the prospect of looking for a gay partner at my age." Ironically this man had advantages (high education, high income, professional position) that would otherwise have contributed to his placement among the most satisfied men in the sample.

Conversely, the fate of men who had left their wives for the gay life might not attract those chafed by marital bonds. Some had found lovers, or at least compatible roommates, but others had floundered from one short gay love affair to another, and now lived alone, regretful and nostalgic for the "security" of married life. This diversity of outcomes meant that for the sample as a whole, there was no relationship between life satisfaction and marital status.

Berger (1982) reports that his older gay men complained about lack of family life. Kimmel (1979:245) says festival holidays are especially difficult for gay men without a family. Marshall (1974) notes that family relationships are sometimes the "last strands" holding the aged person to life. But aging singles — including many gay men — may have learned from years of single adult life how to survive happily alone (Tunstall, 1966). Some sociologists of aging report a surprising noncorrelation of marriage and family life to adjustment with aging. Kutner (1956:59) and Reichard et al. (1962:102) say marital status is "not necessarily a key factor in morale or adjustment to aging." Nor are children and grandchildren necessarily a source of happiness in old age (Cumming and Henry, 1961:60; Simpson and McKinney, 1966:184). My gay sample (like that of Kelly, 1980) appears to support the possibility of a happy but nonfamilial old age: there is no correlation between frequency of contact with relatives and family, and life satisfaction.

Achievement of goals

Each participant was assisted to recall his status, domicile and activities ten years prior to the interview, then asked to recall the important goals that he hoped to achieve in the following ten years — that is, up to the time of the interview. He was then asked how well he had achieved his goals. In the final interview, the men were asked again to recollect their goals *for the period of the study*, and asked how well these goals had been achieved.

The life satisfaction categories varied little in the average number of goals per man (about six, of which financial security, living in a fine home and finding a lover were among the most commonly mentioned). But the men who had achieved a higher proportion of their goals fell into the most satisfied categories. For older gay men, it is clear that life satisfaction can be defined as "progress toward goals" (George, 1979:210).

Crisis competence

There is little that is surprising or controversial in the six factors reported above; except in respect to problems arising from social stigmatization of homosexuality, older gay men seem much like older nongays. But some studies of gay aging (e.g., Francher and Henkin, 1973; Kimmel, 1979; Weeks, 1983) have suggested that gay men may have an advantage in adjusting to any problems brought about by aging itself because their homosexuality has required them to weather crises in adult life that nongay adults are usually spared. The notion of "a crisis competence that buffers a person against later crises" (Weeks, 1983:181) is highly debatable. There is the problem of definition. An event that is considered a "crisis" by one man may be "normal trouble" to another.

In my study, each participant was asked to report stress-causing conditions or events that he had experienced in his adult life, by selecting from a lengthy list I adapted from Huyck (1974:32). The choice ranges from relatively mild stress events (e.g., the death of a pet), to conditions likely to be severely traumatic to anyone (e.g., imprisonment). Some items were gay-specific (e.g., a long period of self-doubt about being gay, or sudden discovery and exposure as a gay person). Selection of such events did not necessarily imply that the respondent considered each a "crisis," but did provide a basis for comparing the presumed "competence" of each man to deal with problems.

Contrary to any theory of "crisis competence," the men who selected the smallest number of stressful events, and generally played down the idea that their lives had involved difficult challenges, were among the most satisfied in their gay old age. Their sentiment was "I got more of the breaks than I ever deserved." Conversely, some men "ricochetted through life, dealing with one crisis after another," as one put it. They survived, but their presumptive "crisis competence" did not make them happy with their lives. These men fell into the least satisfied categories. After the final interview, the number of high-stress events reported by each man *during the study period* was totalled, and showed the same relationship to life satisfaction.

Friends and lovers

A lack of good friends is a tragedy for almost anyone, but particularly so for gay men, say Johnson and Kelly (1979:252), because friends must compensate for lack of family life. Among my sample, almost every man had at least one confidant to whom he could talk freely about his gay life. But the men with two or more close friends were more likely to be satisfied with their aging years. Even more significantly, the men with a close friend nearby, on whom they could call in an emergency, were much more likely to fall in the "most satisfied" categories.

Having "old friends" — friends known for at least five years — also helped increase life satisfaction. It might be argued that the least satisfied men (Categories D and E) were of a higher average age, thus had fewer friends and "old friends," because they were more likely to have outlived them. But when age was controlled, life satisfaction still varied with the number of close friends and old friends.

Having a lover, and especially living with a lover, contributed even more to life satisfaction than friends. Thirteen of the men reported having a lover at some time during the study period, but only eight men in the sample lived with lovers during the study period. Seven of those men fell in the most satisfied categories (A, B), and the eighth was in the middle category (C). Again it would be tempting to explain this difference by age — the men in the least satisfied categories are of a higher average age than the whole sample, and might have a harder time finding a lover in the "youth-oriented" gay subculture. But another finding contradicts any such age-related explanation. The least satisfied men (Categories D, E) were only half as likely as the most satisfied men to have had a lover *at any time in their lives.*

There is no notable relationship between the level of social activity of the men and their satisfaction with life. Almost all the men reported high levels of activity in hobbies, entertainment, homemaking, etc. Nor was there any significant relationship between the overall amount of social time spent alone (e.g., eating dinner alone) and life satisfaction. However, the men who spent major social festivals (e.g., birthday, Christmas, New Year's Eve) alone or with strangers during the four-year study period tended to fall into the least satisfied categories.

Role continuity

One of my hypotheses predicted that older gay men who had experienced substantial role discontinuities in adult life would be less satisfied in old age (cf. Atchley, 1977:70; Rosow, 1974:19). For example, those who had been married for a time, believing themselves heterosexual, then divorced and living with a gay lover, would be less satisfied than those who remained married throughout life (while secretly gay), or those who remained single and gay. My findings do not support this hypothesis. The men who lived most of their adult life alone are the least satisfied in old age. Discontinuous roles (single, with wife, with lover) in whatever order, do not appear to be a significant factor in life satisfaction of my older gay men.

What does appear to bring satisfaction is having had *partners* — whether a wife, a lover, both at once, or each in turn. We have already noted that a wife is no insurance for a gay old age, and that having a lover is related to happy gay aging, but is not easy to achieve. However, the men who had made the attempt to partner, heterosexually or homosexually or both, appeared to feel that their lives had offered a richer and more satisfying variety of experience, even if they were alone now.

It is worth noting that two of the eight men living with lovers found their current lovers during the study period — that is, quite late in life. One man had spent his life happily with a beloved wife and (now-adult) children who knew nothing of his secret gay life. After his wife's death he took a much younger gay lover — whom his adult children have learned to accept and admire. The other man had a lover for forty years and, when that lover died, suffered great distress and considered suicide. But two years later, he began a new relationship with a much younger man. Though he restrains his hopes about the probable duration of this new love, the very fact that he has taken the emotional risks involved brings him new joy in life. These stories remind us that no causal relationship is clear in the happiness of the older gay men with lovers: they may have their lovers because they are otherwise happy with their lives, or may be happy because they have lovers.

Home

Having your own space for the touchstones of memory is a major factor in morale of the elderly (Butler, 1975:103, Atchley, 1977:200). Among gay men, who must often forego or disguise other sources of esteem in the world, the accumulation of valued furnishings in a fine home is often of special importance (Hanson, 1972:266; Silverstein, 1981:126ff). Thus it is significant that none of the ten men in my sample who expressed notable disappointment with their domicile fell in the most satisfied categories, while men who took a special delight in their home surroundings were likely to be among the most satisfied with their lives.

Role entry and gay aging

Gay youths growing up in a heterosexist society face difficult decisions about sexual identity and "coming out" (Dank, 1971; Lee, 1977, 1978). Gay young people must cope with the shock of adjustment from normative (heterosexual) socialization in home, school and peer group to the anxious search for friendship and partner roles in the gay subculture. I hypothesized that men who realized and acted on their gay orientation early in life would make a less wrenching resocialization. Those who came out late in life would face resocialization of deep-set roles and would resent "missed opportunities" of young gay life.

My hypothesis was not supported by this sample. There was no apparent pattern relating the age of first awareness of being gay, or first act of gay sex, or number of years of involvement in the gay community, to the level of life satisfaction.

Relationship with much younger gay men

Much literature argues that people grow old happily by gracefully surrendering any claim to youthfulness, and "finding friends your own age" (cf. Cameron and Cromer, 1974). Roadburg (1985:126), in an assumed-heterosexual sample making no more claim to representativeness than mine, found only 7 percent of 125 elder Canadian males preferred younger company, while 40 percent preferred their own age. I hypothesized the opposite pattern in my study, based on my experience that older gay men with young and attractive partners enjoy more status and power in the gay subculture. (I do not say this *should* be so, but simply that it is, in an ageist gay subculture; cf. Lehne, 1974.)

My sample of 47 men supports my hypothesis. The men who say they prefer sexual partners under 35 are twice as likely to be satisfied with their older years as the men preferring older partners. As to actual behaviour, the men who, during the study period, reported spending at least half of their social time with men at least twenty years their junior, were more likely to be satisfied with their lives than those who spent the majority of their social time with friends closer to their own age. These findings corroborate Berger (1982:171), who argues that psychological health was greater among aging gay males in his small sample who preferred friends at least twenty years younger.

This does not mean an older gay with a lover or friends his own age is necessarily unhappy. But for the majority of older gay men in my sample nothing could seem more "natural" than seeking young associates. "How else am I going to stay lively and keep up with the times?" "I like my older friends, but they're so often old-fashioned!"

Role models of gayness and gay aging

Being actively gay in a heterosexist society is difficult at any age, and is surely made easier with "help from one's friends." I predicted that those with a preference for gay friends, and particularly a personal acquaintance with gay men older than themselves, would be more satisfied with their aging. Both hypotheses are supported by this sample. Given a choice between a heterosexual friend of the same social class or a gay friend of a different social class, the men who chose the gay friend were more likely to fall into the most satisfied categories. Those who knew an even older gay man who could serve as a positive role model of gay aging were also more likely to be satisfied with their lives.

Satisfaction with work life

One factor often taken for granted in a man's assessment of his life is his satisfaction with his job or career (Osgood and Mizruchi, 1982:231). Gay men are no longer stereotyped as exclusively occupied in a few callings such as hairdressing or interior decoration. But Berger (1982:182) demonstrates that the independently employed gay men among his sample are more likely to be integrated into the gay community. The self-employed gay is apparently less anxious about the potential impact of disclosure of his sexual life on his job security. Berger does not cross-tabulate self-employment with life satisfaction among his respondents, but integration into the gay community does correlate positively with life satisfaction in his sample (ibid:179) and in mine.

Among my 47 older gay men, there is a clear relationship between self-employment, or highly independent and secure employment such as university teaching, and life satisfaction. To avoid artifactual outcome, the scores on which the life satisfaction categories are based contain no reference to job or career. Questions on work were asked separately.

If work "even today remains the basis of social identity" (Kart and Manard, 1976:269), higher status work should bring greater life satisfaction among the aged, and this is true of my older gay men. Using Blishen's (1968:741) scale of occupational status, the higher the occupational status of these older gay men, the more likely they are to be satisfied with their lives.

However, work satisfaction is not the same thing as work commitment. Gay men "living in the closet" must be careful not to depend too much on work status for their self-esteem, as there is always the risk of exposure and loss of job. The prudent gay man takes a certain amount of "role distance" from his work, relying instead for self-esteem on friends and fine home, as already noted. Thus, one of my hypotheses predicted that "the less the aging gay man has relied on his work for self-esteem, the less his difficulty with aging." Of course, such a prediction is also congruent with theories of "disengagement" in aging (Cumming and Henry, 1961; Harris, 1975:91). Work commitment was tested by such questions as, "If you won a large lottery prize, would you go on working?" and by noting early retirement. The men reporting low work commitment (but high work satisfaction) were more likely to fall in the most satisfied categories, and these men were the most likely to have taken early retirement by age 60.

Gay community and going public

I began in 1980 with an hypothesis that more satisfying gay aging would come with extent of involvement (but not necessarily duration — see above) in the gay social world. Midway through my four-year study, Berger (1982) reported data supporting this correlation in his American sample. In another hypothesis, I took "gay involvement" a step further. I predicted that gay men who had "gone public" (Lee, 1977) would have reduced the self-denial required by "life in the closet," and therefore would enjoy a happier aging. My findings support the first hypothesis, but not the second.

To the chagrin of this very publicly gay author, being in the closet seems no hindrance to a satisfying gay old age. Some of the most satisfied men had not revealed themselves in such close professional relationships as those with their doctor or lawyer. A capacity for happiness while bearing the stress of a secret life is demonstrated by these men.

Satisfaction with sex life

The importance of sexual satisfaction in old age is said to be often underestimated (Brecher, 1984), but not so often by gay men. It is sexual behaviour that has given these gay men a special sense (often secret) of identity. The cessation of gay sexual activity would, for many of these men, leave little to differentiate them from the general population. Thus, a continued urge to express a gay identity is to be expected. As an 80-year-old participant put it, "that's the only part that still works the way it always did." As expected, the men who were more satisfied with their sex life were more likely to be in the highest life satisfaction categories.

Even gay men with long-term lover relationships are likely to "cruise" occasionally for other sex partners, as total sexual fidelity is rare among gay men (Bell and Weinberg, 1978:75, 85). Of course the men living with wives, with roommates, or alone searched from item to time for partners (with one exception noted earlier). But success in the search for sexual partners declines with age, in both gay and nongay cultures (Brecher, 1984:167, 225). As expected, the men in my sample who reported the highest frequency of "cruising" per month were likely to fall into the lowest life satisfaction categories.

Recent literature on aging has "discovered" the importance of sex to older people. If sex is important to gay men as a means of affirming a master status (even without a partner, through use of pornography) it follows that lack of sexual outlet is likely to be followed by revision of self-image and sense of gay community. Several of the gay men who were no longer sexually successful made observations such as, "Being gay is not the most important thing in my life," or "Gay people only differ from other people in bed."

Summary

This article has reported some findings of the first study of gay male aging in Canada, focussing on factors related to life satisfaction. Many of the findings indicate little difference between the condition and problems of older gay males and their nongay countrymen. A few findings are distinctive, and relate to the problems of adaptation of a largely invisible minority to a majority heterosexual culture.

Despite their problems, the majority of these 47 gay Canadian men, ranging from 50 to 80 years of age, are satisfied with their lives. Changes in the lives of several men during the four-year study period also show that those who are not satisfied may still be able to improve their lot. The apparent route to greater happiness is not easy. Some factors likely to contribute to greater life satisfaction, such as health and income, are difficult challenges for anyone, young or old. Others — such as finding more good friends — are likely to be intimidating enterprises for any older person, gay or nongay. But, as suggested by the few anecdotes that space has allowed, old age is not an insurmountable barrier to the discovery of a new lover, or a self-declaration as a gay person after a lifetime of marriage and child rearing.

This small sample makes no claim to be representative, but the survival of these men demonstrates that Canadians can be happy and gay in old age. The probabilities vary with many factors, of which I have discussed a few. But it is possible to achieve such happiness alone or by sharing life with a lover, even one found late in life. It is even possible to achieve a satisfying gay old age secretly, while cherishing a wife, children and grandchildren.

References

Atchley, Robert
1977   *The Social Forces in Later Life.* Belmont, California: Wadsworth.
Axelrod, Robert
1967   "Structure of public opinion on policy issues." *Public Opinion Quarterly* (Spring):51-68.

Bell, Alan and M.S. Weinberg
  1978   *Homosexualities.* New York: Simon and Schuster.
Berger, Raymond
  1982   *Gay and Gray.* University of Illinois Press.
Blau, Z.S.
  1957   *Old Age: A Study of Change in Status.* University Microfilms.
Blishen, B.R.
  1968   "A socio-economic index for occupations in Canada." Pp. 741-53 in B.R.
          Blishen (ed.), *Canadian Society.* Toronto: Macmillan.
Brecher, Edward M.
  1984   *Love, Sex and Aging.* Boston: Little, Brown.
Bull, C.N. and J.B. Aucoin
  1975   "Voluntary association participation and life satisfaction." *Journal of
          Gerontology* 30(1):73-76.
Butler, R.N.
  1975   *Why survive? Being Old in America.* New York: Harper and Row.
  1977   "Successful aging and the role of the life review." In S.H. Zarit, ed.,
          Readings in Aging and Death. New York: Harper and Row.
Cameron, Paul and A. Cromer
  1974   "Generational homophily." *Journal of Gerontology* 29(2):232-36.
Clark, M. and B. Anderson
  1967   *Culture and Aging.* Springfield, Illinois: Thomas.
Cumming, E. and W.E. Henry
  1961   *Growing Old.* New York: Basic Books.
Dank, Barry
  1971   "Coming out in the gay world." *Psychiatry* 34:180-197.
Francher, J.S. and J. Henkin
  1973   "The menopausal queen: Adjustment to aging and the male homosexual."
          American Journal of Orthopsychiatry 43(4):670-74.
George, Linda
  1979   "The happiness syndrome." *The Gerontologist* 19(2):210-16.
Gough, H.G. and A.B. Heilbrun
  1965   *The Adjective Checklist.* Palo Alto, Calif.: Consulting Psychologists Press.
Hanson, C.
  1972   "The fairy princess exposed." In K. Jay and A. Young (eds.), *Out of the
          Closets.* New York: Pyramid.
Harris, Louis
  1975   *The Myth and Reality of Aging in America.* New York: National Council
          on Aging.
Harry, Joseph
  1978   "Age and sexual culture among gay males." *Archives of Sex Behaviour*
          7:199-208.
Hart, John and D. Richardson
  1981   *The Theory and Practice of Homosexuality.* London: Routledge Kegan
          Paul.
Havighurst, R.J. and R. Albrecht
  1953   *Older People.* New York: Longman Green.

Hoffman, Martin
  1968   *The Gay World*. New York: Basic Books.
Humphreys, Laud
  1970   *Tearoom Trade*. Chicago: Aldine.
Huyck, M.H.
  1974   *Growing Older*. Englewood Cliffs, New Jersey: Prentice-Hall.
Johnson, M.T. and J.J. Kelly
  1979   "Deviate sex behaviour in the aging." In O.J. Kaplan, *Psychopathology of aging*. New York: Academic Press.
Kaplan, H. and Pokorny, A.
  1970   "Aging and self-attitude." *International Journal of Aging and Human Development* 1:241-49.
Kart, C.S. and B.B. Manard
  1976   *Aging in America*. Berkeley, California: Alfred.
Kelly, J.J.
  1977   "The aging male homosexual, myth and reality." *The Gerontologist* 17(4):328-32.
  1980   "Homosexuality and aging." Pp. 176-93 in J. Marmor, ed., *Homosexual Behaviour*. New York: Basic Books.
Kimmel, D.C.
  1979   "Life history interviews of aging gay men." *International Journal of Aging and Human Development* 10(3):239-248.
Kimmel, D.C. and W. Ralph
  1978   "Gay People Grow Old Together: Life Histories of Aging Gay Men." Paper at the Gerontological Society, 14 October.
Kutner, B., D. Fanshel, A. Toga, and T. Langner
  1956   *Five Hundred Over Sixty*. New York: Russell Sage Foundation.
Laner, M.R.
  1978   "Growing older male, heterosexual and homosexual." *The Gerontologist* 18:496-501.
Lee, John Alan
  1973   *Colours of Love*. Toronto: General.
  1977   "Going public." *Journal of Homosexuality* 3(1):49-78.
  1978   *Getting Sex*. Toronto: General.
Lehne, Greg
  1974   "Gay male fantasies." *The Body Politic* 15 (Sept.).
Levy, Herman
  1979   "The middle-aged male homosexual." *Journal of the American Academy of Psychoanalysis* 7(3):405-18.
Lowenthal, M.F. and C. Haven
  1968   "Interaction and adaptation: Intimacy as a critical variable." *American Sociological Review* 33(1):20-30.
Lumby, M.E.
  1978   "Men who advertise for sex." *Journal of Homosexuality* 1:63-72.
Maclean, M.J.
  1983   "Differences between adjustment to and enjoyment of retirement." *Canadian Journal on Aging* 2(1):3-8.

Maddox, G.
1963   "Activity and morale: A longitudinal study." *Social Forces* 42:195-204.
Marshall, Victor W.
1974   "The last strand: Remnants of engagement in later years." *Omega* 5:25-35.
Minnigerode, F.
1976   "Age-status labelling in homosexual men." *Journal of Homosexuality* 1(3):273-75.
Minnigerode, F. and M.R. Adelman
1978   "Elderly homosexual men and women." *Family Coordinator* 27(4):451-56.
Neugarten, B.L., R. Havighurst, and S.S. Tobin
1961   "The measurement of life satisfaction." *Journal of Gerontology* 16:134-43.
Osgood, N.J. and E.H. Mizruchi
1982   "Participation in work, retirement and leisure." In Osgood (ed.), *A Life After Work*. New York: Praeger.
Palmore, E.
1968   "The effects of aging on activities and attitudes." *The Gerontologist* 8:259-63.
Plummer, K.
1975   *Sexual Stigma*. London: Routledge Kegan Paul.
Reichard, S., F. Livson, and P. Petersen
1962   *Aging and Personality*. New York: Wiley.
Roadburg, Alan
1985   *Aging: Retirement, Leisure and Work in Canada*. Toronto: Methuen.
Rosow, Irving
1974   *Socialization to Old Age*. University of California Press.
Saghir, M. and E. Robins
1973   *Male Homosexuality*. Baltimore: Williams and Wilkins.
Silverstein, Charles
1981   *Man to Man: Gay Couples in America*. New York: Morrow.
Simon, William., and J. Gagnon
1967   "Homosexuality: The formulation of a sociological perspective." *Journal of Health and Social Behaviour* 8(5):182.
Simpson, I.H. and J.C. McKinney (eds.)
1966   *Social Aspects of Aging*. Durham: Duke University Press.
Stein, Peter
1976   *Single*. Englewood Ciffs, New Jersey: Prentice-Hall.
Tripp, C.A.
1976   *The Homosexual Matrix*. New York: Signet.
Tunstall, Jeremy
1966   *Old and Alone*. London: Routledge Kegan Paul.
Unruh, David
1983   *Invisible Lives*. Beverly Hills: Sage.
Warren, Carol
1974   *Identity and Community in the Gay World*. New York: Wiley.

Weeks, Jeffrey
   1983   "The problem of older homosexuals." Pp 177-85 in John Hart and D. Richardson, *The Theory and Practice of Homosexuals*. London: Routledge Kegan Paul.
Weinberg, Martin S.
   1969   "The aging male homosexual." *Medical Aspects of Sexuality* 3(12):66-72.
   1970   "The male homosexual." *Social Problems* 17:527-37.
Weinberg, Martin S. and C. Williams
   1974   *Male Homosexuals*. New York: Oxford University Press.
West, D.J.
   1968   *Homosexuality*. London: Penguin.

III
Aging Workers and the Labour Force

The three chapters in this section all deal with the relationship between age and labour-force participation. In Chapter 9, Chen describes the age structure of the Canadian labour force. His analysis is explicitly framed at the level of social structure, rather than at the social psychological level. Age structure has, as a key component in industrialized societies, an age stratification of occupational involvement. Newly created occupations are likely to recruit young workers, rather than retrain older workers. The latter come to be overrepresented in occupations that are decreasingly tied into major industrial production.

Chen conducts a secondary analysis of data from Statistics Canada, testing a theory by Kaufman and Spilerman, which takes the age distribution of occupations as the dependent variable, as that which is to be explained. However, Chen has to adapt and extend that theory in order to account for gender differences.

In Chapter 10, Tindale analyses an occupation that has recently undergone dramatic changes in age structure. Because of declining public-school enrolments due to demographic changes, there has been little opportunity to hire young teachers. Teachers hired during the baby-boom period are still in the teaching labour force, which is an aging labour force. The contracting demand for teachers creates pressures on workers that are differential, depending on their seniority. Seniority, the number of years a teacher has worked, is a very important principle governing the dynamics of age structures in social systems. For individuals, high seniority may protect their jobs, while low seniority may make a person vulnerable to "redundancy" in contracting labour markets.

The reactions to age-group conflict are analysed by Tindale in a theoretical framework that stresses that the dynamics of age-group conflict are conditioned by social class. The same point is evident in Chapter 11, where Stryckman argues that in many industrial sectors and, in particular, in the garment industry, which she has studied, seniority has been rejected by workers as inappropriate to their particular working situation. Work-sharing plans have been developed in an attempt to protect the jobs of older workers in an environment of high unemployment that has particularly adverse effects on the young. From the employer's point of view, older workers are needed for their skills, skills in which few younger workers have been trained. Moreover, there are equity concerns for fairness among age groups (see also Chapter 30 by Neysmith).

In general, the implications of aging in different industrial and non-industrial work settings continues to be an underresearched area in Canada, although the research base has become extended considerably since the first edition of *Aging in Canada*. The proportion of older people remaining in the work force has declined steadily over the past fifty years in Canada and in most other industrialized nations (McDonald and Wanner, 1984). Nonetheless, age-related social conditions such as job insecurity and age discrimination continue to affect many people (Chen, 1980). It is likely that compulsory retirement will be completely abolished in Canada in the near future. While most people will nonetheless probably prefer to retire at or before age 65, some will no doubt wish to exercise their right to continue in employment. A second consideration for the future is that, with the baby-boom generation now largely placed in the labour force, after years of high unemployment in the younger age brackets, the impact of continuing low levels of fertility may soon be seen in a lack of young people to meet labour-force demands. This may create pressures in the future towards keeping older workers in the labour force for longer periods of time. The economic strain of maintaining retirement income adequacy for a growing proportion of retirees (see Chapters 2 and 29) may create similar pressures. Meanwhile, no wholly satisfactory measures of ''functional age,'' to replace age itself as a marker of loss of suitability for employment (due, for example, to declining health, reaction time, etc.), have been found. It is known, however, that on many dimensions, work ability generally increases with increasing age (Koyl, 1977). How all these factors act in the future to affect the environment of the aging worker and to structure the age distribution of the labour force is a topic worthy of continuing investigation.

References

Chen, Mervyn Y.T.
   1980   ''Age and closeness of supervision: A transitional model.'' Chapter 11, pp. 106-112 in V.W. Marshall (ed.), *Aging in Canada: Social Perspectives.* Toronto: Fitzhenry & Whiteside.
Koyl, L.F.
   1977   ''The aging Canadian.'' Pp. 57-79 in Blossom T. Wigdor (ed.), *Canadian Gerontological Collection I.* Winnipeg: Canadian Association on Gerontology.
McDonald, Lynn P. and Richard A. Wanner
   1984   ''Socioeconomic determinants of early retirement in Canada.'' *Canadian Journal on Aging* 3: 105-116.

9

Shaping Factors of Occupational Age Structures of the Female Labour Force in Canada

Mervin Y.T. Chen
Department of Sociology
Acadia University

For a variety of reasons social researchers may be interested in studying the age structures of occupations. In the 1950s a number of studies used age structures in analysing the relationship between age and various aspects of work. For example, Lehman (1953) used age structures extensively in his examination of age and achievement. LeGros Clark and Dunne (1955) used them in their attempt to determine the age at which men are forced to retire by virtue of the nature of the occupation they perform. Belbin (1953, 1955) used age distribution to examine the relationship between old people and heavy work and also to detect some of the difficulties facing old workers. In their analysis of work and occupational skills, McFarland and O'Doherty (1959) also used age structures. In all these studies, age structure of occupations was used as an independent variable. Only in recent years has some effort been made to establish how they arise. Smith (1973), in a study of the determinants of male occupational age structures, argues that an occupation's age structure is the result of the process of matching age-related characteristics (such as physical capacity and previous experience) to the demands of the job. Nelson (1980) argues that old workers are marginal workers, and that there is a match between marginal workers[1] and marginal occupations.[2] That is, there is a high concentration of older workers in marginal occupations such as farmers, farm labourers, service workers, private household workers and sales workers. Kaufman and Spilerman (1982) discuss the mechanisms that generate occupational age distributions and test hypotheses derived from the discussion, using American census data for 100 occupations.

Virtually all the studies reviewed used data for male workers only. Given the fact that women constitute more than 40 percent of the labour force, it is strange that recent studies exclude female workers from their analysis. This paper attempts to remedy this oversight. Using Kaufman and Spilerman's study as a point of departure, I first report their tested hypotheses and reasoning upon which these hypotheses are based, then discuss the mechanisms that may generate female occupational age distributions and, finally, report the findings from an analysis of age structures of selected occupations in Canada.

Kaufman and Spilerman's Hypotheses

With the aim of studying the age structures of occupations "as an alternative to examining job transitions directly," Kaufman and Spilerman (1982:833-34) hypothesized that there were five types of occupational age distributions:

(a) Occupations in which young workers are overrepresented. These should include entry-level positions in job sequences and occupations organized around emergent technologies.

(b) Occupations in which middle-aged workers are concentrated. Senior positions in job sequences (supervisors, foremen, managers) are expected to fall in this category.

(c) Occupations in which the elderly are overrepresented. These should be primarily the sorts of jobs that permit workers flexibility in setting their rate of work and scheduling hours of employment. Contracting occupations are also expected to be in this category.

(d) Occupations with a uniform age distribution. The researchers expect to find the professions and craft occupations here since affiliation with these positions tends to be of long duration, spanning much of an individual's work life.

(e) Occupations with a U-shaped age distribution. These occupations should contain jobs of low desirability, having poor advancement prospects.

While these hypotheses were put in general terms, the reasons upon which they were based, as discussed below, were not always gender-neutral.

Mechanisms That Generate Occupational Age Distributions

1. Physical requirements of tasks

Some manual jobs necessitate daily exertion that can be performed only by the able-bodied. Firefighters, truckloaders and roughnecks are pertinent examples. These occupations have been generally considered as "male occupations." However, mechanization (e.g., forklift) and automation have made many physically demanding jobs much less so. If women are still kept out of these jobs the reasons would not be so much physical demands or strength as the attitudinal sex-typing of occupations.

Some other jobs (e.g., airline pilot) may not be physically exhausting, but require quick reflexes and a high level of motor coordination. Many people (the author *not* being one of them) believe that women lack mechanical aptitude. This is likely more a cultural assumption than a biological fact (Walshok, 1981:4).

Still other occupations appear to require certain physical appearances —

a factor Kaufman and Spilerman did not discuss. For example, the anchor-person on TV news is supposed to project a trustworthy image. However, physical appearance usually is not a requirement of the work per se. Rather, to hire people with certain physical appearances for certain jobs is an employment practice within a certain cultural context. Since, in general, North America is a youth-oriented society and, according to Marcuse (1964:74-75), there is a "large-scale sexual manipulation" of the employee in the business world, the requirement of an attractive and youthful look seems to affect both female and male workers. A well-known case is Christine Craft, an anchorwoman of a TV station, who, at 36, was told by her employer that she was too old. Other obvious examples are models, receptionists and female flight attendants. Whatever the reasons for this requirement, they affect the age structures of many occupations.

2. Retirement rules

Where performance declines sharply with age, retirement rules act to ensure that employees depart from the occupation, rather than reduce their quality of work. Airline pilots and policemen are examples. In some cases, retirement rules have little relevance to the quality of work. Rather, the reasons appear to be: (a) discouraging conflict between age cohorts over the timing of succession, (b) permitting the infusion of young talent and new ideas into an organization, and (c) enabling a firm to divest itself gracefully of workers who have reached an age where illness is likely to take an increasing toll in work regularity (Kaufman and Spilerman, 1982:830).

Obviously, most of these reasons are also applicable to female workers. However, are there considerations unique to women? Kaufman and Spilerman suggest that the combination of entry credentials and retirement rules tend to shape middle-aged occupation (e.g., school administrators, sales managers, airline pilots) and their findings support this hypothesis. This may not be true for "female occupations." Under the regulation of Human Rights laws and the Charter of Rights and Freedoms in the Canadian Constitution, few occupations, if any, have grossly different retirement rules for their male and female workers. For instance, the retirement age for Air Canada flight attendants, both male and female, is 60. However, the upper bound of the age range of such jobs as models or stewardesses appears lower than that for those typically "male occupations." What factors contribute to this pattern? Are there informal practices that discourage women from remaining on their jobs when they reach a certain age, or subtle manipulations that transfer these women to jobs where youthful appearance is not considered important? Or do most of these women change jobs voluntarily when they reach a certain age? In some instances, formal retirement rules may not even be necessary. For example, most models have contractual work. When a model gets fewer and fewer contracts, she is forced to change her career regardless of retirement rules.

Some women retire from paid employment when they become mothers. In recent years, the availability of lengthy and paid maternity leave obviates the necessity somewhat. However, all occupations do not yet have this benefit.

3. Work scheduling

While some occupations compel departure at a certain age, others permit their members to continue their work until a relatively late age. Professions such as law and medicine are perhaps the best examples. The circumstances of these occupations allow elderly workers to vary their working hours and the rate of work flow. Other examples are realtors, insurance salespersons and building janitors, whose work schedules are flexible.

The effect of work scheduling is not gender-neutral, however. While some women with child-rearing and homemaking responsibilities would be more attracted to jobs with flexible work schedules (such as part-time work), others would withdraw from their employment and return some years later. Consequently the age structures of their occupations would be affected.

4. Education and training

As a consequence of education and training, the lower bound of age range for some occupations is higher than that for others. For example, there is a negligible percentage of doctors, lawyers and dentists in the 18-21 age group. Similarly, there is a relatively small proportion of blue collar tradesmen (e.g., tool and die makers) in the 15-18 age group. From the mid-twenties onwards, the age distribution of these occupations tends to be flat. Kaufman and Spilerman's study substantiates this hypothesis with their data on the male labour force.

The effect of education and training alone would be the same for both sexes. However, changing career patterns among women in recent years would result in a concentration of females below 40 in the occupations just mentioned. One would find few women in blue-collar skilled trades and these would be concentrated in the lower age brackets. In the professions, one would also expect a concentration of females at the lower age brackets because there have been more new and young female entrants to these occupations in recent years. Assuming women would continue to enter into professions and there is no dramatic growth or contraction in these professions, the female portion of these occupations may have a more uniform age distribution in the long run.

5. Job linkages

In large industrial organizations, work positions are arranged in hierarchies, with services at one occupational rung a prerequisite for employment at the next higher level. The consequences of the linkages among jobs for occupational age structure is that each position in a job sequence will have a narrow age distribution, with the mean age increasing over the successive positions. Women tend to get "stuck" at the lower rungs of the organizational ladder (Kanter, 1977:138). The age distributions of male and female managers would be quite different, with more women at the lower levels.[3]

6. Additional institutional considerations

Kaufman and Spilerman considered two factors under this heading: the "lifetime commitment" associated with some occupations and the "dual labour market" thesis. I suggest that these factors do not have the same effect on the occupational-age profiles of male and female workers.

The "lifetime commitment" consideration

Kaufman and Spilerman hypothesized that, provided those occupations associated with a "lifetime commitment" are neither expanding nor contracting in employment, their age distributions should be flat, relative to the age distribution of the total labour force. This hypothesis is substantiated by their data on male members of occupations such as carpenters, electricians, plumbers, compositors and typesetters, dentists, doctors and lawyers.

Logically there is no reason why this factor should affect the occupational-age distribution of females differently from its effect on that of males. Historically, however, there have been considerably fewer women in the occupations mentioned above. In recent years increasing numbers of women have been entering into professions such as dentistry, medicine and law (Chen and Regan, 1985:Chapter 7). Since most of them are newcomers to these professions, an overrepresentation of what I call "old-young" age bracket (approximately 26-39) is likely. For similar reasons, one would expect to find most of the female workers in skilled trades in the lower age groups.

It is true that the years 26-39 are the later period of the child-rearing years, when many women stay outside of the labour force. However, the majority of professional women do not. They struggle to continue their careers and fulfill their family responsibilities at the same time. Their families are usually smaller and they are in a better financial position to acquire child-care and domestic services.

The secondary labour market consideration

In their analysis of the American male labour force, Kaufman and Spilerman found that jobs in the secondary labour market tend to have a U-shaped age distribution. That is, there is an overrepresentation of both the old and the young. Older workers in secondary positions are more likely those who embark on a second career when job difficulty compels a job change. Young workers with secondary positions (e.g., gas station attendants, dishwashers, food service workers) are usually new entrants to the labour market and have not committed themselves to a line of work or for other reasons desire intermittent employment.

The distribution of female workers in the secondary labour market is likely widespread, rather than U-shaped. While there are young women who are raising a family and therefore may prefer intermittent employment, there are also middle-aged homemakers who are forced to take part-time jobs. Furthermore, there are women who return to the labour market after their child-rearing years. Many of these middle-aged women lack occupational skills and training and can only find secondary positions. In contrast with the male labour force, I do not expect a low rate of representation of female workers with secondary positions in their prime years.

Hypotheses on Female Occupational Age Structures

Kaufman and Spilerman have shown that systematic forces of a cultural, institutional and demographic nature operate on occupations and are capable of creating a diversity of age patterns. However, from my comments on their discussion of these forces it is evident that these forces do not affect the age distributions of female and male workers in the same manner. From the discussion above, three types of female occupational-age structures may be discerned:

(1) Occupations in which young women are overrepresented. These should include entry-level positions in job sequences, low levels of occupations organized around emergent technologies (i.e., computers, robots and the like) and/or occupations that require an attractive and youthful appearance.

(2) Occupations in which "old-young" women (mid-twenties to late thirties) are concentrated. I expect professions and blue-collar trades fall in this category.

(3) Occupations with a flat age distribution. I expect to find most occupations in which there is a high concentration of women fall in this category.

Methods

Data on all Occupational Unit Groups (4-digit census occupational codes) were obtained from Statistics Canada. The data set consists of information for Canada as a whole, by age and sex for 1981. Occupational age patterns were constructed by using an index or representation in each category. The formula is: $E_{ao} = P_{ao}/P_{at}$, where P_{ao} = percentage of workers in age category a of occupation 0; P_{at} = percentage of workers in age category a of the total sample. Thus, if $E_{ao} > 1.00$, age category a is overrepresented in occupation 0; if $E_{ao} < 1.00$, the age category is underrepresented in the occupation. The age profile of occupation 0 would be

E_{ao}/a = 15-18, 19-21, 22-24, 25-29. . .65 and over

By inspecting the occupational age profiles, the occupations can be classified as young, old-young, middle age, old and so on.

Findings and Discussion

The data appearing in Table 1 illustrate occupations organized around emerging technologies, entrance level jobs and/or occupations that require an attractive and youthful appearance. According to hypothesis one, we would expect that there is a concentration of female workers in the young age groups. Generally, the data support this hypothesis. Comparing the age profiles of females, two distinctive patterns can be identified:

(1) In some occupations the age profiles of female and male workers are quite similar. Occupations in Panel A of Table 1 are such examples. Computer-related occupations such as systems analysts and programmers probably are young people's occupations. Two reasons may be offered to explain this phenomenon. First, the computer is a relatively new technology. Thus, the members of computer-related occupations are, in general, relatively young. Second, and perhaps more important, as a systems analyst's or programmer's career advances, the person is likely to be promoted to a managerial position. Consequently the person is no longer a member of that occupation. In the case of tellers and cashiers, waiters and waitresses and hostesses and stewards (flight attendants and stewards are included in this category), it is likely that the requirement of an attractive and youthful appearance applies to both sexes.

(2) In occupations on Panel B of Table 1, women's age structures differ from those of men. There is a wider concentration of females in the younger age groups (thirties and younger). Typists and clerk-typists are entrance level jobs and are predominantly "female occupations." Due to job changes, career development, or child-rearing responsibilities, there tends to be a high turnover rate among these women. As a result, there is a high concentration of typists in the young age groups. Nationally there were fewer than 3,000 male typists and clerk-typists in 1981. No data regarding the industrial distribution of these men are available. An experienced officer in the Department of Employment and Immigration informed the author that they probably can be found in government agencies, the armed forces and communication industries (e.g., telegraphic typewriter operators). These men usually are not highly qualified. Since their prospects for career development are not particularly bright, they tend to stay in the occupation much longer than their female counterparts. The relatively flat age structure is likely a result of these factors.

The rest of the occupations in Panel B are the ones where women have made tremendous inroads in the past decade. Advertising artists are a very good example. While the number of men in this occupation has had a modest 7.5 percent increment between 1971 and 1981, their female counterparts have enjoyed a 440 percent increase during the same period.[4] The dramatic entry of females in their late teens to mid-twenties into these occupations, by and large, explains their overrepresentation in the age profiles.

Table 2 presents data of some managerial occupations and a number of professions. According to hypothesis two, we would expect a concentration of the "old-young" females (approximately from mid-twenties to late thirties) in these occupations. The data strongly support the hypothesis, although in a few cases the age range of overrepresentation goes beyond the "old-young" as it is defined here (e.g., university teachers [not shown in Table 2]).

The overrepresentation of female lawyers and physicians in age brackets 25-29 and 30-34 merits special comments. The female representation in these age groups ranges from 1.14 to 2.64 times higher than what is expected. These patterns are consistent with the fact that there have been an increasing number of female students in, and female graduates from, graduate schools and professional schools in Canada (Chen and Regan, 1985:53).

When comparing age profiles of males with those of females in these professions, one finds a clear regularity. That is, if the profession is predominately female (e.g., social work), female members of that profession would have a wide-spread age distribution. The same can be said for those predominantly male professions, (e.g., lawyers, physicians and veterinarians).

The exception to the above-mentioned pattern, pharmacy, may be examined in more detail. Clearly most male pharmacists are older individuals, while their female counterparts are younger. This is a nation-wide phenomenon in Canada. According to some extensive studies (Hornosty, 1974, 1980, and 1983; Stieb et al., 1986; Ferguson and Roller, 1985), this profession has been undergoing a process of feminization since the latter part of the Great Depression, particularly in the postwar period. Currently female pharmacy graduates and students outnumber their male counterparts by a factor of two to one. This once male-dominated profession is steadily being transformed into a female one. A number of factors have been suggested to account for this change. Stieb et al. (1985:3) suggest the following factors: "a comparatively enlightened attitude within the profession, the absence of specific prohibitions that existed in other countries and in other health professions; the economic advantages, especially in the rural settings of husband-wife, father-daughter teams, sometimes involving a physician as one of the partners; the manpower situation; and the participation of women in the organizational affairs at an early stage."

While the above-mentioned factors explain well the relatively easy entry

TABLE 1:
Illustrative Age Distribution, Young Age Profiles, Canada, 1981

OCCUPATIONS	Sex	N	MEAN AGE	AGE GROUPS[a]											
				15-18	19-21	22-24	25-29	30-34	35-39	40-44	45-49	50-54	55-59	60-64	65+
A.															
Syst. An. &	F	20,240	28.2	.11	1.01	1.91	2.12	1.40	.77	.41	.25	.29	.16	.09	.01
Comp. Pro.	M	50,615	31.1	.08	.74	1.45	1.87	1.81	1.28	.71	.46	.32	.23	.13	.07
Syst. An. NEC	F	570	24.4	1.97	3.10	1.43	.63	.88	.17	.31	.12	.54	.34	.00	.00
	M	660	30.0	1.72	2.34	1.93	.36	.72	1.26	.86	.74	.69	.58	.17	.00
Tellers	F	286,290	28.3	2.76	1.83	1.17	.81	.69	.70	.66	.63	.59	.49	.46	.24
& Cashiers	M	2,860	27.7	4.83	2.60	1.40	.67	.37	.35	.36	.38	.35	.59	.74	1.02
Waitresses	F	254,155	26.6	3.97	1.77	1.03	.72	.58	.56	.58	.51	.52	.48	.44	.23
& Waiters	M	40,360	26.6	4.13	2.14	1.49	.97	.70	.51	.52	.40	.40	.38	.28	.28
Host. & Stew.	F	6,070	29.2	.41	.57	1.40	2.05	1.78	1.20	.40	.28	.22	.22	.08	.11
(Ex. Food)	M	2,120	30.0	.62	.92	1.07	1.98	1.50	1.32	.89	.49	.34	.18	.05	.00

B.

Typists &	F	128,995	32.2	.69	1.63	1.44	1.09	.94	.85	.77	.78	.75	.67	.68	.39
Clerk-Typ.	M	2,860	37.5	.91	1.26	1.46	1.03	.80	.76	.92	1.13	1.00	.91	1.00	.66
Travel Clerks	F	19,870	30.9	.29	1.22	1.61	1.41	1.13	.92	.77	.70	.66	.64	.36	.37
	M	10,235	37.5	.16	.76	.89	1.21	1.20	1.26	.94	.86	1.18	1.10	.88	.86
Hairdressers	F	63,775	30.9	.82	1.67	1.21	.99	1.31	1.09	.72	.49	.51	.55	.55	.63
& Barbers	M	19,715	40.3	.20	.44	.65	.70	1.30	1.57	1.45	.15	.99	.87	.91	2.02
Advertising	F	8,540	39.4	.26	1.18	1.74	1.90	1.17	.79	.63	.46	.29	.32	.47	.04
Artists	M	9,855	36.0	.22	.76	1.18	1.36	1.27	1.09	.93	.86	1.02	.77	.79	.68
Arch. & Engin.	F	5,125	28.0	.37	1.66	2.54	1.24	.87	.64	.57	.43	.39	.43	.42	.06
Technologists	M	55,615	32.5	.16	1.21	2.02	1.25	1.17	1.04	.91	.78	.69	.54	.44	.17
Medical & Lab	F	33,535	31.1	.08	.66	1.61	1.75	1.49	1.08	.72	.54	.54	.42	.44	.14
Technologists	M	9,095	33.6	.16	.69	1.31	1.42	1.61	1.38	1.00	.73	.46	.56	.33	.30
Insur. Sales.	F	22,185	32.0	.11	.80	1.78	1.65	1.19	.91	.87	.61	.50	.66	.52	.46
& Agents	M	43,325	40.0	.04	.24	.73	1.16	1.32	1.11	1.10	1.09	1.07	1.14	1.27	1.89

NOTE:

[a] Each entry reports the proportion of the occupation's members in the age category, relative to this figure for the total labour force in Canada. Entry>1 indicates overrepresentation of the age group in the occupation; entry<1 indicates underrepresentation. In particular, an entry equal to 2 means twice the representation that is expected; an entry equal to 0.5 means half the expected representation.

Illustrative Age Distribution, Old-Young Profiles, Canada, 1981

OCCUPATIONS	SEX	N	MEAN AGE	AGE GROUPS[a]											
				15-18	19-21	22-24	25-29	30-34	35-39	40-44	45-49	50-54	55-59	60-64	65+
Inspectors &	F	5,090	32.3	.13	.98	1.14	1.67	1.28	.95	.87	.75	.74	.74	.52	.39
Regulatory Off.	M	28,670	42.3	.03	.25	.38	.82	1.13	1.09	1.26	1.26	1.54	1.89	2.03	.48
Mgmt.-Nat.	F	980	33.8	.07	.45	.80	1.08	2.08	2.06	1.07	.75	.55	.49	.34	.00
Sci. & Eng.	M	14,100	41.9	.01	.04	.11	.46	1.24	1.88	1.79	1.66	1.49	1.50	.90	.24
Purchasing	F	2,425	33.5	.11	.52	1.29	1.44	1.32	1.23	.75	.99	.79	1.12	.76	.13
Mgmt.	M	16,360	40.0	.06	.49	.75	.97	1.02	1.13	1.10	1.16	1.43	1.62	1.57	.52
Chemists	F	2,280	31.8	.00	.44	1.28	2.02	1.55	1.16	.92	.56	.51	.59	.37	.00
	M	8,900	36.9	.00	.14	.64	1.37	1.57	1.60	1.24	.81	.82	1.08	.82	.26
Architects	F	175	32.2	.00	.07	1.18	2.16	2.15	1.00	.74	.21	.61	.46	.54	.00
	M	1,740	40.0	.00	.00	.26	1.12	1.60	1.65	1.23	1.23	1.06	1.17	.77	.95
Civil Eng.	F	1,215	32.0	.00	.32	1.62	2.27	1.42	1.07	.38	.39	.57	.64	.28	.54
	M	41,015	37.7	.00	.13	.60	1.38	1.52	1.24	1.36	1.16	.99	.97	.75	.46
Aeronautical	F	65	28.8	.00	.00	2.12	1.52	1.18	1.48	.00	.00	2.37	.00	.00	.00
Engineers	M	2,860	39.4	.00	.06	.41	1.28	1.40	1.04	1.29	1.51	1.31	1.07	1.16	.37
Social	F	23,920	34.7	.00	.09	.69	1.90	1.73	1.17	.98	.81	.94	.85	.79	.26
Workers	M	14,830	35.8	.00	.07	.34	1.67	2.07	1.55	.97	.78	.57	.68	.50	.42
Lawyers &	F	6,230	32.6	.00	.05	.64	2.49	2.14	1.14	.60	.59	.38	.26	.43	.53
Notaries	M	35,380	37.9	.00	.01	.20	1.32	1.99	1.69	1.05	.96	.86	.68	.62	1.31
Physicians	F	8,240	36.0	.00	.02	.63	1.85	1.75	1.25	1.01	.86	.85	.70	.96	1.25
& Surgeons	M	41,300	44.0	.00	.01	.23	.88	1.11	1.38	1.35	1.41	1.31	1.50	1.31	2.59
Veterinarians	F	675	29.0	.00	.00	1.63	2.64	2.22	.78	.34	.01	.00	.28	.00	.49
	M	3,740	38.3	.00	.06	.28	1.18	2.11	1.41	1.15	.59	1.22	.90	.92	.79
Pharmacists	F	7,335	33.2	.00	.19	1.53	2.13	1.33	.94	.93	.50	.63	.63	.55	.72
	M	10,000	44.0	.00	.07	.49	.92	.98	1.17	.95	1.22	1.41	1.69	1.68	3.55

NOTE:
[a] See Table 1.

of women into pharmacy at an early era, some features of the profession itself, some recent trends in the pharmacy industry and the interaction between the two aspects may have also contributed to the steady feminization of pharmacy. In many women's perceptions, pharmacy prepares them for a vocation (Ferguson and Roller, 1985:9). As more women are aspiring for professional status, family responsibilities still loom large in their lives. The availability of part-time employment with a relatively decent income thus provides them with an attractive career option.

Furthermore, considerable expansion of chain pharmacies in recent years has had several effects. First, chain stores provide women with increased opportunities of practising the profession without dealing with the business aspect of it.[5] Second, they offer flexible work scheduling, which is an attractive feature for female pharmacists. Third, it is known that there are male pharmacists who have taken up training in Business Administration to become managers in some of the chain pharmacies, although no statistics are available to show the extent of this shift.[6] In any case, it appears that a number of male pharmacists have been lost to managerial positions. Already there are fewer men entering the profession. The loss of male pharmacists would affect the sex balance of the membership of this profession even further.

It has also been hypothesized that the women of the old-young range would have an overrepresentation in the blue-collar trades. The data do not support this hypothesis (see Table 3). Clearly the age profiles of male tradesmen are flat. This is consistent with Kaufman and Spilerman's finding. The age profiles of females do not seem to have clear patterns. In general, women have not gained much inroad into these occupations. While the number of females has tripled (e.g., carpenters) or doubled (e.g., masons) in some occupations, proportionately it is still very small, ranging from half of one percent to about 4 percent of the total membership of these occupations respectively. In the trades where there have been larger increases of females, for example, carpenters, masons and plumbers, there tends to be an overrepresentation at the young end of the age spectrum. However, this is not a dominant pattern, because there is overrepresentation in older age groups, too. No plausible explanations can be offered at this time. More research beyond the analysis of census data is needed.

Our third hypothesis is to test if the age profiles of most occupations in which there is a high concentration of women are flat. The data support this hypothesis. Table 4 presents illustrations of this pattern. In almost all of these occupations there is a large number of women, and in many there are more women than men. The flat age structures of these occupations are consistent with what we have found earlier, mainly that if an occupation is predominantly female, female members of that occupation tend to have a widespread age distribution.

TABLE 3:
Illustrative Age Distribution of Blue-Collar Trades, Canada, 1981

OCCUPATIONS	SEX	N	MEAN AGE	AGE GROUPS[a]											
				15-18	19-21	22-24	25-29	30-34	35-39	40-44	45-49	50-54	55-59	60-64	65+
Tool & Die	F	35	34.3	.29	.90	.94	1.35	1.34	1.08	1.19	.82	.94	.59	.34	.00
Makers	M	1,725	39.2	.33	.98	.96	.89	.85	1.04	1.03	1.09	1.19	1.55	1.64	.42
Machinists	F	140	34.7	.40	.82	1.54	.57	1.21	1.00	1.17	1.44	1.27	.83	.48	.95
	M	10,455	35.4	.46	1.25	1.21	1.06	1.00	1.08	.93	1.10	1.12	1.20	1.34	.62
Carpenters	F	2,170	31.6	1.33	1.40	1.10	1.00	1.05	.49	1.07	1.08	.78	.76	.47	.92
	M	176,580	36.9	.57	1.05	1.13	1.07	.89	.84	.95	1.10	1.12	1.20	1.34	.64
Construction	F	875	31.2	.72	1.77	1.42	.98	.79	.88	1.00	.92	.88	.66	.19	1.13
Electricians	M	74,870	32.8	.34	1.21	1.47	1.35	1.29	1.07	.82	.71	.64	.59	.53	.32
Masons & Tile	F	290	33.5	.73	1.37	1.11	.57	.80	2.16	.60	1.39	.80	1.00	.00	.00
Setters	M	28,640	36.3	.46	.95	.98	.91	.90	.97	1.29	1.42	1.41	1.09	.69	.30
Pipefit.,	F	525	31.2	.94	1.51	1.40	.81	.81	.92	1.22	.37	.43	1.08	.00	.00
Plumb & Rel.	M	70,520	35.2	.39	1.02	1.12	1.13	1.12	1.06	1.09	.76	.83	.71	.36	.11

NOTE:
[a] See Table 1.

While most of the occupations in Table 4 are customarily female dominated (e.g., librarians, nurses, secretaries, telephone operators and knitting occupations), some are not. Management in social sciences and related fields, administrators in teaching and related fields, and financial management occupations are pertinent examples. The fact that the age structures of women in these occupations are as uniform as those of men, and that the proportions of women in these occupations have increased between 1971 and 1981 (e.g., the percentage of women in management in social sciences increased from 33 to 47) seems to indicate that there are women who have gained advancement in all ranks of management. However, this is by no means a widespread phenomenon. It is still limited to only a few occupational categories. Nor does it mean that women have gained equity with men in these high-status occupations in terms of numbers.

Summary

This paper has discussed the factors that shape occupational-age structures. The findings are summarized as follows:

(1) In occupations organized around emerging technologies, there tends to be a greater concentration of men and women in the young age groups.

(2) There is an overrepresentation of young women in entrance level jobs of traditionally female-dominated occupations and in occupations in which women have made considerable gains in recent years.

(3) There is an overrepresentation of "old-young" females in various professions.

(4) No clear patterns of women's age distribution were found in blue collar trades.

(5) The age profiles of most occupations in which there is a high concentration of women tend to be flat.

Systematic forces of a cultural and institutional nature operate to shape a diversity of age patterns. While some of these factors affect the occupational age distribution of males and females in the same manner, others do not. Women's employment patterns are much more complicated than those of men. For example, intermittent work histories and part-time employment are more common among women. These patterns cannot be revealed by analysing the data used. Therefore, any conclusions that may be drawn from this analysis must be considered tentative. Further research using more refined occupational data and information from other sources is strongly suggested.

TABLE 4:
Illustrative Age Distribution, Uniform Age Profiles, Canada, 1981

OCCUPATIONS	SEX	N	MEAN AGE	15-18	19-21	22-24	25-29	30-34	35-39	40-44	45-49	50-54	55-59	60-64	65+
Mgmt. Occs. in Soc.	F	4,405	39.4	.00	.23	.46	.96	1.44	1.34	1.28	1.66	1.32	1.32	1.64	.98
Sc. & Rel. Fields	M	4,885	41.6	.02	.13	.23	.63	1.47	1.70	1.62	1.18	1.37	1.03	1.38	.95
Admin. in Teach.	F	1,780	42.1	.05	.15	.25	.58	1.14	1.54	1.64	1.73	2.07	1.72	1.61	1.01
& Rel. Fields	M	34,500	42.9	.01	.03	.04	.19	.87	2.14	2.49	1.99	1.67	1.08	.78	.28
Financial	F	15,730	35.8	.02	.21	.86	1.41	1.45	1.41	1.26	1.10	.96	1.00	.73	.44
Mgmt. Occs.	M	52,495	38.3	.01	.10	.47	.97	1.58	1.77	1.49	1.24	1.08	.76	.64	.53
Librarians &	F	15,695	40.4	.00	.53	.26	1.29	1.47	1.34	1.19	1.16	1.35	1.51	1.73	2.28
Archivists	M	3,685	40.0	.00	.62	.44	.87	1.55	1.75	1.17	1.13	1.12	.98	1.31	1.20
Nurs. Grad. Ex.	F	213,730	35.0	.20	.35	1.05	1.46	1.39	1.36	1.21	1.00	.93	.71	.76	.33
Sup. Nurs. in Tr.	M	9,865	35.1	.13	.55	1.19	1.57	1.65	1.21	.82	.70	.70	.61	.59	.34
Stenograph. &	F	452,000	33.2	.33	1.09	1.26	1.20	1.12	1.07	.99	.91	.80	.80	.76	.54

AGE GROUPS[a]

Occupation	Sex														
Secretaries	M	4,585	38.7	.67	.84	.90	1.12	.96	.95	.75	1.05	.93	.99	1.47	2.58
Statistical	F	9,265	35.0	.45	1.02	1.19	1.08	1.05	.95	.92	.97	.90	1.23	1.38	.61
Clerks	M	3,100	33.0	.76	1.57	1.67	1.32	.93	.62	.65	.60	.65	1.09	.96	.55
Office Mach.	F	13,285	31.6	.63	1.57	1.37	1.10	.95	.79	.89	.84	.70	.80	.84	.35
Operators	M	4,205	31.3	.94	2.24	1.46	1.27	1.12	.57	.57	.50	.53	.67	.71	.60
Telephone	F	42,970	33.4	.91	1.44	1.16	.81	.74	.82	1.00	1.12	1.20	1.18	1.06	.59
Operators	M	2,185	34.	1.28	1.99	1.17	1.06	.66	.74	.42	.73	1.40	.98	.94	1.16
Real Estate	F	26,370	39.4	.05	.16	.41	.77	1.24	1.65	1.48	1.62	1.55	1.53	1.27	1.23
Salesmen	M	45,110	42.0	.30	.13	.47	.88	1.12	1.23	1.20	1.25	1.38	1.50	1.62	2.19
Occ. Lab &	F	10,420	33.1	1.21	1.25	.99	.94	.93	.94	.95	1.01	.91	1.02	1.05	.29
Oth. Elem. Wk.	M	19,835	39.7	2.60	2.28	1.64	.93	.66	.62	.67	.55	.57	.52	.79	.33
Textile Spin.	F	1,455	33.6	.63	1.40	.82	1.04	.87	1.03	1.08	.92	1.27	1.13	.46	.00
& Twist.	M	775	32.2	.23	2.14	1.86	.98	1.10	.78	.52	.79	.67	1.19	.30	.27
Knitting	F	2,600	35.8	.99	1.19	.94	.85	1.27	.89	1.14	1.01	.86	1.15	1.23	1.02
Occupations	M	1,655	32.0	.95	1.18	1.41	.98	1.01	1.38	.97	1.01	.63	.60	.49	.51

NOTE:
[a] See Table 1.

Notes

[1] Nelson sets forth three conditions to define "marginal worker" (1980:91-94):
(1) Achieved status: characteristics that are inferior to the achievements of other workers, such as level of educational attainment.
(2) Ascriptive status: assigned characteristics that carry a low status, such as a perceived unwillingness to learn new skills.
(3) Disabilities: physical handicaps and other idiosyncrasies that are viewed as costly to the employer.

[2] Nelson defines marginal occupations in terms of stability and social marginality. For a detailed discussion, see Nelson (1980:94-97).

[3] Unfortunately, since the ranks of administrators and managers are not given in the census data, we are unable to test this hypothesis.

[4] The numbers of workers in these occupations in 1971 are as follows:

OCCUPATION	SEX	N
Advertising Artists	F	1,920
	M	7,940
Arch. & Engin.	F	660
Tech. & Technicians	M	28,520
Medical & Lab	F	17,460
Tech. & Technicians	M	5,255
Travel Clerks	F	5,270
	M	9,185
Insurance Salesmen &	F	4,975
Agents	M	35,505

Source: Statistics Canada, 1971; Census, 4-Digit Occupations, by Age and Sex, Canada and Regions, Special Table.

[5] Hornosty (1980:201) reported that proportionately considerably fewer female than male pharmacy students (29 percent versus 70 percent) aspire to own and operate a pharmacy, while slightly more females than males aspire to manage a pharmacy owned by someone else.

[6] No survey has been done about this change. However, experienced officials in the Department of Employment and Immigration have noticed the trend. This information is obtained from an interview with Mr. Bill Steele, an economist in the Regional Office, CEIC in Halifax, Nova Scotia.

References

Belbin, R.M.
1953   "Difficulties of older people in industry." *Occupational Psychology* 27:177-190.
1955   "Older People and Heavy Work." *British Journal of Industrial Medicine.* 12:309.

Chen, Mervin Y.T.
   1984   "Shaping Factors of Occupational Age Structures of the Female Force: Toronto Metropolitan Area." Paper presented at the 19th Annual Meetings of the Canadian Sociology and Anthropology Association, June 6-9, 1984, University of Guelph, Guelph, Ontario.
Chen, Mervin Y.T. and Thomas G. Regan
   1985   *Work in the Changing Canadian Society.* Toronto: Butterworth.
Ferguson, Joyce A. and Louis Roller
   1986   "Career Aspirations Compared by Gender and Generation Status: Preliminary Analysis of Pharmacy Students. *American Journal of Pharmaceutical Education* 50(1):39-43.
Hornosty, Roy W.
   1974   "A Comparison of Sex Differences Among Pharmacy Students in Canada: 1962 and 1972." Report to the Ontario College of Pharmacy.
   1980   "Implications of feminism for the profession of pharmacy in Canada." *International Journal of Women's Studies* 3(2):183-206.
   1983   "The Pharmacy Student's Trilema: A Response to Professionalization." Paper presented at the Annual Meetings of the Canadian Sociology and Anthropology Association, Vancouver, B.C., June 1-4.
Kanter, Rosebeth Moss
   1977   *Men and Women of the Corporation.* New York: Basic Books.
Kaufman, Robert L. and Seymour Spilerman
   1982   "The Age Structures of Occupations and Jobs," American Journal of Sociology, 87(4):827-51.
LeGros Clark, J. and A.C. Dunne
   1955   *Aging in Industry.* London: Nuffield Foundation.
Lehman, H.C.
   1953   *Age and Achievement.* London: Oxford University Press.
Marcuse, Herbert
   1964   *One-Dimensional Man.* Boston: Beacon Press.
McFarland, R.A. and B.M. O'Doherty
   1959   "Work and occupational skills." In J.E. Birren (ed.), *Handbook of Aging and the Individual.* Chicago: University of Chicago Press.
Nelson, Thomas C.
   1980   "The age structure of occupations." In Pauline K. Ragan, *Work and Retirement: Policy Issues.* The Ethel Percy Andrus Gerontology Center, University of Southern California Press. Los Angeles.
Smith, John M.
   1973   "Age and occupations: The determinants of male age structures — Hypothesis H and Hypothesis A." *Journal of Gerontology* 28(4):484-490.
Stieb, Ernst W., Gail C. Coulas and Joyce A. Ferguson
   1985   "Women in Ontario Pharmacy, 1867-1927." In Commemoration of the Centenary of the First Admission of Women to the University of Toronto, 1984-85. *History and Pharmacy*, 1986 in press.
Walshok, Mary Lindenstein
   1981   *Blue-Collar Women: Pioneers on the Male Frontiers.* New York: Anchor Books.

10

Age, Seniority and Class Patterns of Job Strain

Joseph A. Tindale
Department of Family Studies
University of Guelph

During the past ten years social gerontologists have been paying increasing attention to the question of when and how the variables of class and age interact to affect the well-being of persons in later life. Interest in this area of research has been prompted by twin frustrations. On the one hand much of the social gerontology done in the 1960s and early 1970s was exclusively concerned with age as the criticial independent variable. As such, this kind of work was subject to criticism from sociologists, who argued that structural variables, such as social class, were much more predictive of later life situations. In answer to these criticisms social gerontologists began to address the question of how age and class might interact together to affect later life income, satisfaction, or in this case, intergenerational relations.

This is an examination of the age-based relations between younger and older secondary school teachers in Ontario. Enrolment in Ontario public secondary schools has been falling since the late 1970s as the baby boom cohort moved through the school system. This demographic process has created occupational pressures as school boards have been required to reduce staff levels. At the same time the Ontario Secondary School Teachers' Federation (OSSTF) has worked equally hard to maintain job security for their members. The impact of these enrolment declines on the teachers has been differentiated and at least partially explained by age. The situation is further complicated by the contradictory location of the teachers in the class structure. Teachers possess more day-to-day autonomy on the job than do persons employed in traditional working class occupations. At the same time, they are salaried workers subject to the directives of their school boards first, and second, to those of the provincial Ministry of Education.

What happens to the regard teachers have for one another when persons either are not hired in the first place, or are let go because they have been declared redundant as a result of enrolment declines and shrinking education budgets? And if the organization representing the teachers, the OSSTF, cannot control the situation, but in fact feels compelled to endorse a procedure where the criterion for job security is seniority, what is the cost in terms of relations between younger and older age groups of teachers? These are the questions the following analysis addresses. A theoretical rationale for understanding the interplay between class and age will be presented and then applied. After documenting the extent of the enrolment decline and budgetary restraint, survey data derived from a sample of Ontario secondary school teachers will be examined.

Seniority and the Association Between Age and Class

Seniority is a reference point based on one's birthday, and is used to distinguish the accumulated experience of one person compared to another (Cohen, 1984:244). It may also refer, of course, to a less all-encompassing benchmark; for example, the beginning of one's career employment. In trying to understand how seniority works in terms of its cohesive or divisive character vis-à-vis the teachers as a professional body, one must combine class and age in a dynamic fashion that allows for dissensus as well as consensus.

The data to be presented on the teachers separate them into three groups. In 1980, when these data were collected, the young teachers were 24-34 years (N = 93), those middle-aged were 35-45 (N = 93) and the older teachers were 46-64 (N = 67). This means the oldest cohort are the children of the Great Depression. The middle-aged teachers are the babies of World War II. And the younger teachers are the leading edge of the baby boom group. Each of these statistical artifacts, or age groups, has a biography that is quite unique to its cohort. In each case, their birth period was marked by events their community, and history, have come to consider very significant. However, the present analysis focusses not only on their generational experiences but on their age-group membership and its effects. When the different age groups of teachers interact with one another, they engage in what can properly be termed age-group conflict. Age is not solely a continuous variable, but in this analysis demarcates three discrete interest groups.

The possibility of conflict between generations or between age groups is enhanced at times when class-based strain is evident. Recently Dowd (1986) has made an argument for considering the old to be separated, as a generation, from younger people on the basis of ideological differences derived from biography. The shared biographies of the old are not shared by the young, and as such, the aged are likely to be considered strange. This strangeness can be turned into hostility when class explanations alone are insufficient to explain the dilemma faced by the individual. As Dowd argues (1986:178):

During periods of recession and economic decline, the potential for class conflict increases considerably. Less appreciated, however, is the greater likelihood for age conflict as the recession extends into the occupations dominated by the middle class. Lacking an adequate class explanation for their economic difficulties (it is certainly not the workers from the tight white-collar, service sector labor market), the "explanation" takes on a generational cast. Out-group hostility against non-age group members is the eventual outcome.

The conceptual consideration of class and age interests in the context of later life is relatively recent. Prior to age stratification theory, which began to emerge in the early 1970s, much of gerontological theorizing was characterized by assumptions of a social order thesis (Dawe, 1970; Horton, 1971). Individuals were the focus of attention, and their passive adjustment to normative expectations, as measured by morale and life satisfaction used in studies of disengagement/activity/continuity, was the convention (Marshall and Tindale, 1978-79; Tindale and Marshall, 1980).

A departure from the individualism of disengagement theory, and the beginnings of an understanding of macro social relations in later life are found in the age stratification model. The credit for this theory development goes principally to Matilda White Riley in association with Marilyn Johnson and Ann Foner (Foner, 1974, 1978a, 1978b; Foner and Kertzer, 1978; Riley, 1971, 1976; Riley, Johnson and Foner, 1972). In this perspective, age strata are seen to intercept class strata, providing input to status differentiation by ordering people and roles within age hierarchies (Foner, 1974). Age stratification theorists, however, do not analyse the relationships of economic conditions to social class, and instead focus on the allocation of people to age-graded roles within a division of labour and the socialization of individuals to acceptance of these normatively defined roles.

At about the same time as Riley, Foner and Johnson were developing age stratification theory, Dowd was beginning to articulate a model for the stratification of aging based on exchange theory. Dowd (1975:586-587) presents the basic assumption of the model to be that people will endeavour to maximize rewards. Interaction will be sustained between two actors when it is mutually defined as profitable, and there is a recognition that the rewards accruing to each actor will vary according to who possesses more power.

In focussing on this interaction, Dowd (1980) recognizes there are class differences between actors, where class is defined in nominalist terms as being based on hierarchical access to decision-making authority. This authority, and other personal resources such as income and status, are the basis for any power an actor might wield. Dowd maintains that an individual's access to power is likely to diminish in later life as his stock of personal resources gradually deteriorates. It is this link between class and age that he correctly argues the age stratification theorists miss. He states (1980:33):

. . .there is a major *theoretical* problem with the Riley model — that is, its failure to integrate adequately the effects of class with those of age. It has become evident that, empirically, age variables alone do not totally explain the variance of social-psychological or sociological phenomena.

Dowd would argue that exchange theory is adequate to cover the social-psychological phenomena. He and Bengtson (Bengtson and Dowd, 1980-1981) added structural functionalism to deal with the more sociological phenomena, and together they argue exchange theory and structural functionalism are a complementary match of micro and macro perspectives. On the one hand, however, assumptions of both exchange and structural functionalist theory are normative in nature. They return us to the root assumptions that guided disengagement theory. On the other hand, exchange theory has made a real contribution in better articulating the age and class interaction question than had previously been the case.

What is needed is a framework guided by interpretive assumptions (Marshall, 1980). There must be room in the theoretical perspective for competing values and conflict that is real and involves the meshing of economic conditions with personal life-course opportunities. The framework must also be historically aware in order to grasp the process whereby seniority has come to be a real friction point for teachers because it now involves more than just the salary increments it was associated with in the 1960s and early 1970s. Today seniority is the cutting point criterion for declaring teachers redundant, often terminating their employment, and perhaps their teaching careers.

An interpretive perspective such as this is perhaps best facilitated by combining an understanding of the teachers' class location with one that associates social class and age in terms of the creation of social dependency.

High school teachers fall into a category Hochschild (1975) calls the new middle class, people who exercise decision-making authority over others in their work situation while they are also wage labourers. Wright (1978:36) considers this to be a contradictory class location. And it is illustrated in a very real way by the conflict within the labour organization that represents the bargaining interests of the teachers.

Teachers have a federation (OSSTF), which negotiates on their behalf; yet it is not officially a union. It is a professional association. However, the enmity among teachers over whether the OSSTF should be more or less like a union points up the dilemma teachers find themselves in. They do not work on a fee-for-service basis, nor do they fully control the labour process as traditionally defined professionals have done. They are pressured by boards of education, municipal and provincial governments and to some extent the public to conform to work settings they do not see as advantageous to themselves and/or their students. As a result, many teachers increasingly define themselves in a context that blurs the gap between themselves and industrial workers. And as suggested earlier, this may in part be a function of the circumstances in which young teachers coming into the profession find themselves. The changed circumstances are not something they can live with in the short term in the same way as older teachers perhaps can; younger teachers must confront the external pressures that have an impact on teaching.

The ambiguous class situation these middle-class teachers find themselves in is socially constructed by the interaction between their personal biography and the relationship teachers have with their employers. As was pointed out in the introduction, they are autonomous in terms of many day-to-day decisions, and yet they are salaried public sector workers tied to the directives of school boards and the provincial government.

In a similar vein, Townsend (1981), Walker (1981) and Tindale, Neysmith and Edwardh (1985) argue the dependent status many older persons experience in later life is due to a socially constructed dependency closely related to the class position these older persons have experienced throughout their biography and to the state-legislated social policies that affect them, e.g., those dealing with retirement and pensions.

Taken together, the framework employed here takes seniority as the linchpin in decision making about redundant teachers created by enrolment decline and budgetary restraint. Seniority becomes the age-group cutting point that comes into play because the class situation of teachers is insufficiently clear or powerful enough to give the OSSTF control of the hiring and firing of teachers. Decisions on appointments and dismissals are outside their purview. The consequences are within their sphere of experience, and they involve age-based tension as the seniority factor is played out.

This conceptual framework and the concrete situation of the teachers is illustrated first by documenting the enrolment declines and budgetary restraint and then by considering how these have affected age-group relations among teachers.

Enrolment Decline and Budgetary Restraint

In the final report of the Commission on Declining School Enrolments in Ontario, chaired by Robert Jackson, he predicted (1978:48) that public school enrolment declines would continue until 1985, and that enrolment declines at the secondary school level would persist until 1992 or 1993. The most recent statistics available suggest his estimates were close to being correct. To the extent Jackson was wrong, it was in underestimating the enrolment decline.

Figures released by the Ministry of Education reveal that as recently as 1983 public school enrolment was still declining, as were the number of schools and full-time teachers in the province (Education Statistics, 1983). Table 2 also illustrates the point in its projection of public school enrolments to 1992. Enrolments at this level are now expected to bottom out in 1989, before beginning a modest move back upwards.

Table 1 provides a detailed breakdown of changes in the number of

TABLE 1:
Changes in the Number of Schools, Enrolments, Full-Time Teachers, and the Pupil/Teacher Ratio for Ontario Public Secondary Schools, 1955-1983

Year	Schools	Enrolment	Percentage increase or decrease	Full-time teachers	Pupil/ teacher ratio
1955	375	174,562	—	7,357	23.7
1956	383	185,605	6.3	8,036	23.1
1957	391	203,525	9.7	8,669	23.5
1958	404	222,075	9.1	9,573	23.2
1959	418	237,576	7.0	10,464	22.7
1960	430	262,775	10.6	11,478	22.9
1961	447	299,177	13.9	12,850	23.3
1962	457	331,578	10.8	14,923	22.2
1963	470	364,210	9.8	17,170	21.2
1964	483	395,301	8.5	19,205	20.6
1965	499	418,738	5.9	21,659	19.3
1966	523	436,026	4.1	24,242	18.0
1967	535	463,736	6.4	27,164	17.1
1968	553	500,807	8.0	30,203	16.6
1969	567	530,679	6.0	32,342	16.4
1970	569	556,913	4.9	33,693	16.5
1971	588	574,520	3.2	34,469	16.7
1972	607	583,013	1.5	34,549	16.9
1973	611	585,725	0.5	33,889	17.3
1974	611	589,650	0.7	34,231	17.2
1975	615	605,160	2.6	34,826	17.4
1976	620	613,055	1.3	35,352	17.3
1977	622	613,830	0.1	35,454	17.3
1978	630	611,668	−0.4	35,068	17.4
1979	633	600,084	−1.9	34,513	17.4
1980	639	586,261	−2.3	33,840	17.3
1981	643	568,635	−3.0	33,182	17.1
1982	635	562,013	−1.2	32,741	17.2
1983	632	554,930	−1.3	32,744	16.9

SOURCE: Education Statistics, Table 4.151, Ministry of Education, Ontario, 1983.

public secondary schools, enrolments, full-time teachers and the pupil/teacher ratio for the period 1955-1983 (Education Statistics, 1983). Here it is apparent that, in terms of actual figures, enrolments were still declining as of 1983, while the projected figures presented in Table 2 suggest that enrolments will still be falling in 1992.

TABLE 2:
Projections of Public and Secondary Enrolments in Ontario, 1982-1992

	Public	Secondary
1982 (actual)	658,975	562,013
1983	642,802	552,033
1984	624,425	545,681
1985	610,190	541,340
1986	603,769	533,630
1987	597,820	524,616
1988	594,155	510,915
1989	591,337	504,312
1990	591,706	494,195
1991	591,716	489,322
1992	594,069	483,444

SOURCE: Ministry of Education, Table 4 & 5, Ontario, 1983.

In addition to noting the drop in enrolments evident in Table 1, it is also clear this is not the only area of decline. The number of schools began to drop in 1982, four years after enrolment began to fall in 1978. The figures for number of schools is a net figure, representing the total number of publicly supported secondary schools after new schools have been added and closed schools subtracted.

In terms of the number of full-time teachers, it can be seen that their ranks began to diminish in the same year enrolments began to drop, 1978. On the positive side, the figures presented for the pupil/teacher ratio suggest that student enrolments have been dropping more quickly than teacher positions have been disappearing. In the 1950s this ratio peaked at 23:7; in 1983 it had fallen to 16.9. The teachers who have been able to obtain and keep jobs, on the whole, would seem to be enjoying smaller classes.

In summary, then, enrolment declines were still occurring at both the public and secondary levels as recently as 1983. It is expected secondary school enrolments will continue to fall until the mid 1990s. There have been losses in the number of schools and teachers roughly parallelling the pattern of enrolment declines. Clearly teachers are facing a squeeze on their numbers as a result of enrolment declines.

The situation with regard to budgetary restraint is not quite so obvious, although there are strong indications of a shrinkage occurring in this area, as well. In 1978 Jackson cited Foot (1978:23-28) to argue that after accounting for inflation he expected general grants to school boards to experience a change of − 5.2 percent between 1977 and 1982, and a change of − 8.2 percent between 1982 and 1987.

Figures released by the Ontario government in 1983, and presented in Table 3, show grants from the provincial government as a percentage of school board expenditures between 1969 and 1983. They suggest that the proportion of school board expenditures covered by these grants has been declining at the public and secondary school levels since 1976.

TABLE 3:
Ontario General Legislative Grants (in thousands of dollars) as a Percentage of Public and Secondary School Expenditures 1969-1983

Calendar year	Public			Secondary		
	Expend-iture	Grant	%	Expend-iture	Grant	%
1969	627,902	254,892	40.59	606,079	252,777	41.71
1970	707,278	303,930	42.97	672,581	333,139	49.53
1971	759,178	366,052	48.22	739,531	411,090	55.59
1972	817,619	424,615	51.93	803,309	467,883	58.24
1973	837,233	438,584	52.38	834,653	492,654	59.03
1974	922,735	475,101	51.48	912,901	521,880	57.17
1975	1,109,695	592,514	53.39	1,066,038	628,345	58.94
1976	1,283,071	617,873	48.15	1,260,926	637,805	50.58
1977	1,392,114	669,027	48.06	1,397,449	686,642	49.14
1978	1,474,858	677,120	45.91	1,496,030	713,481	47.69
1979	1,553,304	687,638	44.27	1,617,727	755,882	46.72
1980	1,700,195	734,349	43.19	1,745,597	816,122	46.75
1981	1,893,336	816,471	43.12	1,941,603	896,647	46.18
1982	2,166,763	895,254	41.32	2,158,365	956,631	44.32
1983	2,392,336	945,149	39.51	2,323,734	975,418	41.98

SOURCE: Education Statistics, Table 8.01, Ministry of Education, Ontario, 1983.

Taken together, the estimates of Foot as cited by Jackson, and the available figures on grants as a proportion of board expenditures, are strongly suggestive of budgetary restraint facing teachers and their boards.

Teachers who have been declared redundant and have at least some relative seniority in their board, can sometimes get a new job at another school within their board by "bumping," read displacing, some other teacher with less relative seniority. The result is that as enrolments decline, schools begin to close, and as hiring turns into bumping with only occasional hiring, promotion opportunities for those teachers with some seniority become more difficult to find and those young teachers lacking in seniority have enormous difficulty acquiring job security. The conclusion that can be drawn from this is a very real potential for tension. It is a tension that generally falls along age lines as those with seniority are better protected than those who do not have this security.

Along with reports such as that produced by the Jackson commission on declining enrolments (1978), as early as 1978 editors (*Toronto Star*, May 6, 1978) began to call for early retirement options as an at least partial solution to redundancy strife. Early retirement, though, brings age-related tension full circle. Young teachers are unable to hold on to their jobs. Those with enough seniority to protect their jobs do not have opportunities to be upwardly mobile in the profession because of the no-growth situation, and older, but younger than aged 65 teachers, are encouraged to retire early.

Notwithstanding the multiple age-related tensions that can be pointed to, the context for them is also an integral part of the process. Any existing age-based tensions are exacerbated by the external factors of enrolment declines and budgetary restraint. An added dimension that has not helped relations among teachers, or between them, the boards and the public, is the resentment engendered by teacher/board labour disputes. The burden of carrying this public ill will is borne primarily by the teachers. As recently as November 1985 an extremely bitter strike by public secondary school teachers in the area of Guelph, Ontario, was ended after almost three months by back-to-work legislation passed by the Ontario government. The status of teaching as a profession, and the public prestige it carries, has been under fire since the first teacher strike in 1974.

The Sample

In addition to theory development, the investigation of teachers is an empirical test of the utility of a generational conflict perspective. The data consist of 256 usable cases out of an original sample of 362 (Tindale, 1980). The latter figure represents a 1 percent random sample of the Ontario Secondary School Teachers' Federation (OSSTF) membership. These teachers were administered a questionnaire, and the 256 good cases represents a response rate of slightly over 70 percent. The general hypothesis was that there would be evidence of age-based tension associated with teacher redundancy, and that it could be explained both in terms of age effects and the class location of teachers in the particular historical circumstances in which they find themselves.

As already stated, the sample is divided into three cohorts, where those

24-34 (N = 93) are labelled young, those 35-45 (N = 93) are middle-aged and those teachers 46-64 (N = 67) are the older cohort. This breakdown makes theoretical sense in addition to reflecting three distinct birth periods. The declining enrolments and budgetary restraint have created three distinct, but nevertheless related problems associated with the everyday work world of teachers. The teachers' vulnerability to these problems differs by generational age group. It is the youngest generation who is most likely to be declared surplus and lose their jobs if their relative seniority does not allow them to displace or "bump" a teacher from another school within their board. It is the older members of the youngest age group and those younger members of the middle-aged age group who are most vulnerable to the virtual elimination of promotion opportunities. And logically enough, it is the teachers in the oldest generation who can most be expected to perceive pressure on themselves to retire early.

The teachers were asked a question that specifically sought information on age-based tension, and it was followed by one that asked them to assess the intensity of the tension. The questions dealt with redundancy, promotion opportunity, early retirement and conflict or tension-related issues. In addition, teachers were asked about their class location, including perceived class identity, income, amount of decision-making autonomy on the job and their perception of federal political power. Each of the class location variables provides information on the relative occupational vulnerability of the teachers.

Generational Conflict: As Reality

With respect to age tension in isolation from any other effects, the question put to the teachers was:

> Some people say that in the professions there is tension between younger and older members. Is this the case in the teaching profession?

Forty-six percent of those responding think a tension exists among teachers that is recognizable along age lines. The question about the existence of tension was followed by one asking: "If yes, what is the magnitude of the tension?" Eleven percent (N = 13) think there is a great deal of tension, and more important, 68 percent (N = 78) say there is some tension. This leaves a mere 20 percent who acknowledge tension, but define it as not much. What this suggests, then, is that for the teachers who perceive tension, it is real but not at such high levels as would indicate the inevitability of open and widespread intergenerational conflict. Rather, it is clear a broad segment of the sample have been made aware of a tension that is defined by age.

When age tension is cross-tabulated with age cohort, the results are as found in Table 4. There is near uniformity in perceived age tension across age cohorts, where 51 percent of the younger teachers acknowledge age tension, followed by 46 percent of the older teachers and 41 percent of those middle-aged. The relationship is not statistically significant, and is not so for a good reason. As already noted, the problems besetting the teachers vary by age group in their situational context. Therefore, while a large minority of all teachers perceive age tension, the generations share reasons for perceiving age tension because of a common concern for the welfare of all teachers, at the same time as the perspective of each generation on these issues varies by their particular seniority related vulnerability.

TABLE 4:
The Perception of Age-Based Tension By Age

	AGE		
Perception of Age Tension	Young (24-34)	Middle-Aged (35-45)	Older (46-64)
Yes	50.5%	40.7%	46.2%
No	49.5	59.3	53.8
	100.0	100.0	100.0
N	(93)	(91)	(65)

x^2 = 1.81 with 2df (n.s.) Gamma = .08.

It is not possible in the space available to document the statistically significant associations each generation has between the dependent variable age tension and a set of independent variables reflecting that age group's vulnerability. For this reason, the argument will be limited to that of the older generation.

An explanation of the oldest age group's association with age tension can be initiated by the analysis of the partial relationship between the dependent variable "is there age tension" and the independent variable "tension resulting from bumping," where age is held constant. As Table 5 illustrates, the association is strongly sustained.

The next step in explaining the age tension of each age group, but primarily the older one, is accomplished by an examination of the combination of age tension with pressure to retire early. Table 6 portrays this and in so doing makes clear that the association is strong. Those teachers of any age group who perceive age tension are considerably more likely to think there is pressure to retire early. This is a logical connection in terms of the general argument on vulnerability. When teachers see pressure to retire early, and when the frequency results also show that 72 percent of those who perceive pressure see other teachers as a source, it is not surprising that these teachers are also more likely than others to acknowledge age tension.

TABLE 5:
The Association Between Age Tension and Bumping-Related Tension for the Older Age Group

	BUMPING TENSION			
Age Tension	A Great Deal	Some	Not Much	None
Yes	61.0%	18.8%	33.3%	0.0%
No	39.0	81.2	66.7	100.0
	100.0	100.0	100.0	100.0
N	(41)	(16)	(6)	(2)

$x^2 = 10.57$ with 3df (p < .05), Gamma = .65.

When age tension is related to "pressure for early retirement" while holding age constant, the relationship for the youngest age group disappears, while for the middle-aged group it is basically sustained, and among the oldest generation, it is stronger although not statistically significant (p < .06).

To this point a positive association has been established between the older age group and tension surrounding bumping as a specific source of age tension, as well as with pressure to retire early. And so now the question becomes one of determining the relationship between pressure to retire early

TABLE 6:
The Association Between Age Tension and Pressure to Retire Early for All Age Groups

	PRESSURE TO RETIRE EARLY	
Perceived Age Tension	Yes	No
Yes	52.9%	36.7%
No	47.1	63.3
	100.0	100.0
N	(140)	(109)

$x^2 = 5.81$ with 1df (p < .05), Gamma = .32.

and tension associated with bumping. The point is to show a logical connection between tension resulting from bumping and pressure to retire early. Considering the two variables together, their relationship with each other is reasonable but not statistically significant. The teachers of any age group who think there is pressure to retire early have a greater tendency to think that bumping creates tension than do those who do not think there is pressure on older teachers to retire early.

When the same two variables are explored with controls on age, the association is nonexistent for the youngest generation, but is improved considerably over the original relationship for the middle-aged and older age group. Although the association is not as strong or clear as one might wish, it is sufficient for the present purpose. Table 7 shows the connection between pressure to retire early and tension associated with bumping for the oldest generation of teachers.

TABLE 7:

The Relationship Between Pressure to Retire Early and Tension Associated with Bumping for the Older Age Group

	BUMPING-RELATED TENSION			
Pressure to Retire Early	A Great Deal	Some	Not Much	None
Yes	63.4%	64.7%	33.3%	0.0%
No	36.6	35.3	66.7	100.0
	100.0	100.0	100.0	100.0
N	(41)	(17)	(6)	(2)

x^2 = 5.07 with 3df (n.s.), Gamma = .30.

Conclusion

Older teachers who perceive age tension do so in association with two situations externally motivated by enrolment declines. Teachers of any age who perceive tension around the problem of bumping also are the ones who more often perceive age tension. Some of those teachers are older ones, and the same situation holds for pressure on older teachers to retire early. Both variables are tied to the supply and demand issue in public secondary school teaching right now and in the decade to come. The vulnerability of older teachers does not lie in unachieved position and income; they have made whatever mark they are going to make, and they are adequately compensated for their labour. Their vulnerability lies in both the anxiety and compassion they feel for young teachers being bumped and the knowledge that this redundancy problem has people casting about for ways to alleviate the situation. One of the primary proposals suggested in the press, among teachers and in the Jackson commission report on declining enrolments is early retirement.

Until January, 1986 early retirement was infrequently available to teachers without some kind of financial penalty. They had been able to combine their age and years teaching and come up with a total of 90 + to qualify for a full pension. In the data reported here proposals for an 85 + option, which would enable some teachers to move out sooner without penalty, are widely approved if they come with appropriate protection for the income security of the retiring teachers. At the same time, while a majority of all teachers favour an 85 + option, there is variation by age group. Whereas the younger and middle aged group each support the 85 + option at approximately the 92 percent level, this percentage falls to 79 percent for the older cohort, a drop of 13 percent (P < .05).

The implication of all this is that older teachers have cause to perceive age tension insofar as they feel vulnerable to early retirement pressure as it is a proposed solution to the redundancy issue. The money that goes with a full pension is important, but it is not the complete story. Not all of the older teachers find the prospect of early retirement attractive, and while certainly not all older teachers would be expected to retire early under any such plan, the situation when the data was collected was fraught with uncertainty and is expressed as vulnerability for the older cohort.

The situation has now, temporarily at least, been changed to remove the up front financial penalty for the less than 90 + teachers. An announcement from the Treasurer of Ontario, acting on a recommendation from the Ministry of Education, removed the early retirement financial penalty retroactively to June 1, 1985, and forward to August 31, 1989. During this period a teacher's retirement pension will be a simple calculation of 2 percent of current salary multiplied by the number of years of service. The ministry estimates that 11,000 teachers will be realistically possible participants in this plan, and they expect 5,500, or 50 percent, to take advantage of it (phone interview with Ministry of Education official, March, 1986).

The results will be important for all concerned. If 5,000 or more teachers take an early retirement, it will have a measurable impact on the redundancy problem in Ontario at both the elementary and secondary level. It will free up the avenues of hiring, job retention, and promotion. For all teachers involved at these levels this new four year program is likely to be good news. Among older teachers, however, the responses of the teachers reported on here suggest the news is mixed.

Teachers old enough to be candidates for early retirement will have to weigh the relative adequacy of the money they would receive against the clear inducement/pressure to retire early, and their own feelings of attachment to their work.

The older age group, together with the younger and middle aged groups, is also vulnerable in relation to age tension because of class location. Part of the reason redundancy is such an issue, and therefore why early retirement is being proposed as a partial solution to it, has to do with class location and the inability of teachers to turn the hiring situation around. In other words, the teachers' autonomy vis-à-vis decision making, is limited to the classroom; they do not control hiring, and they did not introduce the early retirement program — the Government of Ontario did that.

If one takes the evidence provided by the teachers and applies it theoretically, it can be seen that indeed there is an association between age and class. In situations like this one, where age-based tensions are associated with redundancy, bumping and job loss related to the pressures created by enrolment decline and budgetary restraint, it is critical that one know the class locations of the people concerned. Teachers are an occupational group trying to present themselves as a professional body at the same time as they are compelled to organize themselves along the lines of an industrial trade union. They are faced with this dilemma because of their ambiguous class location, neither fully autonomous in the workplace nor completely directed by supervisors as production workers typically are.

Insofar as teachers are unable to control the implications of declining enrolments and budgetary restraint, they have been led to turn inwards in conflict with one another intergenerationally because the only presently viable solutions to a presence of surplus teachers are first, redundancy and job termination, and second, pressure to retire early. Each of these options contributes to generational strains that will not be eased until either the demographic and budgetary situation improves, or the teachers gain greater control of their work situation in order to devise a response that is not so internally divisive. Whatever the eventual outcome, and it remains to be seen what effect the new early retirement plan will have on staff members and age tension between younger and older teachers, the relationship between class location, age and biography will remain.

References

Bengtson, Vern and James Dowd
    1980-   "Sociological functionalism, exchange theory and life-cycle analysis: A call
    1981   for more explicit theoretical bridges." *International Journal of Aging and Human Development* 12(1):55-73.

Cohen, Ronald
1984   "Age and culture as theory." Pp. 234-249 in D.I. Kertzer and J. Keith (eds.), *Age and Anthropological Theory*. Ithaca: Cornell University Press.
Dawe, A.
1970   "The two sociologies." *British Journal of Sociology* 21:207-218.
Dowd, James J.
1975   "Aging as exchange: A preface to theory." *Journal of Gerontology* 3(5):584-594.
1980   *Stratification Among the Aged*. Monterey: Brooks/Cole.
1986   "The old person as stranger." In V.W. Marshall (ed.), *Later Life: The Social Psychology of Aging*. Beverly Hills: Sage.
Education Statistics
1983   Table 4.151 and Table 8.01. Toronto: Ministry of Education Ontario.
Foner, Anne
1974   "Age stratification and age conflict in political life." *American Sociological Review* 39 (April):187-196.
1978a   "Age in society: Structure and change." Pp. 13-34 in Anne Foner (ed.), *Age in Society*. Beverley Hills: Sage.
1978b   "Age stratification and the changing family." *American Journal of Sociology* 83: supplement.
Foner, Anne and David Kertzer
1978   "Transition over the life course: Lessons from age-set societies." *American Journal of Sociology* 83(5):1081-1104.
Foot, D.K.
1978   "Resources and constraints: Public education and the economic environment in Ontario, 1978-1987." Working Paper #1, Commission on Declining School Enrolments in Ontario, pp. 23-38, cited in R.W.B. Jackson, *Final Report: Implications of Declining Enrolment for the Schools of Ontario*, p. 29. Toronto: Ministry of Education.
Hochschild, Arlie Russel
1975   "Disengagement theory: A critique and proposal." *American Sociological Review* 40(5):553-569.
Horton, J.
1971   "The fetishism of sociology." In J.D. Colfax and J.L. Roach (eds.), *Radical Sociology*. New York: Basic Books.
Jackson, R.W.B. (Chairperson, The Commission on Declining School Enrolments in Ontario)
1978   *Final Report: Implications on Declining Enrolment for the Schools of Ontario*. Toronto: Ministry of Education.
Marshall, Victor
1980   "No exit: An interpretive perspective on aging." Pp. 51-60 in V.W. Marshall (ed.), *Aging in Canada: Social Perspectives*. Toronto: Fitzhenry & Whiteside.
Marshall, V.W. and J.A. Tindale
1978-   "Notes for a radical gerontology." *International Journal of Aging and*
1979   *Human Development* 9(2):163-175.

Ontario Ministry of Education
  1983   *Ontario Elementary and Secondary School Enrolment Projections,
          1983-1992.* Tables 4 & 5, Catalogue ISSN 0709-4795.
Riley, Matilda White
  1971   "Social gerontology and the age stratification of society." *The Geron-
          tologist* 11(1):79-87.
  1976   "Age strata in social systems." Pp. 189-217 in Robert Binstock, Ethel
          Shanas and Associates (eds.), *Handbook of Aging and the Social Sciences.*
          New York: Van Nostrand.
Riley, Matilda White, Marilyn Johnson and Anne Foner
  1972   *Aging and Society.* Vol. 2. *A Sociology of Age Stratification.* New York:
          Russell Sage Foundation.
Tindale, Joseph
  1980   "Generational Conflict: Class and Cohort Relations." Unpublished doc-
          toral dissertation, York University, Toronto.
Tindale, Joseph A. and Victor W. Marshall
  1980   "A generational conflict perspective for gerontology." Pp. 43-50 in Victor
          W. Marshall (ed.), *Aging in Canada: Social Perspectives.* Toronto: Fitz-
          henry & Whiteside.
Tindale, Joseph, Sheila Neysmith and Joey Edwardh
  1985   "Social dependency: The effects of class and gender in later life."
          Manuscript under review.
Toronto Star
  1978   "Here's how young teachers can get jobs." (editorial) Toronto: *Toronto
          Star* (May 6) C2.
Townsend, Peter
  1981   "The structured dependency of the elderly: Creation of social policy in the
          twentieth century." *Ageing and Society* 1(1):5-28.
Walker, Alan
  1981   "Towards a political economy of old age." *Ageing and Society* 9(1):73-94.
Wright, Eric
  1978   "Class boundaries in advanced capitalist societies." *New Left Review*
          98:3-41.

11
Work Sharing and the Older Worker in a Unionized Setting

Judith Stryckman
Hôpital du Saint-Sacrement
Quebec

In this chapter we will attempt to bring together issues that are, and we believe will continue to be, at the forefront of research in social gerontology concerning the older worker. We will be addressing specifically three questions: Will the older worker be present in the workplace of the future? If so, what, if any mechanisms should be envisioned to accommodate this presence? Finally, what is the impact of unionization in this scenario?

The Future of the Older Worker in the Workplace

Until recently the main preoccupation of the field of industrial gerontology was retirement: preparation for, adjustment to, effect of, etc. But observers of the labour market are increasingly recognizing that the generation of the baby boom may well leave in its wake, because of our declining birth rate, important gaps in the labour market (Harriman, 1982).

As former Minister of Employment and Immigration Lloyd Axworthy pointed out, throughout the sixties and seventies Canada had the best job creation record among the Western industrial countries, but by 1990, we can expect the rate of increase in the labour force to be half of what it was in 1975. And most of the new entrants will be adult women and Native peoples (up to 20 percent in the Prairie Provinces), who likely will not have the skills needed for easy placement in the workplace. Our educational systems across Canada have emphasized, over the past twenty years, general academics and have neglected technical training. "The baby boom generation in general, although highly educated, has been a relatively unskilled generation. . . . High-skill technical work, during this time, was considered unattractive by many high school and college students. So now we have thousands of young people in the labour force who lack the kinds of skills that will be most in demand in the years immediately ahead (Employment and Immigration Canada, 1981).

Thus, despite the fact that we are still plagued with a high level of unemployment, we cannot afford to ignore the possibility that the older worker may become a very precious commodity shortly after the turn of the century. As we have suggested, even now, despite the jobless masses, many fields are short of skilled workers. Obviously immigration may resolve part of the problem, and the chronically unemployed will take up part of the available jobs, but according to Pauline Robinson, former director of the Employment and Retirement Division of the Andrus Gerontology Center at the University of Southern California, "Older workers will not take a significant number of jobs away from the currently unemployed; they will find jobs that are sitting empty because there are not enough skilled workers in the labor force to fill them" (Robinson, 1982).

An additional concern in this area must be the implications of the Equality Act in the Canadian Constitution. Ageism, like sexism or racism, is unjustified discrimination. We would all be very opposed, I believe, to the argument that a woman should be denied the right to work, regardless of her level of need, because there are too many men who are unemployed. By the same token, older workers cannot be pushed out of the labour market because younger workers are jobless. An injustice at one end of the age scale cannot justify an injustice at the other end. In our opinion we must resist such "easy" solutions that deny the basic rights of the individual on the basis of age, or sex, or race.

Persistence of Early Retirement

Once we have affirmed that the older worker must be allowed to keep his place in the labour market because he will be needed in the future, and also because of the equity question, we are still faced with the fact that, when given the chance, he seems to select early retirement rather than a continuation of past work activity. The efforts that are made in the U.S., and here in Canada, to eliminate mandatory retirement and possibly delay retirement age have not had the desired effects, despite the doomsday scenarios that some economists have predicted if workers continue to leave the labour market at such early ages (Equal Opportunities Commission, 1981). Recent Gallup polls in Canada (February 1984) have indicated that 47 percent of the workers interviewed intend to leave the labour market before normal retirement age (65). Twenty-two percent said they intended to retire at 65 and only 4 percent intended to continue beyond 65.

The situation in Quebec can serve as an interesting example. Bill 15 abolished mandatory retirement in Quebec and Bill 20 laid out the program for a 30 percent reduction (6 percent per year before age 65) in the Quebec Pension Plan benefits for those who retire and apply for benefits at 60, and an additional 30 percent (6 percent per year after age 65) for those who apply for benefits at 70. An evaluation of the effects of this law during its first full year of application indicates that flexible retirement for the citizens of Quebec has meant more early retirements. Many more people than were expected chose to take early retirement and applied for QPP benefits before age 65. Forty thousand nine hundred and fourteen people, twice as many as were expected to apply for benefits under the new law in the first year, applied for them during the first six months of 1984. According to Pelchat (1984) most of these individuals were unemployed when they applied for QPP. The Annual Report of the Quebec Pension Plan Board (1985) indicated that less than 2 percent of the contributors choose to retire after age 65, nearly 75 percent retire between 60 and 65, and the remainder retire as soon as they reach 60.

The Equality Act of the Canadian Constitution will apparently provide a legal basis for the generalization of this abolition of obligatory retirement across the country, but given the Quebec example, it is unlikely that many workers will, in fact, choose to modify their plans to retire early.

The Retirement Decision

What is it that encourages workers to retire early? Most agree that it is frequently pension eligibility and higher levels of pension wealth that lead to early retirement (Martin, 1982; Marshall and Tindale, 1980). A study carried out at the Laboratoire de gérontologie sociale at Laval University, not ignoring the importance of economic factors, indicates, however, that a variety of interrelating forces influence this decision according to occupational, physical and social conditions. For example, male workers in the private sector, where pension benefits are not as generous, give as reasons for early retirement poor health and pressure on the part of co-workers and employers. The private sector workers who retire early have had more physically demanding, less prestigious and low wage jobs than those who retire at 65. In the public sector health does not seem to be a determining factor. The early retirees are more often those who have very demanding jobs in which their level of personal responsibility is quite high. This study also indicates that women tend to retire when their husbands do (Baillargeon and Bélanger, 1981). Since they are often three to five years younger than their husbands, they retire early, but often return to the labour market after widowhood.

Obviously our remarks have been referring to voluntary retirement. Given today's labour conditions, however, the older unemployed worker remains jobless for a much longer time than the young unemployed and may often join the ranks of the discouraged, who are no longer included in the official count.

It is also true that the current high levels of unemployment among the younger population creates a certain level of guilt for the older workers, who may decide, with management's and organized labour's support, to "leave in order to empty a spot for a younger person who has a family to support." It is important to respond to this idea that retiring older workers open job possibilities for younger workers. We have already indicated the fundamental injustice of such a position. In addition, it seems that many of the job openings created by retirement simply disappear because the employer wants to cut back on his labour force but could not do so easily because of union contracts (Baillargeon and Bélanger, 1981).

If it is true, as P. Robinson suggests, that the workplace needs, and will continue to need, the experience and expertise of the older worker, retirement of those who are still able to work may well be a waste of talent that our economic system can ill afford. Given the subject of our paper, we are not going to dwell on the question of overburdened pension systems that also add support, according to some analysts, to the view that older workers should be encouraged to delay retirement (Clark and Barker, 1981).

Who would delay retirement, and is he or she the person we need to keep on the job? Retirement has apparently been seen by many as an easy and painless way to get rid of deadwood that only lowers productivity. Martin (1982) suggests, however, that if sufficient income is guaranteed to retirees, only the most highly motivated retiree would delay retirement or want to return to the workplace. That is often precisely the individual the economy needs to retain because of his or her productive possibilities. Given the expectations that have been established among the population concerning retirement possibilities and income replacement, it would be very problematical, although perhaps essential in the long run, to force the older worker to remain on the job with the risk of a seriously deficient level of motivation on his or her part (Martin, 1981). As some have said, this would mean "breaking the social contract" that has been established in our society giving the worker over 65 "the right" to retire. As the rest of our text will indicate, we prefer looking at incentives that will encourage the older worker to remain voluntarily in the work force.

The Possibility of Reversing the Trend: Workplace Accommodation

How could we make it more inviting for the older worker to stay on the job longer? What could be offered or denied that would influence his or her decision? One measure that has been increasingly put forth as a possible incentive is what has been termed "workplace accommodation," in the form of a reduction of time spent in the workplace. One example of such a reduction, work sharing, has particular interest for the older worker. And, as we will see, the presence of a union in the workplace has an impact on the possibility of such an accommodation.

Work sharing: general description

The basic concept of work sharing, i.e., spreading out available work over a large number of employees to avoid unemployment of a few, has been used by industrial societies over a long period of time. In most cases it has been a temporary measure and as such is included as a possibility in about 7 percent of all collective bargaining agreements, but it is concentrated in certain industries. According to a study in Quebec, as of March 1983, 49.7 percent of the collective agreements in the garment industry that were registered with the Labour Ministry included the possibility of work sharing. Other industries where such a possibility was frequent were communications (36.8 percent), bonnetry (31.6) and textiles (30.0 percent) (Lewis and Desjardins, 1985). A similar analysis of union contracts in Ontario indicated that 97.1 percent of the employees in the clothing manufacturing industry were covered by work-sharing provisions (Meltz et al., 1980).

The general tendency to reduce work time (35-hour work week, longer vacations, etc.) has also been perceived as creating jobs for the unemployed. In their push to shorten the work week, unions have traditionally used this argument, in addition, of course, to the need for increased leisure time. As Samuel Gompers, the president of the AFL said in 1887, "As long as we have one person seeking work who cannot find it, the hours of work are too long." The agitation that occurred around the turn of the century and into the thirties to promote a shorter work week referred to Gompers's statement to justify this action (Best, 1981).

During the Depression the work-sharing solution was promoted as a major solution to unemployment and was widely used. Since it often involved major salary cuts, it was perceived as poverty sharing rather than work sharing and was identified with a period of tremendous economic hardship that "many workers viewed as the creation of the business community and the Hoover administration" (Best, 1981:3), what Nemirow (1984) has called the "legacy of ambivalence." In his study (1981), Best provides a detailed history of various forms of work sharing that were used in the U.S. since the Depression. As we mentioned earlier, despite the almost universal reticence of labour unions to use any kind of work sharing that involves pay cuts, this program has been and still is used in some very seasonal industries such as the garment industry, with the blessing of the ILGWU (International Ladies' Garment Workers' Union). This exceptional situation, however, is due to the nature of the industry and the market it addresses, and, to a lesser extent, to the historical background of this union (Stryckman, 1984).

Work sharing as a governmental program: short-time compensation (STC)

A new form of work sharing, also called short-time compensation to distinguish it from its predecessors, was first established as an experimental program in Canada in 1977, in response to a labour market situation in which layoffs were becoming frequent. The program was scheduled to stop in 1979, but was reestablished in 1982, and eventually extended until March

1985 (Lewis and Desjardins, 1985). It was modelled on a West German program that is reported to have reduced the measured unemployment in that country by 17 percent in 1975 (Sadlier-Brown, 1978). A similar program was established in California and has been thoroughly described and analysed by F. Best (1981).

In this program a firm that, because of production slowdown, would normally lay off, for example, 20 percent of its personnel on a temporary basis, applies to the Labour and Immigration Ministry of the Federal Government. The workers in the affected unit or firm, the employer and the Federal Government sign an official agreement by which the firm keeps all its employees on payroll but reduces their work week by 20 percent; for example, they would work, and be paid by their employer, for four days of work instead of five. To compensate for their lost income, due to a temporary modification of the unemployment insurance program allowing for partial payment of benefits, the workers who participate in this program receive a special unemployment insurance allocation for the fifth day, which normally replaces about 82 percent of their lost salary.

An evaluation of the program published in March 1984 indicated that in 1982, 6,714 work-sharing (STC) agreements were signed with the participation of 202,037 employees. In that year 87,000 temporary layoffs were avoided for a total cost of $83.2 million. In 1983, there was a slight increase in the number of agreements signed, 7,835, but the number of participants was quite a bit lower, 93,813, 54 percent less than in the previous year; 34,836 layoffs, 60 percent fewer than in 1982, were avoided at a cost of $83.1 million (Employment and Immigration Canada, 1984).

As this reduction in participation makes clear, the program is fundamentally anticyclical, i.e., employers tend to apply for participation in periods of recession. When the economy picks up, those whose progression is a bit behind the average tend to apply to the program. As we have seen in Canada, particularly in 1983, it was the small and medium-size firms that looked to work sharing as a partial solution to their problem. In Quebec, where the economic upswing has been slower, the size of the firms applying to the program has been larger than in Ontario, for example. Obviously the cost of the program is accordingly higher in that province.

Obviously, too, certain types of firms have more flexibility than others to adjust their work schedules without reducing efficiency or productivity. Such considerations concerning technical and institutional constraints are beyond the scope of this paper. We will, therefore, be referring only to those employers who, we assume, do have the necessary flexibility. As we suggested earlier, seasonal industries such as clothing and textiles have traditionally tended to use work sharing. As one would expect, we see that in Canada these sectors of the manufacturing industry are largely over-represented in the work-sharing program. However, in 1983, there was a notable increase in the number of representatives of commerce, social and cultural services, and business among the applicants (Employment and Immigration Canada, 1984).

Advantages and disadvantages of the work-sharing program

The employer's perspective

For the employer the main advantage lies in the fact that he does not need to recruit and retrain new workers once his normal activity resumes, in the eventuality, of course, that the former employee has found work elsewhere. For example, a 1979 study in Canada showed that it cost from $3,000 to $7,000 to recruit and train a highly skilled worker (Robertson and Humphreys, 1979). As Graham has pointed out, "Employers invest money in any employee they hire. The interviewing and selection process that is part of most staff recruiting is a direct cost because he must pay the recruiting staff. Once a candidate is hired there are costs associated with training" (Graham, 1974). The importance of this element obviously depends on the level of skill required for the work offered (Best, 1981:29).

Again from the perspective of the employer, when a junior employee, generally less well paid, is laid off, the senior employee must sometimes replace him in part of his tasks, usually without a salary cut. This procedure is clearly economically inefficient and would be avoided with work sharing (STC).

Apparently several employers who were involved in the Canadian program felt that the flexibility that the work-sharing program afforded them allowed them to experiment with new marketing or sales tactics and to improve on their production methods (Employment and Immigration Canada, 1984).

An additional advantage is the positive public image such a program gives to the employer and improved labour relations because of the concern expressed for the welfare of the worker. It has been observed in Canada that participation in the work-sharing program has tended to increase the sense of collaboration between management and the employees, thereby contributing to an atmosphere that is potentially much more productive in a given firm (Employment and Immigration Canada, 1984). The employer's ultimate requirement is that it cost him no more to use the work-sharing (STC) program than to lay the employee off.

The only two disadvantages to the employer appear to be a very restricted use of overtime that would need to be included in the work-sharing contract and the cost of certain fringe benefits (e.g., health insurance premiums) that are based on the number of employees and not on the number of hours worked. For high wage earners the employer's contribution to CPP/QPP and unemployment insurance does not change with slightly reduced hours.

The work sharers, therefore, cost the employer relatively more compared to the work supplied (Reid, 1980).

According to interviews with a certain number of employers, the only aspect of the program that should be changed is the large number of forms that need to be filled out for an application. Here, as in so many government programs, the red tape is very onerous (Employment and Immigration Canada, 1984).

The union's perspective

Organized labour's reaction in Canada has been mixed. We already mentioned its basic reticence stemming from the experiences of the Depression. Because the first Canadian program was established during a Wage and Price Control scheme of the government, the CLC was very much opposed to the program, calling it poverty sharing, saying it violated seniority clauses in contracts and that it made layoffs more tolerable and reduced the government's commitment to full employment. Local unions accepted it as a temporary, short-term solution to a very serious problem, as did the major players in the labour movement (Reid, 1980).

The government's perspective

The government's perspective would include considerations of economic efficiency and equity. In a period of recession work sharing is a politically attractive solution that allows the government to avoid the most negative aspects of the employment-inflation trade-off, in particular the indirect social, psychological and medical costs of lengthy unemployment. A disadvantage does result from the adjustments necessary in unemployment insurance legislation, since the normal waiting period for benefits of seven days can no longer apply and since the benefits are slightly higher than for normal unemployment benefits. Also, the duration of benefits may be longer in work sharing (Reid, 1980). One must admit that very careful screening of applicants for work sharing must be made so that the program does not allow incompetent, uncompetitive firms to continue to function when the normal laws of the marketplace would have pushed them out of business.

The employee's perspective

It remains for us to analyse the employees' perspective. Obviously there are two categories of employees to be considered here: those who were designated to be laid off and who have been able to save their jobs thanks to work sharing, and those who were not designated to be laid off but who agreed to reduce their workload. In general, the Canadian program benefited a majority of older skilled workers who had previously had a very stable work history. The program was perceived as a very valid alternative to unemployment, even temporarily. The experience of work sharing did not appear to increase the workers' interest in a permanent reduction in the length of the work week. The employees seemed to be most concerned about their reduced income that was, as we mentioned, partially replaced by unemployment insurance. Almost all the employers involved in the program continued to pay all the fringe benefits of their work-sharing employees, but statistical analysis indicated that the program could be detrimental to the pension plan of one worker in twenty. At any rate, it is clear that unemployment would have a much more devastating effect on fringe benefits and pension plans (Reid, 1980).

Other benefits to the worker who, thanks to work sharing, has been able to avoid unemployment involve avoidance of the social and psychological impact of the loss of a job: alcoholism, family abuse, depression and psychosomatic illnesses due to stress (Reid, 1980). These sorts of benefits are, of course, extremely difficult to measure quantitatively.

The point of view of the worker who was not slated to be laid off is clearly quite different. His income is lowered quite voluntarily. The motivation on his part would have to be based either on a very highly developed sense of solidarity with his fellow workers, or a grasp of the global labour market system in a long-term perspective. The presence of a union could conceivably influence these two conditions.

Case-study: International Ladies' Garment Workers' Union

Historical background

A short description of the development of this union will explain the presence of a work-sharing tradition in the ILGWU.

The union describes itself as an "organization of working people that speaks for employees on behalf of their interests as workers." It traditionally included individuals involved in the various facets of the manufacturing of ladies' and children's apparel: cutters, pressers, operators, finishers, designers, packers, shippers, office workers, etc. (ILGWU, n.d.). The garment industry expanded most rapidly in North America around the turn of the century, due mostly to technological progress and possibilities of large-scale, cheap production. Prior to that time only the very wealthy could afford the products of tailors or seamstresses, and those who could afford these products often used custom tailors or bought in European shops.

There are two main elements in this industry that seem to have favoured the development of the union movement: its technological organization and the influx, around the turn of the century, of liberal Jewish immigrants from Eastern Europe and czarist Russia.

The industry's organization at that time was oriented towards the production of ready-made garments in large "inside" shops, i.e., shops where all stages of the garment manufacturing were carried out together in one place. But with the development of the lightweight sewing machine that could be easily transported, once the cloth was cut the garments were farmed out for completion to contractors. These contractors were often former garment workers themselves who distributed the work among recent immigrants who lived in tenements. In this way it was almost impossible to regulate hours or working conditions. The sweatshop conditions that prevailed at that period nourished the garment workers' consciousness of the need to organize into unions to counterbalance the strength of the employer.

After 1880 there was an influx of liberal Jewish immigrants from Eastern Europe and Russia who settled in New York, New England and Montreal. These individuals, many of whom were former students and intellectuals, found work in the garment trade and formed the early leadership of the union (Laslett, 1970).

The ILGWU was officially established in 1900, but grew slowly in the beginning. The industry was severely affected, as it continues to be even today, by seasonal fluctuations. While the workers were enthusiastic about joining the union in the beginning of the season, when the demand was great, as the season wore on and the competition became ruthless and intense between employers to capture the shrinking market, the workers' interest waned as they feared for their jobs. The labour force was fragmented into small, competing shops.

After a period of rapprochement with the socialist movement and the radical International Workers of the World movement, the ILGWU joined the mainstream union movement. It maintained, however, its role as the conscience of the movement. "What distinguished the ILGWU's socialism and gave it a special character of its own was. . .not so much a preoccupation with the basic elements of Marxist theory. . . . It was, rather, a humanitarian, idealistic and deeply held desire for equality and social justice, which resulted as much from the historic minority position in which the Jews had found themselves in Europe as it did from the specific commitment to Marxist ideology" (Laslett, 1970:119-120).

Work sharing vs. seniority: controlling job security.

A union can affect the employment security of the worker, either old or young, in a variety of ways. If we consider the entry level of a new employee, for example, we see that this is a key point for the union that wishes to intervene in the access of the employer to new labour and of workers to jobs. To the question of *who gets hired?* the union obviously wants to restrict the answer to union members. In the absence of such closed shops, which have been outlawed in most cases, unions have turned to a variety of systems, most of which restrict entry to members of the union or to those who are willing to become members.

Once the individual has entered an enterprise another method of control is seniority. Many union contracts include a provision that jobs must be filled by promotion from within if properly qualified workers are available, and on a basis of length of service. Although this can be seen as an enormous advantage to the older worker, it also imposes important restrictions on the employees, since they must always start at the bottom of the ladder if they change employers or even if they change seniority units within the same enterprise. In addition, as many older workers have discovered, a seniority guarantee is only as good as the solvency of the employer who offers it. In fact, most analysts suggest that the seniority principle serves the employer's interests as much as or more than those of the employee.

For example, it reduces costly turnover (substandard quality and quantity output by inexperienced workers, high rates of work accidents, damage to equipment, infractions against rules, etc.), protects against the adverse effects of arbitrary dismissals and creates an atmosphere of loyalty and discipline. Even in nonunionized settings employers have found it to their advantage to adopt a system of seniority (Gersuny, 1982). However, the older worker generally sees seniority as his only real source of job security, the hard-won workers' advantage that work sharing would eliminate.

The ILGWU and a few other craft unions, however, never relied on seniority to protect the worker from the arbitrary decisions of the employer. As we mentioned earlier, because of the very seasonal nature of the industry and the equalitarian tradition of the union, work sharing was the preferred system. When less work was available on a temporary basis, as was often the case in the widely fluctuating clothing market, the work that remained was divided equally among the workers under the union's supervision. The last worker hired was considered an equal partner in the work-sharing procedure. Only three key individuals in the production process were included automatically; the sample maker, the head cutter and the head presser, because they were essential to any manufacturing. Only in instances of what was called "permanent reorganization," when the employer did not intend "ever" to call back a certain number of employees (at least not within the following six months), did seniority apply. Any plan for permanent reorganization had to be submitted to the union and approved by a committee.

Historically seniority was denounced by craft unions as fundamentally unjust. "The right to work, to live, to be rewarded by the full product of one's labor is a right that cannot be wrested from our economic masters by a law establishing the right of one member to work in preference to another" (taken from a 1912 essay in the International Typographical Union Journal and quoted by Gersuny, 1982:521). As unemployment compensation was established in the aftermath of the Depression, unions generally accepted layoffs according to seniority as "the preferred method of dealing with downturns, since it maximized the income of the group as a whole'' (Willard, 1985:245). Several other developments in the area of industrial organization further undermined work-sharing traditions. Unemployment benefits were often drastically reduced if one worked on a reduced schedule; premium pay encouraged employees to accept overtime work, and fringe benefits paid on a per capita basis made paying overtime cheaper for the employer than having more employees. With a legal work week established at 39.5 hours in 1949, no other work-time reductions for regular employees allowed for flexibility in the system (Willard, 1985).

Rather than resorting to layoffs, the work-sharing (STC) program allows unions to keep more of their members on the job, making an almost full salary, accumulating fringe benefits and paying union dues. Seniority is protected in that the program is always voluntarily established through the mechanism of collective bargaining, and the economic yield of the work force as a whole is maximized.

The future of work sharing

Can work sharing be considered as a real, long-term solution to unemployment? In his article, Reid suggested that a well-developed, well-monitored work-sharing program could reduce unemployment by 1 to 2 percent (Reid, 1983).

It is important to point out, however, that this solution has been and probably will continue to be a temporary one. Two-thirds of the employers who participated in the government's evaluation of the program were of the opinion that it should definitely be limited to periods of recession. Otherwise, they felt, the government could contribute to the support of firms that are poorly managed and would and should fold (Employment and Immigration Canada, 1984). The workers were divided in their opinions concerning the continuation of the program. Many expressed the concern that employers might well abuse the program to their advantage. A union's presence in the work setting seems clearly necessary to assure that the worker's interests be protected.

Very few employers said they would be willing to pay increased unemployment insurance rates in order to maintain the work-sharing program. Two-thirds of the workers, however, expressed a willingness to do so (Employment and Immigration Canada, 1984).

If one judges by the number of layoffs that occurred in the firms that had participated in the program, during the twelve weeks following its expiration, 57 percent of temporary layoffs were actually avoided. Since some of the layoffs were probably due to the economic conjuncture of the time, it has been estimated that the program probably prevented closer to between 74 and 88 percent of the layoffs. From the point of view of the older worker in particular in a unionized setting, we see work sharing as a very effective tool in preventing a precipitous departure from the labour market of older workers who might feel pushed to offer to leave the payroll of a firm because of guilt about youth unemployment. In fact, 87 percent of the workers designated to be laid off had been working for the firm for less than ten years, and 46 percent of those who agreed to share their work voluntarily without having been threatened personally with unemployment had been working for the firm for more than ten years.

The older worker seemed to be quite receptive to the idea of easing into retirement, or simply trying out a reduced workload for a period to see if he really wanted to stop altogether. In the U.S. it has been observed that despite the widespread interest in early retirement, partial involvement (reduced schedule) in the work force is as common as full-time work between the ages of 65 and 69 (Gustman and Steinmeier, 1984). This involvement, however, has meant significantly lower wage rates than those offered to comparable full-time workers, with a final exit from the workplace within a short period. Although this is not at all the intention of the work-sharing (STC) program it could be a secondary outcome that would be quite worthwhile.

Obviously the union must assure that the program be voluntary and that the benefits and status of a full-time worker be provided to the work sharer. If this were not the case the union might be justified in fearing that work sharing would simply be a form of part-time work that has been traditionally characterized by "job insecurity, poor promotion prospects and an absence of fringe benefits" (Equal Opportunities Commission, 1981).

We see work sharing (STC) as building more flexibility into the system, along with other workplace accommodation solutions. It can contribute to providing the span of possibilities that will come closer to fitting the particular situation and preferences of any given worker and his employer. As we have noted, older workers and retirees seem to be very attracted to reduced-time schedules, but other workers, such as members of dual-career families, might well be receptive to work sharing while children are young. Most important, it would reduce the disastrous effect of layoffs.

The presence of a union to negotiate the establishment of the work-sharing (STC) program and to oversee its functioning in the collective interest of the workers is essential. And it would seem that unions are beginning to play their appropriate role.

In 1981 the Executive Council of the AFL-CIO issued a statement favouring work sharing. It remarked that STC "would allow senior workers to elect the shorter work week they may well prefer and at the same time preserve employment opportunities for the recently hired including minorities and women."

On balance, short-time compensation with appropriate safeguards is a worthwhile approach. The AFL-CIO Executive Council urges that in states where short-time compensation is incorporated in the unemployment insurance program, the legislature require (1) adequate funding for the unemployment insurance trust fund to protect the rights of all who are unemployed; (2) where workers are represented by a union, agreement with the union on short-time compensation; (3) wage replacement level of at least two-thirds of each worker's lost pay for up to 40 percent of the work week; (4) full retention of pension insurance or other fringe benefits; and (5) protection against manipulation of short-term compensation that would discriminate against recently hired workers, especially minorities and women (quoted in Willard et al., 1985).

These recommendations would ensure the protection of the workers involved in a work-sharing (STC) program in the most admirable and appropriate tradition of the promotion of the workers' collective well-being.

References

Baillargeon R. and L. Bélanger
  1981　*Travailleurs âgés et prise de retraite hâtive.* Québec: Laboratoire de gérontologie sociale, Université Laval.
Best F.
  1981　*Work sharing: Issues, Policy Options and Prospects.* Kalamazoo, Michigan: W.E. Upjohn.
Clark R. and D. Barker
  1981　*Reversing the Trend Toward Early Retirement.* Washington, D.C.: American Enterprise Institute.
Economic Council of Canada
  1979　*Perspective 2030: The Future of Pension Plans.* Ottawa: Government of Canada.
Employment and Immigration Canada
  1980　*Evaluation of UI Funded Work Sharing in Canada.* Ottawa: Government of Canada.
  1981　*Are We Ready to Change? Canada's Labour Markets in the 1980's.* Ottawa: Government of Canada.
  1984　*Evaluation of the Work-sharing Program in Canada.* Ottawa: Government of Canada.
Equal Opportunities Commission
  1981　Job-sharing: Improving the Quality and Availability of Part-Time Work. London, United Kingdom: Equal Opportunities Commission (July).

Gallup
1984 "Les Canadiens songent à la préretraite." *Le Soleil* (February 2).
Gersuny C.
1982 "Origins of seniority provisions in collective bargaining." *Labor Law Journal* (August):518-24.
Graham, Kathie
1974 "Part-time employment: Another alternative to the traditional work week." *Canadian Personnel and Industrial Relations Journal* 21(1):35-38.
Gustman A. and T. Steinmeier
1984 "Modeling the retirement process for policy evaluation and research." *Monthly Labor Review* 107(July)7:20-33.
Harriman A.
1982 *The Work/Leisure Trade Off: Reduced Work Time for Managers and Professionals.* New York: Praeger.
Laslett, J.H.
1970 *Labor and the Left.* New York: Basic Books.
Lewis, N. and A. Desjardins
1985 *Le travail à temps partiel: le partage du travail comme mesure de sécurité d'emploi et la sous-traitance.* Québec: Centre de recherche et statistiques sur le marché du travail.
Marshall, V. and J. Tindale
1980 "A generational conflict perspective for gerontology." In V. Marshall (ed.), *Aging in Canada: Social Perspectives.* Toronto: Fitzhenry & Whiteside.
Martin, J.K.
1982 "Social policy concerns relating to retirement: Implications for research." Pp. 145-202 in Gloria Gutman (ed.), *Canada's Changing Age Structure: Implications for the Future.* Burnaby, B.C.: SFU Publications.
Meltz, N. et al.
1980 *Sharing the Work: Analysis of the Issues in Work-Sharing and Jobsharing.* Toronto: University of Toronto Press.
Nemirow, M.
1984 "Work-sharing approaches: Past and present." *Monthly Labor Review* 107(9):34-39.
Pelchat, P.
1984 La préretraite ne crée pas de nouveaux emplois." *Le Soleil* (December 1).
Régie des rentes du Québec
1985 *Annual Report 1984-1985.* Québec: Government of Canada.
Reid, F.
1980 "Unemployment and inflation: An assessment of Canadian macro-economic policy." *Canadian Public Policy* (Spring) 6(2):283-99.
1983 "UI Work-sharing as an alternative to layoffs: The Canadian experience. *Industrial and Labor Relations Review* (April) 35(3):319-29.
Robertson, G. and J. Humphreys
1979 *Labour Turnover and Absenteeism in Selected Industries.* Toronto: Ontario Minister of Labour.

Robinson, D.
   1982   "Soon We'll Need the Older Worker." *Los Angeles Times* (April 6).
Sadlier-Brown, P.
   1978   *Work-Sharing in Canada: Problems and Possibilities*. Montreal: C.D.
          Howe Institute.
Stryckman, Judith
   1984   "Union Affiliation and the Older Worker: The ILGWU in the U.S. and in
          Canada." Paper presented at the Annual Scientific and Educational
          Meeting of the Canadian Association on Gerontology, Vancouver, B.C.
Willard, D. et al.
   1985   "Short time compensation, yes; work-sharing, no: Unravelling the
          debate." *Labor Studies Journal* (Winter) 9(3):239-253.

IV

Aging, Leisure and Retirement

The allocation of time to leisure or to work varies considerably over the life course and is thus a phenomenon of interest to social scientists who study aging. Retirement is a social institution that radically structures the allocation of time to leisure or to work. The three chapters in this section focus on aspects of leisure and retirement across the life course and, in particular, in later life. They relate closely to the material presented in Section III, which focussed on age related patterns of behaviour and social structure.

McPherson and Kozlik, in Chapter 12, review recent Canadian data on Canadian leisure patterns over the life course. They note that, while time allocated to work declines with aging, the allocation of discretionary time to leisure activities also declines. Leisure activities that are maintained tend to be more passive and home centred. The data presented by McPherson and Kozlik are interpreted in light of continuity, disengagement and activity theories of aging. They also, however, have important implications for the health status of elderly Canadians, a topic pursued in Section VI. Despite recent gains in fitness activities, older Canadians are highly sedentary, observing rather than engaging in physical activity. The chapter also raises some important questions about the relative importance of social psychological and social structural factors, such as ageism, in causing age-related declines in activity levels.

We now think of the working years as typically ending at age 65. It is easy to forget that retirement is a social institution, an invention if you like. It is not inevitable that the life course should be so structured as to reduce participation in paid labour at age 65. In Chapter 13, Nishio and Lank focus on the labour-force participation of older females. The number of women working past age 65 is anything but trivial. As Nishio and Lank note, among women aged 65 to 69, 7.4 percent worked in 1983. The significance of later-life working patterns for women is greater because this is a demographic category that will increase dramatically in future years.

The central thrust of Nishio and Lank's paper is to emphasize the effects of ageist stereotypes on older female workers. Ageism and sexism are described within the symbolic interactionist perspective as establishing "self-fulfilling prophecies" that marginalize the older female worker. The four hypotheses of labour-market determination that they review should be seen in the context of Chen's analysis of factors shaping occupational age structures, in Chapter 9. Nishio and Lank's analysis differs from that of Chen by turning to a discussion of motivational factors. This discussion is speculative, in the absence of extensive data describing the feelings of older Canadians, whether male or female, about work and retirement.

McDonald and Wanner, as noted by Nishio and Lank, have conducted extensive secondary analysis of existing data sets in Canada and the USA, on issues of retirement. In Chapter 14, they provide detailed data on the "dual labour market" hypothesis that Nishio and Lank discussed in Chapter 13. Their approach is explicitly structural, dealing with "forces external to the individual that may affect retirement." Their theoretical approach is more focussed and more strictly structural than that of Nishio and Lank. McDonald and Wanner draw on the political economy perspective to evaluate the role of economic structures in influencing retirement patterns of both men and women, and, in particular, they look at male and female experiences in the dual economy.

Testing a series of regression models that attempt to predict the number of weeks not worked in a year, they find that a number of socio-economic variables conjointly explain only 12 percent of the variance for men and 5 percent for women. Among these variables, economic sector (tapping the "dual economy" concept) is not itself significant; however, economic sector does appear to influence the impact of other socio-economic variables. Retirement, McDonald and Wanner conclude, "is clearly not a uniform phenomenon, operating in the same way across the economy."

Some people want to keep working; others wish to retire early. Some people even wish to be compelled to retire. Whether work is seen as intrinsically rewarding, and whether the individual foresees the retirement years as carrying the possibility of enjoying leisure while remaining economically secure, ought to affect one's perspective on retirement and retirement age. Canadian research, however, tells us all too little about such issues.

All three chapters in Section IV rely extensively on survey analysis. Moreover, they all employ secondary analysis of survey data not collected by the chapter authors themselves, including Statistics Canada information. Even with the avowed structural approach of McDonald and Wanner, they note that "retirement is far too complex not to include both individual and structural features." However, Canadian research on the social meaning of retirement and patterns of experience at the social psychological level is scarce. The same may be said for leisure research. If, as McPherson and Kozlik point out, the average Canadian aged 65 or older watches 230 minutes a day of television but spends 3 minutes a day in artistic hobbies, how does this pattern of activity contribute to a meaningful old age? With what meanings do older Canadians fill their leisure, as well as their work time? Survey research and secondary analysis of large data sets provide invaluable data about general patterns of leisure and retirement; the meaning of these patterns would be more readily discernible had we more small-scale, ethnographic research about people of different ages at work and leisure.

12

Age Patterns in Leisure Participation: The Canadian Case

Barry D. McPherson and Carol A. Kozlik
Faculty of Human Kinetics and Leisure Studies
University of Waterloo

Whereas leisure was once almost exclusively the domain of children and the retired, today it is an important facet of contemporary lifestyles at all stages in the life cycle. Moreover, with an increasing amount of nonwork time available for most segments of the population in modernized nations, leisure has attained increased importance in the hierarchy of personal and collective goals. That is, leisure has become significant for the expression of personal identity and for enhancing the quality of life throughout adulthood.

This shift towards leisure having an increased value has been precipitated by fewer requirements for long hours at work. Hence, discretionary time has become available to larger segments of the population. The possibility of using this increased discretionary time for leisure has been promoted by the leisure industry, and has been sought by many adults seeking to enhance the quality of their personal life.

Only a few studies have examined the leisure patterns of Canadian adults at different stages in the life cycle. These studies, discussed in this chapter, focus more on older adults than on the stability or change in patterns across the life cycle. Nevertheless, there are a few cross-sectional national studies that support the almost universal finding that the reported frequency of involvement is lower for older age groups in most leisure activities. This pattern seems to hold for sport and physical activities, political participation, voluntary association involvement and attendance at cultural events (cf. McPherson, 1983a:414-417, 1983b; Curtis and White, 1984). Moreover, the evidence to date indicates that leisure activities tend to become more passive with increasing age, and more home centred.

These findings raise the question about whether people disengage (cf. Cumming and Henry, 1961) from social participation, including leisure

We are greatly indebted to Terry Stewart of the Leisure Studies Data Bank of the University of Waterloo for analyses of the data reported in this chapter, and to the Canada Fitness Survey, funded by Fitness Canada, for permission to use the Canada Fitness Survey Microdata Tape.

activities, as they age; whether individuals continue to adhere throughout adulthood to the leisure habits that have resulted from their leisure role socialization experiences prior to late adolescence or early adulthood (i.e., continuity); or whether adults are directly or indirectly induced by the presence of age-related norms to cease participation in specific leisure activities as they grow older. Studies to date have been unable to explain fully the existing patterns due to a reliance on cross-sectional rather than longitudinal data. Nevertheless, the descriptive information in these studies does provide some baseline data concerning the social participation patterns of particular age cohorts in the leisure domain. When other demographic factors are introduced as controls (e.g., gender, ethnicity, education and income) a more definitive picture of adult leisure patterns emerges.

The purposes of this paper are: (1) to raise some methodological and theoretical problems inherent in research on leisure patterns over the life cycle; (2) to review cross-sectional Canadian studies that have examined the leisure pursuits of young, middle-aged and elderly adults; and (3) to provide a secondary analysis of the most recent national survey on the degree and type of involvement in one form of leisure by Canadian adults, namely, physical activity. First, some methodological caveats are introduced.

Classification and Measurement of Leisure Activities

Many descriptive typologies of leisure activities have been proposed and used by program and research personnel in the field of leisure. Some of the more common dimensions include: instrumental-expressive, active-passive, individual-group, family-nonfamily, intellectual-manual and expensive-inexpensive (cf. McPherson, 1983a:408-411). Unfortunately, conceptual or theoretical arguments can be generated to support or refute placing a given leisure activity into almost any category. For example, whereas reading can be considered a passive activity in the physical sense, it is an active form of leisure in the cognitive domain. Therefore, because varying classification systems are used in different studies, it is difficult to compare the results of one study with those of another. Hence, little cumulative and definitive knowledge has been derived about the actual or preferred types of leisure activities at different ages or stages in life.

Similar conceptual problems arise when the frequency or intensity of involvement in leisure activities is reported. In some studies an individual merely reports whether he engages in the activity or not. In others, a wide array of frequency intervals is employed, ranging from daily to weekly, monthly or annually. Furthermore, some of the studies utilize or recode the reported frequencies to qualitative categories such as "never," "sometimes," "regularly," or "as often as possible." This diversity in scaling creates interpretation problems when we attempt to compare patterns within or between countries, across age cohorts, or across time for a given cohort.

Another measurement concern is that the *quality* of the leisure experience is seldom assessed. Moreover, seldom have studies sought to control for period effects (e.g., fads), or important socio-demographic variables (e.g., gender, class, place of residence, ethnicity, education, marital status) that can influence the type and meaning of leisure activities that are selected at different ages or stages in life (cf. McPherson, 1983a:414-419). Finally, it is difficult to compare the patterns among various studies because a variety of quantitative and qualitative age groupings is utilized. Furthermore, many studies include only one category for those "65 years and over." Quite clearly the 65-year-old represents a different birth cohort from the 80-year-old in terms of lifestyle, life chances, health, past leisure and work experiences and present leisure needs and interests.

With these caveats in mind, let us examine three types of studies that describe patterns of leisure participation from young to later adulthood. The first type reports on the time use of Canadian adults, across age groups; the second presents the frequency of leisure involvement for different age cohorts; and the third type examines the time use and leisure patterns of those 65 years of age and over in Canada. Many of these latter studies are regional rather than national in scope. This is an important point, since there seems to be a pattern, from east to west, of increasing social participation in a variety of leisure domains. That is, even when such factors as gender, age, education and ethnicity are controlled, those in British Columbia are more physically active than those in the Prairie Provinces, who in turn are more active than those in Ontario, who in turn are more active than those in Quebec, etc. (cf. McPherson and Curtis, 1986).

Use of Time by Age Cohorts

Time is a central feature of contemporary lifestyles that can influence the duration and sequence of events, and to what extent, why and when we engage in a variety of social acts, including leisure. Surprisingly, little scholarly research has focussed on the similarities or diversities in the use of time by various age cohorts, or on the allocation or use of time across the life cycle. For example, the "problem" of retirement may *not* be that there is a sudden onset of large unallocated blocks of time, but rather that individuals lack experience to make decisions concerning the allocation of this large amount of discretionary time.

Discretionary time is that time which remains on an hourly, daily, weekly, monthly or annual basis after all obligations of work and personal care have been met. Thus, the proportion of time that is allocated to leisure, in general, and to specific leisure activities, is an important lifestyle decision that can have an impact on the form and quality of life of individuals or age cohorts. During childhood, adolescence and young adulthood, a variety of leisure activities may be experienced in family, school and community settings. However, upon marriage and entrance into the labour force, the amount of discretionary time decreases and leisure activities become more limited in number, and more home and family centred.

During middle age, one's career becomes more stable and well established, and children usually leave the nest. Hence, more discretionary time and income may become available for leisure, and leisure may become a more salient facet of one's lifestyle. Generally, the pattern established by middle age continues into the preretirement stage, and subsequently influences the way in which time is utilized in the postretirement years. Thus, it is important to consider the leisure patterns and interests of the middle years when attempting to understand or develop a lifestyle in the retirement years.[1] Moreover, it is important to recognize that each stage in life may have specific, perhaps normative, leisure interests and activities that characterize the needs and demands of that particular stage or age cohort.

In order to understand the actual use of time by adults, a national telephone survey was conducted in October 1981. This study surveyed 2,686 Canadians, 15 years of age and over, concerning their activities in the preceding twenty-four-hour period. Based on the responses to this survey, a snapshot was derived of the relative allocation of time, on one specific day, to work, personal care and a variety of other social activities. Table 1 illustrates the mean number of minutes allocated to work, leisure and personal maintenance for five age cohorts, by sex and language group.

For both males and females, and for both language groups, there is a trend for increasingly older age groups to allocate greater time to maintenance and leisure activities. Not surprisingly, women in all age groups report fewer minutes for work and leisure, and more time for maintenance activities. Among the oldest age cohort (75 +), English-speaking respondents allocate considerably more time to maintenance activities, whereas French-speaking respondents allocate considerably more minutes per day to leisure. Otherwise, there are no significant French-English differences in the allocation of time by age cohort. In data reported elsewhere (McPherson, 1985), it was noted that the relative allocation of time to work, maintenance and leisure varies not only by age cohort and gender, but by marital status, by level of education, by income and by whether the respondent has children at home or not. Similarly, Kinsley and Graves (1983:17), using the same data set, found that 25- to 44-year-olds have the least time for leisure (about 5 hours per day), whereas those over 65 have over 7 hours of leisure per day.

Turning to a more specific examination of how time is allocated to

TABLE 1:
Mean Number of Minutes Per Week Day Allocated to Work, Maintenance and Leisure, By Sex and Language Group[1]

Socio-demographic Variable	Work[2]					Maintenance[3]					Leisure[4]				
	25-34	35-50	51-64	65-74	75+	25-34	35-50	51-64	65-74	75+	25-34	35-50	51-64	65-74	75+
Gender															
Male	476	463	393	118	8	675	713	737	877	954	282	262	308	443	475
Female	286	256	134	28	4	880	917	931	977	976	271	262	372	424	441
Language															
English	378	367	236	71	—	779	805	851	918	958	276	265	348	443	457
French	374	357	227	53	—	785	811	833	948	733	280	268	379	437	707

[1] Data derived from 1981 Canadian Pilot Time-Budget Survey.

[2] Includes 621 respondents who reported 0 minutes of work for the previous day.

[3] Includes: Housework, Shopping, Child Care and Personal Needs and Care.

[4] Includes: Adult Education, Organizations, Social Entertainment, Active Leisure, Passive Leisure.

TABLE 2:
Number of Minutes Per Day Allocated to Cultural Activities*

Activity	15-17	18-24	Age 25-44	45-64	65+
Cultural Spectacles	13	17	8	3	3
Artistic Hobbies	16	7	4	4	3
Reading	22	24	45	59	87
Listening to Radio/ Records, Tapes	114	137	116	123	97
Watching Television	159	144	148	173	230

* Adapted from Kinsley and Graves (1983) and reproduced by permission.

cultural activities, Kinsley and Graves (1983:24-25) found that involvement varies by age (Table 2).

The general pattern appears to be one of older cohorts spending less time attending cultural events outside the home and more time consuming radio and television and reading within the home. In contrast to most leisure activities, the amount of time spent reading appears to be greater by increasingly older age groups. Again, this may be due to cohort or period effects, rather than aging effects. That is, the older cohorts may have always allocated a large part of their leisure time to reading. With respect to what type of programs are watched on television by different age cohorts, those over 65 report higher consumption rates for all types of shows, except movies (Table 3).

For some types of shows there is increased involvement among increasingly older age groups (e.g., news), but for other shows the pattern fluctuates somewhat randomly among age cohorts. It is interesting to note the

TABLE 3:
Number of Minutes Per Day Watching Television*

Program	15-17	18-24	Age 25-44	45-64	65+
High Culture	4	2	4	4	5
Popular Entertainment	66	42	34	42	56
Movies	24	24	26	20	16
News or Information	7	12	18	25	41
Sports	25	15	25	31	46
General	32	49	40	49	65

* Adapted from Kinsley and Graves (1983) and reproduced by permission.

decreased involvement for popular entertainment and sports shows by the 18-to 24-year-old cohort. Does this represent an aging, a period or a cohort effect? Perhaps it is related to added time constraints associated with entrance to the labour force and marriage, two significant role transitions during this stage in life.

Some possible evidence to support an aging effect explanation for apparent age differences in television consumption is provided in a recent panel study of 453 Halifax adults who were interviewed in 1971 and 1981 (Elliott et al., 1984). While all respondents had aged ten years between interviews, each cohort had experienced different life events and role transitions that could influence their use of time. In 1971 there was little age or sex group differentiation in television viewing, but by 1981 those who had moved into their fifties and sixties watched up to forty-five minutes more per day than those in their thirties and forties. Moreover, males in their forties and fifties watched about sixty minutes more per day than females in the same age cohort. Hence, increased television consumption in the fifties and sixties may reflect age-related changes in institutional demands (e.g., a decrease in family responsibilities and work demands); in personal changes in leisure needs, interests and abilities; in role transitions (e.g., women enter the labour force, the empty nest); and in the degree of general social involvement in the later middle years.

Leisure Participation by Age: National Samples

In addition to the 1981 Time Budget survey, there have been three national surveys in Canada that provide cross-sectional information on the leisure activities of varying age cohorts. Based on a secondary analysis of data collected in an appendix to the March 1972 Canadian Labour Force Survey, Milton (1975) analysed the responses of approximately 50,000 adults to determine the degree and type of participation in a variety of leisure activities. He sought to determine the influence on leisure pursuits of age, sex, marital status, level of education, relation to head of the household and attendance at community events. Only the findings pertaining to age as an independent variable are reported here.

For home-centred leisure activities, age was positively related to involvement in television, radio and reading, but inversely related to record listening. For outside the home/low interaction activities, age was inversely related to attendance at paid and free events, to physical activity and to hobbies, although the patterns varied somewhat for those with higher levels of educational attainment. For example, males over the age of 65 with higher levels of educational attainment reported greater involvement in physical activity than the less educated younger groups. This finding stresses the importance of introducing controls into the analysis of leisure behaviour across age groups. That is, even within the same age cohort, life chances and lifestyles may vary because of variations in social status. Finally, for outside the home/high interaction leisure activities, age was inversely related to active sport involvement and to involvement in adult education. Interestingly, only a few Canadians reported involvement in sport for an average of one hour or more per week (18 percent) or in adult education (7 percent). However, these low rates of involvement may reflect a seasonal artifact, since respondents were surveyed during the winter months.

The second major national survey was conducted in October 1976 by Statistics Canada. This study surveyed over 50,000 Canadian adults to determine their frequency of participation in fitness activities, physical recreation and sport. Also included in this supplementary questionnaire to the monthly Labour Force Survey were questions pertaining to the type and frequency of participation in nonphysical leisure pursuits. Some of the findings pertaining to sport and popular culture involvement by age were presented and discussed in the earlier edition of this book (McPherson and Kozlik, 1980). As noted in Table 1 of that chapter, participation rates in all types of sport and exercise activities decline with age, with the most dramatic decreases occurring after 19 years and after age 64 — two points in the life cycle that generally represent, respectively, the beginning and end of involvement in the labour force. It was noted specifically that 37 percent of the adults over 65 engage in some type of exercise. Similarly, the inverse pattern of involvement by age was noted for sport participation as a spectator (cf. McPherson and Kozlik, 1980:Table 2).

The 1980 chapter (McPherson and Kozlik, 1980:Table 3) also examined involvement in popular culture activities by age cohort. Again the pattern of declining involvement by age cohort held for reading books, magazines and newspapers; for engaging in crafts and hobbies; for watching television and movies; and for listening to records. However, within each age cohort there were variations in involvement for specific types of activities by gender, education and income. To illustrate, within all age groups women were reported to be more involved than men in crafts and hobbies, while among all age cohorts those with a university degree reported reading more books than those with lower levels of educational attainment. This stresses the importance of recognizing the heterogeneity within age cohorts as well as between age cohorts with respect to different types of leisure involvement.

In the most recent national survey (1981), over 22,000 Canadians completed the first wave of what is intended to be a continuous study administered by the Canada Fitness Survey. Based on their reported level of involvement in a variety of physical activities, respondents were categorized as "sedentary," "moderately active," or "active."

Table 4 presents the cross-sectional results by age for males and females. Using the "active" respondents as an example, we can see that in com-

TABLE 4:
Age and General Level of Involvement in Physical Activity, By Sex

Age	N	Sedentary[1]		Level of Activity Moderate[2]		Active[3]	
		M	F	M	F	M	F
14-19	2,736	5.0	5.4	21.8	23.7	73.2	70.9
20-24	2,365	4.3	7.7	32.9	35.3	62.8	57.0
25-34	4,495	6.2	8.5	39.3	38.5	54.5	53.0
35-44	3,051	7.9	11.8	42.2	37.9	49.9	50.3
45-54	2,372	11.9	14.2	42.0	35.9	46.1	49.9
55-64	2,107	15.0	16.4	35.6	30.0	49.4	53.6
65-74	1,614	17.3	21.4	26.4	26.7	56.3	51.9
75+	842	25.5	33.9	22.4	16.6	52.1	49.5

[1]Sedentary: Less than three hours of physical activity per week for less than nine months per year.

[2]Moderate: Less than three hours of physical activity per week for at least nine months per year, or an average of at least three hours of physical activity per week for less than nine months per year.

[3]Active: An average of at least three hours of leisure time physical activity per week, for at least nine months a year.

parison with the 1976 survey, the general pattern of declining levels of involvement holds for males and females — but only for the first five age cohorts. Thus, we see that those over 55 are reporting as much or more involvement than younger age cohorts. Moreover, recall that in the 1976 survey only 37 percent of those over 65 reported themselves to be active. Here, based on 1981 data, over 50 percent of the older age cohorts are "active," for both males and females. This suggests that either older age cohorts are becoming more physically active in their later years, or that the current cohorts of older adults have always been more active, and continue to be, than older age cohorts surveyed in earlier studies. It is quite likely that both of these explanations are valid to some degree.

In Table 5 we see that there are activity-specific variations, in terms of *weekly* involvement, in this pattern of declining involvement among increasingly older age cohorts. Of special significance is the higher percentage of 65- to 74-year-olds, especially among males, who are involved in home exercise programs compared to other age cohorts. There are relatively small variations among female age cohorts with respect to home exercising, and there is greater involvement by females over 20 years of age in swimming at a pool.

All respondents were also asked to indicate their self-perceived level of fitness compared to others of the same age and sex.

TABLE 5:
Age and Weekly Level of Involvement In Specific Activities, By Sex[1]

Age	Jogging		Home Exercise Program		Swimming at a Pool	
	M	F	M	F	M	F
14-19	9.3	7.7	9.7	12.4	3.9	3.7
20-24	5.6	3.3	9.4	15.2	2.7	4.9
25-34	3.9	2.4	9.3	11.5	2.8	3.2
35-44	3.6	1.6	7.1	10.5	2.5	3.1
45-54	2.7	0.7	7.9	11.9	2.0	2.6
55-64	1.4	0.2	7.8	11.9	1.2	2.0
65-74	0.1	0.3	9.1	11.6	1.8	1.6
75 +	0.0	0.0	6.5	9.8	—	—

[1] This table presents the results for all respondents who reported that they had been active, at least weekly, in the specific activity.

Table 6 indicates that, increasingly with age, older respondents see themselves as more fit than their peers. However, this may be a halo effect that results from older respondents being more likely to respond to what is perceived to be a more socially acceptable answer. Thus, an accurate and representative measure of the actual fitness level of older respondents is needed. While such a test was conducted by the Canada Fitness Survey, a screening process was used to determine who was ineligible for health reasons from participating in the fitness tests. As a result, a larger percentage of each progressively older age cohort may have been eliminated and not tested. Hence the finding of an increasingly larger percentage of those over 45 who meet the "recommended" level of fitness may be an artifact of the nature of the test situation, namely, the less fit and less healthy respondents were not tested.

Leisure Activities and Patterns of Older Adults

In addition to cross-sectional surveys of a number of age cohorts, many Canadian studies have focussed almost exclusively on the leisure activities of older adults. While it is beyond the scope of this chapter to review these in detail, five recent studies are discussed that illustrate the heterogeneous patterns of leisure within and among subcohorts of older Canadians who may or may not have large blocks of unstructured time.

First, Curtis and White (1984), based on a secondary analysis of the 1976 Statistics Canada Labour Force Survey, reported that the older age categories participate less than other age groups in sport and physical recreation activities. However, they found that among older males and

TABLE 6:
Age and Self-Perceived Fitness Level, By Sex

Age		More Fit	Self-Perceived Fitness Level Less Fit	As Fit
14 - 19	M	21.9	12.3	65.8
	F	12.0	27.3	60.7
20 - 24	M	17.8	19.7	62.5
	F	7.6	33.0	59.4
25 - 34	M	16.8	19.9	63.2
	F	9.7	32.2	58.1
35 - 44	M	18.5	17.0	64.5
	F	12.3	26.2	61.5
45 - 54	M	20.4	15.8	63.8
	F	16.9	22.3	60.7
55 - 64	M	24.3	16.0	59.7
	F	22.2	16.4	61.5
65 - 74	M	30.9	12.7	56.4
	F	32.7	14.1	53.2
75 +	M	47.0	12.3	40.7
	F	47.8	10.4	41.8

females who do participate in these types of activities, the reported frequency of participation was higher than for those who participate among younger age groups. In short, at the older age levels, males and females participate in fewer activities in total; but if they do participate, they are involved more frequently than younger cohorts in these few activities. This perhaps lends some support to an explanation of increased specialization with age, as well as to continuity in a few activities across the life cycle. Thus, as age increases adults may reduce the number and variety of activities in which they are engaged, but increase the frequency of involvement in these fewer, selected activities. Whether this process of reduction and increased specialization reflects personal declines in ability, changing age-related opportunities and norms, or resocialization remains to be explained.

In an ongoing study of 107 males and females between 55 and 83 years of age, Zuzanek and colleagues (Zuzanek and James, 1982; Zuzanek and Mannell, 1983; Larson et al., 1985) randomly "beeped" respondents fitted with a paging device throughout the day. At each "beep" respondents recorded what they were doing, with whom, where they were and their mood at the time. They found that among these respondents, older adults males had more time for leisure; males spent more time consuming mass media events, while women spent more time in social events; most "active" leisure took place in the morning; more media events were consumed in the evening; and most social leisure took place in the afternoon.

Based on open-ended interviews with 352 older adults (61 + ; mean = 75.4 years) included in an opportunistic sample, Roadburg (1985) found that retirees defined leisure differently from working adults. The retirees emphasized enjoyment and relaxation to a greater extent. Interestingly, many of the retired respondents, unlike the working respondents, were unable to define leisure specifically. Perhaps this difficulty depicts a cohort that has had little experience with leisure throughout their lives, or a cohort that is having difficulty arriving at a new definition of leisure that is appropriate to the retirement stage in life.

With respect to the selection of specific leisure activities in the later years, Roadburg found that the nature of the living arrangement and marital status were the most significant variables in terms of what leisure activities were selected. Respondents were asked to indicate their leisure activities as a teenager, during middle age and at present. Those activities that were recalled as having increased or remained unchanged were those pursued

TABLE 7:
Level of Physical Activity Among Older Age Cohorts by Selected Socio-Demographic Characteristics

Socio-demographic Characteristics	Sedentary			Active		
	55-64	65-74	75 +	55-64	65-74	75 +
Marital Status						
Married	15.2	17.5	28.8	50.3	53.5	47.2
Widowed	16.7	23.5	32.4	56.6	54.6	53.4
Div./Sep.	16.7	20.0	—	63.7	60.0	73.3
Never Married	16.9	22.6	34.6	55.9	54.7	46.2
Education						
<High School	17.9	24.1	32.4	48.1	48.4	49.1
Secondary Graduate	56.1	19.3	21.2	58.7	68.3	57.6
University Graduate	11.4	10.3	21.7	59.2	64.6	58.3
Employment Status						
Retired	17.3	18.3	28.6	58.3	55.7	53.2
Employed Full-Time	13.5	19.3	33.3	50.0	45.8	44.4
Employed Part-Time	9.8	16.5	16.7	50.6	54.9	66.7
Homemaker Full-Time	16.2	19.7	28.9	54.3	49.3	47.9

alone, those that did not require physical exertion and those that were low in cost. Activities that declined in frequency over the life cycle were those that required the participation of other people and that involved physical exertion. Finally, activities that tended to peak in middle age in terms of involvement were those that were family oriented. In summary, the activities selected by the particular group of older adults in Roadburg's study tended to be those that occurred indoors, that could be done alone, that were low in cost and that were passive in nature.

The fourth study involves a secondary analysis for this chapter of data collected by the Canada Fitness Survey (1981). This particular analysis focussed on the impact of three variables on the general level of involvement in physical activity by three specific older age cohorts (Table 7). Clearly the data indicate that among all three cohorts of "active" adults, the nonmarried, the better educated and the retired are more likely to report being involved in physical activity on a regular basis. Thus, this provides further evidence that individual differences in socio-demographic factors need to be addressed when attempting to explain patterns of involvement by older adults in specific leisure activities.

The fifth study selected for review focusses on the responses of 846 noninstitutionalized adults (62 +) who were surveyed in 1982 by the United Senior Citizens of Ontario (Hoffman, 1985a, 1985b). Respondents were read a list of 21 activities and were asked about the extent of their involvement in each activity. First, as noted in Table 8, among the oldest residents of Ontario, older age cohorts participate in fewer activities than younger age cohorts.

However, for 8 of the 21 listed activities there were no differences in participation rates across the three older age groups. This suggests that changes, if any, in activity patterns by age must be considered in relation to

---

TABLE 8:
Number of Leisure Activities By Age Cohort For Older Residents of Ontario[1]

Number of Leisure Activities	Age Cohort (%)		
	62-74 (N = 503)	75-84 (N = 276)	85 + (N = 64)
1 - 10	21	33	52
11 - 12	20	22	22
13 - 14	23	28	13
15 +	36	17	13

[1] Adapted from Hoffman, 1985a:26.

the nature and location of the activity itself. Moreover, when asked to cite barriers that kept them from participating in activities to the extent they desired, the reported barriers differed by age cohort. The most frequent barriers cited by the 85 + age cohort, in rank order, were: health, distance to the activity, absence of companions, absence of transportation and a feeling of being too old. For the younger cohort of elderly residents (62-74), the most frequently cited barriers were: being too busy, health, expense and distance to the activity (Hoffman, 1985a:4).

Two other important findings of this Ontario survey merit discussion. First, the respondents, as representatives of the older population, were involved in a wide array of leisure activities, albeit to varying degrees. This reinforces the notion that the elderly are not primarily or exclusively involved or interested in only a few stereotypical leisure pursuits. Second, 94 percent of the respondents identified activities in which they would like to become more involved (Hoffman, 1985b:11). Hence there is a need for further policy and program research to enable older adults to meet their leisure needs and interests.

Discussion

Having described some patterns of leisure participation by middle-aged and elderly adults in Canada, it is now important to consider some possible explanations for these patterns. This review of the leisure patterns of Canadian adults suggests that older cohorts are less involved than younger age cohorts and that different age cohorts are involved in specific activities to varying degrees. What is not clear is why this pattern appears. On the one hand it could be argued that individual and/or institutionalized disengagement occurs, and hence aging leads to decreased social participation. Unfortunately only large-scale longitudinal surveys, or at the least retrospective questions of a particular age cohort concerning their earlier involvement at specific time points,[2] could identify whether there is voluntary or enforced disengagement from leisure activities with increasing age.

Another alternative explanation is that each cohort has undergone unique socialization experiences and almost develops a leisure subculture of its own within the broader social structure. Hence the values, opportunity set and childhood experiences concerning leisure for any given age cohort (e.g., those 25-34) may be quite different from those of earlier age cohorts (e.g., those who are now 55-64). For example, for many of those who are 65 years of age and over in 1986, their early socialization featured an average work week of approximately 50 hours, a high value on work, few vacations, little education beyond elementary school and few opportunities to engage in any form of leisure in their late adolescent or early adulthood years. In view of the support for the "continuity" approach to aging,[3] it might be argued that this cohort never acquired a high value for, or experience with, leisure.

Hence, in the later years they report much less involvement in leisure activities compared to younger age cohorts. It is quite feasible that this older cohort would have reported low involvement in leisure at all ages had they been surveyed at earlier stages in the life cycle.

Projecting ahead, it might be argued that except where declining physical condition or health inhibits involvement in an activity (e.g., sport), those who are in the 25- to 34-year-old cohort today will be considerably more involved in a wider variety of leisure activities when they reach age 65 and beyond than are those in the present 65 + age cohort. Indeed, we have seen that a higher percentage of those over 65 who were surveyed in 1981 report being more physically active than a comparable age group that was surveyed in 1976. However, only longitudinal studies with the same subjects, and at least two or three age cohorts, could explain whether this increase is related to early-life socialization experiences of this cohort that have continued, or to the adoption of contemporary norms and values whereby physical activity is more highly valued.

A third alternative explanation for the apparent pattern of declining involvement by age is derived from the theory of age stratification (Riley, Johnson and Foner, 1972). This perspective suggests that people are socialized for appropriate behaviour in specific age strata and that individuals acquire normative beliefs as to how one should behave while a member of a particular age stratum. The presence of this stratification system is marked by age grading, wherein opportunities, interactions and role responsibilities are related to chronological age. Thus, age discrimination, or ageism, may operate to restrict the opportunity set and to define the normative standards for elderly adults in the leisure domain. More specifically, relatively few opportunities are provided for adults to participate in leisure once they leave the educational setting. Similarly, the record, fashion and movie industries quite clearly direct the content of their product and their marketing approach towards younger age groups. Thus, there is little social reinforcement in the older adult world for the individual who "thinks and acts young," or who wants to be "physically" active, although some changes are taking place concerning adult leisure norms and opportunities within some segments of the middle-aged and elderly population in Canada. In short, this explanation argues that as one gets older specific activities are dropped, or not learned in the first place, because of a lack of opportunity (e.g., facilities, programs, leaders) and because of restrictive behavioural norms based on societal perceptions of age-appropriate behaviour.[4] That is, age discrimination may operate in the leisure domain as it does in other areas of social life.

In summary, while patterns of leisure involvement at different stages in the life cycle have been presented, patterns across the entire life cycle for individuals born at the same point in time have *not* been described. Moreover, a definitive explanation for the apparent inverse relationship between age and leisure involvement is not available because of theoretical and methodological limitations in the studies completed to date. Ideally, a survey by Statistics Canada or the Canada Fitness Survey on a regular basis, with the same subjects, would greatly assist in providing more valid and complete explanations for the patterns described in this chapter.

Notes

[1]   Additional structural and individual correlations of the use of discretionary time are discussed in an earlier paper (McPherson, 1985).

[2]   However, this type of design, (e.g., used in the Roadburg study), has the inherent weakness of the accuracy of recall by the respondents concerning earlier periods of their life cycle.

[3]   This approach argues that as individuals grow older they are predisposed towards maintaining continuity in habits, associations and preferences established in the earlier years. That is, early experiences and lifestyles are maintained as much as possible (cf. Atchley, 1977).

[4]   Some indirect support for this norm-induced behaviour is suggested by the responses of the 85 + age cohort in the recent Ontario study (Table 8), who cited "a feeling of being too old" as a barrier to increased leisure participation.

References

Atchley, R.
   1977   *The Social Forces in Later Life.* 2d ed. Belmont, California: Wadsworth Publishing Co.
Cumming, E. and W. Henry
   1961   *Growing Old: The Process of Disengagement.* New York: Basic Books.
Curtis, J.E. and P.G. White
   1984   "Age and sport participation: Decline in participation with age or increased specialization with age?" Pp. 273-293 in N. Theberge and P. Donnelly (eds.), *Sport and the Sociological Imagination.* Fort Worth, Texas: Texas Christian University Press.
Elliott, D. et al.
   1984   *A Decade Later: Stability and Change in the Pattern of Time Use in the Halifax Panel.* Halifax: Dalhousie University, Institute of Public Affairs.
Hoffman, A.
   1985a *Elderly Residents in Ontario: Age Differences.* Toronto: Minister for Senior Citizens Affairs, Seniors Secretariat.
   1985b *Elderly Residents in Ontario: Leisure.* Toronto: Minister for Senior Citizens Affairs, Seniors Secretariat.

Barry D. McPherson and Carol A. Kozlik   227

Kinsley, B. and F. Graves
  1983   *The Time of Our Lives.* Ottawa: Employment and Immigration Canada.
Larson, R. et al.
  1985   "Being alone versus being with people: Disengagement in the daily experience of older adults." Journal of Gerontology 40(3):375-381.
McPherson, B.D.
  1983a *Aging as a Social Process.* Toronto: Butterworth.
  1983b "Leisure lifestyles, pre-retirement planning and physical activity in the later years of the life cycle." Pp. 52-87 in L. Bollaert (ed.), *Sport, Leisure and Aging.* Brussels: The Free University of Brussels.
  1985   "The meaning and use of time across the life cycle: The influence of work, family and leisure." Pp. 110-162 in E. Gee and G. Gutman (eds.), *Canadian Gerontological Collection V: The Challenge of Time.* Winnipeg: The Canadian Association on Gerontology.
McPherson, B.D. and J.E. Curtis
  1986   *Regional Differences in the Physical Activity Patterns of Canadian Adults.* Ottawa: Canada Fitness Survey Report.
McPherson, B.D. and C.A. Kozlik
  1980   "Canadian leisure patterns by age: Disengagement, continuity or ageism?" Pp. 113-122 in V. Marshall (ed.), *Aging in Canada: Social Perspectives.* Toronto: Fitzhenry & Whiteside.
Milton, B.G.
  1975   *Social Status and Leisure Time Activities: National Survey Findings for Adult Canadians.* Monograph 3. Montreal: Canadian Sociology and Anthropology Association Monograph Series.
Riley, M., M. Johnson and A. Foner
  1972   *Aging and Society.* Vol. 3. *A Sociology of Age Stratification.* New York: Russell Sage.
Roadburg, A.
  1985   *Aging: Retirement, Leisure and Work in Canada.* Toronto: Methuen.
Zuzanek, J. and S. James
  1982   *A Report on the Issues of Time and Leisure by Senior Citizens in the Kitchener-Waterloo, Ontario, Area.* Unpublished study. University of Waterloo, Department of Recreation.
Zuzanek, J. and R. Mannell.
  1983   "Work-leisure relationships from a sociological and social psychological perspective." *Leisure Studies* 2:327-344.

13

Patterns of Labour Participation of Older Female Workers

Harry K. Nishio and Heather Lank
Department of Sociology
University of Toronto

A Statistics Canada report (1984) estimates that 4.6 percent of the women aged 65 and over participated in the labour force in 1983. Among these women, 7.4 percent of those aged 65-69 and 3.1 percent of those over 70 were working (see Table 1). This relatively small but increasingly significant number of older working women in Canada has not been fully explored in terms of the social and family background of the women, their occupational status, their employment needs, income sources, etc.

TABLE 1:
Female Labour Force Participation Rates for Age Groups 65-69 and 70 and Over, 1975-1983

Female Participation Rates in the Labour Force

	65 - 69	70 +	Total 65 +
1975	9.6	2.3	4.9
1976	7.8	2.2	4.2
1977	8.5	2.0	4.4
1978	7.8	2.7	4.6
1979	8.2	1.9	4.2
1980	8.3	2.1	4.4
1981	8.0	2.6	4.5
1982	8.3	2.2	4.3
1983	7.4	3.1	4.6

SOURCE: Statistics Canada Labour Force Annual Averages 1975-1983. Ottawa: Minister of Supply and Services, No. 71-529, 1984. Adapted.

As we advance towards the 2020s, the number of women in this age group is expected to double. Keeping this demographic trend in mind, the present paper intends to shed some light on the underlying social and economic forces of social inequality and inequity that have been affecting the "life chance" of older workers' continuing labour participation beyond their retirement age of 65. Further, in the analysis, we shall limit ourselves primarily to an explanation of the older women workers in Canada, so as to be able to focus our attention on the combined effects of age and sex stereotyping, which are known to "marginalize" their occupational participation in the labour market, consistently more than the participation of their male counterparts.

Thus the basic approach we shall take in this study will be to analyse the effects of stereotypes upon the occupational participation of older female workers. One caution, however, is in order: one must not expect a one-to-one correspondence between what "culture" defines and what is institutionalized in society. After all, "culture" and "society" are interdependent only conceptually, not necessarily in reality. The match may not be perfect. Furthermore, we can observe a significant correspondence only indirectly and inferentially through sociological observation. In the following, then, before turning to the patterns of labour participation, we shall briefly discuss, within the tradition of symbolic interactionism, the social effects of "stereotyping" and its significance to labour participation.

Types of Discrimination Facing Older Women

Age and sex stereotyping

As Herbert Blumer puts it, we live in a symbolic environment in which people are viewed by the general population and are defined by others as well as by themselves to assume certain negative or positive features, traits and characteristics. In other words, to put it loosely, "culture" defines what appears to be the most frequent combination of traits assigned by one group to another (Cox, 1984:15).

"Ageism" is one such example of the most frequent combination of traits assigned by the general population on a daily basis to a group of its elderly members. Often old people are categorized as senile, rigid in thought and manner, old-fashioned in morality, etc. Two consequences are important to remember: (1) by stereotyping the elderly in this way, the younger generations begin to see older people as different from themselves; "thus they subtly cease to identify with their elders as human beings" (Aiken, 1982:166), and (2) the elders in turn are likely to see themselves in light of stereotyped ideas and begin to pursue the "self-fulfillment of the prophecy" by acting like those with such characteristics. Thus stereotyped ideas may influence many individuals in such a way that they begin to assume the assigned characteristics in their everyday lives.

Ageism has a much more subtle and pervasive impact upon the world of work and in the labour market in general. Laws prohibit the practice of age discrimination in recruitment and retention of the older employees, but the practice does not cease to exist, as there are many ways of evading the anti-age-discrimination acts. For instance, the employers can change job qualifications by requesting a longer education that the elderly do not have, or they can institute a system of job rotation requiring older workers to move geographically from one place to another periodically. No doubt one can draw up a lengthy list of practices that result in age discrimination in overt and covert ways (Roadburg, 1985:103-104).

Sexism

A similar "definition of situation" evolved over centuries and generations relating to the generalized characteristics of women and their behaviour. Culture defines, though this has been changing over the past decade or so, and still considers woman to be secondary to man; the role of woman is to be the helpmate of the man, who functions as the breadwinner. In the "natural order," woman is valued in terms of her physical appearance relative to man's appreciation of beauty. These attitudes are not limited to general male-female relationships alone, but are extended to work situations, where the woman's secondary position has been cemented by a variety of legal as well as customary rules. These practices have kept her from jobs with higher wages and status. Often legal legislation, which was designed to safeguard women from unequal treatment at work, functions to reinforce job discrimination derived from sexism (Stolz, 1985:184).

Ageism and sexism combined

Ageism and sexism define and explain how society generally looks at the aged woman. These combined negative effects, which Posner (1977:42) terms the "double whammy," are briefly analysed here. Posner states that traditionally, though gradually less so, the woman's position in society is based upon derived status (Hacker cited in Posner, 1977:43). Seen cross-culturally, women are regarded as objects and men as subjects (though in differing degrees and extent). In this regard, Simone de Beauvoir's view is plainly expressed and direct: aged women are stigmatized in all societies "due to the biological repulsiveness of the aging process" and "their nearness to death." De Beauvoir takes this idea further:

> It is the tendency of every society to live and go on living; society extols the strength and the fecundity that are so closely linked with youth, and it dreads the decrepitude of age (de Beauvoir, 1972:40).

Some may feel that de Beauvoir's analysis is too simplistic, too negative, even misleading, but many may feel it necessary if we are to see a youth-oriented, male-dominated society from the vantage point of the aged woman.

While Posner discusses the status of aging women and their double stigmatization, Susan Sontag opens up a new avenue of thought:

In a man's face lines are taken to be signs of character. They indicate emotional strength, maturity — qualities far more esteemed in men than in women. . . . But lines of aging, any scar, even a small birthmark on a woman's face are always regarded as unfortunate blemishes. . . . A woman's face is prized so far as it remains unchanged (Sontag, 1972:35).

Sontag's message about the double standard of aging is explicit in that "beauty, identified as it is for women with youthfulness, does not stand up well to age" (1972:31) and "converts the life of women into an inexorable march toward a condition in which they are not just unattractive but disgusting" (1972:36). It perpetuates the view of women as objects who have little of importance to offer.

Posner, Sontag and others have attempted in recent years to uncover the deep-seated ageism and sexism in contemporary societies. However, while the "double jeopardy" hypothesis — the additive, negative effects of (1) being old and (2) being a woman — proves to be a useful starting point, we must take one step forward and relate age and gender perspectives to the external structure of the labour market to enable us to see the economic as well as occupational implications of these "defined and perceived realities" affecting the occupational status and the extent of labour participation of the aged women in Canada.

Retirement and Older Working Women

The Institution of compulsory retirement

It is almost a truism to say that there are very few work opportunities for people 65 and over in this country and elsewhere in the industrialized world where the institution of compulsory retirement has been firmly established. The Ontario Status of Women Council (1982:28) has summed up this situation: "As a result of compulsory retirement policies and the lack of work alternatives, the right to work after age 65 barely exists."

While mandatory retirement is not written into the law (Roadburg, 1985:101), and, in fact, its practice is being viewed more and more as "unconstitutional" in light of the Charter of Rights and Freedoms, it will still be a long way before a ban will be imposed upon this practice. Brown, Dulude and Roadburg have argued that one of the major causes of the declining labour force participation of older workers lies in the *increasingly* rigid adherence to compulsory retirement policies (Brown, 1975; Dulude, 1978; Roadburg, 1985).

Financial implications of retirement

As Table 2 shows, employment income for the female age group 65-69 declines from 66 percent to 16 percent and for the female group 70 and over, diminishes to a meagre 3 percent. This decline in the proportion of employment income is compensated for by a substantial increase shown in the category of Transfer Payments (e.g., government pensions such as the Canada Pension Plan and the Old Age Pension), resulting in a sharply increased reliance upon these two sources of income for the older age group.

Also shown in this table is the fact that men aged 70 and older are better able to remain in the labour force than women aged 70 and over: 14 percent as opposed to 3 percent. This is the case despite the fact that women can be expected to live several years longer than men.

We should also remind ourselves of the fact that a large proportion of the women older than 70 have lost (or at least are statistically expected to have lost) their husbands, a fact that adds to their greater reliance upon transfer payments as their sole income source.

TABLE 2:
Sex and Age Composition of Income (1975)

	Total	Employment	Transfer Payments	Other Sources
Males Aged:				
55 - 64	100	83	5	11
65 - 69	100	41	30	29
70 +	100	14	46	40
Females Aged:				
55 - 64	100	66	12	21
65 - 69	100	16	54	30
70 +	100	3	68	29

SOURCE: Statistics Canada Survey of Consumer Finances, cited in L.O. Stone and S. Fletcher, *A Profile of Canada's Older Population*. Montreal. The Institute for Research on Public Policy. 1980. Adapted.

One final observation may be made regarding the varying proportions shown in the category of Other Sources. The older men, but not the older women, are likely to draw funds from this category of income for living as they grow older. Such a financial trend is not shown for the aging women; instead, for those older than 65, a slight reversal is noted, perhaps suggesting a gradual depletion of resources in this category of funds.

The Task Force on Older Women (1983) reports that income is the major problem facing Canada's older women. Their poverty stems from two main sources: one is the inequitable public pension system, and the second is the fact that women work in lower paying jobs (Cohen, 1984:184). Each of these points will be discussed below in some detail.

First, we view the Canadian retirement system as consisting of three sections:

1. Government Pensions: Old Age Security (OAS), Guaranteed Income Supplement (GIS), Spouse's Allowance and, in Ontario, the Guaranteed Annual Income Supplement (GAINS).
2. The Universal Public Pension Scheme: Canada/Quebec Pension Plan (C/QPP), which covers all workers in the labour force.
3. Private employment pensions, Registered Retirement Savings Plan (RRSP) and personal savings.

Many older women are completely dependent on the first level of public benefits for their income. Even with a full government pension (OAS, GIS, GAINS), a single person received less than the level established as the poverty line by the Canadian Council on Social Development in 1981.

The C/QPP theoretically covers the entire work force and provides benefits equal to one-quarter of the individual's salary up to a maximum of 25 percent of the Average Industrial Wage. However, the plan discriminates against women for a number of reasons. Since it is earnings-related, it ensures that women will receive a pension lower than men. After all, women earn only about $0.57 for each $1.00 a man earns (1977). Also, women make up two-thirds (Statistics Canada, 1983) of the part-time workers who earn lower incomes and therefore receive fewer benefits. Benefits for surviving spouses are 60 percent of the husband's earned pension, ensuring lower incomes for wives of lower income workers. Also, there is a maximum that one can contribute to C/QPP, ensuring that high wage earners (usually men) contribute a relatively small percentage of their salaries (Cohen, 1984:129). Women, since they are usually found in lower paying jobs, pay a higher proportion of their salaries and receive small benefits. A further problem is that the C/QPP does not cover people who have not been employed. Homemakers, who make up one of Canada's largest occupational groups, face an impoverished old age. In 1976, only 18 percent of the women 65 and over were receiving C/QPP benefits. This is partially due to women's working patterns (leaving for child rearing, etc.), but also to the fact that since the C/QPP only began in 1966, people who retired before that time get nothing at all.

The position of women with respect to private pensions is no better (Collins and Brown, 1978:105). In 1980, 50.6 percent of employed men and 34.6 percent of employed women were covered by private pensions, while 81 percent of unattached women age 65 and over had no private pension at all (Roadburg, 1985:34). Most pension schemes for women are run by government or Crown corporations. As a result, only 15 percent of women workers in the private sector are covered (Roadburg, 1985:34). Women's concentration in low status, low paid, nonunionized occupations means that they collect fewer pension benefits (Dulude, 1978). These are the jobs in the secondary economic sector. Their high turnover means that even if they are covered by a private scheme, they are likely to lose the benefits — a minimum of ten years is usually required before employee and employer contributions are "vested" or locked in. Given that two-thirds of all women change jobs more than once every five years, they usually lose their employer's contributions (Dulude, 1978). Not surprisingly, the highest work attachment of the older married population is in jobs without employer-sponsored pensions or in situations where they are not yet entitled to this type of pension (McDonald and Wanner, 1982:171).

To summarize, the aged women are poorer than the aged men and have fewer financial resources and alternatives. Many of these women continue to be poor and stay outside the labour market, either voluntarily or involuntarily. Some of these poor women do wish to gain employment to better their financial position, but encounter restrictive social barriers justified on the basis of ageism and sexism. Many of them are thus blocked before entering the labour market.

Occupational, Personal and Financial Characteristics of Older Working Women

As noted earlier, a small fraction of older Canadian women continue to work beyond 65. Less than five out of one hundred women aged 65 and over were still found in the labour force in 1984 in Canada. Who are these women who are still working and what characteristics set them apart from those women who do not work after age 65? What seems to be the motivating factor of their continuing to work? What types of work are they more likely to engage in? Which sectors of the existing occupational structure and of the labour market seem most amenable to the employment of these older women?

To answer these questions, we will briefly outline four major hypotheses available in labour market studies, which have been formulated to explain some of the structural forces operating to determine the occupational positions of older workers. The following four hypotheses are important (Nelson, 1980; Baum and Baum, 1980:122).

Major hypotheses of determination of occupational positions

1) Human capital hypothesis

This hypothesis concerns itself with the extent and mode of "investment" each individual is prepared to make to ascertain his or her future security. "Youth is more likely to invest itself because it has more years to enjoy the fruits of the investment" (Nelson 1980:89). According to this hypothesis, older individuals begin to lose human capital due to obsolescence, depreciation and senescence. "The lesser stock of human capital among the older working force results in older workers occupying jobs that pay a lower return on their accordingly smaller investment" (Nelson, 1980:90).

This hypothesis lacks consideration of important intervening factors such as sex and ethnicity, as well as some structural variables.

2) Dual labour market hypothesis

Doeringer and Piore (1971) have described the labour market as consisting of two distinct sectors: the primary (core) sector as capital intensive, unionized and having high wages, and the secondary (peripheral) sector as labour intensive, less unionized and having low wages. As we shall see below, McDonald and Wanner (1982) recently attempted to test this hypothesis on the dual economy concept. Women and the elderly populate the secondary labour market (McDonald and Wanner, 1985).

3) Marginality hypothesis

T. Sullivan (1978) and Thomas Nelson (1980) have attempted their analysis by focussing on the marginal occupations that are filled by marginal workers, including the young and the old. According to this hypothesis, the marginal workers are old and occupy marginal positions. Nelson, in particular, stresses the match between age group characteristics and occupational requirements and demands.

4) Selective retention hypothesis

This hypothesis assumes that older workers who remain in the labour market beyond the age of 65 are those who are better educated and those who have certain knowledge, experience or skills to be valued in the labour market. The white-collar worker, rather than the blue-collar, is therefore expected to be found in the labour market past retirement.

These four separate hypotheses are sufficient to make us look for certain variables and factors in the labour market that are expected to affect older workers significantly.

Personal and occupational characteristics of older female workers

The labour force participation rates of older women in Canada seem to have become stabilized in recent years, a trend that gives us a basis for suggesting that the social characteristics we are intending to analyse are not likely to alter much in the near future.

In fact, such a stable pattern of older female labour participation has been seen for both age groups (65-69 and 70+) since 1975, with some minor fluctuations caused by the overall economic cycle in Canada (see Table 1).

TABLE 3:
Labour Force Participation Rates for Age Groups 55 - 64 and 65 and Over by Sex, 1953-77

	Males		Females	
Year	55-64	65 +	55-64	65 +
1953	86.5	34.8	12.9	3.6
1954	85.4	33.2	14.0	3.7
1955	86.1	32.3	14.7	3.9
1956	86.4	34.0	15.8	4.5
1957	87.2	34.1	18.2	5.0
1958	87.0	32.1	19.2	5.2
1959	86.8	31.0	20.1	5.2
1960	86.7	30.3	21.3	5.6
1961	86.8	29.3	23.2	5.9
1962	86.1	28.5	23.8	5.6
1963	85.9	26.4	24.6	5.9
1964	86.2	26.8	25.6	6.3
1965	86.4	26.3	27.0	6.0
1966	86.0	26.2	28.4	5.8
1967	85.8	24.7	28.6	5.9
1968	85.4	24.3	29.0	6.1
1969	85.3	23.5	30.2	5.5
1970	84.2	22.6	29.8	5.0
1971	83.3	20.0	30.9	5.1
1972	82.4	18.6	29.7	4.3
1973	81.2	18.1	31.0	4.4
1974	80.3	17.7	29.6	4.3
1975	79.4(80.1)	17.2(18.5)	30.8(29.0)	4.4(4.8)
1976	76.7	16.0	32.1	4.1
1977	76.6	15.5	32.2	4.2

SOURCE: Senate of Canada, 1979:49.

Personal characteristics

McDonald and Wanner (1982), drawing on data from the 1973 Canadian National Mobility Study of more than 6,000 men and women aged 65 and over, suggest the following distinct social characteristics of older people in the work force:

First, older women workers tend to be single and, on the average, younger than those who have withdrawn from the labour force (67.5 compared to 72.7 years of age).

Second, they tend to have more dependent children living at home, compared to those no longer in the labour force.

Third, they enjoy relatively good health.

Fourth, they are generally better educated than those no longer working (10.5 years of schooling compared to 9.1 years). On the average, respondents worked six-tenths of a week more for each additional year of schooling they had.

Employment motives of older women workers

Why do these women continue to work? The motivations for women continuing to work past retirement age are manifold. Some women work because they are committed to their work roles and do not wish to withdraw from the labour force. Vivian, in Cohen's *Small Expectations*, is a public speaker because she enjoys the stimulation and challenge of it. She claims that it has done wonders for her self-confidence and self-esteem (Cohen, 1984:155). For Bertha, taking in boarders has made her feel useful and accepted (ibid:158). There may be hundreds of other personal reasons why they engage in a variety of work.

Although there are motives as discussed above, the principal reasons for women being in the labour force after retirement are financial. According to the National Council of Welfare, one of every four Canadians over the age of 65 is living below the nationally defined poverty line, which was $7,052 for residents of rural areas and $9,538 for those who lived in metropolitan cities during 1984. Indeed, as much as 57.7 percent of the older people who live alone or with nonrelatives were found to be under the poverty line. Many of these happened to be widowed and female. In fact, there are three times as many women aged 65 and over living below the poverty line as there are men in the same age group (Roadburg, 1985:33). Pennings's research (1983) indicates that there is a significant interaction between age and sex such that the lowest incomes are evident among elderly females. Cohen (1984:125) sums up the economic position of older women by saying: "The two poorest groups of people in Canada are women and the old; the poorest of the poor are the old women." By remaining in the labour force after age 65, some women can improve their desperate situation. Those women who work have a higher total personal income than those who have left the labour force. However, when earned income is subtracted from total personal income, the base income (from interest, rents received, pensions, welfare, etc.) is much lower for women who continue to work. Financial incentive is the prime factor motivating labour force participation — base income is by far the most important predictor of labour force activity among older women (McDonald and Wanner, 1982:175-176).

Occupational characteristics

General

These working women can be divided into five main groups: (1) those who continue for a few years with the same employer; (2) those who are self-employed; (3) those who are actually unemployed but are included in the participation rate because they see themselves as still attached to the labour force; (4) those who work part-time; and finally, (5) those who seek and find new full-time employment (Brown, 1975:32-33). While we do not have the exact proportions of women in each of these groups and some of them do overlap, we shall look into the distribution of older women workers in depth.

Age/Sex stereotyping and occupational concentration

McDonald and Wanner (1982:171) have suggested that most older women workers are employed in trade, service and agricultural industries, and in management, technical and professional occupations. What is most conspicuous, however, is the fact that, just as younger women workers, they are heavily concentrated in a narrow range of occupations. This phenomenon of so-called occupation concentration (or occupational segregation — a term that is often used interchangeably in the literature of Industrial Sociology) continues to be the most salient aspect of female employment. Further, the occupational prestige of older women tends to be lower than it was ten years earlier in their career. This seems to reflect broken career lines, and may also be a result of difficult competition with younger women in the marketplace.

The female occupational concentration in this case reflects not only the opportunity structure available for older women, but also their occupational adaptation in fulfilling their financial needs. Perhaps because of their adaptive response to the available occupation opportunity and their personal needs/conveniences, many older women choose to go into "self-employment" (Brown, 1975; McDonald and Wanner, 1982; McPherson, 1983).

Statistics Canada reports that in 1981, 11 percent of older women workers were self-employed, while for all women workers this ratio was only 3.2 percent. Further, the report says that married women showed a slightly greater tendency towards self-employment in all age groups (see Table 4).

In this regard, we do find some interesting changing trends in self-employment among older women in Canada. For instance, in 1966, about 20 percent of older women workers were self-employed, while for all women this ratio was only 5 percent (Podoluk cited in Brown, 1975:34). These were people who were not forced to retire, but neither were they covered by any pension plans. Therefore, it is likely that economic necessity may have forced them to continue working more or less on their own.

With the advent of the Canada Pension Plan and Guaranteed Income Supplement in 1966, there has been a decline in the number of self-employed women aged 65 and over, a fact that seems to reflect the improvement of their economic position.

One of the largest groups of the self-employed appears to be made up of older women involved in agriculture. About two-thirds of the men and women on Canada's farms work beyond the age of 65; they form 21 percent of Canada's workers aged 70 and over (Government of Canada, 1982:33).

Although there has been a moderate decline in self-employment, especially in agriculture, this type of employment still offers the greatest possibilities for older individuals who can, by their own choice, reduce the hours and intensity of the work to a level that best suits them. This enables a more gradual move out of the labour force rather than the more abrupt break that many workers experience (Brown, 1975:34).

TABLE 4:
Distribution of Labour Force Participants into Paid, Self-employed and Unpaid Family Work by Age, Sex and Marital Status, 1981

Canada - Female	Paid Workers	Self-Employed %	Unpaid Family Workers
Total	95.6	3.2	1.2
Married	94.3	4.0	1.7
15 - 19	98.8	.4	.6
Married	98.7	1.0	.3
20 - 24	98.6	1.0	.4
Married	98.0	1.5	.5
25 - 44	95.0	3.6	1.4
Married	94.5	4.0	1.5
45 - 64	93.4	4.7	1.8
Married	92.5	5.0	2.5
65 +	87.0	11.0	2.0
Married	83.0	12.0	5.0
Canada - Male			
Total	90.6	9.1	.3
Married	89.3	10.6	1.0
65 +	67.4	31.9	.7
Married	67.7	31.6	.7

SOURCE: Statistics Canada, 1981 Population Census, Population Labour Force Activity. Ottawa: Minister of Supply and Services, No. 92-915, vol. 1. 1984. Adapted.

Part-time employment of older women workers

The second salient feature in older women's labour participation is that a large proportion are engaged in part-time employment. While only 2.8 percent of women in the part-time labour force are aged 65 and over, they represent 46.9 percent — almost one half — of employed women in that age group. Of married women workers age 65 and over, over half — 52.3 percent — are in the part-time labour force (see Table 5).

TABLE 5:
Distribution of Workers into Full-time and Part-time Employment by Age, Sex and Marital Status, 1981

	Mostly Full-time	%	Mostly Part-time
Canada Both Sexes			
Total	80.8		19.2
Married	84.4		15.6
Males			
Total	89		11.0
Married	94.7		5.3
65 +	66.4		33.6
Married	66.3		33.7
Females			
Total	69.2		30.8
Married	68.7		31.3
15 - 19	42.2		57.8
Married	69.7		30.3
20 - 24	78.8		21.2
Married	80.3		19.7
25 - 44	72.7		27.3
Married	68.8		31.2
45 - 64	67.9		32.1
Married	63.6		36.4
65 +	53.1		46.9
Married	47.7		52.3

SOURCE: Statistics Canada, 1981 Population Census, Population Work Activity in 1980. Ottawa: Minister of Supply and Services, No. 92-915, 1983. Adapted.

Of the 146,000 part-time positions that became available between January 1972 and January 1974, only 1,000 were filled by workers aged 65 and over. This limited access can be attributable to the distribution by industry of part-time employment in relation to all employment (Brown, 1975:38). For instance, Brown comments that while 65 percent of all positions are in the service sector, 85 percent of part-time jobs are found there. On the other hand, production industries represent 30 percent of all positions, but they provided only 8.5 percent of part-time jobs. Therefore, this lopsided distribution of part-time positions in the labour market determines where older women seeking part-time jobs would go and what type of part-time job they would ultimately engage in. There is another important occupational implication that derives from this labour market phenomenon: the older workers are likely to lose the advantages of their experience and industry-related skills and are more likely to be in direct competition with younger workers. Under these conditions, as Brown has feared, judgment is likely to be made on an age basis (Brown, 1975:38). Yet no employers would openly admit the practice of ageism involving labour recruitment.

Marginal jobs in the secondary labour market

Table 5 shows that nearly a half of older working women are part-time workers. As such, they tend to be poorly paid (Dulude, 1978) and rarely receive fringe benefits. These deprived working conditions reveal the typical problems associated with employment in the so-called secondary labour market, one that is characterized by numerous ports of entry, short or non-existent promotion ladders, worker stability discouraged by low wages, few opportunities for advancement, etc. Virtually none of these older women is found in the primary labour market, where working conditions are more than adequate and beneficial to the interest of those who work there. But these old, female workers find themselves being trapped in a small corner of the existing dual labour market. By comparison with the older women who earn their living while self-employed, those who work in small- and medium-sized industries and firms appear to be far more economically and socially deprived (Blau & Jusenius, 1976:196). Thus, it should be remembered that the primary-secondary distinction coincides with social divisions such as sex and age. In this regard, we can hypothesize that the income differences found in retired old people are a direct result of their sectoral location as workers. We might anticipate that women would be more likely to continue working if employed in the secondary sector since their financial situation would be more precarious than those working in the primary sector.

Conclusion

Thus the dual labour market hypothesis helps us to make sense of the patterns of employment of older women workers. However, a number of other conceptual tools are also useful.

One is the "selective retention hypothesis," which argues that some people are allowed to remain in the labour force because "they are less obsolescent than others." Since obsolescence as a concept does not work perfectly (if it did, almost none of the aged would be found at work anywhere), it has to be modified. The modification proposed is that those who continue to work will be higher status, better educated workers (Baum and Baum, 1980:122). Certainly our data suggest that this proposition works quite well for older women workers in Canada. They do tend to be found in white-collar occupations, sometimes in higher status jobs, and many of them are self-employed. Also, the more education they have, the more likely they are to continue working.

Some upper status workers, especially the self-employed, have more control over whether to retire than do lower status workers. Baum and Baum (1980:124-125) suggest that age discrimination might operate more effectively against lower status workers, in part because they are more likely to be subject to bureaucratic decisions. When there are economic shifts and blue-collar workers are laid off, the older worker, especially if unskilled, is likely to have difficulty being reemployed. Many companies are reluctant to hire older workers because of increases in pension costs or ageist orientations. Also, older blue-collar workers often refuse to relocate, to "follow the market," or to change their line of work. Older white-collar workers are more flexible, at least in terms of seeking alternate work, even if it means transferring into a lower paying job in a small business providing services or engaged in the retail trade (Baum and Baum, 1980:125). This helps explain why fewer older women blue-collar workers remain in the labour force compared to white-collar workers.

The selective retention hypothesis, then, has some validity. Alone, however, it is not enough. To understand the position of older women in the labour force, it is essential to consider the combined effects of ageism and sexism. Older women suffer from a "double whammy" of being old and female (Posner, 1977).

This double jeopardy undermines their bargaining power in the labour market. As women, they have faced discrimination throughout their working lives. They have been segregated into female job ghettos and have often been underpromoted and underpaid. They have been forced into the secondary labour market. Those women who have managed to gain seniority and status may be able to maintain their position after age 65 (here the selective retention hypothesis holds). However, most women are not in such a privileged position, and as they age, their position in the labour market weakens. Many are forced to accept poorly paid, part-time, white-collar and service jobs.

The picture we have painted is rather bleak. Many older women who would like to work cannot, and many of those who do, face a difficult employment situation. However, it must be kept in mind that many women withdraw voluntarily from the labour force. Also, there are older women who work in challenging, rewarding positions. Our goal must be to make this an option for all women.

References

Aiken, Lewis R.
1982   *Later Life.* 2nd ed. New York: Holt, Rinehart and Winston.
Atchley, Robert C.
1976   *The Sociology of Retirement.* New York: Wiley and Sons.
1983   *Aging: Continuity and Change.* Belmont, California: Wadsworth Publishing Company.
Baum, Martha and Rainer Baum
1980   *Growing Old: A Societal Perspective.* Englewood Cliffs, New Jersey: Prentice-Hall.
de Beauvoir, Simone
1972   *Old Age.* Trans. Patrick O'Brian. London: Putnam and Sons.
Blau, F.D. and C.L. Jusenius
1976   "Economists' approaches to sex segregation in the labor market: An appraisal." Pp. 181-199 in M. Blaxall and B. Reagan (eds.), *Women and the Work-place.* Chicago: University of Chicago Press.
Brown, Joan C.
1975   *How Much Choice?* Toronto: Canadian Council on Social Development.
Cohen, Leah
1984   *Small Expectations.* Toronto: McClelland and Stewart.
Collins, Kevin and Joan C. Brown
1978   "Canada's retirement policies." *Aging and Work* 1 (Winter):101-8.
Cox, Harold
1984   *Later Life: The Realities of Aging.* Englewood Cliffs, New Jersey: Prentice-Hall.
Doeringer, P.B. and M.J. Piore
1971   *Internal Labor Markets and Manpower Analysis.* Lexington, Mass.: Health Lexington.
Dulude, Louise
1978   *Women and Aging: A Report on the Rest of Our Lives.* Ottawa Advisory Council on the Status of Women.
Government of Canada
1982   *Canadian Government Report on Aging.* Ottawa: Minister of Supply and Services.
McDonald, Lynn and Richard A. Wanner
1982   "Work past age 65 in Canada: A socioeconomic analysis." *Aging and Work* 5(3):169-180.
McPherson, Barry D.
1983   *Aging as a Social Process.* Toronto: Butterworth.
Nelson, Thomas
1980   "The age structure of occupations." Pp. 87-110 in P.F. Ragan (ed.), *Work and Retirement: Policy Issues.* Los Angeles: University of Southern California Press.
Ontario Status of Women Council
1982   *Brief to the Ontario Government on Women and Aging.*

Penning, M.J.
    1983   "Multiple jeopardy: Age, sex and ethnic variations." *Canadian Ethnic Studies* 15(3):81-105.
Posner, Judith
    1977   "Old and female: The double whammy." *Essence* 2(1):41-48.
Roadburg, Allan
    1985   *Aging: Retirement Leisure and Work in Canada.* Toronto: Methuen.
Senate of Canada
    1979   *Retirement Without Tears.* Ottawa: Minister of Supply and Services.
Sontag, Susan
    1972   "The double standard of aging." *Saturday Review* (September 23):29-38.
Statistics Canada
    1983   *1981 Census of Canada Population-Work Activity in 1980.* Catalogue No. 92-916, vol. 1. Ottawa: Minister of Supply and Services.
    1984a   *Labour Force Annual Averages 1975-1983.* Catalogue No. 71-529. Ottawa: Minister of Supply and Services.
    1984b   *1981 Census of Canada.* Population–Labour Force Activity. Catalogue I, 92-915 vol. 1. Ottawa: Minister of Supply and Services.
Stolz, B.
    1985   *Still Struggling: America's Low Income Working Women Confronting the 1980's.* Toronto: D.C. Heath and Company.
Stone, Leroy O. and Susan Fletcher
    1980   *A Profile of Canada's Older Population.* Montreal: The Institute for Research on Public Policy.
Sullivan, Teresa
    1978   *Marginal Workers, Marginal Jobs.* Austin: University of Texas Press.
    1983   *The Task Force on Older Women.*

14

Retirement in a Dual Economy: The Canadian Case

P. Lynn McDonald
Faculty of Social Welfare
University of Calgary

Richard A. Wanner
Department of Sociology
University of Calgary

In Canada, the proportion of older workers remaining in the labour force has been steadily declining for the past fifty years, as in other industrial nations. In 1921, 33 percent of Canadian workers aged 65 years and over were in the labour force, but by 1976 this proportion had dropped to 12.5 percent (Health and Welfare Canada, 1977). Among Canadian men aged 65 to 69, the labour force participation rates dropped from 46.5 percent in 1966 to 21.9 percent in 1981. For women of the same age, the percentage dropped from 10.9 percent in 1966 to 7.8 percent in 1976 and rose again in 1981 to 7.9 percent. While Canadian men appear to be withdrawing from the labour force early, the pattern for women is somewhat different. For those male workers aged 55 to 64, the labour force participation rates have fallen from 86.1 percent in 1966 to 75.1 percent in 1981. In contrast, the labour force participation rates for women of the same age have risen from 28.5 percent in 1966 to 33.7 percent in 1981 (Government of Canada, 1983).

To date, most investigations of these retirement patterns are informed by individualized conceptions of aging. A review of the retirement research quickly indicates that individual factors, such as attitudes to work, leisure and retirement (Health and Welfare Canada, 1977; McPherson and Guppy, 1979; Prothero, 1981; Keating and Spiller, 1983; Roadburg, 1985), the condition of the individual's health (Baillargeon, 1982; Shapiro, 1982), their preparations and planning for retirement (McPherson and Guppy, 1979;

This research was partially supported by an operating grant from the Research Grants Committee of the University of Calgary. The data were acquired through the efforts of the Canadian Association on Gerontology. This is a revised version of a paper presented at the XIIIth International Congress of Gerontology, New York, July 1985.

Bond and Bond, 1980; Stones and Kozma, 1980), the process of retiring (Keating and Marshall, 1980), the impact of retirement (Martin Matthews et al., 1982) and the individual's adjustment to retirement (Keating and Cole, 1980; McPherson, 1980; Krauss, 1981) have gained the attention of many Canadian scholars. Forces external to the individual that may affect retirement have been studied to a lesser extent (Martin, 1982; Tracy, 1982; Myles, 1984; Wanner and McDonald, 1986). Peter Townsend, in a somewhat militant mood, refers to this individualistic bias as " 'acquiescent functionalism' or the kind of theory of aging that attributes the causation of problems to the difficulties of individual adjustment to aging, retirement, or physical decrescence, while acquiescing in the development of the state, the economy and inequality" (Townsend, 1981:6).

More recently, a number of gerontologists have been challenging the individualized conception of retirement. The elderly are not necessarily responsible for the inflation that has eroded their retirement savings (Estes, 1979; Graebner, 1980); they are not responsible for retirement policies that were formulated to facilitate economic development in industrial nations (Estes, 1979; Graebner, 1980); nor are they responsible for inequalities prior to labour force withdrawal that are reproduced in retirement (Walker, 1981; Myles, 1981). Voluntary preretirement or early retirement may be the result of a number of pressures related to a new mythology that workers over a certain age have no right to work (Guillemard, 1983).

The Political Economy of Old Age

This alternative perspective for studying retirement is variously called the political sociology of aging or the political economy of old age. The roots of this framework can be traced to different versions of the conflict model of society that arose in opposition to the structural functional approach underpinning the individualistic studies of aging (see Dowd, 1980; Marshall, 1980; and Estes et al., 1982, for critiques of these "theories"). The major proponents of this approach (Townsend and Walker in Great Britain; Myles in Canada; Cribier, Gaullier and Guillemard in France; Giori in Italy; and Dowd and Estes in the United States) locate the elderly within the prevailing social, political and economic structures of society. Retirement is an integral element in this paradigm. Briefly, retirement is seen as a marginal and dependent position occupied by the aged that is the culmination of the operation of economic, social and political phenomena prior to retirement. These very same structures continue to sustain the positions of the aged in postretirement through the minimization of potential conflict between generations, social classes or interest groups.

For example, Guillemard (1977, 1980, 1983) shows how a state-fostered ideology consistent with "activity theory" has made way for the most current debate between French trade unions and employers about retirement age. The debate, fuelled by the crisis of unemployment and widespread preretirement schemes, is producing a new definition of old age. One is defined as older at a younger age by virtue of a low retirement age, with the implication that the older worker is a "job snatcher" (Guillemard, 1983:84-85). Estes (1979) analyses the implementation of the Older Americans Act and demonstrates how this policy and related programs have resulted in the isolation, stigmatization and general dependency of the aged. Myles (1984), in considering the political economy of public pensions (including those of Canada), argues that the current conflict over the future of old age pensions can be reduced to yet another manifestation of the traditional conflict between labour and capital over the "democratic" control of the state. How the issue is resolved will clearly influence the process of retirement. Walker (1983) argues that age-restrictive policies have been used by the state to exclude older workers from the labour force and to legitimate that exclusion through retirement (Dowd, 1980). Phillipson (1983) suggests that the key to retirement is the political and economic environment within which the institutions of work and retirement are located. More to the point, Dowd (1980) postulates that the differentiation of the industrial sector into a core and peripheral sector has created fundamentally different conditions for employers and workers that will influence the experience of older workers and their retirement.

Following the political economy perspective, the purpose of this chapter is to evaluate the role of economic structures in influencing patterns of retirement of Canadian men and women. Specifically we test the dual economy theory that Dowd (1980) hypothesized should influence the retirement process.

Dual Economy Theory[1]

With the move from competitive capitalism to monopoly capitalism, there has been a differentiation of the industrial sector into two distinct sectors, usually referred to as the core and periphery (Beck, Horan and Tolbert, 1980). The core industrial sector is dominated by large corporate enterprises represented in durable manufacturing, the construction trades and the extraction industries. Firms in the core economy are noted for high productivity, high profits, intensive utilization of capital, a high incidence of monopoly elements and a tendency to have a high degree of unionization. The general result is higher wages, better working conditions and fringe benefits. The career lines of the workers are likely to be orderly, meaning that earnings and occupational prestige increase steadily over time (Spilerman, 1977). The state sector is assumed to be very similar to the core sector in terms of employment (Averitt, 1968).

In contrast, the periphery sector, concentrated in agriculture, nondurable manufacturing, retail trade and subprofessional services, is noted for

TABLE 1.
Means and Percentages for Socioeconomic Characteristics of Men by Age and Economic Sector, Canada, 1981.

Socioeconomic Characteristics	Age 55 to 64		Age 65 or Over	
	Core	Periphery	Core	Periphery
Marital Status				
Married	86.3%	85.4%	81.4%	79.7%
Other	13.7%	14.6%	18.6%	20.3%
Immigrant Status				
Born Elsewhere	25.9%*	22.6%*	29.0%	26.4%
Born in Canada	74.1%*	77.4%*	71.0%	73.6%
Years of Schooling	9.8	9.7	10.0*	9.3*
Occupational Status[1]	45.0*	44.3*	45.3*	42.8*
Class of Worker				
Paid Worker	93.2%*	66.1%*	87.2%*	57.4*
Self-Employed	6.8*	33.9%*	12.8%*	42.6%*
Employment Status				
Full Time	94.5*	88.9%*	69.7%*	64.5%*
Part Time	5.5%*	11.1%*	30.3%*	35.5%*

Hours Worked	32.0*	36.5*	14.7*	22.3*
Unemployment Rate	3.7%	4.0%	2.1*	0.9%*
Weeks Not Worked	7.2*	8.5*	20.0*	16.3%
Wages and Salaries	17989.*	12399.*	8936.*	5147.
Total Income[2]	21774.* *	19989.*	18066.*	16274.*
Base Income[3]	3787.*	7589.*	9131.*	11126.*
Receives OAS	2.0%	1.7%	82.0%*	89.9%*
Receives Other Pension[4]	8.5%	9.5%	39.5%*	30.0%*
Receives Other Transfer Payments[5]	9.2%	9.5%	18.1%	21.0%
Number of Cases	5223	3265	1060	1362

Note: Separate F or x^2 tests for differences in means or percentages across economic sectors were performed. Significant differences at a $< .05$ are indicated by asterisks.

[1]Blishen-McRoberts (1976) scale of occupational status.
[2]Total income from all sources.
[3]Total income from all sources minus earned income.
[4]All regular income received as a result of previous employment of the respondent or a deceased relative.
[5]All other government transfer payments from federal, provincial or municipal governments.

labour intensity, low productivity and profits and intensive product market competition and lack of unionization. These factors are translated into lower wage and fringe benefits and "chaotic" career lines (Spilerman, 1977).

If the sectoral specification of the economic order is correct, then we would expect that there are differences between those working in the core and those working in the periphery, that these differences will reappear in retirement and that retirement patterns should be different between the two sectors. For example, we expect that workers spending their careers in the periphery industries will be less likely to receive private pensions and hence more likely to continue working in later life. Using American data, this was found to be true for men, but the test has not been made in the Canadian context, and never for women (McDonald, 1983).

Retirement in a Dual Economy

The data used to explore these issues come from Statistic Canada's Public Use Sample Tape, which consists of a 2 percent simple random sample of the one-fifth of Canadians age 55 and over who responded to the long form questionnaire in the 1981 Census of Canada. We selected a 50 percent simple random sample of these respondents to yield 45,000 cases for analysis.[2]

The following analysis distinguishes between core and periphery sectors. The measure of economic segmentation was created by assigning the 18 industries represented in the Public Use Sample to core or periphery on the basis of 11 industrial characteristics that were factor analysed according to the procedures used by Beck, Horan and Tolbert (1980). The actual assignment is made on the basis of factor scores and the assignment of workers is made according to past or current industry. Examples of core industries include communication, public utilities, transportation and manufacturing. Periphery industries would include retail trade, forestry, textiles and agriculture.

Table 1 presents the means and percentages for socio-economic characteristics of men by age and economic sector.[3] The table indicates that there are statistically significant differences between sectors on a number of characteristics. Most notably, the core workers have higher educational and occupational status; they are less likely to be self-employed, more likely to work full-time, yet they work fewer hours per week on the average than the periphery workers. The core workers tend to retire more (weeks not worked) and they fare better on most economic variables. They are more likely to receive private pensions and less likely to receive other government transfers such as welfare.

Turning to Table 2, we find similar results for the women. Those women in the core have more education, higher educational prestige, higher wages and total income. Like the men, the women in the core are more likely to receive private pensions. Unlike the men, women who worked in core industries are receiving more government transfer payments, which may be a reflection of the fact that larger proportions of women are single or widowed as they grow older.

Table 3 considers those workers who withdrew from the labour force in 1980 and 1981. Since the census data were not designed to study retirement, no occupation-related variables are available for persons not in the labour force at the time of the survey, with the exception of those who withdrew between January 1, 1980, and the time of the survey. Thus we will use these respondents to ascertain if conditions prior to retirement surface in retirement and if retirement patterns are different between sectors.[4]

It is clear that retirement patterns are different for men across sector, but not for women. Men in the core tend to retire earlier than those in the periphery, they are more likely to retire on time (age 65) and they are less likely to retire late, which is consistent with the notion of an orderly career line. That they are more likely to be paid, full-time workers further supports this finding. Again, their overall income is higher, they more often have recourse to outside pensions and they depend less on other government transfers. All this suggests that conditions prior to retirement do reappear in the postretirement period.

Why there are no sectoral differences for women in retirement patterns is most likely a function of the very different career lines that Canadian women experience (Connidis, 1982) and the less-than-equal benefits they accrue from work as a result (O'Neil, 1979; McDonald and Wanner, 1982, 1984). It is worth noting that on the economic variables, women in the core fare much better in retirement than those women in the periphery, but overall, women are more economically disadvantaged than the men. It is well documented that Canadian women are concentrated in occupations with lower incomes and pensions (O'Neil, 1979), that they experience broken career lines and that women in occupations equivalent to those of men do not receive equivalent pay (Armstrong and Armstrong, 1978). The ascribed status of being female and the concomitant features attached to this position in Canadian society most likely temper the effects of sector.

While we have considerable evidence to this point that the retirement experiences of both men and women in Canada differ depending upon the economic sector in which they spend their careers, we have been looking at no more than a series of bivariate relationships. Table 4 presents a series of regression models in which weeks not worked in the year prior to the 1981 census, our measure of the degree of retirement, is regressed on a dummy variable for sector, coded 1 if the respondent worked in a core industry, 0 in a periphery industry, and a set of other socio-economic variables predicting retirement.[5]

In addition, for each gender category we have added to the main effects

TABLE 2.
Means and Percentages for Socioeconomic Characteristics of Women by Age and Economic Sector, Canada, 1981.

Socioeconomic Characteristics	Age 55 to 64		Age 65 or Over	
	Core	Periphery	Core	Periphery
Marital Status				
Married	59.2%*	68.1%*	35.6%	40.1%
Other	40.8%*	31.9%*	64.4%	59.9%
Immigrant Status				
Born Elsewhere	25.9%	25.5%	20.0%*	27.2%*
Born in Canada	74.1%	74.5%	80.0%*	72.8%*
Years of Schooling	10.6*	10.0*	10.5*	9.3*
Occupational Status[1]	51.8*	45.7*	53.2*	45.0*
Class of Worker				
Paid Worker	98.1%*	87.7%*	94.9%*	84.1%*
Self-Employed	1.9%*	12.3%*	5.1%*	15.9%*
Employment Status				
Full Time	74.2%*	58.3%*	54.2%*	43.4%*
Part Time	25.8%*	41.7%*	45.8%*	56.6%*

Hours Worked	25.4*	23.4*	11.3*	14.7*
Unemployment Rate	3.4%*	3.9%*	2.2%	1.7%
Weeks Not Worked	11.0*	13.2*	19.4	18.1
Wages and Salaries	10498.*	6693.*	4581.*	3859.*
Total Income[2]	12869.*	9436.*	8946.	8462.
Base Income[3]	2370.*	3002.*	7361.	6348.
Receives OAS	9.7%	9.8%	86.4%*	88.6%
Receives Other Pension[4]	8.8%	7.0%	32.5%*	21.5%*
Receives Other Transfer Payments[5]	5.4%	6.0%	84.4%	80.3%*
Number of Cases	2450	2290	550	559

Note: Separate F or x^2 tests for differences in means or percentages across economic sectors were performed. Significant differences at a $< .05$ are indicated by asterisks.

[1] Blishen-McRoberts (1976) scale of occupational status.
[2] Total income from all sources.
[3] Total income from all sources minus earned income.
[4] All regular income received as a result of previous employment of the respondent or a deceased relative.
[5] All other government transfer payments from federal, provincial or municipal governments.

TABLE 3.
Means and Percentages for Men and Women Who Withdrew From the Labour Force 1980-81 by Sector, Canada, 1981

Socioeconomic Characteristics	Men		Women	
	Core	Periphery	Core	Periphery
Age				
55 to 59	19.0%*	19.3%*	31.5%	37.4%
60 to 64	27.6%*	22.3%*	30.4%	29.5%
65	17.7%*	12.7%*	10.9%	7.2%
66 or over	35.7%*	45.7%*	27.2%	25.9%
Birthplace				
Canada	76.3%	79.4%	77.3%	77.1%
Elsewhere	23.7%	20.6%	22.7%	22.9%
Marital Status				
Married	83.9%	81.0%	62.3%	62.9%
Other	16.1%	19.0%	37.7%	37.1%
Level of Education	9.4	9.2	10.4*	9.6*
Occupational Status[1]	44.3	43.3	52.4*	44.8*
Class of Worker				
Self-Employed	7.5%*	27.6%*	2.8%*	12.1%*
Paid Worker	92.5%*	72.4%*	97.2%*	87.9%*
Amount of Work				
Part Time	21.2%*	34.4%*	45.7%*	60.8%*
Full Time	78.8%*	65.6%*	54.3%*	39.2%*
Weeks Not Worked	24.4	26.0	30.1	29.2
Wages	9806.*	6003.*	4452.*	2982.*
Total Income[2]	16806.*	*14841.*	9453.	7161.
Base Income[3]	6999.*	8838.*	5000.	4178.
Receives OAS	45.8%*	52.0%*	61.0%*	61.7%*
Received Other Pension[4]	35.2%*	28.9%*	26.5%*	15.0%*
Received Other Transfer Payments[5]	16.8%*	21.6%*	13.3%	10.7%
Number of Cases	871	606	533	580

Note: Separate F or x^2 tests for differences in means or percentages across economic sectors were performed. Significant differences at a $<$ .05 are indicated by asterisks.
[1]Blishen-McRoberts (1976) scale of occupational status.
[2]Total income from all sources.
[3]Total income from all sources minus earned income.
[4]All regular income received as a result of previous employment of the respondent or a deceased relative.
[5]All other government transfer payments from federal, provincial or municipal governments.

model a set of multiplicative terms capturing differences in the effect of each variable across economic sectors. These are created by multiplying the sector variable by each of the other variables in the model. The slopes associated with these interaction terms are designed to estimate the extent to which the socio-economic factors influence retirement differently in the core and periphery sectors.

The fit of these models is indicated by the square of the multiple correlation coefficient (R^2). In both cases, the R^2s are relatively small, with approximately 12 percent of the variance explained for men and 5 percent for women, though both are statistically significant. While these R^2s are relatively small, possibly due to our inability to include other variables in the model known to affect retirement, our main interest here is the size of the effects.

In neither of the main effects models is the coefficient for sector significant. That is, while for both men and women with jobs in core industries the number of weeks not worked is slightly smaller, we have no evidence that these coefficients are not zero in the population. The factors that do exhibit significant effects on weeks not worked are age, years of graded schooling, occupational status, self-employment and base income. Thus, fewer weeks are worked by older persons, those with fewer years of graded schooling, those with lower occupational status, those who are employed by others and those with lower base incomes.

However, this is not to say that sector is unimportant in understanding retirement. As shown in the two models containing interaction terms, one for males and one for females, the magnitude of the effects of several of these socio-economic variables is different in the core and periphery sectors. Among men, age has a considerably stronger effect on degree of retirement in core industries than in periphery industries. This is consistent with our earlier finding in Table 3 that men in core industries are more likely to retire early or on time than are men in periphery industries. Self-employed men in core industries are also likely to be working fewer weeks than their counterparts in periphery industries. This is certainly consistent with our understanding of the characteristics of firms in the two sectors, since the smaller periphery firms are less likely to generate revenues to permit their owners to retire early. This is further substantiated by a significant difference in the effect of self-employment income in core and periphery on weeks not worked; the effect is substantially weaker for those in core industries. In the case of women no significant age and self-employment interactions are found. Instead we find that women with more years of education are inclined to continue working to a greater extent when employed in core industries, while women in higher ranking occupations work to a lesser extent in core industries.

TABLE 4.
Regressions of Weeks Not Worked on Socioeconomic Characteristics for Men and Women, Canada, 1981

Predetermined Variables	Men		Women	
	Main Effects	Main and Interaction Effects	Main Effects	Main and Interaction Effects
Main Variables				
Economic Sector[1]	− .252	− 12.66*	− .816	− 11.99*
	(− .008)	(− .393)	(− .023)	(− .333)
Age	.605*	.508*	.363*	.324*
	(.209)	(.175)	(.110)	(.098)
Years of Graded School	− .758*	− .678*	− .289*	− .433*
	(− .129)	(− .116)	(− .040)	(− .059)
Years of University	.028	.249	− .038	− .577
	(.003)	(.024)	(− .002)	(− .038)
Occupational Status[2]	− .008*	− .101*	− .123*	− .196*
	(− .072)	(− .082)	(− .080)	(− .128)
Self Employed[1]	− 1.022*	− 1.916*	− 1.763	− 1.343
	(− .026)	(− .048)	(− .026)	(− .020)
Self-Employed Income[3]	− .422*	− .301*	− .559*	− .431*
	(− .216)	(− .154)	(− .104)	(− .080)
Base Income[4]	.316*	.187*	.328*	.110
	(.229)	(.136)	(.113)	(.038)
Interaction Terms				
Sector × Age		.186*		.034
		(.353)		(.058)
Sector × Graded School		− .144		.245
		(− .046)		(.074)
Sector × University		− .354*		− 1..075*
		(− .030)		(− .064)
Sector × Occupation		.014		.113*
		(.021)		(.173)

Table 4 continued

Sector × Self-Employed		3.505*		−.937
		(.046)		(−.006)
Sector × Self-Emp. Income		−.302*		−.356*
		(−.094)		(−.045)
Sector × Base Income		.306*		.520*
		(.145)		(.130)
Constant	−16.91	−10.04	−.138	7.55
R²	.111	.120	.040	.048
Number of Cases	10882	10882	5794	5794

Note: All coefficients are ordinary least-squares estimates; standardized coefficients are in parentheses.
[1]Dummy variables defined as follows: sector, 1 if respondent was employed in a core industry, 0 otherwise; self-employed, 1 if
 respondent was self-employed, 0 otherwise.
[2]Blishen-McRoberts (1976) scale of occupational status.
[3]Metric coefficients multiplied by 1000 for ease of presentation.
[4]Total personal income minus earned income. Metric coefficients were multiplied
 by 1000.
*Coefficients significantly different from 0 at a < .05.

Base income, defined as income from sources other than wages and salaries, has a large and consistent main effect for both men and women. Its effect also differs in core and periphery industries. The main effect is easily understood; those who do not depend heavily on earned income can afford to work less. The interaction with sector is more obscure. Why should base income have a stronger positive effect on weeks not worked for both men and women in core industries? It may be the greater certainty of receiving a private pension in core industries that is operating here. Not only are core workers more likely to retire early or on time and be receiving such pensions, but they may also be anticipating such pensions in scaling down their work involvement before complete retirement.

In sum, we have seen that the importance of incorporating a measure of economic sector into models of retirement is not so much for the main effect it might produce, but for the way in which other variables operate differently in core and periphery industries. Retirement is clearly not a uniform phenomenon, operating in the same way across the economy. Both men and women who work in core firms can anticipate retiring earlier with a greater certainty of receiving a private pension than those who work in periphery firms.

Conclusions

We have attempted to provide some evidence that retirement can be affected by forces outside the individual. In this chapter we have illustrated how one dimension of the structure of Canada's economy can impact upon retirement patterns for men and how conditions prior to retirement can resurface after retirement for both men and women. We also have some evidence to suggest that we require separate models to account for the unique retirement experiences of Canadian women.

The importance of these findings for the individualistic research tradition in retirement indicates that we must consider supraindividual factors or our models of retirement are in danger of being misspecified. This is not to suggest that the political economy perspective is the sole answer to comprehending retirement. Retirement is far too complex not to include both individual and structural features. We simply need to develop the socio-economic and political dimensions to a level at least comparable to those found in individualistic explanations.

Notes

[1] The dual economy theories have developed in opposition to neoclassical economic theories usually labelled the human capital perspective. The human capital perspective subscribes to the view that the socio-economic success of the individual is directly related to the characteristics brought into the market place by the individual worker. Although Walker (1981) alludes to dual economy theory, it was Dowd (1980) who first drew on this theory to supplement the political economy perspective in gerontology.

[2] There are many operational definitions of retirement: a reduction in hours or weeks not worked (Hardy, 1982; Boskin, 1977; McDonald and Wanner, 1984), a reduction in work responsibilities, receipt of social security benefits (Palmore et al., 1982) and a definition of oneself as retired (Health and Welfare Canada, 1977). The measure of retirement used here is number of weeks not worked during the year because it more closely approximates what people do rather than what they say they do (McDonald, 1983).

[3] We note that Statistics Canada collapsed all the manufacturing industries into one category that contains both core and periphery industries. Our results therefore must be interpreted with some caution. Further information about economic assignment is available by writing to the authors.

[4] It must be emphasized that the variables for weeks not worked and wages apply to those men and women who were working between January 1, 1980, and the date of the census in 1981, but retired within this time frame. The results simply support the findings in Tables 1 and 2.

[5] Multiple regression analysis is a widely used technique that estimates the relationship between a continuous dependent variable, weeks not worked in this case, and

one or more independent variables by means of an equation containing a constant representing the value of the dependent variable when all the independent variables equal zero, and a set of regression coefficients, or slopes, representing the number of units the dependent variable changes, on the average, for each unit change in the independent variable. The sign of the regression coefficient indicates the direction of the relationship.

References

Armstrong, P. and H. Armstrong
  1978   *The Double Ghetto.* Toronto: McClelland and Stewart.
Averitt, R.T.
  1968   *The Dual Economy: The Dynamics of American Industry Structure.* New York: Norton.
Baillargeon, R.
  1982   "Determinants of early retirement." *Canada's Mental Health* 30(3):20-22.
Beck, E.M., P.M. Horan and C.M. Tolbert II
  1980   "Stratification in a dual economy: A sectoral model earnings determination." *American Sociological Review* 43:704-720.
Bond, S.L. and J.B. Bond, Jr.
  1980   The impact of a pre-retirement program." *Canadian Counsellor* 14(2):68-71,
Boskin, M.J.
  1977   "Social security and retirement decisions." *Economic Inquiry* 15:1-25.
Connidis, I.
  1982   "Women and retirement: The effect of multiple careers on adjustment." *Canadian Journal on Aging* 1(1):17-27.
Dowd, James J.
  1980   *Stratification Among the Aged.* Monterey, Calif.: Brooks/Cole.
Estes, C.L.
  1979   *The Aging Enterprise.* San Francisco: Jossey-Bass, Inc.
Estes, C.L., J. Swan and L. Gerard
  1982   "Dominant and competing paradigms in gerontology: Towards a political economy of aging." *Ageing and Society* 2:151-164.
Government of Canada
  1983   *Fact Book on Aging in Canada.* Ottawa: Minister of Supply and Services.
Graebner, W.
  1980   *A History of Retirement.* New Haven: Yale University Press.
Guillemard, Anne-Marie
  1977   "The call to activity amongst the old: Rehabilitation or regimentation." Pp. 80-88 in B.T. Wigdor (ed.), *Canadian Gerontological Collection I.* The Canadian Association on Gerontology.
  1980   *La Vieillesse et L'Etat.* Paris: PUF.
  1983   "The making of old age policy in France: Points of debate, issues at stake, underlying social relations." Pp. 75-99 in Anne-Marie Guillemardè (ed.), *Old Age and the Welfare State.* Beverly Hills: Sage.

Hardy, M.A.
1982 "Social policy and determinants of retirement: A longitudinal analysis of old white males, 1969-1975." *Social Forces* 60:1103-1122.

Health and Welfare Canada
1977 *Retirement in Canada: Summary Report.* Social Security Report No. 3. Ottawa: Minister of Supply and Services.

Hodson, R.
1978 "Labour in the monopoly, competitive, and state sectors of production." *Politics and Society* 8:429-490.

Keating, N. and P. Cole
1980 "What do I do with him 24 hours a day? Changes in the housewife role after retirement." *The Gerontologist* 20:84-89.

Keating, N. and J. Marshall
1980 "The process of retirement: The rural self-employed." *The Gerontologist* 20:437-443.

Keating, N. and L.J. Spiller
1983 "Concepts of leisure in retirement: An empirical test." Proceedings of the 3rd Canadian Congress on Leisure Research, Edmonton, Alberta, pp. 567-575.

Krauss, I.
1981 "Individual differences in reactions to retirement." Paper presented at the annual meeting of the Gerontological Society of America, Toronto, November 1981.

Marshall, V.W.
1980 "State of the art lecture: Sociology of aging." Pp. 76-144 in J. Crawford (ed.), *Canadian Gerontological Collection III.* The Canadian Association on Gerontology.

Martin, J.K.
1982 "Social policy concerns related to retirement: Implications for the future." Pp. 154-196 in G.M. Gutman (ed.), *Canada's Changing Age Structure: Implications for the Future.* Burnaby, B.C.: SFU Publications.

Martin Matthews, A., K.H. Brown, C.K. Davis and M.A. Denton
1982 "A crisis assessment technique for the evaluation of life events: Transition to retirement as an example." *Canadian Journal on Aging* 1:28-39.

McDonald, P.L.
1983 "Retirement: A Socioeconomic Analysis." Unpublished doctoral dissertation, Department of Sociology, University of Calgary.

McDonald, P.L. and R.A. Wanner
1982 "Work past age 65 in Canada: A socioeconomic analysis." *Aging and Work* 5:169-180.
1984 "Socioeconomic determinants of early retirement in Canada." *Canadian Journal on Aging* 3:105-116.

McPherson, B. and N. Guppy
1979 "Preretirement lifestyle and the degree of planning for retirement." *Journal of Gerontology* 34:254-263.

McPherson, B.
1980 "Retirement from professional sport: The problems of occupational and psychological adjustment." *Sociological Symposium* 30:126-143.

Myles, J.
1981 "Income inequality and status, maintenance: Concepts, methods and measures." *Research on Aging* 3:123-141.
1984 *Old Age in the Welfare State: The Political Economy of Public Pensions.* Boston: Little, Brown.

O'Neil, M.
1979 "Canada's retirement income system and its impact on women." Pp. 51-94 in G. Gasek (ed.), *Canadian Gerontological Collection II: Retirement Income Systems.* Winnipeg: Canadian Association on Gerontology.

Palmore, E., L. George and G.G. Fillenbaum
1982 "Predictors of retirement." *Journal of Gerontology* 37:733-742.

Phillipson, C.
1983 "The state, the economy and retirement." Pp. 127-139 in Anne-Marie Guillemard (ed.), *Old Age and the Welfare State.* Beverly Hills: Sage.

Prothero, J.
1981 "Retirement expectations and intentions of older workers: Male and female, married and unmarried." Paper presented at the annual meeting of the Gerontological Society of America and the Canadian Association on Gerontology, Toronto, November 1981.

Roadburg, A.
1985 *Aging: Retirement, Leisure and Work in Canada.* Toronto: Methuen.

Shapiro, E.
1982 "Retired and employed elderly persons: Their utilization of health care." *The Gerontologist* 22:187-193.

Spilerman, S.
1977 "Careers, labour market structure and socioeconomic achievement." *American Journal of Sociology* 93:551-593.

Statistics Canada
1976 *Canada's Elderly.* Ottawa: Minister of Supply and Services.

Stones, M.J. and C.A. Kozma
1980 "The components of happiness: Implications for retirement counselling." *Canadian Counsellor* 14:93-96.

Townsend, P.
1981 "The structural dependency of the elderly: Creation of social policy in the twentieth century." *Ageing and Society* 1:5-28.

Tracy, M.B.
1982 "Removing the earnings test for old-age benefits in Canada: The impact on labour supply of men ages 65-69." *Aging and Work* 5:181-190.

Walker, A.
1981 "Towards a political economy of old age." *Ageing and Society* 1:73-94.
1983 "Social policy and elderly people in Great Britain: The construction of dependent social and economic status in old age." Pp. 144-167 in Anne-Marie Guillemard (ed.), *Old Age in the Welfare State.* Beverly Hills: Sage.

Wanner, R.A. and P.L. McDonald
1986 "The vertical mosaic in later life: Ethnicity and retirement in Canada." *Journal of Gerontology*, forthcoming.

V

Family Structure and Social Relationships

As increasing proportions of people live into the later years, the nature of family life changes. Everyone is or has been embedded in some family, and people at all points on the life course are affected by the aging of family members. For this reason, there has been a rich interplay between studies in the area of the family and studies in the social aspects of aging. In everyday affairs, we are accustomed to think of "the family" as a nuclear family of a married couple with a few young children. Gerontologists, however, increasingly focus on three- and even four-generation families and the place of middle-aged and older people in them. The first two chapters in this section, Chapter 15 by Gee and Chapter 16 by Stone and Fletcher, focus on structural changes in the family and in the dwelling unit of some family members, the household.

A major task for social researchers in aging has been to counteract mythology about supposed declines in family life. Among those in the research community, myth destruction has reached the point of acute boredom, yet popular opinion, nourished by the popular media, persists in the view that the family is a social institution near collapse, that family members have abandoned their aged parents and that, compared to earlier times, or some faraway places, North American family life is in bad shape. Such allegations, while not grounded in fact, may have pernicious consequences if used for policy purposes (Aronson, 1985). Rosenthal reviews Canadian evidence about several dimensions of intergenerational family life and finds active relationships between the generations, as indicated by visiting, maintaining other forms of social contact, provision of mutual assistance and moral support. She also points to the need to conceptualize families as complex social units with many members, but she notes the difficulties in doing so.

The family has always provided assistance to its members in need. In recent years, the provision of such assistance to older family members has been referred to as "social support," and this, too, has been a major focus of Canadian social research in aging (see, for example, Chappell, Strain and Blandford, 1986; Krauss, 1984; Storm, Storm and Strike-Schurman, 1985; Wellman and Hall, 1986). Several chapters in this section deal with social-support issues in the family context. It is evident in the "functional solidarity" described by Rosenthal in Chapter 17 and in the social support networks described by Corin in Chapter 19.

Martin Matthews describes a family life-course event experienced by most women and some men: widowhood. Gee notes in Chapter 15 that the average age of widowhood for women in the nineteenth century was in their fifties, whereas today women can expect to experience this event closer to their seventies. In calling widowhood an "expectable life event," she means that it is, compared to many other events experienced by people, relatively scheduled and anticipated. Nonetheless, it is the single event most likely to be experienced as a severe crisis in people's lives (the exception may be dying; while we have not yet managed to secure retrospective data on this event, available data suggest that dying itself is not so severe a crisis [Marshall, 1986]).

Widowhood is an event that triggers a process; it also designates a social status. As Matthews notes, research has focussed more on social supports for people in the status "widowed person" than on changes in the social worlds, including social supports, that accompany the *process* of widowhood. Research is needed to explore more fully the meaning of widowhood as a process in time.

As in earlier sections, the chapters on family structure and social relationships emphasize the importance of the social context in shaping individual experiences. Corin shows that social-support systems in rural areas are not the same as those in urban areas; even a distinction as rural-urban masks other factors such as geographical mobility — a point that Cape also made in Chapter 5. The historical context is also invoked throughout these chapters. For example, Stone and Fletcher identify various living-arrangement passages and suggest that in recent decades the probabilities of experiencing different passages have changed dramatically.

It is always important to consider the historical perspective in which contemporary social patterns have developed, but this may be especially true in the study of aging, where individual lives and relations between the generations have been shaped by history. Surely intergenerational relations and even such single-generational issues as the likelihood of marrying have been affected by the fact that we are a nation of immigrants. Fertility, which for one generation affected the number of children they would have in the later years and for another shaped the number of siblings they would have, was greatly reduced in response to the historical event of the Depression. Increasingly, the family life of older Canadians will be affected by historical changes in divorce legislation that have led to higher divorce rates. These are only selected examples.

While reading the selections about family structure and social relationships, readers should bear in mind that several other selections in the book present data on the family and aging. Marshall discusses health concerns in a family context in Chapter 23, Ujimoto discusses the intersection of family and ethnicity in aging in Chapter 7, and in Chapter 8, Lee discusses a group for whom family life has quite a different character.

References

Aronson, Jane
  1985   "Family care of the elderly: Underlying assumptions and their consequences." *Canadian Journal on Aging* 4 (Autumn) (3):115-125.
Chappell, Neena L., Laurel Strain and A. Blandford
  1986   *Health and Aging: A Social Perspective.* Toronto: Holt, Rinehart and Winston.
Kraus, Arthur S.
  1984   "The burden of care for families of elderly persons with dementia." *Canadian Journal on Aging* 3 (March) (1):45-51.
Marshall, Victor W.
  1986   "A sociological perspective on aging and dying." Chapter 5, Pp 125–146 in V.W. Marshall (ed.), *Later Life: The Social Psychology of Aging. Beverly Hills: Sage.*
Storm, Christine, Thomas Storm and Janet Strike-Schurman
  1985   "Obligations for care: Beliefs in a small Canadian town." *Canadian Journal on Aging* 4 (Summer) (2):75-85.
Wellman, Barry and Alan Hall
  1986   "Social networks and social support: Implications for later life," Ch. 7, pp. 191-231, in Victor W. Marshall (ed.), *Later Life: The Social Psychology of Aging.* Beverly Hills: Sage.

15

Historical Change in the Family Life Course of Canadian Men and Women

Ellen M. Gee
Department of Sociology and
Gerontology Research Centre
Simon Fraser University

The Life Course Perspective

An appreciation of the centrality of age as an important dimension of social structure dates back more than forty years within the discipline of sociology (e.g., Linton, 1942; Parsons, 1942). The changing demographics of Western societies, particularly the increasing proportion of population in the ages 65 and over, led to further sociological interest in old age. In addition, national concerns about the social and economic consequences of population aging resulted in increased funding for social scientific research concerned with the elderly. Thus, the emerging "sociology of aging" focussed its attention on old age.

However, in recent years more emphasis has been placed on the *process* of aging. In this vein, one significant development has been the emergence of the "life course perspective" (e.g., Elder, 1978), itself an offshoot of age stratification theory (Riley et al., 1972). Following Rossi (1980:7), the life course may be defined as "the pathways through the age-differentiated structure in the major role domains of life." These pathways have been studied by researchers in a number of disciplines (including sociology, psychology, demography and history, particularly family history) and, therefore, a variety of theoretical and methodological approaches has been brought to bear on the subject.[1]

From a sociological perspective, two aspects of the life course are important. One is the fact that the pathways that make up the life course are socially created, socially recognized and shared (Hagestad and Neugarten, 1985). The patterning and temporal sequencing of life course pathways are

The author acknowledges support from the Canada Employment and Immigration Challenge '85 Program. Some of the contents of this chapter overlap material presented in "The Life Course of Canadian Women: An Historical and Demographic Analysis," *Social Indicators Research,* forthcoming.

socially regulated (Elder, 1978) and normatively prescribed (Elder and Rockwell, 1976). In other words, the pathways that are experienced by any given population group are not random, but rather are determined, or at least influenced, by the social context in which the population lives.

The second aspect of the life course that is relevant to sociologists concerns the concept of social time. By Elder's (1978) definition, social time refers to the ordering of life course events, and the taking on of social roles, in accordance with age-linked expectations, sanctions and options. One dimension of social time concerns social timetables for life course events or, in other words, transitions to and from major role statuses. Examples of major age-related role transitions include: leaving school, entering (and exiting from) the paid labour force, entering (and exiting from) marriage, the birth of one's first child. Preferred social timetables (e.g., the "best" age to get married, the "best" age to start a family) are erected and, as such, structure the individual's relationship to major social institutions (Neugarten and Datan, 1973). Given that timetables are socially erected, as societies change so does the temporal patterning of life course transitions.

One way to approach the study of the life course is to examine the demographic dimensions of age-related life events and transitions. This approach is taken here, with a particular focus upon historical change in the *occurrence* and *timing* of significant family life events.[2] The relevant questions are: Has the occurrence of a given life event become more or less common over time? Has the age at which a given transition occurs decreased or increased over time? What social, economic and/or historical factors can account for changes in occurrence and timing?

This approach to the study of the life course has been employed in a developing body of American research over the past ten years or so. Representative research in this tradition includes the work of Elder and Rockwell (1976), Glick (1977), Hogan (1981), Modell et al. (1976), Uhlenberg (1974, 1978) and Winsborough (1979). In Canada only one study exists (Rodgers and Witney, 1981).

Methodological Issues

The source of information is aggregate data provided in Canadian censuses and Vital Statistics publications.[3] Due to the nature of the data bases, two types of analysis are performed: *cohort analysis*, in which the differential life course experiences of real cohorts of persons, as traced through successive censuses, are compared; and *synthetic cohort analysis*, in which the differential life course experiences of hypothetical cohorts are constructed from cross-sectional, age specific data. The choice of technique is determined solely by data availability. In the tables that are presented, the term "birth cohort" signifies that cohort analysis has been used; the term "approximate birth cohort" indicates that a synthetic technique has been employed.

Each approach has certain inherent problems. Cohort analysis contains the problem of selective change in the composition of the cohort over time. For example, the birth cohort of 1901 will not consist of identical persons, as it is traced over time in successive censuses. By 1951, for instance, some of the birth cohort will have died and some will have left Canada. In addition, some of the 50-year-olds (in 1951) will consist of immigrants. To the degree that death, in-migration and outmigration are selective for certain characteristics, some of the changes observed to have occurred to the cohort between 1901 and 1951 will not be "real" changes, but rather, will be the result of changes in the social composition of the cohort over time. Particularly relevant to this study is that to the degree that various cohorts are altered over time by different levels of mortality, in-migration and out-migration, intercohort comparisons are affected.

Another problem in cohort analysis is that data relevant to recently born cohorts do not exist. Young persons simply have not lived long enough to experience the whole range of life course events. For example, it is obvious that the cohort born in 1961 is not old enough to have experienced grand-parenthood. The fact that intercohort comparisons are affected by incomplete data for younger cohorts limits the usefulness of cohort analysis for the purposes here.

Synthetic cohort analysis involves the artificial construction of cohorts, using cross-sectional, age-specific data as the basis for the construction. It is based on the assumption that any given set of age-specific rates for a particular behaviour or event is constant over time. To the degree that this assumption is not met, synthetic cohort analysis creates biased estimates. This approach has an advantage over cohort analysis, however, in that estimates of the life course experiences of a wider range of cohorts are possible (within the limitations of the assumption of constancy).

The synthetic cohort approach actually involves a wide range of techniques, depending upon the particular life course event being examined and upon the way the aggregate data are presented in government publications. For general readability, and because readers will vary in their interest in methodological issues, the specific details of the techniques employed are described in the Appendix.

Another set of methodological issues concerns data availability. As one moves back in time, less and less data are available for analysis. In order to present as complete a picture as possible on historical changes in the life course, some of the earlier data presented are estimates only, based on various assumptions. In a similar vein, data for more recent cohorts are also unavailable, because of the above-noted fact that young people have not lived long enough to experience the gamut of life course events. For these more recently born cohorts, projections are provided. Details of the procedures used for the estimations and the projections are provided in the Appendix.

Related to data availability is the fact that geographical coverage of the Canadian population, as provided in censuses, is not uniform over time. The first census after Confederation (1871) enumerated only Ontario, Quebec, New Brunswick and Nova Scotia. In 1881, Prince Edward Island, Manitoba and British Columbia were included, as well, and in 1891, what are now Saskatchewan and Alberta were added. Newfoundland is covered in the censuses from 1951 onwards.

Lastly, the analysis of the timing of family life events here focusses on cohort comparisons of *average* ages at which life course events are experienced. While such information is valuable in itself, it is important to keep in mind that variations exist (in terms of both individuals and subgroups) and one must avoid making the assumption that any cohort is homogeneous with regard to the occurrence and timing of life course transitions (Hogan, 1985).

The Occurrence of Family Life Events

We will first examine historical changes in the occurrence of family life events. Here the relevant questions are: what proportion of a cohort experiences a given family-related event, and how have the proportions changed over time?

Changing mortality

A necessary first step to an understanding of the changing life course of Canadian men and women lies in an appreciation of the major mortality reductions that have occurred. That life expectancy has increased dramatically in the past 100-150 years is well-known. These improvements mean that increasingly larger percentages of birth cohorts can expect to live long enough to experience the full range of life course events. Simply put, one of the most significant changes that has occurred in the life course over time is the increased probability of surviving to ages at which one is at least "eligible" to take on, or exit from, age-related roles.

Let us assume that age 20, age 45 and age 65 are "marker" ages: age 20 is the minimum age for life course changes relating to marriage and family formation; age 45 represents middle age and a reduction in child rearing responsibilities; and age 65 marks the commencement of old age and retirement.[4] We can then ask the question: what changes have occurred in the likelihood that numbers of a birth cohort will survive to these three "marker" ages?

Table 1 presents data relevant to this question for male and female synthetic cohorts born from 1831 to 1981. Of 1,000 persons born in 1831, approximately two-thirds would survive to age 20, approximately one-half to age 45 and substantially less than one-third to age 65. In other words,

TABLE 1:
Survivorship at Ages 20, 45 and 65, Canada, 1831-1981

Males:

Synthetic Cohort	0	Number Alive at Age: 20	45	65
1831	1000	640	472	266
1841	1000	648	492	286
1851	1000	653	503	297
1861	1000	654	544	305
1871	1000	674	522	311
1881	1000	698	554	338
1891	1000	701	561	346
1901	1000	742	609	386
1911	1000	786	663	435
1921	1000	837	721	486
1930-32	1000	862	780	587
1940-42	1000	900	829	619
1950-52	1000	934	879	658
1960-62	1000	953	905	688
1970-72	1000	964	914	700
1980-82	1000	977	935	747

Females:

1831	1000	650	480	302
1841	1000	661	506	328
1851	1000	668	520	342
1861	1000	669	529	354
1871	1000	661	543	361
1881	1000	716	576	391
1891	1000	718	584	401
1901	1000	762	636	448
1911	1000	807	693	504
1921	1000	857	751	557
1930-32	1000	885	794	617
1940-42	1000	920	854	682
1950-52	1000	950	910	755
1960-62	1000	967	940	809
1970-72	1000	976	949	831
1980-82	1000	985	965	861

SOURCES: For 1831-1921; Bourbeau et Légaré (1982); for 1930-32 to 1980-82; Canadian Life Tables.

high mortality levels meant that large numbers of persons simply did not live long enough to experience many life course events. The situation today is radically different. The vast majority of persons survive to ages 20 and 45, and a large percentage (approximately 86 percent of females and 75 percent of males) are alive at age 65.

For all cohorts, women are more likely than men to be alive at the "marker" ages. The female survival advantage increases substantially over time, particularly at age 65. Indeed, it is a well-established fact that the large and increasing female advantage in life expectancy that has occurred in this century results, in the main, from substantial reductions in the mortality of older women relative to that of older men. Research attempting to explicate the sex differential in mortality that favours females includes work by Enterline (1961), Gee and Veevers (1983), Graney (1979), Harrison (1978), Lopez and Ruzicka (1983), Retherford (1975) and Waldron (1976). For the purposes here, the main point is that women's greater survivorship, which is evident in the early cohorts and which becomes more pronounced for later cohorts, means that women have a greater probability of experiencing life course events than do men.

Marriage

A major family life course event is that of marriage, representing an irreversible role change. Once an individual leaves the state of the never married (or singlehood), it is impossible to return to it. When the marriage ends, individuals take on a new role status associated with either widowhood or divorce.

Of course, marriage represents much more than an "irreversible role change." When a marriage occurs, a new economic unit is created, the living arrangements of two people are significantly altered, new kinship ties are formed and a socially approved unit for childbearing and child rearing is established.

Given the significant social and individual consequences of marriage, it is important to know the extent of historical change in the proportion of cohorts who experience this life course event (at least once) and, conversely, the proportion who never marry. Demographers typically measure extent of marriage by examining census data on the percentage of the population that is ever married, and never married, at ages 45-49. As it is rare for first marriages to occur after the age of 50, this measure provides a reasonably accurate estimate of the extent to which persons in a cohort experience the role transition into marriage.

As can be seen in Table 2, the majority of persons in all cohorts marry. The overall trend over time is for marriage to become an increasingly universal life event. For cohorts born between 1862 and 1906, a rather high incidence of nonmarriage occurred, with approximately 14 percent of males and 11 percent of females never marrying. From a global perspective, these percentages are very high, but they are in line with the experience of European and European-origin populations. As first pointed out by Hajnal (1965), European populations, particularly Western European populations, were characterized by a substantial proportion of persons never marrying (often exceeding 15 percent), a pattern that is believed to have commenced in the seventeenth century and that lasted until the 1940s. In contrast, in societies of non-Western European origin, less than 5 percent of the population never marries.

TABLE 2:
Percent Ever Married and Never Married at Ages 45-49

Census Year*	Birth Cohort	Ever Married** Males	Females	Never Married Males	Females
		%	%	%	%
1881	1832-1836	90.8	88.7	9.2	11.3
1891	1842-1846	90.3	90.6	9.7	9.4
1911	1862-1866	84.9	88.0	15.1	12.0
1921	1872-1876	85.9	88.9	14.1	11.1
1931	1882-1886	86.0	89.7	14.0	10.3
1941	1892-1896	85.8	88.8	14.2	11.2
1951	1902-1906	86.9	88.3	13.1	11.7
1961	1912-1916	89.5	90.5	10.5	9.5
1971	1922-1926	90.9	93.0	9.1	7.0
1981	1932-1936	92.5	94.2	7.5	5.8

* No data are available for 1901.
** Consists of married, divorced, separated and widowed at census year.

SOURCES: Computed from data presented in censuses of Canada: 1881 (v. 4, Table G); 1891 (v. 4, Table H); 1921 (v. 2, Table 29); 1931 (v. 3, Table 12); 1941 (v. 3, Table 7); 1951 (v. 2, Table 1); 1971 (cat. 92-730, Table 1); 1981 (cat. 29-901, Table 5).

The reasons for such high levels of nonmarriage are far from clear, but a number of possible causal factors has been suggested. These include: Western family and kinship systems, which encompass the norm of independent household formation upon marriage; a nonlineage kinship system with a corresponding reduced social pressure to marry; nonpartible inheritance (nondivision of land over generations) that makes marriage more difficult for children not inheriting land; and the Christian religion, with the Protestant emphasis upon individualism and the Catholic implicit acceptance of nonmarriage through its idealization of celibacy for church personnel (Gee, 1982).

The trend away from high rates of nonmarriage becomes evident in the 1961 data, i.e., the data relating to cohorts born between 1912 and 1916. These persons would have come to prime marriage age around 1940; thus the Canadian experience is in keeping with that of other populations originating in Western Europe. Further, rather marked declines in never marriage occur among the cohorts born in 1922-26 and 1932-36. These cohorts reached young adulthood in the prosperous post-World War II years, a time when marriage would be "easy" from a financial point of view. This is particularly so for the cohort 1932-36 (the Depression cohort), whose financial prospects in adulthood were particularly favourable given the competitive advantage in the labour market provided by its small size.

While comparative information on more recently born cohorts cannot be provided until they have reached ages 45-49, some speculations can be offered, at least for the baby boom cohorts of 1946-1961. These cohorts have experienced the twin economic disadvantages of a declining economy and a high degree of job competition due to their large size. Therefore, it can be expected that their level of nonmarriage will increase due to these economic factors, coupled with a perhaps related increased social acceptance of "living together." But will it increase to the level experienced by earlier cohorts of Canadians? In 1981, 15.0 percent of males and 10.4 percent of females aged 30-34 (the cohort of 1947-51, the leading edge of the baby boom) had never married.[5] Given that these never-marrieds have another 15 years in which to marry, it would appear that their eventual levels of never-marriage will not be as high as those of the cohorts born between 1912 and 1916.

Childbearing

Becoming a parent is an important life course event. As with leaving singlehood, leaving the state of childlessness is an irreversible role change (except in rare instances), especially for women. Fertility (the production of children) has significant consequences for both individuals and societies. From the point of view of the individual, parenthood signifies a major change in lifestyle, the taking on of major responsibilities, significant investments in time and energy (particularly for mothers), reallocations in household expenditures and the positive experiences associated with child rearing. From the point of view of the society, fertility is a major factor involved in the rate of population growth and in determining the age structure of the population.

What changes have occurred in the proportion of cohorts of Canadian women[6] who have made the transition into parenthood? This question can be answered by examining trends in the incidence of childlessness among ever married women in the postreproductive ages.

Although there is some variation, generally for cohorts born before 1916, the percentage of ever married women who remained childless is in the range of 13-15 percent. The percentage is particularly high (over 15 percent) for women born between 1902 and 1911, women whose childbearing was undoubtedly affected by their historical location in time, i.e., these cohorts reached prime childbearing ages during the Depression.

TABLE 3:
Percent of Childless Ever Married Women

Census Year	Birth Cohorts	Percent Childless
1941	1861-1876	12.8
1941	1877-1886	13.2
1941	1887-1896	12.3
1961	1897-1901	14.6
1961	1902-1906	15.5
1961	1907-1911	15.3
1961	1912-1916	13.1
1971	1917-1921	11.8
1971	1922-1926	9.6
1981	1927-1931	8.4
1981	1932-1936	7.2

SOURCES: Computed from data presented in Canadian censuses: 1941 (v. 2, Table 51); 1961 (cat. 98-507, Table G1); 1971 (cat. 92-718, Table 24); 1981 (cat. 92-906, Table 7).

The incidence of childlessness steadily declines among the cohorts born after 1922 to the degree that the percent of childless ever married women among the cohort of 1932-36 is approximately one-half that of earlier cohorts of women. These more recently born cohorts (i.e., the cohorts born between 1922 and 1936) are the mothers of the baby boom. Hence one aspect of the baby boom was a pronounced trend away from historically established levels of childlessness.

Accounting for trends in childlessness is a complex task, given that the causes of childlessness are twofold, both voluntary and involuntary. It has been estimated that the incidence of involuntary childlessness (i.e., sterility) among Canadian women aged 30-44 in 1961 was approximately 5 percent and that some decreases have occurred over time, due largely to improvements in medical treatment (Veevers, 1972). The levels of childlessness observed for Canadian women, particularly for cohorts born before 1921, are significantly higher than this figure of 5 percent. Even allowing for increases in sterility as one moves back in time, it seems that childlessness was deliberately chosen by some portion of Canadian women throughout the century. Indeed, Veevers (1972) estimates that about 50 percent of childlessness is voluntary, and that this proportion has remained relatively constant over time. It appears that Canadian society, although evaluating childlessness negatively, provided avenues such that some percentage of ever-married women could exercise the option of remaining childless. This finding has been reported for the American population, as well (Tolnay and Guest, 1982). However, it must be kept in mind that higher rates of widowhood at young ages in the past played some role in inflating the incidence of non-sterility-related childlessness.

The levels of childlessness experienced by the cohorts of women who produced the baby boom are exceptionally low. Keeping in mind that some women are married to sterile men, and assuming that sterile women and sterile men do not deliberately seek out one another as marriage partners, virtually every ever-married woman in a union that was not sterile produced at least one child. For reasons that are not clear, voluntary childlessness among these cohorts was virtually nonexistent.

Canadian women currently under the age of 35 exhibit relatively high rates of childlessness (Grindstaff, 1984). These data may indicate trends towards increased childlessness, later childbearing, or both. Experts generally agree that permanent childlessness among today's young women will be in the range of 15 to 20 percent (Veevers, 1985). However, some American researchers predict that as many as 30 percent of recent cohorts of (white) American women will remain permanently childless (e.g., Bloom and Pebley, 1982). If the figure is around 15 percent, the level of childlessness will return to the "traditional" level in Canada; if the figure exceeds 20 percent, childlessness will be higher than experienced by earlier cohorts of women. Factors conducive to increased *voluntary* childlessness include: more effective contraception (including sterilization and abortion); expanded opportunities for women in modern society; and difficult economic times (Grindstaff, 1984). *Involuntary* childlessness may rise due to factors such as: increased incidence of pelvic inflammatory disease, associated with both IUD use and a greater frequency of sexual partners; lower sperm counts, possibly associated with environmental factors such as pesticides; lower fecundity due to prolonged "pill" use; and lower fecundity resulting from delay (Veevers, 1985). However, it is widely held that childlessness will be largely the result of choice (e.g., Bloom and Pebley, 1982; Poston and Kramer, 1981).

Another important dimension of the life course concerns the *number* of children that are born. It is well-known that Canadian fertility has declined substantially. Indeed, this fertility decline is *the* major cause of population aging.

In assessing the magnitude of Canadian fertility decline, both a synthetic cohort measure (the Total Fertility Rate, which gives the number of children that 1,000 women [all marital statuses combined] would bear by the end of their reproductive years if they bore children throughout their lives at the rates observed in a given year) and a cohort measure (the number of children ever born to 1,000 ever married women by the end of their reproductive years) are available. (See the Appendix for further explanation.)

TABLE 4:
Canadian Fertility Trends

(A) TOTAL FERTILITY RATES (per 1,000 women)

Census Year	Approximate Birth Cohorts	Rate
1851	1817-1831	6,562
1861	1827-1841	5,858
1871	1837-1851	5,513
1881	1847-1861	4,975
1891	1857-1871	4,575
1901	1867-1881	4,644
1911	1877-1891	4,396
1921	1887-1901	3,536
1931	1897-1911	3,200
1941	1907-1921	2,832
1951	1917-1931	3,503
1961	1927-1941	3,840
1971	1937-1951	2,187
1981	1947-1961	1,704

(B) NUMBER OF CHILDREN EVER BORN (Per 1,000 ever married women)

Census Year	Birth Cohorts	Number of Children
1941	1861-1876	4,818
1941	1877-1886	4,398
1941	1887-1896	4,167
1961	1897-1901	3,650
1961	1902-1906	3,385
1961	1907-1911	3,154
1961	1912-1916	3,110
1971	1917-1921	3,189
1971	1922-1926	3,315
1981	1927-1931	3,407
1981	1932-1936	3,260

SOURCES: For Total Fertility Rates: 1851-1911, see Appendix; Vital Statistics, 1971 and 1981 (cat. 84-204).
For Children Ever Born: Canadian censuses, 1941 (v. 2, Table 51); 1961 (cat. 98-507, Table G1); 1971 (cat. 92-718, Table 24); 1981 (cat. 92-906, Table 7).

Although the two measures are not strictly comparable, they both indicate the major decreases that have occurred in the number of children that cohorts of women have borne (See Table 4). The Total Fertility Rates cover a greater time period and therefore illustrate more dramatically declines in family size. The cohorts of 1817-31 bore about 6.6 children per woman whereas the cohorts of 1947-61 are expected to bear approximately 1.7 children per woman — a decrease of approximately 75 percent. The cohort measure captures only part of the picture of fertility decline, in that data for the high-fertility early cohorts are not available and the substantial fertility decline of cohorts born after 1936 are not indicated. The two measures also share in indicating the interruption in fertility decline that occurred during the baby boom years. However, it will be noted that the Total Fertility Rate exaggerates this fertility increase.

The overall decline in children born results from the significant changes that have occurred in Canadian society in the past 100-150 years. While space does not allow a detailed examination, a number of interrelated factors can be identified: (a) significant urbanization, which affects the role of children in society, decreasing their economic utility; (b) the emergence and development of a modern economic structure requiring a skilled labour force and thus an extended period of education for children, thereby increasing the costs of child rearing; (c) increased female labour force participation and opportunities for women outside the home, which compete with child rearing; (d) increased levels of education that function to enhance the individual's sense of self and to create people who are more willing, and able, to exercise control over their lives; (e) increasing secularization of society; and (f) increasingly effective contraception, which operates to facilitate smaller family size. As a result of these factors, childbearing and child rearing comprise a much smaller component of the life course than in the past.

Divorce

The rate of divorce in Canada has increased markedly since the liberalization of legal access to divorce in 1968. We have little hard data on the extent of marital breakdown prior to this because: (1) inaccurate data have been provided in vital statistics publications and censuses (Nagnur, 1985); and (2) the difficulty in obtaining a divorce prior to 1968 masked the number of marriages that had broken down in fact if not in law.

Given severe data problems, it is not possible to perform either cohort or synthetic cohort analysis on the life course event of divorce. However, preliminary findings from the Canadian Family History Survey (see note 3) can shed some light on the changing incidence of divorce (Cohn, 1985). Ten percent of Canadians aged 50-64 in 1984 (cohorts of 1920-34) and approximately 15 percent of Canadians aged 30-49 (cohorts of 1935-54) have ever been divorced. These figures reflect an increase in the incidence of divorce among younger cohorts. Yet even among the younger cohorts, the vast majority of people who get married stay married.

The Timing of Family Life Events

One of the major dimensions of the life course is social timetables. Here the concern is with changes that have occurred in the *ages* at which people experience major life course events or role transitions. In turning to this issue, it is important to keep in mind that a sizeable (and variable) minority of cohort members do not ever experience the role transitions we will be discussing here.

Table 5 provides an overview of changes that have occurred in the average ages at which cohorts of Canadian men and women experience the following: age at first marriage; age at birth of first and last child; age at which parents experience the departure of their last child ("empty nest"); and age at widowhood (women only). These data should be viewed as approximates only; the various assumptions made and techniques employed in the calculations are detailed in the Appendix.

For both men and women, significant declines have occurred in age at first marriage. The relatively old age at marriage experienced by cohorts born in the nineteenth century is in keeping with the high percentage of persons never married (see Table 2); both are characteristic of the European marriage pattern (Gee, 1982; Hajnal, 1965). This marriage pattern, termed "restrictive" (van de Walle, 1968), was abandoned when economic and social change made it possible. As argued by Gee (1980:462), an important change occurring in this century affecting lowered age at marriage is increased female labour force participation. Greater proportions of women in the paid labour force have affected the desirability and the feasibility of marriage. The desirability of marriage is a function of the availability of socially rewarding options to marriage (Dixon, 1971). Presumably, increased female labour force participation provides more options for women outside of the traditional sphere of the home. However, given that women working outside the home are concentrated in low-wage clerical and service jobs, their labour force participation has *not* led to a situation in which the worker role is a viable (i.e., socially rewarding) alternative to the wife role for many women. Rather, the occupational role has become supplemental to the familial role — this incorporation of roles implies a loss of alternatives to marriage. The fusion of the worker and familial roles for women has resulted in an opportunity structure that makes marriage *more* desirable by removing, or at least obscuring, alternatives to it.

While the increased labour force participation of women has indirectly, and perhaps paradoxically, operated to increase marriage desirability, it has also functioned to affect the feasibility of marriage. It is more economically

TABLE 5:
Median Ages at Family Life Course Events

				Approximate Birth Cohorts								
	1831-1840	1841-1850	1851-1860	1861-1870	1881-1890	1891-1900	1901-1910	1911-1920	1921-1930	1931-1940	1941-1950	1951-1960
Females:												
Median Age at:												
First Marriage	25.1	26.0	24.9	24.3	25.1	23.4	23.3	23.0	22.0	21.1	21.3	22.5
First Birth	27.1	28.0	26.9	26.3	27.1	25.4	25.0	25.4	23.5	22.9	23.3	24.5
Last Birth	41.0	40.0	38.2	36.2	36.2	33.9	29.1	28.8	29.5	29.1	26.7	26.3
Empty Nest*	61.0	60.1	58.2	56.2	56.2	53.9	49.1	48.8	49.5	49.1	46.7	46.3
Widowhood	58.2	59.5	58.9	58.3	60.1	59.4	61.3	63.0	67.0	67.2	68.8	69.9
Males:												
Median Age at:												
First Marriage	27.9	29.1	29.2	28.0	28.5	28.4	27.0	26.3	24.3	24.0	23.5	24.6
First Birth	29.9	31.1	31.2	30.0	30.5	30.4	28.7	28.7	25.8	25.8	25.5	26.6
Last Birth	43.8	43.1	42.5	39.9	39.6	38.9	32.8	32.1	31.8	32.0	28.9	28.4
Empty Nest*	63.8	63.1	62.5	59.9	59.6	58.9	52.8	52.1	51.8	52.0	48.9	48.4

* Age at which last child is 20 years old.

SOURCES: See Appendix.

feasible to marry, and to marry at younger ages, when two incomes contribute to the setting up of the new household.

There is a slight trend towards older age at first marriage for recent cohorts. Increased incidence of "living together," economic recession and normative change are likely contributing factors. However, it must be kept in mind that age at first marriage remains young when viewed historically.

Age at first birth has declined over time, generally paralleling the declines in age at first marriage. Among cohorts of the nineteenth century, median age at birth of first child for women was about 27; for men, approximately 30. Median age at first birth reached an all time low (22.9 for women) among the cohorts of 1931-40, the mothers of the baby boom, a combination of young age at marriage and a short interval between marriage and first birth. Indeed, decreased age at marriage and accelerated childbearing are major factors accounting for the baby boom (Gee, 1978, 1980; Henripin and Légaré, 1971).

As with age at first marriage, there is a slight increase in average age at first birth among recent cohorts. While much has been made in recent years of delayed parenthood, most people continue to have their first child at relatively young ages (24.5 years for women, 26.6 years for men). Only a two-year interval exists between age at marriage and age at birth of the first child for the most recent cohort. The majority of people who have children continue to have them early in marriage. It seems likely that a class phenomenon is involved: the people who are delaying childbearing are the well-educated, successful middle class — a highly visible and publicized minority.

Age at last birth has decreased dramatically over time. For cohorts born in the middle of the nineteenth century, the last child was born to women when they were approximately 40; for men, the comparable figure is 43. A virtually steady decline over cohorts can be observed, so that for the most recent cohort, the average age for women is 26.3, and for men, 28.4. While decreasing age at marriage is partially responsible for this trend, the major factor involved in declines is the number of children people have, in conjunction with a childbearing pattern in which children are born early in marriage and spaced closely.

The data concerning age at "empty nest," calculated by simply adding 20 years to the age at which the last child is born (and assuming that all last-born children survive to age 20), illustrate the same substantial declines as do the data on age at birth of last child. Whereas cohorts born in the middle of the last century were approximately 60 when the last child left home, this experience is now expected to occur to people in their mid to late forties. This represents a fundamental change in the life course of Canadians, particularly Canadian women. The author has estimated that for female cohorts born between 1831 and 1840, 90 percent of the years lived after marriage were spent rearing dependent children; the comparable figure for the cohorts of 1951-60 is 40 percent. Davis and van den Oever (1982), noting a similar trend among the American population, have argued that the diminution of childbearing and child rearing in women's lives has played a major catalytic role in the feminist movement and in changing gender roles.

The average age at which women become widows has increased quite substantially over time. Whereas women born in the nineteenth century would become widows in their late fifties, their present-day counterparts can expect to be nearly 70 before this life course event occurs. While a narrowing in the male/female gap in age at marriage is partially responsible for this trend, the major factor involved is increased longevity.

Conclusions

The life course perspective, in conjunction with a variety of demographic techniques, provides an overview of the changes and continuities in family-related life events among Canadian men and women.

Major *changes* include the following:

1. Major reductions in mortality have made it increasingly possible for members of birth cohorts to experience age-related family life course events.
2. An increased propensity to marry and to marry at younger ages is evident. Early cohorts of Canadian men and women display the characteristics of the "restrictive" European marriage pattern. In concert with other European-origin populations, this pattern has been abandoned for earlier and more universal marriage. While there has been a recent trend towards later marriage, the median age at marriage for both men and women remains young when viewed with a historical lens.
3. A trend away from childlessness occurs among ever married women, particularly for cohorts born between 1922 and 1936. It is speculated that the incidence of childlessness will return to, and probably exceed, earlier levels, and that the increase will result largely from voluntary factors.
4. Substantial declines in fertility can be observed. A significantly smaller proportion of adult life is devoted to child rearing responsibilities. The median age at birth of the last child decreases dramatically over cohorts, as does the median age at "empty nest."
5. A large increase occurs in the median age at which women become widows, largely the result of improvements in longevity.
   Major *continuities* include:
1. The majority of Canadian men and women marry. There is no trend away from the institution of marriage.
2. There is a continuing trend for married couples who have children to do so early in marriage and to space their children closely. The recent trend

towards delayed child rearing appears to be characteristic of a highly visible minority.

3. While divorce has increased since the legal changes instituted in 1968, the vast majority of Canadian men and women who marry do not divorce.

4. The majority of women can expect to become widows. Indeed, increasing sex differentials in life expectancy favouring women suggest an intensification of this phenomenon.

Last, this analysis points to the atypical life course experience of the cohorts who produced the baby boom. From a historical perspective, they display a young age at first marriage, a low incidence of never marrying, an extremely low incidence of childlessness and a short interval between marriage and birth of the first child. It is easy, even tempting, to look at today's trends in family life course behaviour in light of the experience of these atypical cohorts (who are, for many of us, our parents) and thereby *exaggerate* trends away from marriage, childlessness and early childbearing within marriage. If we cast our net further back, however, the resulting overview of the family life course of Canadians allows for a more accurate, historically based assessment of change.

Notes

1   In psychology, the focus has been on the study of the "life span" rather than the "life course." This difference in terminology reflects an important difference in intellectual focus. Psychologists studying the life span have been concerned with intrapsychic changes that occur to individuals as they age. Sociologists studying the life course have directed their attention to the social determinants of age-related transitions (Hagestad and Neugarten, 1985).

2   Another approach is to focus upon existing variations, rather than historical changes, in the occurrence and timing of age-related events.

3   Another way to study historical change in age-related transitions is to analyse data collected from individuals regarding their life course. In February 1984, Statistics Canada conducted the Family History Survey, which collected retrospective information from 14,000 men and women aged 18-64 concerning the occurrence and timing of family life events. However, at this writing, the survey has yet to be released to nongovernment researchers.

4   These three ages are arbitrarily chosen. Socially created and socially approved "marker" ages, and even the concept itself, are historically and culturally specific. Societies vary in the meaningfulness of such a concept to their members, and within societies in which the concept is relevant, the "marker" ages can change over time.

5   The high percentage of never married women aged 30-34 in 1981 may reflect, to

some degree, what has been termed the "marriage squeeze." These women, born between 1947 and 1951, would typically marry men older than themselves by approximately three years (i.e., the cohorts of 1944-48). As many of these men were born before the baby boom, this cohort of women faces a shortage of available mates.

6   While it is obvious that men are parents, as well, data on fertility are provided in government publications for women only. Therefore this discussion is limited to the fertility of women.

Appendix

Table 1

Life tables are constructed from age-specific mortality data for a given year (or the average of a three-year period). Thus the data relating to any given year contain the assumption that persons born in that year will die off at each age according to the schedule of age-specific death rates experienced during that year. For more information on life tables and their construction, see Barclay (1958), Bogue (1969) and Shryock, Siegel, and Associates (1973).

Table 2

The percentages are computed from data on marital status by age and sex given in Canadian censuses and projected backwards to the appropriate birth cohort. In the 1881 and 1891 censuses, the data are aggregated in ten-year age categories; Aitkens iterative procedure (Shryock, Siegel and Associates, 1973:684) is used to interpolate the data into five-year age categories (i.e., ages 45-49).

Table 3

The percentages are computed from data on number of children ever born to ever married women as provided in the censuses of 1941, 1961, 1971 and 1981. (The census of 1951 does not provide this information.) The data pertaining to a given cohort are sometimes available in successive censuses, e.g., the percent of childlessness among the cohort of 1912-16 appears in the 1961 census (when the women were aged 45-49), in the 1971 census (when they were aged 55-59) and in the 1981 census (when they were aged 65-69). There are small differences in the percentages reported in the three censuses (13.1 percent childless in 1961; 14.5 percent childless in 1971; 14.0 percent in 1981). These differences are due largely to the fact that the composition of the cohort changed somewhat over the years due to mortality and migration effects (although census error is probably partially involved, as well). In order to minimize the distorting effects of mortality and migration, data for the earliest period (in this case 1961) are presented in the table.

The data extracted from the 1961, 1971 and 1981 censuses relate to cohorts of five-year widths. In the 1941 census, the data for women aged 45-64 are aggregated into ten-year categories; hence the cohorts are of a ten-year width. Data for the oldest ages are aggregated at 65 and over in the 1941 census; the assumption made here is that 65 and over is equivalent to 65-80, and hence, the data relate to the cohorts of 1861-76.

Table 4

(a) The Total Fertility Rate (TFR) provides an estimate of the average number of children that 1,000 women, regardless of marital status, will have if they bear children at the age-specific rates observed in a given year. The assumption made here is that the TFR for a given year corresponds most closely to the fertility experience of women aged 20-34 (i.e., the chief childbearing ages) in that year. Thus the TFR for 1981 is assumed to correspond to the fertility of cohorts born between 1947 and 1961. Any fertility differences within these cohorts, therefore, are masked.

The TFRs for 1921-1981 are extracted from Vital Statistics publications. For 1851-1911, the TFRs are computed using Bogue's (1969:661) formula for the estimation of the TFR from the crude birth rate. The crude birth rates used are those estimated by Gee (1978).

(b) Data on number of children ever born to ever married women are provided in the censuses of 1941, 1961, 1971 and 1981. The data pertaining to a given cohort are sometimes available in successive censuses, e.g., the number of children ever born for the cohort 1912-16 appears in the 1961 census (when the women were aged 45-49, in the 1971 census (when they were aged 55-59) and in the 1981 census (when they were aged 65-69). There are slight differences in the number of children ever born to 1,000 ever married women in the three censuses (3,110 in 1961; 3,039 in 1971; 3,131 in 1981). As noted in the comments to Table 3, these differences are due to mortality and migration effects. In order to minimize these effects, data for the earliest period (in this case 1961) are presented in the table.

The data taken from the 1961, 1971 and 1981 censuses relate to cohorts of five-year widths. In the 1941 census, the data for women aged 45-64 are aggregated into ten-year age categories; hence the cohorts are of a ten-year width. Data for the oldest ages are aggregated as 65 and over in the 1941 census; the assumption made here is that 65 and over is equivalent to 65-80, and hence the data relate to the cohorts of 1861-76.

Table 5

(a) Median age at first marriage: data for the cohorts 1831 through to 1890 are singulate mean ages at first marriage calculated using Hajnal's (1953) technique, which utilizes data on marital status by age and sex provided in a given census, and the figures are projected backwards to the appropriate cohort. Data for the cohorts 1891 to 1910 are median ages at first marriage calculated by taking the average of (1) data on all marriages by single age of bride and groom and (2) the singulate mean age at marriage projected backwards. Data for the remaining cohorts are median ages at first marriage as provided in Vital Statistics publications and projecting backwards (e.g., the median age at first marriage for women in 1981 was 22.5, and it is assumed that this figure most closely corresponds to the cohort 1951-1960, women aged 21-30 in 1981).

(b) Median age at first birth: For female cohorts 1901 through to 1960, the figures are computed by applying the standard formula (Shryock, Siegel and Associates, 1973:476) to age-birth order-specific fertility rates provided in Vital Statistics publications, and projecting backwards to the appropriate cohort. For the corresponding male cohorts, the interval between age at first marriage and age at first birth found for females is applied. For earlier cohorts (male and female), a two-year interval between age at first marriage and age at first birth is assumed.

(c) Median age at last birth: For female cohorts 1901 through to 1960, the figures are computed by estimating the average age at first and subsequent births (using the formula provided by Shryock, Siegel and Associates (1973:476)) and applying the Total Fertility Rate. For the corresponding male cohorts, the interval between first and last births calculated for females is applied. For earlier female cohorts, a 2.5-year interval between each birth between first and last is assumed (Potter, 1963), and the appropriate Total Fertility Rate applied. For the corresponding male cohorts, the interval between first and last birth found for females is applied.

(d) Median age at "empty nest": For all cohorts, 20 years is added to the age at birth of the last child. (While 18 years is the more commonly used figure, it is felt that 20 years more accurately reflects real-life family situations.) No childhood mortality is taken into account; it is assumed that the last-born child survives to age 20.

(e) Median age at widowhood: Assuming that (1) all women outlive their husbands, (2) no divorce occurs and (3) the mortality experience of married men is not significantly different from that of nonmarried men, the median age at widowhood is calculated as follows:

Median age at widowhood $= E_{(M)} - \left(MA_{(M)} - MA_{(F)}\right)$

where: $E_{(M)}$ = expectation of life at age at first marriage for males

$MA_{(M)}$ = median age at first marriage for males

$MA_{(F)}$ = median age at first marriage for females

The figures presented in this table differ significantly from those provided by Rodgers and Witney (1981). They use the more common joint survivorship technique for cohorts born from the 1880s to the 1950s, but their estimates do not capture the major longevity increases that have occurred over the period.

References

Barclay, George W.
  1958   *The Techniques of Population Analyses.* New York: John Wiley.
Bloom, David E. and Anne R. Pebley
  1982   "Voluntary childlessness: A review of the evidence and implications."
          Population Research and Policy Review 1:203-24.
Bogue, Donald J.
  1969   *Principles of Demography.* New York: John Wiley.
Bourbeau, Robert et Jacques Légaré
  1982   *Évolution de la mortalité au Canada et au Québec, 1831-1931.* Montréal:
          Les Presses de l'Université de Montréal.
Cohn, Martin
  1985   "Only 1 in 10 married people ever divorced, new study says." *Toronto Star*
          (March 20).
Davis, Kingsley and Pietronella van den Oever
  1982   "Demographic foundations of new sex roles." *Population and Development Review* 8:495-511.

Dixon, Ruth B.
  1971 "Explaining cross-cultural variations in age at marriage and proportions never marrying." *Population Studies* 25:215-33.
Elder, Glen H., Jr.
  1978 "Approaches to social change and the family." *American Journal of Sociology* 84:S1-S38.
Elder, Glen H., Jr. and Richard C. Rockwell
  1976 "Marital timing in women's life patterns." *Journal of Family History* 1:34-53.
Enterline, Philip E.
  1961 "Causes of death responsible for recent increases in sex mortality differentials in the United States." *Milbank Memorial Fund Quarterly* 39:312-28.
Gee, Ellen M.
  1978 "Fertility and Marriage Patterns in Canada: 1851-1971." Unpublished doctoral dissertation. The University of British Columbia.
  1980 "Female marriage patterns in Canada: Changes and differentials." *Journal of Comparative Family Studies* 11:457-73.
  1982 "Marriage in nineteenth-century Canada." *Canadian Review of Sociology and Anthropology* 19:311-25.
Gee, Ellen M. and Jean E. Veevers
  1983 "Accelerating sex differences in mortality: An analysis of contributing factors." *Social Biology* 30:75-85.
Glick, Paul C.
  1977 "Updating the family life cycle." *Journal of Marriage and the Family* 39:5-13.
Graney, Marshall J.
  1979 "An exploration of social factors influencing the sex differential in mortality." *Sociological Symposium* 28:1-26.
Grindstaff, Carl F.
  1984 "Catching up: The fertility of women over 30 years of age, Canada in the 1970s and early 1980s." *Canadian Studies in Population* 11(2):95-109.
Hagestad, Gunhild O. and Bernice L. Neugarten
  1985 "Age and the life course." Pp. 35-61 in Robert H. Binstock, Ethel Shanas, and Associates (eds.), *Handbook of Aging and the Social Sciences*. 2nd ed. New York: Van Nostrand Reinhold.
Hajnal, John
  1953 "Age at marriage and proportions marrying." *Population Studies* 7:111-36.
  1965 "European marriage patterns in historical perspective." Pp. 101-43 in D.V. Glass and D.E.C. Eversley (eds.), *Population in History: Essays in Historical Demography*. London: Edward Arnold.
Harrison, James
  1978 "Warning: The male sex role may be dangerous to your health." *Journal of Social Issues* 34:65-96.
Henripin, Jacques and Jacques Légaré
  1971 "Recent trends in Canadian fertility." *Canadian Review of Sociology and Anthropology* 8:106-18.

Hogan, Dennis P.
   1981   *Transitions and Social Change: The Early Lives of American Men.* New York: Academic Press.
   1985   "The demography of life-span transitions: Temporal and gender comparisons." Pp. 65-78 in Alice S. Rossi (ed.), *Gender and the Life Course.* New York: Aldine.
Linton, Ralph
   1942   "Age and sex categories." *American Sociological Review* 7:589-603.
Lopez, Alan D. and Lado T. Ruzicka (eds.)
   1983   *Sex Differentials in Mortality: Trends, Determinants and Consequences.* Canberra: Australian National University Press.
Modell, John, Frank F. Furstenberg, Jr. and Theodore Hershberg
   1976   "Social change and transitions to adulthood in historical perspective." *Journal of Family History* 1:7-32.
Nagnur, D.
   1985   Personal communication.
Neugarten, Bernice L. and Nancy Datan
   1973   "Sociological perspectives on the life cycle." Pp. 53-69 in Paul B. Baltes and K. Warner Schaie (eds.), *Life-Span Developmental Psychology: Personality and Socialization.* New York: Academic Press.
Parsons, Talcott
   1942   "Age and sex in the social structure of the United States." *American Sociological Review* 7:604-16.
Poston, Dudley L., Jr. and Kathryn Beth Kramer
   1981   *Patterns of Voluntary and Involuntary Childlessness in the United States, 1955-1973.* Final Report to the National Institute of Child Health and Human Development on Contract No. 1-HD-92804.
Potter, Robert G., Jr.
   1963   "Birth intervals: Structure and change." *Population Studies* 17:155-66.
Retherford, Robert D.
   1975   *The Changing Sex Differential in Mortality.* Westport, Connecticut: Greenwood.
Riley, Matilda W., Marilyn E. Johnson and Anne Foner
   1972   *Aging and Society.* Vol. 3. *A Sociology of Age Stratification.* New York: Russell Sage Foundation.
Rodgers, Roy H. and Gail Witney
   1981   "The family cycle in twentieth century Canada." *Journal of Marriage and the Family* 43:727-40.
Rossi, Alice S.
   1980   "Life-span theories and women's lives." *Signs* 6:4-32.
Shryock, Henry S., Jacob S. Siegel, and Associates
   1973   *The Methods and Materials of Demography.* Washington, D.C.: U.S. Printing Office.
Tolnay, Stewart E. and Avery M. Guest
   1982   "Childlessness in a transitional population: The United States at the turn of the century." *Journal of Family History* 7:200-19.

Uhlenberg, Peter
    1974   "Cohort variations in family life cycle experiences of U.S. females." *Journal of Marriage and the Family* 36:284-92.
    1978   "Changing configurations of the life course." Pp. 65-97 in Tamara R. Hareven (ed.), *Transitions: The Family and the Life Course in Historical Perspective.* New York: Academic Press.
van de Walle, Etienne
    1968   "Marriage and marital fertility." *Daedalus* 97:486-501.
Veevers, Jean E.
    1972   "Factors in the incidence of childlessness in Canada: An analysis of census data." *Social Biology* 19:266-74.
    1985   Personal communication.
Waldron, Ingrid
    1976   "Why do women live longer than men?" *Journal of Human Stress* 2:2-13.
Winsborough, Halliman H.
    1979   "Changes in the transition to adulthood." Pp. 137-52 in Matilda White Riley (ed.), *Aging from Birth to Death: Interdisciplinary Perspectives.* Boulder, Colorado: Westview.

16

The Hypothesis of Age Patterns in Living Arrangement Passages

Leroy O. Stone
Population Studies Division, Statistics Canada
Centre on Aging, University of Manitoba

Susan Fletcher
Office on Aging
Health and Welfare Canada

This chapter aims to increase the interest of gerontologists in the dynamic aspects of living arrangements by exploring a hypothesis about patterns of passage from one living arrangement to another and by showing how these patterns change systematically within an aging cohort. A notable feature of this work is its focus on cohorts. The life course perspective is extended to cohorts, where the analogue of the personal life course is the *cohort time trail*. The trail of living arrangement distributions laid down by a specific cohort is followed by tracking the cohort across a series of censuses of Canada.

As a cohort ages it will show a definite pattern of changes in its distribution among different types of living arrangement. Underlying these changes are *systematic age differences in the rate of passage from one living arrangement to another,* e.g., the passage from coresidence with your spouse to living alone.

A systematic age pattern in rates of passage from one living arrangement to another arises partly from the tendency of certain important life events to

The opinions in this paper are personal and are not intended to reflect views of any organization. Responsibility for these opinions and for errors of data processing or interpretation rests with the authors. We are grateful for the support of several persons in the preparation of the paper: Jean Coward for editing and bibliographic work, Claudette Legare for library searching, Vasile Nedelcu for data processing help, Andrew Siggner for assistance with the graphics, and Maureen Anglin and Tracy Waterson for historical data preparation and checking. Thanks are due to Neena Chappell, Mark Novak and Susan McDaniel for their comments on closely related texts.

be concentrated at particular ages. Especially notable among these events are first marriage, divorce, widowhood and remarriage.

The concentration of major life events at particular ages entails substantial age differences in the probability of making *any* living arrangement passage over a given period of time. A further factor that helps to explain these differences is the tendency for wide variation in age, such as that between ages 45 and 65, to be associated with differing propensities to make one particular living arrangement passage in the aftermath of the *same* life event, such as the experience of widowhood.

Key Definitions

Living arrangement distribution

Some people live alone. Others live only with their spouse. Others have a spouse and children at home. Still others have children only in their home. One adult may live with another, and there may or may not have existed some recognized family relationship with the person in question. In other words, we can create types of living arrangement by considering how many are in a household and what kinds of family relationship exist among the members of a household.

The phrase "living arrangement distribution" refers to the proportions of people in different living arrangement categories or types.

Living arrangement passage

In this chapter, the phrases "living arrangement passage" and "living arrangement transition" refer to the movement from one type of living arrangement to another. If your spouse stops living with you and your sister and her son come to live with you, you will have experienced a living arrangement passage.

Private and collective households

In the census of Canada, all the occupants of a designated dwelling are said to form one household. A key breakdown of households by the census is into the categories of "private" and "collective." A private household refers to a person or group of persons who do not have a usual residence elsewhere in Canada and who occupy a structurally separate set of living quarters with a private entrance outside or from a common hallway or stairway inside the building (i.e., the entrance must not be through someone else's living quarters).

In the census, "collective household" refers to a person or group of persons (other than foreign residents) who do not have a usual place of residence in Canada and who occupy a dwelling of an institutional, commercial or communal nature such as hotels, motels, hospitals, dwellings with ten or more persons not related to the household head (e.g., rooming houses), nursing homes or homes for the aged that display indications of a business establishment even though there are fewer than ten persons not related to the head of the household.

A significant subgroup within collective dwellings is the class of "institutions." In the census of Canada an institution is a place where persons receive care or custody, and such a place may be a mental hospital, a home for the aged, a nursing home, etc.

Cohort aging

The concept of the aging of a cohort, or cohort aging, is used frequently in this chapter. Cohort aging means an increase in the average age of the members of a defined cohort.

Support network

Support networks are classified into two groups for this chapter: formal and informal. By "support network" we mean the group that provides an individual with services or commodities to maintain satisfactory life conditions or to correct unsatisfactory life conditions. A formal support network is a group that has been deliberately organized, often as a recognized institution, to deliver a particular class of support (e.g., senior centres, Victorian Order of Nurses, etc.). An informal support network is a group that has become a support network without deliberately intending to create a support organization. Informal support networks can involve family members, other relatives and friends. A family support network consists of persons related by blood, marriage or adoption (e.g., children, siblings, inlaws).

The Hypothesis and Its Importance

If we consider a group of people born in a specific short time period, such as a year or five years — often called a birth cohort — the proportion of the cohort experiencing passage from one specific living arrangement to another (e.g., from living with spouse to living alone) will vary systematically depending on the average age of the cohort. Thus, as a cohort's average age increases, and especially for large age changes, we should look for a definite pattern of shifts in the cohort's rate (or group probability) of experiencing passage among specific living arrangements. This is the hypothesis of systematic age patterns in living arrangement passage or transition.

If the hypothesis holds true for a given cohort it would mean that as the cohort ages, it will show a definite pattern of changes in its distribution among different types of living arrangement. Cross-sectional census data and cohort series constructed from data for a sequence of censuses suggest that definite age differences in living arrangement distribution do indeed exist.

Most discussions of living arrangement and aging allude indirectly to the hypothesis, and statements that almost imply it logically may be found in the work of Lawton (1981:59) and Fillenbaum and Wallman (1984:342). However, our literature review failed to turn up an explicit exposition of the hypothesis, nor did we find stated reflections on its ramifications or related analytical research.

One important ramification of the hypothesis of systematic patterning in living arrangements results from the special needs for informal and formal supports that may arise when a living arrangement passage has to be faced. The passage from one living arrangement to another is not only sometimes a stressful process for those involved, it may also reduce access to natural (informal) helping networks for some of them. This may be particularly important for many of those who pass into living alone from another living arrangement (Beland, 1984:184; Canadian Council on Homemaker Services, 1982:17; Brody, Poulshock and Masciocchi, 1978:560-561; and Morris and Sherwood, 1983-84:89-90).

The weakening of the lines of contact with natural or informal helping networks that may be the result of living arrangement passage can lead to increased reliance upon the formal ones. These are comprised of formal organizations created explicitly as social-service delivery mechanisms. Of special consequence for utilization of public resources is the possibly increased need for formal supports on the part of the subset who move into relatively high-cost institutional care settings (Fillenbaum and Wallman, 1984:348-349).

Even when the living arrangement passage does not lead to increased probability of encountering certain types of formal-support organizations, it may influence the costs or the effectiveness of certain formal supports that were being received prior to the passage. For example, the household composition change might involve the absence of someone who was able to provide crucial transportation to a site where formal-organization services are received, as well as vital in-the-home reinforcement of beneficial behaviours recommended by a formal agency (for example, a physician's instructions about taking medication). In that absence, continuation of the service could be possible only at a new higher plateau of financial outlays, and the loss of the said in-the-home behaviour reinforcement could lead to "backsliding" and consequent reduced effectiveness of the formal supports (Beall, 1984:20; Morris and Sherwood, 1983-84:95; and Brody, Poulshock and Masciocchi, 1978:558-561).

Living arrangement transitions are also important because they often entail a variety of disruptions of customary routines and supportive social relationships (Clifford, Heaton and Fuguitt, 1982:139-140). Especially notable are neighbourhood changes that may reduce ready access to friends and relatives, or community changes that affect access to wanted or needed services.

In addition, the study of living arrangement passages can be helpful in the context of the planning of community design modifications, especially as regards housing, aimed at meeting the needs of a large aging cohort or generation. Particular living arrangement passages are sometimes associated with specific mixes of housing-service needs (Struyk, 1980:46). Forecasting the rates of those particular passages could be important to effective anticipation of the levels of requirement for the pertinent sets of housing services (Mallin, 1984:28).

The analysis of living arrangement passages is also pertinent in the assessment of adequacy of income flows to certain groups, or in anticipating changed requirements for money income related to altered household composition. This can be true when the alteration involves loss or gain of a person whose association with the household substantially affects its ability to acquire certain goods and services.

The foregoing comments take on increased impact in the context of societies in which the state has come to assume a major responsibility for providing certain kinds of supports to persons. In Western societies over the modern era we have first experienced work moving outside the home, then various home economic functions being taken over by business or government organizations, and eventually responsibilities for some aspects of care of persons being taken over progressively by the state (Hareven, 1981:159-160).

In a societal setting where state responsibility for some aspects of the social well-being of elders is legitimized and spreading, living arrangement passages (especially certain sequences of passage) may be so consistently linked with onset of state-financed or state-delivered services to the persons involved that analysis of the passages could become a major aspect of gaining useful knowledge about the risk factors for manifest need of formal-service interventions. In this context, the phenomenon of living arrangement passage is a legitimate focus of scientific study in its own right, quite aside from the already prominent study of particular living arrangements and patterns of distribution of population among them.

Theoretical Basis of the Hypothesis

We have argued that the hypothesis of systematic age patterns in living arrangement passages is worthy of serious scientific study for both academic and practical (public policy) reasons. What is the theoretical foundation for the hypothesis? Given this foundation, what is the range of its applicability over time and space? Should we regard it as a universal law governing the evolution of living arrangement distributions for a cohort? Or should we view its applicability as being constrained by particular historic and geographic (societal) contexts?

A systematic age pattern in rates of passage from one living arrangement to another arises partly from the tendency of certain important life events to be concentrated at particular ages. Especially notable among these events are first marriage, divorce, widowhood and remarriage. We have no estimates on the national or provincial patterns of relationship between such life events and living arrangement *passages*. We do have living arrangement distributions for different marital statuses, by age and sex, but these are seen as *outcomes* of the set of probabilities of passage among the possible living arrangements over given time periods.

Fillenbaum and Wallman (1984:342) remark that: "In looking at change in residential arrangements, information from cross-sectional studies suggest that change in residential arrangements may be occasioned by changes in the life cycle and in environmental circumstances." In their view, what is crucial about the link between life-cycle change and living arrangement is the extent to which the change causes disruption of the preexisting network of mutual supports among the members of a household (Fillenbaum and Wallman, 1984:343 and 348). We might add that in the case of a person living alone, life events or change in life-cycle stage might raise the perceived need for a new network of household-based social supports to the point where a living arrangement passage is sought for the purpose, partially, of achieving the new network of supports.

Similarly, Lawton (1981:59) argues that:

> the usual determinant of how an individual lives is a life-cycle event associated with a normatively influenced choice of how one is to live, moderated by the idiosyncratic needs of the individual or multiperson unit. Thus, children under age 18 or so usually live in a parent's household, most married couples live in a household separate from their parents, and most not presently married (i.e., the never married, widowed, divorced and separated) people live alone. These norm-determined situations are clearly moderated by the flexibility or rigidity of the norms and the pressure of individuals to behave differently.

Major life events or changes in life-cycle stage are not the only important sources of change in living arrangement. In pointing to other factors, Fillenbaum and Wallman refer to "environmental circumstances." These would involve, at least partially, changes in health and income statuses. Although their work deals with living arrangements at a point of time, it is perhaps pertinent to note that Soldo, Sharma and Campbell (1984:492) found that health and income factors were substantial in explaining living arrangement distribution. One might speculate that in a significant proportion of cases, persons sustaining substantial declines in functional capacity and/or income will seek to move in with others so as to gain assistance in coping with perceived personal deficiencies, and that such status changes can be influential in triggering living arrangement passages independently of the arrival of a major life event.

So far we have put the spotlight on major life events, health and income status changes as determinants of the incidence of living arrangement passage. None of that discussion implies a particular age patterning of the probability of a living arrangement passage. We make the connection to the notion of age patterning by asserting that all the factors mentioned above tend to have specific age patterning in their incidence. Moreover, a number of authors (Hareven, 1981; Hogan, 1981; Kohli, 1986; Rossi, 1980) suggest that age patterning of major transitions over the life course has become stronger in our society over the course of this century. This strengthening of pattern is associated with increased age segregation in our society, which may further be linked to a rising propensity to regard government as the appropriate repository of responsibility for the availability of supports under certain circumstances or for special population groups.

Hareven (1981:155-156) suggests that in the late nineteenth century the norms of familial assistance and autonomy were probably stronger than age norms of timing. Up to the early twentieth century "kin served as the most essential resource for economic assistance and security and carried the major burden of welfare functions. . . . Exchange relationships among parents and children and other kin thus provided the major, and sometimes the *only* [our emphasis] base for security" (Hareven, 1981:158-159).

Hareven (1981:155-156) further suggests that since the early twentieth century, demographic changes, "increasing rapidity in the timing of transitions. . .the increasing separation between an individual's family of orientation and family of procreation, and the introduction of publicly imposed transitions, have converged to isolate and segregate age groups in the larger society."

In short, we suggest that major events over the life course are the primary triggers of living arrangement passages. Some of these events now show distinct tendencies towards concentration at particular ages. This concentration helps to provide a cohort-specific age patterning to the probabilities of passing among living arrangement statuses. We further suggest that in recent decades there have developed systematic age differences in the probability of specific passages, such as that from living with a spouse to living with another person. Combined with these trends is the tendency for different ages to have varying propensities to make one particular kind of passage even when the pertinent triggering life event is the same.[1] These considerations, taken together, form the essential rationale for the hypothesis of systematic age patterning of living arrangement passages.

If the hypothesis has a reasonable theoretical foundation, is it universal in scope? Hareven's (1981:155-159) historical research suggests that in the nineteenth century major transitions in the life course were less patterned with respect to age, and that the "popular" living arrangement options did not have the age variation they now show. This means that there existed a societal context that only weakly (compared to the contemporary one) supplied the basis for the hypothesis to be expected to be true. (For a discussion in the Canadian context, see Gee, Chapter 15 of this volume.)

Further evidence of the sensitivity of the hypothesis to historical and socio-economic context may be found in the analysis of the sharp increase, since the 1950s, in the proportion of elders (especially women) who have chosen to live alone. Changes in demographic structure or processes or income growth fail, even when taken together, to explain the greater part of the increase. It appears that basic cultural factors are also involved. If these factors are cohort specific they would imply that we should expect to see intercohort variations in patterns of living arrangement choice (see Mindel, 1979:461; Smith, 1981:103-109; Uhlenberg and Myers, 1981:280-281; Pampel, 1983:433; and Wister, 1984).

Since socio-cultural systems vary widely, we should expect to find societies in which the basis of the hypothesis simply breaks down. This can happen when there is a strong tendency for the same living arrangement to enjoy dominant popularity over a wide range within the life course. It has been suggested at least by implication, for example, that one may expect to find some approximation of this situation in Japanese and Chinese societies (Smith, 1981:96-97).

The socio-cultural variation that might cause the hypothesis to have differing applicability over time and place can be observed even within our own society. For example, within our society there are substantial ethnic group variations as regards certain traditions of family support for elders irrespective of their level of functional capacity (see Thomas and Wister, 1984; Gurland et al., 1983). In ethnic groups where such a tradition of family support is strong, we should expect to find less than impressive evidence favouring the hypothesis, because the same living arrangement options tend to be the dominantly most popular ones across a wide range of the life course.

The hypothesis does not apply equally for men as for women. For example, living with others is the dominant situation across a much wider section of the life course for men than it is for women in North America in the late twentieth century. Partly due to a major gap between men and women in the ages at which widowhood is most likely to be experienced, there are marked male-female differences in living arrangement distribution, as well as (we hypothesize) in the underlying age pattern in rates of passage from one living arrangement to another. We outline a few of these gender variations below.

In sum, the truth value of the hypothesis is highly contingent upon certain features of the pertinent historical, socio-cultural and cohort experiences. Perhaps this high degree of contingency has discouraged exploration of the hypothesis in gerontology. Nevertheless, its applicability to Canada and the United States at this time, and the evidence indicating increased prevalence of its socio-cultural bases, are such that we should not ignore its important ramifications.

Relevant Empirical Analysis

Published research findings tell us little about the extent of support for the hypothesis. The big impediment to pertinent analysis is that we lack longitudinal data for a substantial cohort whose composition is not greatly affected by migration over the period of observation. The period of observation needs to be at least a generation, and ideally would be virtually the lifetime of the cohort being followed. No set of society-level statistics for North America satisfies these requirements. Indeed, we have found no reference to any suitable data set for any society.

In these circumstances, pertinent studies, including this one, have been forced to look at age differences in living arrangement distributions. Rarely do such studies hold the cohort of observation constant. This requires using a consistent classification of living arrangements over a long series of censuses, something that is made difficult by intercensal variations in concept definitions and tabulation practices. Hence, most often inferences for cohorts are mounted on the foundation of observation of age differences at a point of time (i.e., cross-sectional data are used), with the attendant serious prospect for bias (Fillenbaum and Wallman, 1984:348). In spite of this and other problems with the data on living arrangement distributions, let us attempt to gain some useful insights from them.

The cohort perspective

By using a crude living arrangement classification, we are able to find support for the idea that a single real cohort (defined loosely) can be expected to exhibit systematic age-associated variation in living arrangement distribution. To achieve this result we reorganized data for a series of censuses and prepared special estimates when a census failed to provide data for one of our living arrangement classes or did so for an age group wider than the one for which we needed data.

The initial results of this work are shown in Figures 1 and 2. There was a steady increase in the percentage living alone from the age group 65-69

FIGURE 1:
Percent Living Alone or in Institutions, by Sex, Cohort Aged 65-69 in 1961, Canada

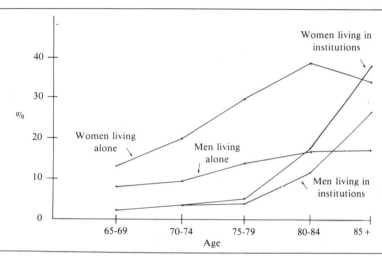

SOURCE: Censuses of Canada, 1961 to 1981, and special estimates by L. Stone.

to that of 80-84, among men and women born between 1892 and 1896 (Figure 1). This percentage peaked for these women in the 80-84 age group, and climbed much more sharply among women than men. It continued to climb among the men into the 85-and-over age group. After the percentage living alone passed its peak for this cohort, there began a sharp rise in the proportion that resided in institutions. In the 85-and-over group 40 percent of the women and 30 percent of the men in the cohort were living in institutions.

The roots of these patterns, and particularly of the marked gender difference shown in Figure 1, reach deeply into the early phases of the cohort's life course as a segment of Canadian society. This point is generally understood, but we have not seen enough commentary on how these "demographic trails" left by aging cohorts clearly reflect profound aspects of the differing acculturation of men and women in modern society. Some of this reflection is provided by Figure 2, which shows proportions living in husband-wife families for men and women aged 25-29 in 1961 (i.e., they were born between 1932 and 1936). This chart permits us to look at this same cohort over five consecutive censuses of Canada.

Although both sexes in the cohort had a sharp increase in the proportion of husband-wife families between the age group 25-29 and that of 30-34, the increase is much more dramatic for the men. After age group 30-34 the proportion of husband-wife families continues to rise gradually for the men up to the age 45-49. In stark contrast, the proportion in husband-wife families began *declining* among the women after age group 30-34!

FIGURE 2:
Percent Who Are Spouses in a Husband-Wife Family,
Cohort Aged 25-29 in 1961, Canada

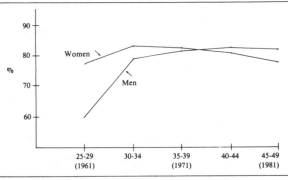

SOURCE: Same as Figure 1.

Thus from quite early in the cohort's life course, we see the groundwork being laid for the major differences in living arrangement distribution that the cohort will likely display when its average age approaches the members' expectation of life, which can reasonably be regarded as the autumn of the cohort's life course. Stone (1985:3-4) has defined "demographic oldness" for a cohort in terms of the proximity of the cohort's attained average age to its members' expected mean length of time.

The cross-section perspective

The data displayed to this point provide us with some basis for making limited inferences about cohorts from the cross-sectional data of the 1981 census. We emphasize that the inferences are limited. For example, while our cohort data indicate that the percentage living alone peaks for women in the 80-84 age group, the 1981 cross-sectional data indicate that the peak is in the age group 75-79.

In spite of the pitfalls in using the cross-sectional data in a paper devoted to discussion about cohorts, we find the temptation to do so irresistible, because we can employ a new and refined classification of living arrangement statuses that we have developed. Our categories are often unduly crude because we had to respect the limitations that flow from the codes on the 1981 Census Public Use Sample file. Let us first consider, then, the more detailed classification.

   (A)   Living in another person's child-nurturing setting:
          Person lives in a couple-headed household that has child at home, is related to Person 1 but is neither Person 1 (in the Canadian census "Person 1" has replaced the concept of "household head") nor his/her spouse.

(B)   Leading one's own child-nurturing setting:
Person lives in a couple-headed household that has child at home, and person *is* Person 1 or his/her spouse.

(C)   Living in a non-child-nurturing family setting:
Person lives in an economic family household that has *no* child at home (in an economic family, census concept, the members are related but are not necessarily related as man and wife or parent and child). Members of this category are broken down into four subclasses as follows.

(C1) person is one of two who live in a couple-only household:
(C2) person lives in a couple-headed household that has other present (i.e., at least three persons live in the household) and person is related to Person 1 but is *neither* Person 1
nor his nor her spouse:
(C3) person lives in a couple-headed household that has others present (i.e., at least three persons live in the household) and person *is* Person 1 or his or her spouse:
(C4) person lives in an economic family household that is *not* headed by a couple:

(D)   Living in a friendship-care setting:
Person lives in household comprised of non-family-related persons (it must be recognized that the depth of mutual caring and commitment among the household members may sometimes be such as to make this setting very similar to a legally constituted family).

(E)   Living alone:
Person lives in a one-person household

(F1)   person is an inmate in a collective dwelling:

(F2)   person is a noninmate in a collective dwelling:

(G)   Not elsewhere specified setting:
person lives in a household not in any of the preceding classes.

On the whole, these living arrangement categories are intended to identify different social contexts of delivery and receipt of care (broadly defined to include such matters as loving care, considerateness).[2] Our focus on care is not intended to deny the obvious — many households are battlegrounds for their members, or stages upon which some members habitually abuse the others. It is equally undeniable, however, that caring in various forms is the dominant factor in joint living of persons (even when they "fight" from time to time.)

Figures 3 to 6 are offered as a simulation of the pattern of shifts in living arrangement distribution as a cohort ages. Since all the data refer to Canada in 1981, and we know that there are major intercohort differences in propensities to choose certain kinds of living arrangement (e.g., the baby boom generation popularized the living arrangement in which a young man and a young woman would live together in a non-legally-married state), we cannot claim that this series of charts portrays accurately what will happen to the future living arrangement distributions of younger Canadians as they age. We do assume, however, that this sequence of charts gives a reasonable approximation of the likely living arrangement distributions of the younger cohorts in the future.

Figure 3 depicts the expected shift in living arrangement distribution from a heavy concentration in the status of being a nonleader of a procreative family at age 10-14 to a situation in which there are high proportions heading such families or comprising members of one-couple settings at age 20-24. Also at 20-24, the proportion living with others in friendship care settings reaches its peak among age groups (at 6 percent for women and 8 percent for men in 1981), and living alone becomes substantial for the first time in the life of the hypothetical cohort (at about 7 percent for each gender).

The next peak is seen, in the 1981 census data, at age group 40-44 for men and 35-39 for women, by which age the proportions in one-couple and friendship-care settings have fallen sharply from earlier high levels and a strong position of dominance (in the living arrangement distribution) is assumed by the setting where the person is a part of the headship of a household that is nurturing young children. In 1981 four-fifths of women age 35-39 and just above three-quarters of men aged 40-44 were in this particular living arrangement.

As a result, largely, of the typical difference in age between brides and their grooms in our society, we begin to notice (no later than age 35-39 for women) the emergence of what will later become a gigantic gender differential in living arrangement distribution at a given age. Indeed, when our hypothetical cohort reaches the next age group where a living arrangement attains a peak value, the sex differential has already become large.

The next notable peak proportion occurs for the living arrangement of being in a one-couple household (two persons only living there). In 1981 this peak is shown for women at age group 60-64, whereas for men it is seen among those age 70-74. About 45 percent of women aged 60-64 were in this living arrangement in 1981, while the corresponding figure for men aged 70-74 was 57 percent. By age 60-64 for women, the death rate of husbands has reached high levels, and partly as a result, the proportion living alone has climbed well above the local peak that it had earlier reached in the age group 20-24 (in 1981 18 percent of women aged 60-64 were living alone). Also creeping up to significant levels by the time age 60-64 is reached is the proportion that lives in a family setting that has no married couple present (3 percent of women aged 60-64 in 1981).

The now widely discussed status of living alone is that for which we see

FIGURE 3:
Percent of Women in Selected Living Arrangement Categories, by Age, Canada, 1981

SOURCE: 1981 Census Public Use Sample.

the next peak proportion. For all Canadian women in 1981 the peak percentage living alone is seen at age group 75-79, with 40 percent. The peak for men is seen in the next age group, 80-84, but it is far lower (at 18 percent) than that for women. At age 80-84, 40 percent of men were still in one-couple two-person-only settings, while the corresponding value for women aged 80-84 had fallen (at 12 percent) far below its earlier peak.

Also by age 80-84, the proportion living in institutional settings has begun to assume substantial values. In 1981 nearly 20 percent of women aged 80-84 were living as inmates of institutions (for the corresponding age group of men the figure was much lower — 12 percent).

In addition, the percentage of persons in this age group who are living in family settings that have no couple present has come up to substantial levels for women. In 1981 just under 7 percent of women aged 80-84 were living in a family setting that had no couple. Also well above their low values reached around age 60-64 was the proportion (7 percent of 1981 women aged 80-84) living as a nonleader (i.e., neither Person 1 nor his/her spouse) in a child-nurturing family setting.

By the time age group 85 and over is reached, cohort attrition has greatly weakened the helping capacity of most of the pertinent informal support networks. The proportion living alone has fallen well below its former peak, while that in institutions has become quite substantial at a value of nearly 40 percent for women and just above 25 percent for men. By the time age 90 and over is reached the proportion in institutional facilities exceeds that living alone by a wide margin (see Stone and Fletcher, 1981:Figure 10).

Hence, although we cannot offer this chart as an accurate representation for a real cohort, it does suggest strongly that as a real cohort traverses its life course, it will experience quite major changes in living arrangement distribution. A potentially useful way of presenting these data is that of displaying the proportions in certain key living arrangement classes (or groups of them) over the age range. This is what Figures 4 and 5 do for the categories of living alone, living in a family-type (including friendship care) setting as part of the household leadership or as another member and living in collective household settings.

The curves for the two family-type settings have a crossover point at age 20-24 for women and at age 25-29 for men. At these respective ages, the curve for those settings where the person is part of the household leadership assumes the higher value for the first time. The next crossover point is seen for women only, at the age group 75-79, where the percentage living alone exceeds that of members of the leadership of a family-type setting for the first time. For men the latter percentage is *not* surpassed on the chart once it assumes dominance around age 25-29. However, if we had detailed ages

FIGURE 4:
Age Profiles for Percentages in Selected Living Arrangement Classes, Women, Canada, 1981

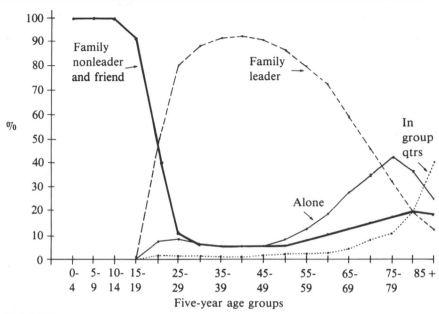

CLASSES:

"Family nonleader and friend" means that the person lives with others, but if the household contains persons who are related by blood, marriage or adoption, the person is neither Person 1 (1981 census concept) nor the spouse.

"Family leader" means the person is either Person 1 or the spouse in a family household (economic family concept — defined implicitly in the preceding note).

"Alone" means the person lives in a one-person household.

"In group qtrs" means the person lives in a collective household (most of which are institutions whose residents are above age 75).

SOURCE: 1981 Census Public Use Sample.

above 85 we might have seen it surpassed by the percentage in collective settings somewhere above age 90.

After age 79 for women, the percentage living alone starts to go down. Among Canadian women aged 80-84 this percentage is equalled by that living in collective households, each being 20 percent. In the age group 85 and over, double this value (40 percent) of women in 1981 were living in collective households. A similar doubling is also observed for men, with the

FIGURE 5:
Age Profiles for Percentages in Selected Living Arrangement Classes, Men, Canada, 1981

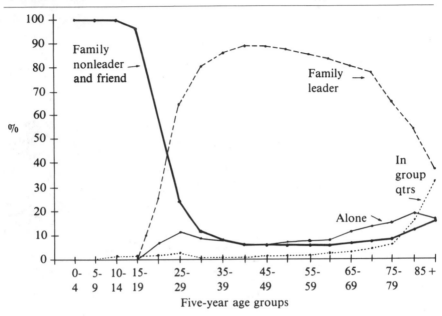

CLASSES:

"Family nonleader and friend" means that the person lives with others, but if the household contains persons who are related by blood, marriage or adoption, the person is neither Person 1 (1981 census concept) nor the spouse.

"Family leader" means the person is either Person 1 or the spouse in a family household (economic family concept — defined implicitly in the preceding note).

"Alone" means the person lives in a one-person household.

"In group qtrs" means the person lives in a collective household (most of which are institutions whose residents are above age 75).

SOURCE: 1981 Census Public Use Sample.

percentage living in collective households going from 14 percent of men aged 80-84 to 30 percent of men aged 85 and over.

Rising percentages living as nonleaders of a family-type setting are notable for both men and women in the older ages, starting from a low of 5 percent for women aged 35-39 and a low of 5 percent for men aged 60-64. From these low points, the percentages rise gradually with each higher age group until a peak of nearly 20 percent is reached for women aged 80-84 and one of 16 percent is reached for men aged 85 and over. Among women, the figure for the 85-and-over age group was just below that for the 80-84 age group in 1981.

Thus, by the time age 90 and over is reached, upwards of one-third of the population is in some kind of collective-type setting. Recent research suggests that the most important factor here is not so much rising functional incapacity, though this is clearly relevant; rather it is the depletion of informal support reserves by the process of cohort attrition (see Stone, 1985, for a review of some ramifications of cohort attrition for support networks, and for related review and pertinent research findings see Brody, Poulshock and Masciocchi, 1978).

FIGURE 6:
Percent Living Alone, By Sex and Age, Canada, 1981

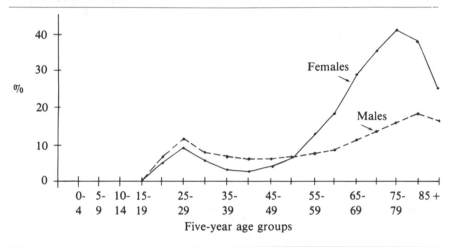

SOURCE: 1981 Census Public Use Sample.

Figure 6 elaborates the major male-female difference that emerges in the percentage living alone as age increases across the 1981 population. Particularly notable is the sharp rise in the percentage of women from the late fifties to the late seventies in age, followed by a dramatic fall thereafter.

These results suggest that we can, with some confidence in the possible utility of our work, go on to construct computer simulations of the sorts of living arrangement transition probability matrices that would have produced the distributional shifts (over statuses of living arrangement) that have been noted. In sum, in the absence of more suitable data, those that we have surveyed have not led us to suggest that the hypothesis be abandoned. The patterns are consistent with those we would expect to see if the hypothesis were correct.

Concluding Observation

The study of living arrangements needs to take into account the pattern of age differences in the rate of passage from one specific living arrangement to another. This pattern arises partly because a number of key life events tend to be concentrated at specific ages and partly because there are age differences in the propensity to make a specific living arrangement passage in the aftermath of the same life event. For example, widowhood of a woman age 45 is much less likely to be followed by prolonged living alone than is widowhood at age 65.

Especially notable among pertinent life events are those that involve family formation and dissolution. The marital status shifts associated with these events often trigger living arrangement passages, and these are not a set of randomly distributed experiences over the age range. The systematic age differences in the concentration of major life events means that we should expect corresponding differences in the probability of making any of the possible living arrangement passages.

Thus, there is a meaningful pattern of age differences in rates and structures of living arrangement passage. The scientific study of these patterns is relevant to the development of a useful understanding of the timing of special needs for informal and formal supports over the whole life course.

Notes

[1]   When that life event is experienced the possible responsive shifts in living arrangement depend upon the choices to which one is exposed (Wister, 1984), as well as upon the extent and character of the person's social network. Both of these variables have prominent age patterns. The range of available choices depends upon income, functional capacity, options that are open in the designs of available housing, and, among other factors, the character of personal ties to significant others who are available as possible co-residents. All of these variables are statistically related to age. The social network is important in yet another way. Membership in a network may entail certain obligations that serve to constrain the decision that is made as regards a change of living arrangement. For example, one may have obligations to children when widowed or divorced at 40; while such obligations may have changed markedly, at least in their character and depth, by the time one becomes 65.

[2]   Gordon Priest (1985) has also published a new detailed classification of living arrangements, one that is oriented towards application in studies of housing consumption. For example, his classification places much emphasis on identifying who is the principal maintainer of a household, which is not deemed to be so important for our work that it needs to enter our classification system.

References

Abu-Laban, Sharon McIrvin
    1981   "Women and aging: A futurist perspective." *The Psychology of Women Quarterly*. Special Issue on Women and the Future.

Alpert, Judith.L.
    1981   "Theoretical perspectives on the family life cycle." *The Counselling Psychologist* 9(4):25-34.

Beall, George Thomas
    1984   "Long-term care cost crisis: Can private insurance bail us out?" *Perspective on Aging* 13(5):20-23.

Béland, François
    1984   "The decision of elderly persons to leave their homes." *The Gerontologist* 24(2):179-185.

Brody, Stanley J., S. Walter Poulshock and Carla F. Masciocchi
    1978   "The family caring unit: A major consideration in the long-term support system." *The Gerontologist* 18(6):556-561.

Canadian Council on Homemaker Services
    1982   *Visiting Homemakers Service In Canada — Survey 1982*. A report on homemaking services, practices and personnel in Canada to the Board of Directors responsible for the study. Ottawa: Department of National Health and Welfare.

Chappell, Neena L.
    1983   "Informal support networks among the elderly." *Research On Aging* 5(March 1983) (1):77-99.

Chudacoff, H. and T.K. Hareven
    1979   "From the empty nest to family dissolution." *Journal of Family History* (Spring).

Clifford, William B., Tim Heaton and Glenn V. Fuguitt
    1982   "Residential mobility and living arrangements among the elderly: Changing patterns in metropolitan and nonmetropolitan areas." *The International Jornal of Aging & Human Development* 14(2):139-156.

Fillenbaum, Gerda G. and Laurence M. Wallman
    1984   "Change in household composition of the elderly: A preliminary investigation." *Journal of Gerontology* 39(3):342-349.

Fletcher, Susan and Leroy O. Stone
    1982   *The Living Arrangements of Canada's Older Women*. Statistics Canada Catalogue 86-503. Ottawa: Minister of Supply and Services.
    1980   "The living arrangements of Canada's older women." *Essence* 4(3):115-133.

Glick, Paul C.
    1979   "The future marital status and living arrangements of the elderly." *The Gerontologist* 19(3):301-309.

Gurland, Barry et al.
    1983   *The Mind And Mood Of Aging. Mental Health Problems of the Community Elderly in New York and London*. New York: The Haworth Press.

Hareven, Tamara K.
  1981   "Historical changes in the timing of family transitions: Their impact on generational relations." Pp. 143-165 in Robert W. Fogel, Elaine Hatfield, Sara B. Kiesler and Ethel Shanas (eds.), *Aging: Stability and Change in the Family.* New York: Academic Press.
  1982   "The life course and aging in historical perspective." In Tamara K. Hareven and Kathleen J. Adams (eds.), *Aging and Life Course Transitions: An Interdisciplinary Perspective.* New York: The Guilford Press.
Harrison, Brian
  1980   "Living Alone in Canada: Demographic and Economic Perspectives." Unpublished paper. Statistics Canada: Social Statistics Field.
Health and Welfare Canada
  1983   *Fact Book on Aging in Canada.* Prepared to serve as a handy statistical resource to participants at the 2nd Canadian Conference on Aging, October 24-27. Joint publication of Health and Welfare Canada and Statistics Canada.
Hogan, Dennis P.
  1981   *Transitions and Social Change: The Early Lives of American Men.* New York: Academic Press.
Kohli, Martin
  1986   "The social construction of the life course." Chapter 9 in V.W. Marshall (ed.), *Later Life: The Social Psychology of Aging.* Beverly Hills: Sage.
Lawton, M. Powell
  1981   "An ecological view of living arrangements." *The Gerontologist* 21(1):59-66.
Lawton, M. Powell, Maurice Greenbaum and Bernard Liebowitz
  1980   "The life span of housing environments for the aging." *The Gerontologist* 20(1):56-64.
Mallin, Dana
  1984   "Housing Canadians: Concerns for the '80s." *Canadian Home Economics Journal* 34(1):27-29.
Mindel, Charles H.
  1979   "Multigenerational family households: Recent trends and implications for the future." *The Gerontologist* 19(5):456-463.
Mooney, Kathleen A.
  1979   "Ethnicity, economics, the family cycle and household composition." *The Canadian Review of Sociology and Anthropology* 16(4):388-403.
Morris, John N. and Sylvia Sherwood
  1983-   "Informal support resources for vulnerable elderly persons: Can they be
  84   counted on, why do they work?" *International Journal of Aging and Human Development* 18(2):81-98.
Novak, Mark and Leroy O. Stone
  1985   "Population Aging and Core Social Institutions." Paper presented to the Canadian Population Society, Montreal, May.
Pampel, Fred C.
  1983   "Changes in the propensity to live alone: Evidence from consecutive cross-sectional surveys, 1960-1976." *Demography* 20(4):433-447.

Priest, Gordon
1985 "Living Arrangements of Canada's Elderly: Changing Demographic and Economic Factors." Occasional Paper Series 85-1. Victoria: Gerontology Research Centre, Simon Fraser University.
Roos, Noralou P., Evelyn Shapiro and Leslie L. Roos
1984 "Aging and the demand for health services: Which aged and whose demand?" *The Gerontologist* 24(1):31-36.
Rossi, Alice S.
1980 "Life-span theories and women's lives." *Journal of Women in Culture and Society* 6(1):4-32.
Siegel, Jacob S.
1981 "Demographic background for international gerontological studies." *Journal of Gerontology* 36(1):93-102.
Siegel, Jacob S. and Maria Davidson
1984 "Demographic and socioeconomic aspects of aging in the United States." Pp. 85-100 in *Current Population Reports, Special Studies*. Series P-23, No 138. U.S. Department of Commerce. Bureau of the Census.
Smith, Daniel Scott
1981 "Historical change in the household structure of the elderly in economically developed societies." Pp. 91-114 in Robert W. Fogel, Elaine Hatfield, Sara B. Kiesler and Ethel Shanas (eds.), *Aging: Stability and Change in the Family*. New York: Academic Press.
Soldo, Beth J., Mahesh Sharma and Richard T. Campbell
1984 "Determinants of the community living arrangements of older unmarried women." *Journal of Gerontology* 39(4):492-498.
Statistics Canada
1981 *Census Public Use Sample Tape.* Individual File. Micro-data file on magnetic tape. Contact CANSIM Division, Statistics Canada, Ottawa, Ontario.
1984 *1981 Census of Canada Profile — The Elderly in Canada.* Statistics Canada Catalogue 99-932. Ottawa: Minister of Supply and Services.
1984 *Living Alone.* Catalogue 99-934. Ottawa: Minister of Supply and Services.
1985 *Population Projections for Canada, Provinces and Territories 1984-2006.* Statistics Canada Catalogue 91-520. Ottawa: Minister of Supply and Services.
Stone, Leroy O.
1985 "Cohort Aging and Support Networks." Paper prepared for the Symposium on Demography and Aging, part of the 13th International Congress of Gerontology, New York, July.
Stone, Leroy O. and Susan L. Fletcher
1981 *Aspects of Population Aging in Canada: A Chartbook.* Ottawa: Minister of Supply and Services.
Streib, Gordon F.
1978 "An alternative family form for older persons: Need and social context." *The Family Coordinator* 27(4):413-420.
Struyk, Raymond J.
1980 "Housing adjustments of relocating elderly households." *The Gerontologist* 20(1):45-55.

Thomas, K. and A.V. Wister
  1984   "Living arrangements of older women: The ethnic dimension." *Journal of Marriage and the Family* 46(2).
Uhlenberg, Peter and Mary Anne P. Myers
  1981   "Divorce and the elderly." *The Gerontologist* 21(3):276-282.
Ward, Russel A.
  1978   "Limitations of the family as a supportive institution in the lives of the aged." *The Family Coordinator* 27(4):365-373.
Wister, Andrew Victor.
  1984   "Living Arrangement Choices Among the Elderly: A Decision-Making Approach." Doctoral dissertation, The University of Western Ontario (October).

17
Aging and Intergenerational Relations in Canada

Carolyn J. Rosenthal
Department of Behavioural Science
University of Toronto

The family is an extremely important source of emotional, social and practical support for older persons and is highly valued by its adult members. Research has destroyed the myths that older people are isolated from and abandoned by their families (e.g., Adams, 1968; Hill et al., 1970; Shanas, 1979; Shanas et al., 1968), that older people were better treated by their families in the past than they are today (Laslett, 1976), and that the elderly are better treated in other, less complex societies than in our own society (Nydegger, 1983). Referring to these negative views of the family relations of older people as "myths" should not be taken to imply that family life is totally positive; because families are emotionally intense environments, conflict is as characteristic of family life as cooperation is (Marshall and Bengtson, 1983).

For most people, kin ties are the most intimate, supportive and enduring relationships over the life course. Most older Canadians are actively involved in family networks in which adult children are central figures. This chapter will concentrate primarily on relations between older parents and adult children. Canadian research on several dimensions of family life is examined, supplemented by reference to U.S. data. I then consider my own research from the Generational Relations and Succession Project, which has sought to expand previous conceptualizations of the aging family. The family is viewed as an organization in which people assume responsibility for specialized tasks in order to maintain familial solidarity.

Some important aspects of family experiences in later life are excluded from the chapter because they are covered elsewhere in the book: widowhood, historical changes in the family life course, ethnic variability, changes in household structure and living arrangements and families as social networks (see Chapters 7, 15, 16, 18 and 19). However, the present discussion should be viewed in the context of these chapters.

Preparation of this chapter was supported by an Ontario Ministry of Health Career Scientist Award to the author.

Conceptualizing Intergenerational Relations

In this chapter, the term "family" is used broadly to denote those persons to whom one is related by blood or marriage. The term "lineage" denotes ranked descent within a family (Bengtson et al., 1985) and encompasses the most significant intergenerational relationships in Canadian families — parents, children and grandchildren. Note that both "family" and "lineage" are terms that refer to family groupings that normally extend beyond the older person's household.

Some years ago, scholars put forth the concept of the "modified extended family" to describe the North American family system in which separate households of related individuals are linked into a wider system by ties of affection, obligation and exchange of goods and services (Litwak, 1960; Sussman and Burchinal, 1962). More recently, scholars have conceptualized and analysed relations among households and kin as social networks (see Chapter 19; Wellman and Hall, 1986).

Intergenerational solidarity

Bengtson and colleagues (Bengtson et al., 1985; Bengtson, Mangen and Landry, 1984; Bengtson, Olander and Haddad, 1976; Bengtson and Schrader, 1982; Marshall and Bengtson, 1983) have conceptualized the social bonds among the generations in terms of solidarity. As Bengtson, Mangen and Landry (1984:63) say: "The concept of solidarity addresses cohesion or integration, as well as implications for potential or actual social support between generations." Six dimensions of intergenerational solidarity are identified: structure, association, affect, exchange, consensus and norms. When these elements are high (or positive), individuals perceive their relationships as having high solidarity.

The dimension of *family structure* includes the number and type of living relatives a person has, including spouse, parents, grandparents, siblings, children and grandchildren. Of particular importance in this chapter is the number of living children. Family structure directly affects the ability of families to provide support to older members and is a precondition for the many other aspects of intergenerational relations. Geographical proximity of relatives is included in the family structure dimension; proximity can facilitate or limit other dimensions of solidarity, particularly association and exchange. Finally, the household structure of the older person is included in this dimension.

Associational solidarity encompasses contact between the generations, whether face-to-face, by telephone or letter, and includes a focus on the frequency of contact and the occasions or reasons around which contact occurs.

Functional solidarity refers to the exchange of assistance and support between generations. This exchange may consist of services, goods, financial aids, or socio-emotional support.

Affective solidarity refers to the perceived quality of interaction. This includes perceived closeness or warmth, understanding, trust and fairness (Bengtson, Olander and Haddad, 1976), or their absence. Bengtson and Black (1973) define this dimension as "mutual positive sentiment among group members and their expressions of love, respect, appreciation and recognition of others."

Consensual solidarity describes the extent to which the generations agree or disagree with one another on general opinions and values, while *normative solidarity* refers to the norms or expectations family members hold of one another and of the family as a social group.

Related concepts: social support and social network

The intergenerational solidarity framework provides a useful way of studying the family as a social support system. The different solidarity dimensions point to different aspects of social support. Kahn (1979:85) defines social support as "interpersonal transactions that include one or more of the following: the expression of positive affect of one person towards another; the affirmation or endorsement of another person's behaviours, perceptions, or expressed views; the giving of symbolic or material aid to another." These elements are also part of the solidarity framework, although Kahn explicitly includes affirmation. Kahn proposes that age-related changes in social support be studied using the concept of the "convoy," the set of significant other people to whom an individual is related by the giving or receiving of social support. The convoy, affected by demographic characteristics, determines the adequacy of social support that in turn determines individual well-being (Kahn, 1979:84-85). Additionally, social support buffers the effects of stress (resulting from such events as widowhood or change of residence) on well-being. Kahn suggests that the convoy characteristics of the elderly are likely to include increasing asymmetry (receiving more than giving), reduced ability to initiate interaction, increased instability (due to loss of members), reduced size (due to narrowing opportunity to replace lost members) and changes in type of interaction (increased direct aid, decreased receiving of affect and affirmation).

The social network approach may also be used to study social support (Wellman and Hall, 1986). Network analysis builds up a composite picture of social ties along which resources or support may flow. Individuals' networks differ in the number and density of ties, and ties differ in content, in reciprocity or symmetry, and strength. Strong ties, characterized by greater intimacy, closeness and interaction, provide more support, but weak ties are useful as well (Granovetter, 1973). Corin describes this approach more fully in Chapter 19.

These approaches share many features and may be viewed as complementary frameworks. This chapter, however, draws primarily upon the solidarity framework that has heavily influenced the author's research.

Empirical Research on Intergenerational Solidarity

In reviewing Canadian research on intergenerational solidarity, this section draws heavily on data from the Generational Relations and Succession Project, conducted in Hamilton and Stoney Creek, Ontario, by the author with Victor Marshall and Jane Synge.[1] In that study, a random sample of 458 persons, stratified by gender and age (the three age categories were 40 to 54, 55 to 69, 70 and older) was interviewed. Questionnaires were sent to all the respondents' adult children if names were provided. (For a description of the sample see Marshall, 1984.)

Family structure

The extent to which a person can have supportive family relationships depends on the availability of kin — whether one has various types of relatives and the distance one lives from them. With some exceptions, nationwide Canadian data on the family structure of older persons are not available. However, data from the Hamilton study (see Table 1) and several other Canadian studies serve to suggest the family structure of older Canadians.

TABLE 1:
Aspects of Family Structure, Respondents Aged 70 + , Hamilton and Stoney Creek, Ontario

Respondent is a member of a family with:	Men		Women	
	%	N	%	N
Spouse	77	(54)	24	(19)
At least one child	81	(57)	80	(64)
At least one grandchild	79	(55)	78	(62)
At least one sibling	79	(55)	80	(64)

N: Men   70
 ·Women   80

Availability of kin

A spouse is one of the most important resources an older person can have. In later life men are advantaged over women in this respect (see Chapter 18). Among Canadians aged 65 and over, about three-quarters of the male population but only about half the female population have a spouse (Minister of Supply and Services Canada, 1983). Even at age 85, when 79 percent of women are widowed, the majority of men still have a spouse (Martin Matthews, 1985).

Most older people have children. As in the U.S. (Shanas with Heinemann, 1982), about 80 percent of older people in the Hamilton study had at least one child. However, 20 percent of the Hamilton respondents had only one child, pointing to some structural fragility in this social support resource. Further, while this chapter focusses on persons who have children, it should be remembered that an important 20 percent of older people have no living children. (For a comparison of the experiences of childless and parent elderly, based on Canadian data, the reader is referred to Rempel, 1985.)

Almost all older people who have children also had grandchildren. In Hamilton, 96 percent of older people with children had grandchildren, and between 23 percent (men) and 38 percent (women) have great grandchildren. In all, about 78 percent of the respondents aged 70+ were members of three or four generation families. Again, these figures are almost identical to those reported for the U.S. (Shanas with Heinemann, 1982).

Siblings can be an important resource in later life, especially among people who do not have a spouse or a child. Most older respondents in the Hamilton study had at least one sibling and, with the exception of persons aged 80 and older, typically two or more siblings.

Today, more and more adults are likely to have a parent alive. Winsborough (1980), referring to U.S. data, suggests that for women, the experience of having their mother die generally occurs in the late fifties and early sixties. However, by the late sixties, very few people have living parents. Shanas found only 4 percent of older people in the U.S. had a parent (typically a mother) alive. Of Hamilton respondents aged 70 and older, none of the men and only 1.2 percent of the women had a living parent. Although these percentages are small, they have serious implications. They denote instances where the parent is very old and likely in need of a high degree of assistance. These parents are very likely to live with their aging adult children (Shanas with Heinemann, 1982).

This review of family structure has shown that most older people have kin. Indeed, among community-dwelling elderly in Manitoba, Chappell (1983) found only 1 percent had no relatives outside their household. However, as Table 1 shows, substantial minorities lack kin in various categories. Older people who do not have children may be in greatest need of formal supports, and the small minority who have neither spouse nor children nor siblings are extremely vulnerable to institutionalization when misfortunes such as serious health losses occur.

Household structure

While the living arrangements of older Canadians are discussed in Chapter 16, a few points bear highlighting here. Like younger adults, older Canadians usually live with a spouse and pre-launched children, if they have them, or alone (for a discussion of ethnic differences, see Thomas and Wister, 1984). Joint households between older parents and adult children have been rare since well before modernization in Canada (Nett, 1981), England (Laslett, 1976) and the U.S. (Dahlin, 1980). The great majority of older people prefer to maintain independent households (Shanas with Heinemann, 1982; Wake and Sporakowski, 1972), but to live near their grown children. In a London, Ontario study of older persons in the community, when respondents were asked where they would prefer to live if they could no longer live alone, most said they would prefer to live elsewhere, rather than with a child (Connidis, 1983). In that study, one-third of the respondents lived alone and 52 percent with a spouse (sometimes including children). Chappell (1983) found almost identical proportions living in these arrangements in Manitoba. In London, 15 percent of the respondents were living with persons other than a spouse, with women being more likely than men to live in nonspousal arrangements or alone (Connidis and Rempel, 1983). Six and one-half percent of the respondents were living with children (Connidis, 1983). In the Hamilton study, among persons aged 70 and older, 3 percent of men and 11 percent of women lived in households that did not include their spouse and that did include a child (Rosenthal, 1986). Béland (1984) studied three groups of community-dwelling older people in Quebec. From 17.3 percent to 29.9 percent of respondents coresided with a child, most commonly with the parent as head of the household. Among Hamilton respondents coresiding with a child, increasing age of parents was associated with an increased likelihood of the household being located in the child's rather than the parent's home (Rosenthal, 1986).

Proximity to children

In the Hamilton study the pattern of geographical proximity between parents and children is similar to that reported in American studies (Cicirelli, 1981; Shanas with Heinemann, 1982). Table 2 summarizes the Hamilton data on proximity. Note that about two-thirds of older respondents who had children lived either in the same household or the same city as a child.

Advanced age and having several children are associated with proximity to children (Shanas with Heinemann, 1982). Since higher social class membership is associated with greater geographical mobility, parents who are middle class, or whose children are middle class, tend to be less

TABLE 2:
Distance from Nearest Child, Respondents Aged 70+ with Surviving Children, Hamilton and Stoney Creek, Ontario, by Gender and Marital Status

					Unmarried				Married			
	Men		Women		Men		Women		Men		Women	
	%	N	%	N	%	N	%	N	%	N	%	N
Same household	7	(4)	13	(7)	22	(2)	16	(6)	4	(2)	6	(1)
Same city	55	(30)	56	(30)	33	(3)	54	(20)	59	(27)	59	(10)
Within 1.5 hours	27	(15)	20	(11)	22	(2)	16	(6)	28	(13)	29	(5)
More than 1.5 hours*	11	(6)	11	(6)	22	(2)	14	(5)	9	(4)	6	(1)
Total	100	(55)	100	(54)	99	(9)	100	(37)	100	(46)	100	(17)

* Categories included same province, other province within Canada, other country.

Missing cases: males   1
females 9

geographically close to children than is true of their working class counter-parts. Nonetheless, most older people, regardless of class, tend to have at least one child living nearby (Shanas et al., 1968:239).

Whereas previous studies have examined how geographically proximate an older parent is to at least one child, the Hamilton study obtained data on all the older person's children. Among respondents aged 70 + who have children, only 11 percent had no children living within one and one-half hours' travel time. Of the remainder, excluding those who still had depen-dent children living at home or who had only one child, 42 percent of per-sons said that all their adult children lived within one and one-half hours' travel time, while 58 percent said some children lived within this distance and some farther away. Thus, the study shows that total family dispersion is very unusual, that partial dispersion is the most common pattern, but also that no dispersion beyond one and one-half hours' travel time is characteristic of a large minority of older families. The relative proximity of these parents to their children may well be related to the urban nature of the sample and to the proximity of Hamilton to Metropolitan Toronto.

Proximity affects other aspects of the parent-child relationship, such as face-to-face interaction and exchange of assistance (Kivett, 1985; Moss, Moss and Moles, 1985; Wolf et al., 1983). Moss, Moss and Moles (1985) suggest that distance beyond about fifty miles might be the point where visiting becomes more difficult. Parents whose children live at a distance communicate regularly with them by telephone or letter and tend to have overnight or more extended visits with them than with more proximate children (Shanas et al., 1968).

Using a subsample of adult children of Hamilton respondents aged 65 +, we compared three proximity groups (same city, within 1.5 hours, more than 1.5 hours) to examine the effects of proximity on interaction, exchange and affect (Marshall and Rosenthal, 1985). While interaction and exchange were strongly related to proximity, affective solidarity was not. Proximity was not associated with variability in feelings of closeness, agreement on values, or feelings of worry about the parent. Affective bonds do not appear to be weakened by distance. The findings concerning the exchange of assistance were more mixed. Exchanges of emotional support, advice, financial help and help in a crisis were not affected by proximity, but distance did limit the exchange of some types of practical help.

Associational solidarity

Available Canadian data suggest that, as in other industrial societies (Can-tor, 1979; Cicerilli, 1981; Marshall and Bengtson, 1983; Shanas et al., 1968; Shanas with Heinemann, 1982), contact between the generations is high. Among the Hamilton respondents aged 70 and older who had living children, over three-quarters had seen a child during the week preceding the interview (see Table 3). Shanas reports almost identical findings for the U.S. (Shanas with Heinemann, 1982). Only a small minority of older people see a child less than monthly. The great majority of older people are in frequent telephone contact with children; about half the older Hamilton respondents had spoken to a child the day of the interview or the day before that (see Table 3).

TABLE 3:
Contact With Children Among Hamilton, Ontario, Respondents Aged 70 + Who Have Surviving Children

	Men		Women	
	%	N	%	N
Last saw a child:				
Today or yesterday	30	(17)	22	(14)
2 - 7 days ago	50	(28)	54	(34)
8 - 30 days ago	14	(8)	10	(6)
More than 30 days ago	5	(3)	14	(9)
Totals	99	(56)	100	(63)
Last spoke on phone to child:				
Today or yesterday	48	(27)	50	(32)
2 - 7 days ago	34	(19)	40	(25)
8 - 30 days ago	7	(4)	3	(2)
More than 30 days ago	11	(6)	6	(4)
Totals	100	(56)	99	(63)

Interaction with children varies according to age, gender and marital status. Although women tend to maintain the ties in families (Bahr, 1976; Bott, 1957:135; Hagestad, 1981:33; Hill et al., 1970; Rosenthal, 1985), research does not unequivocally support the view that older mothers have more contact with children than older fathers do, at least not by virtue of gender alone (Lee, 1980). Age, gender and marital status interact, leading to more frequent contact with children among older, widowed women than among other subgroups. Widowed persons depend more than married persons on the social aspect of contact with children and depend on children, as well, to help out with tasks formerly performed by spouses (Lopata, 1979; Shanas with Heinemann, 1982:261). Higher frequency of contact with children is also associated with having several children rather than only one or two, and having at least one daughter (Shanas with Heinemann, 1982). Some studies have found that contact is more frequent in the working class than in the middle class (Adams, 1970; Warnes, Howes and Took, 1985). This has been attributed to greater proximity among working-class kin, including a greater tendency for coresidence with children (Soldo and Lauriat, 1976). However, Lee (1980), who reviewed this literature, concluded that existing data do not provide a basis for drawing firm conclusions about class and kinship interaction.

The reasons for intergenerational contact, or the activities engaged in when parents and children get together, have been less researched than frequency of contact. Bengtson and Black (1973) identify three dimensions of interaction: informal activities (conversation, talking about important matters, recreation); ceremonial or family ritual activities (getting together for family gatherings, reunions, birthdays, anniversaries, weddings); and exchange of assistance (giving and/or receiving help). In the Hamilton study, we asked respondents how often they engaged in these types of activities with an adult child. Among older respondents, informal activities

---

TABLE 4
Frequency with which Various Types of Activities Form Content of Intergenerational Interaction. Hamilton, Ontario. Respondents, Age 70 + Who Have Surviving Children

Activity	Mean score on a scale of 1 (never or almost never) to 8 (every day)	
	Men	Women
Visiting at either home	5.2	5.4
Talking things over that are important to you	3.2	3.3
Family gatherings for occasions like holidays or birthdays	2.7	3.0
Recreation outside the home such as movies, picnics, sports events	2.3	2.4
Shopping or errands together	2.0	2.9
Getting together to do home repairs or maintenance at either home	1.9	1.9
Religious activities	1.8	1.6

N: Men   56
   Women   63

* Categories included almost never or never, about once a year, several times a year, every other month or so, about 1-3 times a month, about once a week, several times a week, almost every day.

(other than recreation) were the most frequently engaged in, followed by ritual or ceremonial activities (see Table 4). Shared recreational activities and exchanges of assistance were not frequent occasions for intergenerational interaction. Religious activities were the least common occasions for such contact.

Older people maintain contact with siblings (Cicirelli, 1980; Scott, 1983; Shanas with Heinemann, 1982). However, this contact declines with age (Cicirelli, 1980), in part because of decreasing availability related to death and ill health. Among older Hamilton respondents who had surviving siblings, about half the women and just over one-quarter of the men saw a sibling monthly or more often (see Table 5), and higher proportions had phone contact that often. Two points are worth noting. First, women have more sibling contact than men. This finding is consistent with other research documenting the strong ties between sisters (Cumming and Schneider, 1961; Shanas, 1973), the importance of siblings to widows (Martin Matthews, 1985; Chapter 18) and the tendency for women to act as kinkeepers among siblings (Rosenthal, 1985). Second, a substantial proportion of respondents, especially among the men, have infrequent contact with siblings.

Three-quarters of older people who have grandchildren see a grandchild at least once a week (Harris and Associates, 1975). With preadult grandchildren, this contact may occur in conjunction with visits between older parents and adult children. In the Hamilton study, contact between older people and adult grandchildren (aged 18 and older) was investigated. Table 5 shows that about two-thirds of older respondents see a grown-up grandchild once a month or more, with one-third seeing a grandchild as often as once a week or more.

Affective solidarity

Parents and children in the Hamilton study were asked to rate, on a six-point scale ranging from "not close" to "extremely close," how close they felt to one another. Among older respondents, taking the child to whom the respondent felt closest, the mean was 4.4 for men and 4.2 for women. Parents reported somewhat more closeness than their children did (Gesser, Marshall and Rosenthal, 1985). Bengtson and colleagues investigated the degree of understanding, trust, fairness, respect and affection that parents and children felt characterized their mutual relationship. Relatively high levels of perceived solidarity were reported by both parents and children; however, parents perceived a slightly higher level of affective solidarity than children (Bengtson and Treas, 1980). Bengtson and Kuypers (1971) put forth the concept of the "developmental stake" to explain the dynamics underlying such patterned perceptual discrepancy between the generations. They define developmental stake as the need each generation has for the

TABLE 5
Contact With Siblings and Adult Grandchildren Among Hamilton, Ontario Respondents Aged 70+ Who Have Such Kin

| | How often usually see any sibling | | | | How often usually speak on phone to any sibling | | | | How often usually see any adult grandchild | | | |
| | Men | | Women | | Men | | Women | | Men | | Women | |
	%	N	%	N	%	N	%	N	%	N	%	N
Daily	2	(1)	6	(3)	6	(3)	17	(8)	10	(4)	4	(2)
1-2 times per week	6	(3)	20	(9)	6	(3)	28	(13)	23	(9)	30	(15)
1-3 times per month	21	(10)	26	(12)	16	(8)	20	(9)	33	(13)	30	(15)
2-11 times per year	21	(10)	20	(9)	22	(11)	15	(7)	15	(6)	24	(12)
Once a year or less	50	(24)	28	(13)	49	(24)	20	(9)	18	(7)	12	(6)
Totals	100	(48)*	100	(46)*	99	(49)*	100	(46)*	99	(39)	100	(50)

* Note that the Ns for questions on sibling contact are smaller than Ns for questions about children. This is because sibling contact data were not gathered in the interview but by means of a mailed questionnaire which was not returned by every respondent. In addition, one man who returned the questionnaire did not answer the question concerning how often a sibling was usually seen.

other and suggest that differences in the perceptions of parents and children are related to the unique developmental concerns of each generation. The relationship holds different meanings for each generational partner because of different personal goals and life stages. Parents have an investment or stake in establishing continuity through the lineage, and thus may minimize intergenerational disagreement or emotional distance. Children, on the other hand, especially young adults, seek to establish personal independence and autonomy, and may therefore exaggerate the extent of difference between themselves and their parents.

One indicator of affective solidarity in the parent-child relationship is how frequently children serve as "confidants" for parents. In a Manitoba study, older people were asked if there was anyone in whom they could confide or talk to about themselves or their problems (Strain and Chappell, 1982). Next to spouses, children were most commonly identified as such confidants.

Data are fragmentary concerning factors associated with affective solidarity. Marshall and Rosenthal (1985) found no relationship between emotional closeness and geographical proximity. Feelings of closeness also appear to be unrelated to amount of contact (Adams, 1968; Lee and Ellithorpe, 1982). One structural feature influencing affective solidarity is family size; Hamilton parents who had three or more children reported feeling less close to the closest child than parents who had one or two children.

In general, the quality of the parent-child relationship seems to be higher when the parent is in good health and is active in social spheres beyond the family (Johnson, 1978; Johnson and Bursk, 1977); these findings suggest that parental dependence on children has a negative effect on relationship quality. Surprisingly, consensus on values and important matters does not appear to be related to feelings of closeness and affection (Adams, 1968; Troll and Bengtson, 1979). Finally, gender plays a strong role in affective solidarity. The mother-daughter tie is closer than any other parent-child combination, daughters are emotionally closer than sons to parents and female lineages are more cohesive than other types (Troll and Bengtson, 1979).

Research thus shows high levels of affective solidarity in parent-child relationships. This does not mean, of course, that these relationships are characterized solely by positive sentiment. Troll and Bengtson observe that "where affect runs high, it is rarely only positive or negative. . . . Where love is to be found, hate can also be prevalent" (Troll and Bengtson, 1979:151).

Functional solidarity

As in other industrial societies (e.g., Hill et al., 1970; Shanas et al., 1968; Shanas with Heinemann, 1982), Canadian data show older people are

TABLE 6:
Exchange of Help with Children and Adult Grandchildren During Past Year. Respondents Aged 70+, Hamilton, Ontario.

Type of help*	Gave help to adult child				Received help from adult child				Gave help to grandchild aged 18+				Received help from grandchild aged 18+			
	Men		Women		Men		Women		Men		Women		Men		Women	
	%	N	%	N	%	N	%	N	%	N	%	N	%	N	%	N
Provide a home	5	(3)	5	(3)	7	(4)	19	(12)	0	(0)	2	(1)	0	(0)	0	(0)
Child care	23	(13)	27	(17)	4	(2)	13	(8)	0	(0)	2	(1)	0	(0)	0	(0)
Job/occupation	4	(2)	0	(0)	4	(2)	13	(8)	0	(0)	0	(0)	0	(0)	0	(0)
Financial	34	(19)	35	(22)	9	(5)	24	(15)	23	(9)	22	(11)	0	(0)	0	(0)
Advice	61	(34)	40	(25)	29	(16)	37	(23)	20	(8)	18	(9)	0	(0)	0	(0)
Personal services	32	(18)	19	(12)	50	(28)	59	(37)	2	(1)	6	(3)	20	(8)	20	(10)
Household chores	16	(9)	25	(16)	30	(17)	44	(28)	2	(1)	2	(1)	17	(7)	22	(11)
Home repairs	18	(10)	6	(4)	25	(14)	35	(22)	0	(0)	0	(0)	10	(4)	14	(7)
Personal care/ care in illness	7	(4)	14	(9)	23	(13)	37	(23)	2	(1)	2	(1)	7	(3)	2	(1)
Emotional or moral support	54	(30)	49	(31)	54	(30)	70	(44)	20	(8)	16	(8)	17	(7)	8	(4)
No help	16	(9)	29	(18)	20	(11)	16	(10)	51	(20)	52	(26)	48	(19)	56	(28)

N of respondents with adult children: men 56; women 63.
N of respondents with adult grandchildren: men 39; women 50.
* Response categories (with the exception of "no help") were not mutually exclusive; therefore columns do not total 100.

actively involved in reciprocal intergenerational exchanges. Help flows both up and down generational lines, although, with advancing age, there is a decrease in the proportion of older people who provide help to children and an increase in the proportion who receive help. However, even among people aged 75 and over, a majority still report helping children (Shanas with Heinemann, 1982).

In the Hamilton study, 84 percent of older men and 71 percent of older women who had children had given help to children during the year preceding the interview; 80 percent of men and 84 percent of women had received help (see Table 6). On the whole, emotional support was the most commonly identified type of help, testifying to the importance people place on the emotional quality of parent-child relationships.

Table 6 shows the types of help Hamilton respondents had given to and received from children "during the past year." While, in an overall sense, exchange relationships between older parents and their children are reciprocal, some types of help tend to flow down generational lines, from parents to children, while other types flow upwards. In the Hamilton data, for men, emotional support flowed equally up and down the generations. In contrast, more women received emotional support than gave it; this finding is likely related to the increased need for emotional support by widowed women. Older people gave more child care, financial assistance and advice than they received. Children gave more practical assistance, such as help with personal services, household chores, home repairs and personal care.

Cheal (1983) investigated symmetry and asymmetry in intergenerational gift-giving patterns, using both Canadian and U.S. data. Unlike Hill and Associates (1970), Cheal found old people were more likely to give assistance to children than to receive assistance. The elderly gave more in average monetary gifts than either the young or the middle-aged. The young were the largest receivers of gifts, followed by the middle-aged. The old were the smallest receivers.

The generations do not always agree in their reports of how much they help one another. In the Hamilton study, when the reports of older parents and their children concerning help given and received were compared, there was agreement on how much parents helped children. However, parents reported receiving less help from children than children reported providing. Gesser, Marshall and Rosenthal (1985) suggest this discrepancy may be partially explained by a modification of the "developmental stake" concept. They speculate that among older parents the developmental issue of growing dependency, and the fear of such dependency, may lead the parents to downplay the amount of help received from children.

Assistance with health care is an important type of exchange in families. Most routine health-care assistance to older people is provided by families (Brody, 1978; Comptroller General, 1977; Rakowski and Hickey, 1980;

Shanas and Maddox, 1976; Tobin and Kulys, 1980). Kin are also the preferred and most common source of help in a crisis (Hill et al., 1970). In Quebec, Béland (1984) found most respondents (from 72.6 percent to 85.3 percent) had a relative outside their household who was available for help in an emergency. In addition to providing direct service, Sussman (1977) has shown that adult children play an intermediary function in linking their aged parents to the health-care system.

Snider (1981) investigated the involvement of kin in providing health-related advice to older people in Alberta. He found advice from kin was more likely to be sought in emergency than in nonemergency health situations. At the same time, relatively small proportions of older people sought health advice from kin: 26.9 percent in crises and 15.4 percent in noncrisis situations.

While Canadian research has not yet focussed on the impact of social class on intergenerational exchange, U.S. studies suggest the type and frequency of exchange varies by social class (Troll and Bengtson, 1979). Working-class parents receive more help from children than middle-class parents do. Exchanges in the working class tend to take the form of services, while in the middle class they take the form of gifts and money. Reciprocal exchange is more common in the working class, while serial exchange from older to younger generations is typical in the middle class.

Exchange is also patterned by gender. Among older people, because women experience widowhood more commonly than men do, women typically require and receive more assistance from children. This pattern was evident among older Hamilton respondents, in that women received substantially more financial aid, help with chores, repairs, personal care and emotional support than men did (see Table 6). The giving of help is also related to gender. Sons tend to give parents financial assistance and advice, while daughters provide services such as caregiving. Daughters also worry more about their parents' health (Marshall, Rosenthal and Synge, 1983).

Women are the major caregivers to the elderly — as wives to elderly spouses and as middle-aged daughters to aged mothers. Today middle-aged women are increasingly likely to find themselves called upon to provide assistance to aging parents, while also having responsibilities towards children and grandchildren, as well as a spouse. Many women, at this life stage, are in the labour force. The burden on daughters heavily involved in caregiving has been well documented by Brody (1985). The terms the "caught generation," the "sandwich generation" or the "generation in the middle" describe the situation of middle-aged people, usually women, who find themselves torn between such competing obligations.

Concern about the "caught generation" should not obscure the fact that many older people, especially women, provide care. In a Montreal study of elderly caregivers, Marcus and Jaeger (1984) found wives as caregivers experienced more stress than husbands in that role, a disturbing finding in view of the fact that wives are more likely than husbands to be caregivers.

In the Hamilton study, a focus of interest was the concerns of adult children that emanate from and in turn strengthen the caregiving function (see Chapter 23; Marshall, Rosenthal and Synge, 1983). Children recognize filial responsibility for the provision of health care to parents. This leads to a "structuring of concerned watchfulness, a monitoring of parental health and, for most adult children, a readiness to provide care" (Marshall, Rosenthal and Synge, 1983). Such readiness suggests that children may be viewed as a "reservoir" of potential assistance from which help can be drawn if and when parental need arises.

The "reservoir" notion is also applicable to the grandparent-grandchild relationship and is akin to Hagestad's (1985) suggestion that just "being there" for grandchildren is a very important function of grandparents. Bengtson (1985) proposes that simply by "being there" grandparents may act as mediators of or deterrents to familial disruption. Their presence may help provide a sense of family continuity.

"Being there" frequently becomes transformed into concrete assistance in cases of divorce in the middle generation (Hagestad, 1982; Johnson, 1985). In a Canadian study, Gladstone (1985) investigated the impact on grandparents of divorce in the middle generation. In his sample, the grandchildren were aged 12 or younger. Gladstone found grandparents often played an important role in providing support to young grandchildren in the event of divorce, and that the relationship between the grandparent and his or her child strongly influenced the grandparent-grandchild relationship.

In the Hamilton study, exchange of assistance between older people and their adult grandchildren (aged 18 and older) was investigated. Although much less help was exchanged between grandparents and grandchildren than between parents and children, it was found that about half the older respondents reported giving help to and receiving help from adult grandchildren during the past year (see Table 6).

Consensual solidarity

Research points to "selective continuity" in value orientation (Bengtson, 1970) between elderly parents and adult children. The two generations tend to agree on values regarding fatalism and optimism as well as materialism and humanism; on the other hand, generations tend to differ on values towards child rearing and orientations towards collectivism versus individualism (Bengtson, 1975; Hill et al., 1970). Hamilton respondents were asked a global question as to whether, on important matters, they and each of their children agreed "very little, to some extent, a great deal, or completely." Their children were asked the same question concerning agreement with their parent. Both parents and children tended to say they agreed "a great deal" or "to some extent," but parents reported slightly more agreement than children (Gesser, Marshall and Rosenthal, 1985).

In intergenerational living, the "subjective" or perceived agreement or disagreement may be more consequential than "objective" agreement; that is, whether parents and children actually hold similar beliefs. The greater perceived consensus by parents than children in the Hamilton study, as in other studies (Acock and Bengtson, 1980; Bengtson, Mangen and Landry, 1984), may be understood, in part, by referring to the "developmental stake" concept. Parents need to feel they have passed on their values and created "personal heirs," while children need to feel an identity separate from their parents (Bengtson and Kuypers, 1971). These underlying motivations give the older generation a greater "stake" than their children in intergenerational consensus.

Normative solidarity

The expectations each generation has of the other with respect to filial and parental behaviours in family-related domains may be a source of friction or satisfaction in intergenerational life. In general, these expectations may be referred to as norms of familism. Of interest are issues such as filial obligations to visit or support aging parents, attitudes towards multigenerational households and obligations of children to live near their parents. Of course, norms, in isolation from other factors, do not predict behaviour. They are of interest, nonetheless, in that they indicate willingness or opposition to issues such as contributing to parental support. They are consequential, as well, in that unmet expectations may lead to low morale (Seelbach and Sauer, 1977).

It might be predicted that older people, having been socialized in a more traditional era when familial obligations were given greater emphasis, would adhere more strongly than younger people to familistic norms. The data from the Three Generations Study by Bengtson and colleagues support that prediction, both within lineages and in aggregates of different generations (Bengtson, Mangen and Landry, 1984). Not all research, however, supports this pattern. For example, Brody, Johnsen and Fulcomer (1984), in a study of three generations of women, found the oldest generation was the most receptive to formal service provision to the elderly while the youngest generation was the most receptive to family service provision. The youngest generation was also most likely to favour forming joint households with elderly parents.

In a study of women in Maritime Canada, Storm, Storm and Strike-Schurman (1985) examined beliefs concerning obligations to provide physical, financial and psychological support to older people. Although age differences were not marked, young adults tended to be stronger in endorsing children's responsibilities for aging parents than were older people themselves. Perhaps because they are more sensitive to factors making it difficult for families to provide assistance, older people place less responsibility on the family than younger people. This study concluded that the obligation of children to provide care was unambiguous only in the abstract. Considerable ambiguity existed as to when, how much and by what means children should assist parents.

Preliminary analysis of the Hamilton data has focussed on age groups rather than generations. To date, few age differences have been found. In fact, on only one measure and only among women did age prove significant. Middle-aged women were less supportive than older or younger women of the statement: "It is the obligation of children to take care of their aged parents." A substantial minority of men and a majority of women did not feel children should be legally responsible for elderly parents, and a majority felt children should not have to support elderly parents. On the other hand, the vast majority felt children should help out if their parents need it and that children should keep in close contact with their parents. As in other studies, the overwhelming majority agreed that it does not work out well for parents to live with children. Although most people said they preferred to live in the same neighbourhood as children rather than at a greater distance, over 90 percent endorsed the right of children to move away to pursue economic opportunities. As in Connidis's (1983) study, over three-quarters of the sample said even if they could no longer live on their own they would prefer to live elsewhere rather than with children.

In summary, research on norms suggests most families are relatively strong in this domain. While maintaining a commitment to individualism in such respects as the right to move away to pursue financial opportunities, the majority of people are supportive of familistic norms. In this respect, it may be said that in contemporary Canadian society, family members are willing to care for one another in a variety of ways. They may, of course, be limited in their ability to fulfill their perceived obligations because of other factors such as competing commitments or overwhelming needs of parents. A second point is that older people value the affective quality of the parent-child relationship and seek to preserve it. This may be the reason they prefer formal service providers for many types of assistance (Brody, Johnsen and Fulcomer, 1984) and say they would prefer to live apart from children even if they could not live alone.

The Organization of the Family

The solidarity dimensions capture much of the research on intergenerational relations in families, but they do not exhaust the range of theoretically important phenomena in intergenerational life. In the Hamilton study, effort has been directed towards exploring some new dimensions of the intergenerational family (Marshall, 1983; Marshall and Rosenthal, 1982; Rosenthal, 1982, 1983, 1985, 1986, in press; Rosenthal and Marshall, 1986; Rosenthal, Marshall and Synge, 1980).

As was evident in earlier sections of this chapter, most research in intergenerational relations has focussed on dyads, usually an elderly parent and an adult child. The task of studying whole families continues to pose a conceptual and methodological challenge to scholars (Hagestad, 1981). Families, in the sense of networks, can and should be thought of as structures; the structural form of network relationships should be the object of research attention (Wellman, 1981:23). One structural indicator is the extent to which networks have central figures (Wellman, 1981:24).

In the Hamilton study, we have drawn on the network approach in conceptualizing families as structural systems within which people may assume specialized roles. These people are central figures in the family network, and the positions to which their roles adhere are structural features of families. We postulated that families, in their efforts to maintain solidarity over time and generations, might develop a number of specialized roles or status positions. These positions were viewed as comprising a familial division of labour.

We asked respondents to think of their family as all living persons on their side of the family, including brothers, sisters, aunts, uncles, cousins, grandparents and so forth. Thus the boundary suggested was the extended family. Respondents were asked about the existence in their families of five specialized positions (the terms are the researchers' and were not presented as such to respondents): the kinkeeper (the person who works harder than others at keeping family members in touch with one another); the comforter (the person to whom family members turn for advice and comfort, to talk over their troubles); the financial advisor (the person to whom family members turn for advice about money matters); the placement officer (the person in the family who helps other family members find jobs or get started in occupations or business); and the ambassador (the family member who more than others represents the family at events such as funerals of more distant relatives or old family friends). These positions are distinct from their occupants. Individual incumbents may be viewed as passing through the positions, leading to the notion of succession of occupancy through generations.

The head of the family

We investigated headship by asking respondents: "Thinking of your side of the family as including you, your spouse and children and your parents and grandparents, whichever of these people are still alive, is there anyone who is thought of as 'head of the family' on your side of the family?'' Note that this question was structured in terms of the lineage. Follow-up questions asked why the person was considered to be head, how headship was assumed and who would be head in the future.

Two thirds of the respondents named a present head, and another 16 percent who said there was no present head named a former head of the family (see Rosenthal and Marshall, 1986; Rosenthal, in press). The position of ''head of the family'' was thus inferred. The most important activities of heads are advice giving, problem solving and exercising financial responsibility in the family. Being designated head of the family connotes a social recognition that the person plays a definable part in the familial organization of labour. In a minority of cases the position is primarily honorific, but this honour represents a meaningful symbol of familial organization that links the generations.

Headship is primarily a male-dominated position and usually descends in the male line, from father to son to grandson. Less commonly, widowed mothers assume the position for a time. Fathers, if living, tend to be named as lineage heads even into children's middle age, although this tendency gradually declines, as sons come to name themselves and daughters their husbands as head of the family. Thus, as people move through the early phases of the family life course in their own families of procreation, they generally feel a parent remains head of the family. By the time they themselves are middle-aged, there is a shifting of authority in the lineage, evidenced by a weakening of the hold on headship by aging parents and an accession to the position by middle-aged children. Respondents view headship as having moved down from their parents to themselves or their generational peers, yet almost never feel headship has already passed from their own generation to a younger one. Family and individual life course transitions (marriage, death, widowhood) create vacancies in headship into which the respondent's own generation may step. Only death and occasionally ill health are perceived as precipitating succession to the younger generation.

There is not complete consensus in families about headship occupancy and succession. For example, a woman may feel that widowhood propels her into the headship position, while a son may feel he has become the head of the family. Such discrepancies in perception and information management characterize family life and may well contribute to solidarity (Bengtson and Kuypers, 1971; Hagestad, 1981:30; Marshall and Bengtson, 1983). The analysis of headship shows that people view their families as extending beyond the conjugal household. The ability of respondents to name past, present and future family heads indicates people perceive their families as persisting over time, encompassing past, present and future generations. Headship binds members into a lineage unit despite separate households and progression through the life course.

The kinkeeper and other positions in the familial division of labour

Of the positions in the extended family that we investigated, the most commonly identified one was that held by the person who works harder than others at keeping the family in touch with one another, the position we call the "kinkeeper" (Rosenthal, 1982, 1985; Marshall and Rosenthal, 1982). Over half of the interview respondents said there was someone in their extended family who could be considered to be a kinkeeper, and a further 16 percent said there had been such a person in the past but not in the present. The work of kinkeeping consists most commonly of telephoning and writing, visiting and organizing family gatherings. Three-quarters of kinkeepers were women. Note, however, that a significant minority were men. Kinkeepers were most commonly siblings of the respondent, followed by respondents naming themselves. Kinkeeping is most commonly done by women in their fifties and sixties, and may represent another responsibility of the "caught generation."

Occupancy of the position of kinkeeper appears to descend through the maternal line. As a 65-year-old woman said, "My mother used to do this so when she died I took on the job." The most common reasons kinkeepers began their efforts were related to a desire to keep the family together or to the death or ill health of the previous kinkeeper. Often a specific event, such as the death of a parent, was perceived to threaten family continuity (Rosenberg and Anspach, 1973). For example, a 54-year-old man said his family kinkeeper assumed the responsibility because "She wants to keep the family together. She didn't want it to fall apart when our parents died." Parental death removes an important link among kin, leaving a vacuum into which a new kinkeeper may step (Marshall and Rosenthal, 1982). Other threats may be posed by intermarriage, geographical mobility or migration and a sense of personal mortality. Thus kinkeeping becomes more salient in response to a range of specific threats to family solidarity, threats that tend to increase as members move through the family life course. Respondents whose families had kinkeepers were more likely than other respondents to report extended family gatherings, to see extended family members on occasions such as Christmas, to have sentimental objects or heirlooms in the family and to interact with their children on ritual occasions.

Of the other positions, about two-fifths of respondents identified someone in the comforter and ambassador positions. About one-fifth had a financial advisor and a placement officer. We view these positions as comprising a familial division of labour, an aspect of family structure and a mechanism by means of which families counteract threats to solidarity. Three quarters of the families in the study had at least one position, and half had two or more. The number of positions identified may be taken to represent the extent of the division of labour in a respondent's family.

The organization of the family

In the classical Weberian typology, the family is considered to be the opposite of a modern bureaucratic organization. However, it can be theoretically productive to characterize the family as a formal organization with goals to achieve and with a number of positions in a division of labour. Metaphorically we think of the family as a business firm or formal organization. Like organizations, some families are highly differentiated (having many specialized task positions), while others are not. In organization theory, increasing differentiation of function requires the emergence of hierarchy because of a need for someone in authority to coordinate activities. We take the "head of the family" as referring to the presence or absence of such hierarchy, and have investigated how it relates to the degree of differentiation of specialized positions in the familial division of labour. We have found a relationship between vertical organization (headship) and horizontal differentiation (division of labour). The greater the number of horizontal positions, the greater the likelihood of having a head of the family.

Next we constructed a typology of families according to the presence or absence of a head and the number of other task positions. Retaining the metaphor of the formal organization, families with a high division of labour and a hierarchy of authority are "bureaucratic." The second type, with a high division of labour but no hierarchy, is "democratic." The third type, which has a head in command but a low division of labour, is "autocratic." The fourth type, with no head and little or no division of labour, is "anarchic." With increasing age, respondents were less likely to describe their families as bureaucratic and more likely to describe them as anarchic.

The typology shifts the unit of analysis from individuals to types of family structures. It becomes possible, then, to talk about what people in certain social structures might experience in the family (Marshall, 1983). We might inquire, for example, whether people in bureaucratic families receive more support than people in other family types. Typology construction of this type offers a fresh avenue for extending the more conventional analyses of intergenerational solidarity. As another example, we might cross-classify families on two solidarity dimensions such as proximity and amount of exchange, and then inquire as to the causes and consequences of falling into one of the four possible types. Future efforts in such directions would do much to advance the knowledge base represented by the empirical data on the solidarity dimensions reviewed in this chapter.

Conclusion

This chapter has reviewed the small but growing body of Canadian data on the family of later life. Almost all this Canadian research has been conducted since 1980, signifying that the investigation of intergenerational relations in Canada is a field in its early stages of development.

Based on the limited but growing Canadian data on family and intergenerational relations in later life, we have no reason as yet to suggest any great differences between families in Canada and the United States. In fact, the consistencies between the two countries on various measures of solidarity are very striking. It seems unlikely, therefore, that future research will uncover fundamental differences between Canadian and U.S. families. In view of this, it would seem sensible to frame future comparative research in terms of investigating the effects of particular structural or social conditions that differ between the two countries and might influence family life.

The framework for studying intergenerational solidarity has proven useful both in organizing discussions of existing literature and in guiding research. The framework itself has not yet been fully exploited. As Bengtson, Mangen and Landry (1984) point out, research has tended to concentrate on either pure description of the solidarity dimensions or on predictor variables, rather than on the interrelations between the dimensions of solidarity or the consequences of solidarity. The latter issues might be productively investigated using typology construction such as was suggested in the previous section.

Despite its usefulness, the solidarity framework might also hamper future research by restricting conceptualization and investigation to the solidarity dimensions. There is a need for fresh insights into the family life of older people. In part, this might be aided by adopting approaches very different from the intergenerational solidarity framework. The investigation of the organization of the family described in this chapter represented one attempt to break new ground in family research.

The research reviewed in this chapter has relevance for any social policy that would seek to place responsibility for the care of older people on their families. First, the existing data suggest that the family currently provides much support to older members; thus it is unlikely that the family represents an untapped resource whose exploitation could relieve governments of the cost of service provision. Second, while families express willingness to provide care, there are limitations on their ability to do so. Some limitations have to do with family structure. Many older people do not have a spouse to whom they might turn for help. A significant minority of older people have no children or have only one child. Clearly, any policy that relies on family assistance ignores those who lack familial resources. Some limitations stem from broader social change. For example, the trend for middle-aged women to participate in the paid labour force impinges on their ability to provide care to older family members. Third, since women have traditionally performed and continue to perform the work of caregiving within the family, social policy that promotes family care in effect perpetuates the unequal and dependent position of women in our society (Aronson, 1985). Fourth, as Aronson (1985) observes, social policy that promotes family care may serve to make older people dependent on their children, a situation most older people themselves deeply wish to avoid.

Finally, we should place the importance of the family to older people in perspective. Most older people value their intergenerational relationships highly and find personal meaning and satisfaction in them, but the intergenerational family is rarely if ever a person's entire life. Relationships with friends and age peers also have an important place in the lives of older people (Chappell, 1983). Nor should we assume that the more solidarity on any dimension a person reports, the better off that person is; for example, the morale of older people is unrelated to their frequency of contact with children (Lee, 1979). In perspective, however, the family — including intergenerational but also sibling and spousal relationships — continues to be a vital part of the lives of older Canadians.

Note

[1] The study was funded by the Social Sciences and Humanities Research Council of Canada through grant number 492-76-0076-R1. Continuing analysis was supported by the Gerontology Research Council of Ontario. The sample was drawn from the 1979 property assessment list, which is an annual census of all occupants of all dwellings. The sample was stratified into six equal frames of males and females in the age categories 40-54, 55-69 and 70 and over. Attempts were made to contact 1,081 persons, of whom 117 could not be located (30 were known to be deceased and 68 to have moved). Of 964 contacted persons, 116 were ineligible because of insufficient fluency to be interviewed in English and 102 because of poor health. Of 746 eligible contacted persons, 281 refused to be interviewed, yielding a 62 percent response rate. This is comparable to that obtained in similar Canadian community surveys involving an older population (Chappell, 1983; Connidis, 1983). Five respondents who were interviewed in institutions were excluded from ensuing analyses. The study underrepresents the bedfast and very ill elderly. Twenty-five percent of the sample reported annual family income of $8,000 or less, while 22 percent reported $25,000 or more. About half the respondents listed British as their main ancestry, while the next largest groups (Irish, Italian and German) were listed by 7 percent or less of respondents. Recent immigrants are underrepresented because of the criteria that a respondent had to have lived in Canada at least five years and be fluent enough to be interviewed in English.

References

Acock, A. and Vern L. Bengtson
  1980 "Socialization and attribution processes: Actual versus perceived similarity among parents and youth." *Journal of Marriage and the Family* 40(3):501-515.

Adams, Bert
  1968 *Kinship in an Urban Setting.* Chicago: Markham.
  1970 "Isolation, function and beyond: American kinship in the 1960's." *Journal of Marriage and the Family* 32:575-597.

Aronson, Jane
  1985 "Family care of the elderly." *Canadian Journal on Aging* 4:115-125.

Bahr, Howard M.
  1976 "The kinship role." Pp. 61-79 in F. Ivan Nye (ed.), *Role Structure and Analysis of the Family.* Beverly Hills: Sage.

Béland, François
  1984 "The family and adults 65 years of age or over: Co-residency and availability of help." *Canadian Review of Sociology and Anthropology* 21(3):302-317.

Bengtson, Vern L.
  1970 "The generation gap: A review and typology of social-psychological perspectives." *Youth and Society* 2:7-31.
  1975 "Generation and family effects in value socialization." *American Sociological Review* 40:358-371.
  1985 "Diversity and symbolism in grandparental roles." Chapter 1, Pp. 11-25 in Vern L. Bengtson and Joan F. Robertson (eds.), *Grandparenthood.* Beverly Hills: Sage.

Bengtson, Vern L. and K.D. Black
  1973 "Intergenerational relations and continuities in socialization." Pp. 207-234 in P. Baltes and K.W. Schaie (eds.), *Life-Span Developmental Psychology: Personality and Socialization.* New York: Academic Press.

Bengtson, Vern L., Neal Cutler, David Mangen and Victor W. Marshall
  1985 "Generations, cohorts, and relations between age groups." Pp. 304-338 in R.H. Binstock and E. Shanas (eds.), *Handbook of Aging and the Social Sciences.* 2nd edition. New York: Van Nostrand Reinhold.

Bengtson, Vern L. and J.A. Kuypers
  1971 "Generational differences and the developmental stake." *Aging and Human Development* 2:249-260.

Bengtson, Vern L., D. Mangen and P. Landry
  1984 "The multi-generation family: Concepts and findings." Pp. 63-80 in V. Garms-Homolova, E.M. Hoerning and D. Schaeffer (eds.), *Intergenerational Relationships.* New York: C.J. Hogrefe.

Bengtson, Vern L., Edward B. Olander, and Anees A. Haddad
  1976 "The 'generation gap' and aging family members: Toward a conceptual model." Pp. 237-263 in J.F. Gubrium (ed.), *Time, Roles and Self in Old Age.* New York: Human Sciences Press.

Bengtson, Vern L. and S. Schrader
   1982   "Parent-child relations: The measurement of intergenerational interaction and affect in old age." Pp. 115-185 in D. Mangen and W. Peterson (eds.), *Research Instruments in Social Gerontology*, Vol. 2. Minneapolis: University of Minnesota Press.
Bengtson, Vern L. and Judith Treas
   1980   "The changing family context of mental health and aging." Pp. 400-428 in James R. Birren and R. Bruce Sloan (eds.), *Handbook of Mental Health and Aging*. Englewood Cliffs, New Jersey: Prentice-Hall.
Bott, Elizabeth
   1957   *Family and Social Network*. London: Tavistock.
Brody, Elaine
   1978   "The aging of the family." *Annals, American Association of Political and Social Science* 438:13-27.
   1985   "Parent care as a normative family stress." *The Gerontologist* 25(1):19-29.
Brody, Elaine, Pauline Johnsen and Mark Fulcomer
   1984   "What should adult children do for elderly parents? Opinions and preferences of three generations of women." *Journal of Gerontology* 39(6):736-746.
Cantor, M.
   1979   "The informal support system of the inner city elderly: Is ethnicity a factor?" Pp. 153-174 in D. Gelfand and A. Kutzik (eds.), *Ethnicity and Aging*. New York: Springer.
Chappell, Neena L.
   1983   "Informal support networks among the elderly." *Research On Aging* 5(1):77-99.
Cheal, David J.
   1983   "Intergenerational family transfers." *Journal of Marriage and the Family* 45(4):805-813.
Cicirelli, V.G.
   1980   "Sibling relationships in adulthood: A life span perspective." In L. Poon (ed.), *Aging in the 1980s*. Washington, D.C.: American Psychological Association.
   1981   *Helping Elderly Parents: The Role of Adult Children*. Boston: Auburn House.
Comptroller General of the United States
   1977   *Report to the Congress: The Well-Being of Older People in Cleveland, Ohio*. Washington, D.C.: General Accounting Office.
Connidis, Ingrid
   1983   "Living arrangement choices of older residents." *Canadian Journal of Sociology* 8(Fall):359-375.
Connidis, Ingrid and Judith Rempel
   1983   "The living arrangements of older residents: The role of gender, marital status, age and family size." *Canadian Journal on Aging* 2(3):91-105.
Cumming, E. and D. Schneider
   1961   "Sibling solidarity: A property of American kinship." *American Anthropologist* 63(June):498-507.

Dahlin, M.
  1980   "Perspectives on the family life of the elderly in 1900." *The Gerontologist* 20:99-107.
Gesser, Gina, Victor W. Marshall and Carolyn J. Rosenthal
  1985   "A Test of the Generational Stake Hypothesis With an Older Canadian Sample." Paper presented at the 14th annual meeting, Canadian Association On Gerontology, Hamilton, Ontario, October 17.
Gladstone, James
  1985   "A Study of Grandparents Whose Child Has Separated or Divorced." Unpublished doctoral dissertation, Faculty of Social Work, University of Toronto.
Granovetter, Mark S.
  1973   "The strength of weak ties." *American Journal of Sociology* 78:1360-1380.
Hagestad, Gunhild O.
  1981   "Problems and promises in the social psychology of intergenerational relations." Pp. 11-46 in R. Fogel, E. Hatfield, S. Kiesler and E. Shanas (eds.), *Aging: Stability and Change in the Family.* New York: Academic Press.
  1982   "Divorce: The family ripple effect." *Generations: The Journal of the Western Gerontological Society* (Winter):24-31.
  1985   "Continuity and connectedness." Chapter 2, pp. 31-48 in Vern L. Bengtson and Joan F. Robertson (eds.), *Grandparenthood.* Beverly Hills: Sage.
Harris, L. and Associates
  1975   *The Myth and Reality of Aging in America.* Washington, D.C.: National Council on the Aging.
Hill, R., N. Foote, J. Aldous, R. Carlson and R. MacDonald
  1970   *Family Development in Three Generations.* Cambridge: Schenkman Publishing Company.
Johnson, Colleen L.
  1985   "Grandparenting options in divorcing families." Chapter 5, pp. 81-96 in Vern L. Bengtson and Joan F. Robertson (eds.), *Grandparenthood.* Beverly Hills: Sage.
Johnson, E.
  1978   "Good relationships between older mothers and their daughters: A causal model." *The Gerontologist* 18(3):301-306.
Johnson, E. and B. Bursk
  1977   "Relationships between the elderly and their adult children." *The Gerontologist* 17:900-96.
Kahn, Robert L.
  1979   "Aging and social support." Pp. 77-91 in Matilda White Riley (ed.), *Aging from Birth to Death.* Boulder, Colorado: Westview Press.
Kivett, Vira R.
  1985   "Consanguinity and kin level: Their relative importance to the helping network of older adults." *Journal of Gerontology* 40(2):228-234.
Laslett, Peter
  1976   "Societal development and aging." Chapter 4, Pp. 87-116 in R. Binstock

and E. Shanas (eds.), *Handbook of Aging and the Social Sciences*. New York: Van Nostrand Reinhold.

Lee, Gary R.
1979   "Children and the elderly." *Research On Aging* 1(3):335-360.
1980   "Kinship in the seventies: A decade review of research and theory." *Journal of Marriage and the Family* 42(4):193-204.

Lee, Gary R. and E. Ellithorpe
1982   "Intergenerational exchange and subjective well-being among the elderly." *Journal of Marriage and the Family* 44:217-224.

Litwak, E.
1960   "Geographical mobility and extended family cohesion." *American Sociological Review* 25:385-394.

Lopata, Helena
1979   *Women as Widows: Support Systems*. New York: Elsevier.

Marcus, Lotte and Valerie Jaeger
1984   "The elderly as family caregivers." *Canadian Journal On Aging* 3(1):33-43.

Marshall, Victor W.
1983   "The Organization of Family Relationships." Paper presented at the Research Centre for Gerontology, University of Manitoba, April 28.
1984   "Sampling issues in surveys of aging and intergenerational relations." Working paper, Gerontology Research Centre, University of Guelph.

Marshall, Victor W. and Vern L. Bengtson
1983   "Generations: Conflict and cooperation." In M. Bergener, U. Lehr, E. Lang and R. Schmitz-Scherzer (eds.), *Gerontology in the Eighties: Highlights of the 12th International Conference on Gerontology*. New York: Springer.

Marshall, Victor W. and Carolyn J. Rosenthal
1982   "Parental Death: A life course marker." *Generations* 7(2):30-31, 39.
1985   "The Relevance of Geographical Proximity in Intergenerational Relations." Paper presented at the 14th annual meeting of the Gerontological Society of America, New Orleans, Louisiana: November.

Marshall, Victor W., Carolyn J. Rosenthal and Jane Synge
1983   "Concerns about parental health." Pp. 253-273 in E. Markson (ed.), *Older Women*. Lexington and Toronto: D.C. Heath.

Martin Matthews, Anne
1985   "Support systems of widows in Canada." In Helena Z. Lopata (ed.), *Widows: Other Countries/Other Places*. Durham, North Carolina: Duke University Press.

Minister of Supply and Services Canada
1983   *Fact Book on Aging in Canada*. Ottawa: Department of National Health and Welfare.

Moss, M., S. Moss and E. Moles
1985   "The quality of relationships between elderly parents and their out-of-town children." *The Gerontologist* 25(2):134-140.

Nett, Emily
    1981   "Canadian families in social-historical perspective." *Canadian Journal of Sociology* 6:239-260.

Nydegger, C.
    1983   "Family ties of the aged in cross-cultural perspective." *The Gerontologist* 23:26-32.

Rakokwski, W. and T. Hickey
    1980   "Late life health behavior: Integrating health beliefs and temporal perspectives." *Research on Aging* 2:283-308.

Rempel, Judith
    1985   "Childless elderly: What are they missing?" *Journal of Marriage and the Family* 47:343-348.

Rosenberg, G.S. and D.J. Anspach
    1973   "Sibling solidarity in the working class." *Journal of Marriage and the Family* 35:108-113.

Rosenthal, Carolyn J.
    1982   "Family responsibilities and concerns: A perspective on the lives of middle-aged women." *Resources for Feminist Research* (Winter).
    1983   "A New Conceptualization of Family Support for the Elderly." Paper presented at the annual meetings of the American Sociological Association, Detroit, Michigan, August 31-September 4.
    1985   "Kinkeeping in the familial division of labor." *Journal of Marriage and the Family* 47(4):965-974.
    1986   "The differentiation of multigenerational households." *Canadian Journal on Aging* 5(1).

Rosenthal, Carolyn J.
    In press "Generational succession: The passing on of family headship." *Journal of Comparative Family Studies* 18(1).

Rosenthal, Carolyn J. and Victor W. Marshall
    1986   "The head of the family: Social meaning and structural variability." *Canadian Journal of Sociology* 11(2): 183-198.

Rosenthal, Carolyn J., Victor W. Marshall and Jane Synge
    1980   "The succession of lineage roles as families age." *Essence* 4(3):179-193.

Scott, J.
    1983   "Siblings and other kin." Pp. 47-62 in T. Brubaker (ed.), *Family Relationships in Later Life*. Beverly Hills: Sage.

Seelbach, W. and W. Sauer
    1977   "Filial responsibility expectations and morale among aged parents." *The Gerontologist* 17(6):492-499.

Shanas, Ethel
    1973   "Family-kin networks and aging in cross-cultural perspective." *Journal of Marriage and the Family* 35:505-511.
    1979   "The family as a social support system in old age." *The Gerontologist* 19(2):169-174.

Shanas, Ethel with the assistance of Gloria Heinemann
    1982   *National Survey of the Aged*. Administration on Aging, U.S. Department

of Health and Human Services, Washington D.C. DHHS Publication No. (OHDS) 83-20425.

Shanas, Ethel and George Maddox
1976 "Aging, health and the organization of health resources." Ch. 23, Pp. 592–618 in R. Binstock and E. Shanas (eds.), *Handbook of Aging and the Social Sciences*. New York: Van Nostrand Reinhold.

Shanas, Ethel, P. Townsend, D. Wedderburn, H. Friis, P. Milhoj and J. Stehouwer
1968 *Old People in Three Industrial Societies*. New York: Atherton Press.

Snider, Earle L.
1981 "The role of kin in meeting health care needs of the elderly." *Canadian Journal of Sociology* 6(3):325-336.

Soldo, B. and P. Lauriat
1976 "Living arrangements among the elderly in the United States: A log-linear approach." *Journal of Comparative Family Studies* 7(Summer):351-366.

Storm, C., T. Storm and J. Strike-Schurman
1985 "Obligations for care: Beliefs in a small Canadian town." *Canadian Journal on Aging* 4(2):75-85.

Strain, Laurel and Neena L. Chappell
1982 "Confidants: Do they make a difference in quality of life?" *Research On Aging* 4:479-502.

Sussman, M.B.
1977 "Family, bureaucracy, and the elderly individual: An organizational/ linkage perspective." Pp. 2-20 in E. Shanas and M.B. Sussman (eds.), *Family, Bureaucracy and the Elderly*. Durham, North Carolina: Duke University Press.

Sussman, M.B. and L. Burchinal
1962 "Kin family network: Unheralded structure in current conceptualization of family functioning." *Marriage and Family Living* 24(August):231-240.

Thomas, K. and A. Wister
1984 "Living arrangements of older women: The ethnic dimension." *Journal of Marriage and the Family* 46:301-311.

Tobin, S. and R. Kulys
1980 "The family and services." Pp. 370-390 in C. Eisdorfer (ed.), *Annual Review of Gerontology and Geriatrics*. New York: Springer.

Troll, Lillian and Vern L. Bengtson with the assistance of Dianne McFarland
1979 "Generations in the family." Pp. 117-161 in W. Burr, R. Hill, F. Nye and I. Reiss (eds.), *Contemporary Theories about the Family*, Vol. 1. New York: The Free Press.

Wake, S. and M. Sporakowski
1972 "An intergenerational comparison of attitudes towards supporting aged parents." *Journal of Marriage and the Family* 34:42-48.

Warnes, A.M., D.R. Howes and L. Took
1985 "Residential locations and inter-generational visiting in retirement." *The Quarterly Journal of Social Affairs* 1(3):231-247.

Wellman, Barry
1981 "Network Analysis from Method and Metaphor to Theory and

Substance." Working Series Paper 1B, Structural Analysis Program, Department of Sociology, University of Toronto.

Wellman, Barry and Alan Hall
   1986   "Social networks and social support: Implications for later life." In Victor W. Marshall (ed.), *Later Life: A Microsociology*. Beverly Hills: Sage.

Winsborough, H.
   1980   "A demographic approach to the life cycle." Pp. 65-75 in K. Back (ed.), *Life Course: Integrative Theories and Exemplary Populations*. Boulder, Colorado: Westview Press, for the American Association for the Advancement of Science.

Wolf, J., N. Breslau, A. Ford, H. Ziegler and A. Ward
   1983   "Distance and contacts: Interactions of black urban elderly adults with family and friends." *Journal of Gerontology* 38(4):465-471.

18

Widowhood as an Expectable Life Event

Anne Martin Matthews
Gerontology Research Centre and
Department of Family Studies
University of Guelph

The study of life events typically involves the examination of such life-cycle transitions as getting married, having children, the departure of children from the home, retiring from the paid labour force and becoming a widow or widower. Because most events of this sort are linked to the family life cycle, one of their outstanding features is their general predictability. Although, as Pearlin (1980) notes, there is certainly some variation in the timing of life-cycle transitions; they can be viewed as the relatively scheduled and anticipated events of life. Widowhood is such a life event. As such, it differs fundamentally from other life-cycle events such as divorce and illness, which may be widely experienced but nevertheless "not scheduled into our lives as we do the life-cycle transitions" (Pearlin, 1980:351).

This chapter will consider the life event of widowhood as a life-course transition, with attendant "complex patterns of change and stability — or discontinuity and order" (George, 1980). Central to this analysis is Hughes's concept of career, in which he distinguished between *objective career* (a series of social statuses held through the life course) and *subjective career* ("the moving perspective in which the person sees his life as a whole and interprets the meaning of his various attributes, actions and the things that happen to him") (1971:137). This concept has been further elaborated by Hewitt, who observes that:

> Just as an orientation toward the solution of everyday problems and the ongoing negotiation of social order link people and their activities in a "horizontal" way, the activities of individuals are linked "vertically" over time. The concept of "career" captures the nature of this vertical linkage (1976:179).

This chapter will examine how the "objective career" of widowhood has changed historically in Canadian society — in terms of its age-relatedness,

---

The author wishes to acknowledge the assistance of the Gerontology Research Centre, University of Guelph, in the preparation of this chapter.

duration and sex-selective nature. In addition, the nature of widowhood as a "subjective career" will be explored by focussing on four aspects of widowhood: its relative importance as a life-course transition; sources of variability in the perceived impact of the loss of the spouse; the changing nature of the social support mobilized at various points in the widowhood process; and changes in the identity and personal resources of the widowed themselves.

The Objective Career of Widowhood

Patterns of widowhood in Canada have been characterized by both stability and profound change in recent years. In 1981, there were 1,157,670 widowed persons in Canada, representing 6.2 percent of the population aged 15 and over, a proportion that has remained the same for the entire twentieth century. There has also been relatively little alteration in the long-term sex-specific nature of widowhood in Canada. At the time of the 1981 census, only 2.2 percent of males aged 15 and over were widowed, while 9.9 percent of women were (Statistics Canada, 1982).

There have, however, been dramatic changes in the median age of the widowed and other features of this status, such as its duration and age of onset. Overall, two factors now characterize the incidence of widowhood in the Canadian population: its sex-selective and age-related nature. Eighty-two percent of the widowed are women, and their proportion is increasing: for all ages, widows outnumbered widowers by nearly four to one in Canada in 1971; by 1981, the proportion had increased to almost five to one (Statistics Canada, 1982).

This demographic reality accounts for why discussions of widowhood generally focus on women. As Gee indicates elsewhere in this volume, the main reason for this is the differential life expectancy of males and females;

TABLE 1:
Prevalence of Widows and Widowers Aged 65 Years and Over, Canada 1961, 1971 and 1981

	1961 N	1971 N	1981 N	Percent Change 1961-1971	Percent Change 1971-1981
Widowers	137,277	130,235	142,820	− 9.5	+ 9.7
Widows	346,903	475,635	662,210	+ 37.1	+ 39.2

SOURCE: Statistics Canada (1982), *Population: Age, Sex and Marital Status, 1981*, Table 3: Population by marital status and sex, for Canada and Provinces 1921-1981, 3-1.

another reason is the mating gradient, whereby husbands are generally two to three years older than their wives. Yet another factor that influences not the likelihood of being widowed, but the numbers of widowed men and women in the population at any one time is the differential in rates of remarriage for widows and widowers. Not only are men far less likely to *become* widowed, they are also far less likely than women to *remain* widowed. For example, in 1981 the rate of remarriage per 1,000 widowers in Canada was 28.5 per year. The remarriage rate for widows, by contrast, was 6.32 per year (Statistics Canada, 1985b). As a result of all these factors, the relative proportions of male and female widowed in this country are quite different, and this difference is increasing with each decade. As Table 1 illustrates, in the decade 1961 to 1971, the numbers of widows age 65 and

TABLE 2:
Widowed Population 15 Years and Over, By Sex and Age Cohorts, Canada 1981

	Widowers		Widows	
	N	Percentage of Age Cohort*	N	Percentage of Age Cohort*
Total, or 15 + Years	199,530	2.2	958,135	9.9
15-19	320	0.027	600	0.052
20-24	430	0.036	1,350	0.12
25-29	640	0.059	3,225	0.29
30-34	1,215	0.12	5,865	0.58
35-39	1,830	0.22	9,200	1.14
40-44	2,905	0.43	14,580	2.2
45-49	5,280	0.83	25,460	4.1
50-54	9,820	1.6	47,155	7.6
55-59	14,885	2.6	79,500	13.0
60-64	19,395	4.2	109,005	21.1
65-69	26,180	6.7	142,985	31.5
70-74	30,395	10.8	155,290	44.1
75-79	31,285	17.3	145,050	57.5
80-84	26,265	27.7	113,600	70.2
85-89	17,815	40.5	68,675	79.0
90 +	10,880	55.5	36.610	84.7

SOURCE: 1981 Census of Canada, Cat. #92-901, September 1982, Table 4: Population by selected age groups and sex, showing marital status.

* Percentages are my own calculation.

over increased by 37 percent, while the numbers of widowers aged 65 and over actually declined by almost 10 percent (Martin Matthews, 1980a); since then, the increase in numbers of widows has far exceeded that of widowers.

In recent decades, the average age at widowhood has steadily increased, with the proportion of the widowed in each age cohort rising dramatically from age 50 onwards. As a result, widowhood in Canada is associated not only with women, but now also with the elderly. Indeed, most widows in Canada (69.1 percent) are over the age of 65. Table 2 provides data from the 1981 census that indicate the age-related nature of the experience of widowhood in Canada: in the 65-69 age group, 32 percent of women and 7 percent of men are widowed; by age 75-79 this proportion has risen to 58 percent of women and 18 percent of men; and by age 85-89, fully 79 percent of women and 41 percent of men are widowed.

In addition, the years that a widow can expect to live have also increased. Women widowed at age 65 can expect, on average, almost nineteen (18.85) more years of life; those widowed at age 80 can expect an average of nearly nine (8.84) more years of life (Statistics Canada, 1984).

Because most Canadians do marry, the experience of widowhood will be an "expectable" event of later life for most people. Although the Canadian divorce rate has nearly doubled since laws were relaxed in 1968, the current rate of 1125.2 per 100,000 married women aged 15 years and over (Statistics Canada, 1985a:10) still remains about half the American rate. However, figures derived from recent divorce trends in Canada project that nearly one quarter of persons marrying between the ages of 15 and 25 (and born between 1946 and 1956) may be expected to obtain a divorce by the time they reach 75. Nevertheless, these figures indicate that, for the foreseeable future, death of the spouse will be the typical end to the married life of Canadians.

The Subjective Career of Widowhood

Widowhood as a relative life event

A fundamental characteristic of widowhood in Canadian society is its stress-related nature. There is general consensus in the field of life-event scaling that the death of a spouse is among the most, if not *the* most, stressful of role transitions (Holmes and Rahe, 1967; McFarlane et al., 1980). While Pearlin found that most "key transitional life events. . .bring about little or no emotional changes that are sufficiently stable to be discerned," one single life transition raised depression to a higher level than prior to the event: being widowed (1980:352). Evidence of the significant impact of widowhood as a life event also emerged in my own pilot study of the social, emotional, service and economic supports of widowed women living in Guelph, Ontario. In this study, in-depth interviews were conducted with 26 widows, ranging in age from 46 to 86, widowed an average of 8.6 years after having been married an average of 34.3 years. The women were identified through obituary notices appearing in local newspapers over a five-year period.

Included in the structured interview schedule was an assessment of 34 life events, chosen to represent major events that occur in a person's lifetime and ranging from things like "when you left home for the first time" to "the birth of a grandchild." After all experienced life events were sorted into five groups ranging from "did not affect me at all" to "affected me a lot," respondents were asked to rank order, according to impact on their lives, those events that affected them a lot. Without exception, these widows, all a minimum of five and a maximum of ten years into widowhood, indicated that the loss of the spouse had affected them more than any other single life event (Martin Matthews, 1982).

In another study of 450 Ontario men and women aged 61 to 70 and retired an average of 3.5 years, the same method for the evaluation of relative life events was used, and here again the death of a spouse consistently emerged as the life event that had had the greatest impact on respondents. It ranked first of 34 life events in an assessment of crisis; by contrast, retirement ranked 28th of 34 life events, and the end of a marriage through separation or divorce ranked 17th of 34 events (Martin Matthews, Brown, Davis and Denton, 1982). This finding, and similar findings by other researchers, are intriguing, for they indicate that the "predictable" and "scheduled" life event of widowhood has far more significant an impact than events not scheduled and predictable in the life cycle. Given the predictable nature of widowhood and the attendant opportunities for anticipatory socialization, this is not what one would expect. In the rest of this chapter, we shall attempt to consider why this should be so.

Sources of variability in the experience of widowhood

Here we will examine a variety of factors that may serve to exacerbate or minimize the impact of the life event of widowhood. These include age at widowhood and opportunities for anticipatory socialization, gender differences, socio-economic factors and environmental issues.

Age at widowhood.

This chapter, as well as Chapter 15 by Gee, has emphasized how the experience of widowhood has increasingly come to be associated with later life. As Gee notes, women born in the nineteenth century became widows in their late fifties, while their present-day counterparts can expect to be nearly 70 when this life event occurs. Hence, increasingly, old age has come to be viewed as the expectable time for widowhood. Referred to as the "social clock" by Neugarten and Hagestad (1976), this expectation of the typical age at widowhood has implications for how it is experienced by individuals, both in terms of their psychological preparedness and opportunities for anticipatory socialization, and also in terms of the societal resources and supports available to them.

The issue of being "on time" or "off time" in the experience of widowhood has not been systematically investigated by Canadian researchers. However, there is a general recognition in the literature that "The age at which the wife experiences the death of her husband is a very important feature of widowhood because of the way her life is immersed in other social roles" (Lopata, 1973:33; see also Gibbs, 1980:14).

Canadian research has not focussed systematically on individuals whose experience of widowhood is either considerably earlier or quite later than that of their peers. For example, Vachon and her associates have focussed primarily on widowed populations with a mean age of 53 (Vachon, 1981) and aged 55 to 69 (Vachon et al., 1977). Haas-Hawkings et al. (1980) studied a group ranging in age from 49 to 83, with a mean age of 66; Norris (1980) studied a group of women who had been widowed for ten years and whose average age was 70 to 71, but the sample size was only 11; Stryckman's (1981a, 1981b, 1982) sample of widowed "are all at least 55 or over," with the average age at widowhood 62.8. The work of Vachon and her colleagues at the Clarke Institute of Psychiatry is essentially the only investigation of the impact of age per se on the experience of widowhood. In general, this research finds that grief is more intense in the case of a younger death and when death is relatively unexpected (Vachon et al., 1976; Vachon, 1979, 1981). In such cases, of course, there is little opportunity for the anticipatory socialization experienced by older individuals, and patterns of access to a reference group of supportive individuals will be quite different. In addition, the younger the widowed person, the more likely that the presence of dependent children will influence the nature of the transition.

Gender differences in the experiences of widowhood.

Earlier we noted dramatic differences in the likelihood of men and women becoming and remaining widowed. These demographic realities imply differential advantages for men and for women in widowhood. Because widows so outnumber widowers and are, as a group, younger on average, they are more likely to have same-sex widowed friends both prior to and during their own widowhood, who may serve as role models and offer social support. On the other hand, the option to remarry is far more accessible to widowed men.

The greater expectability of widowhood for women than for men frequently becomes translated, at the social-psychological level, into a kind of anticipatory socialization that women more readily express throughout their adult lives. For example, in a study of women's experiences of residential relocation, this author was struck by the frequency with which women in middle age would discuss the prospect of being alone in later life. Such comments as the following were typical: "I don't know where I'd go if something happened to my husband"; "If something happened to my husband, I wouldn't stay here" (Martin Matthews, 1980b:272). It is clear from these comments that for many women, the prospect of widowhood is a reality they recognize and incorporate as part of their "life plan" (Berger, Berger and Kellner, 1973:73). As such, their thinking — if not their overt behaviour — frequently involves a mental rehearsal or anticipation of circumstances associated with becoming and being "unattached" later in life. This is a form of anticipatory socialization for widowhood that — quite realistically — distinguishes men's and women's images of their own aging. Widowhood is an expectable life event for women, but not so for men.

The few studies that consider men's experiences of widowhood have typically focussed on a debate about whether the transition to widowhood is more difficult for women or for men. Berardo (1970), Barrett (1978) and Elwell and Maltbie (1978) are among those who conclude that widowhood is more stressful for men. Atchley (1975), however, found that widowers were better off than widows on all dimensions, particularly in that they have economic supports that for the most part tend to offset the effects of other social and psychological factors. Evidence for the more disadvantaged position of the widower in old age is nevertheless reflected in the findings of higher suicide rates (Bock and Webber, 1972) and a greater increase in the rate of mortality following bereavement (Parkes, Benjamin and Fitzgerald, 1969) in comparison with widows.

However, a more fruitful approach to the examination of this issue lies in exploring the ways in which the experience differs for men and women, rather than merely focussing on "for whom the transition is more difficult." Certainly, in terms of access to social support, there is evidence of substantial male-female differences in the transition to widowhood. Berardo (1970) and Pihlblad et al. (1972) found that widowers are more likely to be isolated and to have fewer emotional ties with their families. Widows, by contrast, apparently become closer to their children, if only for a short time following bereavement. In addition, while older widows have an available group of other widows to provide emotional and social support, widowers by and large lack such supports. Widowers may be especially disadvantaged, because of the tendency for men *not* to develop confidant relationships with others outside their marital relationships, in the way that women frequently do (Lowenthal and Haven, 1968).

To some extent, the lack of Canadian data on widowers is a function of the demography of widowhood. As Fengler and Danigelis (1982) note in their Vermont research, studies of the widowed often result in samples that are only about 13 percent males, "too few cases to make meaningful comparisons" with widows. In my own research, a sample of 115 widowed elderly, derived from a larger community survey, identified 96 widows but only 19 widowers — again an insufficient sample size for comprehensive analysis.

In spite of these limitations, several Canadian studies comparing the experiences of widows and widowers are available. Stryckman (1981a, 1981b, 1982) has studied 475 widowed men and women aged 55 and over, living in urban and rural environments in francophone Quebec. Forty-one percent of the sample was male. Stryckman found no difference between men and women in their identification of widowhood as a painful life event (1982:75), although the sample did not include individuals who had experienced a sudden death of the spouse. The experience of pain did, however, lead to different attitudes towards remarriage, with painfulness linked to the desire to remarry among men and the desire *not* to remarry among women. This difference may be explained by the finding that women had been more actively involved in, and were exhausted by the experience of, a long period of care for an ill spouse; men, on the other hand, tended to rely on other women to help when their wives were terminally ill.

The problems of widowhood differed for men and for women. While loneliness was the major problem for both genders (expressed by 56 percent of the men and 51.5 percent of the women), financial resources were the second major problem for women but not for men. Widowers found problems with completion of daily household tasks and with sexuality to be their areas of concern (Stryckman, 1982:79). An additional difference between the genders was that widows were more likely to report high frequency of contact with children than were widowers (1982:79).

A study by Strain and Chappell in Winnipeg focussed on the maintenance of confidant relationships among the aged, with the widowed comprising a subsample of a larger study. One-fourth had been widowed less than five years, and 17 percent more than 26 years. Significant differences were apparent in the number of confidants reported by the widowed males and females. "The females are more likely than the males to report at least one confidant: 18 percent of the widowed males reported no confidant, but over one-half (54 percent) of the widowed females reported having two or more confidants." This finding corroborates other Canadian research, such as that of Haas-Hawkings (1978) and others who note that "widowed women. . .are more likely to have established intimate relationships outside their marriages" (Strain and Chappell, 1982:489).

Another study by Wister and Strain (1985) examined dimensions of social support among 354 elderly individuals in Manitoba: 42 widowers and 177 widows who use home-care services and 24 widowers and 111 widows who do not. Social support was measured by the variables: number of household members, number of relatives outside the home, number of friends outside the home, number of neighbours and number of confidants, frequency of interaction with relatives, friends and neighbours. Among the nonusers of home support services, the widows had more friends and confidantes and more interaction with relatives and neighbours than did widowers. Among the users of home support services — an older and more functionally disabled group — the widowers had almost twice as many neighbours on whom they could rely than did widows. Other statistically significant differences between the genders emerged on the other support measures when controls were introduced: both for those widowed six years or more and those with high functional ability, widows had more frequent interaction with relatives and with neighbours. In addition, when age was controlled for (comparing those ± 80), widows had more interaction with neighbours and more confidants than did men. For the users of home support services, however, gender overall made very little difference to the availability and utilization of the specified social supports (Wister and Strain, 1985).

These findings suggest a conclusion similar to that recently made by Scott and Kivett (1985). In an examination of the effect of sex differences on the morale of older widowed individuals, they found that economic and physical resources (self-rated health) appear to be more influential determinants of morale. The findings of Wister and Strain similarly suggest that with advancing age and increasing functional disability, the similarities between widows and widowers far outweigh the differences.

Socio-economic factors:

The availability of financial resources has a significant impact on the subjective career of widowhood. My own research has corroborated the finding (Lopata, 1973; Stryckman, 1982) that while loneliness is the widow's most frequently identified problem, financial insecurity is the second. Let us consider the overall financial status of the elderly Canadian widow in order to understand this concern.

Women who are "unattached" in old age (either because they never married, or were widowed, separated or divorced) are financially the worst-off segment of the Canadian population. In 1982, an estimated 60.4 percent of unattached elderly women, most of them widows, were poor, compared to 48.9 percent of unattached men aged 65 and older (National Council of Welfare, 1984). In addition, increasing age raises the risk of poverty for the unattached elderly woman: while just over half (53.9 percent) aged 65 to 69 were poor in 1981, the rate increased to 64.9 percent for unattached women aged 70 years and older, "the highest low-income rate of all age groups in 1981" (National Council of Welfare, 1984:26). Indeed, in 1981, there were more aged unattached women below the poverty line than above it! The main cause of the widow's poverty is the extreme financial vulnerability of most elderly married women, at least one third of whom have no personal income at all. Dulude (1979) notes that: "More than half of all married women aged 55 to 64 have no income at all. When their husbands die, it appears that most of them will inherit nothing other than poverty." These factors have significant implications for the perpetuation of patterns of economic support available to the widowed woman in Canada, and reflect her reliance on savings and other forms of family-generated assistance in order to ensure her livelihood.

In 1982, slightly more than 50 percent of the income of unattached elderly women came from federal old age security or public pension plans, a proportion largely unchanged for more than a decade. In addition, because public pension plans are tied to labour-force participation and benefits depend on the length of time employed and size of contributions, fewer women receive benefits (only 29 percent in 1980) and the benefits they do receive are less than (only 68 percent of) those received by men (Statistics Canada, 1985a:67).

Issues of labour-force participation and rates of unemployment also have a direct bearing on the availability of economic supports in widowhood. While Canada has recently witnessed a significant rate of growth in female labour-force participation, "almost two-thirds of widows in their fifties who are in the labour force hold low-paying, unskilled jobs" (Dulude, 1979:10). Data from the 1981 census show that while the labour-force participation rate for females over the age of 15 as a whole is 51.8, the participation rate for the widowed and divorced female is 31.3 (Statistics Canada, 1984). In addition, while mature women workers have a substantially lower rate of unemployment than their younger counterparts (in 1981 it was 7.0 for widowed and divorced women), the bad news is that "older women suffer longer periods of unemployment than do younger women" (Dulude, 1979:11).

The financial status of the widowed in Canada has also been affected in the past decade by legal reforms in various Canadian provinces, reforms that have fundamentally changed family law. While the legislation associated with such reform is a provincial responsibility, and hence will vary from one province to the next, an overview of legislative provisions in Ontario illustrates several implications of this reform for the widowed. The Succession Law Reform Act in Ontario, for example, governs the right of surviving spouses and other family members on the death of a family member. If a person dies without a will, the surviving spouse receives the first $75,000 of the estate plus half of any remainder if there is one child, or one third of the remainder if there are two or more children. If there are no children, the surviving spouse receives the entire estate. If the deceased left a will, the surviving family members receive the designated bequests. However, if this is inadequate, they can apply to a court for a greater share of the estate. This right is available to the spouse, parents, children, brothers and sisters of the deceased if the deceased was supporting them or was under a legal obligation to support them (Schlesinger, 1979:190).

Environmental factors.

Several researchers (Fengler and Danigelis, 1982; Adams 1975) have noted the particular salience of the environmental context for the aged, the special vulnerability of the elderly widow to environmental influence. While the findings of research in this area are somewhat contradictory, there is evidence that the transition to widowhood may be exacerbated by location in a rural environment. Coward and Kerchoff (as reported in Lassey et al., 1980:28) note that elderly widows in rural areas may be more lonely and isolated because their children may have moved from the region. In addition, they are often geographically isolated from health, recreation and social services. For the rural widowed, lack of public transportation and physical distance from services create physical barriers to a social reconstruction of lifestyle in widowhood. Other researchers suggest, however, that these indicators of isolation are balanced by the higher quality relationships with friends, family and neighbours in the rural environment (Arling, 1976; Fengler and Danigelis, 1982; Harbert and Wilkinson, 1979; Roberto and Scott, 1983). Canadian research comparing the experience of widowhood for men and women living in rural and urban environments is currently underway. Preliminary analyses suggest no significant differences between the rural and urban widowed in terms of a broad variety of indicators of quality of life (Martin Matthews, 1985).

Support systems of widowed women

The findings of Canadian research on the support systems of widowed women present some interesting parallels, but also some notable contrasts, with the findings of U.S. researchers. As described in Chapter 17 in this volume, by Rosenthal, the elderly in Canada are generally actively involved in family networks in which adult children are central figures. Many widowed aged are involved in supportive exchange, either as recipients or providers, within a family support system. One Canadian study that examines the role of children in relation to long-term adaptation to widowhood is the previously cited research by Stryckman (1982). As one measure of social support, relations with children exhibited quite complex, and somewhat contradictory, patterns. For example, while frequency of interaction with children decreased over time in widowhood, these fewer interactions were characterized by the widowed as being more positive; such findings have implications for the many studies that measure social support in terms of frequency of contact only. However, residence with children (itself frequently considered an indicator of social support) did not significantly reduce the emergence of loneliness as a major problem of widowhood. Indeed, 62.7 percent of widowers (n = 51) and 32.8 percent of widows (n = 64) living with children identified loneliness as their major problem (1982:79). Stryckman also found that relations with children constituted the biggest obstacle for those who wished to remarry, particularly so for widows who strongly identified themselves as mothers.

It must be emphasized that exchanges of support between the widowed and their children typically occur between rather than within households. A third (32.2 percent) of women aged 65 and over live alone (Statistics Canada, 1985a:8). In other studies of widowed women, proportions as high as 73 percent living alone (Martin Matthews, 1982) and 78 percent living alone (Martin Matthews et al., 1984) were found. In Stryckman's research, only 22.5 percent were living alone, but fully a third (32.4 percent) were living in quasi-family settings, typically with a sister or a female friend (1982:144-145). It is also important to acknowledge that an estimated 14.6 percent of the ever-married female population aged 65 and over are childless (Statistics Canada, 1983) and will therefore engage in rather different patterns of social support. While Rempel (1985) has found no significant differences between the childless and parent elderly on a variety of quality-of-life measures, Stryckman found that widows who have had children judge their previous marriages more negatively than do the childless. She also found that the childless widowed have developed an important network of social relations to compensate for childlessness, especially with nieces, nephews and siblings (Stryckman, 1981b).

Even though most research on the supports of the widowed has focussed on *inter*generational relationships (particularly those with adult children), there is also evidence that the widowed aged are actively engaged in exchanges of social support with other extended family members. My own research on widowed women in Guelph, Ontario, found stability over time in the contact with adult children, but also found substantial evidence for the support of members of the "family of origin," particularly sisters. These findings are quite in contrast to Lopata's findings in Chicago, where she notes that children are by far the most viable members of the widow's support system (1978; 1979). Siblings, in-laws and other relatives were not actively involved in any of the support systems that Lopata studied. Indeed, 54 percent of the Chicago widows never mentioned a brother or sister in responses to any of the questions, although only 19 percent did not have living siblings. Where widows were involved at all in support systems, they were dependent on their children for all types of support, except economic. In my research, using the same instrument as Lopata, over half the respondents with living siblings saw at least one as frequently as several times a month. More significantly, siblings and other extended kin also emerged as important figures in the social and emotional supports. In all, 54 percent of the widows listed at least one sibling (typically a sister) as being involved in at least one exchange of social support. Sixty-five percent listed an extended kin member (sibling, sibling-in-law, cousin, aunt or niece) as involved in their emotional support system. Half the respondents specifically referred to a sister as one of the three people to whom they felt closest, either currently or in the year before their husband's death.

Findings from this pilot project are necessarily tentative due to limitations of sample size; they are being examined more fully in a major project currently underway (Martin Matthews, 1985). There is presently no ready explanation for the disparate findings in the Guelph pilot study and the Chicago survey. It may be that, because a higher proportion of the Guelph than the Chicago widows grew up in the local area, they have been able to retain more contacts with siblings and extended kin over the years.[1] It may also be that because almost half the Chicago widows have at least one child still living at home (in contrast to 15 percent of the Guelph widows), the presence of children makes them more salient resources than are extended kin at this stage in the life cycle. But this explanation merely raises a question about another curious distinction between the Guelph and Chicago-area widows: since the ages of both samples were comparable, it is intriguing that the American widows were so much more likely than the Canadian to have children at home. This distinction between the two in itself suggests fundamental differences in how the life event of widowhood is experienced, either preceding or following the "empty nest" phase of the life cycle, thus prematurely terminating the postparental period or occurring some years after it.

Other Canadian studies have yielded similar findings to my own on the role of siblings — and other extended family members — in the lives of the elderly. In an Ontario study of the supports of both widowed and non-widowed elderly men and women, respondents were asked a series of questions about qualitative aspects of their family life, and were then asked to indicate who came to mind when they thought of "family." Over half the sample of 453 individuals (53.4 percent) included siblings in their definition of family. In addition, 82 percent of the widowed and 88 percent of the non-widowed reported regular contact with siblings, (Martin Matthews, et al., 1984). In a study of fifty urban Acadian widows in Moncton, New Brunswick, with a median age of 77 and an average six years of widowhood, Arseneault (1985) found fully 22 percent who identified a sister or other extended kin member (niece, granddaughter, cousin or in-law) as *the* person most helpful to the widow. Ten percent specifically mentioned a sister in this role.

Studies of younger widows similarly corroborate the importance of siblings in the lives of the bereaved. Vachon and associates found evidence of the important supportive role of members of the family of origin, although they do not specify whether they were siblings (1977). Similarly, in a current study of decision making among predominantly middle-aged widowed women in Winnipeg, Manitoba, Harvey and Harris found that median contact with siblings is two to three times per month (1985). Ten percent of their sample of 141 women widowed an average of two years have contact with siblings more than once a week, while a further 15 percent have once-weekly contact. Harvey postulates that the residential stability of these women (a median 37 years residence in Winnipeg) may account in part for the extent of sibling involvement in their supports in widowhood.

These data raise questions about the generalizability to the Canadian context of Lopata's conclusions about the limitations of the modified extended kin network in widowhood (1978). The contrasts in the Canadian versus American research are quite striking. In "one of the most unexpected findings of this study," Lopata found that siblings are essentially absent from the emotional support system of widowed women and are generally not sources of psychological closeness (1979:242). While none of the Canadian studies is of the scope and comprehensiveness of Lopata's research, collectively they do point to a notable consistency in the identification of the supportive role played by extended family members in the transition to widowhood. This is most evident in reference to the role of peer family, especially siblings.

There are, in addition, other individuals who may play potentially important roles in the process of negotiating the transition to widowhood. The literature on reference groups well documents their importance in the process of adult socialization. Research by Elias (1977) on elderly widows living in age-segregated apartment complexes in Hamilton, Ontario, emphasizes the importance of neighbours as friends and as social supports to the widowed. She found that most widows had a neighbour who had become a close friend, and the majority had made casual friendships with neighbours who lived on the same floor of the building (1977:62).

Peer relationships other than with neighbours were also important social supports for these elderly widows. The vast majority (92 percent) reported associations limited to other older widows, and 91.8 percent indicated that their closest friend was also a widow, with the friendship originating for the most part (61.6 percent) after bereavement.[2] The importance of the friendship role is also confirmed in the finding that "close relationship was the second best significant predictor of. . .social adjustment" (Elias, 1977:77).

Yet another indicator of the importance of friendship roles in the social support systems of the widowed elderly is the finding that 7.8 percent of a sample of widowed included at least one friend in descriptions of their "family," compared to 4.1 percent of the nonwidowed elderly (Martin Matthews et al., 1984). In another study of widowed women, nearly three-quarters identified neighbours as helpful resources to them in bereavement, and over 80 percent identified friends as being similarly helpful (Martin Matthews, 1982).

The findings of other Canadian research, however, suggest caution in the interpretation of the supportive roles played by friends in widowhood. In a longitudinal study of 162 widows in Toronto, Vachon and associates (1982:1,000) found that "the social support variables were the most important in explaining the level of distress one month after bereavement." Among these, however, the most relevant was the woman's perception that she was seeing old friends less than before the death of her husband. Significantly, in a follow-up of 99 of these widows two years later, low satisfaction with such help at one month was the only social support variable to retain importance in the 24-month regression analysis. This research indicates that friendships were the crucial relationships most likely to change during bereavement. Vachon and associates conclude that families have certain role responsibilities that they are expected to fulfill in interaction with a recent widow. Friendship, on the other hand, based on reciprocity and mutual need fulfillment, will deteriorate or cease to exist if these criteria are not fulfilled. Many widows came to the realization that the significant others they had previously considered to be close friends had not even been seen in several months. From six months after bereavement, half of the women noted a decrease in social relationships.

Findings from the Guelph pilot study similarly indicate some attrition in friendships. Fully 15 percent of the widows indicated that the person who was their closest friend in the year prior to widowhood was no longer a friend at all. When the *processual* nature of social support is considered, we see considerable flux in social support, particularly friendship support, in the transition to widowhood.

Identity and personal resources

It is also important to acknowledge how the personal resources of the widowed influence both the extent of the social supports utilized and the response and attitude towards available social supports. Lopata has recognized that the widow "needs to 'make herself over,' from a dependent person, living vicariously through the husband and children, into an independent person" (1979:32) and that "many of the women are aware of themselves as a resource for supplying supports" (1979:75). To explore this issue further, my pilot study incorporated several questions that allowed for an extensive discussion of the widow's personal supports (Martin Matthews, 1982). These primarily focussed on the issue of how the respondents felt that the years since being widowed had changed them personally. Data collected in response to these questions provided information that proved vital in understanding the context in which changes in the widows' supportive relationships took place. Three quite varied responses

by women who each experienced a contracting of social support in widowhood illustrate this point.

> It made me bitter, awfully bitter. I know now that all those friends
> who came here all those years, all those great parties we had, well,
> they were never *really* our friends, now were they? Oh, we thought
> they were at the time. But where were they when I needed them? The
> kids say I should forget it, but I won't. You can't depend on anybody
> in this life, just your family. That's the lesson I learned the hard way.

> I feel removed from life now. You feel like you're always a third wheel
> at cards. It's not quite the same when you play with another woman.
> You also hesitate to ask couples in, even for dinner. It's a lonelier,
> quieter life. I'm okay. . .I understand that — I can accept it now. But
> it's a different life.

> I'm more independent. I just couldn't keep relying on people. I had to
> stop being dependent on my children and my friends. I had to *force*
> myself to start standing on my own two feet. That wasn't easy, I tell
> you. I did it, though. And I'm proud of myself that I did it, too.

These three comments illustrate distinctly different contexts in which the
change in social support in widowhood takes place, is interpreted, and has
meaning for these widows. These varied responses — embitterment,
resignation and satisfaction — yield quite different interpretations of
changes in the social supports of the widowed and have quite different
implications for strategies of intervention by those working with the
widowed.

In describing how they responded to decreases in contact with friends
after widowhood, these women are also reflecting a rarely acknowledged
aspect of the transition to widowhood: identity change in the widowed
themselves. Such comments reflect the reality that widowhood (paraphras-
ing Berger and Kellner's description of marriage) "involves not only
stepping into new roles, but beyond this, stepping into a new world"
(1970:67). The sociological perspective of symbolic interactionism utilizes
such concepts as meaning, symbols, taking the role of the other, society and
self to explain how our ways of thinking about our world and acting in it
change as the others with whom we interact change themselves or are
replaced (Becker, 1970:290). Changes in the self derive from continual
adjustments in the person's notions of how others will respond to one's
actions and in the meaning an individual gives to his or her own actions
based on the earlier responses of others. This is precisely what is being
described in the observations of these widowed women (see also Martin
Matthews, 1975).

These preliminary findings from a pilot study suggest the need for research to examine more fully the social *meaning* of widowhood and not just the changes in roles associated with it. Lopata's research on Chicago-area widows clearly recognizes this point in the finding that over half the women felt that they personally had been changed by the experience of widowhood (1973). In any study of changes in patterns of social support in widowhood, changes in the widowed themselves as an influencing factor must be considered. This is a point well recognized by widowed individuals when they write of the changes in self and social world that accompany the "progression from wife to widow and back to woman. . ." (Caine, 1974:176; see also Seskin, 1975; Evans, 1971; Wylie, 1976). To focus on identity change in the transition to widowhood is to acknowledge — which widowhood research rarely does — the fundamental centrality of the role of wife in the lives and identities of many women.[3] Canadian research by Norris (1980) found that identity as a wife can be so strong that some elderly women remain committed to the role of wife for as long as ten years following the husband's death. For example, rather than view statements about married life as no longer personally relevant, widowed women frequently expressed strong agreement with the statement "Being married makes my daily activities more satisfying and easy to deal with." A similar pattern was also recently observed in U.S. research on widows (Anderson, 1984).

Outstanding Issues in Widowhood Research in Canada

On the basis of extant Canadian research, we can conclude that younger age, brief final illness of the spouse, being male and having a low income level exacerbate the experience of widowhood as an expectable life event. It is also apparent that tremendous flux characterizes the pattern of social supports in the transition to widowhood, particularly in terms of friendship relations. In contrast to other research findings on widows (Lopata 1978, 1979), however, the role of the extended family in the support system of the widowed is quite striking in Canada. And finally, the importance of the personal resources of the widowed in shaping the reliance upon and response to social supports is supported by Canadian researchers.

While there is a growing body of Canadian research on women in widowhood, in contrast to the situation only six years ago (Martin Matthews, 1980a), this area of research interest is still very much in its infancy. Many outstanding research questions remain. Specific subgroups of the widowed — identified by U.S. researchers as having somewhat distinct experiences of widowhood as a life event (those widowed "off time" and widowed members of minority ethnic groups) — have simply not been systematically studied in Canada. Future Canadian research would also do well to attempt comparative analyses of men's and women's experiences of the transition to widowhood. While their numbers are small, there is preliminary evidence that the issues of relevance to widowed older men are distinctly different from those of women. While some of these differences may be generation specific, it is important to the processes of policy planning and intervention design to understand the particular patterns of social support utilization by elderly widowed men, as compared to women.

Also important to consider are the issues of the context in which widowhood occurs, both environmental and personal. Many features of Canadian society that both contribute to our uniqueness as a nation and add potential complexity to the experience of widowhood (bilingualism, multiculturalism, regional diversity and concentrations of the widowed aged in rural areas) have not been investigated in relation to this life event. Highest priority must be given, however, to the examination of widowhood as a process of transition, rather than merely a status held by most older women. For example, in examining the nature of social support in widowhood, Canadian studies primarily focus on the supportive relationships of those who currently hold the *status* of "widowed person"; there has been relatively little research on the way in which social relationships and support systems are changed by the *process* of becoming widowed. For this, of course, longitudinal research is required. The research findings reported in this chapter have been derived, for the most part, from small, cross-sectional, focussed studies done in a variety of Canadian cities. These have typically examined the "what" and the "how" of the reconstructed social world in widowhood, but not the actual process of reconstruction. Needed is research that more fully addresses the social meaning of widowhood for men and women, the "why." As one of Lopata's own respondents notes: "Maybe the why of things should have been asked more often. Circumstances can change the meaning of answers to some of the questions" (1979:367). The past six years have seen much growth in widowhood research in this country; a realistic and worthwhile goal for the future is the completion of more comprehensive and processually oriented research on widowhood as an expectable life event in Canada.

Notes

[1]   The support systems involving Chicago-area widows (and also examined in the Guelph pilot study) included five economic supports received from others (inflow); five given to others (outflow); the in-and-outflow of ten service supports; the sharing of nine social supports and of thirteen emotional supports received the year prior to the spouse's death and thirteen being received currently. Each respondent could list up to three persons for each type of support, meaning that "each respondent could list up to 30 persons in the economic, 60 in the service, 27 in the social and 78 in the emotional support systems, for a maximum total of 195 persons" (Lopata, 1979:73).

2   While the presence of a supportive reference group may be positively construed, it
    is important to recognize the resentment many widows feel when their social life
    becomes limited to this low-status group (Maddison and Raphael, 1976).
3   This point is made in reference to women; further research is required to deter-
    mine the extent to which this is also true of men.

References

Adams, David L.
    1975 "Who are the rural aged?" Pp. 11-23 in R.C. Atchley (ed.), *Rural
          Environments and Aging*. Washington, D.C.: Gerontological Society of
          America.
Anderson, Trudy B.
    1984 "Widowhood as a life transition: Its impact on kinship ties." *Journal of
          Marriage and the Family* 46(1):105-114.
Arling, Greg
    1976 "Resistance to isolation among elderly widows." *International Journal of
          Aging and Human Development* 7(1):67-86.
Arseneault, Anne-Marie
    1985 "Elderly Acadian Widows: Their Sources of Support." Paper presented at
          the 3rd National Conference on Gerontological Nursing, Hamilton,
          Ontario, June.
Atchley, Robert C.
    1975 "Dimensions of widowhood in later life." *The Gerontologist*
          15(April):176-178.
Barrett, Carol J.
    1978 "Sex Differences in the Experiences of Widowhood." Paper presented at
          the American Psychological Association Annual Meeting, Toronto,
          September.
Becker, Howard S.
    1970 *Sociological Work: Method and Substance*. Chicago: Aldine Publishing
          Company.
Berardo, Felix M.
    1970 "Survivorship and social isolation: The case of the aged widower." *Family
          Co-ordinator* 19:11-15.
Berger, Peter L., Brigitte Berger and Hansfried Kellner
    1973 *The Homeless Mind: Modernization and Consciousness*. New York: Vin-
          tage Books.
Berger, Peter R. and Hansfried Kellner
    1970 "Marriage and the construction of reality." Pp. 49-72 in Hans Peter
          Drietzel (ed.), *Recent Sociology No. 2*. New York: Macmillan.
Bock, E.W. and I.L. Webber
    1972 "Suicide among the elderly: Isolating widowhood and mitigating alter-
          natives." *Journal of Marriage and the Family* 34:24-31.
Caine, Lynn
    1974 *Widow*. New York: Wm. Morrow and Company.

Dulude, Louise
   1979   *Women and Aging: A Report on the Rest of Our Lives.* Ottawa: Advisory
          Council on the Status of Women.
Elias, Brenda
   1977   *Residential Environment and Social Adjustment among Older Widows.*
          Unpublished M.Sc. thesis, Department of Family Studies, University of
          Guelph.
Elwell, F. and A.D. Maltbie
   1978   "Differential Effects of Widowhood: Two Models and Empirical Tests."
          Paper presented at the annual meeting of the Gerontological Society of
          America, Dallas.
Evans, Jocelyn
   1971   *Living with a Man Who is Dying: A personal memoir.* New York: Tap-
          linger Publishing Company.
Fengler, A.P. and N. Danigelis
   1982   "Residence, the elderly widow, and life satisfaction," *Research on Aging*
          4(1):113-115.
Fletcher, Susan and Leroy O. Stone
   1980   "The living arrangements of older women." *Essence: Issues in the Study of
          Ageing, Dying and Death* 4(3):115-133.
George, Linda K.
   1980   *Role Transitions in Later Life.* Monterey, Calif.: Brooks/Cole.
Gibbs, Jeanne M.
   1980   "Family Relations of the Older Widow: Their Location and Importance
          for Her Social Life." Paper presented at the annual meeting of the Geron-
          tological Society of America, San Diego, November.
Haas-Hawkings, Gwen
   1978   "Intimacy as a moderating influence on the stress of loneliness in widow-
          hood." *Essence: Issues in the Study of Ageing, Dying and Death.*
          2(4):249-258.
Haas-Hawkings, Gwen, Michael Ziegler and David W. Reid
   1980   "An Exploratory Study of Adjustment to Widowhood." Paper presented
          at the 33rd Annual Scientific Meeting of the Gerontological Society of
          America, San Diego.
Harbert, A. and Carol Wilkinson
   1979   "Growing old in rural America." *Aging* 291:36-40.
Harvey, Carol D. and Maureen Harris
   1985   "Decision-making during Widowhood: The Beginning Years." Paper
          presented at the Beatrice Paolucci symposium, Michigan State University,
          July 19.
Health and Welfare Canada
   1982   *Pension Plan Coverage by Level of Earnings and Age 1978 and 1979.*
          Ottawa: Planning, Evaluation and Liaison Division, Income Security Pro-
          grams Branch.
   1983   *Fact Book on Aging in Canada.* Ottawa: Minister of Supply and Services.

Hewitt, John P.
   1976   *Self and Society: A Symbolic Interactionist Social Psychology.* Boston: Allyn and Bacon.
Holmes, T.H. and R.H. Rahe
   1967   "The social readjustment rating scale." *Journal of Psychosomatic Research* 11(2):213-18.
Hughes, Everett C.
   1971   *The Sociological Eye: Selected Papers.* Chicago: Aldine-Atherton.
Lassey, W.R., M.L. Lassey, G.R. Lee and N. Lee (eds.)
   1980   *Research and Public Service with the Rural Elderly: Proceedings of a Conference.* Corvallis, Oregon: Western Rural Development Center, Oregon State University Publication no. 4.
Lopata, Helena Znaniecki
   1973   *Widowhood in an American City.* Cambridge, Mass.: Schenkman.
   1978   "Contributions of extended families to the support systems of metropolitan area widows: Limitations of the modified kin network." *Journal of Marriage and the Family* 40(2):355-364.
   1979   *Women as Widows: Support Systems.* New York: Elsevier.
Lowenthal, Marjorie Fiske and Clayton Haven
   1968   "Interaction and adaptation: Intimacy as a critical variable." Pp. 390-400 in Bernice Neugarten (ed.), *Middle Age and Aging.* Chicago, Illinois: University of Chicago Press.
Maddison, D. and B. Raphael
   1976   "Death of a spouse." In H. Grunebaum and J. Christ (eds.), *Contemporary Marriage: Structure, Dynamics and Therapy.* Boston: Little, Brown.
Martin Matthews, Anne
   1975   "Symbolic Interactionism: An Alternative to Role Theory in the Study of Widowhood." Paper presented to the Canadian Association on Gerontology, Annual Meetings, October.
   1980a "Women and widowhood." Pp. 145-153 in Victor W. Marshall (ed.), *Aging in Canada: Social Perspectives,* Toronto: Fitzhenry & Whiteside.
   1980b "Wives' Experiences of Relocation: Status Passage and the Moving Career." Unpublished doctoral dissertation, Department of Sociology, McMaster University.
   1981   "Support systems of widows in Canada." Forthcoming in Helena Z. Lopata (ed.), *Widows: Other Countries/Other Places.* Durham, North Carolina: Duke University Press.
   1982   "Canadian research on women as widows: A comparative analysis of the state of the art." *Resources for Feminist Research* 11(2):227-230.
   1985a *Rural-urban Comparisons of the Social Supports of the Widowed Elderly.* Social Sciences and Humanities Research Council of Canada (Strategic Grants: Population Aging) #492-84-0028.
Martin Matthews, Anne, Kathleen H. Brown, Christine K. Davis and Margaret A. Denton

1982 "A crisis assessment technique for the evaluation of life events: Transition to retirement as an example." *Canadian Journal on Aging* 1(3 and 4):28-39.

Martin Matthews, Anne, Alex Michalos, Anthony M. Fuller, Claude A. Guldner, Joan E. Norris, Joseph A. Tindale, K. Victor Ujimoto, Linda M. Wood and Jacqueline S. Wolfe
1984 *Stability and Change in Assessments of Quality of Life of the Elderly.* University of Guelph Research Board Grant #5089.

McFarlane, A.H., G.R. Norman, D.L. Streiner, R. Roy and D.J. Scott
1980 "A longitudinal study of influence of the psycho-social environment on health status: A preliminary report." *Journal of Health and Social Behaviour* 21:124-33.

National Council of Welfare
1984 *Sixty-Five and Older: A Report by the National Council of Welfare on the Incomes of the Aged.* Ottawa: Minister of Supply and Services.

Neugarten, Bernice L. and Gunhild O. Hagestad
1976 "Age and the life course." In Ethel Shanas and Robert Binstock (eds.), *Handbook of Aging and the Social Sciences.* New York: Van Nostrand Reinhold.

Norris, Joan E.
1980 "The social adjustment of single and widowed older women." *Essence: Issues in the Study of Ageing, Dying and Death* 4(3):135-144.

Parkes, Colin M., B. Benjamin and R.G. Fitzgerald
1969 "Broken heart: A statistical study of increased mortality among widowers." *British Medical Journal* 1:740-743.

Pearlin, Leonard I.
1980 "The life cycle and life strains." Pp. 349-360 in Hubert M. Blalock, Jr. *Sociological Theory and Research: A Critical Approach.* New York: The Free Press.

Pihlblad, C.T., David L. Adams and D.L. Rosencranz
1972 "Socio-economic adjustment to widowhood." *Omega:Journal of Death and Dying* 3:295-305.

Rempel, Judith
1985 "Childless elderly: What are they missing?" *Journal of Marriage and the Family* 47(2):343-348.

Roberto, K.A. and J.P. Scott
1983 "Between Friends: Patterns of Social Involvement and Mutual Assistance of the Rural Elderly." Paper presented at the Annual Meeting of the Gerontological Society of America, San Francisco, November.

Schlesinger, Benjamin
1979 *Families: Canada.* Toronto: McGraw-Hill Ryerson .

Scott, Jean Pearson and Vira R. Kivett
1985 "Differences in the morale of older, rural widows and widowers." *International Journal of Aging and Human Development* 21(2):121-135.

Seskin, Jane
1975 *Young Widow.* New York: Ace Books.

Statistics Canada
  1982 *Population: Age, Sex and Marital Status, 1981.* Catalogue 92-901. Ottawa: Minister of Supply and Services Canada.
  1983 "Population: Nuptiality and Fertility." *1981 Census of Canada.* Catalogue #92-906. Ottawa: Minister of Supply and Services Canada.
  1984 *Life Tables, Canada and Provinces 1980-1982.* Catalogue 84-532, Ottawa: Minister of Supply and Services Canada.
  1985a *Women in Canada: A Statistical Report.* Ottawa: Minister of Supply and Services Canada.
  1985b *Vital Statistics, Volume II: Marriages and Divorces.* Catalogue 84-205. Ottawa: Minister of Supply and Services.
Stone, Leroy O. and Susan Fletcher
  1981 *Aspects of Population Aging in Canada: A Chartbook.* Ottawa: Statistics Canada.
Strain, Laurel A. and Neena L. Chappell
  1982 "Confidants: Do they make a difference in quality of life?" *Research on Aging* 4(4):479-502.
Stryckman, Judith
  1981a "The Decision to Remarry: The Choice and Its Outcome." Paper presented at the joint meeting of the Canadian Association on Gerontology and the Gerontological Society of America, Toronto, November.
  1981b "Childlessness: Its Impact among the Widowed Elderly." Paper presented to the joint meeting of the Canadian Association on Gerontology and the Gerontological Society of America, Toronto, November.
Stryckman, Judith
  1982 *Marriages et mises en menage au cours de la vieillesse.* Université Laval: Laboratoire de gérontologie sociale.
Vachon, Mary L.S.
  1979 "Identity Change Over the First Two Years of Bereavement: Social Relationships and Social Support in Widowhood." Unpublished doctoral dissertation, Department of Sociology, York University, Toronto.
  1981 "The Importance of Social Relationships and Social Support in Widowhood." Paper presented to the Joint Meeting of the Canadian Association on Gerontology and the Gerontological Society of America, Toronto, Canada, November.
Vachon, M.L.S., A. Formo, K. Freedman, A. Lyall, J. Rogers and S. Freeman
  1976 "Stress reactions to bereavement." *Essence: Issues in the Study of Ageing, Dying and Death* 1:23-33.
Vachon, M.L.S., K. Freedman, A. Formo, J. Rogers, W.A. Lyall and S. Freeman
  1977 "The final illness in cancer: The widow's perspective." *Canadian Medical Association Journal* 117:1151-54.
Vachon, M.L.S., W.A. Lyall, J. Rogers, K. Freedman-Letofsky and S.J.J. Freeman
  1980 "A controlled study of self-help intervention for widows." *American Journal of Psychiatry*, 137(11):1380-1384.
Vachon, M.L.S., J. Rogers, W.A. Lyall, W.J. Lancee, A.R. Sheldon and S.J.J. Freeman

1982 "Predictors and correlates of adaptation to conjugal bereavement." *American Journal of Psychiatry* 139(8):998-1002.

Walker, K.N., A. MacBride and M.L.S. Vachon
1977 "Social support networks and the crisis of bereavement." *Social Science and Medicine* 11:35-41.

Wister, Andrew V. and Laurel A. Strain
1985 *Social Support and Well-Being: A Comparison of Older Widows and Widowers.* Publication Series, Centre on Aging, University of Manitoba, Winnipeg.

Wylie, Betty Jane
1976 *Beginnings: A Book for Widows.* Toronto: McClelland and Stewart.

19

The Relationship Between Formal and Informal Social Support Networks in Rural and Urban Contexts

Ellen Corin
Douglas Hospital
Montreal

The concept of social support is becoming increasingly important in the field of health and social services research and practice. It is mainly used in two general frameworks. First, in the field of epidemiology, it has been discovered that the availability of social support is closely linked with well-being and with a positive resolution of health problems, while a lack of support is related to various psychological and physical health problems. Second, in the area of health and social services, practitioners have built models of practice that involve various ways of working with informal support systems: through a mobilization of them in order to help a given person, through the conclusion of an alliance with natural helpers, or through the building or rebuilding of a social support system in a "networking" approach of intervention. This general tendency is presently encouraged by governments, especially in the area of services for the aged.

If we look closely at various publications centred around this theme, we can see that the term "social support" is used in most cases in a very loose way and its meaning varies according to author. I suggest that the very notion of "social support" cannot be taken for granted and that we need to consider more closely the dynamics that underlie the functioning and the use of social support in our society. For this purpose, I propose to enlarge our way of looking at social support and to consider its context in a dual sense: the context of the social relations of a person and the context of a more global field of "support" that encompasses formal as well as informal resources.

To introduce this perspective, I will first consider two major areas of recent criticisms against a too simplistic conception of social support in theory and in practice. On this basis I intend to propose a methodological perspective and theoretical model that could help in reframing studies and practices. This model calls for the necessity to consider personal and socio-cultural variables in studies on social support. To illustrate this I will present data collected on elderly people in the Province of Quebec.

Broadening Current Approaches to Social Support

An emphasis on the social dimension

Studies have been more or less sophisticated in their approach to social support. We can distinguish between three levels of complexity.

At the lowest level the dimension of support attached to specific social relations is taken for granted, so that a measurement of these relations is considered as an estimate of the social support received; e.g., being married, or having relationships with children or friends.

At another level, authors predefine some basic support functions that are thought to be important for everyone. In their review of studies done from this perspective, Mitchell and Trickett (1980) quote four basic dimensions of social support: emotional, instrumental or task specific, communication of expectations or a shared world view, and access to new information and new social contacts. The authors working in this perspective measure the support received or expected according to these dimensions.

This approach has its limitations. It can eliminate certain forms of support that could be important for some groups of the population but that do not fit within the predefinition of support (Garrison and Podell, 1981). Hammer (1981) stresses the interest of doing ethnographic work leading to the identification of relevant areas of support for specific groups. We can give two examples of work done in this direction. In their study of an elderly population located in "single room occupancy hotels" in the Inner City of New York, Sokolovski and Cohen (1978) have collected ethnographic data through field work and participant observation. On this basis they have constructed a grid of significant contents of support relevant for the aged in this specific setting. In Canada, Gottlieb (1978) has initially posed open-ended questions to single mothers with low income. His content analysis of data has allowed him to describe 26 categories of helping behaviours relevant for these women and to construct an instrument to study them in a more systematic way.

At the third level, authors focus their attention first on the social relations. It is only in a second step that they look at their support contents. This was done in the simplest way by authors like Cantor (1975), who asked elderly respondents which types of exchanges they had with children, kin, neighbours and friends. Garrison and Podell (1981) first asked questions intended to build a social network chart (which they name "natural support system"). From this they then asked complementary questions in order to get the names of people who give more specified types of support to the respondents. They label this the "core support" network.

More complex studies were also done from this perspective of social network theory. They consider in which way various properties of social links are related to specific types of support. In Canada, Wellman (1981) and his colleagues (Wellman and Leighton, 1982) have demonstrated how the use of social network theory allows a more specific description of the flux of resources in a specific milieu and how the elements of the social and economic context influence both the way social support flows in the milieu and how people relate with formal resources. These and other authors have shown that the density of links (i.e., the amount of interconnection between social relations) is linked to support (Hammer, 1981, speaks here of a "structural support") and to a reinforcement of social norms (Bott, 1971). We will see later some concrete implications of this process.

More recently authors have emphasized the cognitive dimension of social support and asked for a meaning-centred approach. Simons (1983-84), among others, argues that we need "a theoretical perspective that takes into account the way that psychological needs and social norms determine the meaning inherent in various types of relations."

In our work we have adopted this social network perspective. We have looked at the way the social support system reproduces, or differs from, the general pattern of social links of individuals in various social settings. In the data analysis we have stressed the influence of personal and socio-cultural variables on the meaning attached to social relations in various milieux.

A process perspective of social support: the help-seeking behaviours

A large part of the research on social support stems from the observation that when faced with health and personal problems people do not usually rely on professional resources alone; rather, they also seek help from informal resources. Research done on this topic has been done from two major perspectives.

In the first one authors split the population between "users" and "nonusers" on the basis of their behaviour towards formal resources when faced with a problem. They attempted to find the characteristics that distinguish the two groups. It is interesting for us to note that age was found to be a discriminating factor (Gourash, 1978); Levine and Preston (1970) have suggested that this influence of age can be explained by its relation to the degree of knowledge of formal resources and familiarity with them, and by the general attitude of the elderly towards professional services. Cantor and Mayer (1978) have shown that the general relations of various groups of elderly people with social agencies influences their proneness to use professional resources.

These studies are very interesting, but they have some limitations. They do not explain why some people, or groups of people, are outside the common range of variance (Mechanic, 1978). Neither do they explain the mechanisms underlying the use or the nonuse of formal resources (McKinlay, 1972). They assume that users and nonusers are homogeneous groups, which does not seem to be true; for example, Brown (1978) has established a very relevant distinction between the "reluctant nonseekers of help," who have no personal or social resources, and the "self-reliant nonseekers of help," who have many personal and social resources on which they rely outside of the professional field.

The second line of research stresses the fact that formal and informal resources constitute a global support system (Cantor and Mayer, 1978). In this perspective, we can look at the relations between the two parts of the system. Freidson (1960) has introduced the distinction between the lay and the professional support systems. He has suggested that the degree of congruence between the two systems regarding representations and values influences the probability that lay persons refer the suffering person to formal resources. Suchman (1966) has added the influence of "social group" variables.

In the field of aging, Sussman (1977) has stressed the function that family and other social relations play in helping elderly people relate to formal resources and in dealing with the bureaucracy of formal agencies.

An interesting way of looking at the relations between the two systems is to focus on individuals and to look at their actual behaviour when they are faced with specific problems in daily life.

Social support in the practice of social services

Criticisms against an undiscriminated use of the concept of "social support" also come from the field of the services. They parallel theoretical criticisms in the way they ask for a more complex approach in this area.

In the past ten years, various practitioners have proposed that professionals establish links with informal or "natural" helpers. Froland et al. (1984) and Gottlieb (1981) among others have recently proposed a typology of the models developed in this direction. It is certainly not an accident that this tendency has flourished in a time of economic crisis, when formal agencies are submitted to many constraints. However, in general, the tendency to utilize natural helpers as much as possible has a normative base. Local or "natural" help is perceived as being less alienating, more "humane" and involving less dependency for the users. It encompasses ideological components of "social participation," positively valued by most workers in the social field.

Recently, however, some have called for a more careful approach in this field. Concerning the aged, Lee (1985), for example, criticizes a too fast shift from the general finding that elderly people receive a large part of support from members of their social network to the suggestion that public policy has to acknowledge the help given by informal resources and to give support to them.

This is grounded in various arguments. The availability of social support is very different for various people, so that the use of informal resources cannot be taken as a general principle. At a more qualitative level we have to be aware that not all social relations are supportive. This calls for a distinction between social networks and social support systems. More important, the use of informal resources can go against the positive value attached to autonomy and independency in our North American society and this can have unintended consequences. An indiscriminate call for social support can reinforce dependency on children and family and disturb a very fragile equilibrium. This could be especially important in the area of aging because of the negative stereotypes of the aged in our society.

In this context it seems to be important to begin with an understanding of the way elderly people themselves relate to the various categories of resources, both formal and informal, and which strategies they use to retain some control over the process.

Towards a Dynamic Approach to Social Support

Social support in context: methodological implications

These various studies show that social support is not a separated entity that can be easily grasped in itself. It has to be located in a broader context, which means at least two things:

— If social support is a property that can be attached to the functioning of social relationships, but that is not equivalent to these, we have to look at the relationship between some properties of social relations and their meaning in terms of support for the elderly persons themselves.

— If the social support is only one portion of a larger system of support, we have to consider which place and which function it occupies in the larger framework of strategies that people build when they are faced with concrete difficulties.

In our research, we have taken three methodological options that stem directly from these two ideas:

(1) *A focus on the person:* How he or she uses relationships in the social network enabled us to qualify these in terms of social support; his or her help-seeking behaviour enabled us to describe the relationship between formal and informal resources from the perspective of the person.

(2) *A focus on behaviours:* For the study of the social network we have complemented a "cognitive map" of social relations drawn from questions on various categories of social relations with a "reconstructed week" chart. This shows the importance that these social relations have in the daily life of the person (Corin, 1982, 1984). For the study of social support and the relation between formal and informal resources, we asked questions about the coping strategies

used in four areas: daily life, sense of security, health problems and "varia" (administrative and financial fields); how people perceive the situation; and which types of resources are mobilized.

(3) *A focus on meaning*, i.e., on the implicit representations, norms and values that seem to underlie the use of the various types of resources.

A general model of the help-seeking process

The model that we have built includes three levels of variables: variables that describe the "help-seeking" strategies as such, i.e., the use of various types of resources; variables that describe the help-seeking process, and variables that influence this process.

The "strategies" used by a person when she or he is faced with a situation can be represented as follows:

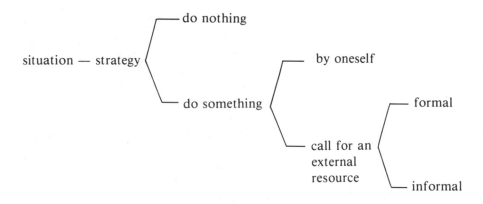

If the help seeking is considered as a process a person can use several of these resources in an attempt to cope with a situation. In order to have enough cases in each category, we have retained a typology with four categories that describe the way of reacting to each situation:

— FR: use of formal resources, alone or in addition to informal resources

    — IR: exclusive use of informal resources in the situation

    — OS: exclusive use of "oneself" or self-resources

    — XR: mixed strategy, joint use of "oneself" and of external resources formal and/or informal

We characterized each person by the predominance of one style of strategy in his or her help-seeking (Corin et al., 1983). Looking at the social support in its context, we can say that the choice of a specified resource is influenced by two sets of variables: variables related to the availability of social relations (social network) and variables related to the availability and knowledge of formal resources.

In addition, we can postulate that the whole process is oriented by the character of the situation (area, gravity, longevity) and by the socio-cognitive variables, i.e., at a socio-cultural level, the "normative expectations" linked with North American society (these could vary according to the milieu), and at an individual level, a personal style of relating to others.

These can be represented in the following diagram:

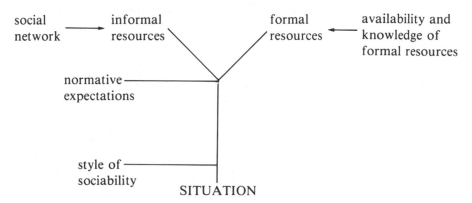

Design of the study

A survey was conducted on a stratified sample of 239 elderly people 65 years old and over. Stratification was done according to age range (65-74, 75 and more), sex and environment (rural, urban middle class (Ste-Foy) and urban deprived area (Inner City)).

The comparison between the environments allows us to construct some hypotheses regarding the influence of the "normative expectations" variable. A parallel project applied the concepts and findings of the study to concrete practices with the elderly (Corin et al., 1983).

A more detailed presentation of our methodology can be found elsewhere (Corin et al., 1983; Corin, 1984; Corin et al., 1984). I will limit myself here to a presentation of data directly relevant to a study of social support in context. I will organize the presentation according to the diagram just presented. The significance levels reported for tabular data are based on chi square.

Social Support in the Context of Social Network

Social network and social support

We have drawn three different maps of the social networks of the people interviewed:

— the Wider Network (WN): all the people quoted in response to questions about categories of social relations

— the Current Network (CN): all persons seen at least once a month

— the Behavioural Network (BN): all persons in touch with the respondent during the past week

At each level, we grouped relationships into three categories: children, siblings and kin, friends and neighbours. Before looking at the relation between social networks and social support, it is interesting to consider the relations between these three levels of network data because it enables us to understand better the dynamics of social life in the various environments.

We can briefly characterize the situation as follows:

Size:

Statistically significant differences exist between the environments, but only for the Wider and Current Network; they disappear when we consider who was actually encountered during the week. Therefore, the apparent disadvantage of the elderly located in the Inner City seems to be compensated for by the concrete functioning of social relations in daily life. If we look at the number of *contacts* through informal relations during the week respondents from Ste-Foy (urban middle class) have the lower rate. This calls for some prudence when we speak about the influence of social class on social life.

Accessibility:

Statistically significant differences exist mainly between rural and urban middle-class respondents. The former have a very significant portion of their social network located in the same village: siblings and kin are less distant there than everywhere else, and almost all friends are located in the immediate neighbourhood. In Ste-Foy the social network is more spread out — particularly siblings and kin, and friends.

Composition:

If we look at the wider network, people from the Inner City differ from those of the other two environments in a very significant way. Their network includes a larger proportion of siblings and kin and a smaller proportion of children. This can be explained by the high percentage of single people (22 percent in men, 34 percent in women) interviewed in this environment (see Table 1).

If we look at the shift that occurs when we change network levels (see the second panel of Table 1), we see that everywhere children tend to occupy a large place in the behavioural network, but this shift is less evident in the Inner City. There is a sharp difference between the rural milieu, where the number of friends and neighbours increases in the behavioural network, and Ste-Foy, where they diminish so that the increase in the proportion of children is more exclusive. The proportion of siblings and kin diminishes everywhere, particularly in the rural environment, when we compare current and behavioural networks. The Inner City is the only place where the relative proportion of siblings and kin in the behavioural network increases.

Therefore, we see that the concrete contacts with people in everyday life do not always reflect the relative importance that each category of social relations has in the cognitive map of social networks. Sometimes the shift seems to be a consequence of objective constraints, as for the urban middle class respondents, whose network is more spread out. We will see that this can be related to their environmental histories. The shift also seems to respond to other rules, such as in the case of the rural milieu, where siblings and kin are less important in daily life than what we would have expected, when we consider their accessibility.

In order to approach the concept of social support more closely, let us look at the people quoted as emotionally "significant" (qualitatively impor-

TABLE 1:
Influence of the Environment on the Dominant Category of Relationship on the Various "Levels" of Social Network*

Environment	Children			Siblings-kin			Friends-neighbours		
	WN	CN	BN	WN	CN	BN	WN	CN	BN
Rural	11	25	39	24	21	7	9	21	31
Inner City	9	21	25	43	20	27	14	23	26
Ste-Foy	15	28	35	25	13	9	19	30	15

WN: "wider" network
CN: "current" network
BN: "behavioural" network

* percentage of persons for which the category of relationship includes more than half of all relationships quoted at this level

Broadness of the Shift

Environment	between WN and BN			between CN and BN		
	Ch	S-K	F-N	Ch	S-K	F-N
Rural	+ 28%	− 17%	+ 22%	+ 14%	− 14%	+ 10%
Inner City	+ 16%	− 16%	+ 12%	+ 4%	+ 7%	+ 3%
Ste-Foy	+ 20%	− 16%	− 4%	+ 7%	− 4%	− 15%

TABLE 2:
Influence of Environment on "Significant" Persons

Environment	Spouse*					Children**					Siblings-kin					Friends-neighbours				
	0	1	2	3	Tot.	0	1	2	3	Tot.	0	1	2	3	Tot.	0	1	2	3	Tot.
Rural	16	12	23	49	(43)	17	25	19	49	(67)	77	0	8	5	(80)	83	6	6	5	(80)
Inner City	46	16	16	22	(32)	22	2	26	50	(50)	52	10	11	27	(79)	65	9	13	13	(79)
Ste-Foy	36	21	33	10	(43)	17	8	14	61	(72)	70	8	7	15	(80)	81	9	7	3	(80)
significance			.01					ns					.01					ns (.08)		

0. Percentage of persons who have quoted nobody in this category.
1. Percentage of persons who have quoted between 1 and 25% in this category.
2. Percentage of persons who have quoted between 26 and 50% in this category.
3. Percentage of persons who have quoted more than 50% in this category.

* percentage adjusted for married people only
** percentage adjusted for people with children only

tant, intimate, advisors). Notice that for the comparison of the relative importance that spouse and children have in various environments, we have taken into account only people who are actually married and people who have children. The differences in milieu are statistically significant for spouse, and for siblings and kin. The spouse is quoted more often in the rural sample and less often in the Inner City, while the siblings and kin are more emotionally present in this latter milieu (see Table 2).

The differences regarding friends and neighbours are just below the threshold of significance (.08), in favour of the Inner City. Differences regarding children are not significant, but people from Ste-Foy tend to mention them more often.

If we look at people involved in the accomplishment of regular activities, the elderly quote their spouses considerably less often in the Inner City even if we look only at married people. Friends and neighbours are quoted more often in the rural milieu, where they share common activities such as participation in associations.

To get a better picture of social support given by informal resources to elderly people we have looked at the strategies adopted in order to cope with four categories of situations as explained above. These data are given in Table 3. Differences between the samples are statistically significant only for two categories of social relations: siblings and kin, and friends and neighbours (both being more present in the Inner City). Spouse and children tend to be mentioned less in this environment, but the difference is not statistically significant. We can also say that people from Ste-Foy tend to rely a little more on their children than those in the rural environment and that respondents from the rural environment tend to rely a little more on their spouse than in Ste-Foy.

If we look at sex differences, women rely significantly more on their children (.001) and on siblings and kin (.01), while men tend to rely more on spouse and a little more on friends and neighbours.

If we consider more global correlations between indices relating to social networks and to social support, we see that the quantitative importance of the social support is not linked to the size of the social network (neither "current" nor "behavioural"). It is nevertheless interesting to note that the importance of social support is significantly correlated with doing regular activities with other people and with an absence of general responses ("everybody" or "nobody," for example) to the questions on significant relationships. This seems to imply a positive orientation towards sociability.

In regard to the composition of the informal support system, we found significant associations between the predominance of each category of social relationships in the following areas:

TABLE 3:
Influence of the Environment on the Natural Support System

Environment	Spouse*						Children**						Siblings-kin						Friends-neighbours					
	0	1	2	3	4	Tot.	0	1	2	3	4	Tot.	0	1	2	3	4	Tot.	0	1	2	3	4	Tot.
Rural	0	9	23	35	33	(43)	12	28	21	19	30	(67)	80	6	3	5	6	(80)	61	27	5	4	3	(80)
Inner City	9	4	37	41	9	(32)	14	12	34	12	28	(50)	58	11	9	5	17	(79)	47	29	13	1	10	(79)
Ste-Foy	0	7	31	36	26	(42)	18	12	17	20	33	(72)	79	11	6	9	3	(80)	66	23	6	4	1	(80)
significance			ns						ns						.01						(.05)			

0. Percentage of persons whose natural support system does not include people from this category.
1. Percentage of persons whose natural support system includes between 1 and 25% of people from this category.
2. Percentage of persons whose natural support system includes between 26 and 50% of people from this category.
3. Percentage of persons whose natural support system includes between 51 and 75% of people from this category.
4. Percentage of persons whose natural support system includes more than 75% of people from this category.

* percentage adjusted for married people only
** percentage adjusted for people with children only

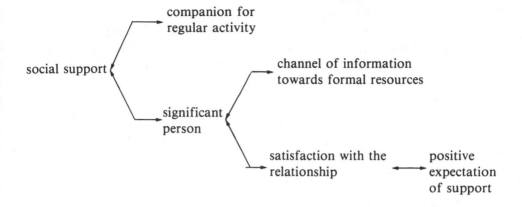

We are therefore justified in speaking about a kind of polarization of emotional and general support in an individual's specific relationships. This could lead to a risk of overwhelming some members of the social support system.

If we return to the differences that exist here between the various environments, we can distinguish two different orientations:

— The first one is centred around the nuclear family with a slight predominance of the spouse in the rural environment and of the children in the urban middle class.
— The second is more oriented towards an extended network and characterizes the Inner City.

We have indications, except in Ste-Foy, that these orientations do not reflect just objective constraints on social relations. In the rural milieu, all social relationships are geographically accessible. Nevertheless, even if friends and neighbours are associated with daily activities, they are seldom included in the significant persons or in the support system. Siblings and kin are almost nonexistent at these various levels. In the Inner City, adjusted responses to questions on significant persons and activities show that the elderly are not oriented towards the nuclear family in this environment. We feel, therefore, entitled to interpret these findings in terms of "normative orientations" linked with the milieu. In the case of the rural environment we have called this a norm of "privatization" of problems.

A nonspecific sense of support related to the environment

In their study of social support, Biegel et al. (1980, 1982) have described the importance of environmental factors in positive mental health. Their study allowed them to distinguish between three levels of social support: direct support, received from members of the social network; indirect support, received through the participation in groups and associations; and what they call "social adjustment," which involves work satisfaction and attachment to the neighbourhood. What interests us is that this last category of support seems to be particularly important to elderly people.

In our study, we have collected interesting data regarding this level of support. If we look first at the general perception of the environment, it is more positive in the rural milieu. This parallels the fact that neighbours were more often quoted as friends, so that the neighbourhood itself seems to be more "friendly." In the urban milieu perceptions were more ambiguous or negative, mainly in the more deprived part of the Inner City. In Ste-Foy, it is interesting to note that present friends were often past neighbours and that present relations with the neighbourhood were positive but limited. This could be a sign of a perceived break in the relation to the milieu due to the environmental history of the respondents in this sample. We will come back later to this issue, which has important consequences for the social support dynamics in this environment.

Our analysis of data regarding reconstructed behaviours of the elderly has shown the importance a global way of relating to the "social milieu" has in some environments. We have labelled as "general sociability" this tendency to go to open or public places (like parks, shopping centres, bars, etc.) in order to be "with people," known or unknown. Correlations between various indices related to this concept indicate that it represents something specific. This type of sociability is characteristic for the rural environment and for the Inner City, especially for men in the latter milieu. They have social contacts through regular "walking" and mention it more than respondents from other milieu as their favourite place for contacts. In contrast, groups and associations are very unpopular in the Inner City, while they are an important source of relationships in the rural environment.

This finding seems to be somewhat contradictory with the negative perception that the aged inhabitants of the Inner City have of their surroundings. It is nevertheless convergent with the fact that people in this environment tend to name more friends and neighbours as significant people in their support system. In the rural milieu, where this "general sociability" is more a support than a substitute for social contacts, we do not find this inclusion of friends or neighbours in the support system.

The question of the relative specialization in the relationship between the "content of support" and the "content of social links"

The question of the relative specialization of support given by formal and informal resources has been widely debated. Are formal resources mainly used in specific situations or are they used mainly by elderly people who lack family or neighbourhood support, or does the support given by formal resources supplant that given by informal resources? What is the relative specificity of the support associated with the various categories of social relations?

We will come back to the first set of questions later. With regard to specialization of informal support relations, we are faced with two main conflicting theses. The "hierarchical compensatory model" by Cantor (1979) says that the elderly tend to ask for help first from their spouse. When this is not available they turn to their children and, if help is still unavailable, to their kin, friends and neighbours, then to formal resources. Litwak and Szelenyi (1969) and Dono et al. (1979) have proposed a "task specific model." They focus their analysis on the way the various primary groups are structurally differentiated in an industrial society. They show that each set of structural characteristics is associated with specific tasks and therefore with specific categories of support. Simons (1983-84) comes to analogous conclusions through an analysis of the various components of social adjustment, each of which relates to the specific "needs" (assistance and security, intimacy, self-esteem). He shows that a "hierarchical compensatory model" exists, but varies according to the various categories of needs.

Our data show that we do not have simple responses to this very complex question. We have considered various indices: the area of problems associated with the support — daily life, sense of security, health problems and "varia"; the degree of regularity of the support given; and the precise content of support that has been associated with each category of social relations in these situations. We have also added the content of services received from various parts of the social network, as an index of implicit daily support.

A comparison between the categories of relations associated with each domain of life shows that the variable "environment" seems to be more important than the variable "domain," but not to the exclusion of this last one:

— Spouse is important in each group but merely for daily life and much less for the sense of security, health problems and varia. Spouse was quoted less often in the Inner City concerning a sense of security, but quoted more often in the rural environment, especially in the area of security.

— Children were important everywhere in the various areas of problems. Elderly from Ste-Foy tended to quote them more exclusively, mainly for the sense of security.

— Siblings and kin, as well as friends and neighbours, were more often quoted in the Inner City.

Two conclusions can be drawn from these data. The categories of persons who are associated with a sense of security tend also to have been quoted in the field of significant person. As we said before, Inner City differs sharply from the other two environments. This can be explained by the fact that more respondents in this milieu were single and childless. In this sense, siblings and kin, as well as friends and neighbours, could be said to have a compensatory function.

Nevertheless this is not entirely true when we consider other indices:

— Siblings and kin support parallels help from children mainly in daily life in the sense that each category of relationship is associated with regular support. Nevertheless, in general, siblings and kin are much less associated with daily life problems, while their action seems to be more important for health problems.

— Friends' and neighbours' support differs from the support given by the other relations. Their assistance is more punctual and nonregular, mainly in the area of health problems, where their intervention is more associated with a crisis than with a long-lasting disability. Receiving help from friends is associated with a use of the strategy "oneself," which suggests that friends can be a complementary source of support for people who remain relatively autonomous (Corin, 1984). Friends and neighbours are also quoted as a source of "security" and as helpers in "varia" situations; in this latter case, they are also more present in the behavioural network.

This shows that we cannot say that friends and neighbours have a compensatory function in the same sense as siblings and kin. Their assistance is associated with more specific circumstances and with a specific milieu: the Inner City.

If we consider the *precise content of the help given* in the various situations, we are struck by the fact that respondents from the different environments differ significantly in the kind of help they say they have received.

In the urban middle class environment there is a strong predominance of instrumental support, and emotional support is mentioned less. In the rural milieu, instrumental help is less dominant, and emotional support is quoted more often. The "reference towards formal resources" mentioned in the two urban samples is almost absent from the rural environment.

We could interpret this predominance of instrumental help in the urban middle class sample from different perspectives: it might be related to norms and values that discourage an expression of emotional dependency; it could be a defense reaction against a too large risk of depending on children who are especially present in the significant network and in the support system, or it could be an outcome of specific environmental histories, in the sense that people have "left behind them" their main sources of emotional support.

In all cases, instrumental support is focussed on the nuclear family:

children and spouse. Inner City people give a larger place to siblings and kin. "Reference" support is strongly focussed on children in Ste-Foy and is sparser between the various categories of social relations in the Inner City. Emotional support is focussed first on children in Ste-Foy and on children and spouse in the rural milieu. It is once again sparser in the Inner City, where siblings and kin parallel friends and neighbours. "Accompanying" support in the rural milieu is associated first with children, followed by spouse, then friends and neighbours.

Later we will look at the relationship between services offered and received as an index of perceived position in the social field. We can say here that services received from children and from neighbours tend to be presented as essentially instrumental, while services received from siblings and kin and from friends encompass a more emotional dimension, mainly through the reception of gifts from siblings and kin, and moral support and visits from friends.

Social Support in the Context of the Help-Seeking Behaviours

Here we shall consider the various types of help-seeking behaviours as they are synthesized in the four classes of our typology: predominance of formal resources, predominance of informal resources, predominance of self-resources, mixed strategy.

We will look first at the association between the preferred strategy and the milieu; then we will examine the relations with the variables presented in our general model.

Inconclusive correlations between preferred strategies and the milieu

When we consider together the whole set of strategies described by our respondents, the differences between the samples are statistically insignificant. Nevertheless significant differences appear in two areas: that of the sense of security and that of "varia."

In the field of security, respondents from the rural sample mention more formal resources, mainly the general practitioner and the Centre local de santé communautaire (C.L.S.C.), while those from the Inner City rely significantly more, and more exclusively, on informal resources. This could possibly be linked to what we have said about their general style of sociability and the place that they give to friends and neighbours in their support systems.

In the field of "varia" (administrative and financial areas), elderly from the rural environment tend once again to use the formal resources available to them in this milieu. Those from the Inner City count a little more on the assistance of their informal network, while people from the urban middle class count more on themselves. This is the only area where this last tendency is manifest.

TABLE 4:
Influence of environment on the type of strategy (in %)

Environment	Daily life			Security			Health			Varia			(Total)
	1	2	3	1	2	3	1	2	3	1	2	3	
FORMAL RESOURCES													
Rural	80	19	1	32	44	24	38	17	45	71	14	15	(80)
Inner City	80	19	1	63	13	24	34	18	48	84	9	7	(79)
Ste-Foy	91	9	—	55	29	16	31	16	53	91	1	8	(80)
Significance	ns			0.000			ns			0.01			
INFORMAL RESOURCES													
Rural	55	35	10	47	40	13	90	10	—	62	5	33	(80)
Inner City	61	29	10	51	18	31	93	6	1	54	15	31	(79)
Ste-Foy	47	34	19	51	35	14	99	1	—	66	13	21	(80)
Significance	ns			0.005			ns			ns			
ONESELF													
Rural	59	39	2	86	14	—	86	10	4	65	15	20	(80)
Inner City	62	34	4	84	15	1	89	7	4	57	23	20	(79)
Ste-Foy	67	29	4	76	20	4	91	5	4	54	10	36	(80)
Significance	ns			ns			ns			0.005			
MIXED STRATEGY													
Rural	65	32	3	96	4	—	87	5	8	85	6	9	(80)
Inner City	78	19	3	95	3	2	96	3	1	85	5	10	(79)
Ste-Foy	62	34	4	96	3	1	95	—	5	90	4	6	(80)
Significance	ns			ns			ns			ns			

[1] Percentage of persons that considered strategy constitutes from 0 to 1/3 of all mentioned strategies in this category.
[2] Percentage of persons that considered strategy constitutes more than 1/3 but not more than 2/3 of all mentioned strategies in this category.
[3] Percentage of persons that considered strategy constitutes more than 2/3 of all mentioned strategies in this category.

It is interesting to note that there is no simple correlation between the number of resources used, the type of strategy privileged and the perceived magnitude of problems in a specific field (Corin et al., 1984). We are justified in saying that in some cases (as in the field of daily life in Ste-Foy) the use of more resources allows for perception of the situation as non-problematic, while in other contexts (as in the field of security in the rural environment) this is insufficient to change the perception that a field is problematic. In the Inner City the mention of informal resources in relation to a sense of security is associated with a positive perception of the field but not in the case of "varia."

It is important to have this in mind when one designs a questionnaire. If a questionnaire focusses too much on "problems" to draw a picture of the support system, it can miss the type of support important in "nonproblematic" areas.

The context of a more global relationship with formal resources

Here we consider the precision of the knowledge that elderly people say that they have of the resources in their milieu; the number of resources they quote in the fields of housing, home services and homes for the aged; the perceptions they have of these resources; and the degree of direct or indirect contacts (through some members of their network) they have with these. The various indices tend to be significantly related. Diverging trends characterize each environment.

At one extreme, urban middle-class people are characterized by a more "global" (versus specific) knowledge; by disinterest, mainly in the area of housing; and by a more negative perception of these resources. They are distributed equally between those with direct, with indirect and with no contact with professional services in these areas.

At the other extreme, respondents from the rural environment show a more precise knowledge of professional services. Their perceptions are split between very positive and very negative, mainly concerning specialized lower income housing and homes for the aged. More of these respondents say that they have had no direct or indirect contact with professional services. Their knowledge of these services seems to be diffused into the community, as friends and neighbours are often quoted as having given the information about the service.

In the Inner City, people are knowledgeable about housing and home services for the aged, but say they have little knowledge about homes for the elderly. They have had more direct contact (two-thirds) with professional services in these fields, but have a more neutral perception of them than elsewhere in our survey.

It is interesting to add that the elderly who live with people from a younger generation tend to know less about professional resources, as if they rely more on their coresidents for this. This parallels the fact that in Ste-Foy, it is mainly the children who act as "referent" for formal resources in the help-seeking process. Their central place in the support system of their parents seems, then, to be accompanied by a general reliance on them. This is less true elsewhere. In general, the spouse is very seldom quoted as a "channel of information" about professional resources.

If we look at the relationship between the social network data and the data regarding the position vis-à-vis formal resources, a large "current" network is negatively associated with a direct contact with formal resources. A large behavioural network is nevertheless associated with the number of resources quoted.

In general, we can say that some people are on the whole positively oriented towards formal resources (direct contact, more resources quoted, precise knowledge, positive perception), while others are globally "distant" from these resources in their knowledge, their perception and their behaviours.

Perceived position in the social field

Authors who have called for a more careful approach to collaboration between the formal and informal resources have stressed the importance that values of independency and autonomy have in our society. These could contribute in a positive way to the self-image in the elderly. Others have suggested that it is better to speak of interdependency than of autonomy in the field of aging. To operationalize the study of this factor we have considered various indirect indices: the degree of symmetry in the content of services received and given; the general position in the giving and receiving of services; and a general attitude towards personal involvement in social relations.

The comparison between the services that the elderly say they have given and received is very instructive. Contents exchanged with friends and neighbours are symmetric. With friends, instrumental (services, transport) and affective (moral support, sociability) services are given and received together. With neighbours, services tend to be mainly instrumental. With siblings and kin, the respondents perceive themselves as receiving mainly instrumental services (services, transport, some money) but as giving both affective (moral support, socialization) and instrumental services. This seems to indicate that they think of themselves as having a significant position in this area of relationships. With children the situation is different. Received services are mainly instrumental and concrete, while return services are mainly instrumental (material aid, watching for children, money) and gifts. It is striking to note that the elderly also quote visits as a service received from, but never given to, their children: as if they had the impression that a conversation with their children is more a burden than a real exchange.

When they express global expectations regarding support given by various categories of relations, this is in the same line as the content of services received from friends (mainly socio-affective expectations) and from neighbours (mainly instrumental), but not from children, for whom they express mainly "socialization" expectations and a wish of "global" support. Expectance of shelter from children is seldom expressed, particularly in the rural environment. The present involvement of the government in the financing and the care of the aged is presented in a positive way as allowing more autonomy for the elderly.

In accordance with Wentowski (1981), we have noticed several ways of "reequilibrating" an asymmetrical gift. We have labelled this "symbolic reciprocity" — when the elderly insist on paying for a service, or when present services are presented as part of a larger reciprocal circle in which the elderly person has taken an active and giving part in the past. Preserving a sense of reciprocity appears to be an important dimension in the flux of services around the aged.

We can also look at the structural position that the elderly perceive they occupy in the social field of exchanges. We have distinguished between: a dominant position, if the person gives services without receiving it; a dominated position, if services are received but not given; a reciprocal position, if services are both given and received; and a "retreat" position, if services are neither received nor given. We have characterized our respondents by the dominant trend that they have expressed in their relations with the various categories of relationships.

The differences between the environments are statistically insignificant. We can nevertheless notice that the tendency to have dominant exchanges is not present in the Inner City, to have dominated exchanges is not present in Ste-Foy, and to have symmetrical exchanges is not present in the rural environment, people there being either in a dominant or in a dominated position. Absence of exchange increases with age, which could be a sign of a perceived marginalization in the social field.

We have looked at the way in which this index correlates with other parallel indices: the direction of contacts mainly given (dominating) or received (dominated) during the past week; the type of response given to the questions on significant others ("general" when people say "everybody" or "nobody," "particular" when they give a name); and the social style of regular activities (mainly alone or mainly with somebody else). We have presented elsewhere (Corin et al., 1984) more detailed correlations between these various indices. It is interesting to note that the data concerning this position in the social field correlate with the social network data:

— A large "current" social network is correlated with a dominant position in the contacts during the reconstructed week and with a "particular" style of response on questions concerning significant persons. These people can be said to occupy an active position in their social field.

— A large "behavioural" social network shows the same correlations. In addition, this is linked to a symmetrical or a dominant position in the exchange of services. The concrete contacts in daily life seem to have a larger relationship on the perceived position in the social field than a more cognitive picture of them.

— A large amount of social support received in the various areas investigated is positively associated with activities with others and with a dominated position in the exchanges and negatively with a dominant position.

According with our theoretical model of the help-seeking behaviour, we have also looked at the relations between these various indices and help-seeking strategies:

— Strategies that are focussed on formal resources are correlated to a positive position regarding formal resources (direct contact, larger number of resources quoted, no disinterest) and to a dominated position in the exchange of services.

— Strategies focussed around informal resources are significantly associated with an active integration in the social field, i.e., negatively correlated to activities alone and with a "general" style of response.

— Strategies centred around oneself are not a "last resource" but are linked with an autonomous position. These people know more formal resources, tend to do their activities alone and tend to have a dominant position in the exchanges.

— People with mixed strategies are somewhat similar. They have had a direct contact with formal resources and have a positive perception of these. They occupy a dominant position in the contacts and a symmetric one in the exchange of services.

Help-seeking as a strategy

The specific relationship between strategies focussed on formal resources and a dominated position in the exchanges can be interpreted in two ways: as a reflection of an objective degree of dependency that could orient people towards professional services, or as a strategy built by people who feel themselves in a dominated position and who turn towards external resources to limit their dependency. In the second hypothesis a perceived position in the social field could be an obstacle for the mobilization of informal resources.

To support this second hypothesis, we have some indirect indices. In Ste-

Foy, where we have seen that people are more centred around one category of social relations (the children) and rely more on them, the expectations expressed for the future focus more than elsewhere on the formal resources. In the Inner City, where people have more direct contacts with formal resources, they tend to put them "at some distance" by having a more neutral perception of them and in focussing their expectations on informal resources. In the rural milieu, where people seem to have very little contact with professional services, they tend to focus their expectations a little more on these. We are faced with a kind of "pendulum" between reality and expectations for the future in what could be an attempt to split dependency on agents who are more diversified.

Factor analysis of our data (see Corin et al., 1984, for a more detailed analysis) shows that both of the hypotheses are plausible and correspond to different "styles" or "strategies" of using resources. One factor associated with a help-seeking style dominated by formal resources includes: having serious problems in the various areas investigated and having chronic ill health; doing few activities alone, being in a dominated position in the exchange of services and having a positive perception of formal resources. Formal resources are less likely to be positively evaluated by respondents living in the Inner City.

A second factor that appears when we isolate the Inner City from the two other environments includes variables that imply a more autonomous style: the person also privileges strategies centred around himself or herself and significantly no strategies centred on informal resources; he or she tends to do regular activities alone. In this case we have no relation between the strategy and the problem level or the size of the social network. We are then justified in thinking that it is more a strategy linked with a personal "style" than an effect of constraints.

Analogous conclusions can be drawn from the factor analysis related to strategies focussed around informal resources. The first factor implies a general context of dependency: the person uses the strategy "oneself" much less, she or he has a large support system, is aged and not in a dominant position in the exchange of services. The two other factors appear when we isolate first the rural environment and second, Ste-Foy. The first one implies an active position in the social field: regular activities done with other people, having a position significantly dominant and nondominated in the exchange of services, living with somebody else and having few mixed strategies. The second of these factors is very similar: significantly few of the three other strategies, few activities alone, receiving much social support and living with somebody. None of these three factors is related to the seriousness of the problems or to the size of the network, and we therefore feel justified once again in saying that this strategy reflects more a style of social integration than external factors or constraints.

The Influence of the Environment: A Complex Question

Our survey data could have been interpreted in quite a different way if we had chosen to emphasize the common trends in social support and in the help-seeking process. We opted for a search for the differences and have tried to explain the diversity in our data. This does not mean that we are returning to the "singularity" of each case. We have to search for some rules that underlie these differences in a specific socio-cultural and temporal context. At several points we have shown that factors related to the environment influence the functioning of the social relations and, in some way, could influence the help-seeking process as much.

To be able to interpret the meaning of these data we have to look more carefully at the mediating factors that could intervene in the various environments. I shall limit myself here to some suggestions regarding the meaning of these environmental correlations.

The rural milieu

The more striking point here is what we have called the "norm of privacy." That means that there is a contrast between the greater availability of various categories of social relations in the proximate environment and the fact that the elderly people tend to rely almost exclusively on their nuclear family, often on their spouse, for emotional and instrumental support. This could be explained by the very high density of the social relations of these people. Because they remain in the same milieu, people of their social network interact in various ways in daily life. If we look at the origins of friendship, the circumstances that are most frequently quoted are: "friend from childhood," "neighbour," "friend of the family," "known at friend's home." Most of the respondents are members of several associations. In this context, the "norm of privacy" could act as a type of defence against the invasion of private space. This could also underlie the positive representation that people have with formal resources, even if they are very rarely in touch with them. In the same line, Coward (1982, quoted in Lee, 1985) has shown that the rural elderly who need assistance and who receive it mainly from a formal agency have the highest scores of life satisfaction. Those who receive it mainly or exclusively from their informal relations get the lowest scores.

The urban middle class

An action of socio-cultural norms is more difficult to show here because of a confusion between personal and environmental variables (Matthews and Vanden Heuvel, 1985). When we look at the history of these people we see that more than elsewhere in our survey, people have moved there relatively recently (39 percent had been there for less than 15 years). Many more people than elsewhere in our survey have moved after 65 years of age. This is true mainly in the case of women who moved in order to be near to their children. The men who moved during their active years often did so in the context of an ascendant work history, as a promotion. In general, elderly from Ste-Foy have moved less often than those in the Inner City, but movers came from farther. They would then be less familiar with the rules governing their present milieu, which could have an effect on their social life (Cape, this volume). This could explain the focus of several of them on their children and their general reliance on them, which is much more evident there than in the other environments. Some indices suggest that this could have been accompanied by a kind of emotional break, at least in some cases, which could reinforce the actual dependence on the children. They have a positive relationship with their environment and they participate in associations, but this remains at a somewhat superficial level and does not imply a deep involvement of the elderly people. We have seen that expectations for the future seem to focus more on formal resources even if their present relationships with these are more indefinite than elsewhere. This could be a strategy in order not to be trapped in too-inclusive social relations. We cannot exclude a parallel action of norms towards a manifest emotional autonomy in these upwardly mobile people.

The inner city

It is in this milieu that the objective constraints on the social relations are the most evident, but we have seen that this milieu promotes a deeper involvement than elsewhere in "extended" social relations with siblings and kin and with friends and neighbours. What could be called "strategies of sociability" built to counter the quantitative deficiencies in social relations are mainly apparent in the single elderly person who is living alone. The factor analysis has shown that this milieu seems to be in some way related to the pattern of use of formal resources in a context of autonomy. Much of the data that we have collected there go in a direction analogous with what Sokolovski and Cohen (1978) have described for their "single room occupancy" dwellers. They have shown that an overinvolvement of formal resources in the life of these people strengthens their attachment to personal autonomy. The importance given to the "general sociability" style might also go in this direction.

Implications

These data confirm the idea that the characteristics of communities are related to the functioning of the social support systems (Oxley et al., 1981). We can then expand the conclusion of Henderson that planning needs for one rural setting are not necessarily transferable to another. Strategies for working with informal resources also have to adjust to the complex dynamics that underlie their utilization by the elderly people in various environments.

In our pilot project we have suggested that we cannot build a model of practice that is universally applicable. What we can do is be conscious of the various levels of variables that mediate relationships between the elderly and the formal and informal resources and try to take them into account in each particular milieu and in each particular case. We need a "grid for looking at and understanding" more than a "grid for precise action."

References

Biegel, D.E., A.J. Naparstek and M.M. Khan
  1980 "Determinants of social support systems." Pp. 111-122 in R.R. Stough and A. Wandersman (eds.), *Optimizing Environments: Research, Practice and Policy*. Washington, D.C.: Environmental Design Research Association.
  1982 "Social support and mental health in urban ethnic neighborhoods." Pp. 21-36 in D.E. Biegel and A.J. Naparstek (eds.), *Community Support System and Mental Health Practice, Policy and Research*. New York: Springer Publishing Company.
Bott, E.
  1971 *Family and Social Networks*. 2nd ed. London: Tavistock Publications.
Brown, B.B.
  1978 "Social and psychological correlates of help-seeking behavior among urban adults." *American Journal of Community Psychology* 6(5):425-439.
Cantor, M.H.
  1975 "Life space and the social support system of the inner city elderly of New York." *The Gerontologist* 15(1):23-27.
  1979 "Neighbors and friends: An overlooked resource in the informal support system." *Research on Aging* 1(4):434-463.
Cantor, M.H. and M.J. Mayer
  1978 "Factors in differential utilization of services by urban elderly." *Journal of Gerontological Social Work* 1(1):47-62.
Corin, E.
  1982 Les stratégies sociales d'existence des personnes âgées: une utilisation dynamique de l'analyse des réseaux sociaux." *Santé mentale au Canada* 30(3):8-14.
  1984 "Manières de vivre, manières de dire: réseau social et sociabilité quotidienne des personnes âgées au Québec." *La culture et l'âge. Questions de culture* 6:157-186.
Corin, E., T. Sherif and L. Bergeron
  1983 *Le fonctionnement des systèmes de support naturel des personnes âgées.* 3 volumes. Québec: Laboratoire de gérontologie.
Corin, E., J. Tremblay, T. Sherif and L. Bergeron
  1984 "Stratégies et tactiques: les modalités d'affrontement des problèmes chez des personnes âgées de milieu urbain et rural." *Sociologie et Sociétés* (numéro spécial sur le vieillissement) 16(2):89-104.

Dono, J.E., C.M. Falbe, B.L. Kail, E. Litwak, R.H. Sherman and D. Siegel
1979   "Primary groups in old age: Structure and function." *Research on Aging* 1(4):403-433.
Freidson, E.
1960   "Client control and medical practice." *American Journal of Sociology* 65 (4):372-382.
Frolands, C., D.L. Pancoast, N.J. Chapman and P.J. Kimboko
1984   *Helping Network and Human Services.* Beverly Hills: Sage.
Garrison, V. and J. Podell
1981   "A practicable 'community support systems assessment' for inclusion in standard clinical interviews." *Schizophrenia Bulletin* 7(1):101-108.
Gottlieb, B.H.
1978   "The development and application of a classification scheme of informal helping behaviours." *Canadian Journal of Behavioural Science* 10:105-115.
Gottlieb, B.H. (ed.)
1981   *Social Networks and Social Support.* Beverly Hills: Sage.
Gourash, N.
1978   "Help-seeking. A review of the literature." *American Journal of Community Psychology* 6:413-423.
Hammer, M.
1981   "Social supports, social networks and schizophrenia." *Schizophrenia Bulletin* 7(1):45-57.
Henderson, J.
1982   "Issues in rural health planning." *Canadian Nurse* 78:30-33.
Lee, G.R.
1985   "Kinship and social support of the elderly: The case of the United States." *Ageing and Society* 5:19-38.
Levine, F. and E. Preston
1970   "Community resource orientation among low-income groups." *Wisconsin Law Review* 1:80-113.
Litwak, E. and I. Szelenyi
1969   "Primary group structures and their functions: Kin, neighbors and friends." *American Sociological Review* 34:465-481.
Martin Matthews, A. and A. Vanden Heuvel
1985   *Methodological Issues in Research on Aging in Rural versus Urban Environments.* University of Guelph, typescript, 22 pp.
McKinlay, J.B.
1972   "Some approaches and problems in the study of the use of services: An overview." *Journal of Health and Social Behavior* 13:115-152.
Mechanic, D.A.
1978   *Medical Sociology* 2nd ed. London: The Free Press.
Mitchell, R.E. and E.J. Trickett
1980   "Task force report: Social networks as mediators of social support. An analysis of the effects and determinants of social networks." *Community Mental Health Journal* 16(1):27-44.
Oxley, D., M. Barbera and E.K. Saralla
1981   "Relationships among community size mediators and social support

variables: A path analytic approach." *American Journal of Community Psychology* 9(6):637-651.

Simons, R.L.

1983-　"Specificity and substitution in the networks of the elderly." *International*
84　*Journal of Aging and Human Development* 18(2):121-139.

Sokolovski, J. and C.J. Cohen

1978　"The cultural meaning of personal networks for the inner city elderly." *Urban Anthropology* 7(4):303-342.

Suchman, E.

1966　"Stages of illness and medical care." *Journal of Health and Social Behavior* 6(1):2-16.

Sussman, M.B.

1977　"Family, bureaucracy and the elderly individual: An organizational/linkage perspective." In E. Shanas and M.B. Sussman, (eds.), *Family, Bureaucracy and the Elderly.* Durham: Duke University Press.

Wellman, B.

1981　*Applying Network Analysis to the Study of Support.* Resource paper no. 3. Centre for Urban and Community Services. Toronto: University of Toronto.

Wellman, B. and B. Leighton

1982　"Réseau, quartier et communauté." *Urban Affairs Quarterly* 14(3):111-133.

Wentowski, G.J.

1981　"Reciprocity and the coping strategies of older people: Cultural dimensions of network building." *The Gerontologist* 21(6):600-609.

VI

Health and Well-Being
in Relation to Age

Most Canadians remain healthy for almost all of their lives. Even very old people, in their eighties and nineties, are for the most part healthy. Popular stereotypes of the aged are so pervasive (even among the aged) that it is important to begin with that point. Moreover, although frequently subjected to criticism, it is also true that the Canadian health-care system has many praiseworthy qualities and may well be considered second to none in an international context. In general, neither the health of older Canadians nor the ways in which they obtain health care differ qualitatively from the situation of young people. Age-related differences in health status, considered in the chapters of this section, rest on an underlying pattern of similarity.

Nonetheless, as Chappell, Strain and Blandford have recently noted (1986:33-34), "One of the major concerns about old age for both the individual and the society is a decline in health. It is, to a large extent, deteriorating health that is associated with individual dependence, or lack of self-sufficiency." Although most older people are in quite good health, aging does generally lead to greater health deficits and limitations in the ability to move freely about, in perception, and in the ability to care fully for oneself.

Chapter 20 Simmons-Tropea and Osborn provides encyclopedia data on mortality and morbidity in relation to age. The data are organized around a central debate in gerontology, the "rectangularization" thesis, which suggests that the shape of the morbidity curve will rectangularize towards a natural limit, assuming a shape very close to a similarly developing rectangularization of mortality. In the best of all worlds, unless one also wished for immortality, one might hope that good health would be maintained until death and that death would come swiftly after a very long life. Simmons-Tropea and Osborn critically examine the arguments around the likelihood of this becoming a typical pattern and offer little hope that it will.

Among the conditions for which little improvement in morbidity is anticipated are the mental disorders. In Chapter 21, D'Arcy examines the relationship between aging and mental health. He first places the very notions of mental health and mental illness into a social framework and also argues that psychiatry and other mental-health treatment processes are inherently social processes. Social factors are thus implicated as causes of psychiatric distress, as mediators between stressful life events and health outcomes in individuals, as contributors to identification and labelling of mental illness and case distribution and in structuring the nature of the mental-health-care delivery system.

While D'Arcy's careful review of Canadian and comparative data shows that many psychiatric disorders that are often thought to be more prevalent in later life are not (one example being depression), nonetheless the meaning and expression of certain disorders may be conditioned by aging and age-related factors. Additionally, the belief that such disorders are increasingly found at advanced ages can be consequential for the ways in which people experience or anticipate their aging and for the treatment they accord to others and to themselves. Gerontologists frequently give the example that forgetfulness, which might be attributed to senility in an eighty-year-old, but might be discounted as merely indicative of commendable preoccupation with business affairs in a forty-year-old.

Simmons-Tropea and Osborn and D'Arcy call attention to the lack of suitable Canadian data on health and aging and the need to make inferences from other, largely U.S. studies. However, the data base is considerably stronger than when the first edition of *Aging in Canada* was published in 1980. These researchers rely on secondary analysis of large national or provincial data sets for some of their concerns. We still lack longitudinal data, as D'Arcy notes. Equally significant, we lack studies that examine the experiences of older people and their families around health matters. It is clear, for example, that self-perceived health status does not closely correspond with actual physiological changes. Perhaps influenced by reference group criteria (Chappell, Strain and Blandford, 1986:52), many older people, despite increasing fragility, aches and pains, take the view "I'm in pretty good shape for the shape I'm in." That is, they set their expectations for health status low because of the widespread stereotypes equating aging with sickness, and thereby feel that they are doing quite well in contrast to "most old people."

Connidis looks at health and more general well-being issues in Chapter 22, focussing on the things people like and dislike about being old and on their reported needs for services in the health and social areas. Her paper is organized around the ambivalent approach to aging and the aged, either focussing unduly on the problems of aging or painting a rosy picture based on atypical, highly successful old people, which is reflected both in popular culture and scientific accounts. Several studies, she notes, show that the aged report higher levels of life satisfaction than the young report.

Community-based studies of the aged do not represent that portion of the elderly who are living in a hospital, nursing home or other long-term care facility. In addition, they underrepresent the community-dwelling elderly in poor health, who are too ill to be interviewed. While proxy data are some-times gathered in such studies, in reality they are rarely analysed. In Chapter 23, Marshall reviews limits to generalizability of several Canadian community studies due to sampling and also measurement features.

While the authors of research reports are generally conscientious in describing exclusions for health and other reasons, their qualifying state-ments are rarely repeated by those who make use of their research reports. Connidis is herself careful to describe her sample, and she indicates that, in addition to excluding a priori the institutionalized elderly, 14 percent of eligible respondents were not interviewed because of their own health.

With her sample of the well elderly in the community, Connidis shows that the need for and the actual use of community-based services is in fact restricted to a small number of individuals. Drawing on other studies, as well, Connidis concludes that the majority of older Canadians enjoy health status sufficient to ensure their avoidance of dependency on formal health services. However, Connidis notes, when people do need services, this need is great. This conclusion is very much in line with data on nursing-home ad-missions reported by Shapiro and Roos in Chapter 26 and the discussion of hospital use, based on Roos, Shapiro and Roos (1984) but which is found in Chapter 27 of this volume. That is to say, the older population is highly dif-ferentiated, even at very advanced ages, in health status and consequent need for services. While most people remain quite healthy throughout their lives or all but a tiny fraction of their lives, it is true that a minority become quite frail or even fragile and that an even smaller minority suffer health deficits that create a large demand for health services.

Differentiation is again a theme in Chapter 23 by Marshall, in which age and gender differences in health status are noted. Moreover, even when the oldest living generation remains in good health, adult children become in-creasingly concerned about their health. A feature of the lives of most peo-ple from their late thirties or early forties on is that they come to "monitor" changes in the health status of their parents. Here medical sociology and the sociology of the family come together, as health becomes a family concern. This chapter can also be read in the context of the discussions of family sup-ports found in Chapters 17 through 19.

As noted earlier, we have very little data on the actual experiences that older people have with their own health. We also have very little data on the experiences of older patients in the context of care (Marshall, 1981, 1986; Rosenthal, et al., 1980). Researchers have made excellent use of nationwide and community-based social survey data, but perhaps not enough attention has been given to gathering qualitative data through focussed interviews such as Connidis used or through participant observation (see, for example, Hanson, 1985). Future research is likely to be heavily informed by theoretical developments in stress research such as D'Arcy describes in

Chapter 21. The life course can be viewed as patterning stressful life events, with major events such as retirement and widowhood being quite predictably located in later life, but with "daily hassles" also variable over different phases of the life course. Researchers are increasingly seeking ways to integrate stress research with life-course research and, in turn, with social support research, all in relation to health (Ryff, 1986; Wellman and Hall, 1986). In that context, the material in this section relates quite strongly to chapters throughout this book.

References

Chappell, Neena L., Laurel A. Strain and Audrey A. Blandford
    1986   *Aging and Health Care: A Social Perspective.* Toronto: Holt, Rinehart and Winston.
Hanson, Barbara Gail
    1985   "Negotiation of self and setting to advantage: An interactionist consideration of nursing home data." *Sociology of Health and Illness* 7(1):21-35.
Marshall, Victor W.
    1981   "Physician characteristics and relationships with older patients." Pp. 94-118 in Marie Haug (ed.), *Elderly Patients and Their Doctors*. New York: Springer.
    1986   "Older Patients in the Acute Hospital Setting." Paper prepared for the conference Health in Aging: Sociological Issues and Policy Directions. State University of New York at Albany, April (published in conference proceedings).
Roos, N.P., E. Shapiro and L.L. Roos
    1984   "Aging and the demand for health services: Which aged and whose demand?" *The Gerontologist* 24:31-36.
Rosenthal, Carolyn J., Victor W. Marshall, A.S. Macpherson and Susan E. French
    1980   *Nurses, Patients and Families: Care and Control in the Hospital.* New York: Springer.
Ryff, Carol D.
    1986   "The subjective construction of self and society: An agenda for life-span research." Chapter 2, Pp. 33-74, in Victor W. Marshall (ed.), *Later Life: The Social Psychology of Aging*. Beverly Hills: Sage.
Wellman, Barry and Alan Hall
    1986   "Social networks and social support: Implications for later life." Chapter 7, Pp. 191-231, in Victor W. Marshall (ed.), *Later Life: The Social Psychology of Aging*. Beverly Hills: Sage.

20

Disease, Survival and Death: The Health Status of Canada's Elderly

Daryl Simmons-Tropea and Richard Osborn
Department of Preventive Medicine
and Biostatistics
University of Toronto

The twentieth century has witnessed exceptional changes in the health status of most populations. In the European, North American and Oceanic countries that largely make up what is called the industrialized or more developed countries, progress has been remarkable. Improved quality of nutrition, control over many communicable diseases of infancy and childhood and increases in the general standard of living have added about twenty-five years to the average length of life of persons born now, compared to those starting life in the year 1900 in both Canada and the United States. Change has been so widespread that we can safely characterize these alterations as revolutionary.

Occurring essentially independently from these health trends have been changes in the size, composition and distribution of the populations of these more developed countries. These changes in age composition are described elsewhere in this volume (see Chapters 2, 15, 28, and 29). These coincidental changes in health status and population structure present significant opportunities to extend the advantages of the improved level of living and quality of life and health to the increasingly larger number of older residents in these countries. As the birth rates and average family size continue to fall, the older elements of the population become proportionally larger, and in the case of those countries that experienced the baby boom, the large number of post-World War II births will themselves become a numerically larger group of older persons beginning sometime after the year 2020. Given the expected association of decline in health with increasing age, this proportional and numerical ascendancy in the population leads to very great interest in the quality of health status of this group of citizens.

In an extremely well-written and influential article done in 1980, a physician from the United States (Fries, 1980) argues that the proportion of people surviving to old age will continue to increase, chronic disease will be confined to a very brief segment of the end of a person's life and the needs for medical care in later life will decrease. Other researchers have been quick to respond critically to this argument and suggest that chronic disease will be present during more years of life as a result of people living longer, and that the needs for medical care are expected to rise (Schneider and Brody, 1983). It is clear that the implications of these positions differ greatly and that to a considerable extent the resolution of this question depends on empirical materials from various populations and subgroupings.

The objectives of this chapter paper are to examine the arguments presented by proponents of these conflicting viewpoints and to review the meagre data available on these concerns from the Canadian population.

The Rectangularization of Mortality and Morbidity

Interest in the effects of improvements in life expectancy on descriptions of mortality/survival curves is not new. In one of the forerunners of modern biostatistics textbooks Pearl (1923) examined this question, and it was later explored in greater depth in gerontological research by Comfort (1964). However, it is later publications that focussed the attentions of the research community on this topic. The questions of patterns, causes and implications differ by whether we are addressing mortality or morbidity, life span or life expectancy, severity of morbidity and other factors.

Life Span

Three models of the potential achievement of human life span emerge from the literature:
1) a fixed life span whose ultimate boundary we are fast approaching;
2) an open life span whose ultimate boundary, as yet unknown, we are approaching slowly;
3) an open life span whose ultimate boundary, as yet unknown, we are approaching rapidly.

Fries supports the theory of a "fixed life span," which is the "average" longevity in a society without disease or accident (Fries, 1983:398). This is not to be confused with "life expectancy," which is the average length of life that we may expect, given current age-specific death rates due to disease and accidents.

In the absence of disease or accidents, Fries calculates that the frequency distribution of the "average" life span (99 percent of all people) would range from age 73 to age 97, with a mean (assuming a normal distribution) of 85 and a standard deviation of 4 years. The difference between a *maximum* life potential of 114 years and *average* longevity in a society without disease or accident is implied by Fries to be a function of genetically determined variations in the aging process, with a range encompassing as much as 30 years. This range is predicted to diminish over time as we control most causes of death.

The basis of Fries's theories is that not only is the life span fixed, but we are also fast approaching its biological limit (Fries, 1980:133). Biological constraints on the length of the human life span are due to species-specific processes of senescence. The decline in function of most organs with aging is the basis of Fries's notion of a "natural death" without disease. A transition from premature death (death attributed to accidents and disease) to natural death occurs as the characteristics of the host's resistance become more important than the specific nature of the insult to the equilibrium of the human body (Fries, 1983:399). More sociologically oriented writers have observed that premature death may also arise from socio-economic factors that are difficult to change (Manton, 1982:188). But as Fries comments, drawing a line between where premature death ends and natural death begins is only a conceptual idea and not a realistic one.

Fries's support of the theory that the "aging process" or senescence limits the life span is based on several arguments. He asserts there has been no historical record of change in the maximum life span and these data show that life expectancy at age 100 changed at most 0.7 years since 1939. However, Myers and Manton (1984:347), utilizing tables from the U.S. Social Security Administration Actuarial Study No. 87 (1982), plotted survival curves for U.S. females by single years of age for the years 1900, 1960 and 1980. Although age misstatement on the death certificate may bias survival values at advanced ages, they provide evidence suggesting a stretching outwards of the survival curves and a shift in maximum lengths of the life span towards higher ages for more recent decades. This increase in maximum life span for subsequent years is not evident in the figures provided by Fries (1980, 1983, 1984) because, as argued by Manton and Myer, "abridged" life tables are used rather than "single year of age" life tables, which are truncated at relatively low ages such as age 85 and older.

For the Canadian population there is evidence of an increased survival rate of the very old. In Table 1 the shift is clearly towards a larger proportion of women alive at the beginning of each successive year. In 1931 50 percent of those alive at age 80 had died by age 85; by 1981 the same proportion reached nearly 88 years. It is also clear from these data that there has not been an upwards shift in maximum length of life span over the time period. To the extent that these data represent an accurate recording of age of death, there is clearly no extension of life to ages beyond the 107 years observed for the 1931 period.

A second piece of evidence in support of a fixed life span is based on the observations of Hayflick (1980). The "Hayflick Limit" indicates that cells from different animal species have the potential for only a fixed number of cell doublings. Although Fries and others have used the "Hayflick Limit" to argue a biologically limited life span, Hayflick himself is careful to emphasize that this phenomenon need not have a simple relationship to the aging of organisms. What occurs in laboratories may have little to do with total human body function. In addition Strekler (1977: 42) points out that there are

TABLE 1:
Percent Surviving from Age 80 to End of Life, Females, Canada, 1931 to 1981

Year	1931	1951	1971	1981
Age				
80	100%	100%	100%	100%
81	89	91	93	95
82	79	82	87	89
83	69	72	80	83
84	59	64	73	77
85	50	55	66	71
86	42	47	59	64
87	35	40	52	58
88	28	33	45	52
89	23	26	38	45
90	18	21	32	39
91	14	16	27	34
92	10	12	22	28
93	8	9	17	24
94	6	7	14	19
95	4	5	10	16
96	3	3	8	13
97	2	2	5	11
98	1	1	4	8
99	.7	.8	3	5
100	.5	.5	2	2
101	.3	.3	1	.6
102	.1	.1	.6	.1
103	.05	.06	.4	

SOURCE: Statistics Canada, Life Tables 1931 to 1981, Catalogue 84-516.

a number of types of cells in the human body, such as cells in the circulatory system, whose ability to reproduce are not defined by the "Hayflick Limit". As emphasized by several critics of the theory, by focussing on only one aspect of the processes that affect mortality, much is being conceptually over-simplified (Sacher, 1980; Gorgon, 1977; Strekler, 1977).

The fixed life span argument is also supported by the hypothesis of a "decline of maximal function of vital organs," which is the basis of the concept of a "natural death" (Fries, 1983). The concept of natural death implies that mortality and morbidity are not necessarily linked and that changing disease risks does not necessarily alter the underlying aging rate of an individual. The organ reserve potential is posited as being greatest in early life, with functional decline that is essentially linear and that is roughly parallel for all major organs (Fries, 1983: 399). This functional decline of the organs results in loss of the body's ability to maintain homeostasis, and finally, in death. Natural death occurs at that point in which homeostasis can no longer be maintained. As Fries explains, this phenomenon of increasing frailty is the very essence of geriatric medicine. Chronic illness is then viewed as a physiological process that accelerates the existing rate of loss of organ reserve. At present, however, there are no data to support the notion of natural death, and given the variances in organ declines within and between individuals, it may be difficult to measure organ reserve potential.

The basis of the model of natural death is a well-known mathematical function often used in models of aging and mortality. Benjamin Gompertz in 1925 noted a linear increase in mortality rates with age when rates were plotted on a logarithmic scale. Mortality rates increase exponentially with age, doubling approximately every eight years. Fries (1980: 131) concluded that "obviously an exponentially increasing mortality rate ensures a finite life span."

Other researchers (Wilkin, 1981; Lew, 1980) provide evidence that application of a Gompertz model may be inappropriate for advanced ages of 90 or more, where mortality rates are much less than would be predicted. At age 100, the mortality hazard is approximately constant (however, the numbers are few).

Manton (1982) criticizes Fries's use of the Gompertz function based on two additional points: (1) Fries mixes Gompertz and normal distributions as models of mortality; (2) a homogeneous population required for predicting mortality risk is in direct contrast to Fries's theory of heterogeneity in mortality risks (a range of 30 years).

Manton (1982) provides an alternative model of the impact of mortality reduction upon life span that depicts increases in life span to be a direct consequence of the control of specific chronic diseases. He suggests that the reduction on severity of chronic disease (or reduced rate of progression) will result not only in reduced mortality, but also increases in life expectancy. This is in contrast to Fries's statement (1983: 403) that "There is no biological reason to assume that any change in genetic longevity characteristics should have occurred merely because we have improved infant mortality, cleaned up water supplies or invented penicillin."

Manton asserts that many of the arguments that control of chronic degenerative disease will have little impact on life expectancy are from over-simplistic use of standard "cause-elimination" life-table calculations. Manton proposes that the use of "cause-delay" calculations as a model of the consequences of mortality reduction, rather than "cause-elimination" calculations, avoids the use of several illogical and unrealistic assumptions. These illogical assumptions clearly articulated in Manton's paper are: (1) all persons have equal susceptibility to death; (2) individuals who are observed not to have died of a given disease at a given age are assumed not to be subjected to any risk from the disease after that age; and (3) the false assumption that death is caused by one set of independently operating diseases. Deaths, especially at advanced ages, are often due to multiple and possibly interacting diseases.

The "cause-delay" model as opposed to "cause-elimination" model indicates the change in survival due to a hypothetical delay of deaths from a chronic disease. As concluded by Manton (1982: 221), "Standard cause-elimination" calculations represent only one aspect of mortality implications of controlling a chronic disease. Controlling a chronic disease among persons susceptible to death from the disease results in large increases in life expectancy for them at advanced ages.

Schneider and Brody (1983) support a third model of potential human life span consisting of an open upper boundary, as yet unknown, towards which we are approaching at a more accelerated rate than that suggested by Manton. Much of their supporting evidence is similar to Manton's, emphasizing the observed increasing life expectancy. Although most authors agree that potential for ultimate human life span is finite, disagreement centres around what the upper boundary may be and what the potential for extension is.

Life Expectancy and Rectangularization of the Survival Curve

Progress in the reduction of mortality or in extending length of life is often measured by "life expectancy at birth." Life expectancy represents the average number of years of life remaining at given ages according to the death rates prevailing at specific dates. Life expectancy at birth is a function of all the death rates from infancy to the oldest ages. At specified older ages the average remaining years of life can be calculated. It is for the older segments that the effects of improvements in health are in dispute. In part this is because this population age group represents the "tail" of the life-table survival curve, where events are rare and estimates less stable.

The life-table survival curve is one graphic illustration of mortality statistics. The percentage of the population surviving at a given age is one way to compare mortality rates between successive decades. Last (1983: 101) defines a survival curve as "a curve that starts at 100 percent of the study population and shows the percentage of the population still surviving at successive times for as long as information is available."

Observations of the changing shape of the survival curve over successive years since the early 1900s has given rise to the concept of "rectangularization" or "squaring" (Fries, 1980, 1983, 1984; Gordon et al 1977, 1980; Comfort 1964).

In the United States in 1900 and in Canada in 1921, mortality occurred at a relatively steady rate throughout the life span. Increases in life expectancy in later decades resulted in the survival curves bending upwards and to the right, becoming increasingly rectangular over the period of observation. The top of the curve has become progressively more flat and the downwards slope increasingly sharp.

As seen in Table 2 the chances of survival increase sharply from 1931 to 1951, and a similarly impressive shift is seen towards improved survival from 1951 to 1981. The gradually sloping survival curve of 1931 increasingly has taken the shape of a rectangle as the proportion surviving to each age increases over the time period. This improvement in life chances is not shared equally by all elements in the population. From the earliest period a distinct female advantage is seen, and this differential has become more pronounced. In 1931 male and female survival curves were relatively similar, but by 1951 the female advantage had widened considerably, and this trend continued until 1981. By the end of the period the male survival curve for 1981 more closely resembles the survival pattern for females in 1951 than that of females in the most recent period. The progress of males in improving survivorship is approximately 30 years retarded compared to females. By way of illustration of the differentials, in 1981 10 percent of the males had died by age 52, whereas the comparable proportion of females occurs at age 60, and 60 percent of the initial cohort of men survive only to age 75, compared to age 82 for women.

Although no one would contest that the changing *graphical* form of the survival curve is one of gradual rectangularization, the theoretical construct proposed by Fries implies the existence of a fixed life span towards which life expectancy is shifting. Thus current discussion of this phenomenon focusses on the quantitative methods used to measure the "tail" of the survival curve that substantiate or refute the hypothesized rectangularization.

Manton (1982) examined U.S. mortality statistics of white females at age 65 from 1950 to 1979. He found no decrease in the *relative* changes in life expectancy from one year to the next, as might be expected if the population were approaching a life expectancy "ceiling." In addition, he examined the change in mortality rates for white females to determine if the reduction was less at extreme ages, which would also indicate the structure was approaching a limit. After 1960, decreases in mortality rates for white females age 85 or more were greater than those aged 55 to 65. Manton concluded (1982: 194): "This evidence indicates that past age 85, mortality rates are decreasing rapidly."

Manton's third piece of evidence was found by examining changes in pat-

TABLE 2:
Percent Surviving at Given Ages, by Sex, for
Selected Census Periods, Canada

Age	1931 Male	1931 Female	1951 Male	1951 Female	1981 Male	1981 Female
0	100 %	100 %	100 %	100 %	100 %	100 %
1	91	93	96	97	99	99
5	89	91	95	96	99	99
10	88	90	94	96	99	99
15	87	89	94	95	98	99
20	86	88	93	95	98	99
25	85	87	83	95	97	98
30	83	85	92	94	96	98
35	82	84	91	93	96	98
40	80	82	90	92	95	97
45	78	79	88	91	94	96
50	75	77	85	89	91	95
55	71	73	81	86	88	93
60	66	68	74	82	83	90
65	59	62	66	76	75	86
70	49	53	55	67	64	80
75	37	41	42	54	50	71
80	23	26	27	38	35	58
85	11	13	14	21	20	41
90	4	5	5	8	9	23
95	.7	1	.9	2	3	9
100	.06	.1	.09	.2	.3	1
105	.002	.01	.003	.01	.007	.04

SOURCE: Statistics Canada, Life Tables for 1931, 1951, 1981, Catalogue 84-516.

terns of the age-specific probabilities of survival from 1940 to 1978, for suggestions of rectangularization.

Survival at age 85 was shown to increase more rapidly in recent years than survival at age 50. Manton suggests that although these data show signs of "approaching an irreducible mortality rate at earlier ages, there are no such indications at age 85." He extends his hypothesis further to suggest that "real increases in the life span are being manifest and the terminal age of the survival distribution is increasing." Schneider and Brody (1983: 855) suggest this "horizontal trend at ages 85 and older is causing a derectangularization of the survival curve."

Fries (1984: 356) finds these conclusions irrelevant and attributes reduction of mortality at advanced ages to changing causes of death in this period and not to the extension of the genetic life span implied by Manton. Fries feels the reduction of mortality at older ages is a short-term trend until an average life span of age 85 is reached and rectangularization results. Manton views this as the beginning of a long-term trend ultimately resulting in increases in the life span towards an upper boundary as yet unknown. Thus, the main differences are not how each is interpreting historical data, but when each projects the future convergence of the "tail" of the survival curve.

Additional evidence (Fries, 1984) of an approaching life-span limit is the changing gap between life expectancy for men and women at various ages. For the United States, at age 100 the differential between men and women is only a few months, whereas at younger ages the differences are large. Fries interprets these reductions as further evidence of rectangularization. Rather than suggesting the existence of a limit, reductions in the life-expectancy gap between men and women more likely suggest a reduction in sex differentials in mortality related to any number of socio-economic characteristics such as lifestyle factors. There is no evidence to suggest that gains will not be made by both sexes equally (or perhaps at different rates) in the future.

The circumstances are very similar in Canada. As is clear from Table 3, at

TABLE 3:
Trends in Life Expectancy, Selected Ages, by Sex, 1921 to 1981, Canada

	At Birth		65 +		85 +	
	Males	Females	Males	Females	Males	Females
1921	60.23*	60.64	12.00**	12.48	3.96***	3.96
1931	60.00	62.10	12.98	13.72	4.10	4.38
1941	62.96	66.30	12.81	14.08	4.05	4.35
1951	66.33	70.83	13.31	14.97	4.27	4.57
1961	68.35	74.17	13.53	16.07	4.46	4.89
1971	69.34	76.36	13.72	17.47	4.74	5.67
1981	71.88	78.98	14.57	18.85	5.14	6.45

*1921 data begin at age 7 because of high mortality rate from birth at age 5

** age 67

*** age 87

SOURCE: Statistics Canada, Life Tables, Catalogue 84-516.

85 years and over, differences by sex were relatively small throughout the period 1921 and 1981. Only in the most recent decade did the females diverge sharply from the males. For the groups aged 65 years and over the sex differential becomes accentuated by 1950 and continues to grow through 1981. By the end of the period of observation the differential is about 4 years for females at ages 65 and over. Not surprisingly this discrepancy is also seen for life expectancy at birth. The advantage in years of life enjoyed by females steadily increases from 1921 to 1941 and begins to increase more rapidly during the succeeding 30 years. By 1981 the differential has narrowed somewhat, but still clearly favours females. The reduction in the differential is due to a rapid improvement of male expectation of life.

Part of the explanation for the discrepancy in expectation of life can be found in the relative importance of diseases that lead to death. Males at ages 65 to 69 are over twice as likely to die from heart disease, and their rate of deaths from cancers in nearly twice that of women (Table 4). Although these differences become less pronounced in the upper ages, and except for male liver disease all rates rise with age, the sex difference for specific causes and for all causes remains evident.

A fifth "measure" of whether rectangularization is occurring is advocated by Myers and Manton (1984). They suggest that the *variance* at the age of death is inversely correlated with increases in life expectancy. As the limits to life span are approached, the variability in the distribution of ages at death will decrease until it reflects only heterogenecity and endowment for longevity. Fries (1984) accepts this approach but disagrees with the actual calculations derived by Manton and Myers. In order to avoid mixing of deaths attributed to infant and child mortality with mortality at older ages, the distribution of deaths that occur at age 60 years and older was examined by Manton and Myers. They found that the standard deviation of age of death rose rather than fell, thus providing evidence that mortality compression did not occur over this time period. Fries (1984) criticizes these findings. He states they are part of a statistical error resulting from truncating the distribution at age 60. As the average life expectancy increases, the artificial lower boundary of the distribution becomes unbounded, permitting standard deviation to increase. This statistical artifact may be more than sufficient to reverse these conclusions, and a more appropriate approach would have been to select a constant proportion of the population for comparison.

Estimates of the increasing proportion of all deaths occurring after age 65 and the increasing mean age of death would be further evidence of increasing longevity. Median estimates of central tendency have not been calculated by any of these researchers, although they are less likely than the mean to be influenced by extreme or rare events in the upper tail of the distribution.

TABLE 4:

Age Specific Death Rates by Sex for Selected Causes, Canada, 1982

	Males				
	65-69	**70-74**	**75-79**	**80-84**	**85+**
	(per 100,000 population)				
Heart disease	1,159.3	1,838.0	2,784.8	4,108.8	7,383.6
All malignant neoplasms	957.5	1,365.7	1,723.3	2,244.8	2,732.7
Respiratory disease	204.1	413.9	691.8	1,266.1	2,619.9
Cerebrovascular disease	174.4	322.8	639.2	1,034.0	2,159.3
Accidental deaths	106.6	133.0	158.9	243.2	525.5
Chronic liver disease	62.5	51.9	41.3	40.2	20.1
Diabetes mellitus	44.3	74.9	120.2	175.8	284.4
Total — All Causes	3,057.6	4,736.9	7,088.0	10,664.5	19,246.6

	Females				
	65-69	**70-74**	**75-79**	**80-84**	**85+**
	(per 100,000 population)				
All malignant neoplasms	539.1	705.1	853.9	1,118.0	1,465.8
Heart disease	489.8	886.9	1,582.2	2,844.7	5,880.0
Cerebrovascular disease	107.3	221.3	461.5	1,004.7	2,221.3
Respiratory disease	80.9	142.9	231.1	415.2	1,222.5
Accidental deaths	46.5	57.3	82.0	154.6	381.6
Diabetes mellitus	44.4	68.6	118.8	179.1	255.0
Chronic liver disease	25.5	25.8	25.8	25.8	16.0
Total — All Causes	1,519.7	2,423.9	3,926.9	6,823.5	14,317.9

SOURCE: Statistics Canada, Causes of Death, Vital Statistics, Volume IV, Catalogue #84-203.

According to the U.S. Current Population Reports P-23 (1984), the proportion of persons surviving from age 65 to 80 years was 3.5 percent in 1929/31, and 54 percent in 1980. The mean age at death at these later ages steadily increased and resulted in a gain of 1.4 years by 1979. The change in mean age at death was 1.8 years for females, twice as great as the male increase of .8 of a year.

Most authors, including Fries, suggest that rectangularization of the survival curve may require decades to achieve, and some authors such as Manton suggest that by that date, procedures for extending human life span may have been developed.

Although the analysis of past and current mortality patterns at advanced ages is subject to the reliability of age reporting and the sparseness of data, the conflicting conclusions reached by several authors have important implications for health and social service development.

The theory of an ultimate life span for humans and subsequent rectangularization of the survival curve is not disputed by most authors. More important, the authors disagree on the future patterns of mortality, what the maximum potential life span is, and whether there is evidence of a maximum life span being reached in the near future supported by rectangularization of the survival curve.

It must be concluded that past and current patterns do not provide evidence in support of a rapidly approaching average life span of 85 years, as postulated by Fries. Given the recent increase in the life expectancy of the very old, the increases in proportion of deaths after age 60, the increase in mean age of death and standard deviation of age of death, it must be concluded that although natural limits to the life span may exist, these limits are as yet unknown.

Compression of Morbidity: Theories and Evidence

Although it is clear that life expectancy is increasing, the implications for the distribution of chronic disease and disability among the aged population is problematic. Two factors underlie interpretations given to the impact of increased levels of survival. The first concerns the rational linking morbidity and mortality in the population, and the second pertains to whether changing disease risks alter the aging rate of humans.

At the centre of the discussion is the theory of the "compression of morbidity." In one formulation this is said to occur if the onset of disease symptoms (and manifestations of aging) can be delayed longer than the rate at which life expectancy is increasing (Fries, 1983). The amount of disability is asserted to decrease as morbidity is compressed into the shorter span between the increasing age at disability onset and the fixed occurrence of death. Postponement of chronic illness/disability results in rectangularization of the mortality curve and the morbidity curve (Fries, 1980: 133).

A natural history of disease is presented in his "Incremental Model of Chronic Disease" (Fries, 1983: 408). The major chronic diseases (atherosclerosis, cancer, emphysema, diabetes, cirrhosis and osteoarthritis) are held to be multifactorial in etiology, to be universal, to have early onset, to be progressive, and are generally characterized by a symptom threshold. In this model, chronic disease progresses from subclinical disease, past a symptom threshold to illicit symptoms (morbidity and disability), again progressing until death due to the disease.

TABLE 5:
Prevalence of Most Common Health Problems, by Sex, Canada, 1978, for Population Aged 65 and Over

Type of Health Problem	Total	Male	Female
Arthritis and rheumatism	42	33	50
Hypertension	29	20	36
Limb and joint disorder	21	22	21
Heart disease	20	21	19
Hearing disorders	17	24	12
Sight disorders	16	11	19
Mental disorders	12	9	15
Digestive disorders	10	9	11
Dental disorders	9	9	9
Diabetes	7	5	8
Bronchitis and emphysema	6	9	4

SOURCE: The Health of Canadians, Canada Health Survey 1978-79, Table 57.

This model implies that the current and future causes of morbidity are also causes of mortality. Mortality and morbidity due to the "major" chronic diseases can be postponed by reducing the slope of progression. Fries states (1983: 409) that "any reduction in the average slope of the lines representing individuals in a population will result in a decrease in age-specific mortality rates. Thus an improvement in the rate of accretion of chronic disease occurs; an effect on morbidity is linked to the effect on mortality." Also, he concludes (1980: 132) "that disability and lowered quality of life due to prevalent chronic diseases are inescapably linked with eventual mortality."

However, the major causes of morbidity are *not* necessarily related to the major causes of mortality. Data from the 1978 Canada Health Survey reinforce this point. Table 4 showed cause of death data for age and sex groups in 1982. It will be recalled that cancer and heart disease were the major killers, with respiratory and cerebrovascular disease far less common, third- and fourth-ranked causes of death.

As data in Table 5, show the most common cause of health problems for the population aged 65 and over is arthritis and rheumatism. In this age group, 42 percent reported this as the cause of a problem, and this was more common among females. A more lengthy comparison of the cause-of-death data with this cause-of-health-problems information makes it abundantly clear that there is very little overlap between these two ranked lists of causes of ill health and death. Data from the United States show an equivalent lack of congruity between causes of morbidity and of mortality. Heart disease, cerebrovascular disease and diabetes appear to be the only diseases responsible for both major causes of morbidity and mortality. To quote McKeown (1976:112): "The diseases that shorten our lives are not usually the ones that diminish their quality from day to day."

It is possible that the comparisons for causes of mortality and morbidity at the upper ages would reveal explanations as to the sources of dissimilarities if the morbidity data could be examined across 5-year age-sex groups comparable to those seen above in cause-of-death data. However, Statistics Canada is unwilling to provide to the research community detailed age data for the sample of elderly residents on the public use sample tape from the Canada Health Survey. Detailed considerations as to age-related effects are therefore not possible.

A second theory of the relationship between increasing longevity and morbidity is provided by Kramer (1981) and Gruenberg (1977). They propose that chronic disease prevalence and disability will increase as life expectancy is increased. Increases in life expectancy are viewed as *not* being accomplished either by reducing the incidence or decreasing the rate of progression of chronic disease (as Fries proposes), but by controlling the fatal consequences of those diseases. The only real improvements are seen in case fatality rates. Thus, the prevalence of certain diseases and their associated disabilities will increase as mortality specific to the disease decreases. A basic epidemiologic relation states that prevalence of disease is mathematically equivalent to incidence of disease multiplied by its duration. Thus if incidence is unchanged, prevalence can only be increased by increasing the duration of disease. Conflicting theories in the literature primarily focus on how *duration* of disease is increased.

Manton (1982) introduces the concept of "dynamic equilibrium." He suggests that improvements in life expectancy can be attributed to retardation of the rate of progression of chronic diseases. Thus, the *duration* of disease is increased by changing the rate of disease progression or severity, as opposed to increasing duration by eliminating lethal sequelae. Though prevalence might increase, severity is decreased. He views chronic degenerative disease as playing an essential role in the process of human aging. Changes in severity and the rate of progression of chronic disease are directly related to mortality changes, so that with mortality reductions there is an associated observed reduction in the rate of aging of the human body. Diabetes mellitus and hypertension are provided as two examples where both the severity and rate of progression of the primary disease has been reduced.

Despite a proliferation of theories regarding the linkage between morbidity and mortality, supporting evidence in the form of comprehensive analyses of the health status of the population, is lacking.

Schneider and Brody (1983: 855) report that vital and health statistics data from the U.S. in 1979 confirm that during the previous decade there was no substantial reduction in the percentage of older populations reporting poor health. They conclude that if the percentage in poor health at specific ages, e.g., 60 or 70, remains the same (or increases) and life expectancy continues to increase, then more people will spend longer proportions of their lives afflicted with chronic disease. Thus, Fries's suggestion that the duration of disease will reduce due to delayed onset against a fixed life span and will result in reduced prevalence is contradicted by the suggestion of an increasing duration due to the unchanging onset of disease, increasing life expectancy and a resulting increase in prevalence.

Manton's review of data from the U.S. Health Interview Surveys of 1972 and 1977 shows the percentage of persons reporting their health as fair or poor decreased only from 31.0 percent to 29.9 percent, and the number of bed disability days due to chronic conditions increased slightly from 14.1 to 14.5 days. An analysis of similar measures for the 1960s produced the same conclusion. Though more people were surviving to advanced ages where chronic diseases should be more prevalent, little evidence existed to suggest that elderly persons of a given age were more disabled than in earlier decades.

Canadian data confirm part of these findings. Data from 1951 and 1978 show an increasing level of short-term disability with age for both males and females. The increases are especially pronounced above 44 years (Table 6) and the number of bed days are somewhat higher for females. Data available from the Canada Sickness Survey permit comparisons over the nearly three decades leading up to the Canada Health Survey. The average number of disability days has changed very little since 1951, and the direction of the observed changes is not consistent. It is tempting to conclude that the causes and effects of short-term disability are relatively constant over time, but become an increasing problem at the older ages and especially above 65 years.

Part of the reason for no increase in disability levels for the noninstitutionalized population could be attributed to an increased rate of institutionalization. The most recent data (1973/74 and 1977) from the U.S. National Nursing Home Surveys indicate that the rate of institutionalization for the population 65 and older increased by approximately 6 percent. For those

414 Disease, Survival and Death

TABLE 6:
Short Term Disability, Canada, by Sex
1951 to 1978, Average Bed Days

Age Group	Males			Females		
	1951	1978	Differences	1951	1978	Differences
0 - 14	5	4	-1	5	4	-1
15 - 24	3	3	0	5	4	-1
25 - 44	4	3	-1	6	5	-1
44 - 64	6	6	0	7	9	+2
65 plus	12	11	-1	16	15	-1
Total	5	4	-1	6	6	0

SOURCE: *Healthfulness of Life,* Wilkins (1983) Table 3.3.

85 years and older, for whom the effects of increases in life expectancy on disability may be greatest, the rate of institutionalization dropped 15 percent from 253.7/1,000 in 1973/74 to 216.4/1,000 in 1977. The gains in life expectancy at age 65 from 1974 to 1977 was 0.8 of a year and 0.7 of a year at age 85. The decline in institutionalization suggests that recent increases in life expectancy at advanced ages does not result in such severe disability that nursing-home care is required (Manton, 1982). Although nursing-home care may imply severity, or lack of social support to supply home care, lack of an increase in total proportion of the population institutionalized does not rule out the possibility of shift in the proportions of disability by levels of severity (see Chapter 26, by Shapiro and Roos, this volume).

Further evidence of changes in health status can be seen by examining trends in the levels of disabling conditions. According to data published by the United States National Centre for Health Statistics, disability increased substantially during the years 1966 to 1976. In the middle age group (45 to 64 years), four causes of disability increased in both sexes: diabetes, musculoskeletal disorders, hypertension and diseases of the circulatory system (other than hypertension and heart disease). In the 65-and-over age group, diabetes and circulatory diseases (excluding heart conditions and hypertension) increased significantly (Colvez and Blanchet, 1981). Although the analysis included severity of disability (both long term and short term), it did not include disability among institutionalized people in the population.

The increase in prevalence of severe limitations among the 45 to 64 age group was statistically significant. For those 65 years and older, the increase in limitations of *major* activity pertained mostly to males. Among women, there was no statistically significant variation.

Over the 10-year period 1966-76 the importance of causes of disability changed. Arthritis and rheumatism took first place as a cause of disability surpassing heart conditions. Combined, these causes of disability accounted for 33 percent of cases of activity limitation. Diabetes moved from 7th to 5th place in importance. These increases are relatively recent, as Sullivan's study between the years 1959 and 1966 noted a slight decrease in both short-term and long-term disability (Sullivan, 1971).

The import of long-term disability in Canada may be different from the United States. Comparisons between 1951 and 1978 show that the disproportionately high levels seen for males in the earlier period have evaporated by 1978. In the most recent survey, female rates are nearly equal to, or may even exceed, male rates in the various age groupings. To reach the overall higher levels of disability seen in 1978 the rate of increase has been much higher for females at all age groups (see Table 7).

TABLE 7:
Long Term Disability, Canada, by Sex
1951 to 1978, in Percentages

	Males			Females		
Age Group	1951	1978	Percent Change	1951	1978	Percent Change
0 - 14	2.4	4.0	67	2.1	3.5	67
15 - 24	2.4	4.0	67	2.1	3.5	67
25 - 44	7.1	7.6	7	5.1	9.8	92
45 - 64	14.7	21.3	45	11.5	21.6	88
65 plus	27.0	38.1	41	23.9	38.3	60
Total	7.9	11.0	39	6.3	12.2	94

SOURCE: *Healthfulness of Life,* Wilkins (1983) Table 3.3.

Long-term disability refers to persons in the noninstitutionalized population who reported currently having a chronic condition (3 months or longer duration) and were limited in their usual activities.

Compared to short-term disability the impact of chronic activity limitation is much more complex and wide reaching. Data summarized in Table 8 show relatively low levels of institutionalization until ages 75 and over. When restrictions in the carrying out of normal daily functions are the criterion for defining activity limitation, then institutionalization is seen as the most severe form of restriction.

TABLE 8:
Severity of Activity Restriction, by Age and Sex
Canada 1978, in percentage

| Age Group | Institutionalized | | Major Activity | | | | Minor Activities Limited | | No Permanent Limitations | |
| | | | Cannot Perform | | Restricted | | | | | |
	M	F	M	F	M	F	M	F	M	F
0 - 14	0.2	0.1	0.0	0.0	2.3	1.4	1.0	0.7	96.5	97.7
15 - 24	0.3	0.2	0.6	0.5	2.2	2.5	1.8	1.9	95.7	94.9
25 - 44	0.3	0.2	1.1	0.4	4.4	6.5	2.0	3.0	92.1	90.0
45 - 64	0.6	0.5	8.2	2.5	10.4	14.9	2.4	4.1	78.5	78.1
65 - 74	2.3	2.6	14.2	3.8	20.4	27.4	1.9	3.9	61.3	62.3
75 plus	11.2	17.5	11.1	5.7	23.2	27.5	2.3	3.7	52.2	45.6
Total	0.7	1.1	3.0	1.1	5.9	8.3	1.8	2.5	88.6	86.9

SOURCE: *Healthfulness of Life*, Wilkins (1983) Table 4.1.

Nearly as severe is the situation where the individual is unable to perform his or her major activities. As reported by the household population of the Canada Health Survey in 1978, the proportion limited in this manner increases with age for both males and females. Relatively few such restrictions are seen before age 45 years, and the level declines somewhat for males at 75 years and over, compared to the 65 to 74 years-of-age prevalence level.

Sex differences in the level of those unable to perform their major activity are quite pronounced. At ages 45 years and above, males are two to three times more likely to report this limitation. At least two explanations can be suggested for these differences. It is possible that disease, trauma and other factors affect males more severely and render them unable to perform normal activities. More likely, however, is an interaction of these causes of limitation with the sex specific nature of the duties and obligations contained in the major activity roles of males and females. For this population, in 1978, most of the females would have defined their major activity as housework. Even if confronted with severe health problems it is often possible to perform housekeeping tasks even if at great personal cost and with difficulty. For those employed outside the home — in this instance, principally males — the need to travel to work and the nature of the work activity should produce a larger proportion of individuals unable to perform normal major activities. In short, if the health problems were equally severe, the impact of these conditions will differ by the demands and expectations of the sex-linked social roles. This explanation would also account for the decline in the males restricted at ages 75 and over. As they would be largely outside the labour force, the out-of-household forces shaping their definition of major activities would be reduced. This would lead to a lower level of limitation for this age group.

At each age level females are more likely than males to be restricted in performance of major activities. The greatest difference is seen at the 65 to 74 age level. If we combine the "cannot-perform" and "restricted in major activity" data for each age-sex group there are only minor differences in the differences by sex for each age group for the reported levels of limitations in major activity. These combined data show clearly the effects of age as the major factor overall. When the data are not combined, the influences of sex-linked social demands are evident.

Few important sex- or age-linked variations in limitations in minor activities are seen in these data. Females are more likely to be so limited, but the results do not vary systematically by age. This is clearly not the case for those who report no permanent limitations. While there are no important sex differences below ages 75 years, there is a persistent and strong effect of age on these data. By ages 45 to 64 years, one-fifth of the population is impaired, and at ages 65 to 74 years nearly 40 percent of the population suffers some limitation. At the highest ages a higher proportion of females is limited. This may reflect both the generally older age structure of the females in this category, as well as the greater burden of illness that they carry into old age.

Health Expectancy: An Index of Health

The conflicting evidence concerning measures of morbidity in the population and the contradictory theories concerning future mortality reductions and the potential human life span emphasizes that human aging, mortality and morbidity are complex interrelated phenomena. To be explained, they must be viewed as dynamic multidimensional processes. A more comprehensive and informative measure of health status than those used by previous authors and one that is based upon measures of mortality and morbidity within the population is essential. Neither life expectancy statistics nor disability statistics, and neither the health status of the noninstitutionalized population nor the institutionalized population, considered separately, clarify our understanding of the relationship between mortality and morbidity.

"Health expectancy" is a comprehensive index of population health status that takes into consideration not only the probability of surviving to a given age, but also the health of survivors in terms of their likelihood of being either free of activity restriction or restricted to a greater or lesser extent (Wilkins, 1983: 3).

Health-expectancy indexes are based on the same life tables used to calculate life expectancy; thus they automatically accord greater importance to deaths at earlier ages, avoiding the arbitrary weighting schemes used by other models.

As first described by Sullivan (1966), the health-expectancy index takes overall life expectancy and breaks it down into years of disabled life by degree of activity limitation, institutionalized disability and years of life with a health condition not resulting in subsequent disability. Sullivan first determined the total volume of disability, including both institutionalized and noninstitutionalized, then calculated the set of age-specific rates of disability and applied these to the hypothetical life-table populations.

Wilkins and Adams (1983) followed this same approach, except that they further subdivided disabled life according to levels of severity and disability. However, they did not classify disability by causes, so it is not possible to distinguish between lethal and nonlethal disease entities. It is this distinction that is required if the link between mortality and morbidity is to be better understood.

Other researchers have incorporated mortality and disability into an index of "life expectancy-free-of-disability." For the noninstitutionalized population in the United States, life expectancy-free-of-disability decreased 0.5 of a year between 1966 to 1976 (56.6 years to 56.0 years) in spite of overall increases of 2.7 years in total life expectancy (Colvez and Blanchet, 1983). Based on these estimates an increasing number of people would be alive, but most of them disabled rather than living limitation-free lives.

The two observation points of 1951 and 1978 are the only available data on the Canadian population as to sickness and disability, and therefore provide only a limited view of morbidity trends. Life expectancy improved by 4.5 years for males from 1951 to 1978 and by 7.5 years for females. Over the same interval the number of years that individuals on the average could expect to live while disabled or suffering long-term activity limitations also increased (3.2 years for males and 6.1 years for females). Only small increases occurred in the average years of disability-free life can be seen from these data.

The absence of continuous monitoring of health status precludes an assessment as to trends in health expectancy. However, these data strongly suggest that the years gained in life expectancy will be largely spent suffering long-term activity limitation. Less than 30 percent of the increased years of life expectancy from 1951 to 1978 can be expected to be free from limitations. Thus the proportions of the population surviving to a given age are growing more rapidly than are the proportions of the population surviving to the same age free from activity limitation. It would be preferable, if not actually required, to calculate the estimates for years of life free from limitation for various age groups. However, the absence of data available to researchers rules out this line of analysis in Canada. It is possible to pursue this with U.S. materials.

Future Trends and Projections

Although the size of the baby-boom birth cohort will largely determine the size of the elderly population, through 2040, assumptions about future mortality trends could have considerable impact upon estimating both size and the rate of increase. A number of different approaches to projecting future mortality trends in the U.S. exist. One is to extrapolate past trends in mortality experience, such as Fries has calculated, to obtain an average life span of 85 years in 2045 (Table 1). But simple extrapolation and use of synthetic assumptions are insufficient for forecasting. Biological and epidemiological-based models of mortality must be developed so changes in trends can be anticipated. Another approach previously discussed in this chapter is Manton's proposal of the use of "cause-delay" calculations rather than "cause-elimination" calculations as a model of the consequences of mortality reduction.

Fries (1984) maintains that projections using this model overestimate future survival gains at advanced ages. The reason for this is that no mathematical function representing senescence is in the equation. This hazard function associated with the aging of the organism is assumed to have relatively minimal force prior to the age of 70, to increase rapidly with age and to dominate disease-related hazard functions over the age of 100.

Rice and Feldman (1983: 362) focussed on the demographic consequences of assumptions of declining mortality and slightly increasing fertility over the next sixty years and what these demographic changes may mean for the nation in terms of health status. Improvements in mortality assumed for projections from 2005 to 2080 were established by considering the following factors: (1) advances in research regarding disease etiology; (2) development of new diagnostic and surgical techniques; (3) presence of environmental pollutants; (4) incidence of violence; and (5) improvements in lifestyle.

For the elderly population, the projected mortality trend is downwards for both men and women, although rates for women are less than men. To estimate morbidity, Feldman and Rice applied age-specific rates of activity limitation to the projected populations under their assumptions of mortality. It is expected that lifestyle factors will affect morbidity. However, the upwards trend in disability and the association between age and the onset of chronic disease do not provide a basis for optimism.

The use of demographic data for projecting trends in health status is usually limited to estimating the effects of the age-sex structure. The effects of other compositional variables are assumed to be negligible. However, the elderly population of the future will differ qualitatively in important ways from preceding cohorts.

Although traditionally the method of projecting population health trends and their impact is by reference to "the informed guesses of experts," Rice and Feldman (1983: 391) suggest that two of several demographic considerations that are detectable now amongst future cohorts of elderly people are:

(1) The rate of childlessness is increasing for cohorts born since the mid 1930s. Elderly people without children may require more long-term care services than those with children due to lack of informal social support.

(2) For at least the next few decades, the numbers of each cohort entering old age will have, on average, more years of education. The more highly educated tend to live longer and be in better health, but use more of some types of health services than the less educated (Simmons-Tropea and Osborn, 1985).

Conclusion

The causal links between morbidity and mortality are complex. Trends in health levels among the elderly population require examination of these causal links by assessing not only lethal and nonlethal disease conditions of the noninstitutionalized population, but also the institutionalized population.

As the sickest elderly are placed in nursing homes and chronic-care facilities the risk of activity limitation (morbidity) among the population remaining at home is selectively changing. Thus it is critically important to assess the institutionalized population simultaneously with the noninstitutionalized.

There is little doubt that rectangularization of the mortality/survival curve is present, and at least for the next few years forces will continue to produce this effect. Whether the life span will become unbounded and cause a change in the shape of the curve for the oldest ages is unclear. The unanticipated improvements in cardiovascular mortality over the past decade provide a signal to all prognosticators that unexpected changes can and will occur. As these are more likely to improve rather than diminish health we cannot overlook the effects of changing mortality on the survival function for the older ages.

The state of knowledge about the morbidity/disability curve is less clear. The proportion of individuals with chronic disease continues to grow over all age groups; long-term disability has continued to increase and these increases have not been confined to the upper age range. In short there appears little evidence that chronic morbidity/disability is rising closer to the increasing age at death. This is largely affected by the continuing and perhaps increasing levels of nonlethal morbidity that have a gradual age at onset and that, as in the case of arthritis and rheumatism, are major causes of disability. While the lethal causes of chronic disease, such as cardiovascular disease, may be subject to control, it does not follow that mental disorders will be amenable to reduction. The most likely future is for increases in nonlethal morbidity and, when combined with reductions in the levels of major causes of death, for the growing aged population to continue to suffer limitations on activities. As the proportion and numbers of the aged increase, more creative and ambitious efforts will be needed to respond to the concerns for maintenance and improvements of quality of life for the aged.

References

Colvez A. and M. Blanchet
   1981   "Disability trends in the United States population 1966-76: Analysis of reported causes." *American Journal of Public Health* 71:464–71.
Comfort, A.
   1964   *Aging: The Biology of Senescence.* New York: Holt, Rinehart and Winston.
Fries, James F.
   1980   "Aging, natural death and the compression of morbidity." *New England Journal of Medicine* 303 (July 17): 130-135.
   1982   "Life expectancy increases but the life span is fixed." *American Journal of Public Health (72).*
   1983   "The compression of morbidity." *Milbank Memorial Fund Quarterly* 61(3): 397-419.
   1984   "The compression of morbidity: Miscellaneous comments about a theme." *The Gerontologist* 24:354-359.
Gordon, T.J., H. Gerjuoy and M. Anderson (eds.)
   1977   *Life Extending Technologies: A Technical Assessment.* New York: Pergamon Press.
Gruenberg, E.M.
   1977   "The failure of success." Milbank Memorial Fund Quarterly/Health and Society 55:3–24.

Hayflick, L.
1980 "The cell biology of human aging." *Scientific American* 242:58-65.
Katz, Sidney et al.
1983 "Active life expectancy." *New England Journal of Medicine* 309 (November 17):1218-1224.
Kramer, M.
1981 "The Increasing Prevalence of Mental Disorders: Implications for the Future." Paper presented at National Conference on the Elderly Deinstitutionalized Patient in the community. Arlington, Va., May 28.
Last, J.M.
1983 *A Dictionary of Epidemiology.* Oxford: Oxford University Press.
Levy, R.
1981 "The decline in cardiovascular disease mortality." *Annual Review of Public Health* 2:49-70.
Lew, E.
1980 "Discussion Comment in Implications of Future Mortality Trends: Follow-up to Ideas Presented at the Chicago Mortality Symposium." Record of the Society of Actuaries, Montreal Meeting, October 20-22, 1980:1365-66.
McKeown, T.
1976 *The Role of Medicine: Dream, Mirage or Nemesis?* London: Nuffield Provincial Hospitals Trust.
Manton, K.G.
1982 "Changing concepts of mortality and morbidity in the elderly population." *Milbank Memorial Fund Quarterly* 60:183-244.
Myers, George C. and K.G. Manton
1984 "Compression of mortality: Myth or reality." *The Gerontologist* 24:346-353.
Pearl, R.
1923 *Introduction to Medical Biometry and Statistics.* Philadelphia: Saunders.
Rice, D.P. and J.J. Feldman
1983 "Living longer in the United States: Demographic changes and health needs for the elderly." *Milbank Memorial Fund Quarterly* 61:430-444.
Sacher, G.A.
1980 *Theory Gerontology, Part 1.* in Vol. 1, Pp. 3-25 in C. Eisdorfer and B. Starr (eds.), *Annual Review of Gerontology and Geriatrics.* New York: Springer.
Schneider, E.L. and J.A. Brody
1983 "Aging, natural death and the compression of morbidity: Another view." *New England Journal of Medicine* 309 (October 6): 854-856.
Shock, N.W.
1977 "Systems Integration." In C.E. Finch and L. Hayflick (eds.), *Handbook of the Biology of Aging.* New York: Van Nostrand Reinhold.
Simmons-Tropea, D.A. and R.W. Osborn
1985 "The Social Composition of Canada's Future Elderly Population." Paper presented at the Canadian Population Society meeting, Montreal, May.
Stern, M.P.
1979 "The recent decline in ischemic heart disease mortality." *Annals of Internal Medicine* 91:630-640.

Strekler, B.L.
 1977   *Time, Cells and Aging*. New York: Academic Press.
Strekler, B.L. and A.S. Meldvan
 1960   "General Theory of Mortality and Aging." *Science* 132:14-21.
Sullivan, D.F.
 1971   "Disability components for an index of health" in Vital and Health Statistics, Series 2, no. 42. U.S. Dept. of Health, Education and Welfare, Washington, D.C..
U.S. Bureau of the Census
 1984   *Demographic and Socioeconomic Aspects of Aging in the United States, Current Population Reports,* Series P-23, No. 138. Washington D.C.: *U.S. Government Printing Office.*
Verbrugge, Lois M.
 1983   "Longer Life but Worsening Health? Trends in Health and Mortality of Middle-Aged and Older Persons." Paper presented at annual meeting of Population Association of America, April.
Wilkin, J.C.
 1981   "Recent Trends in the Mortality of the Aged." Transactions of the Society of Actuaries Vol. 33.
Wilkins, R.
 1983   "The Burden of Ill Health in Canada: Socioeconomic Inequalities in the Healthfulness of Life." Paper presented at the special seminar series on "Population Health and Health Care" McMaster University, Hamilton, April 26.
Wilkins, R. and O. Adams
 1983   *Healthfulness of Life.* Montreal: The Institute for Research on Public Policy.

21
Aging and Mental Health

Carl D'Arcy
Psychiatric Research Division
Saskatchewan Health

Introduction

What is the effect of aging on an individual's mental health? Are the elderly more prone to mental illness? Do they have more psychological impairment than younger age groups? These are the central questions addressed in this chapter.

The questions and their answers are important from a policy and a theoretical perspective. Age grading is a ubiquitous basis for social differentiation and social stratification in societies. Aging is a universal feature of the life cycle. Each age stage has its own pressures and problems, and rights and privileges. Consequently information about the effects of aging has theoretical salience for theories of social organization. The Canadian population is aging and will continue to age for the next several decades. Currently, those over 65 years of age account for 10.3 percent of Canadians. This is expected to increase to 13.5 percent by the year 2000 and 14.2 percent by the year 2006. Because of the effect of the baby boom (those born between 1946 and 1960), the Canadian population will go through a middle-aging process before going through the aging process. The full impact of the aging process will be evident by the 2031 census, when it is estimated that some 23.9 percent of the Canadian population will be over 65 years of age (Statistics Canada, 1985). It should be noted that the aging of the population will become most evident in the growth of those over 75 and 85 years of age. The aged are reported to be high utilizers of health services. The projected population composition figures have already spurred a demand for planning more health and social facilities and services for the aged. It is likely that these demands will increase in the future. Obviously, valid data that allow for more informed estimates of the need and demand for health services in general, and mental health services in particular, will

This work was supported in part by the National Health Research and Development Program of Health and Welfare Canada through a National Health Scholar Award to the author and by continuing support of Saskatchewan Health. The assistance of R. Ryhorchuk and D. Paul for data analysis and preparation is gratefully appreciated. The contents and interpretation of data presented here are solely the responsibility of the author.

be very useful for policy and program planning purposes. Information on the factors associated with successful aging is also of considerable interest in designing policies, programs and facilities.

In laying a groundwork for answering the central questions of this chapter, there is a short introduction to the concepts of mental health/illness and the mental illness processes, and the explication of a conceptual orientation for evaluating and understanding estimates of mental health/illness. The chapter then briefly reviews the literature on aging and mental health/illness, presents some Canadian data on aging and mental health/illness and concludes with a comment on the state of the field and its implications for policy and programs.

Mental Health/Illness — Definitions and Processes

"Health" as defined by the World Health Organization is " . . . a state of complete physical, mental and social well-being, and not merely the absence of disease or infirmity."

"Mental health" is a state in which a person demonstrates his competence to think, feel and (inter)act in ways that demonstrate his ability to deal effectively with the challenges of life. The mentally healthy person is accepting of himself, able to give as well as receive in relationships and, having realistically evaluated his assets and liabilities, has an appropriate level of self-confidence, making decisions based on sound judgment and accepting responsibility for his actions.

"Mental illness(es)" refer to a broad spectrum of disorders of thinking, feeling and doing. They range from a relatively mild but stressful "adjustment disorder," in which "it is assumed that the psychological disturbance will eventually remit after the stressor ceases or, if the stressor persists, when a new level of adaption is achieved" (DSM-III:301), to organic brain syndromes such as "delirium," which sees a clouding of consciousness, perceptual disturbances (including hallucinations), incoherent speech, disorientation and memory impairment, with such symptomatology being judged as organic in origin (DSM-III: 104-109).

Each psychiatric disorder has a different frequency of occurrence and persistence, and a differential impact (burden) upon the individual affected and his immediate social network as well as the larger community. Psychiatric disorders range from relatively rare disorders such as catatonic type schizophrenia, which is marked by stupor or mutism, to much more prevalent simple phobias, which are characterized by an irrational fear of an object or a situation. There may be minor disability and restriction of normal activity in some disorders. Other disorders, particularly the psychoses, are characterized by substantial disability and profound restriction in normal activity.

Some disorders are more successfully treated and/or managed than others. For example, anxiety, panic disorders, phobias and depression can, in contrast to schizophrenia, be reasonably successfully treated (see QAP, 1982, 1983; and Karasu, 1984).

Physical health problems may accompany mental illnesses and vice versa (e.g., Kathol and Petty, 1981).

Mental illnesses are generally seen to have a variety of causes, from the organic to the psychological and social. For example, genetic makeup, organic deterioration, nutrition, stressful life events, continuing life strains, personality, social environment, support networks and coping strategies, and skills and resources have singly or in combination been posited as causes of mental illness in general as well as of specific mental illnesses. Indeed all these factors may be incorporated either as basic risk factors, indicating a propensity or increased likelihood of developing a psychiatric disorder, or as more immediate precipitators, which give rise to a specific disease episode, or as moderators or buffers that protect against mental disorder or limit the negative impact of its occurrence in terms of the severity and duration of symptoms and associated disability (Wing, 1978; Wheaton, 1980; Susser 1973).

The reaction to the signs and symptoms of a disorder depends on a variety of factors such as the precise nature of the disturbed and disturbing behaviour, the social context in which it occurs, the tolerance of the immediate social environment for that deviant behaviour, availability of professional help, the training and ideology of the help provider, etc. (e.g., Rosenhan, 1973; D'Arcy, 1976; Strauss et al., 1964; Hemenway and Fallon, 1985).

It is obvious that in a typical Canadian context a marked and irrational fear of snakes is much less disruptive than a fear of snow or a fear of being contaminated by physical proximity to, or contact with, others.

It is also evident that, in general, communities are relatively tolerant of behaviour that, though strange, is predictable and nonphysically threatening. However, violent and unpredictable behaviour is strongly reacted to with the community seeking to exclude the offender. A good deal of behaviour that mental health practitioners (such as psychiatrists, psychologists, social workers, etc.) may view as aberrant is not seen by the general public as sufficiently bothersome or unusual as to require treatment (D'Arcy, 1981b). Consequently, a substantial amount of behaviour that would be clinically defined as "illness" or "distress" does not come to the attention of treating clinicians. It is not presented for treatment (Shapiro et al., 1984).

What happens to individuals who are brought forth for treatment is further dependent on the health belief of the individual and his immediate social network, whether or not he perceives something as wrong and whether it could benefit from professional attention, the nature and organization of the help/care delivery system, e.g., the type of professional contacted, their orientation, facilities available (beds, hospitals, halfway houses, etc.), policies, payment systems, etc. (Kadushin, 1967; Scheff, 1966; D'Arcy, 1976, 1978; Harris, 1975; Hemenway and Fallon, 1985). The various health professionals are subject to different training and subscribe to different etiological theories. They evolve different professional ideologies and acquire different legal mandates as to what they can do. They have access to different facilities and emphasize different modes of treatment (Strauss et al., 1964).

The practice of psychiatry and the treatment of mental illness are social processes; they have evolved and changed over time. They continue to evolve and change. During the 1950s and 1960s, a number of interrelated clinical events occurred. First, the development of psychotropic medications made it possible to treat many patients in the community rather than in mental hospitals. Second, the very negative effects of prolonged psychiatric hospitalization were more clearly identified. Third, there was increasing recognition by clinicians that the causes and courses of mental illness were influenced not just by physiological and psychological factors, but also by a variety of social, economic and environmental factors.

During the past three decades the advent of more precise and detailed diagnostic systems and new treatment procedures has substantially improved the prognosis for a variety of psychiatric disorders (Karasu, 1984; QAP, 1982, 1983).

A simplification of the mental illness process is diagrammed in Figure 1 as a set of decision/reaction processes and underlying dimensions.

FIGURE 1:
Mental Illness Process(es)

Decision Reaction Processes

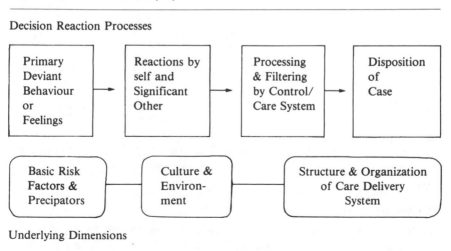

Underlying Dimensions

Getting an Accurate Picture

As the phenomenon of mental health/illness covers a broad spectrum of behaviour/feelings, a variety of data sources, types of information and studies are required to provide a full picture of its occurrence, distribution and correlates in the population.

The iceberg analogy, presented in Figure 2, graphically shows the effects of using different data sources to measure the extent of mental illness in a community, population or group. Indeed, differing data sources may show the same characteristic (e.g., age, sex, socio-economic status, etc.,) as having differing degrees of association/causation with mental illness.

FIGURE 2:
The Iceberg Analogy

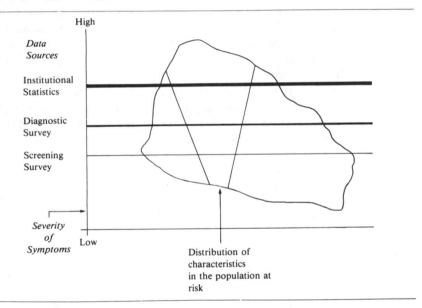

It has been generally found that community surveys will produce much higher rates of occurrence of mental illness as opposed to studies that use more defined criteria, or studies that depend on the filtering effects of the care/control system.

In interpreting statistics and information, one has to be cognizant of their sources and the potential biases inherent in them (Kitsuse and Cicourel, 1963).

Review of Literature

While all age groups are subject to mental ill health, the elderly are generally considered more likely than younger age groups to suffer from psychiatric impairment (e.g., Wasylenki, 1980). A variety of epidemiological studies have shown higher rates of psychiatric disorder among the elderly (see Blazer, 1980, for a summary).

It has been reported that the average incidence of psychosis increases with age, with the increase in new cases most marked after age 70 (Jaco, 1960; Kay and Bergmann, 1980; Cohen, 1977, 1980). Butler (1975) estimates the incidence of psychiatric impairment of all types as: 2.3 per 100,000 in the under 15 age group; 76.3 in the 25 to 34 age group; 93.0 in the 35 to 54 age group and 235.1 in the over 65 age group.

However, these studies fail to distinguish among types of psychiatric disorder. This is a crucial problem for elderly populations, since common psychiatric ailments, such as dementia and depression, are often difficult to differentiate. They have many symptoms in common, particularly memory impairment. However, dementia is usually the product of brain damage that most likely worsens with age. In contrast, depression is an affective disorder that is highly treatable. Depression among the elderly frequently goes undiagnosed or is misdiagnosed. Because depression may be connected to age-specific stresses, such as loss of spouse, declining health, loss of income and independence and diminished social supports, depression among the aged may present itself in forms unlike those found in younger age groups (Cheah, 1978).

The likelihood of age-specific stresses has led to theoretical arguments that the aged are especially prone to depression (Kay et al., 1964; Renner and Birren, 1980; Wilkie et al., 1982). Indeed a variety of studies have indicated higher rates of depression among the elderly (Zung, 1967). The higher suicide rates among the elderly are taken as suggesting increased rates of depression among the elderly. There is also an age gradient in the ratio of successful to unsuccessful suicide attempts, with the elderly having a higher rate of completed suicides.

Though the majority of studies support the contention that the elderly are particularly and increasingly vulnerable to mental ill health, there are other studies that challenge such a conclusion. During a two-year study, Lowenthal et al. (1967) report a lack of marked mental impairment among individuals in their sixties and early seventies, although there was an increased rate of mental illness among the very old. Frerichs et al. (1980), in a Los Angeles survey, report a steady decline in depressive symptoms with age, with those over 65 having the lowest rate. Lieberman (1983) found decreased depression among the elderly over a five-year period. Blazer (1983), looking only at depression, found that the elderly report lower rates as compared to the middle-aged and young adults. Haug et al. (1984), analysing data from Cleveland, Ohio, collected in 1975 and 1976, report that over a one-year period more elderly persons improved or remained stable than declined in terms of self-reported mental health measures.

Among the few studies that provide reasonable data on the prevalence of psychiatric disorders in a Canadian community are the Stirling County studies (of a rural Nova Scotia community) (Leighton, 1959). These studies, looking largely at anxiety and depressive disorders, do not show prevalence increasing with age. The greatest prevalence occurs during middle age. Murphy et al. (1984:996), in reporting on data from the 1952 and 1970 surveys, note that "There is a tendency for the youngest and oldest to have lower prevalence than their age neighbors of the same sex in the same survey year. Mainly, this seems to reflect the fact that among the very young there were few chronic episodes and among the very old few episodes of recent onset." The researchers suggest that cohort effects influence age/sex comparisons over time. The discrepancy in rates of psychiatric disorder between males and females in the middle years decreased between 1952 and 1970. It is stated that in the 40 to 69 age range, the psychiatric disorder rate for men seemed to be catching up to that of women, while the psychiatric disorder rate for women was falling back to that of men with regard to overall rates.

The most recent and comprehensive epidemiological studies that provide data on the incidence and prevalence of psychiatric disorders in the general population are the Epidemiological Catchment Area (ECA) studies conducted in the U.S.A. These studies, conducted at several sites, surveyed some 3,000 sample individuals at each site, and used a structured psychiatric interview, the Diagnostic Interview Schedule (DIS). The DIS allows the determination of a number of discrete psychiatric disorders in terms of the DSM-III classification system. These ECA studies show that the rates for psychiatric disorders are substantially lower for those persons 45 years of age and older, than for younger age groups. The studies also report variations in prevalence rates for each study site (see Table 1). The researchers note that the finding that most disorders other than schizophrenic disorders ". . . have their peak lifetime occurrence in the 25 to 44-year-old age

---

TABLE 1:

Six Month Prevalence of any DIS/DSM III Disorders in the General Population by ECA Site, Age Group and Sex (Percent)

| | | Age Group | | | | |
Site	Sex	18-24	25-44	45-64	65+	Total
New Haven	M	23.8%	18.9%	11.9%	12.3%	16.7%
	F	24.6%	21.2%	10.3%	13.2%	17.1%
Baltimore	M	25.1%	23.5%	18.7%	15.3%	21.1%
	F	26.6%	27.1%	21.5%	17.8%	23.6%
St. Louis	M	18.9%	19.8%	9.4%	8.8%	15.4%
	F	17.8%	17.2%	10.9%	8.8%	14.8%

SOURCE: Myers et al., 1984:964, Table 10.

groups needs further exploration. Clearly it is no accidental finding, because it is replicated in all three sites.'' They describe this finding as the one that most challenged their expectations as older groups, having already passed through as much or more of the age-at-risk than younger groups, should have lifetime rates as high or higher than those of the young (Myers et al., 1984).

Interesting patterns in the occurrence of specific psychiatric disorders are manifest in various àge/sex groups. Table 2 documents the three most frequent psychiatric disorders for specific age/sex groupings in these three ECA sites. Of note is the increasing prevalence of "severe cognitive impairment" — an organic disorder — with age. Also of note is the prevalence of "alcohol and drug addiction and dependence disorders" among males.

TABLE 2:
Three Most Frequent DIS/DIM III Disorders in the General Population by Age and Sex Based on Six-Month Prevalence Rates

		Age Group				
Rank	Sex	18-24	25-44	45-64	65 +	Total
1	M	Alcohol A/D	Alcohol A/D	Alcohol A/D	Severe Cog. Impairment	Alcohol A/D
	F	Phobia	Phobia	Phobia	Phobia	Phobia
2	M	Drug A/D	Phobia	Phobia	Phobia	Phobia
	F	Drug A/D	Major Depressive Episode	Dysthymia	Severe Cog. Impairment	Major Depressive Episode
3	M	Phobia	Drug A/D	Dysthymia	Alcohol A/D	Drug A/D
	F	Major Depressive Episode	Dysthymia	Major Depressive Episode	Dysthymia	Dysthymia

SOURCE: Myers et al., 1984: 965, Table 11.

Taken altogether, the findings from the various studies reviewed do not consistently show a relationship between vulnerability to mental illness and aging. Also noteworthy is the lack of Canadian studies of the effects of aging on mental health.

The inconsistency between study findings reported in the literature may be explained, at least in part, in terms of study design, populations studied and instrumentation. In general, studies that find vulnerability to psychiatric disorder increasing with age have been cross-sectional in design, have used clinical populations, solicited retrospective evidence and utilized "global" measures of mental health. Studies not finding a relationship between aging and mental illness are generally longitudinal in design, have studied general populations and used more structured measures of psychiatric status that allow the determination of discrete psychiatric disorder (Haug et al., 1984).

Only longitudinal studies that disentangle cohort from aging effects can test the notion that aging leads to a decline in mental health. A longitudinal design is also necessary to determine the nature and rate of the decline in mental health, if indeed such a decline exists.

Cross-sectional research has produced a list of factors related to mental health/illness among the elderly. The socio-demographic variables of sex and socio-economic status have been consistently related to mental health/illness. Other social and psychological factors such as social isolation, stress, life events and marital status have also been associated with mental health/illness, although the evidence with regard to the effects of these attributes is more variable. Again, longitudinal designs would permit firmer conclusions about the variety of factors that are associated with positive mental health among the elderly.

Of related interest here are the research studies that have looked at the utilization of general health services. These studies generally report that the elderly on average consume more health services than younger age groups (Schwenger and Gross, 1980; Kane and Kane, 1978). However, Roos et al. (1984), in a detailed examination of health care utilization data for the Province of Manitoba, showed a bimodal pattern of utilization among the elderly. Most of the elderly are healthy and are infrequent users of services. A minority of the elderly are identified as very high users of services (a similar bimodal pattern of service utilization is evident in the examination of psychiatric health care services for the general population of the Province of Saskatchewan [D'Arcy et al., 1979].) Such data raise the issue of whether it is the mental health of the elderly as a whole that declines with age, or particular subgroups of the elderly population that are particularly vulnerable to mental illness with increasing age. If the latter is the case, what are their identifying characteristics?

Some Canadian Data

It should be evident from the preceding discussion that while on the surface a seemingly simple question, the issue of the mental health among the elderly in Canada is indeed more complex. Bearing in mind the foregoing comments and caveats concerning the mental illness processes and data and information sources, the remainder of this chapter reviews a variety of data on mental health/illness among the elderly in Canada.

As noted earlier, there is a paucity of good Canadian studies on aging and mental health. Consequently, straightforward information on the prevalence of mental illness among the elderly in Canada, or indeed among other age groups, is limited. There are few concrete data on the factors associated with positive mental health in the aging transition. There are no studies of comparable scope and quality to the ECA studies in the United States. It is apparent that we as Canadians are relying on others, in other cultures and societies, to provide data of variable applicability to the Canadian context.

In the absence of specific comprehensive data one has to rely upon more fragmented data sources to provide both glimpses of the level of mental health among the elderly in Canada and clues to the factors that may be causally related to positive mental health during the aging transition. The following provides data and commentary on aging and a variety of indicators of mental health, specifically suicide, psychiatric hospitalizations, utilization of physician services for psychiatric services, use of prescribed mood-modifying drugs and reported experiences of a variety of psychiatric symptoms and psychological distress. Each of these variables/events is seen as an indicator of the larger phenomenon of "mental health/illness." The data reviewed are derived from both "official statistics" and epidemiological surveys. They are both national and regional in scope. When reviewing the data one has to be cognizant of the iceberg analogy previously outlined. Each of these sets of data provides us with a glimpse, a view, of the object in question.

Suicide

The literature suggests that suicide rates among the elderly are higher than among other age groups. Figure 3 provides data on suicide rates for Canada for the total population and for males and females separately for the past decade. Figure 4 provides similar data for specific age groups. These data are taken from *Causes of Death*, an annual publication of Statistics Canada. In interpreting these data, one is cautioned that these are "official statistics." The recording of a suicide event is dependent upon the compliance of the immediate family of the deceased and the attending physician signing the death certificate. Social, cultural and practical sensitivities and judgments may influence the recording of a death as suicide. In looking at trends over time or at differences among groups, one has to ask the question, "to what extent are these changes or differences artifacts of 'improvements' in the reporting process or the result of 'real' changes or differences in suicide rates?"

The data reported in Figure 3 show a trend in increasing suicide rates over the past decade, although this trend is more pronounced for males than for females, whose suicide rates have remained relatively static. The female suicide rate was 7.1 per 100,000 in 1973 and 6.9 in 1983. The comparable

FIGURE 3:

Suicides in Canada, 1973-83, by Sex (Rate per 100,000 Population)

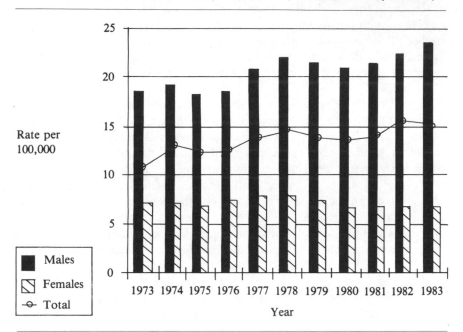

SOURCE: Statistics Canada, *Causes of Death*, and *Population Estimates.*

rates for males were 18.0 and 23.4. Comparable data on age-specific suicide rates presented in Figure 4 show a trend in increasing suicides among the 75 + age group; however, this trend is largely a function of increases in the "Male 75 + " suicide rates. The suicide rate in males 75 + increased from 20.8 per 100,000 population in 1973 to 39.0 in 1983. For females 75 + years of age the suicide rate was 4.4 in 1973 and 6.2 in 1983.

Age/sex differences in suicide rates are more clearly displayed in Figure 5 following, which shows age/sex suicide rates for Canada for 1983. Clearly illustrated here is the fact that sex differences are more significant than age differences in suicide rates. In general males commit suicide three times more frequently than females. For females there is clearly an inverted U-shaped age pattern, with the middle age groups reporting higher suicide rates than older or younger age groups. Among females the highest suicide rate is recorded in the 45 to 54 age group at 12.43 per 100,000 population, with the rate decreasing to 6.24 in the 75 + age group. Among males there is a clearer age gradient. The suicide rate for males increased from 26.67 per 100,000 population in the 34 to 44 age group to 34 per 100,000 in the 75 + age group; the suicide rate in the 25 to 34 age group is also high at 31.87 per 100,000 population.

FIGURE 4:
Suicide Rates for Selected Age Groups and Males 75 +, Canada 1973-83

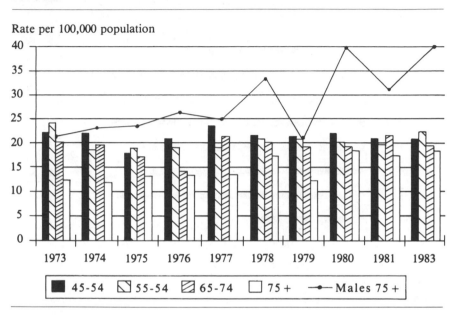

Rate per 100,000 population

SOURCES: Statistics Canada, *Causes of Death*, and *Population Estimates*.

While one might be advised to interpret the trends in increases in reported suicide rates with some caution, the sex and age differences at one point in time can be treated as being more firmly grounded. They are consistent with a variety of other mental health indicators.

Psychiatric hospitalizations

Figure 6 provides age/sex data on separations (discharges and deaths) from designated psychiatric inpatient facilities in Canada over the twenty-year period 1961 - 1981. These data are drawn from the official statistics on mental health compiled by Statistics Canada. The data cover a wide range of facilities such as specialized psychiatric wards of general hospitals, psychiatric hospitals and provincial mental hospitals. Omitted from these data are the considerable volume of hospitalizations for psychiatric disorders in general wards of general hospitals.

As a rule, psychiatric hospitalizations, in contrast to the data on suicides, show a trend in declining admission rates. This is true for the population as a whole particularly since the early 1970s, and especially true for the older age groups. However, consistent with the suicide data are the higher rates of hospitalization for males. The declines in these psychiatric hospitalizations

FIGURE 5:
Suicide Rates by Age Group and Sex, Canada, 1983

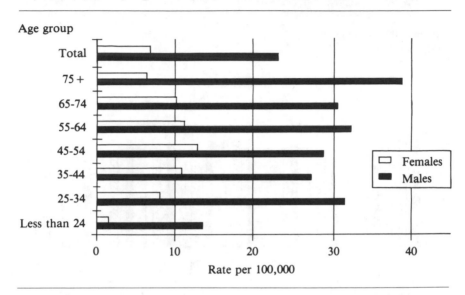

SOURCE: Statistics Canada, *Causes of Death, 1983,* and *Population Estimates.*

are most dramatic in the 80 + age category, which shows a decrease from 563 admissions per 100,000 population in 1961 to 145 per 100,000 in 1979. Such declines in hospitalizations are evident for both males and females. The admission rates for males declined from 614 per 100,000 population in 1961 to 197 in 1979, and for females the admission rates declined from 521 per 100,000 population in 1961 to 116 in 1979.

Rather than indicating tremendous improvements in the mental health of the elderly in Canada, these declines in psychiatric admission rates are generally more reflective of changes in the delivery of mental health services in Canada during the past two decades, as well as changes in the methods of delivery of services to the aged. These changes have seen improvements in the ambulatory (outpatient) treatment of psychiatric disorders and increases in the availability of alternative and more appropriate nursing home facilities for the aged (e.g., D'Arcy,1976).

The data on the diagnoses associated with these hospitalizations by age and sex for 1980-81 show substantial variation in diagnostic patterns be-

FIGURE 6:

First Admissions to Psychiatric Institutions, for Selected Age Groups and Years, Canada, 1961-1979

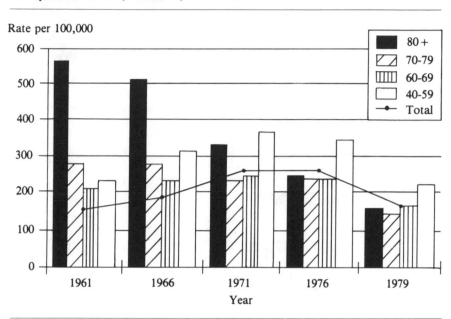

SOURCES: Statistics Canada, *Mental Health Statistics.*

tween age/sex groups (Figure 7). Apparent here is the increase of senile conditions with age, with that increase being more evident in males than females. Also evident are sex differences in diagnostic patterns, with males having a preponderance of alcohol, schizophrenia and personality disorders. Females in comparison have a preponderance of affective (mood) disorders and neurotic disorders. These data parallel the diagnoses-by-sex-and-age data reported by the ECA studies in the United States (see Table 2).

Nonpsychiatric wards of general hospitals account for approximately 40 percent of all admissions/separations from inpatient facilities in Canada (D'Arcy, 1977, 1978; Cardillo, 1980). A key difference between designated psychiatric facilities and nonpsychiatric ward treatment revolves around the issues of voluntary/involuntary and specialized/nonspecialized treatment. *Designated* psychiatric facilities are specialized facilities to which a patient

FIGURE 7:
Diagnoses on Separation, for Selected Age and Diagnostic Groups, Canada, 1980-81, Psychiatric and Mental Hospitals

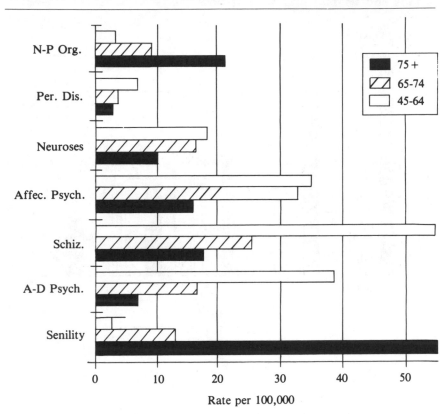

Rate per 100,000

Diagnostic Key: N-P Org.   = Specific Non Psychotic Mental Disorders
                             following Organic Brain Damage (ICDA-9;310)
          Per. Dis.   = Personality Disorders (ICDA-9;301)
          Neuroses   = Neurotic Disorders (ICDA-9;300)
          Affec. Psych. = Affective Psychoses (ICDA-9;296)
          Schiz.   = Schizophrenic Psychoses & Paranoid States
                             (ICDA-9;295, 297)
          A-D Psych. = Alcohol and Drug Psychoses & Dependence
                             (ICDA-9;291, 292, 303, 304)
          Senility   = Senile and Presenile Organic Psychotic Conditions
                             (ICDA-9; 290)

SOURCE: Statistics Canada, *Mental Health Statistics, 1980-81.*

may be involuntarily committed for treatment — although the vast majority of patients in these facilities voluntarily admit themselves for treatment. Specialist qualification is usually required for a practitioner to have admitting privileges. Nonpsychiatric wards are not specialized facilities; all patients in such wards are there voluntarily; general practitioners may admit and treat patients for psychiatric disorders in such facilities.

Data on admissions/separations from general hospital wards show a

FIGURE 8:

Population Use of Any Medical Service for an Explicitly Psychiatric Diagnosis, by Age Group and Sex (Saskatchewan, 1974)

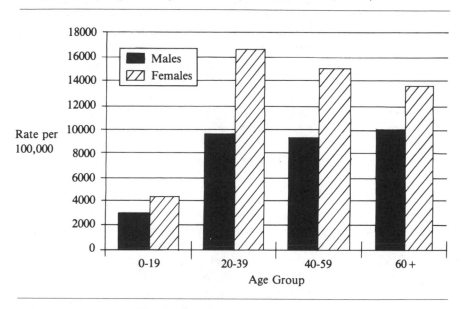

SOURCE: D'Arcy et al., 1979:119, Table VIII.2.

similar age distribution to that for designated psychiatric facilities (as shown in Figure 6); that is, higher rates for the middle-aged group and lower rates for the younger and older age groups. However, in the general hospital wards there is a tendency to concentrate on middle-aged and older age groups. There are relatively few admissions/separations for the younger age group in this type of facilities. Consistent with these age data, diagnostic data show that general wards are more likely to treat alcoholism and neurotic disorders and are less likely to treat personality disorders and various psychoses (including schizophrenia) (Cardillo, 1980; D'Arcy 1977b, 1978).

These admission and diagnostic data do not provide clear information on the functional (role) impairment that afflicts the hospitalized individuals.

However, data on length of hospital stay, a very rough proxy for the disability/impairment associated with a mental disorder, show substantially greater lengths of stay occurring in the older age groups.

Utilization of medical services

Far more people are treated for psychiatric problems on an ambulatory basis than are admitted to hospitals for treatment. Unfortunately there are no readily accessible national data on the use of physician services for psychiatric disorders. However, it is possible, using the unique comprehensive health care data for the Province of Saskatchewan, to look at psychiatric service utilization in the general population. These data cover any "private" fee-for-service physician contacts (both general practitioner and psychiatrist), hospitalizations in general wards and in specialized psychiatric inpatient facilities and contacts with the public specialized psychiatric services branch's facilities and personnel. Figure 8 shows the percent of each age/sex segment of the provincial population using a medical service for the treatment of explicitly psychiatric problems. No obvious age gradient is apparent, the highest psychiatric services utilization occurs in the 20-39 age group for both males and females. Again females' utilization is considerably higher than males'. In contrast to males, females show a greater decline in utilization with age (D'Arcy et al., 1979).

Use of mood-modifying drugs

While there are a variety of methods available for treating psychiatric disorders and psychological distress, e.g., the various psychotherapies, behavioural modification, electro-shock therapy, etc., the dominant method is through the use of mood-modifying psychotropic drugs. Thus, data on the usage of mood-modifying drugs provide further insight into the issue of aging and mental health.

National data on the use of *some* mood-modifying drugs are available from the Canadian Health Survey (CHS). The survey provides a comprehensive snapshot of the health status and health-related practices of Canadians for the year 1977-78. The survey sampled some 32,000 + Canadians coast to coast. (Unfortunately the survey was only conducted for one year, before being terminated in the name of budget restraint.) One of the questions asked in that survey concerned the use of "tranquilizers, medicines for the nerves or medicines to help you sleep" during the past two days. Some 4.93 percent of the Canadians sampled reported using such medications during this time. Figure 9 graphically depicts the age/sex data on usage. Evident is a straightforward age gradient with use increasing with age. Also noteworthy is the substantially higher usage reported by females.

Data on the *actual medical prescription and dispensing* of psychotropic drugs are available for the Province of Saskatchewan. These data complement and provide triangulation for the national CHS self-report data of

FIGURE 9:

Self-reported Use of Mood-Modifying Drugs by Canadians during past two days, by Age Group and Sex

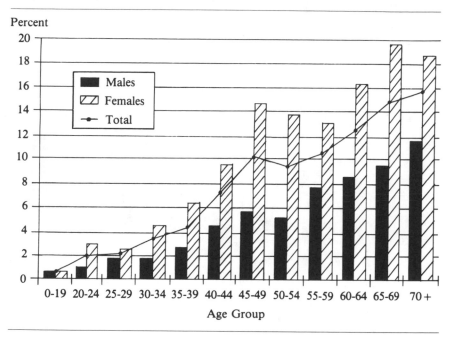

SOURCE: *Canada Health Survey,* Public Use Data Tape.

Figure 9. In Saskatchewan drugs prescribed for a patient's use are covered by the province's health programs. A minimal dispensing fee is charged by pharmacies, but the price of the medication is covered out of public funds. The detailed set of data resulting from this program allow an examination of age and psychotropic drug use. Figure 10 shows age/sex data on the percent of the provincial population receiving a prescription for a mood-modifying drug during the twelve months of 1982. A broad definition of "mood-modifying drug" is used here. Prescription pain relief medicines — analgesics — are included here as mood modifiers. On the other hand, drugs not part of the approved Saskatchewan Formulary are not included in these data. There is a clear and dramatic age gradient in psychotropic drug use. Also evident is the significantly higher usage by females.

Although the levels may appear high, the overall rates of psychotropic drug prescription reported for Saskatchewan are conservative (low) by international comparison (Power et al., 1983). The high levels of psychotropic prescription for women are also evident internationally.

Because of initial concerns with high use of mood-modifying drugs in the older age groups, there has been a concerted attempt provincially to alert

FIGURE 10:
Percent of Population Receiving Prescription for Mood-Modifying
Drugs during a twelve month period, by Age Group and Sex
(Saskatchewan, 1982)

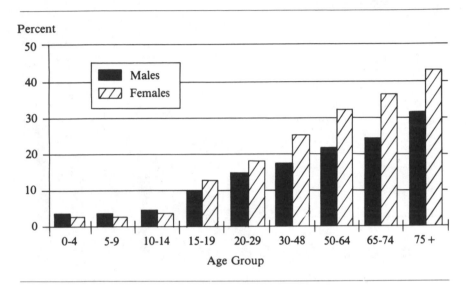

SOURCE: Joint Committee on Drug Utilization (Saskatchewan), 1984, Report No. 8,
p. 3, Table 3.

clinicians to this possible problem and to reinforce the necessity that
psychotropic drugs be appropriately prescribed. This activity has resulted in
decreases in prescriptions for mood modifiers provincially during the past
six years. The majority of the decrease has occurred in prescriptions for
minor tranquilizers, sedatives and hypnotics. The decrease was more pronounced for females than males (JCDU, 1984).

Anxiety and depressive symptoms

Anxiety and depressive disorders are some of the most prevalent psychiatric
disorders encountered in the general population. Unfortunately, we do not
have the appropriate studies to show the prevalence and incidence of these
disorders in the general Canadian population. However, a variety of studies
have used psychiatric screening instruments to assess the prevalence of mental health/illness in the general community and specific subpopulations.
These screening instruments ask about the presence or absence of a variety
of specific symptoms, e.g., "Do you feel weak all over much of the time?"
(HOS — MacMillan, 1957); "Have you recently been thinking of yourself
as a worthless person?" (GHQ — Goldberg, 1978). The symptoms assessed
are usually of an anxiety and depressive nature (Dohrenwend et al., 1980).
Data from two general population studies, one national and the other pro-

vincial in scope, are reported here. The provincial data from the Province of Saskatchewan were collected as part of a survey of stress and well-being in the general population during 1977-78. The screening instrument used was the thirty-item version of the General Health Questionnaire (GHQ-30) (Goldberg, 1972). The data were collected by mail questionnaire and were based on a return sample of 2000 + respondents (53 percent of the original sample) (D'Arcy, 1982). These data, showing the percent of each age/sex group reporting six or more symptoms (Figure 11), reveal a U-shaped age gradient, with more symptoms being reported by youngest and oldest age groups. Reporting six or more symptoms on the GHQ-30 is considered a level of distress warranting professional consultation (Goldberg, 1972). Additional data from a separate study show that late adolescents report even higher levels of distress on the GHQ-30 (D'Arcy and Siddique, 1984).

FIGURE 11:
Percent Reporting Six or more symptoms of Psychological Distress by Age Group and Sex (Saskatchewan, 1976-77)

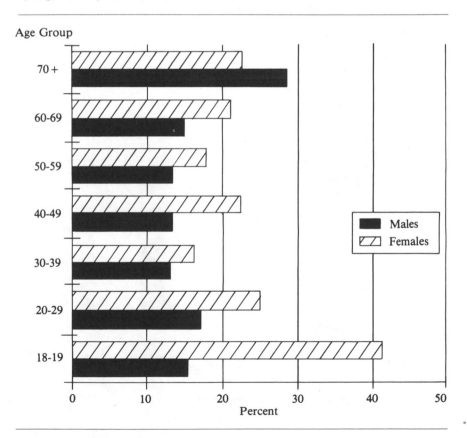

SOURCE: D'Arcy, 1982:319, Table III.

Factor analyses of the GHQ-30 revealed four major factors: (1) anxiety/insomnia; (2) depression/anhedonia; (3) anergia; and (4) social dysfunction. Analysis of the factor structure of the GHQ-30 for each age group revealed differences. Depression/social dysfunction symptoms were most dominant in the 60+ age groups. Anxiety symptoms were more predominant in the middle age categories.

The Canadian Health Survey used as part of its survey battery a sixteen item Health Opinion Survey (HOS). The HOS is a frequently used measure of mental health (Murphy, 1981). Factor analyses of the items used in the CHS showed a single dominant factor. Figure 12 shows the percentage of each age/sex group reporting that they have frequently or very frequently experienced these symptoms (CHS, 1981). A more straightforward age gradient is apparent in these data with the occurrence of symptoms increasing with age. Females reported more symptoms than males. It should be noted that even in the "most distressed" age/sex group, *a full 90 percent of that group did not report any symptoms of anxiety or depression.*

In an attempt to examine the extent to which age was associated with higher levels of psychiatric symptomology, multiple regression analyses were run to look at the extent to which age or some other socio-

FIGURE 12:
Percent Reporting Frequent Symptoms of Anxiety and Depression by Age Group and Sex (Canada, 1978-79)

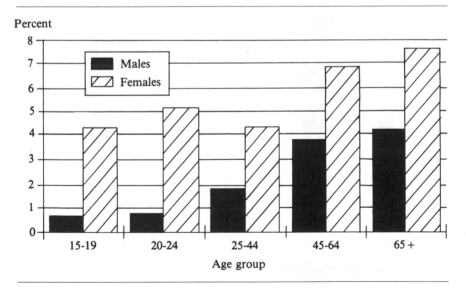

SOURCE: Canada Health Survey, *The Health of Canadians*:134, Table 69.

demographic, health and life-experience variables may account for the variations in HOS scores. This statistical technique is used to see how much of the variation in a dependent variable (the HOS) can be explained by a list of independent variables ("causes"). These regression results show that seven variables: (1) number of health problems during the past year; (2) life events over the past twelve months (e.g., divorce, major illness, etc.,); (3) sex; (4) education; (5) income quintile; (6) age group; and (7) marital status accounted for approximately 25 percent of the variance in the HOS. The other 75 percent of the variance is "unexplained." No doubt most of the variation in HOS scores is a function of other personality and social attributes not captured by the measures used in this study. The number of health problems experienced during the past twelve months is the most significant of the seven variables analysed in the CHS data. Age per se explains a relatively small amount of the variance. However, largely because of the size of the study sample, all seven variable relationships with the HOS scores were statistically significant, although their impact was not large. To explore these sets of relationships further the CHS sample was divided up into five parallel age groups for each sex. Again multiple stepwise regressions were run using the five remaining independent variables. This analysis showed that a greater percent of the variance in HOS scores is explainable in middle-aged and older age groups, than in younger age groups. Evident throughout all age/sex groups is the significance of one's general health in explaining the prevalence of anxiety and depressive symptoms. The importance of "one's general health" in accounting for anxiety and depressive symptoms increases with age.

To a considerable degree these national CHS data parallel the Saskatchewan data presented previously and reported on in more detail elsewhere (D'Arcy, 1981a; 1982). This triangulation provides an added degree of confidence in the findings of these studies.

Concluding Comments

This chapter started off asking, "What are the effects of aging on mental health?" At the end of the chapter it is appropriate to ask, "What can be concluded?" First, it is clearly evident that Canada lacks an adequate knowledge base for rational decision making concerning mental health policies and programs for the elderly. More and more focussed high quality research is needed.

The limited data available provide a mixed picture of the effects of aging on mental health. In terms of severe psychiatric impairment requiring specialist attention and hospitalization, the elderly appear to be less prone to such illnesses than younger age groups, particularly the middle aged. However, organically based psychiatric disorders are much more prevalent among the aged. Data from the Stirling County studies show a greater prevalence of anxiety and depressive disorders in the middle years, with lower rates of disorder in the younger and older age categories. The data on suicide provide a somewhat different picture, with higher suicide rates among the elderly. Data on mood-modifying drug use and prescription show a fairly straightforward increase in use with increasing age. The data on the softer symptoms of distress from general population surveys show much more psychological distress among the elderly, with that distress increasing with age. There are substantial sex differentials readily apparent in all these data, implying substantive sex differences in the experience of the aging process.

The data reviewed also show that there are other points in the life cycle (other than old age and retirement) that are "very stressful." Becoming elderly is not the only role transition associated with age. Adolescence and middle age are also stressful transitions with negative mental health consequences for some segments of the population.

From a policy and program perspective the Canadian population will go through a "middle aging" before an "aging" transition. Although the data do not show the rate of mental illness increasing with age, those same data suggest substantially increased demand for mental health services during the next decades. The rate of illness is only part of the equation generating a demand for services, at the most elemental level; the population base is the other. The increased population, both in percentage and absolute terms, in the middle-aged and older age categories will ensure that the same rate of illness will yield increases in the absolute numbers of patients seeking treatment. To that simple equation of demand must be added, at a minimum, changes in expectations and therapeutic effectiveness.

Clearly evident in the data reviewed is that the substantial majority of the aged appear to be mentally healthy and manifest few mental health problems. This observation leads to a questioning of the characteristics associated with a successful transition to old age in our society. How important is good physical health to good mental health among the aged? How important are education, income, social support, family relationships, interest activities, etc., to positive mental health? We are in need of studies that address such issues.

Finally, the effects of aging need to be clearly delineated from the effects of the historical generational experiences of an age-cohort (Cain, 1967). The advent of the Canada Pension Plan (and its spin-off effects on private pension schemes), medicare and social housing programs in Canada has markedly improved the economic circumstances of the elderly. However, other changes and influences in our economy today may adversely affect younger age-cohorts, making the aging process for them more difficult and stressful.

References

American Psychiatric Association

1980   *Diagnostic and Statistical Manual of Mental Disorders.* 3rd edition (DSM-III). Washington, D.C.; American Psychiatric Association.

Blazer, D.G.

1980   "The epidemiology of mental illness in late life." Pp. 249-271 in Ewald W. Busse and Dan G. Blazer (eds.), *Handbook of Geriatric Psychiatry.* New York: Van Nostrand Reinhold.

1983   "The epidemiology of depression in late life." Pp. 30-50 in Lawrence D. Breslau and Marie R. Haug (eds.), *Depression in the Elderly.* New York: Springer.

Butler, R.N.

1975   "Psychiatry and the elderly: An overview." *American Journal of Psychiatry* 132:893.

Cain, L.D.

1967   "Age status and generational phenomena: The new old people in contemporary America." *The Gerontologist* 7:83-92.

Cardillo, Brenda

1980   *Psychiatric Discharges from Non-Psychiatric Wards of General Hospitals, 1975.* Ottawa: Statistics Canada, Minister of Supply and Services.

Cheah, K.C.

1978   "The depressed elderly patient: Part I. Diagnosis and classification." *Journal of the Arkansas Medical Society* 75: 141-47.

Cohen, G.D.

1977   "Approach to the geriatric patient." *Medical Clinics of North America* 61: 855-866.

1980   "Prospects for mental health and aging." Pp. 971-993 in James E. Birren and R. Bruce Sloane (eds.), *Handbook of Mental Health and Aging.* Englewood Cliffs, New Jersey: Prentice-Hall.

D'Arcy, C.

1976   "The manufacture and obsolence of madness: Age, social policy and psychiatric morbidity in a Prairie Province." *Social Science and Medicine* 10:5-13.

1977a "Patterns in the delivery of psychiatric care in Saskatchewan 1971-72 (11): Types of contacts and some patient characteristics," *Canadian Psychiatric Association Journal* 22 (February): 31-36.

1977b "Patterns in the delivery of psychiatric care in Saskatchewan 1971-72 (111): Patient sociodemographic and medical characteristics," *Canadian Psychiatric Association Journal* 22 (August): 215-224.

1978   "Changing patterns of psychiatric morbidity in Saskatchewan." *Canada's Mental Health* 26:6-12.

1981a "Stress, coping and social support in different age/sex cohorts." Pp. 185-207 in J. Crawford (ed.); *Canadian Gerontological Collection III — The Family in Later Life.* Winnipeg: Canadian Association in Gerontology.

1981b "Opened Rank? Blackfoot Revisited." Pp. 96-108 in D. Coburn et al. (eds.), *Health and Canadian Society: A Sociological Perspective*. Toronto: Fitzhenry & Whiteside.

1982 "Prevalence and correlates of non-psychotic psychiatric symptoms in the general population." *Canadian Journal of Psychiatry* 17(June):316-324.

D'Arcy, C., Janet A. Schmitz and Guin Bold

1979 *Patterns in the Delivery of Psychiatric Care, Saskatchewan 1969-1974*. Service Interface Study Final Report. Saskatoon: Applied Research Unit, Psychiatric Research, July.

D'Arcy, C. and C.M. Siddique

1984 "Psychological distress among Canadian adolescents." *Psychological Medicine* 14(3):615-628.

Dohrenwend, B.P., B.S. Dohrenwend, M.S. Gould et al.

1980 *Mental Illness in the United States - Epidemiological Estimates*. New York: Praeger.

Frerichs, R.R., C.A. Aneshensel and V.A. Clark

1980 "Prevalence of depression in Los Angeles County." Paper presented at the Society of Epidemiological Research, Minneapolis, Minnesota.

Goldberg, D.

1972 *The Detection of Psychiatric Illness by Questionnaire*. London: Oxford University Press.

1978 *Manual of the General Health Questionnaire*. Windsor, Birks. (Eng.): NFER Publishing Co.

Harris, Daniel M.

1975 "An elaboration of the relationship between general hospital bed supply and general hospital utilization." *Journal of Health and Social Behavior* 16:163-172.

Haug, Marie, Linda L. Belgrave and Brian Gratton

1984 "Mental health and the elderly: Factors in stability and change over time." *Journal of Health and Social Behavior* 25 (June):100-115.

Health and Welfare Canada

1981 *The Health of Canadians: Report of the Canada Health Survey*. Ottawa: Ministries of Supply and Services and National Health and Welfare.

Hemenway, D. and D. Fallon

1985 "Testing for physician-induced demand with hypothetical cases." *Medical Care* 23(4):344-349.

Jaco, E.G.

1960 "Depression in the Elderly," *Journal of the American Geriatrics Society* 27:38-42.

Joint Committee on Drug Utilization (Saskatchewan).

1984 *Report No. 8. Use of Mood-Modifying Drugs in Saskatchewan — Update*. Regina.

Kadushin, C.

1967 *Why People go to Psychiatrists*. New York: Atherton Press.

Kane R.L. and R.A. Kane

1978 "Care of the aged: Old problems in need of new solutions." *Science* 200:913-919.

Karasu, Toksoz B.
1984   *The Psychiatric Therapies*. Washington, D.C.: American Psychiatric Association.

Kathol, R.G. and F. Petty
1981   "Relationship of depression to medical illness." *Journal of Affective Disorders* 3: 111-131.

Kay, D.W.K., P. Beamish and M. Roth
1964   "Old age mental disorders in New Castle upon Tyne. Part I: A study of prevalence. Part II: A study of possible social and medical causes." *British Journal of Psychiatry* 110: 146-158, 668-682.

Kay, D.W.K. and K. Bergmann
1980   "Epidemiology of mental disorders among the aged in the community." Pp. 34-56 in James E. Birren and R. Bruce Sloane (eds.), *Handbook of Mental Health and Aging*. Englewood Cliffs, New Jersey: Prentice-Hall.

Kitsuse, J. and A. Cicourcel
1963   "A note on the use of official statistics." *Social Problems* 11:131-139.

Lieberman, M.A.
1983   "Social contexts of depression." Pp. 121-123 in Lawrence D. Breslau and Marie R. Haug (eds.), *Depression in the Elderly*. New York: Springer.

Leighton, Alexander H.
1959   *My Name is Legion: The Stirling County Study of Psychiatric Disorder and Social Environment*. Vol I. New York: Basic Books.

Lowenthal, Marjorie Fiske, Paul L. Berkman and Associates
1967   *Aging and Mental Disorder in San Francisco: A Social Psychiatric Study*. San Francisco: Jossey-Bass.

MacMillan, A.M.
1957   "The health opinion survey: Technique for estimating prevalence of psychoneurotic and related types of disorders in communities." *Psychological Reports* 3:325-339.

Murphy, Jane M.
1981   *Psychiatric Instrument Development for Primary Care Research*. Patient Self-Report Questionnaire. Mimeo. Department of Psychiatry, Harvard Medical School.

Murphy, Jane M., Arthur M. Sobol, R.K. Neff, D.C. Oliver and A.H. Leighton
1984   "Stability of prevalence: Depression and anxiety disorders." *Archives of General Psychiatry* 41(Oct):990-997.

Myers Jerome K., Myrna M. Weissman, G.I. Tischler et al.
1984   "Six-month prevalence of psychiatric disorders in three communities." *Archives of General Psychiatry* 41(Oct):959-967.

Power, Bob, W. Downey and B.R. Schnell
1983   "Utilization of psychotropic drugs in Saskatchewan, 1977-1980." *Canadian Journal of Psychiatry* 28: 547-551.

Quality Assurance Project (QAP)
1982   "A treatment outline for agoraphobia." *Australian and New Zealand Journal of Psychiatry* 16: 25-33.
1983   "A treatment outline for depressive disorders." *Australian and New*

Zealand Journal of Psychiatry 17: 129-146.

Regier, D.A., I.D. Goldberg and C.A. Taube
1978   "The de facto US Mental Health Services System: A public health perspective." *Archives of General Psychiatry* 38: 593-685.

Renner, V.J. and J.E. Birren
1980   "Stress: Physiological and psychological mechanisms." Pp. 310-336 in James E. Birren and R. Bruce Sloane (eds.), *Handbook of Mental Health and Aging.* Englewood Cliffs, New Jersey: Prentice-Hall.

Roos, N.P., E. Shapiro and L.L. Roos, Jr.
1984   "Aging and the demand for health services: Which aged and whose demand?" *The Gerontologist* 24(1):31-36.

Rosenhan, D.L.
1973   "On being sane in insane places." *Science* 179:250-258.

Scheff, Thomas J.
1966   *Being Mentally Ill: A Sociological Theory*, Chicago: Aldine Publishing Co.

Schwenger, C.W. and M.J. Gross
1980   "Institutional care and institutionalization of the elderly in Canada." Pp. 248-256 in V. Marshall (ed.), *Aging in Canada: Sociological Perspectives.* Toronto: Fitzhenry & Whiteside.

Shapiro, Sam, E.A. Skinner, L.G. Kessler et al.
1984   "Utilization of health and mental health services." *Archives of General Psychiatry* 41:971-978.

Statistics Canada
1985   *Population Projections for Canada, Provinces and Territories: 1984-2006.* Ottawa: Minister of Supply and Services
Causes of Death. Ottawa: Publications Division, Statistics Canada.
Population Estimates. Ottawa: Publications Division, Statistics Canada.
Mental Health Statistics. Ottawa: Publications Division, Statistics Canada

Strauss, Anselm, L. Schatzman, R. Bucher, D. Ehrlich, M. Sabshin
1964   *Psychiatric Ideologies and Institutions.* Glencoe, Illinois: The Free Press.

Susser, Mervyn
1973   *Causal Thinking in the Health Sciences: Concepts and Strategies of Epidemiology.* New York: Oxford University Press.

Wasylenki, D.
1980   "Depression in the elderly." *Canadian Medical Association Journal* 122: 525-532.

Wheaton, B.
1980   "The sociogenesis of psychological disorder: An attributional theory." *Journal of Health and Social Behavior* 21:100-124.

Wilkie, F.L., C. Eisdorfer and J. Staub
1982   "Stress and psychopathology in the aged." *Psychiatric Clinics of North America* 5: 131-143.

Wing, J.K.
1978   *Reasoning About Madness.* New York: Oxford University Press.

Zung. W.W.K.
1967   "Depression in the normal aged." *Psychosomatics* 8:287-291.

22

Life in Older Age: The View From the Top

Ingrid Connidis
Department of Sociology
University of Western Ontario

The type of attention paid to the subject of aging often tells more about our view of aging than it does about old age. Most materials, particularly in popular publications, fit into one of two categories. Articles about problems associated with aging, such as illness, widowhood, crime victimization and poverty, show the negative side of growing older. Although solutions are sometimes suggested, the emphasis is on the hazards of aging. A second, "upbeat" category includes articles about the 75-year-old marathon runner, the 80-year-old university graduate, the woman celebrating her 105th birthday, or the couple enjoying their 75th wedding anniversary. While presenting "exceptional seniors" is a positive portrayal of aging, such spectacular successes may threaten the self-esteem of the vast majority, who pale in comparison.

This dichotomy is somewhat less evident in professional research on aging, but even it focusses on the problems of aging with a more recent trend to emphasize the *potential* advantages of older age. This chapter considers the reasons for promoting either a positive or negative stereotype of aging, and the implications of doing so. How older people themselves view their stage of life will then be examined in order to form a more realistic picture of the lives of most older Canadians.

Bad News on Aging: The Problem Orientation

In 1982 an article entitled "Good News and Canadian Sociology" was published in the *Canadian Journal of Sociology*. It reviewed numerous recent studies that indicate that Canadian society is far more just and egalitarian than was thought previously. However, referring to these findings as "good news," the author (Ogmundson, 1982:76-77) concludes:

Findings reported in this chapter are from a study (Grant No. 492-800027) funded by the Social Sciences and Humanities Research Council of Canada, to which the author owes thanks.

The naive reader might imagine that considerations such as these would be greeted with pleasure by Canadian sociologists. . . . However, such is not likely to be the case. Many of us have a vested interest in a previous conventional wisdom that lamented our many woes. . . . We, as sociologists, have a fundamental material interest in the discovery, creation, maintenance and widespread perception of "social problems." Student enrollment, publication opportunities, consulting fees, research money and jobs for our students (to say nothing of ourselves!) very much depend on the success of a continuous effort to convince the public of the existence of a number of social problems requiring sociological expertise. Furthermore, our collective self-esteem is largely based on the belief that our primary motivation is to help others, not ourselves. . . . Consequently, our interests demand "bad news."

This reluctance to accept good news also applies to the area of aging, where it is shared by a variety of professionals involved in the study and care of the elderly. While good intentions often underlie a focus on bad news, or the problems of aging, professional self-interest is an important factor (see Connidis, 1981).

Because funding often relies on documenting the severity of a situation, this emphasis is not surprising. This is especially true among service and care providers, who often work in less than optimal conditions, seeking to meet the needs of more clientel than their budgets can handle. However, theirs is not a broad perspective on the field of aging nor on the lives of the elderly, because their clientele represents only one, usually small, segment of the aged population. In general, we can expect that organizations that provide care and services to the elderly will highlight problems associated with aging in order to ensure their own survival (see Connidis, 1981; Altheide and Johnson, 1980: 26-36; Gardner, 1977; Matthews, 1979: 58). Although the intent is in many respects benevolent (to improve services for the elderly), the vested interests of the professionals involved cannot be denied. The result is a problem orientation to the aging process and the aged.

The dilemma is that the overemphasis on the problems or bad news of aging tends to distort our understanding of the aging process and of old age as experienced by most older people. Worse yet, researchers and practitioners themselves are contributing to the stigma often associated with being old in implicitly equating old age with a litany of problems. In highlighting the problems that *may* accompany aging, this view tends to characterize old age itself as negative, thus bolstering the negative stereotype of old age.

The Negative Stereotype

The Facts on Aging Quiz developed by Palmore (1977), contains 25 statements about physical, mental and social aspects of aging that are assessed to be either true or false. The intended use of this well-known quiz is to provide a stimulus for discussion, a comparative measure of knowledge about aging among different groups, a basis for identifying misconceptions and an indirect measure of bias toward the elderly. Incorrect answers to some questions are assumed to indicate a negative bias, while wrong answers to other items indicate a positive bias. While Palmore (1980) emphasizes that the quiz can only be used as an *indirect* measure of bias, he concludes that "the average person has more anti-aged than pro-aged bias" (Palmore, 1981:435).

Recently, Martin Matthews, Tindale and Norris (1984) assessed the usefulness of Palmore's quiz in Canada. They conclude that the quiz can be applied successfully in the Canadian context "to measure overall levels of information and to identify misconceptions about aging" (Martin Matthews et al., 1984:173). However, they question whether the quiz can be used to measure age bias (see also, Holtzman and Beck, 1979; Romeis and Sussman, 1982; Norris, Tindale and Martin Matthews, unpublished). Ignorance cannot be equated with prejudice or ageism.

Despite such critical examination, the facts on aging quiz is used widely to document the ageist attitudes of North Americans. Indeed, Palmore (1982:333) bases a rallying cry for controlled experiments "to determine which methods of reducing ageism are most effective and efficient" on the presence of "abundant evidence of widespread ageism in our culture, including negative stereotypes and attitudes." However, on closer examination, it appears that some of the "abundant evidence" is a function of selective perception. For example, Bassili and Reil (1981) studied the dominance of old-age stereotypes using a Toronto sample. They found that:

> . . . 70-year-olds were seen by college students and by elderly respondents as traditional, conservative, present oriented, and moral. In addition, the college sample *sometimes* attributed to the 70-year-olds characteristics of dogmatism and rigidity, traits which the elderly sample did not attribute to the older targets. (Bassili and Reil, 1981, emphasis added).

This is Palmore's summary (1982:337) of their findings: "They found that there were over twice as many stereotypes associated with the old groups as with the young, and about *three-fourths* of these were *negative* stereotypes (traditional, dogmatic, cautious, rigid)." The assessment (and quantification) of these traits as negative is Palmore's, not the original researchers'.

What might explain this tendency to interpret findings in order to conclude that a negative stereotype dominates in our society? We have already discussed the vested interests that can be served by focussing on the problems of aging. It would be far more difficult to gain support for research designed to determine how to change attitudes towards the elderly if the attitudes were already positive. In addition, by perpetuating the view that the public holds a negative stereotype of aging, gerontologists can feed both their egos and sense of altruism (Schonfield, 1982). Ego fulfillment rests in playing the role of the educator who can teach the lay person what aging is really like. Altruistic tendencies can be satisfied by encouraging students and others to appreciate and do something about the misunderstood elderly. The key problem is that evidence is often distorted in order to support the view that members of our society hold negative stereotypes of aging and the aged. States Schonfield (1982:272): "When the prevalence of ageism is said to be supported by avowed feelings of greater loss on the death of an 18-year-old than on the death of a 75-year-old, it is time to stop or at least to think again."

When given the opportunity, respondents in Schonfield's Calgary sample frequently note that there are many exceptions to a statement about older people they have just claimed to be true or false. While simplicity is an advantage of using true-false items, the complex issue of attitudes towards aging and the elderly cannot be examined adequately using such tools. The notion that they reflect negative bias towards older people is highly questionable. However, the interpretation that they do serves a number of professional interests.

The Positive Stereotype — And Now, the Good News?

Speaking of ironies regarding the old-age stereotype, Kearl (1981-82:288-89) observes: "And finally, there is the field of gerontology, wherein well-intentioned advocates and service providers . . . seek to debunk such problem-oriented images even though they have, in many ways, served to legitimate and provide economic support for the field." In its more extreme form, the movement to emphasize the positive represents a complete reversal in promoting the glories of older age to the virtual exclusion of the less desirable but nonetheless real aspects of aging. With reference to Palmore's discussion of the advantages of aging (1979), Northcott (1982:72) cautions that this type of positive focus "blunts the youth-is-best perspective, though such attempts to brighten the picture of old age are at best qualified and run the risk of appearing sentimental and apologetic."

Just as the negative stereotype hinders our ability to understand the true nature of aging as experienced by the majority of older people, the positive stereotype denies real aspects of the experience, as well. It is often those who berate others for their ageist views who espouse a positive view so unrealistic that it borders on denial. As Schonfield (1982:271) argues:

. . . the question of dislike of growing old as supporting evidence for ageism must be dealt with. . . . It should be obvious that at least two different attitudes are being combined — attitude toward one's own aging and attitude toward the aged — without any evidence of a positive correlation between them. . . . Holding negative attitudes towards older people merely because they are old is immoral, according to well-nigh universally accepted ethical standards. But is there anything immoral about disliking *some* of the concomitants of aging processes? Is it not reasonable to dislike the idea of reduced eyesight and hearing?

The irony of the positive stereotype is that old age is only positive to the extent that it resembles youth. In an article entitled "Whoever Said Life Begins at 40 Was a Fink, Or Those Golden Years — Phooey," Davis (1980) observes that: "In the area of gerontology current stereotypes indicate growing older can be fun if Americans would only adopt the proper attitude toward aging" (1980:583). This view rests on extending the assumed virtues of youth, fitness, beauty and sex into older age. For those unable to avoid the inevitabilities of older age (virtually all of us) the result of such an emphasis is a sense of failure.

Another assumed advantage of older age according to the positive stereotype is the opportunity to place oneself first. However, Davis (1980:586) questions this notion, arguing that a more likely source of fulfillment is commitment to others. Indeed, in a study of older Manitobans, Novak (1983) finds that those who age successfully share a sense of service to others, from which they derive meaning in later life.

In addition to magnifying a sense of failure, the positive stereotype also heightens the fear of aging. In the words of Davis (1980:586-87): "Perhaps the worst travesty of our new direction is that whatever happens it must be positive. We will not abide with negativism, complaints, and the largest of all sins, unhappiness. . . . (I)n the long run we are increasingly denying and thus enhancing the fear of aging."

Finally, were the positive view to dominate, one can readily foresee a future when funding for services required by those elderly in need could be threatened. It is necessary, then, to assess the realities of aging, to seek a balance between the negative and positive stereotypes that rests on the observations of representative samples of older people. We begin by considering Canadian studies of life satisfaction and well-being among older people.

The Well-Being of Older Canadians

Despite the negative stereotypes of aging, studies find that older people are generally more content than people of younger ages. In a study of 440 Canadians of different ages, Northcott (1982) asked about the pressures and satisfaction experienced in various facets of their lives, including housing, work, standard of living, family life and health. He found that, in general, older people are less likely to feel stress to the degree younger people do, and more likely to feel satisfied with the various domains of their lives. The one exception was health, which older people were more inclined to consider a major source of pressure. Northcott (1982:77) concludes: "In short, the picture one gets of old age is that it is a period of relatively low pressure and relatively high satisfaction, though not without its problems."

Martin Matthews, Tindale and Norris (1984) provide information concerning the actual situation of older Canadians that indicates that older people are not as badly off as we sometimes assume. For example, the majority of Canadians aged 65 and over have incomes above the poverty line, enjoy good enough health to carry out their usual activities and live outside institutions. Indeed, among women up to the age of 75, and men of all older ages, most live in private households with someone else, although this is more common for men than women (Minister of Supply and Services Canada, 1983:68-69; see also Connidis and Rempel, 1983; Schwenger, 1982; Stone and Fletcher, this volume). This difference between the sexes is due primarily to the higher mortality rates among men and consequent higher widowhood rates among women. There are also appreciable differences in income by gender. Martin Matthews et al. (1984:168) state: "The incidence of low income families in which the 'head of household' was 65 years or older was 14.9 percent. . .and 50.3 percent for unattached individuals age 65 and over." Since the majority of "unattached individuals" are women, one can conclude that they are far more likely to be in the low-income category. Thus, while emphasizing that most older people are neither poor nor living alone or in institutions, it is important to note these differences between men and women.

In a survey involving a representative sample of 3,300 Canadians, age is strongly related to overall life satisfaction, with older individuals reporting the highest rates (Atkinson, 1980). Income is another predictor of life satisfaction, but *increases in satisfaction occur with advancing age despite the fact that income decreases at the same time.* Although 61 percent of those 65 and over are in the lowest income group, they exhibit the highest levels of satisfaction" (Atkinson, 1980:278, emphasis added). Within comparable income groups, the elderly are also more satisfied with their incomes than younger age groups. Finally, among the married and unmarried with no current relationship, older people are more satisfied with their romantic life than their younger counterparts. A problem in interpreting this pattern is the probability that most younger people "with no current relationship" either have never married or are divorced, while the older individuals in this category are most likely widowed. Thus, the elderly may have the memories of a long and successful marriage to sustain a sense of romantic satisfaction, while the younger have either never had the experience or have tried and failed.

The lack of relationship between life satisfaction and income among the aged is an anomaly that Atkinson (1980:278) seeks to explain by two factors. First, he argues, the hopes and goals of older people are more confined to their current situation because the likelihood of altering it substantially is limited. Unlike younger people, the elderly are therefore less inclined to contrast their present circumstances with anticipated future improvements, only to find themselves wanting. Second, the increased leisure time enjoyed by older individuals is assumed to enhance their general satisfaction with life.

In his study of life satisfaction among 428 Edmontonians aged 65 and over,

Snider (1980) found that only 7 percent reported that they were "not very satisfied" with life on the whole, while the remainder said they were either "fairly satisfied" (47 percent) or "very satisfied" (45 percent). He also found that life satisfaction is related to subjective health; that is, to how respondents evaluate their own health. This echoes Northcott's finding that health is one factor that stresses older people more than their younger counterparts. Like Atkinson, Snider also found income to be unrelated to the high levels of satisfaction reported by his sample.

Finally, two studies concerning the institutionalization of older people indicate that even among those elderly whom many would consider worst off (namely, those in institutions), high levels of satisfaction are the norm. Using data collected in Manitoba, Myles (1979) studied whether institutionalization leads to isolation and disengagement of the residents. Comparing institutionalized individuals with older persons residing in the community, he discovered that those *in* the institutions interacted more with friends and neighbours and derived more satisfaction from these relationships than the noninstitutionalized (Myles, 1979). At a broader level, Chappell and Penning (1979) examined levels of overall well-being among three groups of older Manitobans: those living in the community, in subsidized housing for seniors and in care institutions. While they found that those living in the community reported the highest levels of well-being (65 percent rated good or excellent) and those in care institutions the lowest, the fact remains that a slim majority (51 percent) of the care institution residents also fall in the good to excellent categories.

In sum, these studies indicate that older people tend to perceive their lives in very positive terms. However, with the exception of Northcott's work, they do not provide much detail concerning the experience of older age as perceived by most older people, or of their concerns about aging. Indeed, their lack of detail could foster complacency about the situation of older people, because they appear to be so content with their lives. While these studies force us to question the validity of the negative stereotype, it remains necessary to obtain more information about the lives of older people, as perceived by them.

In an attempt to fill some of these gaps, I turn to data from my own study of 400 persons aged 65 and over. First, I examine the service use and needs of older persons living in the community in order to ascertain their more immediate or pressing concerns, concerns that can be addressed most readily by public policy. Second, I consider interview data about what older people like and dislike about being their age, and any worries they may have about further aging.

The London Community Study

In 1981 interviews were conducted with 400 community-dwelling Londoners aged 65 years of age and older.[1] A stratified random sample was employed in order to ensure that the sexes were represented according to their actual distribution in the population (40 percent male and 60 percent female) and that older age groups (85 and over) were overrepresented so that there would be large enough numbers for some statistical analysis. The sample was restricted to those living in the community, because the objective of the study is to create a comprehensive profile of aging as experienced by those who do not live in institutions. The sample thus represents over 90 percent of all persons aged 65 and over living in London. London (population: 265,000 at the time of interviewing) is a representative Canadian city and is, therefore, used extensively for marketing research (Vender, 1979; Dhalla, 1966). Thus, there is some basis for assuming that findings from this study will apply to cities in other parts of the country. At the same time, it should be noted that London tends to be somewhat better off economically and to have less of an ethnic mix than some other urban areas in Canada.

Potential respondents were first contacted by letter and then telephoned to seek their cooperation. Those who participated were interviewed in their homes for an average of one hour and forty-five minutes on a number of topics, including living arrangements (see Connidis, 1983a; Connidis and Rempel, 1983), health, well-being (see Connidis, 1984), work and retirement, familial relationships, friends, marriage and views on aging. The data, both quantitative and qualitative, complement one another (see Connidis, 1983a; 1983b). Additional qualitative data were obtained in interviews conducted by the author with a purposive sample of 40 of the original sample.

The Service Needs of Community-Dwelling Elders

An essential part of the negative stereotype of old age is the assumption that old age can be equated with dependency. At its worst this means institutionalization. In less severe cases, it means living at home while dependent on help from others to get through the essentials of daily living. There is limited documentation concerning the actual use of and need for services among older persons who live in the community. Several questions on the subject were included in the study (see Connidis, 1985). Respondents were asked: "Are there any community services from which you now receive help?" "Are there any community services from which you have received help in the past?" And, "Are there any services which you require but cannot find or cannot afford?" If respondents answered affirmatively they were asked which services applied.

Of the 400 respondents, 46 (12 percent) had used community services at some time in the past. These covered quite a broad range, including physiotherapists, meals-on-wheels and house-cleaning services. The service used most frequently was the homemaker service, which was needed for temporary, follow-up care after release from hospital.

Only 28 of the respondents (7 percent) were using any form of community service at the time of the interview. These included public health nurses, Victorian Order of Nurses, Homemaker Services and library services. As well, 15 individuals could not find services they required, one person could neither find nor afford a needed service and another could not afford a necessary service. This means that just over 4 percent of the sample are in need of a service they can either not find or not afford. There are some respondents who are currently using one or more services *and* require additional ones. Correcting for this duplication, we find that 9 percent of the older persons in this study need the support of a community service. This refutes the notion that being old is synonymous with dependency on formal social services.

It should be noted that a substantial proportion of those individuals initially contacted refused to participate in the study for reasons of poor health. This could have the effect of deflating the number of respondents who report the use of and need for community services. At the same time, the majority of those who refused to participate did so because they were "too busy," suggesting that these nonparticipants were healthier than average. It may be that the net effect of health ineligibles and preoccupied refusals is a fairly representative sample with respect to health. In a 1981 survey of Old Age Security recipients (Minister of Supply and Services, 1983:64-65) conducted by Health and Welfare, respondents reported service use as follows: meal services, 8 percent; special transportation services, 3.5 percent: homemaker, 4.3 percent; assistance for shopping or banking, 4.3 percent and nursing or other medical care at home, 3.7 percent. Because the proportion of respondents using more than one service is unknown, the amount of duplication cannot be computed and a direct comparison with the data reported here drawn. However, it does seem that both studies support the conclusion that the extent of service use and need is limited.

One can thus conclude that the majority of older Canadians are able to function without the aid of community services. However, it is essential to note two things. First, given the growing number of older people, expenditures for the maintenance of existing programs will escalate. Added to this is the need for *new* services to meet the needs of an older population. Recall that 4 percent of this sample could not find or afford a necessary service. Second, although the proportion of older citizens requiring formal support services is small, when the need is there it is often great, making several services essential if community dwelling is to continue.

Finally, when queried about the need for additional services for seniors, respondents highlight the salience of very basic support services. One woman of 65 noted the importance of services provided by the local Community Home Support Program saying, "I think it is a good idea, because it helps people stay at home." In her case, her husband was unable to perform household chores that involved lifting.

An 81-year-old man replied:

I wish that it was like the old days, where you could phone a doctor up and he would come out to see you. You have to be half dead before they will come. . . . They used to come when we were up north. They would drive for miles to see you if you had pinkeye. I know a doctor who drove fifteen miles to see you. That was their job. . . . And then they would come back tomorrow or the next day to see how you were getting on. . . . Yes, after a certain age I think they should come to you.

In this case, a once standard practice is seen as a route to improving the lives of older people. Another dying practice is mentioned by a woman aged 74:

I drove for meals-on-wheels for many years and I think that is a fine thing, but I think that even more important than meals-on-wheels would be some sort of a service so that you could get groceries. . .or just general shopping. A lot you can do by phone, but it is getting to the point where it is practically impossible to do any grocery shopping by phone. . . . This (respondent's apartment building) is kind of a halfway house to the undertaker's. . . . We have a great many old people who are just not able to get around. . .and it is very difficult to just get your ordinary groceries. . . . I don't think that there is anyone that doesn't want to feel that they are independent, and when you just simply can't get out on the street, it is really poor.

These comments highlight the importance of providing support for routine needs — household chores, grocery shopping, and medical care — if older people are to stay in their own homes. The general desire to do so is emphasized by a 67-year-old man: "I think that older people are much happier in their own homes, and I think that every provision should be made or any angle considered to leave the older people there who want to stay there as long as possible."

Apart from these suggestions, the overwhelming response when asked if any changes should be made in services for older people was no. Many comments were emphatic, as the following sampling illustrates: "I think the senior citizens are certainly being coddled" (woman of 75); "Personally, I think that older people have never been so well off as they are today. Today they are well looked after. They are provided with entertainment and a lot of things that older people never thought of having. . . . I think the old people are well looked after" (woman of 80); "I think myself, as far as Canadians are concerned, we have it made really. . . . I am of the firm opinion that Canadian old people — or retired people, I should say, as I don't think that I am old yet — but retired people in Canada are certainly well taken care of. . . I don't feel that people should have everything dropped in their lap. I think you have to work for what you want in this world, and if you don't work for it, then things shouldn't be basically quite as easy as they should be for some people who have worked for it and saved for it" (man of 68); "Older people never had it so good. It gripes me to hear people say, 'we want this, we want that.' You've got to earn things for yourself" (man of 70); and, "It seems to me that there is an awful lot being done to make life happier for seniors. Every time you pick up the paper there is something that is being done for them. What more do seniors want? Pretty soon they will not want to take care of themselves. . . . I think that seniors are treated wonderfully. I haven't got very much patience with the complainers" (woman of 84).

At the same time as making these claims, however, a number of respondents distinguished between the majority of older people and those in need. Thus, while speaking of "coddled" seniors the 75-year-old woman above notes that "on the other hand, if you are living on a fixed income it (reduced prices and benefits for seniors) is extremely important". Similarly, the woman of 80 who believes the elderly are "well looked after" also observes, "I think that some of those government subsidies for old people are ridiculous. . . A lot of government projects could be done with a lot less funds if they were only done for the people that need them. . . I wouldn't go back to the old days, where you had absolutely nothing or you weren't subject to the old-age pension, for instance." Similarly, the 70-year-old man above noted that there was too much for some seniors and not enough for others. He believed that for those who lost everything in the Depression and consequently could not save for the future, subsidies, reduced fares and other seniors' benefits were a good thing. Finally, a man of 66 is clearly disconcerted by the stark contrast between the poverty of some elderly persons and our wealthy society:

There are always improvements needed for the needy. Social gatherings for people who can afford to go places is nothing to be improved. . .but people in need — there is always room for a big improvement. . . . I don't like to see people along the street just waiting for the end. You can see that. That is miserable. That is a pity. The old sitting there in front of a bank or something — it is a shame — just waiting. Because they haven't got a dime, but that shouldn't be. Not in a country like this. This is one of the richest — we have everything — and there are no reasons for anyone to be poor in this country. Nobody.

In addition to distinguishing between different levels of need, some respondents noted different interests among seniors in similar circumstances. For example, a female respondent of 75 said: "I am not interested in going to senior citizens' groups and playing cards. It drives me up the wall. . . . Some people find amusement in certain ways and others aren't interested. . . I think that senior citizens' groups are marvellous for some people, but as far as I am concerned, I couldn't care less." This woman draws our attention to the diversity among old people, a diversity that has direct policy implications concerning service provision for the elderly.

In summary, while we observe that the vast majority of older persons do not require services at a given point in time, those who do may have multiple-service needs and limited finances. It is also interesting to observe the impact of past experience. Several respondents appear to assess the current situation of older people in a historical context, concluding that older people "never had it so good." Upcoming generations will have acquired a different set of expectations for old age and may be less likely to evaluate circumstances similar to those of the present older generation in such positive terms.

The Pros, Cons and Worries of Aging: The View of Older People

We turn now to consider the observations of the London sample on the assets and liabilities of their age and their concerns about growing older. This exploration provides a basis for forming a more realistic picture of older age as actually experienced by older individuals. In considering those things that respondents like and dislike about their age it is possible to assess the relative appropriateness of the negative and positive views of aging.

Respondents were asked: "At each stage of life there are usually some things that people like about being the age they are. What do you like about being your age? By this I mean the things you think are good about this stage of your life and the things you enjoy about being the age you are now." The corresponding question about dislikes was: "Each stage of life has its troubles and problems. What things do you dislike about being your age? By this I mean the things you find difficult about this stage of your life, the problems you may have at the age you are now and the ways other people treat you that you don't like." For both questions, interviewers were instructed to probe for additional information. Concerning worries, respondents were asked: "When you look ahead, are there any worries or concerns you have about growing older?" Respondents who answered yes were asked; "What are they?"

In the second interview with the subsample of 40, individuals made comments pertinent to this discussion, as well. These were sometimes in direct response to questions such as: "Do you feel you have changed as you have grown older?" or, "Are there any other things you think we should talk about?" They sometimes merely arose in the course of conversation. The following discussion is based upon responses to the three questions answered by all 400 respondents in the first interview, and comments made in the second interview.

The vast majority of the respondents — 90 percent — like something about their stage of life. The remaining 10 percent claim to like nothing about their age, with some saying they preferred being younger. In contrast, 34 percent of the sample state that there is nothing they dislike about being their age, and 62 percent say they have no worries about growing older. While men and women are similar in their propensity to like and dislike aspects of old age, women (44 percent versus 28 percent of men) more often voice worries about growing older, which may be a function of their greater likelihood of doing so. These findings suggest that older people are more inclined to focus on the positive aspects of aging.

The fact that 10 percent of the sample like nothing about being their age is disturbing. Analysis was conducted to determine what distinguishes those who like various facets of aging from those who do not. The two groups differed significantly in age, expectations and self-assessed health. Thirty percent of those 85 and over report there is nothing they like, compared to 5 percent of those aged 65 to 74 and 12 percent of those 75-84. They more often state that their stage of life is worse than they had expected it to be, while those who like something about their age claim it is better than or similar to what they had anticipated. Finally, 35 percent of those who assessed their health as poor like nothing about their age, compared to 6 percent of those with good or excellent health. These findings suggest that it is only when one reaches very old age, experiences health problems and finds expectations of older age are not met that the negative stereotype of older age applies. For the remainder, old age has positive aspects.

Indeed, there are a number of things older people like about being their age. Because many respondents (22 percent) mentioned more than one positive aspect of older age, the unit of analysis is responses rather than individuals for this discussion. The features of older age that respondents enjoy are listed in column 1 of Table 1. An appreciation for the increased freedom and relaxation due to decreased responsibility and worry that accompany older age is readily apparent in over half of all comments that fit this category. Respondents noted that there were fewer obligations and more time for engaging in chosen pursuits. Women were more inclined to mention freedom from familial obligations, while men more often emphasized the autonomy of retirement, a difference that reflects the division of labour by sex more typical of this age group. This opportunity to pursue objectives unencumbered by children and work distinguishes old age from earlier stages. As well, perceived freedom is frequently a function of the self-confidence that accompanies the maturity of older age. In the words of a 65-year-old man: "I feel I don't have to worry about making impressions. I can be myself." Thus, one of the *unique* aspects of older age is also a positive one.

The general contentment of older age is described by a man of 68 in the second interview:

Your life is not as cluttered when you are older, because you are going more of an even pace. . . . I never think about my age. When I was 65

TABLE 1:
Percentage Distribution of Respondents' Likes, Dislikes and Worries of Older Age (Unit = Responses)

LIKES	%	DISLIKES	%	WORRIES	%
Greater Freedom; Fewer Worries	53	Physical Effects	60	Poor Health and Its Effects	69
— General freedom; reduced responsibilities	(24)[4]	— Limits on Activities	(28)[4]	— Health	(34)[4]
— Freedom from work	(14)	— Poor Health	(19)	— Dependency	(23)
— Freedom from familial responsibility	(5)	— Physical Restrictions	(13)	— Institutionalization/ Giving Up Home	(12)
— Reduced Pressure	(9)	Concerns: Health of Spouse/Impact of Widowhood/ Being Alone/Dependency	9	Being Alone/ Loss of Spouse	9

Old age pension; Financial security	9	Short Time Left/Getting Older	8	Worries About Spouse	7
General contentment/ satisfaction	8	Treatment by Others	7	Finances/Expenses	6
Good health	7	Other[2]	16	Death/Limited Time Left	5
Family	7			Other[3]	4
Respect from others	5				
Other[1]	11				
Total	100.0 (n = 444)		100.0 (n = 278)		100.0 (n = 195)

1   Includes any item accounting for less than 5% of all responses. Of greatest frequency are: friends (11), reminiscing and good memories (9), and maturity (7).

2   Includes any item accounting for less than 5% of all responses. Of greatest frequency are: not working (10), loss of others (10), and financial situation (7).

3   Includes any item accounting for less than 5% of all responses. Of greatest frequency is: not wanting to live any longer (3).

4   Percentages in parentheses are subcategories and should not be included when calculating the total.

my wife said, "How does it feel to be 65?" And I said, "The same as when I turned 40." I remember when I cried when I hit 40. I actually cried, you know. But if anything, the quality of your life is going to be that much greater, because if you have matured going through life, you are just going to love people more and understand more. And all the little things, the things that are so, well, tremendously important sometimes — and shattering — when you are young? When you are older you just sort of know that you are going to go right through it. You know, it is very pleasant from that sense. It is great. I love being alive and being old.

For this man, past experience is a basis for a more relaxed approach to life. This comment exemplifies the 8 percent of all responses that referred to the general contentment and satisfaction of old age. Women were twice as likely as men to make such comments. Men more often commented on good health and the pleasure of "having lived this long." This may reflect their awareness of their shorter life expectancy.

Surprisingly, 9 percent of the comments related to financial security and receipt of the old-age pension as benefits of older age. This may reflect the fact that Londoners, as a group, are relatively well-off. However, it may also be a function of receiving a form of financial assistance that older people can remember was once nonexistent.

Finally, 7 percent of the responses indicate that family is a major source of pleasure in old age. The satisfaction takes two forms. In the first, older people enjoy witnessing their children as successful adults. Speaking of her children, a 66-year-old woman says: "I can sit and listen to them talking, and feel a pride in them, because I see the way that they have grown. I see the characters that they have developed and things like that. It makes me feel good inside. And I think to myself, I was a part of all that, you know."

In the second form, respondents enjoy the additional time they can spend with family members. Speaking of her husband's relationship with their children, another woman of 67 observes:

I would have liked him to have been more involved with them, and I find that he is more involved with the grandchildren. He plays ball with his grandchildren, and he never would have played ball with his own sons. And he fishes with one little grandson who loves to fish. But I think that it is because his life is more relaxed now. He has the time, not only the physical time, but the mental relaxation enough to enjoy this now, where he couldn't before, you know. Because he was too tired.

The things respondents dislike about older age are summarized in column 2 of Table 1. Recalling that only two-thirds of the sample expressed any dislikes, it remains striking that 60 percent of the comments concern the physical effects of aging. Although both sexes dislike the physical effects of aging, women are more concerned about poor health, while men are more inclined to emphasize physical restrictions, often due to declining strength.

Another striking difference between men and women is their level of concern about dealing with the future versus having one. Men (12 percent) focus more than women (6 percent) on getting older and the short time left, while women (14 percent) emphasize the potential and actual problems of coping alone more than men (1 percent). Related to the dislike of there being a short time left is the feeling that there is little left to look forward to.

> The other stages (of my life) were more satisfying, you know, because you felt that you were useful and you were accomplishing something, and now, as I say, I am just burning life's tape at the close. . . . I can recall — this is probably quite a few years ago — when there were advances to look forward to with such great anticipation. You think, "Oh, no, I can't wait for the day when that event will take place." Quite simple things, probably. And, you know, now I can't think of any event that I look forward to with that anticipation. I suppose that after you have seen and done so many things, why it becomes an old story (woman aged 65).

Another dislike of older age discussed by 20 respondents (7 percent of all responses) is the way older people are treated by others. A man of 76 dislikes "the fact that some people have the tendency to discount your ideas as being too far over the hill. They think you're living in the past". A woman of 67 claims, "People are less tolerant of old people and sometimes judgmental of their liabilities," while another aged 81 says, "I resent people saying, 'We know what's best for you.' "

These comments are in marked contrast to those of 22 respondents who said that respect from others was one of the things they *liked* about being their age (see column 1, Table 1). A 76-year-old woman likes "the way people treat me. People are very kind and helpful to me." Another woman, aged 84, finds, "Everybody seems to like you. Babies smile at you and people help you." A 78-year-old woman enjoys "the little favours shown old people, like opening doors, letting me on the bus first, little kindnesses, especially from younger people. My grandchildren have me on a pedestal, and I love that." It is difficult to know whether this discrepancy is based on differences in actual experience or differences in perception.

The worries about aging expressed by those respondents (38 percent) who claimed to have some are listed in column 3 of Table 1. They are quite similar to those aspects of older age respondents dislike. Hence, 69 percent of the comments describe concern about future poor health and its implications. An additional 9 percent of the responses denote worry about losing one's spouse and being alone, and another 7 percent express apprehension about the health of spouses and their future welfare if widowed. Men and women share the same general worries, although women are more likely to worry about becoming dependent. Again, this may be related to the experience or anticipation of widowhood.

Although poor health is a major worry, death tends not to be. Regarding the nature of death, a 74-year-old woman made the following observation during the second interview: "I think that people worry so much about older people, about finding them dead in their apartments. I don't think that bothers the older people at all. I think that the younger people are feeling guilty about it, and that is the difficulty." However, for another woman of 79, "no one finding me after I die" is a key concern, demonstrating once more the diversity among older people.

Only 12 respondents (6 percent of all responses regarding worries) express any anxiety about their future financial situation. This was unanticipated, especially among women, who so often experience economic hardship in old age.

In summary, a much larger proportion of older individuals in this study like aspects of being their age rather than dislike features of their age. A surprising majority also report having no worries about growing older. This suggests that older people tend to take a positive view of their stage of life. There appear to be some unique elements of older age that are enjoyed by older individuals: reduced responsibility, greater freedom and maturity gained from experience.

At the same time, large numbers of the sample document some negative aspects of older age, most notably failing health, physical decline and the consequences of dependency and widowhood that often follow. This indicates an awareness of the very real setbacks that may accompany older age. In short, older people tend to combine a positive view of their stage of life with a realistic grasp of its detriments.

Conclusion

The preceding discussion has presented a picture of aging based on the actual experiences and perceptions of older people. A key objective in doing so was to offset reliance on either a positive or negative stereotype as an accurate portrayal of aging. Some researchers have argued that acceptance of a negative stereotype can be functional for older people, who can consider themselves advantaged relative to the poor expectations of old age which such stereotypes establish (see e.g., Bultena and Powers, 1978; Kearl, 1981-82). The comments by several respondents in this study make such an assertion questionable. For example, a woman of 71 says, "I don't like to be classed as a 'senior citizen' — a part of a group. I feel I'm an individual. Getting fom 69 to 70 was very traumatic. It really bothered me. I know I always felt people who were 70 were old — so I felt terrible.''

In the close of her article about positive stereotypes of aging Davis (1980:588) concludes:

> In brief, when a person faces a crisis, false assurance does not diminish anxiety or aid performance. Neither is excessive overconcern with the total details of possible morbid outcomes helpful. Such excessively graphic descriptions may also arouse fears of incomprehensible proportions. The manner most conducive to adequate coping is: (1) confront the crisis — recognize the realities, (2) confront the crisis in manageable doses — take respite as needed, (3) locate the facts — the unknown is more frightening than the known, (4) don't blame others, (5) accept help from others.

In many respects this logic can be extended to the societal level. In order to overcome the problems of aging and an older population we must first recognize what they are. However, just as individuals should avoid "excessive overconcern," so, too, there is a point at which emphasizing the problems of aging can make them appear so overwhelming as to be insurmountable. Barring total revolution, society, too, must deal with an aging population in "manageable doses," accepting responsibility for the problems its policies have often created and offering solutions for the actual problems confronted by substantial numbers of older Canadians. Finally, researchers and practitioners have a role to play in providing the facts about aging, positive and negative, in order to inform future policy directives in the private and public sectors.

Note

[1] In order to obtain a total of 400 completed interviews, we attempted to contact 983 persons, drawing randomly selected matched (by age and sex) cases as needed. We could not contact 182 of these persons. Of the 801 contacted persons, 26 (3.2 percent) were ineligible due to language and 142 (17.7 percent) were deemed ineligible for health reasons. The latter category includes 107 refusing the interview for reasons of their own health, 25 for spouse's or other family member's health, 6 incomplete interviews and one sudden illness. There remained 633 eligible contacted persons, of whom 233, or 36.8 percent refused and 400, or 63.2 percent responded. While the loss of cases through nonresponse and ineligibles is most unfortunate, its extent is comparable to other surveys in Canada (see e.g., Chappell, 1983; Marshall, Rosenthal and Synge, 1983; and for a discussion, Marshall, 1984).

References

Altheide, D.L. and J.M. Johnson
  1980   *Bureacratic Propaganda.* Boston: Allyn and Bacon.
Atkinson, Tom
  1980   "Public perceptions on the quality of life." *Perspectives Canada III.* Ottawa: Minister of Supply and Services Canada, 277-292.
Bassili, John N. and Jane E. Reil
  1981   "On the dominance of the old-age stereotype." *Journal of Gerontology* 36(6):682-688.
Bultena, Gordon L. and Edward A. Powers
  1978   "Denial of aging: Age identification reference group orientations." *Journal of Gerontology* 33(5):748-754.
Chappell, Neena L.
  1983   "Informal support networks among the elderly." *Research on Aging* 50(1):77-79.
Chappell, Neena L. and Margaret J. Penning
  1979   "The trend away from institutionalization: Humanism or economic efficiency?" *Research on Aging* 1(3):361-387.
Connidis, Ingrid
  1981   "The stigmatizing effects of a problem orientation to aging research." *Canadian Journal of Social Work Education* 7(2):9-19.
  1983a "Living arrangement choices of older residents: Assessing quantitative results with qualitative data." *Canadian Journal of Sociology* 8(4):359-375.
  1983b "Integrating qualitative and quantitative methods in survey research on aging: An assessment." *Qualitative Sociology* 6(4):334-352.
  1984   "The construct validity of the Life Satisfaction Index A and Affect Balance Scales: A serendipitous analysis." *Social Indicators Research* 15:117-129.
  1985   "The service needs of older people: Implications for public policy." *Canadian Journal on Aging* 5(1):3-10.
Connidis, Ingrid and Judith Rempel
  1983   "The Living Arrangements of Older Residents: The Role of Gender, Marital Status, Age, and Family Size." *Canadian Journal on Aging* 2(3):91-105.
Davis, Ann E.
  1980   "Whoever said life begins at 40 was a fink or, those golden years — phooey." *International Journal of Women's Studies* 3(6):583-589.
Dhalla, N.
  1966   *These Canadians.* Toronto: McGraw-Hill.
Gardner, Bonny
  1977   "Rethinking Services for the Elderly." An occasional paper for the Center for Social Work Research, School of Social Work, University of Texas at Austin.
Holtzman, J.M. and J.D. Beck
  1979   "Palmore's Facts on Aging Quiz: A reappraisal." *The Gerontologist* 19(1):116-120.

Kearl, Michael C.
  1981- "An inquiry into the positive personal and social effects of old-age
  82   stereotypes among the elderly." *International Journal of Aging and Human
         Development* 14(4):277-290.
Marshall, Victor W.
  1984   "Sampling Issues in Surveys of Aging and Intergenerational Relations."
         Prepared for the symposium Methodological Issues in the Study of Aging
         and Intergenerational Relations, Gerontology Research Centre, University of
         Guelph, Guelph, Ontario, June 7.
Marshall, Victor W., Carolyn Rosenthal and Jane Synge
  1983   "Concerns about parental health." Chapter 11, Pp. 253-273 in Elizabeth W.
         Markson (ed.), *Older Women*. Toronto: D.C. Heath.
Martin Matthews, Anne, Joseph A. Tindale and Joan E. Norris
  1984   "The Facts on Aging Quiz: A Canadian validation and cross-cultural com-
         parison." *Canadian Journal on Aging* 3(4):165-174.
Matthews, Sarah H.
  1979   *The Social World of Old Women: Management of Self-Identity*. Beverly
         Hills: Sage.
Minister of Supply and Services
  1983   *Fact Book on Aging in Canada*. 2nd Canadian Conference on Aging, Oc-
         tober 24-27, 1983, Ottawa.
Myles, John F.
  1979   "Institutionalization and disengagement among the elderly." *Canadian
         Review of Sociology and Anthropology* 16(2):171-182.
Norris, Joan E., Joseph A. Tindale and Anne Martin Matthews
         "Psychometric Properties of the Facts on Aging Quiz." Unpublished.
Northcott, Herbert C.
  1982   "The best years of your life." *Canadian Journal on Aging* 1(3&4):72-78.
Novak, Mark
  1983   "Discovering a good age." *International Journal of Aging and Human
         Development* 16(3):231-239.
Ogmundson, Richard
  1982   "Good news and Canadian sociology." *Canadian Journal of Sociology*
         7(1):73-78.
Palmore, Erdman
  1977   "Facts on Aging: A short quiz." *The Gerontologist* 17:315-320.
  1979   "Advantages of aging." *The Gerontologist* 19(2):220-223.
  1980   "The Facts on Aging Quiz: A review of findings." *The Gerontologist*
         20:669-672.
  1981   "Facts on Aging Quiz: Part two." *The Gerontologist* 21(4):431-437.
  1982   "Attitudes toward the aged: What we know and what we need to know."
         Research on Aging 4(3):333-348.
Romeis, James C. and Marvin B. Sussman
  1982   "Cross-cultural differences on the facts on Ageing Quiz: Additional com-
         ments on age bias." *Ageing and Society* 2(Part 3):357-370.

Schonfield, David

  1982   "Who is stereotyping whom and why?" *The Gerontologist* 22(3):267-272.

Schwenger, Cope W.

  1982   "Professionalization of health care for the aged." *Canadian Journal on Aging* 1(1 and 2):66-71.

Snider, Earle L.

  1980   "Explaining life satisfaction: It's the elderly's attitudes that count." *Social Science Quarterly* 61(2):253-263.

Vender, Eric

  1979   "Columbus Helps Merchandizers Discover America, We Guide Them to Canada." London, Ontario: *London Free Press* (October 13).

23

The Health of Very Old People as a Concern of Their Children

Victor W. Marshall
Department of Behavioural Science
University of Toronto

Aging may be considered at many different levels. At the level of the population we speak of the "greying of nations" to refer to an increase in the proportion of the population falling into the later years and a rise in the average age of the population. In the Western industrial societies and beyond them in the relatively nonindustrialized societies, population aging is reflected in an increased proportion of people living not just to the age of 60 or 65 and beyond, but into the late seventies and eighties. At the level of the individual, the phenomenon of population aging means that many people are finding they have lived beyond the time they thought they would.

In this chapter I explore some of the implications of population aging and of the fact of individual longevity as these come together in the context of the family. Aging, it might be said, is a "family affair." Any individual grows older in the context of one or more other family members — a spouse, parents, children, grandchildren and so forth — who are growing older at the same time. To consider aging in the family context introduces additional complexity to any analysis, but this complexity is required in order to understand many aspects of aging.

The particular interest of this chapter is the implications for family members of health changes, or the increasing likelihood of health changes, as some family members enter very advanced age.

The Health of the Old and of the Very Old

If more and more people are living to be very old, then people must be, on the whole, healthier than in former years. The general pattern is that people re-

Data from the Generational Relations and Succession Project described in this paper were gathered under grant no. 492-79-0076-R1 from the Social Sciences and Humanities Research Council of Canada; V.W. Marshall, C.J. Rosenthal and J. Synge, investigators. Additional support has been provided by the Gerontology Research Council of Ontario to C.J. Rosenthal and me. In addition, I am grateful for support as a National Health Research Scientist by Health and Welfare Canada and for an award from the Laidlaw Foundation. An earlier version of this chapter was published in French (Marshall, 1983).

main quite healthy and vigorous into their seventies, but that many people become quite frail late in their lives. This is apparent in the greatly increased rates of institutionalization within the age 65 plus category, in utilization data and in surveys of the aged in their communities. My objective in this chapter is not to describe the health status of the aged in detail, but only to overview the age and sex differences within the aged group within a demographic framework.

Institutionalization of the aged in Canada is high compared to any other jurisdiction in the world, with the sole exception of the Netherlands. We institutionalize over 8 percent of our age 65 plus population, and 39 percent of our age 85 plus population (Large, 1981). Institutionalization is related to the fact that women usually outlive men. Using a definition of "collective dwelling," which is broader than the concept "institution" and which includes not only nursing homes and hospitals, but any dwelling of an institutional, commercial or communal nature in which ten or more persons unrelated to the household head dwell, Fletcher and Stone (1981, and Chapter 16 of this volume) show that increases in the propensity to live in such a household occur earlier for females than for males. This is because, no doubt, so many of the females are widowed, with no one to care for them at home. Moreover, children are not always available or, if available, not always willing to provide a home for an aged parent. People in their eighties and nineties often have children who themselves are in or about to enter the later years.

There are now several community studies in various parts of Canada that show age differences in health status. The overall pattern of these studies is remarkably similar. These are interview studies conducted in the community, and exclude both those institutionalized and a large number of people in the community who might be too ill to be interviewed. They therefore exaggerate the good health and underreport the health problems of the community-dwelling aged (Streib, 1983).

Tilquin et al (1980) of the University of Montreal interviewed over 2,000 people on the South Shore of the St. Lawrence near Montreal, and asked if they required partial or total help with the following five Activities of Daily Living (ADL) items: rising and going to bed, daily personal hygiene, walking around inside the house, bathing, and shopping in summer. The proportion reporting a need for some assistance with at least one of these activities was just 16 percent for those aged 65-69, but rose to 33 percent for those aged 75 and over.

Dr. Ronald Cape (1980), in a community study in London, Ontario, and the rural counties of Grey and Bruce, asked the same type of question for four activities: dressing, walking indoors, bathing and climbing stairs. His sample size was 385 persons over age 65. The proportion unable to perform at least one of these four activities was just 5.5 percent for those aged 65-69, rising to 35.5 percent for those aged 85 or more. In Cape's study there was a great increase in need for assistance after the age of 85, because while 35.5 percent in that category reported need for assistance with at least one of the four items, only 9.4 percent of respondents aged 80-84 did so. Cape's data are roughly comparable to those of Tilquin and associates on corresponding items. He finds, overall, less disability, because he did not ask, as did Tilquin and associates, about the ability to shop in summer, an activity that requires both energy to walk and ability to lift parcels.

Other studies, in British Columbia, Manitoba, Kingston and Hamilton, using some of the same items and some different ones, come up with roughly the same results: on various individual items 1 to 5 percent of people over the age of 65 and living in the community will report that they need assistance with some activity of daily living, and for older respondents, especially over the age of 85, the proportions may rise to over 10 percent on individual items. The proportion requiring help with *at least one* activity of daily living can rise to between 30 and 50 percent (see Gutman, 1980; Marshall, Rosenthal and Synge, 1983).

The items used on these various versions of the ADL Scales are mundane. They refer to everyday necessities: the ability to get dressed, to prepare and eat meals, to go to the toilet or to bathe, the very ability to get up and walk around one's house. They measure a need for help, and in every instance, they measure help received from some individual or some health or social-service institution. If it is a male who reports these needs for assistance, the chances are reasonably good that the assistance is in fact being provided by a spouse — a spouse who keeps better health for five years or more longer, on average, than her husband (Havens, 1980). If it is a female who reports this need for assistance, the chances are that there is no husband alive to provide it, and she must look elsewhere for help (Marshall, Rosenthal and Synge, 1983).

Another indication of the patterns of health changes by age and sex is found in data from the Generational Relations and Succession Project, which was conducted in Hamilton and Stoney Creek, Ontario, in 1986 (see also the data reported by Rosenthal, Chapter 17 of this volume). This study is based on interviews with a stratified random sample of 468 persons aged 40+, with roughly equal numbers of males and females in the three age groups 40-54, 55-69 and 70+.

We asked respondents: "Is there any physical condition, illness or health problem that bothers you *now*?" The proportion of males replying that there was rose from 38 percent of men in their forties to 64 percent of men aged 80 or more. For females, the proportion reporting such a condition rose from 44 percent in their forties to fully 85 percent of those in their eighties or older. The vast majority of respondents referred to their condition as chronic (see Table 1).

More important, however, than reporting a health problem is finding that

TABLE 1:
Selected Health Indicators, by Age and Sex,
of Initial Interview Respondents (Parents)

		Age Group: Percent Falling in Response Category					
		40-49	**50-59**	**60-69**	**70-79**	**80+**	**Row Total**
See health as	m	10	27	32	36	50	29
fair to poor	f	17	26	42	37	42	32
Health now	m	15	20	16	30	50	23
worse than 3 years ago	f	22	27	22	20	46	25
Physical condition	m	38	52	63	63	64	55
or illness now	f	44	62	67	75	85	65
Health problem stands in way:							
a great	m	5	15	18	36	29	20
deal	f	9	13	20	18	42	18
not at	m	75	61	50	41	21	54
all	f	70	57	49	47	27	53
5 or more days	m	5	14	13	16	29	14
hospital in past year	f	0	6	4	19	23	10
Needs help over	m	0	5	3	9	36	7
long period due to illness	f	0	6	9	4	19	6
No. of Males		40	66	38	56	14	214
No. of Females		46	68	45	57	26	242

Missing observations: 12

Within each sex, increasing age is significantly related to lowered health status, at the .05 level or usually well beyond, using Tau C.

problem interfering with one's ability to do as one likes. We asked: "How much do health problems stand in the way of your doing the things you want to do. . .not at all, only a little, or a great deal?" For men, the proportion saying, "A great deal," tripled from 5 to 18 percent between the forties and the sixties, then doubled again to 36 percent in the seventies. For women, the proportion replying yes fluctuated between 9 and 20 percent in the decades of the forties through the seventies. The big jump in perceived interference with activities due to a health problem came only in their eighties. Whereas just 18 percent of women in their seventies said there was a great deal of interference, the proportion rose to 42 percent for those in their eighties.

When we asked: "Are you yourself currently in a position where you *usually* need help over a *long period of time* because of your health?" we found a similar pattern. For males, the large increase in the proportion saying they required such continuous, regular help rose from 9 percent for those in their seventies to 36 percent for those in their eighties. Less than 20 percent of women in their eighties said they required such help.

In all these community studies, it must be stressed that the very ill are usually not interviewed. The state of our information concerning the health of the elderly is that we have a great deal of information on the institutionalized, a modest amount of information on the well elderly at home in the community, and virtually no information about people in the community who are not well. American studies suggest that while about 5 percent of people over the age of 65 are homebound and cannot leave their homes without assistance, about 2 percent of the elderly, or 40 percent of the homebound, are also bedfast and cannot leave their beds without assistance (Shanas, 1980). Because it is the very old, and not those in their sixties or early seventies, who are most likely to be bedfast, homebound, or in some more minor way dependent upon others, the demographic implications are again quite clear: the highest dependency group is also the one that is increasing at the greatest rate as a component of our population.

It is quite obviously ridiculous to talk about "the aged," referring to all people over the age of 65. Just as obvious, it is ridiculous and even a bit dangerous to use a cavalier distinction between the so-called young-old and the old-old, if this is defined on the basis of age alone. That distinction, increasingly used in research reports and everyday parlance by people in the aging field, is not useful, because the older population does not divide up so cleanly. Analysing the aging in a Manitoba survey of unmet needs of the elderly, Havens (1980:221) found that if two categories were used to break up the older population, sex differences were very important, and the cutting point would have to be at age 85 for females but age 80 for males, in order to classify people usefully in terms of unmet needs for health and social services and economic, social and cultural supports. She says: "This contrast calls attention to and warns the researcher that age-category analysis should be expanded to age/sex category analysis in order to be adequate." Needless to say, the same injunction applies to those planning or delivering any kind of services to the elderly.

With the patterns of health decline, a new buzz word has entered the professional vocabulary: the "frail elderly." We point with pride to the healthy aged and to the ability of people to maintain active and vigorous lives into their seventies and even in many cases into their eighties. But the ordinary state of health for most people towards the very end of their lives is frailty, if not fragility. With better nutrition, housing and health care, we have produced a great victory over disease and death. The result has been to place the locus of needs later in the life cycle than it has been before. Who is to meet these needs? The answer to that question will involve a consideration of the family.

Family Support

The demographic changes that have produced our current age structure, with its high proportion of old and very old people, have concomitantly affected the family situations of those entering the later years. It is important to understand the general nature of the family situation of the aged and its variability, because American studies (on which I draw in the absence of comparable Canadian information) suggest that perhaps 70 to 80 percent of the assistance received by the aged does not come from the formal service sector. The majority of health and social-support services provided to the elderly come from family, friends and neighbours (Brody, 1978:18; Comptroller General, 1977; Maddox, 1979; Shanas et al., 1968:428-9; Tobin and Kulys, 1980).

We are moving increasingly towards a situation where families will have a fragile structure in terms of ability to provide support. We often now have not just one, but two generations in retirement.

The childbearing experiences of women who are now in their seventies, and the hard core of our elderly, were such that they had on average 2.8 to 2.9 children. If the first child were a son, because of the difference by sex in mortality and longevity, there is an 18 percent chance the mother will outlive the son (Neugarten, 1978). With an average of less than three children, it must be remembered that some women had no children. About 10 percent of women never marry and 14 percent have no children, so that about 18 percent or so of people over the age of 65 are found to have no children alive. Any claim that the needs of the aged should be met in whole or in part by their children should bear in mind that many older people have no children.

Nor is it clear, in any case, that older people or people in general wish to have to rely on children. In our Hamilton study, we asked a number of questions about people's feelings concerning the obligations of family members to one another. For 404 respondents over the age of 40, we found that 45 percent disagreed either a little or a lot with the statement "It is the obligation of grown children to take care of their elderly parents." Men and women in the age range 55-70, who are most likely to be providing such care or to have already done so, were most likely to disagree. Half the men and two-thirds of the women in this age range disagreed that childen have this obligation, and about a third disagreed strongly.

About three-fourths of all respondents and four-fifths of men over the age of 70 agreed that "It usually doesn't work out too well for older people to live with their children and grandchildren." We asked if people agreed with the statement "When parents get older, their children should help support them if they need it." Endorsement of this view was far from enthusiastic. Just 23 percent said they "agree a lot" with that sentiment, 46 percent "agree a little," 17 percent "disagree a little" and 12 percent said they "disagree a lot."

These are value statements and they are abstract for most of our respondents. However, one-third of our respondents were over the age of 70, with another third between the ages of 55 and 69. On many of these value statements the youngest and oldest respondents are roughly equal in moderate levels of support for statements endorsing responsibility of children to aged parents. On most of the items, however, respondents in the middle group, and especially the women who are most likely to be somewhat hard pressed in actually feeling and taking such responsibility, show less enthusiastic support for statements about their obligations to parents. This is not to say that such support is withheld; rather, it points to the fact that there seems to be some feeling of being overburdened or overtaxed, especially among women in their late fifties and sixties.

I have focussed on the issue of support from children because of the demographic situation that suggests that those most in need will be very old widows, with no husbands to care for them. From a structural point of view, given the differential between men and women in mortality and life expectancy, it is not reasonable for women to count on their husbands for help in their later years. At the age of 65, 80 percent of men but only 55 percent of women in our sample are still married and living with spouse. Of people aged 70 or more, 67 percent of men but only 31 percent of women are still married.

There is now no longer any question about the willingness of family members to care for one another. Much research has shown that, where the older person has family, help will be forthcoming almost all the time. However, from a purely structural or demographic point of view, the family will often be nonexistent or under considerable strain in its ability to care for its very old members (see Rosenthal, Chapter 17 of this volume).

About three out of four people over the age of 65 have grandchildren, making them members of three-generation families, and about 40 percent have great-grandchildren, making them members of four-generation families. Increasingly, the family of the older person is multi-levelled (Shanas, 1981). But the number of persons at any one level varies considerably and, compared to earlier eras, is smaller in number. Structurally, then, we have a long and thin family, which is in many instances fragile. Two of these levels might themselves be in the retirement years, with the economic constraints common among the retired. Or the second or third oldest level might consist in some instances of what has been called the "caught generation," sandwiched between one or two older generations and their own children and perhaps even grandchildren, still concerned about launching their children and emptying their nest, while increasingly concerned about the health status or the economic status of their parents, parents-in-law and a grandparent or two.[1]

Looking at the services that are in place to meet the social and health needs of the aged, the Canadian situation must be somewhat like that of the Americans: we must rely on the informal support system — family, friends and neighbours — for 70 to 80 percent of our care. If this is so, and given the fragility of the family structure of so many of our old people, then the informal support network, including as its most important component the family, must be sorely overtaxed. Nonetheless, data from our research in Hamilton, Canada, do suggest that the family is willing, if not always able, to provide support for its very old family members as they increasingly suffer deficits in their health status.

Worries About the Health of the Parent

In one sense the family can be seen as a set of structured relationships of concern or worry. Mothers of young children watch over them and monitor their health. No one knows better the health of a person than does that person's spouse. And there is a point at which even quite young children become aware that their parents are not always healthy. As children grow older, they watch their parents age and, ultimately, die. Little attention has been given by investigators in the health field to the phenomenology of concerns about health in a family context; yet the family is undoubtedly the single most important context in which health care is provided.

Of respondents with living children, about a third claimed to have received help from at least one child in a time of health crisis over the previous ten years. Health crisis help was not patterned by age or sex. Help of a more ongoing nature for routine or chronic health problems was, however, patterned by age and sex. Of those who claimed to require such long-term help, about a quarter are in their seventies and another 30 percent are aged 80 or more.

Turning to reports from the children of our interview respondents (gathered by mailed questionnaire), 20 percent of children who had parents in their sixties or seventies said they had provided help with personal care in a time of illness to the parent we had interviewed, but 46 percent of children with parents aged 80 or older reported having done so. Mothers were more likely to be the recipients of this help (31 percent) than were fathers (21 percent).

I would like to focus, however, on a dimension of family life to which less attention has been given, namely the feelings of worry or concern that children have about health changes in their parents. We asked the children of our interview respondents the question "How much do you worry about problems that might arise in the future should your parent become seriously

TABLE 2:
Concerns About Parent's Future Health,
by Age and Sex of Child and of Parent

How much do you worry about problems that might arise in the future should your parent become seriously ill or unable to look after himself or herself. Would you say. . .

	Not At All		Only A little		A Great Deal		Row Total	
	son	daugh	son	daugh	son	daugh	son	daugh
Age of Child*								
50+	16	25	37	14	47	61	19	28
40-49	15	18	39	46	46	36	33	50
30-39	30	7	51	53	20	40	61	73
less than 30	21	14	52	49	27	37	89	148
	45	42	97	139	60	118	202	299
Age of Parent**	moth	fath	moth	fath	moth	fath	moth	fath
80+	30	17	20	33	50	50	30	18
70-79	18	9	48	44	34	47	44	57
60-69	23	11	42	68	35	21	66	38
50-59	21	13	45	55	34	32	104	101
40-49	17	27	50	55	33	18	36	11
N =	60	28	120	118	100	79	280	225

* The relationship without controlling for sex shows significant age differences (Chi Square = 14.52, df = 6, sign. = .03), and a trend towards greater concern expressed by older children (Tau C = .055; sign. = .077, with n = 501). Controlling for sex, a significant age difference persists for daughters only, but there is a trend for both daughters and sons for increased age to be associated with increased concern. For sons, Chi Square = 10.98, df = 6, sign. = .09; Tau C = .090, sign. = .070. For daughters, Chi Square = 16.59, df = 6, sign. = .01; Tau C = .040, sign. = .207.

** Without controlling for sex, Chi Square = .03. For fathers, Chi Square = 13.72, df = 8, sign. = .09; Tau C = .122, sign. = .02. For mothers, Chi Square = 8.09. df = 8, sign. = .43; Tau C = 0.18; sign. = .367.

ill or unable to look after himself or herself. Would you say. . .not at all, only a little, or a great deal?'' Seventeen percent of the children of our initial interview respondents said they worried "not at all," but on the other hand, 36 percent said they worried "a great deal" (see Table 2).

Because the age of a child is loosely related to the age of a parent, the concerns that children have can be seen to change in a related way. We found not much concern about the health of mothers until the mother reached the age of 80 or older, while concern about the fathers became greater as the fathers were in their seventh decade. Daughters are slightly more likely to worry about a parent's health than are sons when considering children of all ages (39 percent versus 30 percent), but breaking down the children into age groups shows that if women in their forties are excluded, the differences are stronger. In the forties, sons worry more about parental health (46 percent worry a great deal) than do daughters (36 percent worry a great deal), but if the child is 50 years of age or older, daughters worry more than do sons (61 percent versus 47 percent). It may be that the daughters in their forties are less worried about their parents because they are preoccupied with raising their own children (an example of the "caught generation"), but this age patterning is in need of more detailed investigation before any strong conclusions can be made.

The general pattern, however, is for daughters to worry more than sons, and for fathers to be more worried *about* than mothers. If the former pattern reflects traditional sex-role stereotyping, which tends to place the "wife and mother" in a nursemaid role in the family, the latter finding perhaps reflects realistic concerns about the father in light of the actual mortality experiences, which lead to relatively shorter life expectancy for men.

It is important to note that children who said they were very concerned about future health changes in their parents were more likely to describe their relationship with the parent as close or extremely close, on a six-point scale of closeness, than were those who reported no or little concern. They were also more likely to be in frequent contact with the parent, either in person or by telephone. For example, of the 36 percent of the children who claimed to worry "a great deal" about what should happen if a parent became ill, 48 percent claimed to have seen this parent "today or yesterday," and 60 percent said they usually saw the parent once or twice a week or more. Telephone contact was even more pervasive. Forty percent of highly concerned children had been in telephone contact with their parent during the past two days, and 70 percent during the past week.

While the relationships between children and their parents were described, generally, as close by most of our respondents regardless of the health of the parent, and while interaction patterns linked the generations in close contact, concern about the parent's health was associated with even more contact and reported feelings of being closer to the parent. In a cross-sectional study it is impossible to speak definitively about the direction of causation among the factors of closeness, interaction and concern for the parent's health. No doubt the three factors are mutually reinforcing.

Because we gathered questionnaire data from adult children anywhere in Canada and the world, we know that children who are not in geographical proximity to their parents tend to be anxious because they cannot closely monitor changes in the health of their parents and because they feel ignorant of the health-care system that their parents might need in the case of a health change or emergency. We think of concern about the parent as a kind of watchfulness that develops in children as their parents grow older and, perhaps, begin to experience illnesses and hospitalization more frequently. Children frequently keep one another informed as to the health of the parent, and such collective monitoring may play an important part in sibling interaction during the middle years. In an indirect way, therefore, the illnesses of advanced age, and the increased potential for those who are still healthy to become ill, may contribute to solidarity within the younger generations of the family.

Conclusion

This chapter began by considering the increasing likelihood that people in the advanced years will experience health difficulties and require assistance from a family member. Concern about these changes is systematically patterned by the ages of the parents and child. It would be useful to know more about the extent to which concern about the parent's health is shared by siblings or assumed by just one of the children, such as the one child who lives closest to the parent. Our data suggest that concern exists regardless of proximity, but we do not know the extent to which a child might alter his or her own behaviour because of this concern. More needs to be known about the patterning of such concern by age and sex. One American study using similar measures (Lieberman, 1978) found concern not highly patterned by these variables, in contrast to our data. Would a child move to be closer to a parent, take a parent into the home, sacrifice his or her career interests in order to provide health care for the parent? Would women be expected to sacrifice more than men in these matters?

Where public policies for the support of the aged turn increasingly to the family as the locus of responsibility (as in jurisdictions such as the United States, where drastic budget cuts in state-supported services are being experienced, or as in Canada, where home-care programs are becoming increasingly popular), the way in which such concern might be activated in families and the capacity of family structures (many of which are extremely fragile) to take action based on such concerns become critical issues in our ability to provide health care to the community-dwelling older population (Treas, 1977; Ward, 1976).

Note

1 Current analysis, by C. Rosenthal, S. Matthews and myself suggests that fewer people are actually "caught" in situations of competing obligations than much gerontological literature suggests.

References

Brody, Elaine
  1978 "The aging of the family." *Annals, American Academy of Political and Social Science* 438:13-27.
Cape, Ronald D.T.
  1980 "Old patients need hope, personal planning, care." *Ontario Medical Review* (January):11-16.
Comptroller General of the United States
  1977 *Report to Congress: The Well-Being of Older People in Cleveland, Ohio.* Washington, D.C.: General Accounting Office.
Fletcher, Susan, and Leroy O. Stone
  1981 *Living Arrangements of Canada's Older Women and Their Implications for Access to Support Services.* Ottawa: Statistics Canada.
Gutman, Gloria, M.
  1980 "The elderly at home and in retirement housing: A comparative study of health problems, functional difficulties and support service needs." Chapter 18, Pp. 189-203, in Victor W. Marshall (ed.), *Aging in Canada: Social Perspectives,* Toronto: Fitzhenry & Whiteside.
Havens, Betty
  1980 "Differentiation of unmet needs using analysis by age/sex cohorts." Chapter 20, Pp. 212-221, in Victor W. Marshall (ed.), *Aging in Canada: Social Perspectives,* Toronto: Fitzhenry & Whiteside.
Large, Mary-Jane
  1981 "Services for the elderly." *Ontario Medical Review* (January):38-41.
Lieberman, G.
  1978 "Children of the elderly as natural helpers: Some demographic differences." *American Journal of Community Psychology* 6 (Autumn):489-498.
Maddox, George L.
  1979 "Sociology of later life." *Annual Review of Sociology* 5:113-135.
Marshall, Victor W.
  1983 "La santé des grands vieillards, sujet de préoccupation de leurs enfants." Pp. 99-112 in *Mieux vivre pour bien vieiller.* Paris: Centre international de gérontologie sociale.
Marshall, Victor W., Carolyn J. Rosenthal and Jane Synge
  1983 "Concerns about parental health." Chapter 12, Pp. 252-273, in Elizabeth W. Markson (ed.), *Women and Aging.* Toronto: D.C. Heath and Company.

Neugarten, Bernice L.
  1978 "Aging in the future." Pp. 2-26 in Blossom T. Wigdor (ed.), *Canadian Gerontological Collection I*. Winnipeg: Canadian Association on Gerontology.
Shanas, Ethel
  1980 "Self-Assessment of physical functions: White and black elderly in the United States." Pp. 269-281 in S.G. Haynes, M. Feinleib and Associates (eds.), *Second Conference on the Epidemiology of Aging*. Bethesda, Maryland: National Institute on Aging.
  1981 "Old Parents: Middle-Aged Children." Paper presented at the meetings of the International Association of Gerontology, Hamburg, Germany, July 11-17.
Shanas, E., P. Townsend, D. Wedderman, H. Friis, P. Milhoj and J. Stehouwer
  1968 *Old People in Three Industrial Societies*. New York: Atherton Press.
Streib, Gordon F.
  1983 "The frail elderly: Research dilemmas and research opportunities." *The Gerontologist* 23(1):40-44.
Tilquin, C., C. Sicotte, T. Paquin, F. Tousignant, G. Gagnon and P. Lambert
  1980 "The physical, emotional and social condition of an aged population in Quebec." Chapter 21, Pp. 222-231, in Victor W. Marshall (ed.), *Aging in Canada: Social Perspectives*. Toronto: Fitzhenry & Whiteside.
Tobin, Sheldon S. and Regina Kulys
  1980 "The family and services." Chapter 15, Pp. 370-399, in Carl Eisdorfer (ed.), *Annual Review of Gerontology and Geriatrics*. Vol. 1. New York: Springer Publishing Company.
Treas, J.
  1977 "Family support systems for the aged: Some social and demographic considerations." *The Gerontologist* 17(6):486-499.
Ward, Russell A.
  1976 "Limitations of the family as a supportive institution in the lives of the aged." *The Family Coordinator* 27, 4 (October):365-373.

VII

Health Care

In an ideal society, the nature of health care would be determined by the need for it. Health care is not, however, organized in that manner. Among the factors that produce a lack of fit between needs for health services and its provision are the pressures of population aging. The Canadian health-care "system" may be briefly characterized as: heavily slanted towards medical, rather than health-care; physician-dominated; acute-hospital centred; based on advanced technology; and delivered primarily on a fee-for-service basis. In these respects, it is not very different from the health-care system in the United States. However, most Canadians if asked what they prefer about Canada when compared to the United States would answer: our health-care system.

Its major distinguishing feature is the means of payment. Hospital and health-care insurance is nationwide. Chappell and Schwenger, in Chapters 24 and 25, outline the historical struggles that brought this system to its present state (see also Andreopoulos, 1975; Coburn et al., 1986; Taylor, 1978). Hospital insurance came into force nationwide only in 1957 and insurance coverage for physician services became nationwide only in 1972. Full universal accessibility is likely to exist in all provinces by 1987, as the last provinces comply with federal requirements. This will benefit the aged, because the evidence is compelling that both the aged and the poor suffer when physicians "opt out" of full participation in medicare (Badgley and Smith, 1979).

Canadian constitutional history dictates that health care is largely a provincial matter. Nonetheless, Schwenger describes in Chapter 25 no less than eight ways in which the National Department of Health and Welfare impacts on the health and well-being of older Canadians. Historically, one major means to impact on health care was through grants in support of hospital and health-care institution construction, including nursing homes. The impact of this policy is evident in the chapters by both Chappell and Schwenger. A well-supported law in the health-services field, referred to as Roemer's Law (Roemer, 1961), holds that "a built bed is a filled bed" (see Evans, 1984:85-6). This law asserts that supply generates demand. As Chappell notes, hospital costs account for about half of health-care costs in Canada, and physicians control about 80 percent of total health-care costs.

In Chapter 26, Shapiro and Roos review three studies they conducted in Manitoba that identify predictors and patterns of nursing-home use and that assess the impact of nursing-home residency on hospital use. Health needs are not the sole determinants of nursing-home use. Such social characteristics as availability of a spouse and being female have an impact. An important finding is that health status, as indexed by an ADL measure, has decreasing importance with advancing age, which seems to "wash out" the effect of health variability itself.

Age is a major factor in nursing home entry, with four of five new admissions to nursing homes being 75 years of age or older. There is differentiation among the nursing home population. For example, while half of an entry cohort will have died within four years of institutionalization, a small group of survivors remain for a relatively long time; those who do not die are likely to deteriorate.

Shapiro and Roos raise the question "Do nursing home beds reduce hospital bed consumption?" and answer that, when age, sex and survivorship are taken into account, nursing-home utilization does decrease hospital-bed utilization, but that this effect is specific to the advanced ages (75 +). However, in a finding relevant to Chapter 27 by Aronson, Marshall and Sulman, nursing homes are found to have no significant impact on length of stay of persons once hospitalized.

The major need for health services by an aging population is for chronic rather than acute care. In Chapter 27, Aronson, Marshall and Sulman describe the competing interests that conspire to create a truly pathological manifestation of acute hospital-centred care in which older patients who no longer need it cannot find appropriate placement at less intensive levels in the long-term care system. This problem is partly due to the low level of development of programs to assist the frail elderly to remain in their own homes, leaving too many of them inappropriately placed in a nursing home setting that is at too intensive a level of care for them; it partly is due to a failure to rehabilitate the geriatric patient.

Limited attention is given by Aronson, Marshall and Sulman to the experience of hospitalized elderly patients. In fact, little is known about the life of the elderly patient in the acute hospital, in the nursing home or elsewhere on the long-term care spectrum (see also Marshall, 1986). While most older Canadians spend little or no time in the acute hospital setting and indeed, most spend little time in long-term care facilities, significant minorities do or will spend significant portions of their lives in such settings, and most of these will die in such settings. We would do well to investigate their impact on the lives of patients and residents.

Other chapters in this book relate to health-service utilization. In particular D'Arcy presents extensive utilization data in the mental health field in Chapter 21, and in Chapter 22 Connidis shows the generally low demand for health and social services emanating from the community-dwelling aged. The economic implications of health services for an aging society are examined in Chapter 28, by Denton, Li and Spencer.

When the first edition of this book appeared in 1980, there was little research in the area of health care for the aged. The growing significance of the issues is indicated by the fact that we now have a large and growing research base and, indeed, a textbook in the area (Chappell, Strain and Blandford, 1986). The growing body of research makes it increasingly possible, and desirable, to compare the policy implications of the Canadian health-care delivery system to other systems. Our society's capacity to provide adequate health care for the elderly is a test of our commitment to basic human values. It is probably the case that no society provides a higher quality and greater accessibility of health care to its aged than does Canada. The chapters in this section, however, remind us both that the system is not without its weak points and that the good we have has come only through struggle. The struggle continues as the system, with its present benefits, is always under threat both from political interest grounds and from the danger of failing to adapt to changing needs. Indeed, needs themselves are not adequately measured. There is thus no room for complacency about health care for the aged.

References

Andreopoulos, Spyros (ed.)
  1975   *National Health Insurance: Can We Learn from Canada?* Toronto: John Wiley.
Badgley, Robin F. and R. David Smith
  1979   *User Charges for Health Services.* Toronto: Ontario Council of Health.
Chappell, Neena L., Laurel Strain and Audrey Blandford
  1986   *Aging and Health Care: A Social Perspective.* Toronto: Holt, Rinehart and Winston of Canada.
Coburn, David, Carl D'Arcy, George M. Torrance and Peter New (eds.)
  1986   *Health and Canadian Society: Sociological Perspectives.* 2nd edition. Toronto: Fitzhenry & Whiteside.
Evans, Robert G.
  1984   *Strained Mercy: The Economics of Canadian Health Care.* Toronto: Butterworth.
Marshall, Victor W.
  1986   "Older patients in the acute hospital setting." Paper presented at a conference, Health in Aging: Sociological Issues and Policy Directions, Albany, New York.
Roemer, Milton I.
  1961   "Bed supply and utilization: A natural experiment." *Hospitals: Journal of the American Hospital Association* 35:35-42.
Taylor, Malcolm G.
  1978   *Health Insurance and Canadian Public Policy.* Montreal: McGill-Queen's University Press.

24

Canadian Income and Health-Care Policy: Implications for the Elderly

Neena L. Chappell
Centre on Aging and Department of Sociology
University of Manitoba

This chapter presents a brief historical overview of the development of social policy at the national level in Canada. This history is restricted to a discussion of legislation related to elderly persons in the income and health-care areas and the working assumptions reflected in this legislation. It also includes a discussion of some of the consequences of this legislation for elderly individuals. Many other issues, such as the role of voluntary agencies, housing policy, familial support systems, etc., which are also relevant to the societal condition of elderly persons, are not discussed.

It was not until well into the 1900s that the Canadian government entered the area of social security in a significant way. However, activity by others in the areas of both income and health care is evident a century before. For example, the beginnings of home care were evident in Canada in 1838 with the formation of the Grey Nuns and the visitation of the sick in their own homes. In 1898 the Victorian Order of Nurses was established to provide home nursing services (Wilson, 1982). Worker's compensation laws were adopted in most provinces between 1851 and 1928.

In 1867 at the time of Confederation, neither income security nor social service programs had been an issue. The British North America (BNA) Act made no mention of welfare measures, and the government's minimal contribution was limited to poor relief administered at the local level. Those in need were left to rely mainly on private charities or religious organizations. This reflected the working assumption of the time: individuals are responsible for their own resources, for obtaining and retaining employment and for providing for the contingencies of life, including old age and health services.

The BNA Act did assign responsibility for quarantine centres and marine hospitals as well as for "special" groups (such as the armed forces and veterans) to the federal government, and responsibility for other hospitals,

This research was conducted while the author was a National Research Scholar (#6607-1340-48), funded through Health and Welfare Canada. For a comprehensive discussion of the arguments found here see Chappell et al., 1985.

asylums, charities and charitable institutions to the provinces (Bryden, 1974:20-22; Government of Canada, 1970:18-20). The particular significance of this allocation lay in the fact that any jurisdiction not specifically assigned federal responsibility necessarily fell within the provincial domain. Since health and welfare were not specifically mentioned, they would be considered provincial areas when they arose as issues later.

The market ethos, which left each individual family to care for itself, prevailed into the 1920s. The few exceptions that did exist were either limited or implemented for reasons other than social welfare. For example, the Annuities Act of 1908 had little effect, as few people took advantage of it as a means of saving towards their old age. Worker's compensation was instituted less as a social security measure than as a means to end lawsuits against employers of injured workmen. Custodial care for the mentally ill was used primarily to remove the "insane" from the community (Government of Canada, 1970:34). The 1920s, however, did see the federal government's first major intervention in old-age income security.

Income Security

Despite lobbies against such a program by private insurance industries (Bryden, 1974:58-59), the 1927 Old Age Pensions Act established a national, noncontributory, means-tested plan providing for $20.00 a month at age 70 (Barber, 1972:11; National Health and Welfare, 1974:9). The passage of this act established the principle of public responsibility for ensuring that aged persons receive a basic subsistence allowance, and represented the first major federal intervention into the social-welfare field. It did so while establishing the principles of federal/provincial cost sharing, national program standards and provincial administration of old-age pensions. These principles reflect the federal/provincial divisions of authority and the decentralized governmental system in Canada, which contrasts with more centralized systems found elsewhere, for example, in Britain.

Once Canada entered the welfare field in this area, legislation evolved fairly regularly. During the economic depression of the 1930s, with heavy unemployment and agricultural distress, the financial resources of the municipalities became unable to provide relief. This, together with at least partial recognition that the causes of unemployment and declining income were national and international, led the federal government to greater involvement in national income provisions. Assistance came as special grants-in-aid made on an ad hoc year-to-year basis. Although Ottawa funded at least half the costs, it continued to insist that unemployment and other relief expenditures were primarily the responsibility of the provinces (Barber, 1972:11; Government of Canada, 1970:36). It was, however, in 1930 that the federal share of old-age pensions increased to 75 percent because some of the poorer provinces could not pay.

The 1930s also brought a change in the working assumption of policy makers. It was recognized that individuals could become destitute through the exigencies of life and through no fault of their own. The values of independence and self-sufficiency were nevertheless still dominant, reflected in the belief that, while it was the public's responsibility to provide for those who could not work (such as the aged, the blind, the disabled), such provision should not discourage the incentive to work and to save for one's own retirement (National Health and Welfare, 1973:4-6,17,20). It was, in other words, the Depression that demonstrated the social nature of human need (Irving, 1980). According to Bryden (1974:75-76), poverty among the aged was so acute, widespread and chronic during the twenties that it simply could not be ignored. It was after the Depression and the two World Wars, in a climate of postwar prosperity, that this new assumption was implemented and the so-called welfare state introduced.

In 1951, an amendment to the BNA Act resulted in old-age security payments to all persons age 70 and over, irrespective of means (later lowered to age 65), supplemented if necessary by means-tested old-age assistance starting at age 65. In 1960, the Guaranteed Income Supplement program gave additional funds to old-age pensioners whose income was less than $1,620.00 a year. In 1964, the income-tested supplement was extended to survivors' disability benefits, irrespective of age. Further evolution took place in 1965 with the development of contributory social insurance matched with income-tested supplementation. Canada's system has been described in terms of tiers, with new forms of assistance generally added to rather than replacing those already in existence.

Health Care

As was evident when discussing the development of income-security legislation, volunteer organizations such as the Victorian Order of Nurses and the Grey Nuns provided services in Canada long before the federal government entered the area of health-care service provision. It is equally true that there are instances of local government involvement prior to major efforts, especially national efforts, in the provision of services. Examples include: medical services; hospital outpatient departments for the indigent and near indigent; public clinics for venereal disease, tuberculosis, etc.; and health plans operated by numerous industries. Furthermore, public effort was most effective in the area of public health or preventive medicine, such as the collection of vital statistics; sanitary inspection; supervision of water, milk and food; and the disposal of sewage and garbage.

Since the development of the formal health-care system in Canada is tied to the development of the medical profession, it is important to recognize that most writers place the inception of the public acceptance of medicine around the late 1800s and early 1900s (Brown, 1979; Enos and Sultan, 1977:188-196).

It was in the late 1800s that Pasteur discovered that each disease had its own micro-organism and Lister advanced techniques for sterilizing operating procedures. It was also at this time that the vaccine for smallpox was used and that the stethoscope, clinical thermometer, hypodermic syringes, etc. were invented. In the first two decades of the twentieth century medical licensing laws were passed, medical schools were standardized, restrictions on entry into the medical field were enforced and the income and status of the medical profession increased.

The Depression of the thirties demonstrated the vulnerability of private schemes, exposing the social nature of human poverty. With the Depression, thousands could not afford care. The lack of standardized services from one local area to another and the lack of central coordination became evident. Social services were unable to meet the growing demand (Bryden, 1974:15-21). This was also a time when private enterprise dominated the health field. Doctors, dentists and nurses sold their services privately. Drugs and medications were sold on the market. This was, however, well after the public acceptance of medicine had begun. An increased interest in health insurance became visible in Canada within this climate.

According to Granatstein (1975:249-278), Mackenzie King's decision to stay on as Prime Minister of Canada in the forties was related to his dream of making a complete program of social security. He wanted to add health insurance to old-age pensions and unemployment insurance (the latter was passed at the beginning of World War II). In addition, individuals in government civil service and industry feared possible dislocations in returning to peacetime: massive unemployment and popular unrest. After the prosperous wartime years, people would not willingly return to the conditions of the thirties. Social-welfare legislation could dampen unrest and possibly aid in the reelection of the Liberals.

In 1940, Prime Minister Mackenzie King requested the Rowell-Sirois Commission to study the economic problems of Canada and the nature of federal/provincial relations. That commission recommended medical care stay a provincial responsibility with the federal government sharing the costs, because the provinces were not subject to wide, internal variations in demands, while inter-provincial variability was higher. The risks were relatively easy to establish, relatively constant, not subject to cyclical fluctuations or sudden emergencies. Regional differences in delivery of medical care added support for leaving it a provincial responsibility.

A Committee on Reconstruction was established in 1941, with Leonard C. Marsh appointed Research Director. It argued that the basic soundness of social security is that the universal risks of sickness and invalidity in old age were underwritten by the community as a whole. The first suggestion was for a national health-insurance scheme. Implementation began in 1945, with half of Marsh's main points acted upon. Both a research and training program and assistance in hospital construction were implemented (Marsh, 1975:xxii). It was not, however, until 1957 that the Hospital Insurance and Diagnostic Services Act ensured hospital care for the entire population through a fiscal policy in which the federal government agreed to share the costs of running hospitals (excluding tuberculosis hospitals and sanitoria, institutions for the mentally ill and care institutions, such as nursing homes and homes for the aged). The Medical Care Act was passed in 1965/66 and implemented in 1968, providing a national insurance scheme for physician services.

The 1966 Canada Assistance Plan provided social assistance for anyone in need, irrespective of age or reason for lack of income. This plan was designed to fill gaps, paying for health-care services not covered by hospital insurance and medical care, such as homes for the aged and nursing homes. Based on income, it replaced the 1956 Unemployment Assistance Act, Old-Age Assistance and blind and disabled persons' allowances. However, each province administers its social assistance programs, and there is no uniformity between them (Lee, 1974; Leclair, 1975).

By 1972 all provinces and the territories had joined the federal government's cost-shared comprehensive medical insurance program. To be eligible for federal cost sharing, any provincial health plan must include universal coverage, reasonable access to services, portability of benefits, comprehensive services and nonprofit administration by a public agency. Prior to 1977, federal/provincial cost sharing was fifty-fifty, with the federal government matching every dollar the provinces spent on approved services. This in effect meant the provinces controlled overall health expenditures. This was changed in 1977 to a system of cash grants from the federal to the provincial governments based on population, gross national product and the transfer of specific taxing powers to the provinces. By divorcing funds from specific health expenditures, the rate of growth of federal costs was limited. It also gave provinces more control over health expenditures within their own territory, since transfers were no longer dependent on the use of specified services.

In addition, much debate has arisen around extra billing by physicians (additional charges to patients over and above the payment schedule) and hospital user fees within provinces to help finance their share of health-insurance costs. The concern arose that "reasonable access" was threatened. This resulted in federal government legislation and the passage of the Canada Health Act in 1984. This act provides for a reduction in federal financial contributions to provincial health plans by the amount of extra billing and user charges implemented in the province.

Implications of Canadian Social Policy

The many policies enacted in both the income and health-care areas in the period 1940-1970 were aided by the efforts of various interest groups (such as trade unions, welfare associations and the aged and their children), all of whom helped to make income and social security a political issue. The recognition of these issues was reflected in the establishment of the federal Department of National Health and Welfare in 1945. The legislation that evolved was primarily directed towards universal rather than group-specific benefits, although some legislation was aimed explicitly towards the aged.

By the end of its first century, Canada had evolved what Collins (1978:61) calls "six layers" of provision for the elderly: old-age security payments, guaranteed income supplements, Canada/Quebec Pension Plan and different forms of provincial supplements (including decreased property taxes and health premiums, decreased transportation costs, etc.), as well as private pension plans and private savings. In addition, hospital and physician services were ensured, and the Canada Assistance Plan provided for some services not included in these two. In 1980/81, income and social security programs totalled 11.9 percent of GNP (Statistics Canada, 1982, 1984; Evans, 1984).

Despite this growth in public programs, the 1970s brought increasing dissatisfaction on the part of the elderly, with welfare organizations, both provincial and federal governments, and others. One reason was the low incomes of elderly persons generally. The average yearly income for elderly males and females has not been striking. It was only $4,053 and $2,213 respectively, in 1971 (Statistics Canada, 1973), rising to $14,221 and $8,678 respectively in 1981 (Statistics Canada, 1982). Fully half (53 percent) of all persons age 65 and over had sufficiently low incomes to receive the GIS in 1979 (Statistics Canada, 1982). The low level of benefits from public programs on which most elderly depend accounts for their economic situation.

Few have income from private sources. Private pension plans are available only to those who work in the paid labour force, excluding most women, especially among those who are elderly today. For those who are employed, private pensions are scaled to earnings (C/QPP operates in the same way). Many do not provide spouse's benefits, and those that do, often provide minimal levels that are terminated on the death of the husband. In addition, few Canadians can afford to save. Dulude (1978) estimates only the top 20 percent of income groups between the ages of 45 and 64 have sufficient income to save after meeting basic needs. In other words, despite the existence of many programs, the benefits are insufficient to keep most elderly out of poverty. This has led to a general questioning of the country's income-security program.

The low level of benefits reflects the belief that payments that are too high will discourage younger persons from saving for their own retirement and older persons from accepting paid employment. While this can be viewed as consistent with the market ethos, it ignores the fact that few Canadians earn sufficient money to save during their younger years, and once they reach age 65 there is compulsory retirement in all provinces except Manitoba (private sector only) and New Brunswick and a general discrimination against hiring older persons across the country. The extent to which the Constitution and the Bill of Rights will change this situation is not yet known. There is no evidence that the general discrimination against hiring older persons is likely to change quickly.

The changing market conditions have not helped this dilemma. In 1921, fully 59.6 percent of men 65 and over and 6.6 percent of women were employed in paid labour. These figures dropped to 14.3 percent for men and remained more or less stable at a low 7.8 percent for women in 1981 (Long Range Planning, 1973:D-6). Most of the employed men in 1921 were working on farms, an employment area that has shrunk considerably over the years to be replaced by employment in business, where there is more likely to be compulsory retirement. These figures demonstrate the ability and willingness of the elderly to work in paid employment when the opportunity is provided. Said another way, the working assumptions behind current legislation have not changed significantly since the Depression. They still maintain the values of self-sufficiency, but in a society that does not provide the opportunity for such independence.

The concession to the market ethos has also resulted in the maintenance of the gap between the haves and havenots, leaving almost unchanged income inequalities among Canadians. While income redistribution resulting from transfer payments does involve *intergenerational* distribution, Bryden (1974:206-210), Collins (1978), and Pesando and Rea (1977:75,97-99,113-117) all come to the conclusion that *class* redistribution is minimal. The public pension system is progressive; that is, the amount of wealth transferred increases as permanent income increases, at the bottom of the income scale only. The system is regressive; that is, the amount of wealth transferred decreases with permanent income, in the upper ranges.

The main burden, therefore, is on those in the lower middle-income range and below to assume a disproportionate share of income maintenance for those who have been reduced by age to the bottom of the income scale. Women, of course, are the dominant fraction of poorly paid workers who subsidize both the state and private pension systems. Although old-age security payments, guaranteed income supplements and provincial supplements alter the regressivity of C/QPP somewhat, the total package is progressive only at the lower levels. Old-age tax exemptions are even less progressive, since they provide more savings for those with more money.

Turning to health-care policy, the independence of the provinces in this jurisdiction makes generalization to the entire country difficult. Nevertheless, the major focus in the Canadian health-care system is medical. Evans (1976) demonstrates the major role of physicians in cost figures. He estimates they control approximately 80 percent of health-care costs. Even though only about 19 percent of total health-care expenditures in Canada go directly to physicians, this group largely controls hospital utilization (accounting for about half of all health-care costs), prescribing of drugs, etc. That is, the decision to use expensive health-care services is not made primarily by the individual patient or client. The decision is made primarily by medical doctors. They are the major gatekeepers to utilization of the system. Physicians and other providers have expert knowledge not shared by patients and make decisions on patients' behalf.

The focus on physician-centred services (insured in a national scheme in 1965/66) reflects an acceptance of a medical model of health and illness. There is a tendency to equate good health with proper medical care, to identify health with medicine, and therefore to imply that an extension and expansion of health-care services will be accompanied by rising health levels within the population (Mishler et al., 1981). The central role played by physicians and the medical emphasis are evident within the very naming of our health-care system as Medicare. This biomedical perspective focusses largely on cure and acute care rather than on chronic illness and coping with permanent conditions. Indeed, some argue it has resulted in old age itself being defined as a problem considered solvable through the receipt of services, essentially medical services, at the individual level (Estes, 1979).

Concomitant with the rise of a physician focus and with the development of medicine as a profession has been the development of an institutional bias within our health-care services, especially short-term institutional services and specifically hospitals. In Canada, it was after World War II that hospitals developed as a central focus of health care and signalled a break with home care, where illness had traditionally been treated. By this time hospitals were viewed not as places where the poor went to die but where skilled medical specialists practised and complex diagnostic technologies were utilized (Coburn et al., 1983). As already noted, hospital growth in Canada was federally supported in the forties and fifties through contributions towards their construction.

The growth of hospitals encouraged the development of hospital insurance, since the high costs could be devastating for an uninsured patient. As the number of hospitals increased, physicians became increasingly specialized, hospital minded and accustomed to expensive therapies, for which dollars flowed readily from the public purse (Tsalikis, 1982). The public financing of hospitals reinforced the move from the patient's home and doctor's office to hospitals as a major place for treatment. It also gave rise to the growth of paramedical workers to assist in the tasks performed in this milieu. Ultimately it was a major factor in transforming doctors from independent entrepreneurs to participants in a complex medical industrial institution.

While physicians are central to the system, hospital costs represent about half of the total health-care expenditures in this country. Increased utilization is often cited as the reason for these increasing costs. However, Bennett and

Krasny (1981) estimate that, in Canada, it took 6 percent more hospital workers and 80 percent more drugs, X-ray films and other supplies to treat the average hospital patient in 1975 than it did in 1965. Furthermore, there was a levelling off of both physician and hospital-worker salaries during the 1970s. Hospital space and resources have been relatively stable since that time, as well. The number of physicians, in comparison, has grown rapidly, with a resultant increase in pressure for hospital capacity (Evans, 1984:176). The extent to which physician practices can be disentangled from independent hospital utilization is not clear. Physicians play major roles in the use of hospitals. Patients usually have access to hospital benefits only if admitted by a physician.

While the focus in the system is on hospitals, thereby reinforcing short-term acute care, it is well-known that the major illnesses of old age are chronic in nature. Elderly persons tend to suffer more from chronic than acute illnesses, and the chronic illnesses they suffer from are not necessarily the cause of their death. The most frequent chronic conditions are heart disease, arthritis and chronic rheumatism, and hypertension (Neugarten, 1982). The leading causes of death among the elderly are heart disease, cancer and cerebrovascular disease. That is, they need services to help them cope with chronic conditions and functional disability. Long-term institutions, referred to variously as nursing homes, personal-care homes, etc., are the major service provided for such needs. Funding for long-term institutional services is still not uniform, although in some provinces, such as Ontario, they are now covered by the Canada Assistance Plan.

A national scheme covering community-based care similar to that for physician and hospital services does not exist. As of the early 1980s, three provinces (British Columbia, Manitoba and Saskatchewan) had coordinated home care and community-support systems (Robertson, 1982), which included homemaker services, home nursing, therapy services, medical services, social workers, meals-on-wheels and some handyman services. Even here recent political developments in British Columbia suggest this is no longer true in that province. Other provinces offer some such services on an ad hoc basis.

Community services have not achieved the same place within national legislation for health care, as is true of traditional medical services. The first national insurance scheme determined a short-term institutional focus. As Schwenger and Gross (1980) point out, Canada has opted for the two most expensive forms of care: institutional care and medical care. Because of the historical development of formal care in Canada, community-based programs have tended to develop as "add-ons" to existing institutional and medical care.

That is, the major focus on medical and institutional care in our society means that the provision of community care, including home care, and of broader health, but traditionally nonmedical, services has been neglected. An awareness of this situation has developed at a time when the costs of both the income and health-care aspects of our national social-security system continue to escalate. From 1970 to 1975, the growing population of elderly people, cost of living increases and improvements in benefits have all contributed to a substantial increase in expenditures for Old Age Security, Guaranteed Income Supplement and Spouse's Allowance. Health costs were increasing annually, costing 8.4 percent of the GNP in 1982.

As well as growing concern over increasing costs, there has also been mounting dissatisfaction among the provinces with federal interference in provincial jurisdictions. The provinces still formally maintain responsibility for the health area and administer the programs, but the federal government had taken the initiative in income maintenance during the expansion years. Ottawa's responsibility for statistics permitted it to develop uniform standards for benefits, thereby influencing planning and development. In addition, Ottawa's power to finance allowed it to specify the requirements to be met for the provinces to receive health-care funds. Ottawa, for example, defined the institutions and services for which costs would be shared in the hospital-insurance program, as well as the formula for sharing. The provinces did not have an opting-out arrangement agreed to in 1964, but the financial advantages generally meant they opted in.

The national health-insurance plans, which were cost shared at the federal level, had resulted in an expansion of the traditional medical view of health and health care. More than ever, the personal health-care system was oriented to treating existing illness, rather than developing alternative forms such as preventive, custodial and home care (Lalonde, 1974:12,25). The coverage provided by both hospital and medical insurance resulted in this development; the former provides for care in hospitals, outpatient clinics and medical and nursing schools. Services by nonmedical personnel are covered only if the facility is listed as a hospital. The latter provides for services by or under the supervision of a physician. Andreopoulos (1975) and Leclair (1975) have demonstrated the profound effect this public policy has had on medicalizing our health and welfare system. Because hospital insurance began first, every town and city was encouraged to build hospitals and physicians were given an incentive to hospitalize their patients. Then Medicare committed funds to "sick" care, without the resultant decrease in the number of physicians predicted by some.

While both the federal and provincial governments espouse support for the position that a patient should not be hospitalized unless absolutely necessary, cost sharing with other facilities such as nursing homes (unless the patient is on welfare) or health professionals who are not working with physicians has not been established. Direct expenditures on health are mostly physician centred, including medical care, hospital care, laboratory tests and prescription drugs. Adding dental care and the services of those such as optometrists and chiropractors, the personal health-care system can be seen as mainly oriented to curing what in many cases could have been prevented. It was estimated in the early 1970s that for each physician the system incurred about $50,000 in expenses for his or her services and about $100,000 for hospital care, laboratory testing, special nursing care, etc. (see Andreopoulos, 1975:5).

As Havens (1977) points out, available residential resources are best able to meet the needs of the elderly at the extremes, either the very sick or the very well, but are less able to meet the needs of those in the intermediate range. Similarly, Dulude (1978:92) notes that 45 percent of the over 100,000 elderly in nursing homes in 1975 were in self-sufficient or Level I care, and therefore most were probably able to live in the community if support services were available. Although the Department of National Health and Welfare established a committee to develop pilot home-care programs as early as 1957, there were only twenty-six programs operating in six provinces by 1967. While today most communities have Victorian Order of Nurses, Canadian Arthritic and Rheumatism Society, Canadian Red Cross Society and visiting homemaker services, few provide universal home-care programs, and some provinces still require medical authorization. As already noted, the lack of nonmedical services, notably community care, is particularly relevant for the elderly.

Conclusions

Despite the fact that the 1970s saw a critical review of existing income-security and social-welfare programs that affect the elderly, neither system has changed dramatically, and costs continue to escalate. Specifically in terms of the income-security program, payments are too minimal to provide an adequate standard of living; they maintain income differences between the haves and havenots; and they suggest a stagnation of the working assumption behind such programs since the 1930s, rather than a recognition of societal changes that have decreased the opportunities for self-maintenance among the elderly. The cost of income and health-care programs to both the federal and provincial governments has continued to increase, and the provinces have become increasingly dissatisfied with federal interference within areas of provincial responsibility. Finally, public policy instituted primarily at the federal level has expanded the medicalization of the health-care system to the neglect of nonmedical aspects.

Despite such awareness and concern, there is little evidence that either program is going to change substantially. Turning first to income payments, it seems clear that cost considerations will prevent any significant improvement from the public purse. An address by the then federal Minister of Health and Welfare (Bégin, 1978) saw a policy of economic independence for the elderly praised, but it was also noted that since government pensions are not sufficient to maintain the elderly in our society, private pensions should be more accessible and equitable. There is no indication that the current federal government is about to change substantially from this position at the present time. The initial plans of the 1985 federal budget (eventually shelved) to decrease indexing associated with old-age pensions suggests few improvements can be anticipated.

It was as a result of the review undertaken in the early 1970s and expressed provincial dissatisfaction, together with the federal government's concern over cost escalation, that the bloc-funding approach for health-care services was adopted in 1977. As mentioned earlier, Ottawa agreed to provide the provinces with a lump-sum payment for such services, freeing them from having to shape their health care to federal cost-sharing criteria. However, this came only after a very large, a very expensive and a very powerful medical industrial complex of health-care services was already in place.

The ability of the current system to change sufficiently to meet the needs of an aging population is questionable. As so convincingly argued by Evans (1984:85-86, 196-207), no one part of the formal care system has responsibility for ensuring either cost effectiveness or treatment effectiveness. Neither physicians nor hospital management nor other sectors within the system have any incentive or pressure to adopt less costly types of care. Increased capacity tends to lead to increased utilization without corresponding price decreases. Bed capacity seems to be the best single predictor of hospital utilization. Once hospitals are built they are seldom closed or reduced in capacity. Innovations that free capacity have the same effect. They induce more utilization. New procedures that become implemented because they are less expensive, less effective, less dangerous, or more comfortable, become utilized to meet capacity. The result is increased overall costs. For example, one frequently hears the argument that the provision of more extended care for elderly persons and those chronically ill would reduce pressure on acute-care facilities. As such facilities are built, both they and acute-care hospitals remain full.

Despite the billions of dollars spent each year to improve the health of its citizens, no systematic effort is made either to measure results or to account for costs in terms of outcomes. Canada does not even conduct periodic national health surveys, as does the United States. Despite the frequently made assumption that more dollars spent on health care will lead to better health status, no good evidence exists to support this claim. As the nature of illness has shifted away from infectious diseases to chronic conditions, as well as accidents and other lifestyle-related causes, the effectiveness of more dollars spent on the current medical-care system is limited and very expensive. As a society we have not yet dealt with the issue, especially during old age, when decline is inevitable, or when health-care servicing is inappropriate or too much.

Finally, much is heard today, given cost concerns surrounding the existing system and sentiment in favour of more community and chronic-care services, that implementing more community and social programs at this time simply represents "add-ons" to an already expensive system. If, in fact, the current medical-care system remains as it is or continues to grow, there is good reason to expect that new community and social services might well represent additional cost. This is because the current system operates on provider demand creating additional need for utilization of the system. This is evident in variation of surgical rates, for example, by the interest, preferences and beliefs of the local medical community.

However, the provision of more community and social services need not represent add-ons to the system. A revamping of the system, incorporating a broader definition of health and a greater focus on community and social services, with a decreased emphasis on physician and hospital services, could result not only in no additional costs, but could also help stem the tide of increases currently being experienced in the cost of formal health care. It must be emphasized that appropriate community and social services are considered a necessity in the provision of adequate care in an aging society. A move to deinstitutionalize without adequate community support is not a viable alternative. The change, however, must be global, not partial. If substitutes for inpatient care are introduced, corresponding components of inpatient capacity must be withdrawn simultaneously.

Part of the problem lies in the many health-care interventions that have not been evaluated at all or only improperly. Despite the billions of dollars spent on health care, little goes into adequate research. The assessment of treatment has to be made in terms of its effectiveness in preventing, postponing, or lessening morbidity or mortality. Even if it delays death or some illness, side effects and decreases in quality of life have to be considered. But evaluations must include population-based experience and comparisons with proper control groups. The system must then have a mechanism for change based on the effectiveness and ineffectiveness of various interventions.

This chapter has directed attention towards a brief discussion of the historical development of public policy relating to the elderly in both the income-security and health-care legislation areas. The intent has been to provide sufficient background for an understanding of the types of policies that we have today and their implications for the aging population. Current policy in both areas is considered in need of change and improvement to meet adequately the needs of an aging Canadian society.

References

Andreopoulos, S.
  1975   *National Health Insurance: Can We Learn from Canada?*
          Toronto: John Wiley.
Barber, C.L.
  1972   *Welfare Policy in Manitoba.* Winnipeg: Report to the Planning and
          Priorities Committee of the Province of Manitoba.
Bégin, M.
  1978   "Federal Social Policies on Aging." Address by the federal Minister of
          Health and Welfare to the Canadian Association on Gerontology,
          Edmonton.
Bennett, J.E. and J. Krasny
  1981   "Health care in Canada." Pp. 40-66 in D. Coburn, C. D'Arcy, P. New and
          G. Torrance (eds.), *Health and Canadian Society: Sociological Perspectives.*
          Toronto: Fitzhenry & Whiteside.
Brown, E.R.
  1979   *Rockefeller Medicine Men: Medicine and Capitalism in America.* Berkeley,
          Calif.: University of California Press.
Bryden, K.
  1974   *Old Age Pensions and Policy-making in Canada.* Montreal: McGill-Queen's
          University Press.
Canadian Council on Social Development
  1973   *Social Security for Canada: A Report of the Task Force on Social Security.*
          Ottawa.
Chappell, N.L., L.A. Strain and A.A. Blandford
  1985   *Aging and Health Care: A Social Perspective.* Toronto: Holt, Rinehart and
          Winston.
Coburn, D., G.M. Torrance and J.M. Kaufert
  1983   "Medical dominance in Canada: The rise and fall of medicine." *International Journal of Health Services* 13:407-432.
Collins, K.
  1978   *Women and Pensions.* Ottawa: The Canadian Council on Social
          Development.
Dulude, L.
  1978   *Women and Aging: A Report on the Rest of Our Lives.* Ottawa: Advisory
          Council on the Status of Women.
Enos, D.D. and P. Sultan
  1977   *The Sociology of Health Care: Social, Economic and Political Perspectives.*
          New York: Praeger Publishers.
Estes, C.L.
  1979   *The Aging Enterprise.* San Francisco: Jossey-Bass.
Evans, R.G.
  1976   "Does Canada have too many doctors? Why nobody loves an immigrant
          physician," *Canadian Public Policy* 2:147-160.

1984   *Strained Mercy: The Economics of Canadian Health Care.* Toronto: Butterworth.

Government of Canada
1970   *Income Security and Social Services: Government of Canada Working Paper on the Constitution.* Ottawa: Queen's Printer.

Granatstein, J.
1975   *Canada's War: The Politics of the Mackenzie King Government, 1943-1945.* Toronto: Oxford University Press.

Havens, B.
1977   "Social Planning Implications of Needs Assessment." Paper presented at the World Conference on Aging: A Challenge to Science and Social Policy, Vichy, France.

Health and Welfare Canada
1976   *Basic Facts on Public Retirement Income Programs.* Ottawa: Queen's Printer.

Irving, A.
1980   "The development of income security in Canada, Britain and the United States, 1908-1945: A comparative and interpretive account." Publication series, working papers on social welfare in Canada, University of Toronto, Faculty of Social Work.

Lalonde, M.
1974   *A New Perspective on the Health of Canada.* A working document. Ottawa: National Health and Welfare.

Leclair, M.
1975   "The Canadian health care system." Pp. 11-93 in S. Andreopoulos (ed.), *National Health Insurance: Can We Learn from Canada?* Toronto: John Wiley.

Lee, S.S.
1974   "Health insurance in Canada: An overview and commentary." *New England Journal of Medicine* 290:713.

Long Range Planning, Welfare
1973   *Early Retirement: A Preliminary Analysis.* Ottawa: Government of Canada, Publication SWP-7302.

Marsh, L.
1975   *Report on Social Security for Canada.* Toronto: University of Toronto.

Mishler, E.G., L.R. Amarasingham, S.T. Hauser, S.D. Osherson, N.E. Waxler and R. Liem (eds.)
1981   *Social Contexts of Health, Illness and Patient Care.* Cambridge: Cambridge University Press.

National Health and Welfare
1973   *Working Paper on Social Security in Canada.* 2nd Edition. Ottawa: Queen's Printer.

1974   *Progress Report of the Working Party on Income Maintenance.* Ottawa: Information Canada.

Neugarten, B.L. (ed.)
1982   *Age or Need? Public Policies for Older People.* Beverley Hills: Sage.

Pesando, J. and S. Rea
   1977   *Public and Private Pensions in Canada: An Economic Analysis.* Toronto:
         Ontario Economic Council.
Robertson, D.
   1982   "Establishing new services: Canada as a case study." Pp. 199-216 in D.
         Coakley (ed.), *Establishing a Geriatric Service.* London, Eng.: Croom Helm,
         Ltd.
Schwenger, C.W. and J.M. Gross
   1980   "Institutional care and institutionalization of the elderly in Canada." Pp.
         248-256 in V.W. Marshall (ed.), *Aging in Canada: Social Perspectives.*
         Toronto: Fitzhenry & Whiteside.
Statistics Canada
   1973   *Income Distributions by Size in Canada, 1971.* Ottawa: Minister of Industry,
         Trade and Commerce, May.
   1982   *Old Age Security, Guaranteed Income Supplement and Spouse's Allowance,
         1982.* Ottawa: Minister of Supply and Services, June, CS86-509.
   1984   *Canada and Quebec Pension Plans, 1984.* Ottawa: Minister of Supply and
         Services, March, CS86-507.
Tsalikis, G.
   1982   "Canada." Pp. 125-162 in M.C. Hokenstad and R.A. Ritvo (eds.) *Linking
         Health Care and Social Services.* Beverley Hills: Sage.
Wilson, L.
   1982   "Historical perspectives: Canada." Pp. 3-18 in W.M. Edwards and F. Flynn
         (eds.), *Gerontology: A Cross-national Core List of Significant Works.* Ann
         Arbor: University of Michigan.

25

Formal Health Care for the Elderly in Canada

Cope W. Schwenger
Programme in Gerontology
University of Toronto

This chapter provides a brief account of the evolution of health insurance and the funding of long-term care in Canada. Also included will be an outline of the role of the federal and provincial/territorial governments in the care of the elderly, and finally, a critique of some of these activities as evidenced in a recent study that the author has done for Health and Welfare Canada. The main focus will be on formal government services. The extensive voluntary sector will be dealt with only peripherally.

Evolution of Health Services

At the time of Confederation, practices in New Brunswick and Nova Scotia reflected the strong influence of the Elizabethan Poor Law Legislation of 1601. In Quebec (Lower Canada), meeting the needs of the poor, sick, orphaned and aged was left to the religious orders. Ontario passed legislation in 1792 that shifted responsibility from the public domain to the individual, family and private philanthropy. Prince Edward Island, both before and after entry into Canada, tended to administer poor relief and related measures itself. In the case of what was to become the four western provinces, municipal organization was either nonexistent or, at best, only rudimentary, resulting in a greater degree of provincial responsibility (Wilson, 1982).

The constitutional authority for the delivery of health services in Canada as a whole was established in 1867, when the division of powers between the federal and provincial governments was carefully laid out in the British North America Act. Canada became a federated system, with all matters of national and international concern ascribed to the federal government and matters of more local interest such as health, housing, social services, recreation and education declared to be provincial responsibilities. The federal government, however, has had an enormous impact on health services in Canada, especially over the past thirty years, because it is in receipt of the major tax

The material for this chapter was prepared for a study done in 1984 for Health and Welfare Canada (Health Care for Elderly Canadians, 1985).

revenues (e.g., income tax), which it has used as financial incentives to the provinces to encourage nationwide programs.

In the last analysis, however, it is up to the provinces to determine the health schemes they will initiate, such as the innovative insurance schemes and long-term care systems that were developed originally in the prairie provinces of Saskatchewan and Manitoba. It is also up to the provinces to decide whether they will join federal master plans. These, however, have proven eventually to be almost irresistible.

Prepaid health-care financing goes back a very long way in Canada. The seeds of health insurance were first planted by Etienne Bouchard in 1655 in Montreal, the city that also saw the inception of Canada's first home-care plan under the Grey Nuns in 1733 (Wilson, 1982). It was in Western Canada (which saw the development of "municipal doctors" and "union hospitals" in the early twentieth century) that more widespread insurance schemes developed to assure basic health services to small and scattered populations living under harsh economic conditions. Similar reasoning led to the Newfoundland Cottage Hospital and Medical Care Plans (Taylor, 1978).

Finally, in 1958, the federal government instituted a national hospital insurance plan, and ten years later, a Canada-wide medical insurance scheme, both of these based on already existing models established by the Province of Saskatchewan.

Almost from the beginning there has been increasing concern (first by the federal and then by provincial governments) with the rising costs of the national schemes. In 1969 there was the Task Force Report on the Costs of Health Services. The 1970s saw a growing sense of political identity and power by the wealthier provinces, with a demand for more flexibility and less federal control. Two trends were occurring: (1) a gross overbuilding of our hospital system, and (2) an unprecedented increase in the number of physicians (Taylor, 1986).

As a result, in 1977 came the *Established Programs Financing* (EPF) Act in which, in place of the previous open-ended ("50¢ dollars") system, the federal government gave up a significant number of personal income and corporate tax points to the provinces and gave them, instead, block grants with an equalization formula bringing low-income provinces up to the total average (Hastings and Vayda, 1986).

In addition, the federal government introduced the *Extended Health-Care Services* (EHC) Program, which consisted initially of $20.00 per capita, escalated annually, to assist the provinces in providing less expensive alternatives to hospitalization, including extended care, residential care, home care and ambulatory care. By 1984 this amounted to over $1 billion. The only condition of payment is that the provinces and territories provide the Ministry of National Health and Welfare "with such health services information as is reasonably required for its international obligations, for the planning and achieving of national standards and for mutually useful exchanges of information between the federal government and the governments of the provinces and territories.'' The federal government has thus far asked for very little of such information.

Another crucial additional piece of legislation is the *Canada Assistance Plan* (CAP), introduced in 1966 and aimed at consolidating federal support for public assistance recipients, including financial help to the provinces for health services beyond universal benefits. In terms of the aged this has meant means-tested assistance not only for basic requirements of food, shelter and clothing, but also for travel and transportation, funerals and burials, clothing and comfort allowances in institutions, care in homes for the aged and nursing homes, rehabilitation services, casework and counselling, assessment and homemaking services, etc.

Health and Welfare Canada

General departmental responsibilities are said to focus on six areas: income security for individuals and families; essential social services, particularly for socially and economically disadvantaged Canadians; universal access for all Canadians to quality health services; protection against disease and environmental hazards; promotion of healthy lifestyles; and excellence in amateur sport (Canada, 1984).

The main strategies through which the department carries out its general responsibilities are transfers to individuals, transfers to provincial and territorial governments, regulation and surveillance, research, direct service to specific groups, advice, consultation, information and promotion.

The role of Health and Welfare in aging has been examined, and the activities divided into seven subdivisions as follows (Wilson, 1983):

(1) *Programs* — (a) Direct-Income Security (CPP, OAS, GIS, Spouse's Allowance); New Horizons.

(b) Indirect (through the provinces) — Medical Services, Hospital Services, Extended Health Care (EHC), Canada Assistance Plan (CAP).

(2) *Policy Development* — Formulating specific legislation, analysis of effect of aging on social policies.

(3) *Advisory, Consultative, Liaison and Information* — Federal/provincial coordination, standards and guidelines, research (internal and external).

(4) *Evaluation* — New Horizons, social programs; projects and research proposals for funding; medical devices.

(5) *Regulatory* — Medical devices, food and drugs.

(6) *Coordination within department* — Office on Aging.

(7) *Advisory to Minister* — National Advisory Council on Aging (NACA).

Provincial/Territorial Long-Term Care Systems

There is a considerable variety of *delivery systems for both health and social services* in Canada. The relationship between them is especially important in regard to the elderly. An attempt has been made to coordinate these services centrally, regionally and locally with varying degrees of success. In two of the provinces (Quebec and Prince Edward Island) and the two territories, there are (1984) unitary departments with a single minister and deputy minister. Health and social services are separated in seven of the other provinces. In New Brunswick, there has been active consideration of a unitary department. This has happened several times before in this province, but almost inevitably, it seems, separation reoccurs. Manitoba also experienced a unitary central department for a number of years, only to see it again divided. Even when there is a unitary department, the degree of coordination between health and social services can still be minimal.

Alberta has a unique model in which social services and community health have been joined into one department where they face the combined giant resources of hospitals and medical care, which have been joined into another department. A report by the Interdepartmental Committee on Long-Term Care has recently been published with a strong plea for a coordinated assessment and placement service for Alberta, with a single point of entry, first of all into the Home-Care Program (under the Department of Social Services and Community Health) and then to a Regional Institutional Placement Panel (under the Department of Hospitals and Medical Care) for institutional placements (Alberta, 1984).

Varying attempts have been made in several provinces to coordinate health and social services at a regional level, two of the most successful of these occurring in Quebec and Manitoba.

Manitoba was the first province to attempt a much more *systematized approach to long-term care,* including a closer coordination of home care and long-term institutional care for the elderly throughout the province. This so-called *Manitoba model* of delivery, which has since been dubbed "continuing care," has been adopted (with some revisions) first by British Columbia and later by Saskatchewan. Many other provinces have also examined this model. It is interesting, for example, in Ontario in November 1984 that nursing homes and home care were brought more closely together under the same executive director in the Ministry of Health.

Another aspect of the Manitoba model has been the diminution of the role of the physician in home care and a greater emphasis placed on the importance of social factors in long-term care. This has been termed a "social model," in contradistinction to the so-called medical model in Ontario and Alberta, where access to the system (including home care) is physician controlled.

Even in the Yukon and the Northwest Territories a system of long-term-care delivery is developing, and a surprising number of services and facilities are already available, at least in urban areas. Interesting in this regard are the reports to the Government of the Yukon (Resources Management Consultants, 1983) and to the Government of the Northwest Territories (Willis, 1983).

In the Atlantic Provinces, departments of social services have traditionally had the major responsibility for long-term care (both institutional and community) and still do in Newfoundland and Nova Scotia (1984). Notable new developments have included the new Division of Aging and Extended Care in Prince Edward Island, which has drawn together administration of chronic hospitals, manors (homes for the aged and nursing homes) and community-based services. An interesting needs study has been completed on the elderly in Prince Edward Island (Fryer, 1981). New Brunswick has established its unique Extra Mural Hospital (EMH) Program, physician controlled and fully insured (Ferguson, 1984). This acute home-care program is separate from the public-health home-care program (community health nurses) and from the community-based services in the Department of Social Services (homemakers and meals-on-wheels). It has been recommended that Newfoundland transfer responsibility for nursing homes from the Department of Social Services to the Department of Health (Newfoundland, 1984).

Home care is very recent and still quite underdeveloped in the Atlantic region, where the demand, however, is increasing rapidly. Long-term care is much more fully organized in New Brunswick than elsewhere. There is a particular dearth of coordinated services in Nova Scotia, where, however, there is an interesting new report that recommends expansion of their Home Life Supports Program. This includes a considerable increase in the number of homemakers; initiation of a demonstration project of $200,000 for innovative, self-help, intergenerational community volunteer projects; and a municipal social-assistance program allowing up to $400/month for families (caregivers) in need, where the older person would otherwise require more costly institutional placement (Nova Scotia, 1984).

Apart from medical services and institutional facilities, there was, in 1984, a considerable variation in the availability of *insured services for the elderly* in various parts of the country. Prescription-drug plans (generally called Pharmacare) are found in all provinces and territories with the exception of Prince Edward Island. Dental-care plans for the elderly exist only in Alberta and the Yukon — this program was briefly available in British Columbia, but has since been discontinued. Hearing aids are provided as a benefit in British Columbia, Saskatchewan and Alberta. Health-care aids and appliances are more readily available in some provinces than others. A new province-wide community chiropody program has been instituted in Saskatchewan.

There is a variation in the availability of certain private *nonprofit services* in Canada. The Victorian Order of Nurses has, for example, never been available in Prince Edward Island. Their bedside nursing activities were taken over by Quebec and also by the provincial government of British Columbia in 1977. Rumours have it that this could happen imminently in certain other provinces. Generally speaking, there is sentiment favouring private non-profit services, both institutional and community based, in most parts of Canada, providing cost-effective services can be offered. This may be especially true in the Atlantic Provinces.

Privatization of long-term care services, however, has increased in popularity in certain parts of the country — particularly in British Columbia, Alberta and Ontario. This has included commercialization both of the institutional and home-care sectors. In Ontario, for example, in 1983 over one-half of Ontario's beds for elderly people were provided "for profit" (compared with 27 percent in the rest of Canada), and one-half of the contracts for homemaking services purchased by Ontario's local Home Care Programs were with commercial agencies (Social Planning Council of Metropolitan Toronto, 1984).

Interdepartmental coordination at the provincial level in 1984 includes the Alberta Interdepartmental Coordinating Committee on Long-Term Care (Departments of Hospitals and Medical Care, Social Services and Community Health, and Housing). This is chaired by the Deputy Minister of Hospitals and Medical Care. In Saskatchewan, the Standing Interdepartmental Coordination Committee on Aging (SICCOA) composed of representatives of twenty-one government departments and agencies is chaired by the Provincial Gerontologist (Saskatchewan, 1984). Manitoba also has a Liaison Officer's Committee, representing every department of government, which gets together one-to-two times a year. An Interagency Committee on Support Services to Seniors (IACSSS) meets every three weeks and brings together the Departments of Health, Housing and Community Services and Corrections, as well as the Manitoba Health Services Commission and the Federal Canada Mortgage and Housing Corporation (CMHC) (Manitoba, 1984). Both of these committees in Manitoba are chaired by the Provincial Gerontologist. Ontario and Nova Scotia both have Seniors Secretariats. In Ontario, this has been under the jurisdiction of the Secretariat for Social Development. In Nova Scotia, in 1984, it is headed by a former Deputy Minister of Social Services.

Departmental offices and consultants in 1984 include the long-standing Senior Citizens Bureau in Alberta and the recently established Seniors Bureau in Saskatchewan, headed by the Provincial Gerontologist (a former Deputy Minister of Health). Both of these are under the jurisdiction of the Department of Social Services and Community Health. In Manitoba, the Provincial

Gerontologist is in the Department of Health (Minister's office). British Columbia had, at one time, consultants both in gerontology and geriatrics (positions not filled in 1984). In Nova Scotia, the Director of the Seniors Secretariat is frequently referred to as the Provincial Gerontologist.

Finally, the following five *provincial advisory councils and commissions* (1984), composed largely of senior citizens, are appointed by the respective provincial governments: the Alberta Provincial Senior Citizens Council, the Saskatchewan Provincial Senior Citizens Council, the Manitoba Council on Aging, the Ontario Advisory Council on Senior Citizens and the Nova Scotia Senior Citizens Commission. These bodies provide a measure of participation of older people in planning and advising on the delivery of services and facilities for the elderly in their particular provinces. Their counterpart at the federal level is the National Advisory Council on Aging (NACA).

The following material was collected from a study carried out under contract with Health and Welfare Canada involving interviews with a variety of individuals in different parts of the country to elicit their views on two questions:

(1) What are regarded as priority health-care needs of the elderly in Canada?
(2) What leadership role(s) should the Department assume in helping to respond to these needs?

Between July and October 1984, consultations were held with over two hundred individuals and small groups in all provinces and territories. Over one-half of the interviews were with senior provincial and territorial government officials. Other contacts included the Victorian Order of Nurses, the Canadian Red Cross Society and the St. John Ambulance, the Canadian Medical Association, the Canadian Nurses Association, the Canadian Association of Social Workers and the Canadian Council on Homemaker Services. Also included were twenty-six clinicians in the field of geriatrics and geriatric psychiatry, and ten gerontologists and key elderly informants.

Two reports were produced in 1985: A detailed 206-page report for Health and Welfare, and a 24-page summary of the conclusions and sixty recommendations under the title *Health Care for Elderly Canadians*. The following are a few of the conclusions arrived at as a part of the study:

A National Framework

Canadians, as usual, have very little confidence in themselves or in their own health-care system. As far as long-term care is concerned, they have far more conviction about the U.K. National Health Service, the European Office of WHO, the U.S. Rand Corporation or the National Institute on Aging. We need to examine what has been happening in our own country to discover some of the most interesting, innovative and promising developments in long-term-care delivery in the world.

This quotation from a Canadian gerontologist, elicited in this study, points to our tendency to look elsewhere rather than in our own country for answers to our own problems in spite of the fact that others are finding answers here (Kane and Kane, 1985). Part of this tendency is reflected by an internal parochialism called "provincialism." It is quite extraordinary how oblivious certain provinces seem to be to what is going on in other provinces, even adjacent ones.

Information in this rapidly growing field is increasingly available provincially — some provinces are in fact models of international renown. There have not been enough examples of mutual help between the provinces — it is felt that this should be provided more on a regional basis and much more actively encouraged and supported by Health and Welfare.

Provincial and territorial authorities have been forced by rapidly changing circumstances to develop a variety of increasingly effective health-care delivery systems for the elderly. Consideration should be given to an exchange program between certain senior federal civil servants and those in the field, including provincial health and social-service employees, officials of voluntary and professional organizations and selected university professors. This would make federal employees more aware of recent issues and solutions at provincial and local levels. It would also lead to more understanding of financial and other constraints on the federal government and of approaches taken by federal civil servants.

The Long-Term Care System

There is a widespread recognition throughout the country that the system is *heavily institutionalized* and very costly as a result. Examples of inappropriate placement and bed blockage occur in most institutions; the most common complaints concern general hospitals (see Chapter 27, this volume). Noted by many is the deteriorating health status of patients in long-term care. A frequently expressed need is for more chronic and extended-care facilities. Day care, day hospitals, respite and hospice beds are in very short supply. So much money is being spent on hospital care and the rapidly increasing technology of hospitals (see Chapter 26, this volume), that alternatives to hospitals, case finding, adequate assessment and social programs are starved for funds. Inappropriate use of drugs is a serious problem. Concern is expressed about high surgical rates for the elderly in some areas.

Competition between provincial departments of health and social services, or between the *medical and social models* (even where the departments are amalgamated) is described as destructive and a terrible waste of time. Health services are criticized by social services as being insufficiently imbued with a philosophy of community care. The social model is described by those on the health side as having an image of poverty and a means-test mentality. Lip service is given to the various so-called home support services in this country.

Programs such as meals-on-wheels, friendly visiting and even visiting homemakers (home helps) are considered to be almost frills by many respondents in departments of health. They are referred to as "soft services," not in any way as important as the "harder" medical, nursing and other health-care therapies provided in the home. It is not generally recognized that these "soft" services are also keeping older people out of institutions and that they may even be more cost-effective.

Most of the western provinces have progressed further than elsewhere in Canada in rationalizing their systems of long-term care. This has involved the adoption of a social model with increasing recognition that social admissions are frequently more important than medical admissions. Control of the medical profession over the system has decreased, and an attempt has been made to deprofessionalize home care. Continuing care has brought together provincial authorities responsible for long-term care both at home and in institutions. Case management, assessment and a single point of entry are all emphasized.

There is a general expression of agreement on the necessity for an overall *systems approach* to long-term care. The provinces have a great deal to learn from one another, i.e., from those provinces that have installed a systems approach. In the case, however, of most provincial governments and of the federal government itself, activities are too fragmented, with little relationship (sometimes even competition) between those responsible for hospital care, long-term care facilities and care at home. There is said to be too little support at all government levels for care outside of institutions and still too little interest in alternatives. A genuine commitment to the value of long-term care needs to be made at provincial/territorial and federal levels.

The Health Care Work Force

Similar to the concerns expressed about the high rate of institutional care for elderly Canadians, there is consensus almost everywhere of the dangers of *too much power wielded by too many physicians* on the long-term health-care system. Medicalization was described as working in collusion with institutionalization — for example, an alliance is seen to be forged between boards and medical staff. On the other hand, it is obvious, due to maldistribution, that some provinces and territories are suffering from too few, and not enough of the right categories, of physicians to care for the elderly.

Somewhat disquieting is the number of reports indicating physicians' relative lack of expertise or even interest in dealing with elderly patients. Physicians' attitudes were described as unfortunate and discouraging. It was felt by some that an increasing number of younger physicians are more enlightened. Several spoke of the hope that more women in medicine might help change the attitude of physicians towards the elderly and the treatment of chronic illness.

Virtually everyone in this survey in all parts of the country referred disparagingly to the lack of recognition in all medical schools in Canada of the demographic imperative of an aging population and of the unwillingness to change undergraduate and postgraduate curricula accordingly. Medical schools are described as being very slow to adapt to changing health-care demands.

Nursing leaders and organizations of *nurses* have been inveighing against the medical model for several years. Concern for medicalization of health care for the elderly is voiced by many, but is probably expressed most forcefully by nursing. There is uneasiness about what is described as a "struggle for turf," which has the potential to damage the health-care system, including care of the elderly. This problem does not as yet seem to be reflected at the actual patient-care level (according to my contacts), although concern is expressed about the present trends.

There were numerous complaints about the overprofessionalization, poor preparation and lack of concern of many nurses for the elderly, although their reputation seemed somewhat better in this regard than physicians. It was suggested that the highly professionalized nurse might price her/himself out of the market with what was described as an obsession with university degree qualifications. It was felt by some that we should be wary of replacing medicalization with "nursingization" or the horse-and-buggy doctor by the horse-and-buggy nurse.

Where long-term care is delivered according to a social rather than a medical model, *social workers* are considered more useful, necessary and even essential. This is certainly the case where institutional and home care (support) are under the aegis of social services. Criticism was directed at other members of the health team for not understanding and for not incorporating the social worker more frequently into the health team and for not recognizing the advantage of a generally more sensitive, nonjudgmental and less directive approach. Criticism of social workers included their overprofessionalization, sense of timelessness, restrictiveness and overconcern with sharing information.

One of the manpower issues most frequently expressed by government officials and others throughout Canada (more often on the health, but also on the social services side) is the unavailability of *rehabilitation therapists* in almost all parts of the country. This is part of the widespread underemphasis on the rehabilitation potential of the elderly. First and foremost is the expressed need for physiotherapists almost everywhere. Not far behind is the need for occupational therapists. Less well recognized, but expressed in several provinces, is the need for speech therapists and audiologists.

Problems expressed regarding *homemakers* included the difficulties of getting agreement on the definition of a homemaker as opposed to a home help; disagreement on their cost effectiveness; and their restriction in a highly medicalized, inflexible and unduly sophisticated health system. Professionalization of homemaking and the danger of decreasing standards due to increasing privatization were also said to be issues.

Cost Constraints and Funding

There is no doubt that the rising costs of health care for the elderly already pose a real crisis for some provinces. For those with a smaller economic base, there is little reserve for expansion, and it is difficult to redistribute resources away from the more traditional forms of health care when these services already fall below the national standard (for example, in the Atlantic Provinces). Where expansion of long-term care has taken place, this has sometimes occurred too quickly and unanticipated costs have had to be sustained (for example, in British Columbia). Provincial governments are very loath to cut back on long-term care services that are already in place, particularly with the increasing political clout of the aged.

Questions were asked about cost-control measures such as the following: In the process of *deinstitutionalization* are institutions available when really needed? In the *deprofessionalization* of health services, is there a sufficient number of professionals available to maintain quality? In the context of attempts at disease *prevention* are sufficient care facilities available for essentially non-preventable conditions such as Alzheimer's? Are people being held too long in *housing alternatives* before being admitted to institutions? In the urge to encourage *self-care by older persons* or use of her/his *informal networks,* is formal care available when necessary?

Caution was advised regarding additional methods of controlling burgeoning health costs. *Local autonomy,* for example, is a fine principle going back a long way in Canadian history. It doesn't make a great deal of sense, however, if the local areas are insufficiently organized or have too little money available. It can be used as an excuse by financially strapped provinces, unwilling to take their rightful responsibility and simply passing the actual costs back to the municipal level.

"Extra billing" and "user fees" were emotionally charged words in many parts of Canada at the time this survey was carried out (1984). In this study the main reaction against extra billing and user fees came from senior citizens, both individually and collectively, whether or not they had been personally involved.

Targetting or selectivity was mentioned as an issue by provincial authorities in all provinces but one and is felt to be inevitable by many. It is much less acceptable to social-service personnel than to those on the health side, who were, however, more enthusiastic about selectivity in the softer social services than in the harder health services. Arguments against selectivity include: administrative costs, demeaning aspects of the means (or even the needs) test and the very important matter of loss of social solidarity between the classes.

Privatization is a concept that is discussed by a great many in different parts of Canada. Increasing reliance on the commercial sector in at least three provinces raises questions of accountability to services users (and government), cost of enforcement of regulations, questionable influences on public policy, maintenance of quality of services, equality of access and increase in total costs of services (combined public and private).

There were many more criticisms about *federal funding arrangements* than anything else in this study. These included the recently enacted Canada Health-Care Act, the effect of provincial priorities being steered by federal funding, the dangers of relying on seed money and the general requirement for more money for burgeoning institutional and community health-care costs of an aging population.

It would seem reasonable to provide funding of long-term care on a more equalized economic basis (which might, for example, relate to the average annual income of the elderly in the province). Similarly, it would be fairer to fund Extended Health-Care Services, not just on a provincial per capita basis, but also to recognize the reality of demographic changes and give more to those provinces with a higher proportion of needy elderly (for example, those 75 years of age and over).

Data Collection and Research

There is complete agreement throughout the country on the desperate need for federal leadership in improving the collection of *data on long-term care.* This includes deciding on definitions of just what is to be collected, actual collection itself, analysis of data and comparisons (for example, international and interprovincial), publication in easily interpreted forms and periodic revision (keeping the data up-to-date).

There is a general recognition of the relative wealth of data on hospitals and physicians collected provincially and in turn federally. This reflects the bias of the system. They are, however, still insufficiently available for various age subcategories of the elderly (65-74, 75-84, 85 +).

There were complaints from almost everywhere about the absence of data on institutional care other than hospitals, and manpower services other than medical. Long-term care utilization data (including home care) and data on housing are either nonexistent or incomplete. Where they do exist, they are generally inaccurate.

Although a lot of work has been done on definitions of long-term institutional care, there is still concern about the appropriateness of existing levels of care and confusion regarding terms used in various parts of the country. Concern is also expressed about the accuracy of data collected on "extended care," and "residential care," and it is felt that not enough attempt is made to improve the response rate and ensure the completeness and accuracy of data collected on "homes for special care." We rely often on optimal long-term bed-per-population ratios for Great Britain or Western Europe. Because of differences in climate, distances and our social structure, such comparisons are not always appropriate, and we need to put more effort into developing made-in-Canada guidelines.

Canadian data on care at home were described by many in this study as almost completely useless. Data on home-support services are even more unreliable than for organized home care, which, although better, are relatively narrowly defined and payment oriented. It is felt that Health and Welfare must provide leadership in improving provincial and national data in this area.

Finally, better and more detailed data are needed both nationally and provincially on changing lifestyle patterns and health-care needs of the elderly. There is general agreement on the short-sightedness of discontinuing the Canada Health Survey. In several places the need was also expressed for better local data on elderly health-care needs.

Government officials generally felt that although *research* was necessary, the more practical geriatrically oriented research seemed to be of more use than the more academic, theoretical, gerontological type of research. The clinicians interviewed tended to emphasize the need for services rather than more research, unless it is on the basis of demonstration projects. They felt that what was needed was much more action on the provision of already well-proven services and facilities. Gerontologists, on the other hand, put a much higher premium on the value of research and (not surprisingly) justified the need for more basic research. They are, however, aware of the bias of government officials and practitioners, and are making an earnest attempt to provide more practical types of projects.

A combination of theoretical and practical research appears to be a pressing need, including, for example, more joint research by behavioural scientists, epidemiologists and geriatricians. Also important is multidisciplinary research crossing the borders of health, social services and housing. Finally, studies of the effectiveness and efficiency of home care are considered almost everywhere to be a top priority. There are some very sceptical people throughout the country who still assume that home care, and particularly home support, are not cost-effective, despite studies to the contrary in the United States and the United Kingdom.

References

Alberta, Government of
1984   *An Assessment/Placement Model for Long-Term Care Services in Alberta.* Interdepartmental Committee on Long-Term Care.

Canada, Government of
   1984   *Health and Welfare Canada 1984-85 Estimates Part III (Expenditure Plan).*
           Ottawa: Minister of Supply and Services.
Ferguson, G.
   1984   "Putting It All Together — The New Brunswick Extra Mural Hospital."
Fryer, M.L.
   1981   *Towards Meeting the Needs of Senior Citizens in Prince Edward Island.*
           Prince Edward Island Department of Health and Social Services.
Hastings, J.E.F. and Vayda, E.
   1986   "Health services organization and delivery: Promise and reality." Forth-
           coming, in R.G. Evans and G.L. Stoddard (eds.), *Medicare at Maturity:
           Achievements, Lessons and Challenges.* Toronto: Irwin.
Kane, R.L. and R.A. Kane
   1985   *A Will and a Way: What the United States Can Learn from Canada about
           Caring for the Elderly.* New York: Columbia University Press.
Manitoba, Government of
   1984   *Resources and Support Services to Seniors.* Interagency Committee on Sup-
           port Services to Seniors.
Newfoundland, Government of
   1984   *Royal Commission on Hospital and Nursing Home Costs.* Report to the
           Government of Newfoundland and Labrador.
Nova Scotia, Government of
   1984   *Home Life Supports Manual.* Department of Social Services.
Resources Management Consultants, Ltd.
   1983   *Survey of Geriatric Rehabilitation Needs.* Report to Government of the
           Yukon.
Saskatchewan, Government of
   1984   *Towards a Full and Vigorous Old Age.* Saskatchewan Interdepartmental
           Coordination Committee on Aging (SICCOA).
Schwenger, C.W.
   1985   *Health Care for Elderly Canadians (A New Role for Health and Welfare
           Canada).* (a) complete report — 206 pages, (b) summary of conclusions and
           recommendations — 24 pages. Health and Welfare Canada.
Social Planning Council of Metropolitan Toronto
   1984   *Caring for Profit — The Commercialization of Human Services in Ontario.*
Taylor, M.G.
   1978   *Health Insurance and Public Policy,* Montreal: McGill-Queens University
           Press.
   1986   "The Canadian Health Care System." In R.G. Evans and G.L. Stoddard
           (eds.), *Medicine at Maturity: Achievements, Lessons and Challenges.* Toron-
           to: Irwin.
Willis, L.
   1983   *Long-Term Care for the Elderly and Disabled in Yellowknife and the Ter-
           ritories.* A review for the Government of the Northwest Territories (revised
           December 1983).

Wilson, L.
    1982   "Historical perspectives — Canada." In *Gerontology: A Cross-National Core List of Significant Works* (with historical perspectives from Canada, the United Kingdom and the United States). Institute of Gerontology, University of Michigan.
    1983   "Health Care of the Aged from a Federal Aspect." Mimeo-lecture to M.H.Sc. students at University of Toronto.

26

Predictors, Patterns and Consequences of Nursing-Home Use in One Canadian Province

Evelyn Shapiro and N.P. Roos
Department of Social and Preventive
Medicine
University of Manitoba

Health policy making and program planning require information on the kinds of persons likely to use a specific service (predictors of use), the length of time persons will use the service (utilization patterns) and the effect its use will have on the consumption of other related resources. Predictors of use permit decision makers to calculate how many persons will consume a particular resource and to decide which of these persons might be more appropriately or more economically served by alternate programs. Utilization patterns reveal the rate at which a given quantity of a resource will accommodate new users. The effect of use on the utilization of other resources discloses whether the service substitutes for or adds to the cost of health care.

Despite growing awareness that the number of the very elderly (the major consumers of nursing-home care) is growing and that the cost of nursing-home care is increasing more rapidly than inflation.[1] Canadian research designed to address these questions relative to nursing-home use has been scarce. This chapter summarizes and discusses the findings of three studies that used Manitoba data to identify the predictors and patterns of nursing-home use and to assess the impact of nursing-home residency on hospital use.

Predictors of Nursing-Home Use (Shapiro and Tate, 1985)

Twenty-eight socio-demographic, health and health-care utilization variables from the Manitoba Longitudinal Study on Aging (Mossey et al., 1981) were used to address two questions: (1) What characteristics of the elderly predict nursing home use? (2) Do these characteristics or the size of their effect differ in the short run (within two and a half years of the interview) when compared with the long run (seven years)?

This research was supported by Grant number 607-1157-46, Research Programs Directorate, Health and Welfare Canada.

TABLE 1:
Factors Associated with the Risk of Becoming a User Relative to a Nonuser of a LTC Facility in the Short Run and Over Full Seven Years (Final Multiple Logistic Regression Model)

Variable	Short-Term Admission			Long-Term Admission		
	Relative Odds Estimate	95% Confidence Interval	Significance (p value)	Relative Odds Estimate	95% Confidence Interval	Significance (p value)
Age 85+/64-74	6.69	(3.80, 11.78)	.0001	8.34	(5.64, 12.33)	.0001
Age 75-84/65-74	3.21	(2.04, 5.06)	.0001	3.97	(3.03, 5.21)	.0001
No spouse/spouse living in household	2.66	(1.73, 4.09)	.0001	1.64	(1.25, 2.15)	.001
Residency/nonresidency in S. C. housing unit	2.64	(1.70, 4.09)	.0001	2.61	(1.92, 3.62)	.0001
Admitted/not admitted to hospital in 1971	2.42	(1.64, 3.57)	.0001	2.19	(1.68, 2.85)	.0001
1+/Zero disabilities in basic ADL	2.38	(1.34, 4.24)	.003	1.63	(1.05, 2.54)	.03
Fair or poor/satisfactory comprehension	1.72	(1.11, 2.67)	.01			
Fair to bad/excellent or good Self-rated health				1.48	1.15, 1.89	.002
Problem/no problem Remembering names of friends or relatives				1.44	(1.06, 1.96)	.02
Steady/less than steady state of mind				1.42	(1.01, 1.99)	.03
Male/Female				0.62	(0.48, 0.81)	.001
More frequent/less frequent or no contact with relatives				0.85	(0.74, 0.97)	.02

Model Chi Square = 217.96, df = 7, p = .0001

Model Chi Square = 483.35, df = 11, p = .0001

Table 1 summarizes the results of the analyses. In the short run, advanced age was the most significant predictor of nursing-home use. Persons over age 85 had almost seven times and those age 75-84 just over three times the odds of becoming users relative to the youngest elderly. Two social characteristics, residency in senior citizens' housing and living without a spouse at home, were next in importance to age, each increasing the odds of institutionalization over 2 and one-half times. Mental impairment, a hospital admission in the interview year and having one or more problems with basic activities of daily living (ADL) also contributed to institutionalization.

The key predictors of nursing-home use in the short term retained their significance over the full seven-year period. The impact of advanced age increased, while that of the other characteristics, such as the presence of a spouse in the household and having one or more problems with basic ADL, declined. In addition, being female, having low self-rated health and having frequent contact with relatives were significant predictors of institutional placement.

Three-factor interactions of admissions with pairs of significant variables disclosed a significant interaction between admission, age and basic ADL in both the short and long run. The impact of ADL problems on admission decreased substantially with age: the odds of institutionalization for 65 to 74-year-olds with one or more ADL problems were almost nine times those of persons with no problems, for 75 to 84-year-olds almost three times and for 85-year-olds only one and a half times, suggesting that the importance of having one or more problems with ADL declined with advancing age.

In the long run, the type of residence and the basic ADL measure showed significant interaction with admission. The elderly senior-citizen housing residents who reported one or more ADL problems were only slightly more at risk of admission than those with no disabilities (relative odds = 1.2). On the other hand, the relative odds of admission for similar persons in other types of community dwellings was 3.9 times those with no disabilities. This suggests that, while residents of retirement housing are more likely to enter a nursing home than their peers, living in such units helps to "protect" them from institutionalization when they have one or more disabilities.

Nursing-Home Utilization Patterns (Shapiro and Webster, 1984)

All persons admitted to nursing homes each year from 1974 through 1981 were followed until the end of 1981. In 1974, Manitoba had 6,825 nursing-home beds or 166 beds/1,000 persons aged 75 or more. By 1981, the number of beds had increased 11 percent to 7,606, or at the same rate as the increase in population aged 75 and over.

As expected, age was a major factor in nursing-home entry. Despite some variations from year to year, advancing age raised the admission rate from 3/1,000 persons aged 65 to 69 to about 65/1,000 persons aged 90 or more (Table 2). Eighty percent of the new admissions each year were 75 years old or

TABLE 2:
First Admissions per 1,000 Population in Each Age Group

Age Group	1974	1975	1976	1977	1978	1979	1980	1981
<65	.11	.11	.09	.07	.08	.10	.08	.11
65-69	2.68	2.48	2.61	2.38	2.49	1.83	1.64	3.13
70-79	11.73	11.12	10.28	8.33	8.75	8.34	8.81	11.19
80-89	42.82	43.44	38.95	31.88	37.73	31.55	37.18	43.84
90+	61.18	60.50	60.41	53.28	57.53	59.06	64.36	71.89

older, 15 percent were 65 to 74 years old and 5 percent were under age 65. The percentage of each age group among new admissions was stable over the eight years.

Men and women under age 75 had the same admission rate per thousand population, but the admission rate of women over age 75 was higher than that of males. From 1974 to 1981 just under 40 percent of new admissions were males. The stability of the ratio of male to female admissions may reflect the increased risk of females being institutionalized, but it probably also reflects the predominance of double-room occupancy and shared washrooms. When rooms and bathrooms are shared, the sex of the person to be admitted is often determined by the sex of the resident already occupying the premises.

The level of care distribution among new admissions is shown in Table 3. The percentage of admissions who required Level 1 care (the lightest level of care) was remarkably stable, ranging from 19 percent to 23 percent until 1981, when it dropped to 14 percent. Since 1981 was the year with the largest increase in the number of beds and with the highest number of new admissions, this sudden decrease in the percentage of Level 1 admissions appears to be due primarily to a change in policy regarding the allocation of new beds to higher levels of care rather than to the redistribution of existing beds or a change in admission practices by the previously operating institutions.

The percentage of first admissions at Levels III and IV (the heaviest levels of care) increased steadily from 22 percent in 1974 to about 40 percent in 1978 and remained about the same for the next three years. However, this increase appears to have taken place primarily at the expense of Level II rather than of Level I admissions. The percentage of Level II admissions fell from a high of 55 percent of all admissions in 1974 to only about 40 percent by 1978 and thereafter.

Since 96 percent of nursing-home admissions die in the nursing home or shortly after transfer to hospital, the analyses treated the term "separation" as synonymous with death and made no distinction between persons who died in the nursing home and those who were transferred to hospital before death. Table 4 shows the cumulative percentages of deaths at the end of each year for each admission cohort.

Despite the fact that individuals can be admitted to a facility at any time during the year, about 15 percent of first admissions were deceased by the end of the year in which they were admitted. Approximately one-third of each cohort died by the end of the second and over one-half were dead by the end of the fourth year. On the other hand, almost 20 percent of the 1974 cohort were still in the institution after eight years and the data suggest that the same would apply to subsequent cohorts. The decline in the separation rate each year, and especially after the sixth year, reveals that a small cohort of survivors remains in the nursing home for a relatively long time.

Mortality rates for males were consistently higher than for females in each age and level of care category. Persons admitted at higher levels of care died sooner than those who required less care. To compare the mortality rates of

Table 3:
Level of Care Distribution of First Admissions, 1974-81

Level of Care	1974	1975	1976	1977	1978	1979	1980	1981
% Level I	23	20	20	22	20	21	19	14
% Level II	55	53	48	41	40	35	40	48
% Level II and IV	22	27	32	37	40	44	41	38

Table 4:
Cumulative Percentage of Each Cohort Separated, 1974-81

Year Admitted	n	% Separated								% Still in Program
		1	2	3	4	5	6	7	8	
1974	1,801	17	36	47	56	65	72	77	81	18
1975	1,800	18	38	48	57	65	72	78	x	23
1976	1,688	16	31	44	56	63	70	x	x	29
1977	1,408	13	32	44	55	64	x	x	x	36
1978	1,658	15	30	44	55	x	x	x	x	45
1979	1,517	15	33	46	x	x	x	x	x	54
1980	1,625	13	31	x	x	x	x	x	x	69
1981	2,064	13	x	x	x	x	x	x	x	87

the cohorts, all deaths among the succeeding cohorts at the end of Years 2 and 4 were standardized on the age, sex and level of care distribution of the 1974 cohort. The data indicate that mortality rates among first admissions declined in 1976 but remained stable thereafter. Furthermore, the declines in mortality among the 1976 and later cohorts were more marked by the end of Year 2 than by the end of Year 4, suggesting that early gains tended to disappear over time.

Most people who are admitted to nursing homes die or deteriorate over time, especially if they require heavy care upon admission. However, some persons' functional status actually improves and others remain at the same level of care for a considerable length of time. Of Level I admissions who remained alive, approximately 25 percent of each cohort required more care by the end of the second year, 40 percent by the end of the fourth year and 50 percent by the end of the sixth year. Nevertheless, almost half the level I survivors in the 1974 admission cohort still required Level I care after eight years in the facility.

Among Level II admissions who survived, more than one third had deteriorated by the end of the second year, almost one half were in worse health by the end of the fourth year and slightly more than half were worse after six years. Here again, however, 45 percent of the surviving 1974 cohort of Level II admissions remained at Level II after eight years. Furthermore, a small minority (5 percent to 14 percent) of each Level II admission cohort required less care at the end of each of these time periods than they did when they were admitted.

Less than 20 percent of the people entering at the two heaviest levels of care survived six years. Eighty percent of these survivors remained classified as Levels III and IV. The rest of the survivors (15 percent to 20 percent, depending on the cohort) enjoyed better health than when they entered the facility. For example, at the end of the sixth year approximately 15 percent of one admission cohort were designated as needing Level II care and a small number improved enough to be classified as Level I.

The Effect of Nursing Homes on Hospital Use (Shapiro et al., 1985)

The use of the term "alternate care" facility to describe nursing homes assumes that these institutions serve a significant number of persons who might otherwise require hospital care. The following study was, therefore, designed to test the hypothesis that nursing-home beds reduce hospital bed consumption.

The data from the Manitoba Longitudinal Study on Aging were used to build four-year hospitalization histories for three groups: (1) new entrants to nursing homes during 1972-76; (2) long-term residents of nursing homes, i.e., those interviewed in these facilities in 1971 and still resident as of July 1, 1972; and (3) community residents who were never admitted to a nursing home up to the end of 1976. The histories of new admissions were constructed to identify hospital use during the two years before and the two years after they entered an institution. Histories of long-term nursing-home residents and community dwellers summarized use for the two years before and after July 1, 1974 (the pivot date) because this date is approximately the mid-point of the period for which data were available for new entrants. The age of the individuals in the three groups is their age at the pivot date.

Table 5 illlustrates the marked differences in the age and sex distribution of the three groups in the year before the pivot date. The most striking difference is in the proportion of elderly aged 85 or more: 58 percent of long-term nursing-home residents were in that age category as compared to 36 percent of persons about to be admitted to nursing homes and 10 percent of community residents. Over 80 percent of elderly new admissions and long-term residents of nursing homes were 75 years old or more in contrast to just over half of the community residents. Females were overrepresented in both groups of nursing home users, and over 40 percent of the long-term nursing home residents were women 85 years of age or older.

TABLE 5:
Age and Sex Characteristics of the Three Groups

Age	Sex	New Admissions	Long-Term Nursing Home Residents	Community Residents
65-74	M	5.2%	4.5%	25.2%
	F	11.0%	7.0%	23.5%
75-84	M	13.2%	10.2%	20.1%
	F	34.6%	20.1%	20.8%
85 +	M	15.3%	16.3%	5.2%
	F	20.8%	42.0%	5.2%
N		327	443	2993

Table 6 shows the odds of new admissions and long-term nursing-home residents being admitted to hospital prior to the pivot date relative to their peers living in the community. Despite the exclusion of decedents (by definition) in the new admissions group, the relative odds of hospital admission for the 65 to 74-year-olds who would enter a nursing home were already three and one-half times that of their community peers two years before their admission, and their relative odds of being hospitalized increased dramatically to 26.9 in the year before their pivot date. These "young" elderly were already much sicker than their community peers at least two years before using long-term facility care.

TABLE 6:
Relative Odds of Hospitalization Before Pivot Date Among New Nursing Home Admissions and Long-Term Nursing Home Residents as Compared to the Elderly Who Continue Living in the Community

Age	Two Years Before Pivot[1]		One Year Before Pivot[2]	
	New Admissions	Long-Term Residents	New Admissions	Long-Term Residents
65-74 years	3.4	0.8	26.9	1.0
75-84 years	1.6	1.3	5.2	0.9
85+ years	1.4	0.7	3.0	0.5

[1] Best fitting log-linear model was HAG, SAG (Goodness of Fit Chi Sq. = 8.18, p = .5160, df = 9) in which A represents age, S sex, H hospitalization, and G group.
[2] Best fitting log-linear was HS, SAG, HAG (Goodness of Fit Chi Sq. = 7.41, p = .4929, df = 8) wih letters representing the same variables as above.

The hospitalization pattern of those over age 75 who were to enter a nursing home appeared to be quite similar to that of their community counterparts until the year before their nursing-home admission, when their relative odds rose from about 1.5 to 5.2 and from 1.5 to 3 for the 75 to 84-year-olds and those of 85+, respectively.

During each of the two years before their pivot date, the odds of the very elderly long-term nursing home residents being admitted to hospital were about a half to two-thirds those of their community counterparts despite the higher mortality rate of the institutionalized (see Table 7).

TABLE 7:
Mortality Rates by Age for Community Residents, New Nursing Home Admissions and Nursing Home Residents in Each of the Two Years After Pivot Date

Age	One Year After Pivot			Two Years After Pivot		
	Community	New Admissions	Long-Term Residents	Community	New Admissions	Long-Term Residents
65-74	2.9%	18.9%	6.5%	4.5%	9.3%	7.0%
75-84	5.4%	21.2%	9.1%	6.6%	9.1%	14.8%
85+	15.3%	20.3%	24.4%	11.1%	20.4%	15.9%

The early manifestation of special problems among the youngest elderly who become nursing-home users was also reflected in their hospital day use. Two years before placement, their relative odds of high use (using 31 or more hospital days if admitted) were almost five times those of their community peers. Persons over age 75 did not show similar signs of impending institutionalization so early.

In the year before entering a nursing home, the relative odds of using 31 or more days when hospitalized increased substantially for all age groups. While some of this increase could be attributable to the time they wait for a nursing home after acute care is no longer required, the consistency with which the relative odds decreased with age (from 6.7 to 4.9 to 2.5) suggests that this high use also reflects the very serious health problems of the youngest elderly. In fact, about one-half of the 65 to 74-year-olds entered the nursing home from hospital rather than from the community, in contrast to only a third of those aged 75 or more.

The mortality rates of all three groups in each of the two years after their pivot date are shown in Table 7. In the first year, all new nursing home admissions had higher mortality rates than their community peers, but the youngest admissions also had about the same death rate as older admissions (about 20 percent of each group died). In marked contrast, the percentage of decedents among community residents and long-term nursing home residents increased with advancing age. During the second year after their pivot date, age was a factor in survival for all three groups although both institutionalized samples continued to have higher mortality rates than their community peers. Not only were new and long-term nursing home residents generally sicker than the elderly in the community, but new facility entrants, especially those under age 85, were at a particularly high risk of dying in the first year of institutionalization.

Table 8 presents the expected and observed number of hospital admissions for new nursing-home entrants and long-term residents relative to their community peers. When age, sex and survivorship are taken into account, nursing homes play a significant role in reducing hospital admissions after the elderly have been institutionalized for more than one year. Among the long-term residents, based on the experience of the elderly living in the community, 116 persons should have been hospitalized in the year after their pivot date. Instead, only 76 were hospitalized (p = < .001). Of new admissions, 63 were hospitalized, in contrast to the expected 79 during their second year in a long-term care facility (p < .05). Also, in this second year after the pivot date, 74 long-term nursing home residents were hospitalized when one would have anticipated 94.

This substantial reduction in hospital admissions occurs primarily as a result of the high proportion of elderly over age 75, but especially over age 85, in long-term care facilities. There was no significant difference between the

TABLE 8
Expected and Observed Number of Persons Admitted to Hospital[1]

	One Year After Pivot		Two Years After Pivot	
	New Admissions (p value)	Long-Term Residents (p value)	New Admissions (p value)	Long-Term Residents (p value)
Age 65-74				
N Expected	16 (NS)	11 (NS)	10 (NS)	10 (NS)
N Observed	17	9	11	7
Age 75-84				
N Expected	52 (NS)	33 (NS)	34 (NS)	33 (NS)
N Observed	48	30	29	26
Age 85+				
N Expected	43 (NS)	72 (<.001)	35 (<.05)	51 (NS)
N Observed	40	37	23	41
Total				
Expected	111 (NS)	116 (<.001)	79 (<.05)	94 (<.05)
Observed	105	76	63	74

[1] Level of Significance (p value) = Chi Sq. with 1df with Chi Sq =
$\frac{(\text{Expected} - \text{Observed})^2}{\text{Observed}}$

observed and expected number hospitalized among the 65 to 74-year-old new or long-term nursing home residents.

While nursing homes reduce the number of elderly admitted to hospital, they appear to have no significant impact on reducing higher-than-average hospital day use once individuals are hospitalized. For persons admitted to hospital, the number of new admissions and long-term residents who used 18 or more days was similar to what would have been expected had they resided in the community. This may be because the illnesses for which they are hospitalized are more serious than those of community dwellers or because the facilities are no better at accommodating early discharges than are families or the home care program.

Discussion

Two recent U.S. studies (Branch and Jette, 1982; Weissert and Scanlon, 1983) also used representative samples and similar analytic methods to identify the predictors of nursing-home use. One or both confirm that age, living alone or without a spouse at home (the type of residence was not included in these studies) are the strongest predictors of nursing-home use, with mental impairment and ADL dependency also significant contributors to institutionalization, especially when ADL dependency is high. The use of ambulation aids, a variable used only by Branch and Jette (1982) as well as living in a cold climate, a variable used only by Weissert and Scanlon (1983), were also found to be a positive predictor of institutional placement.

Since the factors that significantly increase the risk of nursing-home use in the short run continue to exert a major influence over a considerably long time, the identification of potential users can occur relatively early. Further investigations within the Canadian context are needed, but it is not too soon to consider how the information on predictors could be used. As Branch (1984) demonstrates by testing the sensitivity and specificity of each risk factor, screening that would use individual risk factors as a signal for intervention would be of questionable value. However, the analyses by Weissert and Scanlon (1983) suggest a more practical and economical approach. By calculating the probability of institutionalization for persons with specific constellations of traits, persons would not be classified as high risk simply because they are old or dependent or alone, but because the combination of these and/or other factors would make it highly probable that they would enter a nursing home. Health and other professionals in contact with the elderly might use these "constellations" to help them identify those most at risk. Furthermore, the constellation of characteristics that signal high risk could help in evaluating whether interventions to change the outcome were effective.

The significantly greater impact of socio-demographic variables than health status variables on nursing-home admission raises questions about the credibility of "snapshot" studies on nursing home residents (most of whom are the very old). Such studies rely exclusively or primarily on basic ADL assessments to identify the individuals who, it is then reported, do not really "need" to remain in the facility. This is especially true when the impact of ADL dependency on institutionalization appears to decline sharply with age and with time. In fact, this study's findings suggest that the current importance generally attributed to basic physical functioning status relative to nursing-home use may well be overrated.

Despite some ambiguities in current research results, the information currently available on predictors of institutional placement can be useful for policy-making, planning and practice as long as its limitations are taken into account. As indicated, more Canadian data are needed and all the data on which the research findings of this and other studies are based reflect policies and usage during the 1970s. Therefore, changes in usage during the 1980s (independent of or as a result of changes of the policies and practice of other health-care services such as hospitals and home care) that affect admissions could change both determinants and the size of their impact. This problem may, however, be inevitable due to the lag in the availability of data for research and the time it takes for research to be completed.

For planning purposes, it is now possible to make rough estimates of the number of elderly who will be institutionalized in the near future by using currently available data to identify elderly with constellations of traits signalling a high probability of their using a nursing home. It must be emphasized again, however, that it is prevalence of a combination of risk factors rather than prevalence of a specific risk characteristic that needs to be used in making such estimates.

From a program perspective, the findings provide a basis for targetting specific programs to the elderly at greatest risk of institutionalization and for testing the efficacy of these programs in reducing nursing-home use. Thus far, the main thrust has been in the direction of providing home care or components of home care (e.g., adult day care) with or without restrictive eligibility criteria. Home care may indeed be appropriate for many elderly who would otherwise require a nursing-home bed. However, for some high-risk elderly such as men over age 80 who live alone and have a mental functioning problem, the cost of home care may be higher than that of a nursing home and they might be less safe at home. Furthermore, such men may not be able to be sustained in the community with home-care programs that restrict eligibility to those in need of a medical service.

It might, therefore, be useful to increase the variety of responses designed to reduce or delay nursing-home admission and to evaluate the potential of these programs for meeting this objective. Encouraging small groups of elderly who live alone to share living quarters might help to develop a mutual support system as a bulwark against future institutionalization. Offering practical guidance to families who are finding it difficult to cope with mentally impaired relatives might forestall or delay nursing-home admission.

The constellation of factors that increases the probability of nursing-home use also raises questions about the restrictive criteria that now apply in some jurisdictions to home care. These constellations strongly suggest that many of those most at risk need help that is primarily nonmedical. It might, therefore, be useful to reassess current policies that, although meant to substitute home care for nursing-home care, may actually have little effect in reducing or delaying institutional use.

The results of the study on the utilization patterns of nursing homes indicate that Manitobans enter nursing homes at a much older age and remain in these institutions longer than persons in the United States (Liu and Manton, 1983; Vincente et al., 1980-81). This is probably because Manitoba's admission, payment and home-care policies have resulted in persons entering on the basis of need and as a "last resort" when their advanced age, combined with other factors, make community care no longer a viable alternative. In the U.S., the source of payment is the most significant determinant of length of stay (Liu and Manton, 1983).

The turnover rate of beds in Manitoba, i.e., the rate at which new users can be accommodated, depends largely on the age, sex and care level of admissions. Concern about an impending bed "crisis" because of the growth in the proportion of the very old is not supported by the data on nursing-home utilization patterns or on hospital use. Although the nursing-home admission rate for this age group is the highest and it accounts for about one-third of each admission cohort, it is the smallest in actual number and its members die the fastest even when they require only minimal care on admission. Furthermore, the hospital use of the very elderly who are in nursing homes as compared to their community counterparts suggests that their institutionalization produces real savings in hospital-bed utilization.

The study's findings also show that new bed construction does not automatically ensure increased bed availability for new admissions. Manitoba had a comparatively generous supply of beds in 1974, the growth in bed supply kept pace with the growth of the population over age 75 and the beds were kept full. Nevertheless, fewer new people were accommodated from 1976 to 1980 than in 1974 or 1975. This was at least partly because the short-term gain in survival rate after 1976 contributed to a drop in the number of new entrants. As these early gains in survival rates almost disappeared, the number of new admissions in 1980 and 1981 rose by 108 and 339 respectively, despite a loss of 30 beds in 1980 and a gain of only 114 beds in 1981.

Although no one is admitted to a Manitoba nursing home without having been assessed as requiring such care, nursing homes can influence turnover rates by their right to decide whom they will admit. The minimal results achieved by government efforts to encourage the voluntary redistribution of existing resources in favour of heavy-care admissions illustrates the difficulty governments can encounter in trying to change the pattern of health care delivered by autonomous facilities that can select whom they will admit even when they are almost totally dependent on public funding. It is, therefore, surprising that so little attention has been paid to the contribution of nursing-home admission practices to overall utilization patterns and that so little discussion has been devoted to considering whether nursing homes should retain their control over admissions.

To a minor extent, the need to alter some buildings originally designed to provide only minimal care constitutes a barrier to change. In addition, some homes, especially those delivering all four levels of care, try hard to retain their proportion of Level I residents because these persons contribute activity and vitality to the ambience of the facility. Furthermore, caring for Level I residents may be more profitable, despite the per diem differentials paid for heavier levels of care in Manitoba. Concern for staff satisfaction may also encourage the maintenance of the status quo.

The data on lengths of stay and changes in health status over time for successive nursing-home admission cohorts provide several interesting insights into what happens to persons who are institutionalized. The mortality rate of new admissions at the beginning of their nursing-home stay was higher than in subsequent years. Two other findings indicate that the excess of deaths shortly after admission cannot be explained simply by assuming that a group of very sick, terminally ill persons were admitted each year. First, although higher-level-of-care admissions died faster than those requiring less care, the mortality rates during this early period was higher than subsequently among all first admission cohorts at all four levels of care. Second, the greatest deterioration in health status (as measured by increase in level-of-care requirement) among Level I and II admissions who survived also occurred during this time. It is possible that new admissions at every care level include a proportion of medically unstable persons with undiagnosed and untreated illnesses. Also, the decision of some functionally impaired persons to seek admission may reflect a prescience of subtle changes in health that are not yet clinically detectable. Furthermore, placement itself may be associated with some increased risk of deterioration or death, although the literature indicates that this question is still unresolved.

Some survivors maintained and even improved their ability to function, although most deteriorated or died. Almost half of the Level I survivors and only a slightly smaller proportion of Level II survivors who were admitted in 1974 still required the same level of care at the end of eight years. At the same time, almost 10 percent of the surviving Level II admissions needed less care than when they entered the facility. Perhaps the consistency with which a group of each cohort of survivors maintained or enhanced their health status reflects the "hardiness" of survivors, but it may also be a result of Manitoba's policy of making regular quality-of-care assessments of nursing homes.

The traditional expectation of never returning home and the added burden of paying even modest per diem charges while maintaining a home mean that almost all elderly persons relinquish their home and major belongings when they enter a nursing home regardless of their level-of-care requirement on admission. Although their age and previous type of living arrangement might preclude most of them from returning home, the current situation reinforces the inability of institutions to discharge persons whose health improves. Reducing the effects of these barriers to change may help encourage better use of a scarce and expensive resource.

The evidence from the study on the hospital use of new and long-term nursing home residents shows that elderly persons entering or living in these institutions are sicker than their community counterparts (also see Goldstein et al., 1984), and that, when age, sex and mortality rates are taken into account, nursing homes significantly reduce the hospitalization rate of their elderly residents to below that of their community peers. The savings in hospital usage may, in fact, be greater than the data show. Even though institutionalization of the youngest elderly does not appear to decrease their hospital admission rate, their particularly problematic health status (as indicated by their high hospital use before and high mortality after nursing-home admission) would likely have resulted in higher hospital-bed consumption than their peers if they had remained in the community. Clearly, the higher the hospital-bed occupancy rates in an area, the more important the role played by nursing homes as an alternate care facility. Reduced hospital usage also benefits the elderly institutional residents themselves because they are less often subjected to the stress accompanying hospital admission and to the adverse consequences of hospitalization (Gillick et al., 1982).

The significant reduction of the hospital admission rate of the elderly in nursing homes is not matched by a similar reduction in longer-than-average stays once they are admitted to hospital. This apparent anomaly may reflect the capacity of nursing homes to care for the dying or for those with relatively minor acute episodes of illness for which the community elderly may be hospitalized so that when hospitalization occurs, the problems may be particularly serious or complex. It is also possible, however, that long-term-care facilities may not be any better at accommodating early discharges from hospital for elderly persons with serious or complicated illnesses than families or community care programs.

Finally, it is important to note that the decrease in hospital use as a result of institutionalization should not be interpreted to mean that the supply of nursing-home beds or the number of users should be increased. First, providing nursing-home care, although less expensive than hospital services, is also costly. Second, real savings through the reduction of hospital use may not be achieved unless hospital beds are closed or no new beds are added to accommodate growth in the general population or in the number of elderly. Furthermore, institutionalization is neither the most desired nor the most desirable living arrangement. Most elderly prefer to remain at home and in control of their own lives. Community care can provide many of them with this option if the policies of the program are consistent with their needs. Besides, the reduction in hospital consumption is only one measure of social value. The value of home, familiar surroundings, personal preference and other factors also need to be taken into account. Furthermore, there are no Canadian studies that compare the effectiveness of nursing home and home care in reducing hospital use.

Nevertheless, public policy must take account of the interrelationship between the use of hospital and nursing home beds in order to plan effectively for the future. Policies affecting nursing-home bed construction and admissions that fail to recognize the interdependence of acute and long-term institutional resources will create problems that could have been anticipated.

Note

[1]   While the number of nursing-home beds in Manitoba increased by 11.4 percent (from 6,825 to 7,606) between 1974 and 1981, public expenditures for nursing-home

care more than tripled, growing from just under $30.5 M to almost $99.5 M in 1981. The province's net operating cost per bed increased by 184 percent, about double the inflation rate as measured by the CPI. (The basic per diem room-and-board charge paid by each resident also increased from $4.50 to $14.35.)

References

Branch, L.G.
  1984   "Relative risk rates of nonmedical predictors of institutional care among elderly persons." *Comprehensive Therapy* 10(7):33-40.

Branch, L.G. and A.M. Jette
  1982   A prospective study of long-term care institutionalization among the aged. *American Journal of Public Health* 72(12):1373-1379.

Gillick, M.R., N.A. Serrell and L.S. Gillick
  1982   Adverse consequences of hospitalization in the elderly." *Social Science in Medicine* 16:1033-1038.

Goldstein, R.L., E.W. Campion, A.G. Mulley et al.
  1984   "Nursing home patients admitted to a medical intensive care unit." *Medical Care* 22(9):854-862.

Liu, K. and K.G. Manton
  1983   "The characteristics and utilization pattern of an admission cohort of nursing home patients (I)." *The Gerontologist* 23(1):92-98.

Mossey J., B. Havens, N.P. Roos and E. Shapiro
  1981   "The Manitoba longitudinal study on aging: Description and methods." *The Gerontologist* 21(5):551-558.

Shapiro, E. and R. Tate
  1985   "Predictors of long-term care facility use among the elderly." *Canadian Journal on Aging* 4(1):11-19.

Shapiro, E., R. Tate and N.P. Roos
  1985   "Hospital utilization patterns among nursing home residents prior and subsequent to their admission." Paper presented at the International Congress on Gerontology, New York, July.

Shapiro, E. and L.M. Webster.
  1984   "Nursing home utilization patterns for all Manitoba admissions, 1974-1981." *The Gerontologist* 24(6):610-617.

Vincente L., J.A. Wiley and R.A. Carrington
  1980- "Duration of stay and other aspects of nursing-home use." *International*
  81   *Journal on Aging and Human Development* 12(4):301-311.

Weissert, W. and W.J. Scanlon
  1983   "Determinants of institutionalization of the aged." Chapter 1 in Scanlon (ed.), *Project to Analyze Existing Long-Term Care Data*, Vol. 3. *Long-Term Care Service Utilization & Outcomes*. Washington, D.C.: The Urban Institute.

27

Patients Awaiting Discharge From Hospital

Jane Aronson and Victor W. Marshall
Department of Behavioural Science
University of Toronto

Joanne Sulman
Department of Social Work
Mount Sinai Hospital, Toronto

In recent years, the growing phenomenon of elderly patients awaiting discharge from acute-care hospitals has received increased attention in the medical and health literature and from governments and the media. Typically, we are told, such patients enter hospital with acute conditions but, when the indicated treatment is completed, remain hospitalized because suitable care is not available elsewhere. For some elderly patients, an episode of acute illness is associated with decrements in their ability to return to the same level of independence in their living situation. However, a full program of active rehabilitation to counteract these losses is rarely available for them in acute-care hospitals. Hospital social workers are often involved in assessing such patients' current needs, assisting them and their families in making their way through what may seem a confusing array of services and application procedures. These difficulties are compounded by a lack of coordination of service delivery and scant community support services, which often result in long delays in discharge.

Patients awaiting discharge from hospital are frequently presented as the unfortunate consequence of population aging: the health-care system is portrayed as not having adjusted to an increased demand for services caused by increases in the population of very old people, an increased proportion of

Jane Aronson's work on this paper has been supported by a doctoral fellowship from the National Health Research Development Program of Health and Welfare Canada. Victor Marshall's research is supported by a National Health Scientist Award from the same program. The project from which this paper emanates is supported by an award to Victor Marshall from the Laidlaw Foundation.

elderly women and, derivatively, of widows and single old people with fewer younger family members able or willing to care for them. Underlying this rhetoric may be found a political and economic background of recession, government concerns to constrain medical-care expenditures and reliance on the private, profit-motivated sector to provide much long-term care.

Accounts of this group of waiting patients in the research literature and in the media are not, generally speaking, sympathetic to them. They are depicted as medically uninteresting, as frustrating to the smooth flow of patients through acute-hospitals, as unwarranted consumers of expensive health-care resources and as a threat to acutely ill patients who have stronger claims to the beds they occupy. They are seen as "bed-blockers" (McAlpine, 1979), "inappropriately placed patients" (Metropolitan Toronto District Health Council, 1984), "misplaced patients" (Gross and Schwenger, 1981) and "placement problems" (Fisher and Zorzitto, 1983). The "extra" days of hospital care they consume are seen as "administratively necessary days" (Markson, Steel and Kane, 1983). Such terms give primacy to the hospital organization and health-care resources rather than to patients' needs.

The tone and ingredients of such definitions are more explicit in the following:

If a hospital is to function efficiently for the treatment of acute medical and surgical conditions, there is no place in it for geriatric medicine; its presence within the walls of the hospitals acts like dry rot eroding the very fabric of the institution. Old people must be got out of acute hospitals (Lawrence, 1979:19).

In a Toronto newspaper article entitled "Shortage of Beds in Hospitals Nearing Crisis, Doctor Testifies" (Polanyi, 1984), a doctor is quoted as saying that ". . . Canadian hospitals have become 'baby-sitting' services for elderly patients who need chronic care." Another article (McNenly, 1984) refers to the needs of a "deluge" of old people and suggests that: "Ironically, at a time when the government is trying to hold down rising health costs, the cost of providing care for patients who shouldn't be in acute-care hospitals is staggering." Under a headline "Bed-blockers' Blamed for Emergency Ward Crunch" (Grant, 1985), a quoted source indicates that: "The Problem. . .is how to take care of these long-term care patients who seem to be 'imposing' on the system. Nobody wants them. The hospitals don't. The families don't and certainly the government doesn't."

This chapter focusses on the definition of elderly patients awaiting discharge, critically examines the accuracy and implications of definitions such as those noted above and considers alternative ways of understanding the predicament of these patients. Concentrating on meanings and definitions does not alter the reality that some elderly people do consume a substantial share of public expenditures on health care, including the costs generated by their apparently disproportionate occupancy of acute beds. However, we will argue that the definition of elderly patients awaiting discharge is framed in images that reflect certain social and political interests. Observations that are presented as inevitable, factual features of this patient population, we view as aspects of a socially constructed reality reflecting social and political interests.

We address three key questions in this chapter:

(1) *The Scale of the Problem.* How many people wait long periods prior to discharge? How costly are they? Do they pose a crisis for the health-care system?

(2) *Alternative Constructions of Patients Awaiting Discharge.* How are they constructed by different participants and interest groups in the health-care system, such as physicians, other service providers, hospital administrators, government? What does a long waiting period mean for the patients themselves?

(3) *The Consequences of Alternative Definitions.* What ramifications do different definitions have at the levels of professional practice, hospital organization and policy making?

The Scale of the Problem

As reflected in the quotations above, common definitions of the problem of elderly patients awaiting discharge suggest a large population that imposes high costs on the health-care system. Both dimensions of scale, size and costliness, present difficulties in measurement.

Estimates of the extent of the problem are usually expressed in terms of bed occupancy. For Canada as a whole, Paget (1983) estimates that between 10 percent and 20 percent of acute hospital beds are occupied by patients waiting for long-term placement. Gross and Schwenger (1981) estimate the figure for Ontario at 12.7 percent, while a recent study sets the figure for Toronto at 13.9 percent (Metropolitan Toronto District Health Council, 1984).

Bed occupancy is an easily available statistic but not a very useful one. Gross and Schwenger (1981) note that bed occupancy figures are at times based on arbitrary limits of legitimate hospital stay, usually 30 days in the Canadian context, which may obscure cases where a much shorter, or longer, stay was medically necessary. Alternatively, bed occupancy estimates may rely on a simple primary diagnosis as the basis for evaluating legitimate length of stay, being insensitive to the multiple conditions that characterize typical geriatric patients. Others raise additional questions about the use of the bed, rather than the patient, as the unit of analysis. Bed-based analysis implies that all beds generate equal consumption of hospital resources. This is a highly doubtful assumption because long-stay elderly patients currently receive less expensive hospital services than acutely ill patients (LeTouzé, 1984).

By tracking a sample of elderly people over a five-year period, Roos, Shapiro and Roos (1984) were able to produce patient-based, rather than bed-based, figures. Contrary to common belief, they found that, while the aged as a whole are heavy consumers of acute hospital services, high bed occupancy figures are accounted for by a very small proportion who are admitted frequently and for long stays. Their Manitoba data suggest that less than one-fourth of the elderly are hospitalized in any given year and that just 5 percent of the elderly consume fully 59 percent of the hospital days used by the elderly. A five-year follow-up showed that 35 percent of the elderly had no hospitalization, while 9 percent used 57 percent of all acute and chronic hospital patient days (see also Roos and Shapiro, 1981; Shapiro, 1980; Shapiro and Roos, Chapter 26 in this volume). In fact, the vast majority of elderly patients admitted to acute-care hospitals are treated and discharged rapidly.

The image of a threatening deluge of old people bearing down on the hospital system (an image recently found in a major Canadian Medical Association report, [1984]) can be more accurately replaced by one of a small group of patients who can potentially be targetted for special preventive or service delivery measures.

Although the size of the patient population appears debatable and perhaps partly an artifact of measurement, fairly consistent findings describe the type of patient involved in the specific problem of discharge delays. Elderly patients awaiting discharge tend to be over age 75, women, waiting transfer to heavy-care facilities (rather than to alternative destinations), suffering from a variety of conditions and functional impairments, with a high incidence of dementia (Fisher and Zorzitto, 1983; Markson, Steel and Kane, 1983; McArdle, Wylie and Alexander, 1975; Rubin and Davies, 1975).

There are regional differences in length of stay in acute hospitals. In Winnipeg, a city relatively well endowed with institutional resources, the average wait for nursing-home transfer in 1976 was 71.2 days (Shapiro and Roos, 1981). Recent Toronto data (Metropolitan Toronto District Health Council, 1984) indicate much longer waiting periods, ranging from 57.1 days for residential care to 124.3 days for chronic care. The latter data underestimate the problem by including palliative care and special rehabilitation figures, both of which have much shorter waiting times. Reports of patients waiting for periods between two and three years are not uncommon.

As noted above, a number of studies question the extent to which additional costs can be related to the bed occupancy of patients awaiting discharge. Such patients are, explicitly, no longer receiving treatment for acute conditions and it is likely that they consume relatively fewer hospital services than the typical hospital patient (LeTouzé, 1984). Hutton states that it is ". . . erroneous to consider a long-stay patient in an acute medical bed as occupying an 'expensive' bed. She requires only board, lodging and nursing care and makes no demands on expensive diagnostic and therapeutic services'' (Hutton, 1976).

Challenging the assumption that geriatic patients pose unwarranted financial demands on the system, Roos, Shapiro and Roos (1984:33) ask, "Whose Demand for Service?" Rejecting the notion that ". . . the patient and his medically defined 'needs' directly determine hospital and surgical patterns," they suggest that physician behaviour contributes independently to the generation of costs. Evidence for physician-generated demand consists of variations found in practice patterns, rates of surgery and diagnostic procedures. The general argument that physicians play a major role in creating "demand" for their services is well put by Evans (1984:84-91), who also applies it to the hospital setting:

> . . .the direct influence of providers on use is reflected in the universal observation that bed availability is the principal determinant of bed use — a built bed is a filled bed — sometimes referred to as Roemer's Law (Roemer 1961). . . . Overall bed capacity emerges from study after study as the single most important factor influencing hospital inpatient utilization, and the level of bed capacity at which use would appear to stop responding to increases is double or triple current capacity or need estimates (Evans, 1984: 85-86).

Once hospitalized, patients provide a stimulus through which demand may be created by others. Fisher and Zorzitto note this phenomenon and deplore its effects on patients (1983:331-332):

> The very presence of the patient, even though he or she may only be awaiting transfer, can prompt investigations for the sake of completeness. . . . The acute care medical setting encourages such patients to be passive and dependent while the necessary investigations and treatments are undertaken, since the emphasis is on diagnosis, treatment and cure, rather than on rehabilitation.

In summary, prevailing images of a deluge of old people imposing staggering costs on the hospital system are overdrawn. That such patients are nonetheless designated as a threat to the health-care delivery system alerts us to the socially constructed nature of the "bed-blocking" crisis. Estes (1983:446) notes that ". . .the less the knowledge base for a particular problem is empirically grounded, the greater the influence of social and political factors in the interpretation and acceptance of information as knowledge." She and other writers from a social construction of reality perspective suggest that the construction of crises reflects prevailing structures of power rather than non-political, "objective" states of affairs (Edelman, 1968; Marshall, 1981a; Minkler, 1983). In this view, alarmist information about demographic causation of a health-care crisis, the tendency to blame the victims for the problem, the arousal of public anxiety and the creation of a climate of public opinion in which sacrifices are called for should be seen as rhetoric that serves political interests.

Alternative Constructions of Patients Awaiting Discharge

We have noted that older patients awaiting discharge are frequently viewed negatively. Shapiro and Roos (1981) consider the constructions of these patients put forth by a number of relevant "constituencies," including physicians, hospital adminstrators, governments and the public. The interests of these groups can be inferred from the medical literature and from the media and these are briefly reviewed here. Patients must be added to the list of interested constituencies, although their interests find less direct expression.

Most definitions of this patient population turn on the needs of hospitals and the health-care system rather than on the needs of patients. Hall and Blytheway's data from a British sample of hospital authorities' definitions of the "blocked bed" problem underline the organizational definition of patients (1982:1987): ". . . blockage is identified with a failure of movement within the organization: the failure of the patient rather than the services to move."

Medical practitioners' frustrations at the inability to admit and treat acutely ill patients creates pressures on administrators and governments. This frustration embodies numerous complex elements: the acute, curative orientation of Canada's health-care system; the socialization of physicians and other health-care providers that stresses cure and values heroic, scientific medicine (Marshall, 1981b); the fact that the elderly are seldom the preferred patients of health professionals (Williams, 1981); and reimbursement mechanisms that render the treatment of older patients less financially rewarding. Beds filled by long-stay patients are unavailable for patients requiring elective and non-emergency procedures and treatment. The higher the physician-bed ratio, the more likely will physicians define this situation as a crisis.

Presumably, hospital administrators experience contradictions in their conception of this patient population. They are pressured by interest groups within the hospital and by government. On the other hand, as noted earlier, their own interests are served by having relatively inexpensive patients in acute-care beds, who effectively subsidize the hospital by compensating for the higher costs of acutely ill patients.

There is a counterthread of sentiment against the view that the aged patient is interfering with more appropriate acute care (Lawrence, 1979; McArdle et al., 1975). Especially in the British literature, such views are tempered with a more patient-centred and critical stance that recognizes that the existing boundaries between acute and chronic institutions and between medical and social care do not serve patients well (Isaacs, 1981). An additional strain of self-criticism notes, for example, the damaging consequences of negative labelling and the pejorative language used to describe elderly patients in acute beds:

> Defamatory language is accompanied by the symbols of medical exasperation: the cot sides, the barrier chair, the catheter bag and the massive usage of sedatives. These to me do not represent the needs of patients, but rather the frustration of the doctors who have been unable to perform the effective transactions with their patients on which their professional satisfactions are based (Isaacs, 1981:146; see Fisher and Zorzitto, 1983, for a similar view expressed in the Canadian context).

The term "bed blocker" is increasingly seen in not only the media but also in professional literature. It subtly connotes a motivated, active involvement of patients in their situation. Suggestions that families are to blame for the acute-bed shortage are another way of holding the victims of the situation responsible. There is evidence that families provide care even though their resources, time and energy may be taxed (see Chapters 17, 19 and 23 in this volume). However, when these resources are exhausted, families correctly perceive the acute-care hospital as the only immediate alternative.

Isaac's (1981) allusion to the signs of medical exasperation are echoed in several studies that examine the meaning of long waiting periods for patients themselves. In a Boston study, Gillick, Serrell and Gillick (1982) applied the concept "social iatrogenesis" to the process of hospitalization and studied four specific symptoms of psychophysiologic dysfunction, unrelated to the acute problems for which patients were originally admitted. They found these symptoms (confusion, falling, not eating, incontinence) in 40.5 percent of the elderly patients studied. Of that group, 47.1 percent of the symptoms were found to be subject to related medical interventions (psychotropic medications, restraints, nasogastric tubes, Foley catheters). A number of other studies and commentaries confirm this picture (Fisher and Zorzitto, 1983; Sloane et al., 1981). As will be discussed more fully below, patients awaiting discharge in acute hospitals do not generally receive the stimulation and therapy that is likely to maximize their functioning and prevent deterioration. For example, hard-pressed nursing staff find it easier to do things for patients than to help them to do those things themselves. Arrangements for meals, bladder and bowel control and sleeping patterns tend to be organized around institutional needs, such that patient self-care abilities and potential for self-direction and autonomy are not reinforced (Fisher and Zorzitto, 1983; Glaser and Strauss, 1968; Sloane, Redding and Wittlin, 1981).

Consequences of Alternative Constructions of the Problem

We have seen how the different interests of those involved in the situation of elderly patients awaiting discharge are reflected in their definitions of the problem. It is important to establish whether the attitudes embodied in these definitions affect professional practice, hospital organization and social policy.

Geriatrics has not been a preferred or prestigious area of medical practice (Coe, 1967; Feldbaum and Feldbaum, 1981). A general devaluation of the older patient population (Marshall, 1981b), coupled with their designation as undesirable anomalies in acute hospital beds inevitably has an impact on their treatment. A participant observation study of four wards in a Hamilton, Ontario, hospital found that the most common nursing staff adaptations to "career patients" were to avoid them, to avoid enactment of a detailed nursing care plan and to complain to the doctors:

> . . .especially on one of the four study wards, some of the problems concerning imputations that patients did not belong on the ward stemmed from the difficulty in finding other placements for older patients. On the one ward where such placement problems were most acute, many of the staff came to think of their ward almost as a geriatric ward . . . despite the fact that the average age of patients was not significantly higher on this ward. . . . The difference in perception of the age of patients apparently arose from the presence in this ward of a very small number of patients who were difficult to place and whose length of stay was inordinately long (Rosenthal, Marshall, Macpherson and French, 1980:37).

Looking specifically at stroke patients in Montreal, Eakin-Hoffman (1974) emphasizes the lack of fit between their needs and hospital routines. Evers's observations of geriatric wards in a British hospital (1981:584) similarly reveal the consequences of negative definition of patients: "The labelling of patients as 'long-stay' often appears to be in effect a one-sided 'disengaging' of old people from their social roles by the institutions in which they find themselves."

The construction of elderly patients awaiting discharge as blockages in the smooth turnover of bed occupancy has some impact on institutional practices. Although not formalized in any way, efforts to keep potentially long-stay patients out of hospital beds are increasingly reported. Physicians are reluctant to admit elderly patients through emergency departments (Eakin-Hoffman, 1974; Grant, 1985; Hart and Hutton, 1976). Accusations that families are "dumping" their elderly relatives and efforts to persuade family members to remove them from hospital are not infrequently heard. The conflicting budgetary concerns within acute hospitals have been discussed above.

Unfortunately we cannot give equal attention to the impact of long stays on patients and their families, due to a lack of research and the absence of an effective collective expression of their concerns. Many patients are too debilitated to speak for themselves, and in any case, they or their families may fear adverse consequences of complaining about excessive length of stay. Moreover, patients and families often prefer the acute-hospital environment. Press accounts of problems in nursing homes understandably frighten family members. Patients themselves see transfer to a long-term-care institution as "the end of the road" and find this fact difficult to accept.

Finally, whatever their views, patients and families have less power to influence the definition of the situation than staff, hospital administration and governments (Coe and Prendergast, 1985; Marshall, 1981b). Moreover, they, like the general public, are exposed to the rhetoric of crisis discussed earlier.

Identification of the definitions and consequent actions of governments is difficult, in part because of the many levels of administration involved. Several government reports on the future needs for hospital care have been spawned by combined concern about present hospital utilization patterns by the aged, rising health costs and demographic projections (Lefebvre, et al., 1979; Rombout, 1975). Shapiro and Roos (1981) set out four policy responses to the problems of patients awaiting discharge: (1) building more beds of all types; (2) central screening mechanisms; (3) formally designating some acute beds for chronic patients; and (4) doing nothing. To these possibilities, we would add the development of enhanced and coordinated community supports and, even more important, the provision of intensive rehabilitative services within the acute hospital, and also within chronic hospitals, that are designed to facilitate discharge. Robertson (1982) provides a useful description of such developments in Canada.

All these solutions have been attempted in different jurisdictions, but a review of the limited evaluative evidence is beyond the scope of this chapter. However, from the social construction of reality perspective we have employed, the results of inertia and nonintervention are seen to have a profound impact. Effectively this response means that a system of care is perpetuated in which the interests of the most powerful prevail and in which the phenomenon of elderly long-stay patients is cast as an insoluble problem.

Conclusion

In this chapter we have argued that the situation of elderly patients awaiting discharge must be understood as a social construction rather than as an unambiguous, objectively definable problem. As such, the critical factors in affecting change or amelioration lie in the political arena. Research can contribute greatly by challenging definitions, articulating their consequences and providing a basis for social policy that knowingly and explicitly balances the varied interests of patients, families, health-care providers, adminstrators and governments.

References

Canadian Medical Association
1984 "Health: A need for redirection." *A Task Force on the Allocation of Health Care Resources.* Ottawa: Canadian Medical Association.

Coe, R.
1967 "Professional perspectives on the aged." *The Gerontologist* 7:114-119.

Coe, R.M. and C.G. Prendergast
1985 "The formation of coalitions: Interaction strategies in triads." *Sociology of Health and Illness* 7(2):236-247.

Eakin-Hoffman, J.
1974 "Nothing can be done: Social dimensions of the treatment of stroke patients in a general hospital." *Urban Life and Culture* 3(1):50-70.

Edelman, M.
1968 *The Symbolic Uses of Politics.* Urbana: University of Illinois Press.

Estes, C.L.
1983 "Social security: The social construction of a crisis." *Millbank Memorial Fund Quarterly* (Health and Society) 61(3):445-461.

Evans, R.G.
1984 *Strained Mercy: The Economics of Canadian Health Care.* Toronto: Butterworth.

Evers, H.
1981 "The creation of patient careers in geriatric wards: Aspects of policy and practice." *Social Science and Medicine* 15A: 581-588.

Feldbaum, E.G. and M.B. Feldbaum
1981 "Caring for the elderly: Who dislikes it least?" *Journal of Health Politics, Policy and Law* 5(4):62-72.

Fisher, R.H. and M.L. Zorzitto
1983 "Placement problem: Diagnosis, disease or term of denigration?" *Canadian Medical Assocation Journal* 129 (August 15):331-334.

Gillick, M.R., N.A. Serrell and L.S. Gillick
1982 "Adverse consequences of hospitalization in the elderly." *Social Science and Medicine* 16:1033-1038.

Glaser, B.G. and A.L. Strauss
1968 *Time for Dying.* Chicago: Aldine.

Grant, D.
1985 " 'Bed-Blockers' Blamed for Emergency Ward Crunch." Toronto: *Globe and Mail* (February 18):16

Gross, M.J. and C.W. Schwenger
1981 "Health care costs for the elderly in Ontario: 1976-2026." Occasional Paper 11, Ontario Economic Council, Toronto, 1981.

Hall, D. and B. Blytheway
1982 "The blocked bed: Definition of a problem." *Social Science and Medicine* 16:1985-1991.

Hart, C. and P.W. Hutton
1976 "Geriatric patients in acute medical wards." *British Medical Journal* 5:41.

Hutton, P.W.
   1976   "Correspondence" British Medical Journal, January 3,5:41.
Isaacs, B.
   1981   "Ageing and the Doctor." In David Hobman (ed.), *The Impact of Ageing*. London: Croom Helm.
Lawrence, M.
   1979   "Geriatric Cuckoo." *World Medicine* 25:19-20.
Lefebvre, L.A., Z. Zsigmond and M.S. Deveraux
   1979   *A Prognosis for Hospitals: The Effects of Population Change on the Need for Hospital Space, 1967-2031*. Ottawa: Statistics Canada.
LeTouzé, D.
   1984   "Hospital bed planning in Canada: A survey analysis." *International Journal of Health Services* 14(1):105-126.
Markson, E.W., K. Steel and E. Kane
   1983   "Administratively necessary days: More than an administrative problem." *The Gerontologist* 23(5):486-492.
Marshall, V.W.
   1981a   "Societal toleration of aging: Sociological theory and societal response to population aging." Pp. 85-104 in *Adaptability and Aging I*. Paris: International Centre for Social Gerontology.
   1981b   "Physician characteristics and relationships with older patients." Pp. 94-118 in M.R. Haug (ed.), *Elderly Patients and Their Doctors*. New York: Springer Publishing Company.
McAlpine, C.J.
   1979   "Unblocking beds: A geriatric unit's experience with transferred patients." *British Medical Journal* 2:646-648.
McArdle, C., J.C. Wylie and W.D. Alexander
   1975   "Geriatric patients in an acute medical ward." *British Medical Journal* 4 (December 6):568-569.
McNenly, P.
   1984   "Controversy Goes on about Hospital Bed Situation." *Toronto Star* (September 2).
Metropolitan Toronto District Health Council
   1984   *Long Term Care Bed Needs in Metropolitan Toronto*: Metropolitan Toronto District Health Council.
Minkler, M.
   1983   "Blaming the aged victim: The politics of scapegoating in times of fiscal conservatism." *International Journal of Health Services* 13(1):155-167.
Paget, A.G.
   1973   "Acute care hospitals: Their role in long-term care." *Dimensions in Health Service* 60(11):28-29.
Polanyi, M.
   1984   "Shortage of beds in hospitals nearing crisis, doctor testifies." Toronto: *Globe and Mail* (August 16).
Robertson, D.
   1982   "Establishing new services: Canada as a case study." Pp. 199-216 in Davis Coakley (ed.), *Establishing a Geriatric Service*. London: Croom Helm.

Rombout, M.

1975   *Health Care Institutions and Canada's Elderly, 1971-2031*. Ottawa: Department of National Health and Welfare.

Roos, N.P. and E. Shapiro

1981   "The Manitoba longitudinal study on aging: Preliminary findings on health care utilization by the elderly." *Medical Care* 19:644-657.

Roos, N.P., E. Shapiro and L.L. Roos

1984   "Aging and the demand for health services: Which aged and whose demand?" *The Gerontologist*, 24:31-36.

Rosenthal, C.J., V.W. Marshall, A.S. Macpherson and S.E. French

1980   *Nurses, Patients and Families*. London: Croom Helm. New York: Springer.

Rubin, S.G. and G.H. Davies

1975   "Bed-blocking by elderly patients in general hospital wards." *Age and Ageing* 4:142-147.

Shapiro, E.

1980   "The reality and the myths of 'geriatric bed-blocking.' " *Essence* 3(3):179-184.

Shapiro, E. and N.P. Roos

1981   "The geriatric long-stay hospital patient: A Canadian case study." *Journal of Health Politics, Policy and Law* 6(1):49-61.

Sloane, P.D., R. Redding and L. Wittlin

1981   "Longest-term placement problems in an acute care hospital." *Journal of Chronic Disease* 34:285-290.

Williams, T.F.

1981   "The physician viewpoint." Pp. 42-46 in M.R. Haug (ed.), *Elderly Patients and Their Doctors*. New York: Springer.

Wilson, L.A.

1980   "Blocked Beds." *The Lancet* (December 6):1255.

VIII
Political, Economic and Social Implications of Population Aging

In the media, age-related issues are all too often seen solely in terms of the threat of an increased economic burden to society. The three chapters in this concluding section place the consideration of economic costs in a broader context. At the societal level, cost is a measure of the impact of population aging. In the following chapters, population aging is viewed as one aspect of very complex demographic, social and economic changes, and costs are seen not in a purely economic framework but in the context of debates over Canadian social values. The economic implications of aging in Canada are examined in Chapter 28 by Denton, Li and Spencer, and in Chapter 29 by Messinger and Powell. In the concluding chapter of the book, Neysmith examines the policy process and the dilemmas of policy making.

Denton, Li and Spencer focus on the implications of population aging for health care, and their chapter follows from those in the previous section. While we would not wish to be content with the present level of health care provided to Canadians of any age, it is useful to inquire what the future costs would be if we were to maintain the same level of care, but with an aging population. In particular, Denton, Li and Spencer ask: "Is there likely . . . to be a demographically induced 'crisis'?" Their answer is no. They provide five alternative population projections based on varying assumptions about fertility and mortality, incorporating a large set of variables. The same demographic variables that describe population aging are also associated with changing labour-force participation and with economic growth patterns. In that wider context, population aging is cause for concern about the provision of health care, but does not justify a crisis mentality.

Demographic factors, the authors note, are not the only causes of health-care costs. Medical technology, changes in the organization and delivery of health care (such as increased use of nurse practitioners) and changing expectations for appropriate care levels all may impact on health-care costs.

If there is no cause for a crisis mentality, why are there signs of one? Economic issues are never totally isolated, but rise and fall in a political and social context. A crisis, whether over health costs, the provision of income security, or some other issue, may be at least partly a social construction, a move in a political game. For example, private-sector economic interests may find it useful to advocate an image of crisis concerning the Old Age Security or Canada/Quebec Pension Plan, as this view may foster public opinion supportive of increased private control over pensions.

Health-care costs are much lower in Canada than in the United States, which devotes roughly 25 percent more per capita for health care than does Canada and which has less to show for it (i.e., higher age-specific mortality rates, higher morbidity rates and a wider gap between the upper and lower classes in the health care received). This suggests that the social organization of health care and not just population dynamics or technological changes may have profound effects on its costs. Population aging will, Denton, Li and Spencer inform us, occur at a pace that makes judicious planning possible. The added costs of health care that they project as an implication of population aging are not inordinate in an international context, but they do imply that careful organizational planning is crucial.

Messinger and Powell also caution against overreacting to demographic changes. They argue that "while the demographic factor will bring about significant changes to the structure of our society and economy, the very long lead time allows private and public sectors to adjust adequately, and that in any case demographic issues are not likely to be the major factors shaping public policy debates." Their focus is complementary to that of Denton, Li and Spencer in that they deal with social expenditures. They emphasize that the economy is likely to grow more rapidly than the demographic pressures caused by population aging, and they predict that individual productivity will also increase. A number of sociologically interesting hypotheses are embedded in their argument. For example, they suggest that declining elementary school enrolments will lead to an improved quality of education, which will in turn lead to increased productivity per worker. If average family size decreases, parents may find it easier to assist all their children in attaining a university education. These are cast by Messinger and Powell as reasonable arguments; they are in fact testable with available data.

Neysmith, in the concluding chapter of this book, also looks towards the future of aging in Canada. She returns us to some of the themes of earlier chapters. For example, she reminds us that we have an increasing diversity in our older population, but points out that our social policies tend to ignore or obliterate such diversity. She raises the important policy question of whether we ought to target our social policies towards the aged population, thereby risking an increased marginalization and stereotyping of the aged and reinforcement of age stratification, or whether we should design social policies to meet generic needs, even if the majority of persons with such needs happen to be old. This question is being answered in the context of a society that is based to a greater extent on individualistic than on collectivistic values, as Chappell pointed out in Chapter 24. But Neysmith points out that even within the area of income security for the aged, our social policies reflect a conflict of values. For the most part, decisions pertaining to the resolution of such conflicts reflect the intrinsic relationship of economic interests to social values.

Neysmith concludes her chapter by recognizing the inherent tension between economic and social policies and predicting that the nature of the resolution of this tension is the factor that will shape the "new social order" of aging in Canada. Finally, she reminds us of what should be obvious, but what often escapes our view: that we are all in this together, makers of our history as well as made by it. This is a fitting sentiment with which to end the book.

28
How Will Population Aging Affect the Future Costs of Maintaining Health-Care Standards?

Frank T. Denton, S. Neno Li and Byron G. Spencer
Department of Economics
McMaster University

The population of Canada is slowly "aging," a characteristic that it shares with the populations of the United States and many other developed nations. The average age of Canadians is rising, the proportion of old people is growing and the proportion of young people is declining. If fertility rates remain at their current low levels, the population aging process will continue for many decades. Indeed, even if fertility rates were to move up very sharply in the next few years — a development that available evidence gives no reason to expect — the proportion of people 65 and over would continue to increase for perhaps half a century. The problems that society and its governments must cope with in the future as a result of the aging of the population thus cannot be avoided; they can only be anticipated.

One of the problems associated with aging is that of providing adequate health care. At the level of the individual, a lucky person may live out his or her life span without serious illness or health disability, but for the population as a whole, average health-care costs rise increasingly rapidly with age after midlife. Other things being equal, a population with a larger fraction of older people will require more health-care services than a population with a smaller fraction. The future aging of the Canadian population will thus tend to raise aggregate health-care requirements and the associated annual expenditures, assuming that present health-care standards are to be maintained.

Some have envisioned a future crisis in health care resulting from the aging of the population. Is there likely, in fact, to be a demographically induced "crisis"? Prospective changes in the age distribution will certainly tend to increase health-care costs, and thereby increase the burden of such

The work on which this paper is based has been supported by the Social Sciences and Humanities Research Council of Canada under its grant program in the field of population aging. We acknowledge with gratitude the support of the SSHRCC and the computing and related assistance of Christine H. Feaver and Rosanna Giordano.

costs on the national economy. But they will have other effects on the economy, as well, and these are often neglected. In particular, they will affect the size and age distribution of the labour force, and hence the economy's ability to generate output and income. The economic base on which health-care costs must be financed will thus be altered by the same demographic forces that will be operating to increase those costs. To look only at the effects of population change on the costs is therefore to look at but one aspect of the situation with which Canadian society will be confronted. A full understanding requires that the effects of population change on Canada's productive capacity also be considered.

The purpose of this paper is to assess the likely impact of population aging on health-care costs, both in isolation and in the broader economic setting. We begin by presenting estimates of the average male and female age profiles of health-care costs. We then consider these profiles in the context of an overall economic-demographic model, so that demographic influences on both health-care costs and national productive capacity can be studied jointly. The model is used to project the time paths of health-care costs per capita and as a proportion of the gross national product. A "standard" or "baseline" projection is provided first, and then some alternative projections that make different assumptions about the future courses of fertility and mortality rates, in order that the degree to which projections depend on the underlying demographic assumptions can be studied. While demographic influences are the subject of present interest, other influences on health-care costs may be as important or more important, and we note some of these subsequently. We conclude the paper with an overall evaluation of the results presented and return to the question of whether a demographically induced health-care "crisis" is to be expected.

Age Profiles of Annual Average Health-Care Costs

The manner in which health-care expenditure varies with age is depicted in Figure 1. Separate age profiles are shown for men and women. We have derived these profiles using estimates of total hospital, physician, dental, drug, and other health-care costs, and various available series that reflect the age-sex distributions of the totals.[1] The profiles should be viewed as approximations, since of necessity they are estimated rather than observed directly. However, their general shapes are no doubt reliable representations of actual age-cost patterns in Canada in recent years.

The series plotted in Figure 1 represent *relative* average costs at different ages rather than dollar expenditures. The units in which the series are expressed are arbitrary, relative costs being all that we require for present purposes. Dollar expenditures will vary through time, but the relative age patterns are likely to remain much the same. Also to be noted is the fact that the relative costs we are measuring are those associated with health-care delivery, however paid for: they include privately financed expenditures,

Figure 1:
Relative per Capita Costs of Health Care for Males and Females, by Age

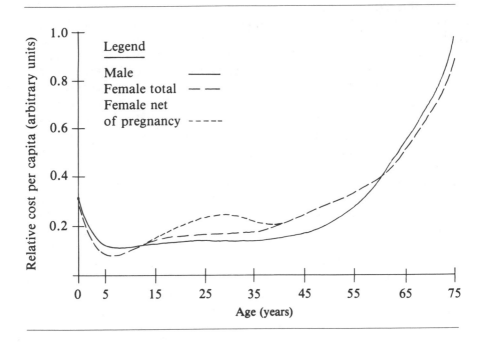

public expenditures financed by general taxation and expenditures covered by public or private health-insurance plans, but do *not* include the premiums paid under insurance plans. They thus represent the average actual costs incurred by society in providing health care to people of different ages, rather than the costs as they might appear to an individual person or household.

The profiles for both sexes reflect the high average costs associated with infancy, followed by the relatively low costs of children beyond the infant stage. For males, average cost rises continuously with age after childhood, first gradually, during youth and middle age, and then with increasing rapidity in old age.[2] The profile for females is generally similar to that of males, except for costs associated with pregnancy and childbearing, which are reflected in higher female levels in the age range from late teens to early forties. The cost profile for females is shown in Figure 1 for all costs and also "net of pregnancy" (i.e., excluding costs associated with pregnancy and childbearing). The importance of considering separately those costs associated with pregnancy and childbearing in the context of the present analysis lies in the fact that they can be expected to vary with the level of fertility that is assumed in projecting the population.

Health-Care Costs in a Macro-Economic-Demographic Model

It is an essential aspect of this study that changes in health-care costs are to be considered in a general economic-demographic setting. We thus require a model that captures those features of the economy and the population that are important for the assessment of long-term demographic effects. In practice this means a model that pays special attention to changes in the size and composition of the labour force, the rates of saving and investment, the growth of the stock of capital and the consequent changes in the economy's capacity to generate output and income. A relation representing specific influences of population changes on health-care costs is embedded in the larger macro-economic-demographic model. The complete model can then be used to trace out simultaneously the future time paths of health-care costs and overall national product under alternative demographic assumptions.

The broad features of the model are as depicted in Figure 2.[3] At the left side of the figure are three rectangles, representing the three basic demographic flows that determine how the population changes: births, deaths, and migration (including both immigration and emigration). Births and deaths are themselves determined by underlying fertility and mortality rates interacting with the age distribution of the population. The population age distribution, in conjunction with rates of participation, also determines the size and composition of the labour force. If rates of unemployment are given, the numbers of people employed are then determined, and hence the input of labour into production of the national output. (Labour input is weighted within the model to reflect age differences in productivity; the age distribution of the population thus interacts, also, with the age-related productivity weights in determining the national output.)

The age profiles of health-care costs shown in Figure 1 are assumed to hold in every year in the model, and these combine with the changing age distribution of the population and numbers of births to determine total annual health-care cost. For purposes of the model, this total cost is treated as a "tax" on the national output. Much of the cost may in fact be paid for out of public funds, including both those raised by general taxation and those collected in the form of public insurance premiums. However, if we assume (for present purposes) that fixed health-care standards must be met, then even the privately paid portion of the total cost is unavoidable and may be viewed as a "tax." In any event, it is convenient to think of taxes being levied on the national output (or equivalently, the national income) in the exact amount required to pay the total health-care bill. To put it differently, it is convenient to think of health care as imposing a first claim on the national product, with what is left being regarded as the disposable portion of the product — or disposable income, as it is labelled in Figure 2.

Figure 2:
Schematic Outline of the Model

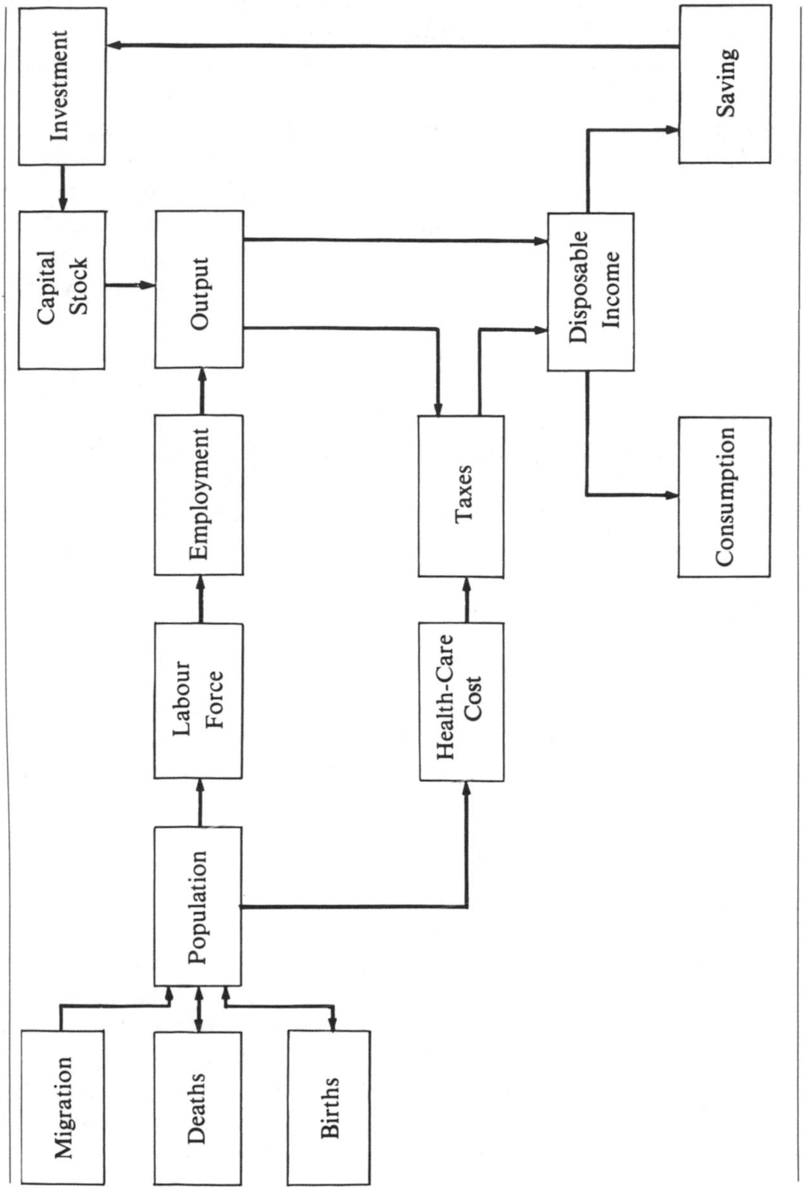

Disposable income — the total national income or product not claimed by health care — is divided between consumption and saving. The level of saving in the economy determines the level of investment, and this in turn determines the rate at which the capital stock grows. Of course, the capital stock (the stock of buildings, machinery, etc.) depreciates each year, and a substantial fraction of total investment may be required simply to maintain the stock, so that only some of the investment will represent actual growth. The capital stock joins with employment to generate the national product, and thus a well-known circuit in the working of the macro-economy is completed — from output to disposable income to saving to investment to capital stock and finally back to output.

This, then, is the basic framework within which our model operates. The actual model takes the form of a computer program, and this program can be used to simulate or project the population and the economy year by year from a given starting point, thus generating the time paths of those variables in which we are interested for as long a period as we wish. In the present case, the variables of special interest include health-care cost expressed per capita and as a percentage of the gross national product. Some basic demographic variables are also of interest from the point of view of interpreting the changes in the health-care variables.

Long-Term Projections

The model has been used for purposes of this paper to make five projections under alternative demographic assumptions.[4] All the projections start from the 1981 Canadian census population and go to the year 2051. That is a very long projection period. However, if the implications of current fertility levels for future health-care costs are to be assessed it is desirable to look far into the future, for the children of the 1980s will not reach old age until the middle of the twenty-first century.

The five projections differ with regard to their assumptions about future fertility and mortality rates, but share common assumptions about migration: the actual migration rates of 1981-84 are assumed for those years; thereafter, immigration of 120,000 and emigration of 40,000 per annum are assumed to the end of the projection period. (These latter figures are close to recent actual average levels). The parameters on the economic side of the model are given more or less realistic values based on historical Canadian experience, and these values remain the same from one projection to another. In each projection, allowance is made for likely future changes in the labour force participation rates of males and females in different age groups, based on Canadian historical experience.

Projection 1 (Standard): This may be regarded as a "standard" or "baseline" projection. The total fertility rate is set at 1.7 children per woman, which is approximately the actual rate at the present time, and it remains at that level. (Note that 1.7 is well below the level of 2.1 required for natural long-run replacement of the population.) Individual age-specific fertility rates also remain constant. Age-sex-specific mortality rates are assumed to decline from their 1981 levels, but more and more slowly, until by the year 2031 they have stopped declining altogether. (The initial annual rates of decline are set equal to the 1961-81 average rates.)

Projection 2 (Low Fertility):   In this projection the total fertility rate is assumed to fall from 1.7 to 1.4 by 1996, and then to remain at its new level. All age-specific fertility rates fall in the same proportion. Other assumptions are the same as in Projection 1.

Projection 3 (High Fertility):   The total fertility rate rises from 1.7 to 3.0 by 1996 in this projection, and then remains constant. All age-specific fertility rates rise in the same proportion. Other assumptions are the same as in Projection 1.

Projection 4 (Low Mortality):   Mortality rates decline until 2051 (instead of 2031). Other assumptions are the same as in Projection 1.

Projection 5 (High Mortality):   Mortality rates decline only until 2011, remaining constant thereafter. Other assumptions are the same as in Projection 1.

Interpretation of the Results

The projection results of present interest are displayed in Tables 1 to 5 at ten-year intervals. The first five columns of results relate to the population, its age distribution and the life expectancies of males and females at birth. The last two columns present the projected health-care costs in per capita form (indexed with base value 100.0 in 1981) and as percentages of the gross national product.

The standard projection of Table 1 shows the population increasing in every decade from 1981 to 2031 and then starting to decline. By 2001 it has increased by almost 20 percent, and by 2031 it has increased by almost 32 percent over its 1981 level. As the population grows, the proportion aged 0-19 falls and the proportion 65 and over rises. These shifts in age distribution are quite pronounced. They continue through the first four decades of the next century; only by the middle of the century does the distribution appear to have stabilized.

The life expectancies of newborn children increase in the standard projection until 2031, in consequence of our assumption that mortality rates generally will continue to decline over the first half-century of the projection period. The male expectancy was 71.9 years in 1981; by 2031 it is 74.9, an increase of three years. The female life expectancy was 79.0 years in 1981 — some seven years greater than the male expectancy — and by 2031 it has

TABLE 1:
Future Population Characteristics and Health-Care Costs Based on Projection 1 (Standard)

	Population total and age distribution			Life expectancy at birth		Health-care costs	
	Total (millions)	0-19 (percent)	65 +	Male (years)	Female	Per capita index	% of GNP
1981	24.3	32.0	9.7	71.9	79.0	100.0	7.6
1991	27.0	27.6	11.7	73.1	80.8	109.9	8.2
2001	29.1	25.6	13.3	73.9	82.2	121.3	8.8
2011	30.6	22.9	15.2	74.4	83.2	133.8	9.8
2021	31.7	21.7	19.4	74.8	83.7	146.9	11.1
2031	32.0	21.0	23.8	74.9	83.9	166.2	12.9
2041	31.6	20.4	24.5	74.9	83.9	182.3	14.3
2051	30.9	20.5	24.4	74.9	83.9	184.3	14.4

risen to 83.9. The male-female differential is thus maintained, and in fact increased under our assumptions, which is consistent with the patterns of mortality change of recent decades.

Now let us look at the consequences of these demographic developments for health-care costs. The overall per capita cost (in constant dollars, i.e., abstracting from price inflation) rises in every decade in the standard projection, and rises at a substantial pace throughout almost all of the seventy years covered by the projection. This is almost entirely a result of the changes in the age distribution of the population. From 1981 to 2001, the per capita cost index rises by more than 21 percent; over the whole of the period from 1981 to 2051, it rises by more than 84 percent.

When health-care costs are expressed as a proportion of the gross national product the increases are again apparent, although the pattern is somewhat different. In the long run — over the full seventy years — the GNP share rises in about the same proportion as per capita costs. In the first few decades, however, it rises at a somewhat slower pace. From 7.6 percent of the GNP in 1981 (as estimated by Health and Welfare Canada), the fraction spent on health care rises to 8.8 percent by 2001, to 11.1 percent by 2021 and to 14.4 percent by 2051. The growth of the GNP offsets some of the health-care increases in the earlier decades, but in the long run the GNP share and the level of health-care costs rise at pretty much the same pace.

There are perhaps three important points to emphasize in light of the foregoing. First, health-care costs will rise markedly in the future, if demographic influences alone are taken into account. Second, growth of the GNP will offset the health-care increases to some extent in the first few decades, but not in the longer run. Third, the increases in health-care costs will be spread over a fairly long period: they will not all occur in the next few years, as popular discussion sometimes seems to imply, but in the next several decades. There is thus considerable time for the social and economic adjustments needed to cope with the cost increases to be planned and implemented. A fourth point to bear in mind is that we are considering only the hypothetical increases in health-care costs that would occur if present technology and institutions were frozen. "Necessity is the mother of invention," as the saying goes, and it is very likely that innovations will occur to offset the demographically induced cost increases, at least in some measure — that technology and institutions will adapt as the problem becomes more pressing. One only has to look back to the 1930s and note the changes that have taken place in the Canadian health-care system since then to appreciate the likelihood of major innovations in the next half century. What we are doing in this paper is simply asking the hypothetical question: "What if only demographic changes mattered in the future?" We are certainly not suggesting that that will be the case.

How sensitive are our projections to the underlying assumptions about fertility and mortality? The answer is, "very sensitive to fertility, much less sensitive to mortality." If the total fertility rate is assumed to drop from its present level of 1.7 children per woman to 1.4 children by 1996, as in Table 2, the population still increases until two decades into the next century, but then it starts to decline. The proportion of young people falls and the proportion of old people rises more sharply. Health-care costs increase faster, both per capita and as a fraction of the gross national product. The differences are relatively small for several decades, but then become more pronounced; by 2051, 15.8 percent of the GNP is going to health care in Table 2, compared with 14.4 percent in Table 1. All this is a result of a drop of only 0.3 children per woman in the total fertility rate.

The sensitivity to fertility becomes much more obvious in Table 3, where the projection assumes an increase in the total fertility rate from 1.7 to 3.0 children per woman. The fertility rise induces a massive increase in population in the next century, and instead of falling, the proportion of young people rises. The proportion of old people continues to increase until 2031, but then declines. Health-care costs per capita rise much more slowly in this "high" fertility scenario, commencing in the 1990s, and by the end of the projection period they have actually started to decline. The fraction of GNP going to health care is somewhat higher for several decades in Table 3 than in Table 1, but after fifty years the situation is reversed. By 2051, 11.5 per-

TABLE 2:
Future Population Characteristics and Health-Care Costs Based on Projection 2 (Low Fertility)

	Population total and age distribution			Life expectancy at birth		Health-care costs	
	Total (millions)	0-19 (percent)	65 + (percent)	Male (years)	Female (years)	Per capita index	% of GNP
1981	24.3	32.0	9.7	71.9	79.0	100.0	7.6
1991	26.9	27.2	11.8	73.1	80.8	109.8	8.1
2001	28.4	23.8	13.6	73.9	82.2	122.6	8.7
2011	29.3	19.9	15.9	74.4	83.2	137.1	9.6
2021	29.6	18.5	20.8	74.8	83.7	153.0	11.1
2031	29.0	17.2	26.3	74.9	83.9	177.3	13.3
2041	27.7	16.4	28.0	74.9	83.9	199.6	15.1
2051	25.9	16.4	29.1	74.9	83.9	207.1	15.8

cent of the GNP is going to health care under the "high" fertility assumption, compared to 14.4 percent under the standard assumption of a continuation of the present fertility level. A total fertility rate of 3.0 seems very high by current standards, but it should be kept in mind that this level is not assumed to be attained until 1996 and that during the postwar "baby boom" of the 1940s and 1950s the rate achieved much higher levels than 3.0.

The "low" mortality projection of Table 4 shows somewhat greater increases in life expectancy than the standard projection of Table 1, and somewhat greater increases in health-care costs, both per capita and relative to the GNP. The differences in costs between Table 4 and Table 1 are negligible in the first few decades, and quite minor until some three or four decades into the next century. On the whole, the consequences of changes in mortality rates are seen to be much less important than the consequences of changes in fertility rates. This is apparent again from Table 5, where "high" mortality is assumed. Health-care costs rise less rapidly in Table 5 than in Table 1, over the projection period as a whole, but again the differences are not large, especially in the earlier decades.

Other Issues

We have been examining the possible future effects of population aging on health-care costs. It should be emphasized again that we have *not* been attempting to forecast what will actually happen to health-care costs. There

TABLE 3:
Future Population Characteristics and Health-Care Costs Based on Projection 3 (High Fertility)

	Population total and age distribution			Life expectancy at birth		Health-care costs	
	Total (millions)	0-19	65+ (percent)	Male	Female (years)	Per capita index	% of GNP
1981	24.3	32.0	9.7	71.9	79.0	100.0	7.6
1991	27.6	29.1	11.5	73.1	80.8	110.2	8.4
2001	32.1	32.4	12.1	73.9	82.2	116.3	9.3
2011	36.3	33.3	12.8	74.4	83.2	122.3	10.3
2021	41.7	33.5	14.7	74.8	83.7	126.4	11.3
2031	47.9	35.4	15.9	74.9	83.9	130.8	12.3
2041	54.5	35.6	14.2	74.9	83.9	131.7	12.3
2051	62.8	36.2	12.1	74.9	83.9	123.6	11.5

TABLE 4:
Future Population Characteristics and Health-Care Costs Based on Projection 4 (Low Mortality)

	Population total and age distribution			Life expectancy at birth		Health-care costs	
	Total (millions)	0-19	65+ (percent)	Male	Female (years)	Per capita index	% of GNP
1981	24.3	32.0	9.7	71.9	79.0	100.0	7.6
1991	27.0	27.6	11.7	73.1	80.9	109.9	8.2
2001	29.1	25.5	13.4	74.0	82.4	121.6	8.9
2011	30.7	22.8	15.3	74.7	83.6	134.6	9.8
2021	31.8	21.6	19.6	75.2	84.5	148.5	11.2
2031	32.2	20.8	24.3	75.6	85.2	169.4	13.3
2041	32.1	20.2	25.3	75.8	85.6	188.4	14.9
2051	31.4	20.2	25.5	75.9	85.7	192.8	15.3

TABLE 5:
Future Population Characteristics and Health-Care Costs Based on Projection 5 (High Mortality)

	Population total and age distribution			Life expectancy at birth		Health-care costs	
	Total (millions)	0-19 (percent)	65 +	Male (years)	Female	Per capita index	% of GNP
1981	24.3	32.0	9.7	71.9	79.0	100.0	7.6
1991	27.0	27.6	11.7	73.0	80.7	109.8	8.2
2001	29.1	25.6	13.2	73.6	81.7	120.8	8.8
2011	30.5	22.9	15.0	73.8	82.0	132.1	9.6
2021	31.4	21.8	18.9	73.8	82.0	143.2	10.7
2031	31.5	21.2	23.0	73.8	82.0	160.3	12.3
2041	31.0	20.7	23.4	73.8	82.0	173.9	13.4
2051	30.2	20.9	23.2	73.8	82.0	174.6	13.4

are many factors that will bear on these costs in the coming years and decades. Population change is one, but only one. Other factors may be just as important or more important than population change. They are not the subject of investigation in this paper, but it is worth taking note of them.

Technology is obviously a major consideration in relation to future health-care costs. We have deliberately assumed away the effects of technological change in order to focus on strictly demographic influences, but undoubtedly such change will occur, both in health care and in the economy at large. Advances in health-care techniques can be thought of as either reducing costs for given standards of care, or as raising the standards. Advances in the technology of production in the economy at large can serve to increase the nation's capacity to produce output and income, and hence, among other things, the size of the economic base available to support future health-care costs. Technological change and associated increases in productivity may thus play a major role in offsetting the effects of population aging on the costs of health care.

There are resource-saving possibilities available today that might serve to offset demographically induced cost increases in health care, quite aside from whatever innovations the future may bring. One example is the more efficient use of hospital and special-care facilities in the treatment of elderly patients and others not in need of acute care. This is a current concern in health-care policy. The desirability of transferring patients from acute-care to lower cost chronic-care hospitals and from chronic-care hospitals to nursing homes and similar less costly facilities, is recognized (assuming, of course, that the levels of care required by individual patients would permit this). The possibilities for more extensive provision of health care in patients' own homes is also a policy concern. Any policies designed to shift patient treatment from higher cost to lower cost facilities (while still maintaining standards) will, of course, improve the efficiency of the health-care system as a whole, and thereby help to offset the cost-increasing effects of population aging.

A second example is the more extensive use of nurse practitioners. It has been determined that nurse practitioners can perform a variety of routine procedures that are normally now provided by physicians, and that they can do so both effectively and safely. It seems likely that nurse practitioners could provide a substantial portion of medical services required by elderly ambulatory patients. A study by Denton, Gafni, Spencer and Stoddart (1983) has indicated that greater use of nurse practitioners could provide some measure of offset to demographically induced health-care costs.

There are institutional factors and patterns of behaviour to be considered. The extent to which cost reductions can be effected in the health-care delivery system depends not only on the availability of lower-cost alternatives but also on the degree to which the alternatives will be accepted by the system's managers and practising physicians. If the use of nurse practitioners were simply superimposed on the existing system, for example, costs might well rise rather than fall. It has been argued by Evans (1980, 1984) and others that physicians (collectively) are able to control the demand for their services to a significant degree, and that the increasing stock of practising physicians in Canada thus tends to raise the aggregate demand for their services so as to maintain their average income levels. Considerations such as this are clearly important in assessing the potential for offsetting future demographically induced increases in health-care costs. However, the failure of the system to adopt available measures that would offset such increases should be blamed on the system, not the population aging process.

It has been argued, also, that induced increases in the demand for health care are apt to be greatest for the older population. As Evans (1984) puts it:

. . .age-sex specific utilization rates are themselves changing, in such a way as to increase substantially the *relative* utilization of the elderly. Extensions of technological possibilities and increases in available manpower and facilities translate into increased intensity of health-care servicing. And these increases occur to a greater extent among the elderly, as they are on average 'sicker.' It is easier to justify interventions as the organism slowly deteriorates — there is always something wrong. (p.309)

Our own work supports the view that shifts of age-cost profiles in the past decade or two towards the older end of the age spectrum have made total health-care costs in Canada more sensitive to population aging: the present study, which uses recent data, suggests considerably more sensitivity than earlier ones, which were based on health-care utilization data for the late 1960s or early 1970s. Our analysis assumes that present standards of health care — as represented by per capita costs — will be maintained, and that only the population will change. But the standards themselves have been changing, and they may well continue to change. That is an important issue, but again one that must be distinguished from the issue of how the aging of the population, as such, will affect the costs of health care in the future.

Conclusion

Health-care costs are sensitive to the age structure of the population, and prospective changes in age structure will tend to drive up costs in the coming decades. Our projections make that clear. The increases are likely to be offset in part by higher levels of gross national product in the next few decades, in consequence of the same demographic forces that will be operating to raise health-care costs. However, in the longer run, population change is likely to have a much greater effect on health-care costs than on the productive capacity of the economy. No one can say with any certainty what will happen to fertility and mortality rates in the next twenty, thirty or fifty years, and that has a bearing on the issue of how much health-care costs will grow. But almost certainly they will grow, both per capita and as a proportion of the GNP, as the population aging process continues.

Is there likely to be a "crisis"? We suggest that the answer is "no." At least there *need* not be one. The demographically induced increases in health-care costs will not all occur tomorrow. The population aging process, even if inexorable, is slow. There is much time to foresee the problems and plan to deal with them. The Canadian society and the Canadian economy coped with the postwar baby boom and baby bust; there is no reason that they cannot cope, also, with the much more gradual population aging process.

Notes

[1]   Estimated total costs are from Health and Welfare Canada (1984). Series used to allocate individual cost totals by age and sex include the most recent available tabulations of overall days of hospital care, numbers of residents in special-care facilities, payments to physicians, consultations with dentists, payments to optometrists and chiropractors, users of prescription and nonprescription drugs, users of hearing aids, and days of hospital care for women classified to the

category "complications of pregnancy, childbirth, and puerperium" in the official morbidity statistics. (In spite of its name, the largest component of this category is "delivery without mention of complication.") These series are from various Statistics Canada sources or from tables published by the Saskatchewan Medical Care Insurance Commission.

2 It should be stressed that the male and female profiles represent *average* costs at different ages. It has been noted by Roos and Shapiro (1981) that the high costs for the elderly population are associated largely with a small fraction of that population. To some extent the same observation may also apply at other ages.

3 For other applications and technical descriptions of economic-demographic models of the kind used in the present study, see Denton and Spencer (1973, 1975a, 1975b, 1979, 1983a, 1983b). Particular attention is given to demographic influences on health-care costs in Denton and Spencer (1975a, 1983a, 1983b). Studies that deal with demographic influences on health-care costs in Canada but not in the context of an overall economic-demographic model include Boulet and Grenier (1978), Lefebvre, Zsigmond and Deveraux (1979), Stone and Fletcher (1980) and Gross and Schwenger (1981). For a recent study of the latter kind in the United States, see Russell (1981).

4 On the setting of assumptions and the technical procedures in demographic projections, see Denton, Feaver and Spencer (1980).

References

Boulet, Jac-André and Gilles Grenier
  1978 "Health Expenditures in Canada and the Impact of Demographic Changes on Future Government Health Insurance Program Expenditures." Discussion Paper 123, Economic Council of Canada.
Denton, Frank T., Christine H. Feaver and Byron G. Spencer
  1980 *The Future Population and Labour Force of Canada: Projections to the Year 2051.* Ottawa: Economic Council of Canada.
Denton, Frank T., Amiram Gafni, Byron G. Spencer and Greg L. Stoddart
  1983 "Potential savings from the adoption of nurse practitioner technology in the Canadian health-care system." *Socio-Economic Planning Sciences* 17 (4): 199-209.
Denton, Frank T. and Byron G. Spencer
  1973 "A simulation analysis of the effects of population change on a neoclassical economy." *Journal of Political Economy* 81 (2): 356-375.
  1975a "Health-care costs when the population changes." *Canadian Journal of Economics* 8 (1): 34-48.
  1975b *Population and the Economy.* Westmead, England: D.C. Heath Ltd.
  1979 "Some economic and demographic implications of future population change." *Journal of Canadian Studies* 14 (1): 81-93.
  1983a "Population aging and future health costs in Canada." *Canadian Public Policy* 26 (2): 155-163.

1983b "The sensitivity of health-care costs to changes in population age structure." In Christopher Garbacz (ed.), *Economic Resources for the Elderly: Prospects for the Future.* Boulder, Colorado: Westview Press.

Evans, Robert G.
1980   "Review" of Boulet and Grenier (1978). *Canadian Public Policy* 6 (1): 132-133.
1984   *Strained Mercy: The Economics of Canadian Health Care.* Toronto: Butterworth.

Gross, John M. and Cope W. Schwenger
1981   *Health Care Costs for the Elderly in Ontario: 1976-2026.* Toronto: Ontario Economic Council.

Health and Welfare Canada
1984   *National Health Expenditures in Canada, 1970-1982.* Ottawa.

Lefebvre, L.A., Z. Zsigmond and M.S. Deveraux
1979   *A Prognosis for Hospitals: The Effects of Population Change on the Need for Hospital Space, 1967-2031.* Ottawa: Statistics Canada.

Roos, Noralou P. and Evelyn Shapiro
1981   "The Manitoba longitudinal study on aging." *Medical Care* 19 (6): 644-657.

Russell Louise B.
1981   "An aging population and the use of medical care." *Medical Care* 19 (6): 633-643.

Stone, Leroy O. and Susan Fletcher
1980   *A Profile of Canada's Older Population.* Montreal: Institute for Research on Public Policy.

29

The Implications of Canada's Aging Society on Social Expenditures

Hans Messinger and Brian J. Powell
Department of National Health and Welfare

The average age of the Canadian population is rising. The combination of low mortality and fertility rates along with relatively low immigration inflows has combined to produce an aging process that it has been estimated, will continue gradually for the next several decades. More significantly, when the baby boomers reach retirement age in the second and third decades of the next century, our population structure will have changed dramatically from the present. The proportion of those aged 65 and over will have more than doubled, such that there will be at least four elderly for every ten working-age individuals in Canada by the year 2031, compared with less than two today.

The economic implications of these demographic changes have become matters of increasing debate over the past few years, with, sometimes, shrill expressions of alarm being expressed over the long-term health of the economy and, in particular, the ability to increase further or even maintain living standards as the working-age population is faced with the economic burden of supporting the elderly.

It is the thesis of this chapter that, while demographic factors will bring about significant changes to the structure of our society and economy, the very long lead time allows the private and public sectors to adjust adequately to meet the needs of the elderly. In addition, the "burden" of social expenditures will not likely necessitate radical policy changes. Social policy will change over the coming decades for a variety of reasons, but purely demographically driven problems are unlikely to be the major concern.

To support this contention, the first section of this chapter examines projected demographic trends to the year 2031, clearly showing the continuing aging trend as well as the shrinkage of the working age population after the year 2011. It is these two predicted phenomena that generate a cause for concern with regard to the future financing of social expenditures. The second section looks at the sources of income for the elderly, indicating the importance of government programs. The third section develops projections of social spending and economic growth based purely on demographic factors. These forecasts indicate that the "burden" (i.e., proportion of

GNP) of financing social expenditures is relatively constant until the year 2011 and then rises sharply as the baby boomers reach retirement age. The fourth section discusses other factors that affect economic growth. A comprehensive forecast of economic growth indicates that the economy (GNP) will grow much more rapidly than reflected in the demographics. In the light of this, the burden of financing social spending falls well below today's levels. The final section, however, looks at non-demographic factors that will affect social spending, concluding that collectively they will generally serve to raise the level and growth, but not likely to alarming proportions of GNP.

Demographic Factors

Some courage is required to project, for policy purposes, some fifty years into the future. Indeed, were there to have been projections made in 1935 of economic conditions today, we would not be surprised to find some degree of error. However, demographers are likely to be more accurate in their field than other social scientists are in theirs because of the slower changes in society with respect to fertility and mortality rates and the inevitability of the aging of the baby boomers.

Starting with the medium growth scenario of Statistics Canada's population projections,[1] Table 1 highlights the aging trend. The young and elderly age groups can be seen to be moving in opposite directions. The aged, who made up 10.2 percent of the population in 1984, will grow to approximately 13 percent by the turn of the century and, in the following thirty years, will grow rapidly to reach 24 percent of the population. In absolute terms, the 65-and-over group will represent more than 7 million Canadians by 2031 and will have grown from the present by approximately 180 percent. On the other hand, the young, aged 0 to 17, will decline in both relative and absolute terms. The absolute decline is not as dramatic as the increase of the elderly, but as a proportion of the population they will drop from 26.3 percent in 1984 to less than 20 percent in 2031.

The traditional working-age group, 18-64, will continue to grow as a proportion of the population until about 2010. In the following two decades, the working-age population will decline, reflecting the retirement of the baby boomers. By 2031, however, the work force will still be, in absolute terms, about 7 percent larger than at present. This serves to emphasize that the "demographic problem," if indeed it exists as a serious problem, would be well into the future, and provides ample time for both the private and public sectors to plan, in a rational fashion, strategies and policies to cope with its consequences. Further, we are not without evidence of how other societies deal, successfully or not, with large elderly populations; at present there are ten European countries with populations containing 13 percent or more aged 65 or over (Organization for Economic Cooperation and

TABLE 1:
Population Projections for Selective Age Groups
Canada
Thousands

Year	0-17		18-64		65 +		Total
1984	6,611	26.3	15,956	63.5	2,556	10.2	25,123
1991	6,622	24.7	16,986	63.4	3,173	11.9	26,781
2001	6,464	22.7	18,181	63.7	3,884	13.6	28,529
2011	5,927	20.1	19,055	64.5	4,544	15.4	29,526
2021	5,780	19.2	18,374	61.2	5,871	19.6	30,025
2031	5,537	18.6	17,114	57.5	7,128	23.9	29,779

NOTE: Projection 3 assumes a fertility rate of 1.66 children per woman, net immigration of 50,000 and 1 fe expectancy at birth to increase to 74.9 for males and 81.6 for females by the year 1996.
SOURCE: Statistics Canada, Medium Growth — Projection 3.

Development 1984a). We shall not achieve such a state until the turn of the next century.

Sources of Income for the Elderly

The production and allocation of goods and services in Canada are predominantly determined within the private sector, but the government plays a highly visible role in the provision of services and the redistribution of income generated in the private economy.

One of these roles is to provide assistance to those in financial need. From the individual's point of view, in the absence of government intervention, the economic problem of aging is associated with the ability to choose an appropriate pattern of work/leisure and savings/consumption over his or her lifetime (for a detailed discussion of the early development of economic theory, see Barro, 1977; Feldstein, 1974; and Lucas, 1972). To ensure that individuals can optimally satisfy their lifetime choices, the market system must be effective in terms of labour markets and savings and investment institutions, and the public at large must be aware of the opportunities available and the relevant constraints.

However, because of equity considerations, market rigidities, the apparent short-term horizons of most individuals, the complexity and cost of obtaining the information available, the cyclical impacts of the economy, the inability of the least productive to earn sufficient income for current consumption, let alone to save for the future, and the increased tendency for families to expect the state to care for the less fortunate through the tax/expenditure system rather than via intrafamily transfers, governments have increasingly become involved in the reallocation and redistribution of the gross national product. Thus, from a national perspective, the important economic problems associated with an aging society are first, to determine the slice of the GNP pie that is allocated to older members of society via taxation and government expenditures; and second, to establish the degree to which governments need to intervene by way of regulation to ensure that individuals are more able to exercise choices that will both serve themselves and society (O.E.C.D., 1984b).

With respect to providing for retirement income, the generally held expectation in Canada is that this should be a matter of individual responsibility. However, as can be seen from Table 2, governments have found it necessary to provide a substantial proportion of the income flowing to those over the age of 65.

TABLE 2:
Sources of Income for the Elderly in 1982

SOURCE	INCOME	RECIPIENTS
	%	%
OAS/GIS/SPA	33.9	98.1
CPP/QPP	9.4	58.8
Private Pensions/Annuities	12.2	33.3
Investment	28.1	66.1
Earnings	12.3	15.6
Other	4.1	47.0

NOTE: An elderly unit is defined to be one in which at least either the head or spouse is 66 + .

For the purpose of this table, 66 + is used to define the elderly, because many individuals work for part of their 65th year. This gives a distorted picture of the importance of "earnings" as a source of income for seniors.

SOURCE: Statistics Canada — Special Tabulations, Census Family Micro data type, Survey of Consumer Finances, 1983.

Private Pensions

The relatively low share of income in the form of private pensions flowing to the elderly is the result of several factors. First, the employer-sponsored pension plan system has been slow in developing. For instance, by 1960 only 31 percent of workers participated in such plans. However, coverage has now risen to include almost half the work force.

Second, because of the high mobility of workers between jobs, combined with historical pension portability obstacles and traditionally long periods before pensions are vested, even if individuals participated in pension plans with various employers, they may have ended up with little or no pension income benefits. In a similar vein the limitations of survivor benefits in many pension plans have resulted in widows typically suffering considerable economic hardship. In fact, among the elderly in Canada who live in poverty, single women have primarily been victims. However, as a result of several studies by both the private and public sectors over the past decade, the government has recently introduced legislation to improve the private pension system by removing many of these problems.[2] These measures will likely increase future benefits for the present working generation.

Not all problems have been resolved in the private pension market. Workers still appear to be relatively uninformed about various mechanisms available for retirement and about the pros and cons of such mechanisms. For instance, most employees are in defined-benefits plans, with the benefits being a function of the last few years of service. Plans of this kind tend to favour those who remain with one particular employer, and while recently introduced legislation with respect to improving portability and vesting will significantly reduce this inequity, there will continue to be problems if deferred benefits are not indexed to protect them from erosion due to inflation. (Government of Canada, 1982; House of Commons, 1983; Treasurer of Ontario, 1984).

Investment income

With respect to income from investments flowing to the elderly, the greatest problems facing governments is that even though savings rates in general are considered to be high in Canada, relative to other countries, the wealth accumulated is more unequally distributed among Canadians than the distribution of income. Thus, while the aggregate wealth of the elderly might be considerable, its distribution is such that many of the elderly have little or no income-producing assets.

Over the past decade, tax incentives associated with Registered Retirement Savings Plans (RRSPs) have undoubtedly led to an increase in retirement oriented savings for a broader class of individuals. Table 3 shows the recent dramatic increase in the buildup of RRSPs. Further, an important component of savings is the buildup of equity in the homes of families. This aspect of wealth of the elderly is not reflected in the income statistics, even though it contributes to their well-being.

Finally, considerable saving takes place via the life-insurance system. About one million life-insurance policies are purchased each year. Although life insurance may not be explicitly intended to provide retirement income, with over 87 percent of widows and widowers aged 55 and over, it is

TABLE 3:
Assets Held by Financial Institutions

Assets of $ billions

	Trustee Pension Plans[1]	Life Insurance Co. Assets[2]	RRSP Savings[3]
1975	21.2	23.6	N.A.
1979	42.3	38.4	N.A.
1980	51.1	43.7	14.5
1983	82.7	63.4	27.5

NOTES: [1] Does not include life insurance plans.
   [2] Assets held on behalf of Canadian policy holders.
   [3] Accumulated gross contributions plus accrued interest less withdrawals.
   Data are not available prior to 1980 on a consistent basis.
SOURCE: Statistics Canada; Department of Insurance, Canada.

reasonable to assume that a larger portion of benefits flow to the elderly. Table 3 shows how the assets of life-insurance companies have increased, and is an indicator of another source of increased private income for future elderly cohorts.

Earned income

With respect to earned income flowing to the elderly, Table 2 shows that it represents only 12 percent of total income. It can be expected, however, that age 65 will gradually cease to be the "normal" retirement age. Flexible retirement arrangements, allowing those with sufficient income to choose to retire early, will undoubtedly continue, but as the age structure of the population changes, it can also be expected that employers will change hiring practices to induce older individuals to remain in the work force.

Government programs (Health and Welfare Canada, 1985)

To compensate for the limited income generated privately for retirement purposes, Table 2 also shows the large degree to which governments provide income to the elderly. The public retirement-income system can be described in terms of demogrants, income-tested assistance and work-related pensions:

(i) Demogrants

The Old Age Security program provides a flat benefit to everyone aged 65 and over who has met certain residence requirements. In December

1985, monthly payments to each individual were $282.94. These are adjusted quarterly to the cost of living as measured by the Consumer Price Index. The total cost of the progam in 1984/85 was $8.2 billion.

(ii) Income-Tested Programs

The Guaranteed Income Supplement provides extra benefits to low-income pensioners, with benefits being reduced one dollar for every two dollars of other family income in most cases. Total benefits paid to low-income elderly Canadians under this program in 1984/85 were $2.9 billion. In 1984/85 about 50 percent of pensioners were receiving GIS benefits.

The Spouses Allowance is another income-tested program, providing benefits to those aged 60 to 64 whose spouses are old-age pensioners.

Further, provinces augment these income-tested programs in a variety of ways, such as the Guaranteed Annual Income System (GAINS) in Ontario.

(iii) Work-Related Pensions

The Canada Pension Plan and the Quebec Pension Plan are the twin earnings-related pension plans that cover virtually everyone in the labour force. The maximum retirement benefit will eventually be about 25 percent of average wages and salaries. These plans have none of the portability problems currently associated with private pension plans. Further, the plans provide for survivors' "pensions," and all benefits are indexed to compensate for increases in the cost of living.

These income programs, at the federal level, provided $17 billion to the elderly in 1984, which represents about 4 percent of the GNP. However, it is not only these costs that are of concern when the demographic changes are under study. The other major component of social security is the health-care system. Medical and hospital services are heavily utilized by older people, and although they made up about 10 percent of the population in 1984, it is estimated that health-care expenditure on their behalf amounted to almost one-third of total health spending: this is more than 2 percent of GNP and equivalent to nearly one-third of the cash income of the aged (Boulet and Grenier, 1978).

Projecting Social Spending and the Implications for Its Financing

Having examined the projected demographic changes and government social programs for the elderly, in this section we shall project the implications of these demographic changes on social spending to the year 2031. Because there will be some trade-off between spending on the young and elderly, we have included education expenditure and child-benefit expenditure (Family Allowances and the Child Tax Credit). Further, because we are dealing with the total population, we have included Unemployment Insurance paid to the working-age population as well as the social assistance payments provided jointly by the federal government through the Canada Assistance Plan and the provinces.

Projections based solely on demographic factors

In the projections of social spending shown in Table 4 it is assumed that real per capita benefits and program utilization rates remain unchanged. Thus it is implicitly assumed that changes in per capita benefits are identical with the rate of inflation. It is further assumed that in forecasting economic growth, capital/labour ratios are fixed and that there is no impact on economic growth from changes in the unemployment rate, labour-force participation rates and productivity. Zero productivity growth assumes no change in inputs of capital per worker, work-force skills and technology. Thus the social spending and economic growth forecasts in this table are affected only by changes in age structure and the total size of the population. The demographic assumptions are the same as those outlined in Table 1 based on Statisitics Canada's medium growth projection.

The spending estimates under this projection show that over the entire period social spending will increase by 44 percent, while the total population will grow by less than 19 percent. This clearly demonstrates that an aging population, holding constant real per capita benefits and program utilization rates, generates a definite upward impact on social spending. This is particularly evident between the years 2011 and 2031, when social spending will increase by 17 percent. During the same period the total population will rise by only 1 percent. On examining the various expenditure categories, we see that elderly income benefits increase almost threefold, while health costs rise by nearly 80 percent. Those costs associated with Canada's young population, child benefits and education fall by less than 20 percent and do little to offset the pressures of meeting the needs of the aged.

While a small proportion of the elderly will be contributing to the economy as a result of work or capital investment, the financial burden of social expenditure will fall mainly on the non-elderly work force. At present, 21 percent of GNP is required to support the social programs included in Table 5. If GNP is projected on the same assumptions underlining Table 4 the share of social spending changes very little between 1984 and 2001 (about 1 percent), but rises sharply to almost 30 percent in 2031.

Basing these forecasts on alternative high or low population growth scenarios represented by Statistics Canada (Projections 5 and 1), the absolute expenditures levels show marked differences as indicated in Table 5.[3] These alternative assumptions, however, also affect economic growth such that in terms of share of GNP, social spending varies only slightly (between

TABLE 4:
Projected Social Expenditures: Implications of the Aging Population ($ 1984 billions)

	Elderly Benefits[1]	Health	Child Benefits[2]	Education	Labour Force[3]	Social Assistance[4]	Total	GNP
1984	16.8	25.4	3.8	23.9	12.4	5.1	87.4	420.9
1991	20.9	28.8	3.9	23.2	13.2	5.4	95.4	448.1
2001	25.5	33.2	3.8	22.4	14.1	5.8	104.8	479.6
2011	29.9	38.7	3.4	21.0	14.8	6.1	113.9	502.6
2021	38.6	42.1	3.3	20.2	14.3	5.9	124.4	484.7
2031	46.9	45.4	3.2	19.4	13.3	5.5	133.7	451.5

NOTES: [1] Includes OAS/GIS/SPA and CPP/QPP
[2] Includes Family Allowances and Child Tax Credit.
[3] Includes Unemployment Insurance Benefits and Worker's Compensation Benefits.
[4] Includes cash benefits only.
SOURCES: 1991-2031, Projections Messinger and Powell 1984 values, Statistics Canada.

28.2 and 29.6 percent in 2031) across all three projections. The impact of higher fertility rates and immigration levels underlying Projection 5 do little to offset the economic burden of financing social spending during the twenty-year period that follows the year 2010.

TABLE 5:
Projected Social Expenditures: Alternative Population Growth Scenarios

	Social Expenditures ($ 1984 billions)			Proportion of GNP (percentage)		
	Low[1]	Medium[2]	High[3]	Low[1]	Medium[2]	High[3]
1984	87.4	87.4	87.4	20.8	20.8	20.8
1991	94.1	95.4	96.5	20.9	21.3	21.3
2001	101.1	104.8	111.5	21.0	21.9	22.5
2011	108.0	113.9	125.7	21.7	22.7	23.4
2021	116.8	124.4	142.8	25.2	25.7	25.5
2031	122.6	133.7	160.4	29.5	29.6	28.2

NOTES: [1] Low-growth scenario is based on Statistics Canada population projection 1, which assumes a fertility rate of 1.4, net immigration of 50,000 and a life expectancy of 74.9 for males and 81.6 for females by 1996.
[2] Medium-growth scenario is based on Statistics Canada population projection 3 (see note: Table 1).
[3] High-growth scenario is based on Statistics Canada population projection 5, which assumes a fertility rate of 2.2, net immigration of 100,000 and a life expectancy of 74.9 for males and 81.6 for females by 1996.
SOURCES: 1919-2031 Projections, Messinger and Powell; Statistics Canada, 1984.

A broader view of economic growth

The restrictive assumptions included in the preceding projections do produce results that may generate causes for concern. But to what extent are they realistic?

While the theory of economic growth is not the clearest aspect of the discipline, it is safe to say that future changes in gross national product will be affected by more than just demographic factors. Complex economic forecasting models use historic information as well as established structural relationships and assumptions about external factors to predict future economic growth.

First, because of the relatively slow growth of the absolute size of the work force and the improvements to the pension system noted above, as well as the tax incentives that should increase long-term savings rates, we can expect that the capital/labour ratios will increase, making each worker more productive. The demand for goods and services is not likely to diminish, even though the composition of consumer preferences may change. The slow nature of this change will permit the private suppliers to adjust to changing demand. Indeed, the adjustment of producers to the needs of the baby boomers has already been observed as they moved from their youth into their thirties.

Besides this potential for growth as more capital is available for each worker, one must also consider the quality of the labour force, or, in economic terms, the availability of human capital. First, because of the falling numbers of the school-age population, it is not unreasonable to believe that the quality of education will rise, or at least not fall. Further, the reduced number of youth to the working population would indicate that a greater proportion of parents will be able to assist in financing post secondary education for their children. Finally, as the work force ages, productivity increases can be expected from "experience." Several studies — especially those related to the mandatory retirement age issue — have shown that increased job experience and general maturity exert a positive influence on productivity throughout one's employed lifetime. Research results indicate that in most cases productivity does not peak until after age 50, frequently at age 60, and declines from that peak very slowly (Palmer and Gould, 1986).

Finally, technological change, although always difficult to predict, has traditionally been the primary engine of economic growth that has enabled living standards and social conditions to improve. As we look forward to slower entry of young cohorts into the work force, it could be expected that producers in Canada will have greater incentives to seek out technologically superior methods of production and to devote more resources to innovative techniques. At the same time, because of a slower-growing labour force, we can expect that unemployment rates will fall from their currently high levels.

Having discussed some of the factors that affect long-term economic growth, it is clear that demographics, albeit an important element, cannot be used as the sole independent variable in a reasonable forecast. A comprehensive forecast based on Informetrica's national economic forecasting model (TIM) yields an average growth rate of 2.8 percent until the year 2005 (Informetrica Ltd., 1985).[4] At that point, the level of real GNP will be almost 50 percent higher than the estimate based on the simplistic demographic assumptions. Moreover, unlike in the previous section, the unemployment rate, which stood at 11.3 percent in 1984, decreases steadily as the economy grows. The rate based on Informetrica's forecast stabilizes at about 5 percent in the mid 1990s. This, of course, has the effect of lowering expenditures on unemployment insurance benefits. In addition, expenditures on Canada Pension Plan benefits will outpace the growth of the elderly population due to continued maturing of the plan, real earnings growth and increasing labour-force participation.

The forecasts in Table 6 reveal a significantly different picture to those produced by the projections based only on demographic factors. While the costs of providing income security and health services remain high because of the undeniable aging factor, the increased "fiscal burden," expressed as the portion of GNP required to finance social expenditures, is eliminated. In fact, given no changes in social programs, the "fiscal burden" will be substantially reduced up to the year 2010 and will only increase over the following two decades, but to levels that will be far more manageable than at present.

TABLE 6:
Forecast of Economic Growth (Informetrica[1])

	GNP[2] $ 1984	Social Spending[3] $ 1984	Social Spending as a Proportion of GNP %
1984	420.6	87.4	20.8
1991	543.4	92.5	17.0
2001	675.2	103.3	15.3
2011	794.4	114.8	14.5
2021	844.4	127.9	15.1
2031	870.6	139.6	16.0

NOTES: [1] Informetrica, Ltd., is an economic forecasting and analysis company focussing on medium and long-term issues.
[2] GNP projection from 2006 to 2031 is based on productivity trends (output per worker) and growth of the working-age population based on Statistics Canada population projection 3.
[3] Social-spending projections are those from Table 4, adjusted for lower unemployment rates and higher Canada Pension Plan benefits based on the Informetrica forecast.
SOURCES: GNP 1984 to 2005, Incormetrica, Ltd.; GNP 2006–2031, Messinger and Powell; Social Spending, Messinger and Powell

As shown in Table 6, the proportion of social spending to GNP drops sharply from 20.8 percent to 15.3 percent at the turn of the century. About 1 percent of this decline is due to a projected reduction in unemployment. Although the proportion rises from 14.9 percent to 16.0 percent during the twenty years representing the period of retirement of the baby boomers, this is far less dramatic than the increase shown by the demographic projections (i.e., 21.7 to 27.9 percent). In summary, a more comprehensive forecast of economic growth indicates that social programs can even be enhanced in the coming years without placing an increased burden on the working-age population.

Nondemographic Factors Affecting Social Spending

Just as economic projections based only on demographic factors were deemed to be overly simplistic, similarly, additional factors should be considered in forecasting social expenditures. Economic developments and social preferences result in both positive and negative forces on social spending. Some of these will be examined in terms of social security, child benefits, education, benefits to the working-age population and health expenditures. No attempt is made to estimate a comprehensive forecast of social spending, although particular examples will be illustrated to indicate the degree to which social spending projections can vary.

Social security

The aging of the population will beyond any doubts result in a sharp growth in income transfers to the elderly. Clearest in this is Old Age Security, a demograms to which almost all Canada's elderly are entitled.

While the private pension system has been improved in the sense of providing greater coverage and removing obstacles to portability, there still remain a number of concerns as to how private pension benefits will be affected, both in terms of growth and distribution. At present only 50 percent of the working population is covered by private pensions, and these generally tend to be higher-paid workers. On the other hand, lower paid workers, who basically have difficulty in saving for their retirement, are often in occupational groups or work for small firms where pension plans are either non-existent or slow in developing. In addition, many private pensions do not provide full inflation protection. Although this is not a major issue with currently low inflation rates, it leaves much uncertainty as to the future real value of private pension benefits. Moreover, pension plan assets are often invested in instruments that do not necessarily yield the most favourable returns. In summary, it appears that improvements in the private pension system will alleviate some of the upwards pressure of GIS spending, but the magnitude is unclear.

Finally, it was assumed that real per capita benefits for the elderly will remain constant. This means that their incomes will be protected against inflation such that living standards for the aged will remain unchanged. The Informetrica forecast, however, indicates that real incomes, and hence living standards for the non-elderly, will rise on average by about 1 percent per annum over the next twenty years. To the extent that the elderly share in future economic prosperity, in order to keep their living standards relatively in line with the rest of the population, additional upwards pressure will be placed on social spending. For example, a 1 percent-per-year rise in real elderly benefits by the year 2031 will require additional expenditures equivalent to 3 percent of GNP.

Child benefits and education

The federal budget of May 1985 announced that Family Allowances and the Child Tax Credit would only be indexed by the amount that the annual cost of living exceeded 3 percent. This has the effect of eroding real benefits by 3 percent each year. If this trend is continued over the entire forecast period, child benefits by 2031 will be reduced to about one-quarter of their present value. Although this policy is unlikely to continue indefinitely, for the years it does, child benefits will be lower than projected. Furthermore, rising family incomes will reduce the eligibility for the income-tested Child Tax Credit and further lower expenditures on child benefits.

As mentioned earlier in the chapter, the need for a higher-skilled work force is imperative to maintaining economic growth as expansion of the labour force slows. In this regard, even though enrolment in educational institutions continues to decline, there will be pressures to increase the amount of real spending per student in an effort to provide higher quality education in a more capital intensive and technologically complex environment.

Benefits to the working-age population

As indicated earlier, the economic forecasts show that unemployment rates will fall significantly and thus reduce unemployment-insurance expenditures. These effects have already been included in the social spending projections. In addition, the economic recession of the early 1980s resulted in a dramatic increase in the number of "unemployed employables" on social assistance. Improved economic opportunities will attract some of these individuals into the work force and thus alleviate some of the spending pressures in this area.

Health

Society places, and will continue to place, a high priority on the quality of health-care services. Over the past decade it was estimated that new technology has added from 1 to 3 percent in real health spending (Klarman). If these trends continue, health expenditures will be considerably higher than projected by 2031. The conservative estimate of a 1 percent per annum increase by 2031 raises health cost by 60 percent and the proportion of social spending to GNP from 16.0 to 19.1 percent. Assumptions of 2 and 3 percent will boost this ratio to 24.0 and 31.7 percent respectively, with the latter increasing health costs by fourfold. Also, to the extent that technological advancements in medicine may increase life expectancy, further upwards pressure will be placed on social-security spending.

In summary, we have demonstrated that there are many nondemographic factors that will undoubtedly affect the growth and levels of social expenditures. The example of the impact of technology on health costs has demonstrated how critical these factors can be in terms of predicting the future burden of financial social spending. Overall, taking these factors into account, the future situation still does not appear to be one of doom and gloom, as portrayed by the demographers.

Conclusions

The purpose of this chapter has been to look objectively at the implications of aging in Canada on social spending and the burden this is likely to place on the working-age population, or, more specifically, the slice of the GNP pie required to finance Canada's social programs. The projections based solely on population dependency ratios and demographically extrapolated social-spending and economic-growth estimates, indicate that as the baby-boom cohorts reach retirement age the economic burden of financing Canada's social programs will rise.

However, a more reasonable forecast, that takes into account both demographic changes and economic factors, indicates that the social spending required to support an increasing proportion of elderly in the future may actually take a smaller slice of the economic pie. This scenario, however, can change significantly due to nondemographic factors that could dramatically alter the level and growth of social spending, particularly in the area of health care. In addition, economic growth may not materialize as projected, and government spending priorities may change in response to issues such as the environment or national security. In summary, policy changes may well be required to respond to the needs of Canada's aging society.

As a final note, although it appears that the economy can sustain the current social spending network, there is scope for continued improvement to the retirement income system. The high incidence of poverty among single elderly is a clear example that further initiatives are required. To the extent that there are barriers to Canadians providing for themselves, the government's role in providing income security for the aged will remain prominent. Further, it is impossible to predict how generous future generations will be with regard to Canada's elderly citizens. In light of the uncertainties that surround the well-being of Canada's aging society, it is important, as a safeguard, that individuals be encouraged to accumulate wealth in the private sector to provide for their retirement.

Notes

[1] Medium growth, Projection 3, assumes a fertility rate of 1.66 children per woman, net immigration of 50,000 and a life expectancy at birth that increases to 74.9 for males and 81.6 for females by the year 1996.

[2] Recently introduced legislation in the federal budget of May 23, 1985, delivered by the Honourable Michael H. Wilson, Department of Finance, "Improved Pensions for Canadians."

[3] Low growth, Projection 1, assumes a fertility rate of 1.4 children per woman, net immigration of 50,000 and a life expectancy at birth that increases to 74.9 for males and 81.6 for females by the year 1996.

High growth, Projection 5, assumes a fertility rate of 2.2 children per woman, net immigration of 100,000 and a life expectancy at birth that increases to 74.9 for males and 81.6 for females by the year 1996.

[4] Informetrica, Ltd., is an economic forecasting and analysis company focussing on medium and long-term issues.

References

Barro, Robert
  1977   "Social security and private saving — evidence from the U.S. time series." Mimeograph, University of Rochester.

Boulet, Jac-André and Gilles Grenier
  1978   "Health expenditures in Canada and the impact of demographic changes on future government health insurance program expenditures." Discussion paper no. 123, Economic Council of Canada.

Feldstein, Martin
  1974   "Social security, induced retirement and aggregate capital accumulation." Journal of Political Economy 82 (5): 905-26.

Government of Canada
  1982   *Better Pensions for Canadians.* Ottawa: Minister of Supply and Services Canada, Catalogue No. CP 45-28/1982E.

Health and Welfare Canada
  1985   *Basic Facts on Social Security Programs,* January.

House of Commons
  1983   Report of the Parliamentary Task Force on Pension Reform. Ottawa: Queen's Printer for Canada.

Informetrica, Ltd.
  1985   *Reference Forecast: Post-Workshop I-85,* National Forecasting Service.

Klarman, Herbert E
          "Observations on health care technology: measurement, analysis and policy" in *Medical Technology: The Culprit Behind Health Care Costs?*

Stuart H. Altman and Robert Blendon (eds)., DHEW Publication no. (PHS) 79-3216, U.S. Government Printing Office.

Lucas, Robert E., Jr.

1972   "Expectations and the neutrality of money." *Journal of Economic Theory* 4 (April): 103-24.

Organization for Economic Cooperation and Development

1984a Working Party on Social Policy, *The Changing Population Age Structure: Demographic Trends to 2025.* Paris: October.

1984b Working Party on Social Policy, *Problems of Social Security Retirement Pension Schemes.* Paris: October.

Palmer, John L. and Stephanie Gould

1986   *Economic Consequences of an Aging Society.* Daedalus 115 (1) Winter: 295-324.

Statistics Canada

1985   *Population Projections in Canada, Provinces and Territories 1984-2006.* Ottawa: Catalogue No: 91-520.

Treasurer of Ontario

1984   *Ontario Proposals for Pension Reform.* Toronto: Queen's Printer for Ontario.

30

Social Policy Implications of an Aging Society

Sheila M. Neysmith
Faculty of Social Work
University of Toronto

This chapter, like the two others in the final section, discusses some of the likely consequences for Canada of population aging. It stands in the present while trying to view the future. The lessons of history give fair warning of the precariousness of such an undertaking. At the very least, forecasting assumes that there will be a future, that Canada in cooperation with other nations will build mechanisms for averting nuclear warfare so that Canadians can age and continue to contribute to the development of their society. This chapter, of necessity then, is written in an optimistic vein. It examines *how* Canadians are responding to emerging issues that should remain or magnify in importance over the coming years, other things being equal. By responses, I mean those policy and programmatic choices that we make that affect people as they age.

In one form or another many writers have noted that increased life expectancy has led to considerable diversity within the elderly population (Government of Canada, 1984; Government of Canada, 1983; Neugarten, 1982:33-37; Denton, Feaver and Spencer, Chapter 2, this volume). That is, the increasing number and proportion of the population over 65 has dramatized the necessity to recognize and respond to intragroup variability. An aging native Canadian trapper who prospects for gold in the Yukon to supplement his income bears little resemblance to the housebound widow contemplating a move into a long-term care facility in Montreal, yet we develop income security policies at the federal level that must meet the needs of both these individuals. Health programs are set primarily at the provincial level, but urban-rural and ethnic differences within each province are frequently greater than those between provinces. Disparate program jurisdictions and funding sources mean that service delivery at the local level usually entails coordinating public, voluntary, proprietary and family resources. Although this diversity has been well documented, there is little consensus on why these differences exist, which should be perpetuated and how social policies and programs should respond.

Generic Versus Age-Based Services

Because living into old age is now the norm rather than the exception, advanced age per se has lost its claim to special status. One of the consequences has been a questioning of the validity of using age as a basis for social allocation. Age, like gender and race, is a descriptive attribute that says nothing about people outside of the social context that infuses it with meaning. Any rationale for using such factors as criteria in resource distribution has to be anchored in an analysis that argues that they are reliable indicators of a particular social condition, that gender, age and race are important determiners of the quality of life of people. It is this connection that justifies their use as a basis for entitlements or rights. Ultimately we must ask whether we want specific social policies for the elderly.

For instance, we have decided that families with members under 18 warrant special provision. Our various child benefits (Family Allowance, the Child Tax Credit, child tax exemptions) are a recognition that parents are making a significant contribution to Canadian society by raising the next generation. In addition, they have costs that nonparent taxpayers do not have. Therefore, it is only fair that they receive extra resources. (For a detailed discussion of the differential impact of these various programs, see Government of Canada, 1985.) If age alone is being questioned as a legitimate criterion for making claims on some of society's resources, what are the alternatives? In answering this question, inevitably there will be disagreement around the specifics, but among those concerned about future policy directions there is some consensus that *need* should remain paramount. Such a position, however, if it is to be more than rhetoric, calls into question the legitimacy of many of our current policies. In addition, it has value implications that are difficult to reconcile with others that Canadians hold dear.

A careful reading of the literature advocating *need* as the criterion for resource allocation suggests that most writers are concerned about promoting fairness or equity (Hardy, 1981; Miller, 1976; Neugarten, 1982; Plant et al., 1980; Smith, 1980). Therefore, the following discussion places the concept of need within this larger context. The possibilities for using need as a vehicle to further such social goals are examined and compared against policies that emphasize reward arising from contributions, efforts or compensation. In the second part of the chapter it is argued that distributing social resources so that fairness and equity are maximized will inevitably encounter serious opposition. Such policies would have to coexist with a definition of freedom which stresses the importance of choice and non-interference. The former may be central to the existence of a welfare state, but the latter is more compatible with the functioning of a market economy. The following section sets the stage by defining what is social policy.

What is Social Policy

There is no single agreed-upon definition. The parameters of the subject have changed over the years, resulting in several different substantive threads today. A current Canadian writer defines social policy as

". . . those social arrangements, patterns and mechanisms that are concerned with the distribution of resources in accordance with some criterion of need" (Mishra, 1981; xi). Many distinguish social policy from economic policy, the former being concerned with the welfare of individuals, the latter on promoting the welfare of the nation (see A. Walker, 1981, for a summary of definitional differences and current debates). A well-known U.S. analyst states that:

> The study of social policy is basically concerned with the range of human needs and the social institutions created to meet them . . . . Policies are in fact interdependent systems of: (1) the abstract values we cherish; (2) the operating principles which give these values form in specific programs and institutional arrangements; (3) the outcome of these programs which enable us to contrast ideals and reality; (4) the often weak linkages among aims, means and outcomes; and (5) the feasible strategies of change this pattern suggests (Rein, 1976:6;141-142).

Both of these definitions refer to need and a *collective* responsibility for meeting it. Many of our programs, however, use criteria such as merit for resource allocation or stress *individual* responsibility for meeting need, or do both. Our income security policies are a good example of mixed criterion usage, in that they provide a minimal economic baseline as a collective good, but assume the exercise of individual initiative to provide full adequacy of income.

In the opening pages of the report by the recent Parliamentary Task Force on Pension Reform it was stated that:

> Three main principles underlie the legislation currently governing the Canadian pension system. The Government of Canada believes that these same principles should continue to provide the basis for reform. Simply stated, they are:
> — Elderly Canadians should be guaranteed a reasonable minimum income.
> — The opportunities and arrangements available to Canadians to provide for their retirement should be fair.
> — Canadians should be able to avoid serious disruption of their pre-retirement living standards upon retirement (Government of Canada, 1983:11).

Note that the last point recommends that differences in income prior to retirement shall be retained or preserved after retirement. Despite this mixing of objectives within a given policy arena, I will argue in the following pages that one can make demands, establish entitlement and/or rights on *either* merit or need, but not on both, because they are essentially contradictory. Income security policy is being used only as an illustrative arena because its high profile over the past few years ensures familiarity with the main arguments on the part of most readers.

Equity: A Much Abused Concept

Fairness and equity are frequently presented as the guiding principles for formulating policy, but there the agreement ends. Debate really starts with determining how fairness is to be judged. Each of the earlier statements on income security contain the word "should." They are prescriptive declarations with assumptions underlying each. If these assumptions were made explicit, the statements would read something like the following:

— Elderly Canadians have basic needs that must be met. Therefore they are entitled to a minimal income (a *right* is clearly implied).
— Since retirement is a social institution affecting all Canadians, the opportunity to save must be available to all. (The emphasis is on assuring that the rules of the game are non-discriminatory, i.e., equality of opportunity, although outcomes can vary, i.e., equality of condition.)
— Before retirement the value of a person's contribution to society was reflected in level of income. People deserve to have this differential evaluation continue in retirement (past contributions, i.e., merit, deserve to be rewarded).

Establishing rules of the game that apply across the board to everyone has a long and respectable history in North American social policy. From such a perspective, more popularly known as equality of opportunity, any differences in outcome are assumed to be due to differences in competences of the contestants. The classic critique of this position is that in non-egalitarian societies the starting positions of people differ. Institutions that treat all alike will therefore perpetuate rather than mitigate existent inequalities. However, equality of opportunity is the most widely accepted form of fairness in our society. It regulates formal competitions and the majority of our social programs. Those who win or qualify while abiding by the rules are defined as deserving of reward. From such a premise it can be argued that if pension plans are to be the vehicle for saving for retirement, in order to be fair their terms and conditions must not be discriminatory. Such arguments have been successful recently in lowering vesting requirements that discriminated against younger and mobile workers.[1] By unrealistically defining permanent employees as only those over 40 with ten years attachment to the firm, many employers retain their contribution, while geographically mobile or otherwise nonpermanent employees (who often are women) lose this contribution to later-life security.

The value empowering equality of opportunity is individualism, with its emphasis on personal freedoms and private responsibility (see Chappell, Chapter 24 of this volume, concerning the "market ethos"). The existence of Registered Retirement Savings Plans (RRSPs)[2] reflects this value. They are frequently admired because they encourage the individual to assume the responsibility of saving for his/her retirement without restricting freedom, whereas public pensions are seen as foreclosing choice because all must contribute. Differences in outcome do not enter the argument. Obviously these two perspectives contain inherent conflicts. One emphasizes freedom of the individual, ensuring opportunities for resource accumulation over a lifetime and building social structures that guard against discrimination in the application of rules. The other focusses on some desired outcome, emphasizes the collective responsibility for achieving a goal and concerns itself with building mechanisms for redistributing resources between persons, groups and institutions. Historically, the latter perspective argued that if we wish to change the social conditions of disadvantaged groups, then need, not achievement, has to be the basis for entitlement to resources. Before examining how the concept of need has been used in Canadian social policy, a brief look at the usage of the term *rights* will clarify some of the discussion.

Translating Merit and/or Need into Rights

Either of these concepts of fairness can be used as a basis for entitlement. A right is simply a claim that is institutionalized and thus recognized. Unfortunately, establishing a need or acknowledging that a reward is deserved does not lead automatically to a right. We may wish to reward effort, but if the rules reward only achievement, then proving the existence of effort does not mean that one's rights have been violated. Assigning grades is one example; occupational pensions are another. A person may have contributed to pension schemes all his or her working life but violate the rules by changing jobs or dropping out to raise children. According to current rules, such individuals have no right to a pension. Now, if the case can be made that those who deserve to get benefits (on some other ground) are being excluded, then the rules have to be changed so that new definitions of "deserving" become the basis for claiming benefits (Miller 1976:83-120).

Assessing Need-Based Policies

"Need" is a term with considerable definitional ambiguity. Despite substantial (and substantive!) theoretical debates, "need" has usually been equated with "means" when programmatic operational definitions of the concept are examined. Thus, in many of our social programs eligibility is determined by income. It is argued that limited resources are targetted only to the "most needy." The Guaranteed Income Supplement (GIS) provincial top-off programs and welfare schemes that cover people in poverty are examples of such programs. These residual programs have been praised or damned depending on the analytical perspective of the assessor.

An alternative approach is to develop programs that are universal — meaning that they cover everyone in a given category regardless of income. Usually when we talk of universality it refers to the lack of a means test. Examples of such programs are the Old Age Security (OAS), Family Allowances and health services covered by the Canada Health Act. Such programs, it is argued, are nonstigmatizing and equitable. Targetting is achieved via the tax system; i.e., everyone receives the same benefit and the personal income-tax system is used as a vehicle for recovering that portion that goes to higher income earners. The essential difference is on which side of the ledger the emphasis is put. It should be noted that both sides can make excellent theoretical claims for efficiency and effectiveness; both claims are based on need not merit, and, alas, both use income as the operational definition of need.

In the final analysis one has to examine how the concepts get translated into actual programs. Today the OAS is set so low that half of the elderly qualify for the Guaranteed Income Supplement (GIS) (House of Commons, 1983:22). Historically, we have taken the route of increasing GIS when constituent pressure has mounted:

> In recent years, the program has evolved in a way that ensures that new resources directed at the elderly are received by those in greatest need. For example, the three benefit increases provided to the elderly since 1979, other than by regular indexation, have been directed only to recipients of the GIS (Department of Finance, 1984: 75).

As presently set up, the GIS is simple enough to apply for, with a straightforward eligibility criterion — level of income. However, the onus is on the individual to apply, and poverty has to be declared. Second, the measurement of need does not include other financial assets or expenditures.

Ultimately, the fairness of programs comes down to substantiating the validity and reliability of their eligibility criteria. Universal programs are attractive because they eliminate front-end proof of necessity according to a set of criteria. The tax system is used as a mechanism for assessing total income. Child benefits, discussed earlier, are an example of three different types of programs all using the tax system. Unfortunately, universal programs that pay benefits directly are a constant focus for attack, especially in times of economic restraint. Their "image" problem seems to be their high visibility at the point of resource allocation and the publicly invisible role of tax recovery — the very features that make for non-stigmatizing programs.

There is also the justifiable argument that loopholes make the progressive structure of our tax system less than perfect. Thus, in before-tax programs like the Family Allowance, upper income groups tend to reap greater benefits than they do in after-tax programs like the Child Tax Credit.

Given that resources are limited no matter what the state of the economy, there is little reason to believe that our national preference for selectivity in programs will decrease as the number of elderly increase. However, this is probably less of a concern than our tendency to conceptualize programs as social safety nets rather than social provisions. Such a perspective means that exclusion rather than inclusion guides the rules of allocation. This necessitates regulations that at a minimum are effective in determining who does *not* qualify for a service. Need does not have to be equated with means testing. Programs can be universal in *application* and selective in *impact*. Once again, the Child Credit is a good example of such a program.

In the opening pages of this chapter it was suggested that age may be a poor indicator of a social condition. But if current definitions continue, need may not be the hoped-for substitute. Our belief in individual responsibility has resulted in programmatic rules that emphasize assessing the individual (e.g., ensuring that resources go only to the "most needy") rather than assessing the collective impact of a policy (e.g., have the social conditions of a particular group improved). Unless meeting need is defined much more broadly than rescuing individuals, the social conditions of disadvantaged groups in our society will not change and the dire straits of a few will become a tool for curtailing benefits to a wider segment of the elderly. The attempt in 1985 to deindex partially Old Age Security is an example. The well-off elderly would not have been affected by such a policy, but low and middle-income groups would have — they would then have had to prove "need" to receive a supplementary benefit for the poor. Under current tax structures the net effect would probably have been a redistribution of resources to the well-off and poor from middle-income groups (for an analysis using U.S. data see Nelson, 1983).

Balancing Equity and Freedom

The goal of a policy may be to maximize the choices or options available to the elderly: to work or to retire; to spend today or to invest so as to increase one's retirement income; to have a variety of living arrangements.

The increased variability that will occur among the elderly of the future emphasizes the importance of options. Choice is an important value in North American society. We see it as crucial if freedom is to have any meaning. However, in any given program, maximizing choice can conflict with the pursuit of equality (Hardy, 1981:93). The idea of personal freedom is closely linked to individual responsibility, whereas an emphasis on equity is more congruent with collective obligations. Legislation that eliminates mandatory retirement practices obviously increases personal freedom. The question is, does the benefit accrue equally to all? Studies of retirement decisions show that health as a precipitating reason for early retirement is found more frequently among lower income workers (for a summary of Canadian studies, see McPherson, 1983:Chapter 10). There are also differences in the retirement patterns of men and women, although they have been studied less (see Sizinovacz, 1982; and Chapters 13 and 14, this volume). What this research seems to indicate is that the "choice" to retire or not has been and will continue to be subject to other facets of a person's life situation.

The same types of dilemmas are encountered when assessing income mechanisms for those no longer in the labour force. In 1983 the Parliamentary Task Force on Pension Reform stated:

> We approach this task from a perspective that assumes a twofold role for government in the retirement-income system. First, to provide a basic safety net to ensure an adequate level of income for all elderly Canadians through the OAS and GIS, and second, to ensure, on a uniform, equitable basis, adequate individual opportunities to provide, through personal effort and individual decisions and through public plans like the C/QPP, for the maintenance or continuity of personal living standards into retirement. We therefore emphasize both the general social responsibility to ensure that the basic needs of the elderly are met and the appeal to self-reliance — dependence on individual initiative — to provide for the maintenance of living standards beyond agreed minimum levels (House of Commons, 1983:8).

In the 1985 federal budget, RRSP contributions were increased so that "starting in 1986, the limits on RRSP contributions will increase each year until 1990, at which time equity will be restored between RRSPs and other types of pension plans" (*Globe and Mail*, May 24, 1985:13).

Given that half of retired Canadians have incomes so low that they qualify for GIS payments, that occupational pensions cover only one-third of women workers and that at the time of the statement OAS was being partially deindexed, one wonders how the word "equity" was being used in the above statement. The conflict between expanding opportunities to save for those who have the means to take advantage of them (individual responsibility) and developing mechanisms to ensure that resources flow to disadvantaged groups (social responsibility) is evident in programmatic outputs even if policy statements like the above two are ambiguous.

Linking Social and Economic Policy

Basing the distribution of resources on rights, definitions of merit and/or need have all been put forward as ways for promoting social justice. As we have seen, however, need and merit claims are inherently contradictory, although both may be transformed into rights and argued as being fair — depending on whether the primary concern is with process or outcome.

I have argued that although the literature has emphasized the responsibility of the state to meet individual need, there has been a tendency for program regulations to stress individual proof of need rather than the social obligation to ensure that need is met. In the latter type of programs there would have to be a readiness to acknowledge that subgroups in our society may require differential resources. The policy goal would stress some desired outcome. Thus, for example, programs of affirmative action are consistent with the pursuit of equity — defined as pursuing equality of condition. I would suggest that these types of programs are regularly attacked because they challenge the efficacy of equality of opportunity; their very existence testifies to the presence of structured inequalities within our society. A policy position, however, that emphasizes equality of condition rather than equal opportunity leads to all kinds of difficulties around defining need, the policy outcomes desired and the programmatic structures required to "match" need and resources. As the elderly population becomes more diverse, so will these issues.

Notwithstanding the complexity of the analytical task facing us, I do not think that defining need is where the policy battles are going to rage in the next decade. Rather they will centre on the relationship of social to economic policy. It is helpful at this point to return to the multiple definitions of social policy outlined earlier. Although social policy (health, education, housing, income security, etc.) focusses on the distribution of benefits to people, there is increasing concern that it cannot be isolated from economic policy. Such a separation results in the subordination of social policy to economic policy. This is evident, for example, in a report presented by the Minister of Finance, which concludes: "Difficult choices face the government. . . . Deficits must be reduced. Government intervention in the marketplace must be reduced. Investment must be encouraged. Confidence must be restored" (Department of Finance, 1984:91). With these choices already in place for economic policy, the options for social policy are extremely limited.

Making socially visible the relationship of social policy options to economic decisions has radical implications. It recognizes that economic policy has social effects and reflects social priorities. For example, in order to help *individuals* plan for their retirement, the transfer of private pension schemes among firms is currently being encouraged. The form of the "encouragement" is economic incentives, e.g., favourable tax treatment of these pension dollars. The outcomes will be social. If successful, such incentives should lead to wider coverage of workers by private pensions. An indirect outcome will undoubtedly be removal of some of the demand to expand the public pension (CPP) system that already covers all paid workers. However, throughout the pension debate the social policy concern about coverage has been secondary to the economic concern of loss of investment dollars to the private sector, which is seen as the motor that keeps the economy growing. The hegemony of the private enterprise economic model and strength of its lobby are reflected in the following conclusion by the 1983 Task Force on Pension Reform: "In part, this (recommending the expansion of occupational pensions rather than the CPP) represents a decision to give the private sector a further opportunity to demonstrate that coverage of adequate scope and depth can be achieved without recourse to a universal public plan" (House of Commons Canada, 1983:71). When private occupational pensions and RRSPs are discussed in an explicitly social context, however, economic concerns are downplayed. Rather the emphasis is put on maximizing opportunities to save for one's old age, of increasing choice while not reducing individual freedom. This perspective would limit state responsibility to catching those that fall "between the cracks;" not guaranteeing that cracks do not exist — even if it means major structural changes.

A preference for equality of opportunity, expansion of choice and freedom from interference are all values that mesh with a market economy. Need, except as a safety-net concept, does not. If we were truly to have social policies based on it, our economic model would have to be challenged. One of the difficulties in trying to blend welfare-state social policies with a market economy is that the assumptions clash. In times of economic restraint the inherent contradictions just become more obvious.

Social Justice — An Elusive Goal

What does this discussion of the constraints on social policy mean for the future aging of the Canadian population? Without being prescriptive, I think that a few guideposts can be demarcated:

1. If we believe that people should be allowed to retire after so many years in the labour force, then income mechanisms are needed. The guarantee of an adequate income will continue to exist with or without mandatory retirement. Such income must be defined as a right if socially constructed dependency is to be avoided (Townsend, 1981). "Safety net" programs, with their reliance on means testing, will increase, not decrease, dependency. It seems that an Old Age Tax Credit, along the lines of the Child Tax Credit, would be equitable as well as meeting the twin goals of effectiveness and efficiency. It is an after-tax allocation, and thus would selectively impact on the low-income elderly. Since it is universal in application, it would be nonstigmatizing.

2. People do not suddenly become isolated from society as they get old —

although there are certain practices that may accentuate such feelings. The great variability among the old reflects over a half century of accumulated advantages and disadvantages. Therefore, the impact of social policies must be viewed across a lifetime. For example, home-care policies affect the aging of a 50-year-old caring daughter as surely as they do her 80-year-old mother (Land, 1978; Neysmith, 1981; Finch, 1984).

3. In our society economic and social policies will more often conflict than mesh. Although the domination of New Right ideas in the 1980s makes the conflict more obvious, the inherent contradictions are always there. Recognizing the conflicts rather than masking them is the first step in defining a new social order.

Thus it is hoped that the ideas discussed in this chapter contribute to an ongoing social analysis in which our needs, rights and freedoms as individuals are weighted against our collective responsibility.

Notes

[1] Vesting is a legal mechanism by which an employer's contribution to an employee's pension plan is deemed to become the property of the employee. Typically this occurs only after some period of employment.

[2] The nature of RRSPs and other aspects of the Canadian income security apparatus (Old Age Security, Guaranteed Income Supplement, Canada/Quebec Pension Plan) is described elsewhere in this volume (Chapters 24 and 29).

References

Department of Finance
    1984 *A New Direction for Canada: An Agenda for Economic Renewal.* Presented by the Honourable Michael H. Wilson, Minister of Finance. Ottawa.
Finch, J.
    1984 "Community care: Developing non-sexist alternatives." *Critical Social Policy* 9:6-18.
Government of Canada
    1983 *Better Pensions for Canadians.* Ottawa: Minister of Supply and Services Canada.
    1983 *Fact Book on Aging.* Ottawa: Minister of Supply and Services Canada.
    1984 *Sixty-five and Over* A Report by the National Council of Welfare on the Incomes of the Aged. Ottawa: Minister of Supply and Services Canada.
    1985 *Opportunity for Reform.* A Response by the National Council of Welfare to the Consultation Paper on Child and Elderly Benefits. Ottawa: Minister of Supply and Services Canada.

Hardy, J.
1981   *Values in Social Policy: Nine Contradictions.* London: Routledge and Kegan Paul.
House of Commons Canada
1983   *Report of the Parliamentary Task Force on Pension Reform.* Ottawa: Canadian Government Publishing Centre, Supply and Services Canada.
Land, H.
1978   "Who cares for the family?" *Journal of Social Policy* 7(3):32-42.
McPherson, B.
1983   *Aging As A Social Process.* Toronto: Butterworths.
Miller, D.
1976   *Social Justice.* Oxford: Clarendon Press.
Mishra, R.
1981   *Society and Social Policy.* London: Macmillan .
Nelson, G.
1983   "Tax expenditures for the elderly," *The Gerontologist* 33(5):471-478.
Neysmith, S.
1981   "Parental care: Another female family function?" *Canadian Journal of Social Work Education* 7(2):55-64.
Neugarten, B.L. (ed.)
1982   *Age or Need? Public Policies for Older People.* Beverly Hills: Sage.
Plant, R., H. Lesser and P. Taylor-Gooley.
1980   *Political Philosophy and Social Welfare: Essays on the Normative Basis of Welfare Provision.* London: Routledge and Kegan Paul.
Rein, M.
1976   *Social Science and Public Policy.* Middlesex, England: Penguin.
Sizinovacz, M. (ed.)
1982   *Women's Retirement: Policy Implications of Recent Research.* Beverly Hills: Sage.
Smith, G.
1980   *Social Need: Policy, Practice and Research.* London: Routledge and Kegan Paul.
Townsend, P.
1981   "The Structured dependency of the elderly: Creation of social policy in the twentieth century." *Ageing and Society* 1(1):5-28.
Walker, A.
1981   "Social policy, social administration and the social construction of welfare." *Sociology* 15(2):225-250.

NAME INDEX

SUBJECT INDEX